W9-BUL-360

Fourth Brief Canadian Edition

Business Communication
Process & Product

Mary Ellen Guffey
Professor Emerita of Business, Los Angeles Pierce College

Dana Loewy
Business Communication Program, California State University, Fullerton

Kathleen Rhodes
Faculty Emerita, Durham College

Patricia Rogin
Durham College

NELSON EDUCATION

NELSON / EDUCATION

Business Communication: Process and Product, Fourth Brief Canadian Edition

by Mary Ellen Guffey, Dana Loewy, Kathleen Rhodes, and Patricia Rogin

Vice President, Editorial Higher Education:
Anne Williams

Acquisitions Editor:
Anne-Marie Taylor

Marketing Manager:
Terry Fedorkiw

Senior Developmental Editor:
Linda Sparks

Photo Researcher and Permissions Coordinator:
Melody Tolson

Senior Content Production Manager:
Natalia Denesiuk Harris

Production Service:
MPS Limited, a Macmillan Company

Copy Editor:
Dawn Hunter

Proofreader:
Jennifer A. McIntyre

Indexer:
Sonya Dintaman

Senior Production Coordinator:
Ferial Suleman

Design Director:
Ken Phipps

Managing Designer:
Franca Amore

Interior Design:
Lou Ann Thesing

Interior Design Modifications:
Sharon Lucas

Cover Design:
Johanna Liburd

Cover Images:
Olix Wirtinger/Corbis (foreground images); Pokki/VectorStock (background vector)

Compositor:
MPS Limited, a Macmillan Company

Printer:
RRDonnelley

Library and Archives Canada Cataloguing in Publication Data

Business communication : process & product / Mary Ellen Guffey ... [et al.]. — 4th brief Canadian ed.

Includes bibliographical references and index.
ISBN 978-0-17-650358-1

1. Business communication.
2. Business writing. I. Guffey, Mary Ellen

HF5718.3.G82 2012
651.7   C2012-900225-9

ISBN-13: 978-0-17-650358-1
ISBN-10: 0-17-650358-7

Dear Business Communication Students:

We are proud to present to you the **Fourth Brief Canadian Edition** of *Business Communication: Process and Product*. In an effort to bring you the latest information and tools to succeed in today's increasingly interconnected workplace, we have made innumerable revisions and enhancements, a few of which are highlighted here:

- **Integrated, cutting-edge coverage of digital tools and social media.** The Fourth Brief Canadian Edition prepares you to become accomplished communicators in today's digital workplace. A new Chapter 7, *Electronic Messages and Digital Media*, is solely dedicated to digital media. Every chapter has been thoroughly researched and updated to acquaint you with the latest trends in workplace communication technology.

- **More figures and model documents.** To demonstrate the professional use of the latest business communication tools, the Fourth Brief Canadian Edition has been enhanced with numerous new figures and model documents that show the use of Twitter, instant messages, podcasts, blogs, and wikis.

- **Independent Grammar Review.** Grammar/mechanics exercises in every chapter present a structured review to guide you through all of the rules.

In the preface that follows, we illustrate key features of the **Fourth Brief Canadian Edition** that highlight both the process and products of business communication. We welcome your comments and suggestions.

Cordially,

Mary Ellen Guffey   *Kathleen Rhodes*
Dana Loewy   *Patricia Rogin*

Dr. Mary Ellen Guffey

A dedicated professional, Mary Ellen Guffey has taught business communication and business English topics for over thirty years. She received a bachelor's degree, summa cum laude, from Bowling Green State University; a master's degree from the University of Illinois, and a doctorate in business and economic education from the University of California, Los Angeles (UCLA). She has taught at the University of Illinois, Santa Monica College, and Los Angeles Pierce College.

Now recognized as the world's leading business communication author, Dr. Guffey corresponds with instructors around the globe who are using her books. She is the founding author of the award-winning *Business Communication: Process and Product*, the leading business communication textbook in this country and abroad. She also wrote *Business English*, which serves more students than any other book in its field; *Essentials of College English;* and *Essentials of Business Communication*, the leading text/workbook in its market. Dr. Guffey is active professionally, serving on the review board of the *Business Communication Quarterly* of the Association for Business Communication, participating in all national meetings, and sponsoring business communication awards.

Dr. Dana Loewy

Dana Loewy brings extensive international expertise, broad business communication teaching experience, and exceptional writing skills to this edition. Dana Loewy earned a magister artium (MA) degree in English, linguistics, and communication from Rheinische Friedrich-Wilhelms-Universität Bonn, Germany, where she also studied Slavic languages and literatures and took business administration courses. Before receiving a master's degree and PhD from the University of Southern California, Dr. Loewy expanded her teaching experience in freshman writing at USC. She also taught at Loyola Marymount College Palos Verdes and Glendale Community College. Since 1996 Dr. Loewy has taught both graduate and undergraduate business communication classes at Cal State Fullerton. As a guest lecturer, she regularly travels to Germany.

A longtime professional translator of film subtitles, writer, and brand-name consultant, Dr. Loewy has published several books, articles, and translations, both poetry and prose, most notably *The Early Poetry of Jaroslav Seifert* (1997) and *On the Waves of TSF* (2004). In addition to German, Dr. Loewy is fluent in her native tongue, Czech, and understands many Indo-European languages. To broaden her consulting and business expertise, Dr. Loewy has become a business etiquette consultant certified by The Protocol School of Washington.

The Canadian Team: Kathleen Rhodes and Patricia Rogin

Kathleen Rhodes and Patricia Rogin have enjoyed a writing partnership through numerous editions of *Business Communication: Process and Product*. With close to 60 years of combined experience at Durham College, they have seen a lot of changes in higher education. Both qualified teachers, Rhodes and Rogin have witnessed firsthand the impact of technology on both students and the learning environment. Through their work on *Business Communication: Process and Product*, they have kept students updated and aware of the changes in the workplace, thus preparing them for the ever-evolving world of work. They have not only delivered material to college students but also worked with school boards and industry professionals to share their passion for the value of excellent communication skills. By using *Business Communication: Process and Product* in their classrooms, they have been able to gauge student feedback and responses and are proud that students use this text as a learning tool; students also report that the text is a valuable reference tool in the workplace. Although students and technology have changed over the years, Rhodes and Rogin believe that excellent communication skills will always be required for success.

Brief Contents

Contents

Unit 2: The Writing Process   78

Unit 3: Workplace Communication 143

Chapter 10: Persuasive and Sales Messages   **234**

Unit 4: Reports, Proposals, and Presentations   265

Chapter 11: Report and Research Basics   **266**

Unit 5: Employment Communication   404

PREFACE

The unrivalled market leader, ***Business Communication: Process and Product*** delivers the most current and authoritative communication technology and business communication concepts available. This renowned leader is hands down the most up-to-date and best researched text on the market, and the exciting Fourth Brief Canadian Edition is bursting with new, interactive student resources and comprehensive coverage of workplace technology.

A premier business communication and workplace technology text, the Fourth Brief Canadian Edition of *Business Communication: Process and Product* breaks new ground with a host of innovations to create the most complete business communication authority available. With its up-to-the-minute coverage, riveting examples, hands-on applications, and lively writing, the Fourth Brief Canadian Edition gives you a truly engaging text that equips you with the skills and technology prowess you need for effective communication throughout your career.

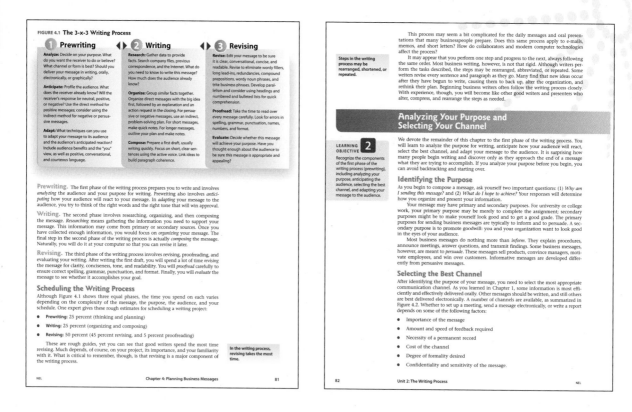

INNOVATIVE FEATURES

Springboard to Discussion boxes begin every chapter and create opportunities to stimulate vigorous in-class or online discussion of chapter topics.

springboard to discussion

The 2010 Winter Olympics in Vancouver introduced a new patriotism to Canada with the bold and unprecedented Canadian "Own the Podium" campaign. This unique confidence was seen as a defining moment in Canadian sport and created a new perception of Canada on the world stage. The classic Canadian stereotypes of Mounties and mountains, and hockey players and hosers, are part of our national identity; however, should we rethink and redefine Brand Canada? How do you define Canada?

PLUGGED IN

Using Technology to Edit and Revise Collaborative Documents

Collaborative writing and editing projects are challenging. Fortunately, Microsoft Word offers useful tools to help team members edit and share documents electronically. Two simple but useful editing tools are **Text Highlight Color** and **Font Color**. These tools, which are found on the **Home** tab in MS Office 2007, enable reviewers to point out errors and explain problematic passages through the use of contrast. However, some projects require more advanced editing tools, such as **Track Changes** and **Comment**.

Track Changes. To suggest specific editing changes to other team members, **Track Changes** is handy. The revised wording is visible on screen, and deletions show up in callout balloons in the right-hand margin. Suggested revisions offered by various team members are identified and dated. The original writer may accept or reject these changes. In Office 2007 you will find **Track Changes** on the **Review** tab.

Comment. Probably the most useful editing tool is the **Comment** function. This tool allows users to point out problematic passages or errors, ask or answer questions, and share ideas without changing or adding text. When more than one person adds comments, the comments appear in different colours and are identified by the writer's name and a date/time stamp. To use this tool in Word 2007, click **New Comment** from the drop-down **Review** tab. Then type your comment, which can be seen in the Web or print layout view (click **View** and **Print Layout** or **Web Layout**).

Completing a Document. When a document is finished, be sure to accept or reject all changes on the **Review** tab, a step that removes the tracking information.

Expansive coverage of digital tools and media carefully explains and illustrates how to use these tools professionally in an increasingly connected workplace. For example, a new Chapter 7 is dedicated solely to digital media, acquainting you with the latest trends in workplace communication technology. In addition, all chapters have been enhanced to reflect the use of new digital tools.

Numerous new figures and model documents illustrate the professional uses of the latest digital media at work, including the use of Twitter, instant messages, podcasts, blogs, and wikis.

FIGURE 7.3 Instant Message for Brief, Fast Communication

Figure 7.3 shows a brief IM exchange between a supervisor and a subordinate. Both are using a computer-based IM program. Texting is a convenient tool that enables team members to locate quick information and answers in solving immediate problems even when they are apart.

Ryan Mlodzik · Conversation

File Edit View Actions Help

To: Ryan Mlodzik <mlodzik@armour.com>

Camille Montano says:
Hi, Ryan, are you free for a quick question?

Ryan Mlodzik says:
Sure thing. What have you got?

Camille Montano says:
I just finished my meeting with the folks at Zymak Enterprises, and they've agreed to terms we discussed yesterday, but they want 45-day terms instead of 30.

Ryan Mlodzik says:
Did they agree to a 2-year or 3-year contract?

Camille Montano says:
3-year.

Ryan Mlodzik says:
OK, let's go with it. I approve the 45-day adjustment. Good work!

Block · Font · Emoticons

Send

Last message received on 8/4/14 at 1:26 PM.

INNOVATIVE FEATURES

Chapter Review

1. Why is intercultural communication increasingly important, and what must business communicators do to succeed? (Obj. 1)
2. Why is geographic location virtually irrelevant for many activities and services today? (Obj. 1)
3. What is culture and how is culture learned? (Obj. 2)
4. Describe five major dimensions of culture. (Obj. 2)
5. Briefly, contrast high- and low-context cultures. (Obj. 2)
6. How do the words *backward, advanced, primitive,* and *sophisticated* relate to ethnocentrism? (Obj. 3)
7. How is a stereotype different from a prototype? (Obj. 3)
8. Name techniques for bridging the gap between cultures and achieving intercultural proficiency. (Obj. 3)
9. When interacting with people who do not use your language, why is it important to learn the words for *please, yes,* and *thank you* rather than relying on gestures? (Obj. 4)
10. What should you assume about the level of proficiency in nonnative speakers of English? (Obj. 4)
11. Describe five specific ways you can improve oral communication with someone who speaks another language. (Obj. 4)
12. Describe five specific ways you can improve written communication with someone who speaks another language. (Obj. 5)
13. What categories of ambiguous expressions should be avoided because they could confuse readers for whom English is a second language? (Obj. 5)
14. Name three groups that benefit from workforce diversity and explain why. (Obj. 6)
15. Describe six tips for improving communication among diverse workplace audiences. (Obj. 6)

Critical Thinking

1. Queen Elizabeth II once said, "Stereotypes wither when human contacts flourish."[26] What does this statement mean? Have you found this to be accurate in your own experience? (Objs. 1, 3)
2. Because English is becoming the world's business language, why should Canadians bother to learn about other cultures? (Objs. 1, 2, and 6)
3. Cultural expert John Engle complained that his North American students resist references to cultural generalizations. He asserted, "Thoughtful generalizations are the heart of intercultural communication, allowing us to discuss meaningfully the complex web of forces acting upon individuals that we call culture."[27] Do you agree or disagree? Why? (Objs. 2, 3)
4. Some economists and management scholars argue that such statements as "diversity is an economic asset" or "diversity is a new strategic imperative" are unproved and perhaps unprovable assertions. Should social responsibility or market forces determine whether an organization strives to create a diverse workforce? Why? (Obj. 6)
5. **Ethical Issue:** You know that it's not acceptable to make ethnic jokes, least of all in the workplace, but a colleague of yours keeps invoking the worst ethnic and racial stereotypes. How do you respond? Do you remain silent and change the subject, or do you pipe up? What other options do you have in dealing with such a co-worker? Consider whether your answer would change if the offender were your boss. (Obj. 6)

Activities

3.1 Trouble on a Global Scale: Analyzing Intercultural Blunders (Objs. 1–3)

INTERCULTURAL

As business organizations become increasingly global in their structure and marketing, they face communication problems resulting from cultural misunderstandings.

Your Task. Based on what you have learned in this chapter, describe several broad principles that could be applied in helping the individuals involved understand what went wrong in the following events. What suggestions could you make for remedying the problems involved?

a. During a festive dinner for a delegation from Singapore visiting the government of the Czech Republic, the conversation turned to the tasty main course they were eating. One of the Czech hosts explained to the inquiring foreign guests that they were enjoying a Czech specialty, rabbit, known for its light white meat. The Singaporeans' faces showed shock, embarrassment, and irritation. As inconspicuously as possible they put down their silverware. Only later did the Czech delegation learn that a rabbit is a pet in Singapore much like the house cat in European or North American households.[28]

b. An advertising agency manager, new to his post in Japan, gathered his team for an old-fashioned brainstorming session in the boardroom. A big presentation loomed, and he expected creative ideas from his staff. Instead, he was met with silence. What went wrong? How could he coax ideas from his staff?[29]

74

Get more practice at **www.guffeybrief4e.nelson.com**

NEL

End-of-chapter Activities offer the most complete, descriptive, understandable, and relevant activities on the market.

Model documents with callouts enable you to better understand strategies highlighted in the text. New intercultural communication model documents help you readily see differences in cultural adaptation.

FIGURE 10.4 **Claim (Complaint) Letter**

ARTE INTERNATIONAL FURNISHINGS
141 Rue Champlain, Gatineau, QC J8T 3B9 (819) 496 3500

February 16, 2014

Customer Service
ZTech Electronics
87 Emilie Simard Avenue
Edmundston, NB E3V 3B9

Dear ZTech Customer Service Representative:

Your VoIP Expandable Telephone System came highly recommended and seemed to be the answer to increasingly expensive telephone service. Here at Arte International Furnishings we were looking for a way to reduce our local and long-distance telephone charges. The VoIP system was particularly attractive to us because it offered Internet phone service with unlimited calling within Canada and to the United States. Our business in fine furnishings and unique objet d'art requires us to make and receive national and international calls.

On February 8 we purchased two VoIP systems (SGU #IP7402-2) for our main office here in Gatineau and for our showroom. Each system came with two cordless handsets and charging docks. Although we followed all the installation instructions, we discovered that an irritating static sound interfered with every incoming and outgoing telephone call.

This static is surprising and disappointing because the product description promised the following: "You will experience excellent signal clarity with Frequency Hopping Digital Spread Spectrum (FHDSS) transmission and a frequency of 5.8 GHz. Ninety-five channel auto-search ensures a clear signal."

On February 10 we filled out a Return Merchandise Authorization form at your Web site. However, we are frustrated that we have had no response. We're confident that a manufacturer with your reputation for reliable products and superior customer service will want to resolve this matter quickly.

Please authorize return of these two systems and credit our account for $877.24, which represents the original cost plus taxes and shipping. Enclosed is a copy of the invoice with our credit card number.

Sincerely,

Marilyn Easter

Marilyn Easter
President

Enclosure

Begins with compliment; keeps tone objective, rational, and unemotional

Provides identifying data and justifies claim

Explains why claim is valid and suggests responsibility of receiver

Expresses disappointment and appeals to receiver's reputation and customer service

Tells what action to take

Tips for Making Complaints
- Begin with a compliment, point of agreement, statement of the problem, or brief review of action you have taken to resolve the problem.
- Provide identifying data.
- Prove that your claim is valid; explain why the receiver is responsible.
- Enclose document copies supporting your claim.
- Appeal to the receiver's fairness, ethical and legal responsibilities, and desire for customer satisfaction.
- Describe your feelings and your disappointment.
- Avoid sounding angry, emotional, or irrational.
- Close by stating exactly what you want done.

NEL

Chapter 10: Persuasive and Sales Messages

245

3-x-3 writing process provides you with a proven three-step strategy for developing effective communication.

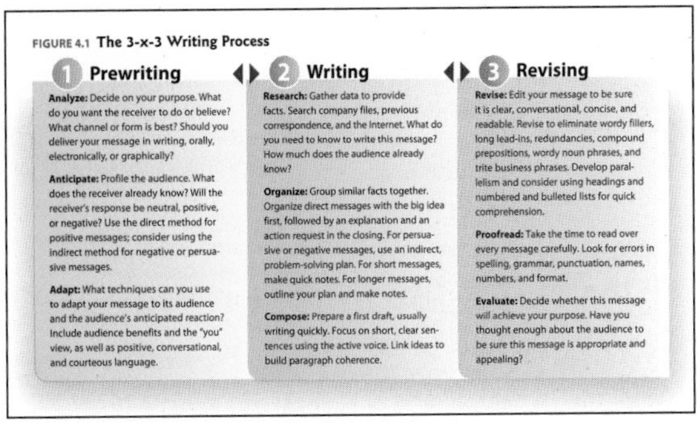

FIGURE 4.1 **The 3-x-3 Writing Process**

1 Prewriting

Analyze: Decide on your purpose. What do you want the receiver to do or believe? What channel or form is best? Should you deliver your message in writing, orally, electronically, or graphically?

Anticipate: Profile the audience. What does the receiver already know? Will the receiver's response be neutral, positive, or negative? Use the direct method for positive messages; consider using the indirect method for negative or persuasive messages.

Adapt: What techniques can you use to adapt your message to its audience and the audience's anticipated reaction? Include audience benefits and the "you" view, as well as positive, conversational, and courteous language.

2 Writing

Research: Gather data to provide facts. Search company files, previous correspondence, and the internet. What do you need to know to write this message? How much does the audience already know?

Organize: Group similar facts together. Organize direct messages with the big idea first, followed by an explanation and an action request in the closing. For persuasive or negative messages, use an indirect, problem-solving plan. For short messages, make quick notes. For longer messages, outline your plan and make notes.

Compose: Prepare a first draft, usually writing quickly. Focus on short, clear sentences using the active voice. Link ideas to build paragraph coherence.

3 Revising

Revise: Edit your message to be sure it is clear, conversational, concise, and readable. Revise to eliminate wordy fillers, long lead-ins, redundancies, compound prepositions, wordy noun phrases, and trite business phrases. Develop parallelism and consider using headings and numbered and bulleted lists for quick comprehension.

Proofread: Take the time to read over every message carefully. Look for errors in spelling, grammar, punctuation, names, numbers, and format.

Evaluate: Decide whether this message will achieve your purpose. Have you thought enough about the audience to be sure this message is appropriate and appealing?

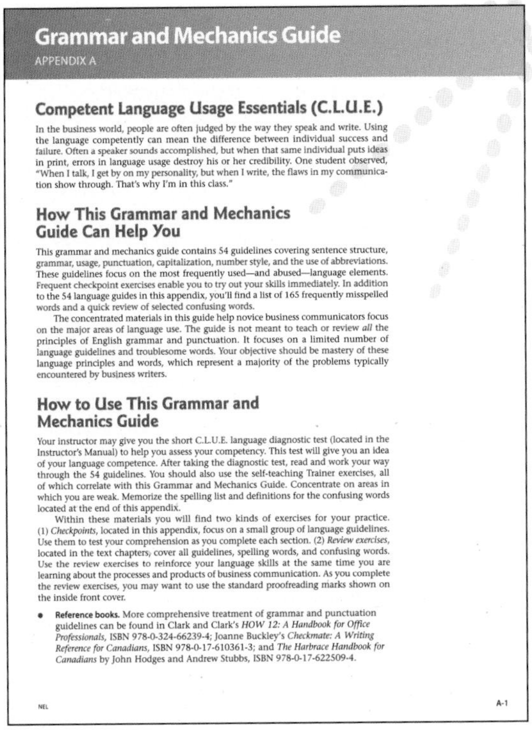

Grammar and Mechanics Guide
APPENDIX A

Competent Language Usage Essentials (C.L.U.E.)

In the business world, people are often judged by the way they speak and write. Using the language competently can mean the difference between individual success and failure. Often a speaker sounds accomplished, but when that same individual puts ideas in print, errors in language usage destroy his or her credibility. One student observed, "When I talk, I get by on my personality, but when I write, the flaws in my communication show through. That's why I'm in this class."

How This Grammar and Mechanics Guide Can Help You

This grammar and mechanics guide contains 54 guidelines covering sentence structure, grammar, usage, punctuation, capitalization, number style, and the use of abbreviations. These guidelines focus on the most frequently used—and abused—language elements. Frequent checkpoint exercises enable you to try out your skills immediately. In addition to the 54 language guides in this appendix, you'll find a list of 165 frequently misspelled words and a quick review of selected confusing words.

The concentrated materials in this guide help novice business communicators focus on the major areas of language use. The guide is not meant to teach or review *all* the principles of English grammar and punctuation. It focuses on a limited number of language guidelines and troublesome words. Your objective should be mastery of these language principles and words, which represent a majority of the problems typically encountered by business writers.

How to Use This Grammar and Mechanics Guide

Your instructor may give you the short C.L.U.E. language diagnostic test (located in the Instructor's Manual) to help you assess your competency. This test will give you an idea of your language competence. After taking the diagnostic test, read and work your way through the 54 guidelines. You should also use the self-teaching Trainer exercises, all of which correlate with this Grammar and Mechanics Guide. Concentrate on areas in which you are weak. Memorize the spelling list and definitions for the confusing words located at the end of this appendix.

Within these materials you will find two kinds of exercises for your practice. (1) *Checkpoints*, located in this appendix, focus on a small group of language guidelines. Use them to test your comprehension as you complete each section. (2) *Review exercises*, located in the text chapters, cover all guidelines, spelling words, and confusing words. Use the review exercises to reinforce your language skills at the same time you are learning about the processes and products of business communication. As you complete the review exercises, you may want to use the standard proofreading marks shown on the inside front cover.

● **Reference books.** More comprehensive treatment of grammar and punctuation guidelines can be found in Clark and Clark's *HOW 12: A Handbook for Office Professionals*, ISBN 978-0-324-66239-4; Joanne Buckley's *Checkmate: A Writing Reference for Canadians*, ISBN 978-0-17-610361-3; and *The Harbrace Handbook for Canadians* by John Hodges and Andrew Stubbs ISBN 978-0-17-622509-4.

NEL   A-1

Numerous examples and applications illustrate how business communication concepts are applied in the workplace, giving you a better understanding of today's digital work environment and business communication strategies.

Grammar/mechanics exercises in every chapter present a structured review to guide you through all the rules.

IMPROVEMENTS: What's New in *Business Communication: Process and Product,* Fourth Brief Canadian Edition

This new edition incorporates the use of technology in areas related to teamwork, research, document creation, and the job search. Each chapter begins with a new discussion topic to guide discussion to relevant topics in the chapter. Each chapter ends with completely updated C.L.U.E. reviews.

Chapter 1 — Effective and Ethical Communication at Work

- Related the importance of communication skills to finding a job in today's tight job market so that students recognize the value of this course and improving their business communication skills.
- Added new figures illustrating information flow in organizations, so that students better understand the functions and flow of organizational communication.
- Introduced practical guidance in how to respond to workplace gossip.
- Updated as well as added new end-of-chapter activities that provide engaging opportunities to apply chapter concepts.

Chapter 2 — Professionalism: Team, Listening, Nonverbal, and Etiquette Skills

- Focused chapter on professional workplace skills to help students make a smooth transition from the classroom to the business world.
- Distinguished between face-to-face and virtual meetings, emphasizing the latter because virtual meetings reduce travel costs, lessen employee fatigue, and connect remote workers.
- Added instructions and Web screenshot illustrating the use of digital calendars to schedule meetings so that students will know how to use this electronic tool.
- Added Web screenshot to illustrate e-mail meeting summary template so that students see how savvy companies are using digital tools to summarize key points and note action items to monitor.
- Provided many tips and specific ground rules on how to plan and interact professionally during virtual meetings.
- Emphasized the importance of soft skills and professionalism in regard to being hired and promoted.

Chapter 3 — Intercultural Communication

- Added end-of-chapter social media assignments to ensure that students acquire business-relevant technology skills.

Chapter 4 — Planning Business Messages

- Reorganized the chapter to introduce the writing process earlier so that students immediately grasp the three-phase process and its importance in planning business messages.
- Strengthened Figure 4.1 describing the writing process so that it is more specific and contains more details to enhance student comprehension.
- Expanded the discussion of channel selection by adding media richness theory.
- Added discussion regarding customer live chat so that students recognize the importance of communication skills in expanding technology applications in the workplace.
- Updated discussion of student collaboration tools, including Google Docs and revised commands for Word 2007 Comment and Track Changes functions.
- Provided new Chapter Review and Writing Improvement Exercises so that instructors have a fresh set of these popular chapter reinforcement and application exercises.

Chapter 5 — Organizing and Writing Business Messages

- Strengthened discussion of effective sentences by adding coverage of fragments, comma splices, and run-ons so that students will avoid this common set of writing faults.
- Expanded discussion of active voice and passive voice and added a figure illustrating the use of each to help business communicators better understand how to implement these tools effectively.
- Streamlined coverage of techniques that build paragraph coherence.

- Revised the Chapter Review and Writing Improvement Exercises to give instructors and students fresh reinforcement material.
- Prepared new Document for Analysis to enable students to apply many writing techniques covered in the chapter.

Chapter 6 — Revising Business Messages

- Reorganized coverage of revision techniques to improve chapter flow and enhance coverage of revision techniques.
- Expanded coverage of document design so that students learn about white space, margins, typefaces, and fonts to prepare them for today's workplace, where they will be expected to design effective, readable messages.
- Added Figure 6.1 showing students how to make revisions manually and digitally because writers today increasingly edit on screen.
- Added Figure 6.2 comparing typefaces so that students recognize font personalities and appropriate use.
- Added Figure 6.3 with before/after illustrations showing how the readability of an e-mail message can be greatly improved with document design.
- Added Figure 6.4 showing revisions on PDF files because many messages today are exchanged in this format and revisions must be done using markup software.
- Provided new Writing Improvement Exercises offering fresh opportunities to apply and reinforce chapter content.

Chapter 7 — Electronic Messages and Digital Media

- Created a new chapter dedicated solely to digital media to acquaint students with the latest trends in workplace communication technology.
- Emphasized business uses of digital media so that readers will recognize their professional, rather than social, applications.
- Updated coverage of e-mail with special focus on format and message components to ensure that college and university graduates understand how business messages differ from personal e-mail messages.
- Introduced discussion of blogs, instant messaging, text messaging, podcasts, blogs, wikis, and social networking so that students see how these communication channels function in the workplace and comprehend the risks associated with their use.
- Covered RSS feeds and social bookmarking sites to help readers to share and manage information online efficiently.
- Provided a Plugged-In feature about cloud computing so that students glimpse future trends.
- Presented end-of-chapter activities for students that reinforce the use of new digital media.

Chapter 8 — Positive Messages

- Reorganized chapter to combine positive e-mails, interoffice memorandums, and business letters in one place so that students can recognize similarities in content and strategies regardless of channel choice.
- Explained the primary uses of interoffice memos and how they differ from e-mail messages so that students can make appropriate choices in selecting channels for these important workplace messages.
- Discussed the significance, primary functions, and value of business letters, regardless of the popularity of e-mail.

- Added discussion of how to write messages that describe instructions, a common workplace task.
- Illustrated the difference between indicative verbs and imperative (command) verbs to help readers prepare instructions.

Chapter 9— Negative Messages

- Reorganized chapter to give more emphasis to the possible use of the direct strategy for delivering bad news so that students can use either direct or indirect strategy depending on the context.
- Streamlined the goals in communicating negative news to make them easier to comprehend and retain.
- Added specific real-world examples to illustrate how the writing process is applied to the delivery of negative news.
- Added coverage of managing negative news on Facebook, Twitter, and other Web sites to enable readers to be able to deal with unhappy customers in cyberspace.
- Added new section announcing rate increases and price hikes, including a blog model document to show students that companies today are using new channels to deliver negative news.
- Streamlined the checklists for conveying negative news into one comprehensive list so that students have all the tips in one handy place.
- Changed some end-of-chapter activities so that students and instructors have new or fully revised activities to apply their skills in relation to new chapter content.

Chapter 10 — Persuasive and Sales Messages

- Streamlined chapter by combining related learning objectives and checklists to enhance readability and comprehension.
- Reorganized chapter to combine coverage of persuasive favour requests, claims, and complaints to simplify presentation and allow students to apply similar writing techniques.
- Moved coverage of internal communication (persuasive messages within organization) so that it follows the discussion of external communication (favour requests, claims, and complaints) for a more unified presentation.
- Added model document showing the use of a cover e-mail with an attached memo to help students see how businesspeople combine e-mail and attachments.
- Strengthened coverage of sales messages by adding e-marketing so that readers understand basic techniques for preparing successful e-mail sales messages.
- Illustrated media releases and effective writing techniques with a new model document featuring the Antique and Classic Boat Society – Toronto Chapter.

Chapter 11 — Report and Research Basics

- Expanded the discussion of scope and limitations to clarify for students how to establish the scale and extent of their research assignments.
- Added or changed at least several of the end-of-chapter activities to provide students and instructors with new and up-to-date examples demonstrating chapter content.
- Incorporated technology, for example by introducing SurveyMonkey and Zoomerang, wherever feasible to aid students in understanding how modern communication technology affects research and report writing.
- Created current end-of-chapter activities to which students can relate to help them stay engaged.

Chapter 12 — Informal Reports
- Replaced many end-of-chapter activities to present students with fresh activities, cases, and business scenarios.
- Introduced a new figure showing a periodic (activity) report in bullet form sent by e-mail to reflect the latest technological trends in workplace communication.

Chapter 13 — Proposals, Business Plans, and Formal Business Reports
- Reorganized the content to make the chapter easier to grasp and easier to retain for students.
- Introduced new model documents that provide a glimpse of current business practices in proposal and report writing to readers.
- Added end-of-chapter activities to practise executive summaries as requested by reviewers to meet instructor and student needs.

Chapter 14 — Business Presentations
- Emphasized cutting-edge concepts in presentation software to demonstrate to students the trend toward less text and more reliance on images.
- Provided authentic coverage from business practitioners such as venture capitalist Guy Kawasaki to create interest and familiarize readers with current best practices in business slide presentations.

Chapter 15 — The Job Search, Résumés, and Cover Letters
- Updated section on today's workplace to provide information about cutting-edge employment trends.
- Added current statistics about the effectiveness of searching for a job online, and modified list of job boards to include those most widely used by today's job seekers.
- Expanded list of employment sites to include social media sites, which are widely used by both employers and job seekers today.

- Added a new section covering tips for conducting a safe and effective online job search, including strategies for avoiding identity theft.
- Expanded tips for using online networking to tap into the hidden job market by adding advice for using Twitter during the job search.
- Strengthened section about using technology to optimize one's résumé by including information on the latest trends.
- Included information about the ethics of using hidden keywords in online résumés.

Chapter 16 — Interviewing and Following Up
- Added information about online interviews, which often take place using webcams.
- Expanded the "Before the Interview" section to include tips for ensuring professional telephone techniques and for making the first telephone conversation with a prospective employer impressive.
- Updated company research section to include strategies for using Facebook, Twitter, and other social media sites to gather information about prospective employers.
- Enhanced section on digital dirt to provide specific examples of online information that could be looked at negatively by employers. Also added list of techniques for cleaning up one's online presence.
- Expanded the "During the Interview" section to include tips for travelling to and arriving at the job interview.
- Added a new Career Coach feature that provides techniques for fighting fear during the job interview.

Resources for Instructors

The Nelson Education Teaching Advantage (NETA) program delivers research-based instructor resources that promote student engagement and higher-order thinking to enable the success of Canadian students and educators.

Instructors today face many challenges. Resources are limited, time is scarce, and a new kind of student has emerged: one who is juggling school with work, has gaps in his or her basic knowledge, and is immersed in technology in a way that has led to a completely new style of learning. In response, Nelson Education has gathered a group of dedicated instructors to advise us on the creation of richer and more flexible ancillaries that respond to the needs of today's teaching environments.

The members of our editorial advisory board have experience across a variety of disciplines and are recognized for their commitment to teaching. They include

Norman Althouse, Haskayne School of Business, University of Calgary

Brenda Chant-Smith, Department of Psychology, Trent University

Scott Follows, Manning School of Business Administration, Acadia University

Jon Houseman, Department of Biology, University of Ottawa

Glen Loppnow, Department of Chemistry, University of Alberta

Tanya Noel, Department of Biology, York University

Gary Poole, Director, Centre for Teaching and Academic Growth and School of Population and Public Health, University of British Columbia

Dan Pratt, Department of Educational Studies, University of British Columbia

Mercedes Rowinsky-Geurts, Department of Languages and Literatures, Wilfrid Laurier University

David DiBattista, Department of Psychology, Brock University

Roger Fisher, PhD

In consultation with the editorial advisory board, Nelson Education has completely rethought the structure, approaches, and formats of our key textbook ancillaries. We've also increased our investment in editorial support for our ancillary authors. The result is the Nelson Education Teaching Advantage and its key components: NETA Engagement, NETA Assessment, and NETA Presentation. Each component includes one or more ancillaries prepared according to our best practices, and a document explaining the theory behind the practices.

NETA Engagement presents materials that help instructors deliver engaging content and activities to their classes. Instead of Instructor's Manuals that regurgitate chapter outlines and key terms from the text, NETA Enriched Instructor's Manuals (EIMs) provide genuine assistance to teachers. The EIMs answer questions like *What should students learn?, Why should students care?*, and *What are some common student misconceptions and stumbling blocks?* EIMs not only identify the topics that cause students the most difficulty, but also describe techniques and resources to help students master these concepts. Dr. Roger Fisher's *Instructor's Guide to Classroom Engagement* (IGCE) accompanies every Enriched Instructor's Manual. (Information about the NETA Enriched Instructor's Manual prepared for *Business Communication: Process and Product*, Fourth Brief Canadian Edition, is included in the description of the IRCD below.)

NETA Assessment relates to testing materials: not just Nelson's Test Banks and Computerized Test Banks, but also in-text self-tests, Study Guides and web quizzes, and homework programs like CNOW. Under NETA Assessment, Nelson's authors create multiple-choice questions that reflect research-based best practices for constructing effective questions and testing not just recall but also higher-order thinking. Our guidelines were developed by David DiBattista, a 3M National Teaching Fellow whose recent research as a professor of psychology at Brock University has focused on multiple-choice testing. All Test Bank authors receive training at workshops conducted by Professor DiBattista, as do the copyeditors assigned to each Test Bank. A copy of *Multiple Choice Tests: Getting Beyond Remembering*, Professor DiBattista's guide to writing effective tests, is included with every Nelson Test Bank/Computerized Test Bank package. (Information about the NETA Test Bank prepared for *Business Communication: Process and Product* is included in the description of the IRCD below.)

NETA Presentation has been developed to help instructors make the best use of PowerPoint® in their classrooms. With a clean and uncluttered design developed by Maureen Stone of StoneSoup Consulting, NETA Presentation features slides with improved readability, more multimedia and graphic materials, activities to use in class, and tips for instructors on the Notes page. A copy of *NETA Guidelines for Classroom Presentations* by Maureen Stone is included with each set of PowerPoint slides. (Information about the NETA PowerPoint® prepared for *Business Communication: Process and Product* is included in the description of the IRCD below.)

IRCD

Key instructor ancillaries are provided on the Instructor's Resource CD (ISBN 978-0-17-662888-8), giving instructors the ultimate tool for customizing lectures and presentations. (Downloadable web versions are also available at www.guffeybrief4e.nelson.com.) The IRCD includes

- **NETA Engagement:** The Enriched Instructor's Manual was written by Esther Griffin, Georgian College. It is organized according to the textbook chapters and addresses key educational concerns, such as how to actively engage students in the classroom and in an online learning environment. The manual focuses on student engagement strategies and making the content relevant to all learners. It includes interactive discussion questions and classroom and online delivery activities, as well as a Reflections on Teaching section for faculty. Other features include *Answers to Chapter Review Questions, Critical Thinking,* and *Activities.*

- **NETA Assessment:** The Test Bank was also written by Esther Griffin of Georgian College. It includes over 900 multiple-choice questions written according to NETA guidelines for effective construction and development of higher-order questions. Also included are over 600 true/false questions and over 50 essay-type questions. Test Bank files are provided in Word format for easy editing and in PDF format for convenient printing whatever your system.

  The Computerized Test Bank by ExamView® includes all the questions from the Test Bank. The easy-to-use ExamView software is compatible with Microsoft Windows and Mac. Create tests by selecting questions from the question bank, modifying these questions as desired, and adding new questions you write yourself. You can administer quizzes online and export tests to WebCT, Blackboard, and other formats.

- **NETA Presentation:** Microsoft® PowerPoint® lecture slides for every chapter have been created by Katherine Ferguson of Seneca College of Applied Arts and Technology. There are between 20 and 30 slides per chapter, many featuring key figures, tables, and photographs from *Business Communication: Process and Product.* NETA principles of clear design and engaging content have been incorporated throughout.

Image Library: This resource consists of digital copies of figures, short tables, and photographs used in the book. Instructors may use these jpegs to create their own PowerPoint presentations.

- **DayOne:** Day One—Prof InClass is a PowerPoint presentation that you can customize to orient your students to the class and their text at the beginning of the course.

CourseMate   CourseMate

Nelson Education's Business Communication CourseMate brings course concepts to life with interactive learning and exam preparation tools that integrate with the printed textbook. Students activate their knowledge through quizzes, games, and flashcards, among many other tools.

CourseMate provides immediate feedback that enables students to connect results to the work they have just produced, increasing their learning effectiveness. It encourages contact between students and faculty: You can choose to monitor your students' level of engagement with CourseMate, correlating their efforts to their outcomes. You can even use CourseMate's quizzes to practise "Just in Time" teaching by tracking results in the Engagement Tracker and customizing your lesson plans to address their learning needs.

Watch student comprehension and engagement soar as your class engages with CourseMate. Ask your Nelson representative for a demo today.

Video Resources

New to this edition! Enhance your classroom experience with the exciting and relevant videos of the DVD prepared to accompany *Business Communication: Process and Product*. This video resource is designed to enrich, support, and bring chapter concepts to life in class.

Resources for Students

 The more you study, the better the results. Make the most of your study time by accessing everything you need to succeed in one place. Read your textbook, take notes, review flashcards, watch videos, and take practice quizzes—do it all online with CourseMate. All of these extra learning materials will help you to review for tests and prepare for class.

This Business Communication CourseMate includes

- An interactive eBook with highlighting, note taking, and an interactive glossary

- Interactive learning tools, including

  - Quizzes

  - Flashcards

  - Videos

  - Additional model documents

  - Cases

  - Chapter summaries

  - And much, much more!

Go to NelsonBrain.com to access these resources for your text in Business Communication CourseMate.

Acknowledgments for the Canadian Edition

We are very pleased to present the Fourth Brief Canadian Edition of *Business Communication: Process and Product*. As always, we owe a huge debt of gratitude to Dr. Mary Ellen Guffey, whose authoritative, market-driven texts and ancillaries, now written in conjunction with Dr. Dana Loewy, form the foundation and framework of this Canadian edition. In addition, we continue to appreciate the support from the team at Nelson Education Ltd.: Anne-Marie Taylor, Linda Sparks, and Natalia Denesiuk Harris.

We particularly appreciate those instructors and students who continue to choose *Business Communication: Process and Product,* especially those who provide both formal and informal feedback. Those who had a specific impact on the content of this edition include the following:

Denise Blay, Fanshawe College

Jay Buis, Lethbridge College

Rhonda Dynes, Mohawk College

Marissa Fleming, Georgian College

Gerta Grieve, NAIT

Gail Rees, Canadore College

Binod Sundararajan, Dalhousie University

The support of colleagues and friends at Durham College and other institutions continues to play an important part in our work. We thank you all.

Finally, as always, we thank our families for their unswerving support.

Kathleen Rhodes, Patricia Rogin

UNIT 1

Communication Foundations

Chapter 1
Effective and Ethical
Communication at Work

Chapter 2
Professionalism: Team,
Listening, Nonverbal,
and Etiquette Skills

Chapter 3
Intercultural
Communication

Simon Potter/Getty Images

CHAPTER 1

Effective and Ethical Communication at Work

OBJECTIVES

After studying this chapter, you should be able to

1. Understand the importance of communication skills in relation to career success and explain the need for thinking critically and taking charge of your career.

2. Recognize significant trends in today's dynamic workplace and how these trends increase the need for excellent communication skills.

3. Analyze the process of communication and understand how to use it effectively.

4. Recognize barriers to interpersonal communication and examine specific strategies for overcoming those barriers.

5. Understand the internal and external functions of communication in organizations and compare and contrast the advantages and disadvantages of oral and written communication.

6. Examine critically the flow of communication in organizations and understand how to overcome typical barriers and respond ethically to office gossip.

7. Analyze ethics in the workplace, understand the ethical goals of business communicators, and apply tools for doing the right thing.

Purestock/Getty Images

With the increase in technology and the ability to work from satellite locations, individual office space has declined from an average of between 45 and 65 m² per person in the 1960s and 1970s to 19 m² per person today. The decrease has happened not only to reduce real estate costs but also to acknowledge flexibility in the workplace. In 2015, when millennials will compose more than half of the workforce, the focus will be on performance and output, not physical office space.[1] How has technology changed the perception of the office? What size of workspace is reasonable for you?

Communication Skills and You

Developing excellent communication skills is extremely important to your career success, whether you are already working or are about to enter today's workplace. Such skills are particularly significant at a time when jobs are scarce and competition is keen. During an economic downturn, many candidates vie for fewer job openings. Those candidates with exceptional communication skills will immediately have an edge over others. In this chapter you will learn about the importance of communication skills, the changing world of work, the process of communication and its barriers, and ethical goals and tools to help you do the right thing. Each section covers the latest information about an issue. It also provides tips and suggestions that will help you function successfully in today's dynamic workplace.

LEARNING OBJECTIVE 1

Understand the importance of communication skills in relation to career success and explain the need for thinking critically and taking charge of your career.

The Importance of Communication Skills to Your Career Success

Surveys of employers consistently show that communication skills are critical to effective job placement, performance, career advancement, and organizational success. In making hiring decisions, employers often rank communication skills among the most requested items. Many job advertisements specifically ask for excellent oral and written communication skills. In several polls of recruiters, oral and written communication skills were by a large margin the top skill set sought. When executives were asked what they looked for in a job candidate, the top choices were general communication skills, interpersonal skills, and teamwork skills. The majority of employers also said that communication skills are at least as important as technical skills for entry-level and management positions.[2]

When we discuss communication skills, we generally mean reading, listening, nonverbal, speaking, and writing skills. In this book we focus on listening, nonverbal, speaking, and writing skills. Chapters are devoted to each skill. Special attention is given to writing skills because they are difficult to develop and increasingly significant.

Communication skills are critical to your job placement, performance, career advancement, and organizational success.

Writing Skills Are More Important Than Ever

Writing skills are especially important today. Technology enables us to transmit messages more rapidly, more often, and more widely than ever before. Writing skills are also significant because many people work together but are not physically together. They stay connected through spoken and written messages. Writing skills, which were always a career advantage, are now a necessity.[3] They can be your ticket to work—or your ticket out the door. "Rightly or wrongly, people judge their colleagues based on their writing ability," says R. Craig Hogan, director of the Business Writing Centre and author of *Explicit Business Writing*. "Those who write poorly are viewed as less intelligent, less educated and less competent. Those who are articulate are seen as intelligent, educated and capable."[4]

The ability to write opens doors to professional employment. People who cannot write and communicate clearly will not be hired. If already working, they are unlikely to last long enough to be considered for promotion. In fact, business professionals may not realize how much poor writing skills can impede their careers. "It's a silent killer," Hogan says.[5]

Communication Skills Must Be Learned

You are not born with the abilities to read, listen, speak, and write effectively. These skills must be learned. Thriving in the demanding work world depends on many factors, some of which you cannot control. But one factor that you do control is how well you communicate. The goals of this book and this course are to teach you basic business communication skills, such as how to write a memo or letter and how to make a presentation. You will also learn additional powerful communication skills that will help you now and throughout your career. This book and this course may well be the most important in your entire curriculum because they will equip you with the skills most needed in today's dynamic workplace.

Thriving as a Knowledge Worker in the Information Age

Regardless of economic downturns and recoveries, we continue to live in an economy based on information and knowledge. The computer, the mobile phone, and the Internet are all instrumental in the continuing development of the Information Age. Previously, in the Industrial Age, raw materials and physical labour were the key ingredients in the creation of wealth. Today, however, wealth depends on the development and exchange of knowledge. Individuals in the workforce offer their knowledge, not their muscles. *Knowledge workers,* a term first coined by management guru Peter Drucker, get paid for their education and their ability to learn.[6] Statistics Canada defines knowledge-based jobs as those that have high relative wages and require people to possess university degrees or some level of postsecondary education.[7] Regardless of the terminology, knowledge and information workers engage in mind work. They deal with symbols: words, figures, and data. Estimates suggest that knowledge workers outnumber other workers in North America by at least four to one.[8]

What Does This Mean for You?

As a knowledge and information worker, you can expect to be generating, processing, and exchanging information. Whether you work in the new economy of *m-commerce* (mobile technology businesses) or the old economy of *bricks-and-mortar* companies, nearly three out of four jobs will involve some form of mind work. Jobs that require thinking, brainpower, and decision-making skills are likely to remain plentiful. To be successful in these jobs, you will need to be able to think critically, make decisions, and communicate those decisions.

Learning to Think Critically

Management and employees work together in such areas as product development, quality control, and customer satisfaction. Whether you are an executive or a subordinate, you will be asked to think creatively and critically. Even in factory production lines, workers are part of the knowledge culture.

Thinking creatively and critically means having opinions that are backed by reasons and evidence. When your boss or team leader says, "What do you think we ought to do?" you want to be able to supply good ideas. The accompanying Career Coach box provides a five-point critical-thinking plan to help you solve problems and make decisions. Having a plan, however, is not enough. You also need chances to try out the plan and get feedback from colleagues and your boss (your instructor, for the time being). At the end of each chapter are activities and problems that will help you develop and apply your critical-thinking skills.

Thinking critically means having options that are backed by reason and evidence.

Taking Charge of Your Career

In today's workplace, you can look forward to constant training to acquire new skills that will help you keep up with evolving technologies and procedures. You can also expect to exercise greater control over your career. Many workers today will not find nine-to-five jobs, predictable pay increases, lifetime security, or even conventional workplaces. Don't presume that companies will provide you with a clearly defined career path or planned developmental experiences. In the private sector, you can expect to work for multiple employers, moving back and forth between work and education and between work and family responsibilities.[9] Whether you are currently employed or about to enter the constantly changing work world, you must be willing to continually learn new skills that supplement the strong foundation of basic skills you are acquiring in college or university. The most successful businesspeople are willing to become lifelong learners.

Constantly changing technologies and work procedures mean continual training for employees.

Using This Course to Advance Your Career

This book is filled with model documents, practice exercises, procedures, tips, strategies, suggestions, summaries, and checklists—all meant to ensure that you develop the superior communication skills that are vital to your success as a businessperson.

Remember, communication skills are not inherent; they must be learned. Remember, too, to take advantage of the unique opportunity you now have. You have

This book, this course, and your instructor can help you develop the skills you need to succeed in today's challenging workplace.

career coach

Sharpening Your Skills for Critical Thinking, Problem Solving, and Decision Making

Gone are the days when management expected workers to do only as they were told. As a knowledge worker, you will be expected to use your brain in thinking critically. You will be solving problems and making decisions. Much of this book is devoted to helping you learn to solve problems and communicate those decisions to management, fellow workers, clients, the government, and the public.

Faced with a problem or an issue, most of us do a lot of worrying before separating the issues or making a decision. All that worrying can become directed thinking by channelling it into the following procedure.

1. Identify and clarify the problem. Your first task is to recognize that a problem exists. Some problems are big and unmistakable, such as failure of an air-freight delivery service to get packages to customers on time. Other problems may be continuing annoyances, such as regularly running out of toner for an office copy machine. The first step in reaching a solution is pinpointing the problem.

2. Gather information. Learn more about the problem. Look for possible causes and solutions. This step may mean checking files, calling suppliers, or brainstorming with fellow workers. The air-freight delivery service, for example, would investigate the

tracking systems of the commercial airlines carrying its packages to determine what went wrong.

3. Evaluate the evidence. Where did the information come from? Does it represent various points of view? What biases could be expected from each source? How accurate is the information gathered? Is it fact or opinion? For example, it is a fact that packages are missing; it is an opinion that they are merely lost and will turn up eventually.

4. Consider alternatives and implications. Draw conclusions from the gathered evidence and pose solutions. Then weigh the advantages and disadvantages of each alternative. What are the costs, benefits, and consequences? What are the obstacles, and how can they be handled? Most important, what solution best serves your goals and those of your organization? Here's where your creativity is especially important.

5. Choose the best alternative and test it. Select an alternative and try it out to see if it meets your expectations. If it does, implement your decision. If it doesn't, rethink your alternatives. The freight company decided to give its unhappy customers free delivery service to make up for the lost packages and downtime. Be sure to continue monitoring and adjusting the solution to ensure its effectiveness over time.

an expert who is willing to work with you to help improve your writing, speaking, and other communication skills. Many organizations pay thousands of dollars to communication coaches and trainers to teach employees the very skills that you are learning in this course. Your instructor is your coach. Take advantage of this opportunity and get your money's worth! With this book as your guide and your instructor as your coach, this course, as we mentioned earlier, could be the most important in your entire postsecondary curriculum.

Trends Affecting You in Today's Dynamic Workplace

LEARNING OBJECTIVE **2**

Recognize significant trends in today's dynamic workplace and how these trends increase the need for excellent communication skills.

Today's workplace is undergoing profound changes. As a businessperson and especially as a business communicator, you will undoubtedly be affected by many transformations. Some of the most significant trends include global competition, flattened management hierarchies, and team-based projects. Other trends include constantly evolving technology; the "anytime, anywhere" office; a diverse workforce; and an emphasis on ethics. The following overview of trends reveals how communication skills are closely tied to your success in a demanding, dynamic workplace.

Heightened Global Competition

Many of the changes in today's dynamic workplace make communication skills a key to your success.

Small, medium, and large companies increasingly find themselves competing in global rather than local markets. Improved systems of telecommunication, advanced forms of transportation, and saturated local markets—all these developments have encouraged companies to move beyond familiar territories to emerging markets around the world.

Communication is more complicated among people who have different religions, customs, and lifestyles.

Doing business in far-flung countries means dealing with people who may be very different from you. They may have different religions, follow different customs, live different lifestyles, and rely on different approaches in business. Now add the complications of multiple time zones, vast distances between offices, and different languages, and you can see the importance of understanding diversity.

Successful communication in these new markets requires developing new skills and attitudes. These include cultural knowledge and sensitivity, flexibility, and patience. Because these skills and attitudes may be difficult to achieve, you will receive special communication training to help you deal with intercultural business transactions.

Flattened Management Hierarchies

Flatter organizations demand that every employee be a skilled communicator.

In response to intense global competition and other pressures, businesses have been cutting costs and flattening their management hierarchies for years. This flattening means that fewer layers of managers separate decision makers from line workers. In traditional companies, information flows through many levels of managers. In flat organizations, however, where the lines of communication are shorter, decision makers can react more quickly to market changes.

Progressive organizations are in the midst of changing from "command and control" to "coordination and cultivation" management styles. This means that work is organized to let people use their own talents more wisely.[10] But today's flatter organizations also bring greater communication challenges because frontline employees and managers participate in decision making. Nearly everyone is a writer and a communicator. Nearly all employees have computers and write their own messages.

Expanded Team-Based Management

Along with flatter chains of command, companies are expanding team-based operations to increase employee involvement in decision making and to improve communication.

When companies form cross-functional teams, individuals must work together and share information. Working relationships can become strained when individuals don't share the same background, knowledge, or training. Some companies must hire communication coaches to help existing teams get along. They work to develop interpersonal, negotiation, and collaboration techniques. But companies prefer to hire new workers who already possess these skills. That is why so many advertisements for new employees say "must possess good communication skills."

Innovative Communication Technologies

New electronic technologies are dramatically affecting the way workers communicate. We now exchange information and stay in touch by using e-mail, instant messaging (IM), text messaging, personal digital assistants (PDAs), fax, voice mail, wireless networking, cellphones, powerful laptop computers, satellite communications, wireless networks, and even tweeting. Through teleconferencing and videoconferencing, we can conduct meetings with associates around the world. The rapid development of social software, such as weblogs, wikis (multiuser weblogs), and peer-to-peer tools, makes it easier for workers to communicate online and wirelessly almost instantaneously. One complaint about e-mail is that messages and documents with pertinent information are limited to senders and receivers.[11] The latest software, however, enables people in different offices to work on projects by using a single Web calendar, a to-do list, and online discussion rooms. To share information graphically, presenters use sophisticated presentation software.

All businesspeople today rely heavily on the Internet and the Web to collect information, serve customers, and sell products and services. Figure 1.1 illustrates many new technologies you will see in today's workplace.

To use these new resources most effectively, you, as a skilled business communicator, must develop a tool kit of new communication skills. You will want to know how to select the best communication channel, how to use each channel safely and effectively, and how to use online search tools efficiently. All of these topics are covered in upcoming chapters.

"Anytime, Anywhere" and Nonterritorial Offices

Today's work environments are also changing profoundly. Thanks largely to advances in high-speed and wireless Internet access, thousands of workers no longer report to nine-to-five jobs that confine them to offices. They have flexible working arrangements so that they can work at home or on the road. The "anytime, anywhere" office requires only a mobile phone and a wireless computer.[12] In 2009, it was estimated in that about 800,000 Canadians telecommuted almost daily, and about 2 million to 2.5 million workers telecommuted at least one day a week; this number increases annually.[13] To save on office real estate, a growing number of industries provide "nonterritorial" workspaces. Also known as "mobile platforms" and "hot desks," these unassigned workspaces are up for grabs. The first to arrive gets the best desk and the corner window.[14]

Even in more traditional offices, employees work in open spaces with flexible workstations, shared conference rooms, and boomerang-shaped desks that save space. Moreover, many workers are part of virtual teams that complete projects without ever meeting each other. Such tools as e-mail, instant and text messaging, file sharing, conferencing software, and wireless networking make it easy for employees to collaborate or complete their work in the office, at home, or on the road.

As more and more employees work separately, communication skills become increasingly important. Staying connected involves sending messages, most of which are written. This means that your writing skills will constantly be on display. Those who can write clear and concise messages contribute to efficient operations and can expect to be rewarded.

Increasingly Diverse Workforce

Changes in today's work environments include more than innovative technology, team management, and different work environments. The Canadian workforce is becoming

FIGURE 1.1 **Communication Technologies: Reshaping the World of Work**

Communication Technologies: Reshaping the World of Work

Today's workplace is changing dramatically as a result of innovative software, superfast wireless networks, and numerous technologies that allow workers to share information, work from remote locations, and be more productive in or away from the office. We're seeing a gradual progression from basic capabilities, such as e-mail and calendaring, to deeper functionality, such as remote database access, multifunctional devices, and Web-based collaborative applications. Becoming familiar with modern office and collaboration technologies can help you be successful in today's digital workplace.

Telephony: VoIP

Savvy businesses are switching from traditional phone service to Voice over Internet Protocol (VoIP). This technology allows callers to communicate using a broadband Internet connection, thus eliminating long-distance and local telephone charges. Higher-end VoIP systems now support unified voice mail, e-mail, click-to-call capabilities, and softphones (phones using computer networking). Free or low-cost Internet telephony sites, such as the popular Skype, are also increasingly used by businesses.

Multifunctional Printers

Stand-alone copiers, fax machines, scanners, and printers have been replaced with multifunctional devices. Offices are transitioning from a "print and distribute" environment to a "distribute and print" environment. Security measures include pass codes and even biometric thumbprint scanning to make sure data streams are not captured, interrupted, or edited.

Open Offices

Widespread use of laptop computers, wireless technology, and VoIP have led to more fluid, flexible, and open workspaces. Smaller computers and flat-screen monitors enable designers to save space with boomerang-shaped workstations and cockpit-style work surfaces rather than space-hogging corner work areas. Smaller breakout areas for impromptu meetings are taking over some cubicle space, and digital databases are replacing file cabinets.

Handheld Wireless Devices

A new generation of lightweight, handheld devices provide phone, e-mail, Web browsing, and calendar options anywhere there's a wireless network. Devices such as the Black-Berry and the Palm Treo now allow you to tap into corporate databases and intranets from remote locations. You can check customers' files, complete orders, and send out receipts without returning to the office.

Company Intranets

To share insider information, many companies provide their own protected Web sites called intranets. An intranet may handle company e-mail, announcements, an employee directory, a policy handbook, frequently asked questions, personnel forms and data, employee discussion forums, shared documents, and other employee information.

Voice Recognition

Computers equipped with voice recognition software enable users to dictate up to 160 words a minute with accurate transcription. Voice recognition is particularly helpful to disabled workers and to professionals with heavy dictation loads, such as physicians and attorneys. Users can create documents, enter data, compose and send e-mails, browse the Web, and control the desktop—all by voice.

Electronic Presentations

Business presentations in PowerPoint can be projected from a laptop or PDA or posted online. Sophisticated presentations may include animations, sound effects, digital photos, video clips, or hyperlinks to Internet sites. In some industries, PowerPoint slides ("decks") are replacing or supplementing traditional hard-copy reports.

Collaboration Technologies: Rethinking the Way We Work Together

Global competition, expanding markets, and the ever-increasing pace of business accelerate the development of exciting collaboration tools. New tools make it possible to work together without being together. Your colleagues may be down the hall, across the country, or around the world. With today's tools, you can exchange ideas, solve problems, develop products, forecast future performance, and complete team projects any time of the day or night and anywhere in the world. Blogs and wikis, part of the so-called Web 2.0 era, are social tools that create multidirectional conversations among customers and employees. Web 2.0 moves Web applications from "read only" to "read-write," thus enabling greater participation and collaboration.

Blogs, Podcasts, and Wikis

A *blog* is a Web site with journal entries usually written by one person with comments added by others. Businesses use blogs to keep customers and employees informed and to receive feedback. Company developments can be posted, updated, and categorized for easy cross-referencing. When the writer adds audio, the blog becomes a *podcast*. A *wiki* is a Web site that allows multiple users to collaboratively create and edit pages. Information gets lost in e-mails, but blogs and wikis provide an easy way to communicate and keep track of what's said.

Voice Conferencing

Telephone "bridges" allow two or more callers from any location to share the same call. *Voice conferencing* (also called *audioconferencing*, *teleconferencing*, or just plain *conference calling*) enables people to collaborate by telephone. Communicators at both ends use enhanced speakerphones to talk and be heard simultaneously.

Videoconferencing

Videoconferencing allows participants to meet in special conference rooms equipped with cameras and television screens. Groups see each other and interact in real time although they may be far apart. Faster computers, rapid Internet connections, and better cameras now enable 2 to 200 participants to sit at their own PCs and share applications, spreadsheets, presentations, and photos.

Web Conferencing

With services such as GoToMeeting, WebEx, or Microsoft LiveMeeting, all you need are a PC and an Internet connection to hold a meeting (*webinar*) with customers or colleagues in real time. Although the functions are constantly evolving, Web conferencing currently incorporates screen sharing, chats, slide presentations, text messaging, and application sharing.

Presence Technology

Presence technology makes it possible to locate and identify a computing device as soon as users connect to the network. This technology is an integral part of communication devices including cell phones, laptop computers, PDAs, pagers, and GPS devices. Collaboration is possible wherever and whenever users are online.

Video Phones

Using advanced video compression technology, video phones transmit real-time audio and video so that communicators can see each other as they collaborate. With a video phone, people can videoconference anywhere in the world over a broadband IP (Internet Protocol) connection without a computer or a television screen.

increasingly diverse. Projections report that by 2017 about one in five Canadians will be a member of a visible minority group, compared with 13 percent in 2001 and less than 5 percent of the Canadian population in 1981.[15] Predictions are that by 2015, 48 percent of Canada's working population will be between the ages of 46 and 64, compared with 29 percent in 1991.[16] As a result of these and other demographic trends, businesses must create a work environment that values and supports all people.

Communicating in this diverse work environment requires new attitudes and skills. Acquiring these new employment skills is certainly worth the effort because of the benefits diversity brings to consumers, work teams, and business organizations. A diverse staff is better able to read trends and respond to the increasingly diverse customer base in local and world markets. In the workplace diversity also makes good business sense. Teams made up of people with various experiences are more likely to create the products that consumers demand. Customers also want to deal with companies that respect their values. Learning to cooperate and communicate successfully with diverse co-workers should be a major priority for all businesspeople.

Understanding the Process of Communication

Because communication is a central factor in the emerging knowledge economy and a major consideration for anyone entering today's workforce, we need to look more closely at the total process of communication. Just what is communication? For our purposes communication is the *transmission of information and meaning from one individual or group to another*. The crucial element in this definition is meaning. Communication has as its central objective the transmission of meaning. The process of communication is successful only when the receiver understands an idea as the sender intended it. Both parties must agree not only on the information transmitted but also on the meaning of that information. How does an idea travel from one person to another? We engage in a sensitive process of communication, discussed here and depicted in Figure 1.2.

FIGURE 1.2 The Communication Process

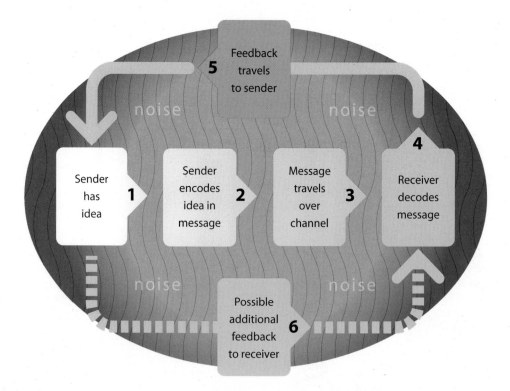

Sender Has Idea

The process of communication begins when the person with whom the message originates—*the sender*—has an idea. The form of the idea will be influenced by complex factors surrounding the sender: mood, frame of reference, background, culture, and physical makeup, as well as the context of the situation and many other factors. The way you greet people on campus or on the job, for example, depends a lot on how you feel, whom you are addressing (a classmate, a professor, a colleague, or your boss), and what your culture has trained you to say.

The form of the idea, whether a simple greeting or a complex idea, is shaped by assumptions based on the sender's experiences. A manager sending an e-mail announcement to employees assumes that they will be receptive, whereas direct-mail advertisers assume that receivers will give only a quick glance to their message. The ability to accurately predict how a message will affect its receiver and the skill in adapting that message to its receiver are key factors in successful communication.

Sender Encodes Idea in Message

The next step in the communication process involves encoding. This means converting the idea into words or gestures that will convey meaning. A major problem in communicating any message verbally is that words have different meanings for different people. When misunderstandings result from missed meanings, it is called *bypassing*. Recognizing how easy it is to be misunderstood, skilled communicators choose familiar words with concrete meanings on which both senders and receivers agree.

In selecting proper symbols, senders must be alert to the receiver's communication skills, attitudes, background, experiences, and culture: How will the selected words affect the receiver? Because the sender initiates a communication transaction, he or she has primary responsibility for its success or failure. Choosing appropriate words or symbols is critical to a successful message.

Message Travels Over Channel

The medium over which the message is physically transmitted is the channel. Messages may be delivered by computer, telephone, cellphone, letter, memorandum, report, announcement, picture, spoken word, fax, or Web page, or through some other channel. Because communication channels deliver both verbal and nonverbal messages, senders must choose the channel and shape the message carefully. A company may use its annual report, for example, as a channel to deliver many messages to stockholders. The verbal message lies in the report's financial and organizational news. Nonverbal messages, though, are conveyed by the report's appearance (showy versus bland), layout (ample white space versus tightly packed columns of print), and tone (conversational versus formal).

Anything that interrupts the transmission of a message in the communication process is called *noise*. Channel noise ranges from static that disrupts a telephone conversation to typographical and spelling errors in a letter or e-mail message. Such errors damage the credibility of the sender. Channel noise might even include the annoyance a receiver feels when the sender chooses an improper medium for sending a message, such as announcing a loan rejection via postcard or firing an employee by e-mail.

Receiver Decodes Message

The individual for whom the message is intended is the *receiver*. Translating the message from its symbol form into meaning involves *decoding*. Only when the receiver understands the meaning intended by the sender—that is, successfully decodes the message—does communication take place. Such success, however, is difficult to achieve because no two people share the same life experiences and because many barriers can disrupt the process.

Decoding can be disrupted internally by the receiver's lack of attention to or bias against the sender. It can be disrupted externally by loud sounds or illegible words. Decoding can also be sidetracked by semantic obstacles, such as misunderstood words or emotional reactions to certain terms. A memo that refers to groups of individuals as "baby-boomers" or "Gen Xers" for example, may disturb its receivers so much that they fail to comprehend the total message.

Feedback Travels to Sender

Asking questions encourages feedback that clarifies communication.

The verbal and nonverbal responses of the receiver create *feedback,* a vital part of the communication process. Feedback helps the sender know that the message was received and understood. If, as a receiver, you hear the message *How are you?* your feedback might consist of words (*I'm fine*) or body language (a smile or a wave of the hand). Although the receiver may respond with additional feedback to the sender (thus creating a new act of communication), we concentrate here on the initial message flowing to the receiver and the resulting feedback.

Senders can encourage feedback by asking questions, such as, *Am I making myself clear?* or *Is there anything you don't understand?* Senders can further improve feedback by timing the delivery appropriately and by providing only as much information as the receiver can handle. Receivers can improve the process by paraphrasing the sender's message with comments, such as, *Let me try to explain that in my own words.* The best feedback is descriptive rather than evaluative. For example, here's a descriptive response: *I understand you want to launch a used golf ball business.* Here's an evaluative response: *Your business ideas are always weird.* An evaluative response is judgmental and doesn't tell the sender whether the receiver actually understood the message.

Overcoming Interpersonal Communication Barriers

LEARNING OBJECTIVE **4**

Recognize barriers to interpersonal communication and examine specific strategies for overcoming those barriers.

The communication process is successful only when the receiver understands the message as intended by the sender. It sounds quite simple. Yet it is not. How many times have you thought that you delivered a clear message, only to learn later that your intentions were totally misunderstood? Most messages that we send reach their destination, but many are only partially understood.

Obstacles That Create Misunderstanding

You can improve your chances of communicating successfully by learning to recognize barriers that are known to disrupt the process. The most significant barriers for individuals are bypassing, differing frames of reference, lack of language skill, and distractions.

Barriers to successful communication include bypassing, differing frames of reference, lack of language or listening skills, emotional interference, and physical distractions.

Bypassing. One of the biggest barriers to clear communication involves words. Each of us attaches a little bundle of meanings to every word, and these meanings are not always similar. *Bypassing* happens when people miss each other with their meanings.[17] Bypassing can lead to major miscommunication because people assume that meanings are contained in words; however, meanings are actually in people. For communication to be successful, the receiver and sender must attach the same symbolic meanings to their words.

Miscommunication often results when the sender's frame of reference differs markedly from the receiver's.

Differing Frames of Reference. Another barrier to clear communication is your *frame of reference.* Everything you see and feel in the world is translated through your individual frame of reference. Your unique frame is formed by a combination of your experiences, education, culture, expectations, personality, and other elements. As a result, you bring your own biases and expectations to any communication situation. Because your frame of reference is different from everyone else's, you will never see things exactly as others do. Wise business communicators strive to prevent miscommunication by being alert to both their own frames of reference and those of others.

Lack of Language Skill. No matter how extraordinary the idea, it won't be understood or fully appreciated unless the communicators involved have good language skills. Each individual needs an adequate vocabulary, a command of basic punctuation and grammar, and skill in written and oral expression. Moreover, poor listening skills can prevent people from hearing oral messages clearly and thus responding properly.

Distractions. Other barriers include emotional interference, physical distractions, and digital interruptions. Shaping an intelligent message is difficult when one is feeling joy, fear, resentment, hostility, sadness, or some other strong emotion. To reduce the influence of emotions on communication, both senders and receivers should focus on the content of the message and try to remain objective. Physical distractions, such as faulty acoustics, noisy surroundings, or a poor cellphone connection, can disrupt oral communication. Similarly, sloppy appearance, poor printing, careless formatting, and typographical or spelling errors can disrupt written messages. What's more, technology doesn't seem to be helping. Knowledge workers are increasingly distracted by multitasking, information overload, conflicting demands, and constant digital availability digitally. Clear communication requires focusing on what is important and shutting out interruptions.[18]

Overcoming Communication Obstacles

Careful communicators can conquer barriers in a number of ways. Half the battle in communicating successfully is recognizing that the entire process is sensitive and susceptible to breakdown. Like a defensive driver anticipating problems on the road, a good communicator anticipates problems in encoding, transmitting, and decoding a message. Effective communicators also focus on the receiver's environment and frame of reference. They ask themselves such questions as, *How is that individual likely to react to my message?* or *Does the receiver know as much about the subject as I do?*

Misunderstandings are less likely if you arrange your ideas logically and use words precisely. But communicating is more than expressing yourself well. A large part of successful communication is listening. Effective communicators create an environment for useful feedback. In oral communication this means asking such questions as, *Do you understand?* and *What questions do you have?* as well as encouraging listeners to repeat instructions or paraphrase ideas. As a listener it means providing feedback that describes rather than evaluates. In written communication it means asking questions and providing access: *Do you have my phone numbers in case you have questions?* or *Here's my e-mail address so that you can give me your response immediately.*

> To overcome obstacles, communicators must anticipate problems in encoding, transmitting, and decoding.

> Good communicators ask questions to stimulate feedback.

Communicating in Business Organizations

Until now you've probably been thinking about the communication you do personally. But business communicators must also be concerned with the bigger picture, and that involves sharing information in organizations. On the job you will be sharing information by communicating internally and externally.

Understanding Internal and External Functions

Internal communication includes exchanging ideas and messages with superiors, co-workers, and subordinates. When those messages must be written, you will probably choose e-mail (see Figure 1.3). When you are communicating externally with customers, suppliers, the government, and the public, you may send letters on company stationery.

Some of the functions of internal communication are to issue and clarify procedures and policies, inform management of progress, develop new products and services, persuade employees or management to make changes or improvements, coordinate activities, and evaluate and reward employees. External functions involve answering inquiries about products or services, persuading customers to buy products or services, clarifying supplier specifications, issuing credit, collecting bills, responding to government agencies, and promoting a positive image of the organization.

> **LEARNING OBJECTIVE 5**
>
> Understand the internal and external functions of communication in organizations and compare and contrast the advantages and disadvantages of oral and written communication.

> Internal communication often consists of e-mail, memos, and voice messages; external communication generally consists of letters.

FIGURE 1.3 Functions of Business Communication

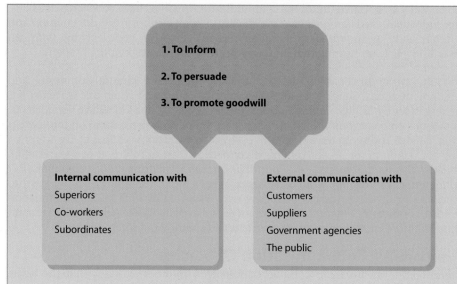

1. To Inform

2. To persuade

3. To promote goodwill

Internal communication with
Superiors
Co-workers
Subordinates

External communication with
Customers
Suppliers
Government agencies
The public

Organizational communication has three basic functions: to inform, to persuade, and to promote goodwill.

In all of these tasks, employees and managers use a number of communication skills: reading, listening, speaking, and writing. As postsecondary students and workers, you probably realize that you need to raise these skills to the proficiency level required for success in today's knowledge society. This book and this course will provide you with practical advice on how to do just that.

Look back over the preceding discussion of internal and external functions of communication in organizations. Although there appear to be a large number of diverse business communication functions, they can be summarized in three simple categories, as Figure 1.3 shows: (1) to inform, (2) to persuade, and (3) to promote goodwill.

Shifting to Interactive, Mobile, and Instant Communication

Communication media are changing from one-sided, slow forms to more interactive, fast-results forms of communication.

The flattening of organizations, coupled with the development of sophisticated information technology, has greatly changed the way we communicate internally and externally. One major shift is away from one-sided, slow forms of communication, such as memos and letters, to more interactive, fast-results communication. Speeding up the flow of communication are e-mail, instant messaging (IM), text messaging, smartphones, voice mail, cellphones, and wireless fidelity (Wi-Fi) networks. Wi-Fi lets mobile workers connect to the Internet without cables at ultrafast speeds.

Many workers can't imagine their lives without instant and text messaging. *Instant messaging* is a type of communications service that allows you to create a private chat room to communicate in real time over the Internet. Typically, the instant messaging system alerts you when someone on your private list is online. *Text messaging* involves sending short text messages usually to a wireless device, such as a cellphone or PDA. Many companies issue smartphones, notably the BlackBerry, to staff members who travel but must stay in connect with customers.

Other forms of interactive communication include intranets (company versions of the Internet), Web sites, video transmission, videoconferencing, and Web chats. You will learn more about these forms of communication in other chapters. Despite the range of interactive technologies, communicators are still working with two basic forms of communication: oral and written. Each has advantages and disadvantages.

Understanding the Advantages and Disadvantages of Oral Communication

Nearly everyone agrees that the best way to exchange information is orally in face-to-face conversations or meetings. Oral communication has many advantages. For one thing, it minimizes misunderstandings because communicators can immediately ask questions to clarify uncertainties. For another, it enables communicators to see each other's facial expressions and hear voice inflections, further improving the process. Oral communication is also an efficient way to develop consensus when many people must be consulted. Finally, most of us enjoy face-to-face interpersonal communication because it is easy, feels warm and natural, and promotes friendships.

The main disadvantages of oral communication are that it produces no written record, sometimes wastes time, and may be inconvenient. When individuals meet face to face or speak on the telephone, someone's work has to be interrupted. And how many of us are able to limit a conversation to just business? Nevertheless, oral communication has many advantages. The forms and advantages of both oral and written communication are summarized in Figure 1.4.

> Oral communication minimizes miscommunication but provides no written record.

Understanding the Advantages and Disadvantages of Written Communication

Written communication is impersonal in the sense that two communicators cannot see or hear each other and cannot provide immediate feedback. Most forms of business communication—including e-mail, announcements, memos, faxes, letters, newsletters, reports, proposals, manuals, instant messages, Web sites, blogs, wikis, and résumés—fall into this category.

Organizations rely on written communication for many reasons. It provides a permanent record, a necessity in these times of increasing litigation and extensive government regulation. Writing out an idea instead of delivering it orally enables communicators to develop an organized, well-considered message. Written documents are also convenient. They can be composed and read when the schedules of both communicators permit, and they can be reviewed if necessary.

Written messages have drawbacks, of course. They require careful preparation. Words spoken in conversation may soon be forgotten, but words committed to hard or soft copy become a public record—and sometimes an embarrassing or dangerous one. E-mail and text-messaging records, even deleted ones, have often become "smoking guns" in court cases, revealing insider information that was never meant for public consumption.[19]

Another drawback to written messages is that they are more difficult to prepare. They demand good writing skills, and we are not born with these skills. But writing

> Written communication provides a permanent record but lacks immediate feedback.

> Written messages demand good writing skills, which can be developed through training.

FIGURE 1.4 Comparing Oral and Written Forms of Organizational Communication

	Forms	Advantages	Disadvantages
Oral Communication	Telephone call, conversation, interview, meeting, conference	Provides immediate feedback, can be adjusted to audience, can be delivered quickly, supplies nonverbal cues, may create warm feeling, can be forceful	Lacks permanent record, may contain careless or imprecise expression, may be inappropriate for formal or complex ideas, does not promote easy recall
Written Communication	E-mail, memo, letter, fax, instructions, procedures, policy, report, proposal, manual, newsletter, instant message, Web site, blog, wiki, résumé	Creates permanent record, is convenient to distribute, may be economical, promotes comprehension and recall, allows precise and uniform expression, gives audience flexibility in when and how to receive content	Leaves paper trail, requires skill and effort to produce, lacks verbal cues and warmth, cannot be immediately modified based on audience feedback, may seem impersonal

proficiency can be learned. Because as much as 90 percent of all business transactions may involve written messages and because writing skills are so important to your business success, you will be receiving special instruction in becoming a good writer.

Improving the Flow of Information in Organizations

LEARNING OBJECTIVE 6

Examine critically the flow of communication in organizations and understand how to overcome typical barriers and respond ethically to office gossip.

Information within organizations flows through formal and informal communication channels. A free exchange of information helps organizations respond rapidly to changing markets, boost efficiency and productivity, build employee morale, serve the public, and take full advantage of the ideas of today's knowledge workers. Barriers, however, can obstruct the flow of communication.

Formal Communication Channels

Formal channels of communication generally follow an organization's hierarchy of command. Information about policies and procedures originates with executives and flows down through managers to supervisors and finally to lower-level employees. Many organizations have formulated official communication policies that encourage regular open communication, suggest means for achieving it, and spell out responsibilities. Official information among workers typically flows through formal channels in three directions: downward, upward, and horizontally.

Formal communication channels follow an organization's chain of command.

Downward Information Flow. Information flowing downward generally moves from decision makers, including the CEO and managers, through the chain of command to workers. This information includes job plans, policies, and procedures. Managers also provide feedback about employee performance and instil a sense of mission in achieving the organization's goals.

Obstacles to Downward Flow. One obstacle that can impede the downward flow of information is distortion resulting from long lines of communication. The longer the lines of communication, the greater the chance that a message will be distorted.

Job plans, policies, instructions, feedback, and procedures flow downward from managers to employees.

Improving Downward Information Flow. To improve communication and to compete more effectively, many of today's companies have restructured and reengineered themselves into smaller operating units and work teams. Rather than being bogged down with long communication chains, management speaks directly to team leaders, thus speeding up the entire process. Management is also improving the downward flow of information through newsletters, announcements, meetings, videos, blogs, podcasts, and company intranets. Instead of hoarding information at the top, today's managers recognize the importance of letting workers know how well the company is doing and what new projects are planned.

Upward Information Flow. Information flowing upward provides feedback from nonmanagement employees to management. Subordinate employees describe progress in completing tasks, report roadblocks encountered, and suggest methods for improving efficiency. Channels for upward communication include phone messages, e-mail, memos, reports, departmental meetings, and suggestion systems. Ideally, the heaviest flow of information should be upward, with information being fed steadily to decision makers.

Feedback from employees forms the upward flow of communication in most organizations.

Obstacles to Upward Information Flow. A number of obstacles can interrupt the upward flow of communication. Employees who distrust their employers are less likely to communicate openly. Employees cease trusting managers if they feel they are being tricked, manipulated, criticized, or treated unfairly. Downsizing, cost-cutting measures, the use of temporary workers, discrimination and harassment suits, outsourcing, outrageous compensation packages for chief executives, and many other factors have lessened the feelings of trust and pride that employees once felt toward their employers and their jobs. Other obstacles include fear of reprisal for honest communication, lack of adequate communication skills, and differing frames of reference. Imperfect communication results when individuals are not using words or symbols with similar meanings, when they cannot express their ideas clearly, or when they come from different backgrounds.

Improving Upward Information Flow. To improve the upward flow of communication, some companies are (a) hiring communication coaches to train employees; (b) asking employees to report customer complaints; (c) encouraging regular meetings with staff; (d) providing a trusting, nonthreatening environment in which employees can comfortably share their observations and ideas with management; and (e) offering incentive programs that encourage employees to collect and share valuable feedback. Companies are also building trust by setting up hotlines for anonymous feedback to management and by installing ombudsman programs. An *ombudsman* is a mediator who hears employee complaints, investigates, and seeks to resolve problems fairly.

Horizontal Information Flow. Lateral channels transmit information horizontally among workers at the same level. These channels enable individuals to coordinate tasks, share information, solve problems, and resolve conflicts. Horizontal communication takes place through personal contact, telephone, e-mail, memos, voice mail, and meetings. Most traditional organizations have few established regular channels for the horizontal exchange of information. Restructured companies with flattened hierarchies and team-based management, however, have discovered that when employees combine their knowledge with that of other employees, they can do their jobs better. Much information in these organizations travels horizontally among team members.[20]

Workers coordinate tasks, share information, solve problems, and resolve conflicts through horizontal communication.

Obstacles to Horizontal Information Flow. Obstacles to the horizontal flow of communication, as well as to upward and downward flow, include poor communication skills, prejudice, ego involvement, and turf wars. Some employees avoid sharing information if doing so might endanger their status or chances for promotion within the organization. Competition within units and an uneven reward system may also prevent workers from freely sharing information.

Improving Horizontal Information Flow. To improve horizontal communication, companies are (a) training employees in teamwork and communication techniques, (b) establishing reward systems based on team achievement rather than individual achievement, and (c) encouraging full participation in team functions. However, employees must also realize that they are personally responsible for making themselves heard, for really understanding what other people say, and for getting the information they need. Developing those business communication skills is exactly what this book and this course will do for you.

Informal Communication Channels

Most organizations today share company news through consistent, formal channels, such as e-mail and staff meetings, a recent survey shows. However, as many as 20 percent do not provide consistent channels to share company news.[21] Even within organizations with consistent formal channels, people still gossip about company news. The grapevine is an informal channel of communication that carries organizationally relevant gossip. This powerful but informal channel functions through social relationships; people talk about work when they are lunching, working out, golfing, and carpooling, as well as in e-mails, texts, and blogs. At one time gossip took place around the water cooler. Today, however, a study of office workers reveals that gossip usually takes place in the office break room (36 percent), at a co-worker's desk (33 percent), or in e-mails and instant messages (10 percent).[22]

Using the Grapevine Productively. Researchers studying communication flow within organizations know that the grapevine can be a powerful, pervasive source of information. In some organizations it can account for as much as two thirds of an employee's information. Is this bad? Well, yes and no. The grapevine can be a fairly accurate and speedy source of organization information. Studies have demonstrated accuracy ratings of nearly 80 percent for many grapevine transmissions.[23] When employees obtain most of their company news from the grapevine, management is not releasing sufficient information through formal channels.

Managers can influence the grapevine by (a) respecting employees' desire to know, (b) increasing the amount of information delivered through formal channels, (c) sharing bad and good news, (d) monitoring the grapevine, and (e) acting promptly to correct misinformation.[24] The truth is that most employees want to know what's going on. In fact, one study found that regardless of how much information organization members reported receiving, they wanted more.[25] Many companies today have moved away from a rigid authoritarian management structure in which only managers were allowed to see vital information, such as product success and profit figures. Employees who know the latest information feel like important members of the team.[26] Through formal lines of communication, smart companies are keeping employees informed.

Responding Ethically to Office Gossip. To many of us, gossip is fun and even entertaining. It encourages social bonding and makes us feel close to others who share our trust. We feel a part of the group and that we can influence others when we share a significant tidbit. We might even argue that gossip is good because it can help people learn how to behave and how to respond to social miscues faster and less awkwardly than if they made the mistakes themselves.

However, not all gossip is harmless. Someone known as an office gossip can be viewed as untrustworthy and unpromotable. Even more damaging, malicious gossip spread in e-mails or text messages can be used in defamation cases. It can also become evidence against employers in supporting charges of harassment or a maintaining a hostile work environment. Unfounded gossip can ruin careers and harm companies. In addition, employers look upon gossip as a productivity drain. The time spent gossiping reduces the time spent working.

How can you respond ethically to gossip or reduce its occurrence? Workplace ethics expert Nan DeMars offers several helpful pointers on her Internet ethics Web site (**www.office-ethics.com**):

- **Run, don't walk, away from anyone who starts to gossip.** Even if you don't contribute to the conversation, just being present indicates consent.

- **End rumours about others.** If you overhear something that is untrue, step up and say so. People will respect your integrity.

- **Attack rumours about yourself.** Be aggressive and determine who originated the remark, if possible. Always follow with documentation explaining what really happened.

- **Keep confidences.** Become known as someone who is close-mouthed.

- **Limit the personal tidbits you share about yourself and keep them on the light side.** Too much information may be blown out of proportion or become tempting for someone else to expand on. Trust only those who have earned your confidence.

- **Avoid any form of co-worker belittlement.** Today's co-worker may be tomorrow's senior vice president.

- **Build co-workers up; don't tear them down.** If you must use the grapevine, use it to praise co-workers. They will remember.[27]

Examining Business Communication Ethics

Recent media reports seem to increasingly focus on workplace or business ethics. Reports centre not only on issues of workplace corruption, fraud, influence peddling, and cronyism but also on ethical questions relating to policies on human rights, animal welfare, genetic engineering, relations with developing nations, and the environment.[28] As a business communicator, you should understand basic ethical principles so that you can make logical decisions when faced with dilemmas in the workplace. Professionals in any field must deal with moral dilemmas on the job. However, just being a moral person and having sound personal ethics may not be sufficient to handle the ethical issues that you may face in the workplace.

LEARNING OBJECTIVE **7**

Analyze ethics in the workplace, understand the ethical goals of business communicators, and apply tools for doing the right thing.

What Is Ethics?

Ethics refers to conventional standards of right and wrong that prescribe what people should do. These standards usually consist of rights, obligations, and benefits to society. They also include virtues, such as fairness, honesty, loyalty, and concern for others. Ethics is about having values and taking responsibility. Ethical individuals are expected to follow the law and refrain from theft, murder, assault, slander, and fraud.

In our discussion of ethics, we will examine ethics in the workplace, study goals of ethical business communicators, and learn tools for doing the right thing.

Examining Ethics in the Workplace

On the job you will face many dilemmas, and you will want to react ethically. To help their employees make the right decisions, many organizations have codes of ethics and training programs in place. In a recent survey conducted by KPMG on ethics training in Canadian organizations, 81.5 percent of respondents were implementing initiatives to promote ethical practice, and 70.6 percent provided ethics training.[29]

Determining the right thing to do, however, is not always an easy task. Despite workplace policy document, few solid rules guide us. For some people, following the law seems to be enough. They think that anything legal must also be ethical or moral. Most people, however, believe that ethical standards rise to a higher level. What are those standards? Although many ethical dilemmas have no "right" answer, one solution is often better than another. In choosing that solution, keep in mind the goals of ethical business communicators.

Goals of Ethical Business Communicators

Taking ethics into consideration can be painful in the short term. But in the long term, ethical behaviour makes sense and pays off. Dealing honestly with colleagues and customers develops trust and builds stronger relationships. Many businesses today recognize that ethical practices make good business sense. Ethical companies endure less litigation, less resentment, and less government regulation. Although the following guidelines hardly constitute a formal code of conduct, they will help you set specific ethical goals and maintain a high ethical standard.

> Goals of ethical communicators include abiding by the law, telling the truth, labelling opinions, being objective, communicating clearly, using inclusive language, and giving credit.

Abiding by the Law. Know the laws in your field and follow them. Particularly important for business communicators are issues of copyright law. Don't assume that Internet items are in the public domain and free to be used or shared. Internet items are covered by copyright laws. If you are in accounting, financial management, investing, or corporate management, you should be aware of the restrictions set forth by legal and professional organizations. Whatever your field, become familiar with its regulations.

Telling the Truth. Ethical business communicators do not intentionally make statements that are untrue or deceptive. We become aware of dishonesty in business when violators break laws, notably in advertising, packaging, and marketing.

Facts are verifiable;
opinions are beliefs held
with conviction.

Labelling Opinions. Sensitive communicators know the difference between facts and opinions. Facts are verifiable and often are quantifiable; opinions are beliefs held with confidence but without substantiation. Assertions that cannot be proved are opinions, and stating opinions as if they were facts is unethical.

Being Objective. Ethical business communicators recognize their own biases and strive to keep them from distorting a message. Honest reporting means presenting the whole picture and relating all facts fairly.

Communicating Clearly. Ethical business communicators feel an obligation to write clearly so that receivers understand easily and quickly. Some organizations have even passed "plain language" policies that require policies, warranties, and contracts to be written in language comprehensible to average readers. Plain language means short sentences, simple words, and clear organization. Communicators who intentionally obscure their meaning with long sentences and difficult words are being unethical.

Using Inclusive Language. Strive to use language that includes rather than excludes. Do not use expressions that discriminate against individuals or groups on the basis of their sex, ethnicity, disability, or age. Language is discriminatory when it stereotypes, insults, or excludes people.

Giving Credit. Ethical communicators give credit for ideas by (a) referring to originators' names within the text, (b) using quotation marks, and (c) documenting sources with endnotes, footnotes, or internal references. Don't suggest that you did all the work on a project if you had help. In school or on the job, stealing ideas, words, graphics, or any other original material is unethical.

Members of the International Association of Business Communicators (IABC) have developed a code of ethics with 12 guidelines (articles) that spell out criteria for determining what is right and wrong for members of its organization. You can see the IABC Code of Ethics for Professional Communicators at **www.iabc.com/about/code.htm**.

Tools for Doing the Right Thing

In composing messages or engaging in other activities on the job, business communicators can't help being torn by conflicting loyalties. Do we tell the truth and risk our jobs? Do we show loyalty to friends even if it means bending the rules? Should we be tactful or totally honest? Is it our duty to make a profit or to be socially responsible? Acting ethically means doing the right thing given the circumstances. Each set of circumstances requires analyzing issues, evaluating choices, and acting responsibly.

Business communicators
can help resolve ethical
issues through self-
examination.

Resolving ethical issues is never easy, but the task can be made less difficult if you know how to identify key issues. The following questions may be helpful.

- **Is the action you are considering legal?** No matter who asks you to do it or how important you feel the result will be, avoid anything that is prohibited by law.

- **How would you see the problem if you were on the opposite side?** Looking at all sides of an issue helps you gain perspective. By weighing both sides of the issue, you can arrive at a more equitable solution.

- **What are alternative solutions?** Consider all dimensions of other options. Would the alternative be more ethical? Under the circumstances, is the alternative feasible? Can an alternative solution be implemented with a minimum of disruption and with a good possibility of success?

Discussing an ethical
problem with a co-worker
or colleague might lead
to helpful alternatives.

- **Can you discuss the problem with someone whose advice you trust?** Suppose you feel ethically bound to report accurate information to a client even though your manager has ordered you not to do so. Talking about your dilemma with a co-worker or with a colleague in your field might give you helpful insights and lead to possible alternatives.

- **How would you feel if your family, friends, employer, or co-workers learned of your action?** If the thought of revealing your action publicly makes you uncomfortable, your choice is probably unwise. Losing the faith of your friends or the confidence of your customers is not worth whatever short-term gains might be realized.

Perhaps the best advice in ethical matters is contained in the platinum rule: *Do unto others as they would like to have done unto them*. The ultimate solution to all ethics problems is treating others fairly and doing what is right to achieve what is good. In succeeding chapters you will find additional discussions of ethical questions as they relate to relevant topics.

Summary of Learning Objectives

1 **Understand the importance of communication skills in relation to career success and explain the need for thinking critically and taking charge of your career.** Communication skills are critical to job placement, performance, career advancement, and organizational success. These skills include reading, listening, speaking, and writing. They are not inherent; they must be learned. Writing skills are particularly important because messages today travel more rapidly, more often, and to greater numbers of people than ever before. In today's dynamic workplace, you can expect to be a knowledge worker; that is, you will deal with words, figures, and data. You must learn to think critically and develop opinions backed by reasons and evidence. Because technologies and procedures are constantly evolving, you must be flexible and willing to engage in lifelong learning. You should expect to take charge of your career as you work for multiple employers. The most important foundation skill for knowledge workers is the ability to communicate. You can improve your skills by studying the principles, processes, and products of communication provided in this book and in this course.

2 **Recognize significant trends in today's dynamic workplace and how these trends increase the need for excellent communication skills.** The workplace is undergoing profound changes, such as the emergence of heightened global competition, flattened management hierarchies, expanded team-based management, innovative communication technologies, "anytime, anywhere" offices, an increasingly diverse workforce, and a renewed emphasis on ethics. Nearly all these changes require that businesspeople have strong communication skills to be able to make decisions, exchange information, stay connected with remote colleagues, and meet ethics and accountability requirements.

3 **Analyze the process of communication and understand how to use it effectively.** The sender encodes (selects) words or symbols to express an idea. The message is sent verbally over a channel (such as a letter, e-mail message, or telephone call) or is expressed nonverbally, perhaps with gestures or body language. "Noise"—such as loud sounds, misspelled words, or other distractions—may interfere with the transmission. The receiver decodes (interprets) the message and attempts to make sense of it. The receiver responds with feedback, informing the sender of the effectiveness of the message. The objective of communication is the transmission of meaning so that a receiver understands a message as intended by the sender.

4 **Recognize barriers to interpersonal communication and examine specific strategies for overcoming those barriers.** Bypassing causes miscommunication because people have different meanings for the words they use. A person's frame of reference creates a filter through which all ideas are screened, sometimes causing distortion and lack of objectivity. Weak language skills and poor listening skills impair communication efforts. Emotional interference—joy, fear, anger, and so forth—hampers the sending and receiving of messages. Physical distractions—noisy surroundings, faulty acoustics, and so forth—can disrupt oral communication. Multitasking, information overload, and constant digital availability also make it difficult to focus. You can reduce or overcome many interpersonal communication barriers if you (a) realize that the communication process is imperfect, (b) adapt your message to the receiver, (c) improve your language and listening skills, (d) question your preconceptions, (e) plan for feedback, (f) focus on what is important, and (g) shut out interruptions.

5 Understand the internal and external functions of communication in organizations and compare and contrast the advantages and disadvantages of oral and written communication. Internal functions of communication include issuing and clarifying procedures and policies, informing management of progress, persuading others to make changes or improvements, and interacting with employees. External functions of communication include answering inquiries about products or services, persuading customers to buy products or services, clarifying supplier specifications, and so forth. Oral communication provides immediate feedback, can be adjusted to receivers, can be delivered quickly, supplies nonverbal cues, may create a warm feeling, and can be forceful. Written communication creates a permanent record, is convenient to distribute, may be economical, promotes comprehension and recall, allows precise and uniform expression, and gives receivers flexibility in what and how to receive the content.

6 Examine critically the flow of communication in organizations and understand how to overcome typical barriers and respond ethically to office gossip. Formal channels of communication follow an organization's hierarchy of command. Information flows downward from management to workers. Long lines of communication tend to distort information. Many organizations are improving the downward flow of communication through newsletters, announcements, meetings, videos, and company intranets. Information flows upward from employees to management, thus providing vital feedback for decision makers. Obstacles include mistrust, fear of reprisal for honest communication, lack of adequate communication skills, and differing frames of reference. To improve upward flow of communication, companies are improving relations with staff, offering incentive programs that encourage employees to share valuable feedback, and investing in communication training programs. Horizontal communication is among workers at the same level. Obstacles include poor communication skills, prejudice, ego involvement, competition, and turf wars. Techniques for overcoming the obstacles include (a) training employees in communication and teamwork techniques, (b) establishing reward systems, and (c) encouraging full participation in team functions. Informal channels of communication, such as the grapevine, deliver unofficial news—both personal and organizational—among friends and co-workers.

7 Analyze ethics in the workplace, understand the ethical goals of business communicators, and apply tools for doing the right thing. The goals of ethical business communicators include abiding by the law, telling the truth, labelling opinions, being objective, communicating clearly, using inclusive language, and giving credit. When faced with a difficult decision, the following questions serve as valuable tools in guiding you to do the right thing: (a) Is the action you are considering legal? (b) How would you see the problem if you were on the opposite side? (c) What are alternative solutions? (d) Can you discuss the problem with someone whose advice you trust? (e) How would you feel if your family, friends, employer, or co-workers learned of your action?

Chapter Review

1. What does the expression *communication skills* include? (Obj. 1)

2. In today's workplace can you expect to be exercising more or less control of your career? Why? (Obj. 1)

3. Who are knowledge workers? Why are they hired? (Obj. 1)

4. Fewer layers of management mean greater communication challenges for frontline workers. Why? (Obj. 2)

5. What technologies enable workers to have "anytime, anywhere" offices? (Obj. 2)

6. What are the five steps in the process of communication? (Obj. 3)

7. How can business communicators overcome some of the inevitable barriers in the communication process? (Obj. 4)

8. What are the three main functions of organizational communication? (Obj. 5)

Get more practice at **www.guffeybrief4e.nelson.com**

9. Why is oral communication considered more effective than written communication? Why doesn't everyone use it exclusively? (Obj. 5)

10. Why is written communication important in business, and why doesn't everyone use it exclusively? (Obj. 5)

11. Compare formal and informal channels of communication within organizations. Which is more valuable to employees? (Obj. 6)

12. Who is generally involved and what information is typically carried in downward, upward, and horizontal communication channels? (Obj. 6)

13. How can you control or respond ethically to office gossip? (Obj. 7)

14. What are seven goals of ethical business communicators? (Obj. 7)

15. When you are faced with a difficult ethical decision, what questions should you ask yourself? (Obj. 7)

Critical Thinking

1. Communication skills are frequently listed among the desired qualifications for job candidates. What do these skills consist of? How would you rate your skills? (Obj. 1)

2. Recall a time when you experienced a problem as a result of poor communication. What were the causes of and possible remedies for the problem? (Objs. 2 and 3)

3. Critics complain that e-mail is reducing the amount of face-to-face communication at work and that this is bad for business. Do you agree or disagree? Support your position. (Objs. 3–5)

4. How are the rules of ethical behaviour that govern businesses different from those that govern your personal behaviour? (Obj. 7)

5. **Ethical Issue:** Josh in the Accounting Department tells you that he heard from a reliable source that 15 percent of the staff will be released within 120 days. You would love to share this juicy news with other department members, for their own defence and planning. Should you? Why or why not? (Obj. 7)

Activities

Note: All Documents for Analysis may be downloaded from **www.guffeybrief4e.nelson.com** so that you do not have to rekey the entire message.

1.1 Online Communication Skills Assessment: How Do You Rate? (Objs. 1–3)

WEB

This course can help you dramatically improve your business communication skills. How much do you need to improve? This assessment exercise enables you to evaluate your skills with specific standards in four critical communication skill areas: writing, reading, speaking, and listening. How well you communicate will be an important factor in your future career—particularly if you are promoted into management, as many postsecondary graduates are.

Your Task. Either here or online at **www.guffeybrief4e. nelson.com,** select a number from 1 (indicating low ability) to 5 (indicating high ability) that best reflects your perception of your skills. Be honest in rating your skills. Think about how others would rate you. When you finish, see a rating of your skills. Complete this assessment online to see your results automatically!

Writing Skills	Low				High
1. Possess basic spelling, grammar, and punctuation skills	1	2	3	4	5
2. Am familiar with proper e-mail, memo, letter, and report formats for business documents	1	2	3	4	5
3. Can analyze a writing problem and quickly outline a plan for solving the problem	1	2	3	4	5
4. Am able to organize data coherently and logically	1	2	3	4	5
5. Can evaluate a document to determine its probable success	1	2	3	4	5

Reading Skills	Low				High
1. Am familiar with specialized vocabulary in my field and with general vocabulary	1	2	3	4	5
2. Can concentrate despite distractions	1	2	3	4	5
3. Am willing to look up definitions whenever necessary	1	2	3	4	5
4. Am able to move from recreational to serious reading	1	2	3	4	5
5. Can read and comprehend college-level or university-level material	1	2	3	4	5

Speaking Skills	Low				High
1. Feel at ease in speaking with friends	1	2	3	4	5
2. Feel at ease in speaking before a group of people	1	2	3	4	5
3. Can adapt my presentation to the audience	1	2	3	4	5
4. Am confident in pronouncing and using words correctly	1	2	3	4	5
5. Sense that I have credibility when I make a presentation	1	2	3	4	5

Listening Skills	Low				High
1. Spend at least half the time listening during conversations	1	2	3	4	5
2. Am able to concentrate on a speaker's words despite distractions	1	2	3	4	5
3. Can summarize a speaker's ideas and anticipate what's coming during pauses	1	2	3	4	5
4. Provide proper feedback, such as nodding, paraphrasing, and asking questions	1	2	3	4	5
5. Listen with the expectation of gaining new ideas and information	1	2	3	4	5

Total your score in each section. How do your skills rate?

22–24	Excellent! You have indicated that you have exceptional communication skills.
18–21	Your score is above average, but you could improve your skills.
14–17	Your score suggests that you have much room for improvement.
10–13	You recognize that you need serious study, practice, and follow-up reinforcement.

Where are your skills strongest and weakest? Are you satisfied with your present skills? The first step to improvement is recognition of a need. The second step is making a commitment to improve. The third step is following through, and this course will help you do that.

1.2 Getting to Know You (Objs. 1, 2)

E-MAIL

Your instructor wants to know more about you, your motivation for taking this course, your career goals, and your writing skills.

Your Task. Send an e-mail or write a memo of introduction to your instructor. See Chapter 7 for tips on preparing an e-mail message. In your message include the following:

a. Your reasons for taking this class

b. Your career goals (both temporary and long-term)

c. A brief description of your employment, if any, and your favourite activities

d. An assessment and discussion of your current communication skills, including your strengths and weaknesses

1.3 Small-Group Presentation: Getting to Know Each Other (Objs. 1, 2)

TEAM

Many business organizations today use teams to accomplish their goals. To help you develop speaking, listening, and teamwork skills, your instructor may assign team projects. One of the first jobs in any team is selecting members and becoming acquainted.

Your Task. Your instructor will divide your class into small groups or teams. At your instructor's direction, either (a) interview another group member and introduce that person to the group or (b) introduce yourself to the group. Think of this as an informal interview for a team assignment or for a job. You will want to make notes from which to speak.

Your introduction should include information such as the following:

a. Where did you grow up?

b. What work and extracurricular activities have you engaged in?

c. What are your interests and talents? What are you good at doing?

d. What have you achieved?

e. How familiar are you with various computer technologies?

f. What are your professional and personal goals? Where do you expect to be five years from now?

To develop listening skills, team members should practise good listening techniques (see Chapter 2) and take notes. They should be prepared to discuss three important facts and to remember details about each speaker.

1.4 Communication Skills: What Do Employers Want? (Obj. 1)

TEAM   **WEB**

What do employers request when they list job openings in your field?

Your Task. Individually or in teams, check the listings at an online job board. Visit a job board, such as Monster, Workopolis, Career Builder, or Yahoo! HotJobs. Use your favourite search engine to locate their sites. Follow the instructions to search job categories and locations. Study the jobs listed. Find five or more job listings in your field. If possible, print the results of your search. If you cannot print, make notes on what you find. Study the skills requested. How often do the ads mention communication, teamwork, and computer skills? What tasks do the ads mention? Discuss your findings with your team members. Prepare a list of the most frequently requested skills. Your instructor may ask you to submit your findings or report to the class.

1.5 Language Skills: Who Me? I Won't Need to Write on the Job.

Some job candidates experience a disconnect between what they expect to be doing in their career fields and what they actually will do.

Your Task. In teams or as a class, discuss the following statements. Are they myths or facts?

a. No one really writes anymore. They just text and send e-mails.

b. Because I'm in a technical field, I will work with numbers, not words.

c. Technical writers do most of the real writing on the job.

d. Today's sophisticated software programs can fix any of my writing mistakes.

e. I can use form letters for most messages.

1.6 Customer Service: Tech Skills Not Enough (Objs. 1–3)

TEAM

"One misspelled word and customers begin to doubt the validity of the information they are getting," warns Mary

Jo Lichtenberg. She's director of training, quality, and career development at a leading retailer and reseller of computer hardware and software. One of her big problems is training service agents who have weak communication skills. "Just because agents understand technically how to troubleshoot computers or pieces of software and can walk customers through solutions extremely well over the telephone doesn't mean they can do the same in writing," she complains. "The skill set for phone does not necessarily translate to the skill set needed for writing e-mail." As more and more of its customers choose e-mail and Web chat sessions to obtain service and support, the organization's service reps are doing more writing.[30]

Your Task. In teams, discuss what communication skills are necessary for service agents who are troubleshooting computers and software at large computer retailers. How are the skill sets different for answering phones and for writing e-mail responses? What suggestions could you make to a trainer preparing customer service reps for chat and e-mail responses?

1.7 Communication Process: Avoiding Misunderstanding (Obj. 3, 4)

Communication is not successful unless the receiver understands the message as the sender meant it.

Your Task. Analyze the following examples of communication failures. What went wrong?

a. David Brooks ran a family business selling T-shirts to young people at athletic events. To get permission to sell at one event, he spoke to a tournament committee member, who said the committee wasn't "concerned." Delighted, he began to make travel and staffing plans. In a follow-up call, however, he learned that "not concerned" to this committee member means "not enthusiastic."[31]

b. Team leader Tyson said to team member Alicia, "I could really use your help in answering these customer inquiries." Later Alicia was resentful when she found that he expected her to answer all the inquiries herself.

c. The following statements actually appeared in letters of application for an advertised job opening. One applicant wrote, "Enclosed is my résumé in response to Sunday's *Calgary Herald*." Another wrote, "Enclosed is my résumé in response to my search for an editorial/creative position." Still another wrote, "My experience in the production of newsletters, magazines, directories, and online data bases puts me head and shoulders above the crowd of applicants you have no doubtedly been inundated with."

1.8 Miscommunication in Organizations: Understanding the Boss (Objs. 3–6)

> **TEAM**

Sales representative Tim Pearson was underperforming. However, the vice president was unaware of this. At a busy sales reception where all of the sales reps were milling about, the CEO pulled the vice president aside and said, "Why is Pearson still a sales rep?" The vice president assumed that the CEO wanted Pearson promoted. Unwilling to question the CEO, the vice president soon thereafter sent down orders to promote Pearson. Later, when the CEO learned what had happened, he "came out of his chair like a Saturn rocket." He meant to say, "Why is that guy still on the payroll?"[32]

Your Task. In teams, discuss the factors contributing to this miscommunication. What went wrong in the process of communication? What role did feedback play?

1.9 Document for Analysis: Barriers to Communication (Objs. 3–5)

The following memo is from an exasperated manager to her staff. Obviously, this manager has no administrative assistant to clean up her writing.

Your Task. Comment on the memo's effectiveness, tone, and potential barriers to communication. Your instructor may ask you to revise the memo, improving its tone, grammar, and organization.

Date:	Current
To:	All Employees
From:	Albertina Sindaha, Operations Manager
Subject:	Cleanup!

You were all supposed to clean up your work areas last Friday, but that didn't happen. A few people cleaned their desks, but no one pitched in to clean the common areas, and you all saw what a mess they were in!

So we're going to try again. As you know, we don't have a big enough custodial budget anymore. Everyone must clean up himself. This Friday I want to see action in the copy machine area, things like emptying wastebaskets and you should organize paper and toner supplies. The lunchroom is a disaster area. You must do something about the counters, the refrigerator, the sinks, and the coffee machine. And any food left in the refrigerator on Friday afternoon should be thrown out because it stinks by Monday. Finally, the office supply shelves should be straightened.

If you can't do a better job this Friday, I will have to assign individuals to a specific cleaning schedule. Which I don't want to do. But you may force me to.

1.10 Information Flow: What's the Latest Buzz? (Obj. 6)

All organizations provide information to the public and to members through official channels. But information also flows through unofficial channels.

Your Task. Consider an organization to which you belong or a business where you've worked. How did members learn what was going on in the organization? What kind of information flowed through formal channels? What were those channels? What kind of information was delivered through informal channels? Was the grapevine as accurate as official channels? What barriers obstructed the flow of information? How could the flow be improved?

Grammar and Mechanics C.L.U.E. Review 1

Each chapter includes an exercise based on Appendix A, Grammar and Mechanics Guide: Component Language Usage Essentials (C.L.U.E.). This appendix is a business communicator's condensed guide to language usage, covering 50 of the most used and abused language elements. It also includes a list of frequently misspelled words and a list of confusing words. In the first ten chapters, each exercise will focus on a specific set of grammar and mechanics guidelines. In the last six chapters, exercises will review all the guidelines as well as spelling and confusing words.

Sentence Structure

Study sentence structure in Guides 1–3 of Appendix A beginning on page A-2. Some of the following sentences have sentence faults. On a sheet of paper, write a correct version and identify the fault and the relevant guide. If a sentence is correct, write C. Avoid adding new phrases or rewriting sentences in your own words. You may need to change or delete one or more words. However, your goal is to correct the sentence with as few marks as possible. When finished, compare your responses with the key beginning on page Key-1.

1. Whether you are already working or about to enter today's workplace. Communication skills are critical to your career success.

2. Surveys of employers consistently show that communication skills are important to job success, job advertisements often request excellent oral and written communication skills.

3. Technology enables us to transmit messages more rapidly, more often, and more widely than ever before.

4. We cannot predict future jobs, however they will undoubtedly require brainpower and education.

5. Face-to-face conversations have many advantages. Even though they produce no written record and sometimes waste time.

6. A vital part of the communication process is feedback, it helps the sender know that the message was received and understood.

7. Knowledge workers must be critical thinkers they must be able to make decisions and communicate those decisions.

8. Management uses many methods to distribute information downward. Such as newsletters, announcements, meetings, videos, and company intranets.

9. Ethical companies experience less litigation, and they also receive less resentment and less government regulation.

10. You may be expected to agree to a company's code of ethics, you will also be expected to know the laws applying to your job.

Endnotes

1 Nelson, J. (2011, January 19–February 14). Office space gets the squeeze. *Canadian Business, 84*, p. 23.

2 George Brown College. (2010). Back-to-school wake-up call: Gen Y, employers diverge on importance of knowledge economy skills [press release]. Retrieved November 22, 2010, from http://www.newswire.ca/en/releases/archive/September2010/10/c8490.html; Engineers Canada and the Canadian Council of Technicians and Technologists. (2008). 2007 engineering and technology employer survey. Retrieved November 22, 2010, from http://www.engineerscanada.ca/etlms/media/2007%20Employer%20Survey%20Report1.pdf; Keith, J. (2005). BCIT survey highlights importance of oral communication skills. Retrieved November 22, 2010, from http://www.johnkeithcommunications.com/listening/prof/BCITGradSurvey.html

3 Messmer, M. (2001, January). Enhancing your writing skills. *Strategic Finance, 82*(7), 8–9. See also Staples, B. (2005, May 15). The fine art of getting it down on paper, fast. *The New York Times*, p. WK13(L).

4 Hoffman, A. (n.d.). IT workers improve your writing skills. Retrieved April 20, 2009, from http://career-advice.monster.ca/career-development/education-training/it-workers-improve-your-writing-skills/article.aspx

5 Ibid.

6 Drucker, P. (1989, May). New realities, new ways of managing. *Business Month*, pp. 50–51.

7 Luciw, R. (2003, October 30). Canada's work force in the know. *Globe and Mail Update*. Retrieved April 22, 2009, from http://www.theglobeandmail.com/servlet/story/RTGAM.20031030.wbwork1030/BNStory/Business

8 Haag, S., Cummings, M., & Phillips, A. (2003). *Management information systems for the information age* (3rd ed.). New York: McGraw-Hill.

9 O'Toole, J., & Lawler, E. E., III. (2006). *The new American workplace*. New York: Palgrave Macmillan, p. 17.

10 Malone, T. W. (2004). *The future of work*. Cambridge: Harvard Business School Press, p. 32.

11 Miller, C. C. (2008, June 2). Higher office. *Forbes*, p. 62. See also Shinkle, K. (2008, March 10). Running an office by wiki and e-mail. *U.S. News & World Report*, p. 50.

12 Holland, K. (2008, September 28). The anywhere, anytime office. *The New York Times*, p. 14 BU Y.

13 Telework—Issues and concerns for organizations and workers. (2009, January). *Healthy Organizations Newsletter, 3*. Retrieved November 23, 2010, from http://healthyorganizations.net/newsletters.aspx

14 Holland, K. (2008, September 28). The anywhere, anytime office. *The New York Times*, p. 14 BU Y.

15 Belanger, A., & Caron Malenfant, E. (2005). Ethnocultural diversity in Canada: Prospects for 2017 (Catalogue No. 11-008). Retrieved August 17, 2009, from http:// www.statcan.gc.ca/pub/11-008-x/2005003/article/8968-eng.pdf

Get more practice at **www.guffeybrief4e.nelson.com**

16 Minigail, H. (2004, September 29). Wise ways for retraining older workers. *The Globe and Mail,* p. C8.

17 Sullivan, J., Karmeda, N., & Nobu, T. (1992, January/ February). Bypassing in managerial communication. *Business Horizons, 34*(1), 72.

18 McGirt, E. (2006, March 20). Getting out from under: Beset by interruptions, information overload, and irksome technology, knowledge workers need help: A survival guide. Fortune, 88.

19 E-mail becoming crime's new smoking gun. (2005). *USA Today.* Retrieved October 11, 2006, from http://www. usatoday.com/tech/news/ 2002-08-15-email-evidence_x. htm

20 Sims, R. R., Veres, J. G., III, Jackson, K. A., & Facteau, C. L. (2001). *The challenge of front-line management.* Westport, CT: Quorum, p. 10.

21 Steelcase Inc. (2007, August 9). Steelcase workplace index survey examines "water cooler" conversations at work. Retrieved May 4, 2009, from http://www.prnewswire.com/ news-releases/steelcase-workplace-index-survey-examines- water-cooler-conversations-at-work-58006482.html

22 Ibid.

23 Karathanos, P., & Auriemmo, A. (1999, March–April). Care and feeding of the organizational grapevine. *Industrial Management, 41*(2), 26. Retrieved January 2, 2007, from InfoTrac College Edition database.

24 Goman, C. K. (2006, June). *I heard it through the grapevine.* Paper presented at the International Association of Business Communicators, Vancouver, Canada. Retrieved October 22, 2006, from http://www.communitelligence. com/clps/clitem.cfm?AdsID=329

25 Zimmermann, S., Davenport, B., & Haas, J. W. (1996, April). A communication metamyth in the workplace: The assumption that more is better. *Journal of Business Communication, 33*(2), 185–204.

26 Nelson, B. (1997, October). How to energize everyone in the company. Bottom Line/Business, 3.

27 DeMars, N. (2008). *What you can do when you're the latest topic on the rumor mill.* Retrieved May 4, 2009, from http:// www.office-ethics.com/columns/gossip.html

28 Saner, M., & von Baeyer, C. (2005). *Workplace and policy ethics: A call to end the solitudes* (Policy Brief No. 24). Ottawa: Institute on Governance. Retrieved November 24, 2010, from http://www.workplaceethics.ca/brief24.pdf

29 KPMG. (2002). Ethics and social responsibility survey. Montreal: KPMG. Quoted in Singh, J. B. (2006). Ethics programs in Canada's largest corporations. *Business and Society Review, 111*(2), 119–136. Retrieved November 24, 2010, from http://cronus.uwindsor.ca/users/j/jang/main. nsf/inToc/FA648AB46DBAF1758525708900706D95

30 Do your reps' writing skills need a refresher? (2002, February). *Customer Contact Management Report*, 7.

31 Sandberg, J. (2008, January 19). Global-market woes are more personality than nationality. *The Wall Street Journal*, p. B1.

32 Sandberg, J. (2006, September 18). What exactly was it that the boss said? You can only imagine. *The Wall Street Journal,* p. B1.

CHAPTER 2

Professionalism: Team, Listening, Nonverbal, and Etiquette Skills

OBJECTIVES

After studying this chapter, you should be able to

1. Explain the importance of professionalism, soft skills, and teamwork in today's workplace.

2. Understand how you can contribute positively to team performance, including resolving workplace conflicts, avoiding groupthink, and reaching group decisions.

3. Discuss effective techniques for planning and participating in face-to-face workplace meetings.

4. Describe effective practices and technologies for planning and participating in virtual meetings.

5. Explain and implement active listening techniques.

6. Understand how the functions and forms of nonverbal communication can help you advance your career.

7. Enhance your competitive edge by developing professionalism and business etiquette skills.

LWA/Getty Images

Although workers spend an average of 5.6 hours each week in meetings, 69 percent of them feel meetings aren't productive.[1] A recent poll of senior executives also revealed that 45 percent thought that employees could be more productive if meetings were banned one day a week.[2] Do you think that it would be a good idea for companies to ban meetings one day a week? Why or why not?

Becoming a Team Player in Professional Groups

Most businesses seek a workforce that gets along and delivers positive results that enhance profits and boost a company's image. As a budding business professional, you have a stake in acquiring skills that will make you a strong job applicant and a valuable employee.

LEARNING OBJECTIVE 1

Explain the importance of professionalism, soft skills, and teamwork in today's workplace.

What Do Employers Want?

When you look for a job, employers will typically want to know about four key areas: education, experience, hard skills, and soft skills. Hard skills refer to the technical skills in your field. Soft skills, however, are increasingly important in our knowledge-based economy. These include both oral and written communication skills, which you learned about in Chapter 1. Soft skills also include other competencies, such as listening proficiency, nonverbal behaviour, and proper business etiquette. Employers also want team players who can work together efficiently and productively. They want managers and employees who are comfortable with diverse co-workers, who can listen actively to customers and colleagues, who can make eye contact, who display good workplace manners, and who are able to work in teams. These skills are immensely important not only to being hired but also to being promoted.

Hiring managers expect you to have technical expertise in your field. Such skills and a good résumé may get you in the door. However, your long-term success is greatly influenced by your ability to communicate with your boss, co-workers, and customers, as well as your ability to work as an effective and contributing team member. Even in technical fields, such as accounting and finance, employers are looking for soft skills.

This chapter focuses on developing team, meeting, listening, nonverbal, and etiquette skills. These are some of the soft skills that employers seek in today's increasingly interconnected and competitive environments. You will learn many tips and techniques for becoming a good team member and to expand and perfect your listening, nonverbal, and etiquette skills.

Soft skills—including team, listening, nonverbal, and etiquette skills—are key in hiring and promotion processes.

Preparing to Work With Groups and Teams

As we discussed in Chapter 1, the workplace and economy are changing. In response to intense global competition, businesses are being forced to rethink and restructure their operations. They must find new and faster ways to develop advanced products and bring them to market efficiently and profitably.[3] Many are turning to teams to innovate, share knowledge, and solve problems. The reasoning behind this thrust is that many heads are better than one.

As a result, today's workplace is teeming with teams. You might find yourself a part of a work team, project team, customer support team, supplier team, design team, planning team, functional team, or cross-functional team. You might be assigned to a committee, a task force, a steering group, a quality control circle, a flat team, a hierarchical team, an advisory team, an action team, or some other group. All these teams are formed to accomplish specific goals.

Why Form Groups and Teams?

Businesses are constantly looking for ways to do jobs better at less cost. They are forming teams for the following reasons:

- **Better decisions.** Decisions are generally more accurate and effective because group and team members contribute different expertise and perspectives.

- **Faster response.** When action is necessary to respond to competition or to solve a problem, small groups and teams can act rapidly.

- **Increased productivity.** Because they are often closer to the action and to the customer, team members can see opportunities for improving efficiency.

- **Greater buy-in.** Decisions arrived at jointly are usually better received because members are committed to the solution and are more willing to support it.

- **Less resistance to change.** People who have input into decisions are less hostile, aggressive, and resistant to change.

- **Improved employee morale.** Personal satisfaction and job morale increase when teams are successful.

- **Reduced risks.** Responsibility for a decision is diffused, thus carrying less risk for any individual.

Despite the current popularity of teams, however, they are not a panacea for all workplace problems. Some critics complain that they are merely management fads while others charge that teams are a screen behind which management intensifies its control over labour.[4] In addition, some companies found that teams slowed decision making, shielded workers from responsibility, and reduced productivity.[5] However, in most models of future organizations, teams, not individuals, function as the primary performance unit. In fact, many organizations evaluate managers on how well they develop teamwork among their employees.

Virtual Teams

The days when you could expect to work with a colleague who sat near you are long gone. Today you can look forward to collaborating with fellow workers in other cities and even in other countries.[6] In such collaborations, called virtual teams, a group of people work interdependently with a shared purpose across space, time, and organization boundaries by using technology.[7]

Virtual teams may be local or global, and work is increasingly viewed as *what you do* rather than a place you go. In some organizations remote co-workers may be permanent employees from the same office or may be specialists called together for temporary projects. Regardless of the assignment, virtual teams can benefit from shared views and skills. However, not all teams automatically work well together and are productive. The suggestions in the accompanying Plugged In box offer helpful strategies for avoiding pitfalls.

Four Phases of Team Development

Small groups and teams may be formed to complete single tasks or to function as permanent bodies. Regardless of their purpose, successful teams normally go through predictable phases as they develop. In this section we discuss four phases of team development. You will learn how team members can perform positively or negatively in achieving the group's goals. You will also study the role of conflict and how to apply a six-step plan for resolving conflict.

Organizations are forming teams for better decisions, faster response, increased productivity, greater buy-in, less resistance to change, improved morale, and reduced risks.

Some companies rejected teams because they slowed decision making, shielded workers from responsibility, and reduced productivity.

Virtual teams are groups of people who work interdependently with a shared purpose across space, time, and organization boundaries by using technology.

PLUGGED IN

How to Form and Participate in Effective Virtual Teams

Virtual team members must overcome many obstacles not faced by groups that can meet in person. The following recommendations help members form virtual teams and interact effectively.

- **Select team members carefully.** Choose team members who are self-starters, good communicators, and experts in areas needed by the team.

- **Invest in beginnings.** If possible, meet face to face to work out procedures and to bond. Spending time together initially expedites reaching consensus about goals, tasks, and procedures.

- **Redefine "we."** Encourage behaviour that reflects unity, such as including one another in decisions and sharing information. Consider having a team photograph taken and made into something used frequently, such as a mouse pad or computer wallpaper.

- **Get the maximum benefit from technology.** Make use of speakerphones, collaborative software, e-mail, teleconferencing, videoconferencing, blogs, wikis, and instant messaging. But be sure that members are well trained in their professional use.

- **Concentrate on building credibility and trust.** Encourage team members to pay close attention to the way others perceive them. Acting consistently, fulfilling promises, considering other members' schedules, and responding promptly to e-mail and voice messages help build credibility and trust.

- **Establish responsibilities.** Identify expectations and responsibilities for each member. Make rules about e-mail response time and sharing information with all team members.

- **Keep track of information.** Capture information and decisions in a shared database, such as a wiki. Make sure all messages define expected actions, responsibilities, and timelines. Track to-do items and follow up as necessary. Expect messages to be more formal than in traditional same-time/same-place teams.

- **Avoid misinterpreting messages.** Because it is easy to misunderstand e-mail messages, be careful about responding quickly and negatively. Always take time to question your reactions.

When groups are formed, they generally evolve through four phases, as identified by psychologist B. A. Tuckman. These phases are *forming, storming, norming,* and *performing.* Some groups get lucky and move quickly from forming to performing. But most struggle through disruptive, although ultimately constructive, team-building stages.

> Successful teams generally go through four phases: forming, storming, norming, and performing.

Forming. During the first stage, individuals get to know each other. They often are overly polite and feel a bit awkward. As they search for similarities and attempt to bond, they begin to develop trust in each other. Members will discuss fundamental topics, such as why the team is necessary, who "owns" the team, whether membership is mandatory, how large it should be, and what talents members can contribute. A leader functions primarily as a traffic director. Groups and teams should resist the efforts of some members to dash through the first stages and race to the performing stage. Moving slowly through the stages is necessary in building a cohesive, productive unit.

Storming. During the second phase, members define their roles and responsibilities, decide how to reach their goals, and iron out the rules governing how they interact. Unfortunately, this stage often produces conflict, resulting in *storming.* A good leader, however, should step in to set limits, control the chaos, and offer suggestions. The leader will be most successful if she or he acts like a coach rather than a cop. Teams composed of dissimilar personality types may take longer to progress through the storming phase. Tempers may flare, sleep may be lost, and leaders may be deposed. But most often the storm passes, and a cohesive group emerges.

Norming. Once these conflicts have been resolved, teams and groups enter the *norming* stage. Tension subsides, roles are clarified, and information begins to flow

FIGURE 2.1 Why Teams Fail: Typical Problems, Symptoms, and Solutions

Problems	Symptoms	Solutions
Confused goals	People don't know what they're supposed to do	Clarify team purpose and expected outcomes
Mismatched needs	People with private agendas working at cross-purposes	Get hidden agendas on the table by asking what people personally want from the team
Unresolved roles	Team members are uncertain about what their jobs are	Inform team members of what is expected of them
Senseless procedures	The team is at the mercy of an incomprehensible employee handbook	Throw away the book and develop procedures that make sense
Bad leadership	Leader is tentative, inconsistent, or foolish	Leader must learn to serve the team and keep its vision alive or give up the role
Antiteam culture	The organization is not committed to the idea of teams	Team for the right reasons or don't team at all; never force people onto a team
Poor feedback	Performance is not being measured; team members are groping in the dark	Create a system of free flow of useful information from all team members

Source: Reprinted with permission of the publisher. From *The New Why Teams Don't Work*, © 2000 by Harvey Robbins & Michael Finley, Berrett-Koehler Publishers, Inc., San Francisco, CA. All rights reserved. www.bkconnection.com

In the norming stage, tensions subside, roles are clarified, and information flows among team members.

among members. The group periodically checks its agenda to remind itself of its progress toward its goals. People are careful not to shake the hard-won camaraderie and formation of a single-minded purpose. Formal leadership is unnecessary because everyone takes on leadership functions. Important data are shared with the entire group, and mutual interdependence becomes typical. The group or team begins to move smoothly in one direction. Members make sure that procedures are in place to resolve future conflicts.

Performing. In Tuckman's team growth model, some groups never reach the final stage of *performing*. Problems that may cause them to fail are shown in Figure 2.1. For those that survive the first three phases, however, the final stage is gratifying. Group members have established routines and a shared language. They develop loyalty and a willingness to resolve all problems. A "can-do" mentality pervades as they progress toward their goal. Fights are clean, and members continue working together without grudges. Best of all, information flows freely, deadlines are met, and production exceeds expectations.

Analyzing Positive and Negative Team Behaviour

LEARNING OBJECTIVE 2

Understand how you can contribute positively to team performance, including resolving workplace conflicts, avoiding groupthink, and reaching group decisions.

Team members who are committed to achieving the group's purpose contribute by displaying positive behaviour. How can you be a good team member? The most effective groups have members who are willing to establish rules and abide by those rules. Effective team members are able to analyze tasks and define problems so that they can work toward solutions. They offer information and try out their ideas on the group to stimulate discussion. They show interest in others' ideas by listening actively. Helpful team members also seek to involve silent members. They help resolve differences, and they encourage a warm, supportive climate by praising and agreeing with others. When they sense that agreement is near, they review significant points and move the group toward its goal by synthesizing points of understanding.

Not all groups, however, have members who contribute positively. Negative behaviour is shown by those who constantly put down the ideas and suggestions of others. They insult, criticize, and aggress against others. They waste the group's time with unnecessary recounting of personal achievements or irrelevant topics. The team joker distracts the group with excessive joke telling, inappropriate comments, and disruptive antics. Also disturbing are team members who withdraw and refuse to be drawn out. They have nothing to say, either for or against ideas being considered. To be a productive and welcome member of a group, be prepared to perform the positive tasks described in Figure 2.2. Avoid the negative behaviours.

Negative team behaviour includes insulting, criticizing, aggressing against others, wasting time, and refusing to participate.

FIGURE 2.2 Positive and Negative Team Behaviours

Positive Team Behaviours	Negative Team Behaviours
Setting rules and abiding by them	Blocking the ideas and suggestions of others
Analyzing tasks and defining problems	Insulting and criticizing others
Contributing information and ideas	Wasting the group's time
Showing interest by listening actively	Making inappropriate jokes and comments
Encouraging members to participate	Failing to stay on task
Synthesizing points of agreement	Withdrawing, failing to participate

Six-Step Procedure for Dealing With Conflict

Conflict is a normal part of every workplace and every team. Although the word alone is enough to make your heart begin to thump, conflict is not always negative. When managed properly, conflict can improve decision making, clarify values, increase group cohesiveness, stimulate creativity, decrease tensions, and undermine dissatisfaction. Unresolved conflict, however, can destroy productivity and seriously reduce morale. You will be better prepared to resolve workplace conflict if you are able to implement the following six-step procedure for dealing with conflict.[8]

1. **Listen.** To be sure you understand the problem, listen carefully. If the other person doesn't seem to be listening to you, you need to set the example and be the first to listen.

2. **Understand the other's point of view.** Once you listen, it is much easier to understand the other's position. Show your understanding by asking questions and paraphrasing. This will also verify what you think the other person means.

3. **Show a concern for the relationship.** By focusing on the problem, not the person, you can build, maintain, and even improve the relationship. Show an understanding of the other person's situation and needs. Show an overall willingness to come to an agreement.

4. **Look for common ground.** Identify your interests and help the other person identify his or her interests. Learn what you have in common and look for a solution on which both of you can agree.

5. **Invent new problem-solving options.** Spend time identifying the interests of both sides. Then brainstorm to invent new ways to solve the problem. Be open to new options.

6. **Reach an agreement based on what's fair.** Seek to determine a standard of fairness that is acceptable to both sides. Then weigh the possible solutions and choose the best option.

> Following an effective six-step procedure can help resolve conflicts through collaboration and cooperation.

Avoiding Groupthink

Conflict is normal in team interactions, and successful teams are able to resolve it by using the methods you just learned. But some teams avoid conflict. They smooth things over and in doing so may fall victim to *groupthink*. This is a term coined by theorist Irving Janis to describe faulty decision-making processes by team members who are overly eager to agree with one another. Several conditions can lead to groupthink: team members with similar backgrounds, a lack of systematic procedures, a demand for a quick decision, and a strong leader who favours a specific decision. Symptoms of groupthink include pressures placed on any member who argues against the group's mutual beliefs, self-censorship of thoughts that stray from the group's agreement, collective efforts to rationalize, and an unquestioned belief in the group's moral authority. Teams suffering from groupthink fail to check alternatives, are biased in collecting and evaluating information, and ignore the risks of the preferred choice. They may also neglect to work out a contingency plan in case the preferred choice fails.[9]

> Groupthink means that team members agree without examining alternatives or considering contingency plans.

Effective teams avoid groupthink by striving for team diversity—in age, gender, background, experience, and training. They encourage open discussion, search for relevant information, evaluate many alternatives, consider how a decision will be implemented, and plan for contingencies in case the decision doesn't work out.

Reaching Group Decisions

The way teams reach decisions greatly affects their morale and commitment, as well as the implementation of any team decision. In North American culture, the majority usually rules, but other methods, five of which are discussed here, may be more effective. As you study these methods, think about which would be best for routine decisions and which would be best for dealing with emergencies.

- **Majority.** Group members vote and a majority wins. This method results in a quick decision but may leave an alienated minority uncommitted to implementation.

- **Consensus.** Discussion continues until all team members have aired their opinions and, ultimately, agree. This method is time consuming, but it produces creative, high-quality discussion and generally elicits commitment by all members to implement the decision.

- **Minority.** Typically, a subcommittee investigates and makes a recommendation for action. This method is useful when the full group cannot get together to make a decision or when time is short.

- **Averaging.** Members haggle, bargain, wheedle, and negotiate to reach a middle position, which often requires compromise. With this method the opinions of the least knowledgeable members may cancel the opinions of the most knowledgeable.

- **Authority rule with discussion.** The leader, boss, or manager listens to team members' ideas, but the final decision is his or hers. This method encourages lively discussion and results in participatory decision making. However, team members must have good communication skills. This method also requires a leader who is willing to make decisions.

Characteristics of Successful Teams

The use of teams has been called the solution to many ills in the current workplace.[10] Many teams, however, do not work well together. In fact, some teams can actually increase frustration, lower productivity, and create employee dissatisfaction. Experts who have studied team workings and decisions have discovered that effective teams share some or all of the following characteristics.

Small Size, Diverse Makeup.
Teams may range from 2 to 25 members, although 4 or 5 is optimum for many projects. Larger groups have trouble interacting constructively, much less agreeing on actions.[11] For the most creative decisions, teams generally have male and female members who differ in age, ethnicity, social background, training, and experience. Members should bring complementary skills to a team. The key business advantage of diversity is the ability to view a project and its context from multiple perspectives. Many of us tend to think that everyone in the world is like us because we know only our own experience.[12] Teams with members from different ethnicities and cultures can look at projects beyond the limited view of one culture. Many organizations are finding that diverse teams can produce innovative solutions with broader applications than homogeneous teams can.

Agreement on Purpose.
An effective team begins with a purpose. Working from a general purpose to specific goals typically requires a huge investment of time and effort. Meaningful discussions, however, motivate team members to buy into the project.

Although time consuming, consensus decisions generally produce the most team commitment.

Small, diverse teams often produce more creative solutions with broader applications than homogeneous teams do.

Agreement on Procedures. The best teams develop procedures to guide them. They set up intermediate goals with deadlines. They assign roles and tasks, requiring all members to contribute equivalent amounts of real work. They decide how they will reach decisions by using one of the strategies discussed earlier. Procedures are continually evaluated to ensure movement toward the attainment of the team's goals.

Ability to Confront Conflict. Poorly functioning teams avoid conflict, preferring sulking, gossiping, or bickering. A better plan is to acknowledge conflict and address the root of the problem openly by using the six-step plan outlined earlier. Although it may feel emotionally risky, direct confrontation saves time and enhances team commitment in the long run. To be constructive, however, confrontation must be task oriented, not person oriented. An open airing of differences, in which all team members have a chance to speak their minds, should centre on the strengths and weaknesses of the different positions and ideas—not on personalities. After hearing all sides, team members must negotiate a fair settlement, no matter how long it takes. Good decisions are based on consensus: all members agree.

Use of Good Communication Techniques. The best teams exchange information and contribute ideas freely in an informal environment. Team members speak clearly and concisely, avoiding generalities. They encourage feedback. Listeners become actively involved, read body language, and ask clarifying questions before responding. Tactful, constructive disagreement is encouraged. Although a team's task is taken seriously, successful teams are able to inject humour into their interactions.

> Good teams exchange information freely and collaborate rather than compete.

Ability to Collaborate Rather Than Compete. Effective team members are genuinely interested in achieving team goals instead of receiving individual recognition. They contribute ideas and feedback unselfishly. They monitor team progress, including what's going right, what's going wrong, and what to do about it. They celebrate individual and team accomplishments.

Acceptance of Ethical Responsibilities. Teams as a whole have ethical responsibilities to their members, to their larger organizations, and to society. Members have a number of specific responsibilities to each other. As a whole, teams have a responsibility to represent the organization's view and respect its privileged information. They should not discuss with outsiders any sensitive issues without permission. In addition, teams have a broader obligation to avoid advocating actions that would endanger members of society at large.

Shared Leadership. Effective teams often have no formal leader. Instead, leadership rotates to those with the appropriate expertise as the team evolves and moves from one phase to another. Many teams operate under a democratic approach. This approach can achieve buy-in to team decisions, boost morale, and create fewer hurt feelings and less resentment. But in times of crisis, a strong team member may need to step up as leader.

The Checklist box on page 36 provides tips for ensuring team effectiveness.

Planning and Participating in Face-to-Face Workplace Meetings

As you prepare to enter the workplace, you can expect to attend meetings—lots of them! Estimates suggest that workers spend from five to eight hours a week in meetings.[13]

Meetings consist of three or more people who gather to pool information, solicit feedback, clarify policy, seek consensus, and solve problems. However, as more and more people work separately, the character of meetings in today's workplace has changed. People are meeting regularly, but not always face to face. To be able to exchange information effectively and efficiently, you should know how to plan and participate in face-to-face and other kinds of meetings.

LEARNING OBJECTIVE 3

Discuss effective techniques for planning and participating in face-to-face workplace meetings.

Checklist

Developing Team Effectiveness

- **Establish small teams.** Smaller teams are thought to function more efficiently and more effectively than larger teams.

- **Encourage diversity.** Innovative teams typically include members who differ in age, gender, ethnicity, and background. Team members should possess technical expertise, problem-solving skills, and interpersonal skills.

- **Determine the purpose, procedures, and roles.** Members must understand the task at hand and what is expected of them. Teams function best when operating procedures are ironed out early and each member has a specific role.

- **Acknowledge and manage conflict.** Conflict is productive when it motivates a team to search for new ideas, increase participation, delay premature decisions, or discuss disagreements. Keep conflict centred on issues rather than on people.

- **Cultivate good communication skills.** Effective team members are willing and able to articulate ideas clearly and concisely, recognize nonverbal cues, and listen actively.

- **Advance an environment of open communication.** Teams are most productive when members trust each other and feel free to discuss all viewpoints openly in an informal atmosphere.

- **Encourage collaboration and discourage competition.** Sharing information in a cooperative effort to achieve the team purpose must be more important than competing with other members for individual achievement.

- **Share leadership.** Members with the most expertise should lead at various times during the project's evolution.

- **Create a sense of fairness in making decisions.** Effective teams resolve issues without forcing members into a win–lose situation.

- **Lighten up.** The most successful teams take their task seriously, but they are also able to laugh at themselves and interject humour to enliven team proceedings.

- **Continually assess performance.** Teams should establish checkpoints along the way to determine whether they are meeting their objectives and adjust procedures if progress is unsatisfactory.

Making Face-to-Face Meetings More Productive

Despite their regular occurrence, meetings are almost universally disliked. Typical comments include, "We have too many of them," "They don't accomplish anything," and "What a waste of time!" One writer called them "the black holes of the workday."[14] In spite of their bad reputation, meetings are not going away. Our task, then, as business communicators is to learn how to make them more efficient, satisfying, and productive. The following suggestions will be especially helpful in face-to-face meetings, but most of the advice applies to virtual meetings as well.

Although meetings are disliked, they serve another important purpose for you. They represent opportunities. Because meetings are a prime tool for developing staff, they are career critical. Why are meetings so important to your career? At meetings, judgments are formed and careers are made. Therefore, instead of treating meetings as thieves of your valuable time, try to see them as opportunities to demonstrate your leadership, communication, and problem-solving skills. So that you can make the most of these opportunities, here are techniques for planning and conducting successful meetings.

Deciding Whether a Meeting Is Necessary. No meeting should be called unless the topic is important, can't wait, and requires an exchange of ideas. If the flow of information is strictly one way and no immediate feedback will result, then don't schedule a meeting. For example, if people are merely being advised or informed, send an e-mail, text message, memo, or letter. Leave a telephone or voice mail message, but don't call a costly meeting. Remember, the real expense of a meeting is the lost productivity of all the people attending. To decide whether the purpose of the meeting is valid, it is a good idea to consult the key people who will be attending. Ask them what outcomes are desired and how to achieve those goals. This consultation also sets a collaborative tone and encourages full participation.

Selecting Participants. The number of meeting participants is determined by the purpose of the meeting, as shown in Figure 2.3. If the meeting purpose is motivational,

> Meetings enable three or more people to pool information and solve problems, but they also represent great opportunities for you to distinguish yourself and advance your career.

> Call meetings only when necessary and invite only key people.

FIGURE 2.3 Meeting Purpose and Number of Participants

Purpose	Ideal Size
Intensive problem solving	5 or fewer
Problem identification	10 or fewer
Information reviews and presentations	30 or fewer
Motivational	Unlimited

then the number of participants is unlimited. But to make decisions, according to studies at 3M Corporation, the best number is five or fewer participants.[15] Ideally, those attending should be people who will make the decision and people with information necessary to make the decision. Also attending should be people who will be responsible for implementing the decision and representatives of groups who will benefit from the decision.

Distributing Advance Information. At least two days before a meeting, distribute an agenda of topics to be discussed. Also include any reports or materials that participants should read in advance. For continuing groups, you might also include a copy of the minutes of the previous meeting. To keep meetings productive, limit the number of agenda items. Remember, the narrower the focus, the greater the chances for success. A good agenda, as illustrated in Figure 2.4, covers the following information:

- Date and place of meeting
- Start time and end time
- Brief description of each topic, in order of priority, including the names of individuals who are responsible for performing some action
- Proposed allotment of time for each topic
- Any premeeting preparation expected of participants

Using Digital Calendars to Schedule Meetings. Finding a time when everyone can meet is often difficult. People have busy schedules, and telephone and e-mail messages sent back and forth to find an open time can be frustrating. Fortunately, digital calendars now make the task quicker and more efficient. Two of the most popular digital calendaring programs are Google Calendar and Yahoo Calendar. Microsoft Outlook also provides a calendar program, as shown in Figure 2.5. Online calendars enable you to make appointments, schedule meetings, and keep track of daily activities. To schedule meetings, you enter a new meeting request, add the names of attendees, and check the availability of each attendee on their calendars. You select a date when all are available, enter a start and end time, and list the meeting subject and location. Then the meeting request goes to each attendee. Later you check the attendee availability tab to see a list of all meeting attendees. As the meeting time approaches, the program automatically sends reminders to attendees.

Getting the Meeting Started. To avoid wasting time and irritating attendees, always start meetings on time—even if some participants are missing. Waiting for latecomers causes resentment and sets a bad precedent. For the same reasons, don't give a quick recap to anyone who arrives late. At the appointed time, open the meeting with a three- to five-minute introduction that includes the following:

- Goal and length of the meeting
- Background of topics or problems
- Possible solutions and constraints
- Tentative agenda
- Ground rules to be followed

Problem-solving meetings should involve five or fewer people.

A meeting agenda, showing topics to be discussed and other information, should be distributed before the meeting.

Meetings should start on time and open with a brief introduction.

FIGURE 2.4 **Typical Meeting Agenda**

AGENDA

Quantum Travel International
Staff Meeting
September 4, 2014
10 to 11 a.m.
Conference Room

I.   Call to order; roll call

II. Approval of agenda

III. Approval of minutes from previous meeting

		Person	Proposed Time
IV.	Committee reports		
	A. Web site update	Jared	5 minutes
	B. Tour packages	Lakisha	10 minutes
V.	Old business		
	A. Equipment maintenance	John	5 minutes
	B. Client escrow accounts	Alicia	5 minutes
	C. Internal newsletter	Adrienne	5 minutes
VI.	New business		
	A. New accounts	Garth	5 minutes
	B. Pricing policy for Asian tours	Minh	15 minutes

VII. Announcements

VIII. Chair's summary, adjournment

A typical set of ground rules might include arriving on time, communicating openly, being supportive, listening carefully, participating fully, confronting conflict frankly, and following the agenda. More formal groups follow parliamentary procedures based on *Robert's Rules of Order*. After establishing basic ground rules, the leader should ask if participants agree thus far. The next step is to assign one attendee to take minutes and one to act as a recorder. The recorder uses a computer and projector or stands at a flipchart or whiteboard and lists the main ideas being discussed and agreements reached.

Moving the Meeting Along. After the preliminaries, the leader should say as little as possible. Like a talk show host, an effective leader makes "sure that each panel member gets some air time while no one member steals the show."[16] Remember that the purpose of a meeting is to exchange views, not to hear one person, even the leader, do all the talking. If the group has one member who monopolizes, the leader might say, "Thanks,

FIGURE 2.5. Using Calendar Programs

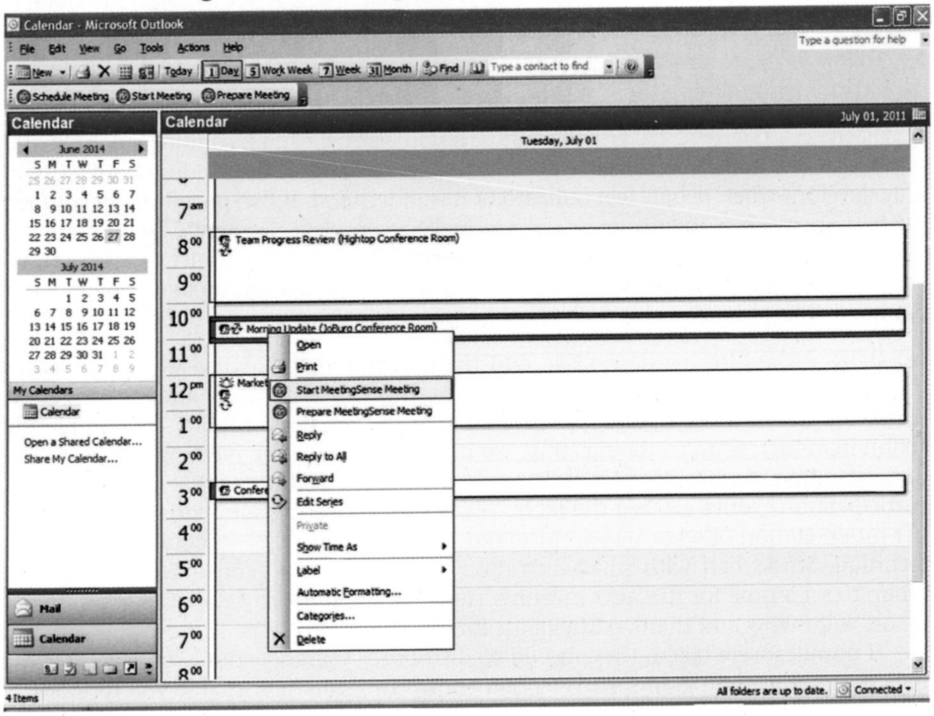

Calendar programs ease the frustration of scheduling meetings for busy people. The program allows you to check colleagues' calendars, locate a free time, schedule a meeting, send out an initial announcement, and follow up with reminders.

Michelle, for that perspective, but please hold your next point while we hear how Ryan would respond to that." This technique also encourages quieter participants to speak up.

To avoid allowing digressions to sidetrack the group, try generating a "parking lot" list. This is a list of important but divergent issues that should be discussed at a later time. Another way to handle digressions is to say, "Folks, we are getting off track here. Forgive me for pressing on, but let's return to the central issue of. . . ." It is important to adhere to the agenda and the time schedule. Equally important, when the group seems to have reached a consensus, is to summarize the group's position and check to see whether everyone agrees.

> Successful leaders keep the meeting moving by avoiding issues that sidetrack the group.

Participating Actively and Productively. Meetings are an opportunity for you to showcase your abilities and boost your career. To get the most out of the meetings you attend, try these techniques.[17]

> To benefit from meetings, arrive early, be prepared, contribute positively and respectfully, stay calm, give credit to others, don't use your cell phone or laptop, help summarize, express your views in the meeting (not after), and complete your assignments.

- **Arrive early.** You show respect and look well organized by arriving a little early.

- **Come prepared.** Bring the agenda and any distributed materials. Study the topics and be ready with questions, comments, and good ideas.

- **Bring a positive attitude.** Use positive body language; speak energetically.

- **Contribute respectfully.** Wait your turn to speak; raise your hand to be recognized.

- **Wait for others to finish.** Show respect and good manners by not interrupting.

- **Keep your voice calm and pleasant, yet energetic.** Avoid showing anger, as this focuses attention on your behaviour rather than on your ideas.

- **Give credit to others.** Gain allies and enhance your credibility by recognizing others in front of peers and superiors.

- **Put the cellphone and laptop away.** Focus your attention on the meeting, not on answering e-mail or working on your computer.

- **Help summarize.** Assist the meeting leader by reviewing points you have noted.

- **Express your views in the meeting.** Build trust by not holding postmeeting "sidebars" with criticism and judgments.
- **Follow up.** Send the signal that you are efficient and caring by completing the actions assigned to you.

When a conflict develops between two members, allow each to make a complete case before the group.

Handling Conflict in Meetings. As you learned earlier, conflict is natural and even desirable. But it can cause awkwardness and uneasiness. In meetings conflict typically develops when people feel unheard or misunderstood. If two people are in conflict, the best approach is to encourage each to make a complete case while group members give their full attention. Let each one question the other. Then the leader should summarize what was said, and the group should offer comments. The group may modify a recommendation or suggest alternatives before reaching consensus on a direction to follow.

Ending and Following Up. End the meeting at the agreed time. The leader should summarize what has been decided, who is going to do what, and by what time. It may be necessary to ask people to volunteer to take responsibility for completing action items agreed to in the meeting. No one should leave the meeting without a full understanding of what was accomplished. One effective technique that encourages full participation is "once around the table." Everyone is asked to summarize briefly his or her interpretation of what was decided and what happens next. Of course, this closure technique works best with smaller groups. The leader should conclude by asking the group to set a time for the next meeting. He or she should also assure the group that a report will follow and thank participants for attending.

If minutes were taken, they should be distributed within a couple of days after the meeting. Software programs, such as that shown in Figure 2.6, enable you to follow a structured template that includes brief meeting minutes, key points and decisions, and action items. It is up to the leader to see that what was decided at the meeting is accomplished. The leader may need to call people to remind them of their assignments and also to volunteer to help them if necessary.

Effective meetings end with a summary of accomplishments with a follow-up reminding participants of their assigned tasks.

FIGURE 2.6 E-Mail Meeting Minutes

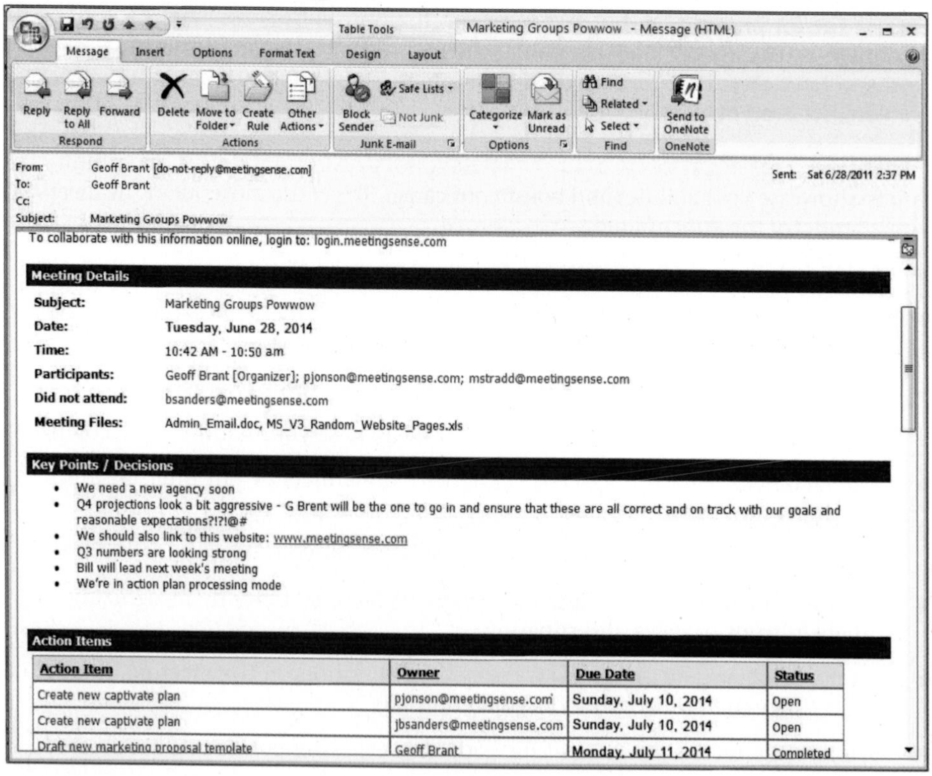

Meeting proceedings are efficiently recorded in a summary distribution template that provides subject, date, time, participant names, absentee names, meeting files, key points, decisions, and action items.

Using Effective Practices and Technologies in Virtual Meetings

One of the major trends in today's workplace is the rise of virtual meetings instead of face-to-face meetings. *Virtual meetings* are gatherings of participants who are connected technologically. As travel costs rise and companies slash budgets, many organizations are cutting back on meetings that require travel.[18] In addition, more and more people work together but are not located in the same spot. Instead of meeting face to face, people have found other ways to exchange ideas, brainstorm, build consensus, and develop personal relationships. They may meet in audioconferences by using telephones or in videoconferences by using the Internet. Steady improvement in telecommunications networks, software, and computer processing continues to fuel the shift to virtual meetings. These meetings have many purposes, including training employees, making sales presentations, coordinating team activities, and talking to customers.

Saving travel costs and reducing employee fatigue are significant reasons for the digital displacement of business travel. Virtual meetings are possible through the use of a number of efficient tools, including audioconferencing, videoconferencing, and Web conferencing.

Audioconferencing

Among the simplest collaboration tools is *audioconferencing* (also called teleconferencing, conference calling, or phone conferencing). One or more people in a work area use an enhanced speakerphone to confer with others by telephone. To make a call, a company engages a telecommunications carrier and participants dial a given number. They enter a pass code and are admitted to a conference bridge. This kind of audioconferencing enables people at both ends to speak and be heard simultaneously. Thanks to mobile phones, people can even participate in an audioconference from an airplane or the beach. Although audioconferencing is not as sophisticated as other collaboration tools, it is the mainstay of the entire teleconferencing industry.

Audioconferencing enables collaborators to confer with each other by telephone.

Videoconferencing

If meeting participants need to see each other or share documents, they may use *videoconferencing*. This tool combines video, audio, and communications networking technologies for real-time interaction.

At the high end of videoconferencing systems are *telepresence rooms*. These specially designed conference rooms are the next best thing to being there. Telepresence rooms typically are equipped with three huge curved screens, custom lighting, and advanced acoustics. Sharper than the best high-definition television sets, images may be magnified to scrutinize even the microcircuitry on new electronic products. Multiple high-definition monitors deliver life-size images so real that the next time you see a participant, you feel as if you've met that person before, says one proponent.[19] Whether using high- or low-end conferencing tools, participants do not have to journey to distant meetings. Organizations reduce travel expenses, travel time, and employee fatigue.

Videoconferencing combines video, audio, and software to connect collaborators in real time.

Web Conferencing

Web conferencing is similar to videoconferencing but may work with or without the transmission of pictures of the participants. Attendees use their computers to access an online virtual meeting room where they can present PowerPoint slides or share spreadsheets or Word documents, just as they might do in a face-to-face meeting. Web conferencing is particularly useful for team meetings, training, and sales presentations. Participants can demonstrate products and make changes in real time during a meeting.

Features of Web conferencing programs typically include slideshow presentations, live or streaming video, tours of Web sites in which users may participate, meeting recording, whiteboard with annotation capabilities, screen sharing, and text chat. GoToMeeting, a reasonably priced commercial conferencing tool, enables people to launch meetings by sending instant messages to attendees, who click on an embedded link to join the group. Participants are generally connected to a phone conference call.

Web conferencing enables collaborators to use their computers in sharing documents, data, and slideshows.

On their computers, attendees see the presenter's desktop and all the actions performed there—from viewing Web pages to advancing through a presentation. They participate with each other by using instant messaging in a chat window. WebEx offers a richer Web conferencing tool, including whiteboarding and other advanced functions.

Skype, a virtually free conferencing tool popular with students and expatriates, is also used by businesspeople. It allows conferencing with or without a camera. All that is needed is a laptop, a headset with a microphone, and a Web camera. Constantly evolving, Web conferencing is changing the way businesspeople work together.

Planning Virtual Meetings and Interacting Professionally

Because people are not physically together, virtual meetings and teleconferences require special awareness and planning. Although the same good meeting management techniques discussed for face-to-face meetings prevail, additional skills and practices are important. A major problem when people are not facing each other is that any small infraction or miscue can be blown out of proportion. Words and tone can be easily misinterpreted. In addition, bandwidth and technology issues can create chaos in virtual meetings. To help you plan and participate professionally in efficient virtual meetings, we present the following suggestions gathered from experienced meeting facilitators.[20]

Before starting a virtual meeting, decide what technology will be used and ensure that everyone is able to fully participate.

Premeeting Considerations.
A virtual meeting or teleconference will be more successful if you address a number of premeeting issues. Most important, decide what technology will be used. Check to be sure that everyone is able to participate fully by using that technology. If someone can't see what is happening on screen, the entire meeting can be disrupted and delayed. A few participants may need coaching before the session begins so that they can interact comfortably. Set the time of the meeting, preferably by using Coordinated Universal Time (UTC) so that participants in different time zones are not confused. Be particularly mindful of how the meeting schedule affects others. Avoid spanning a lunch hour, holding someone overtime, or making someone arrive extra early.

Important virtual meeting ground rules include ensuring that participants understand how questions will be asked and answered.

For global meetings decide what language will be used. If that language may be difficult for some participants, think about using simple expressions and repeating major ideas. Before the meeting distribute any materials that will be shared. If documents will be edited or marked during the meeting, be sure participants know how to use the online editing tools. Finally, to avoid panic at the last minute, encourage participants to log on 15 minutes early. Some programs require downloads and installations that can cause immense frustration if not done early.

Ground Rules for Virtual Meetings.
During virtual meetings, establishing a few ground rules achieves the best results. For one thing, explain how questions may be asked and answered. Many meeting programs allow participants to "raise their hand" with an icon on a side panel of the computer screen. Then they can type in their question for the leader and others to see. Unless the meeting involves people who know each other well, participants in audioconferences should always say their names before beginning to comment.

One of the biggest problems of virtual meetings is background noise from participants' offices or homes. You might hear dogs barking, telephones ringing, and toilets flushing. Meeting planners disagree on whether to require participants to put their phones on mute. Although the mute button reduces noise, it also prevents immediate participation and tends to deaden the conference. If you decide to ask participants to mute their phones, make it part of your ground rules and include a reminder at the beginning of the session. In addition, remind people to turn off cellphones and smartphones. As a personal ground rule, don't allow yourself to multitask—and that includes not checking your e-mail—during virtual meetings. Giving your full attention is critical if the meeting requires engagement and interaction.

Techniques for Collaborating Successfully in Virtual Meetings.
Collaborating successfully in virtual meetings requires awareness of limitations and techniques for overcoming those limitations. For example, when individuals meet face to face, they usually can recognize blank looks when people do not understand

something being discussed. But in virtual meetings participants and presenters cannot always see each other. "They [participants] will lose place, lose focus, and lose attention to the meeting," one meeting expert noted.[21] He also warned that participants won't tell you if they are lost. As a result, when presenting ideas at a virtual meeting, you should be as precise as possible. Give examples and use simple language. Recap and summarize often. Confirm your understanding of what is being discussed. If you are a presenter, project an upbeat, enthusiastic, and strong voice. Without eye contact and nonverbal cues, the best way to keep the attention of the audience is through a powerful voice.

To encourage participation and avoid traffic jams with everyone talking at once, experts suggest a number of techniques. Participants soon lose interest if the leader is the only one talking. Therefore, encourage dialogue by asking questions of specific people. Often you will learn not only what the person is thinking but also what others feel but have not stated. Another technique that promotes discussion and gives everyone a chance to speak is "around the table." Even though the table is merely symbolic, the image works. Go through the list of participants, inviting each to speak for 30 seconds without interruption. If individuals have nothing to say, they may pass

> Prevent participants from getting lost during virtual meetings by being precise, confirming your understanding of what is being discussed, encouraging dialogue by asking questions, and allowing time before and after the meeting for small talk.

Checklist

Planning and Participating in Productive Meetings

Before the Meeting

- **Consider alternatives.** Unless a topic is important and pressing, avoid calling a meeting. Perhaps an e-mail message, a telephone call, or an announcement would serve the purpose better.

- **Invite the right people.** To make a decision, invite those people who have information and authority to make the decision and implement it.

- **Distribute an agenda.** Prepare and distribute an agenda that includes the date and place of meeting, the start and end times, a brief description of each topic, the names of people responsible for any action, and a proposed time allotment for each topic.

- **Use a calendaring program.** If it's available, use calendaring software to set a meeting date, issue invitations, and send the agenda.

- **Train participants on technology.** Especially for virtual meetings, be sure participants are comfortable with the conferencing software.

During the Meeting

- **Start on time and introduce the agenda.** Discuss the goal and length of the meeting, provide background of topics for discussion, suggest possible solutions and constraints, propose a tentative agenda, and clarify the ground rules for the meeting.

- **Appoint a secretary and a recorder.** Ask one attendee to make a record of the proceedings and ask another person to record discussion topics on a flipchart or whiteboard.

- **Encourage balanced participation.** Strive to be sure that all participants' views are heard and that no one monopolizes the discussion. Avoid digressions by steering the group back to the topics on the agenda. In virtual meetings, be sure participants identify themselves before speaking.

- **Confront conflict frankly.** Encourage people who disagree to explain their positions completely. Then restate each position and ask for group comments. The group may modify a recommendation or suggest alternatives before agreeing on a plan of action.

- **Summarize along the way.** When the group seems to reach a consensus, summarize and see whether everyone agrees.

Ending the Meeting and Following Up

- **Review meeting decisions.** At the end of the meeting, consider using "around the table" to be sure everyone understands what has been decided. Discuss action items and establish a schedule for completion.

- **Distribute minutes of meeting.** A few days after the meeting, arrange to have the secretary distribute the minutes. Use an e-mail template, if available, to distribute meeting minutes.

- **Remind people of action items.** Follow up by calling people to see whether they are completing the actions recommended at the meeting.

when their names are called. A second "around the table" provides another opportunity to speak. Leaders should avoid asking leading questions, such as, *Does everyone agree*? Remote attendees cannot answer easily without drowning out one another's responses.

One final suggestion involves building camaraderie and trust. For teams with distant members, it helps to leave time before or after the scheduled meeting for small talk. A few moments of chat builds personal bonds and establishes a warm environment. Even with larger, unfamiliar groups, you can build trust and interest by dialling in early and greeting others as they join the group.

Virtual meetings are the wave of the future. Learning to plan and participate in them professionally will enhance your career as a business communicator. The Checklist box on page 43 summarizes helpful techniques for both face-to-face and virtual meetings.

Listening in the Workplace

LEARNING OBJECTIVE 5

Explain and implement active listening techniques.

According to the Conference Board of Canada, listening is a critical employee and management skill. Listening skills are part of the soft skills that employers seek when looking for well-rounded candidates who can be hired and promoted.

But, you may be thinking, everyone knows how to listen. Most of us believe that listening is an automatic response to noise. We do it without thinking. Perhaps that explains why so many of us are poor listeners. In this chapter we explore the importance of listening, the kinds of listening required in the workplace, and how to become a better listener. Although many of the tips for improving your listening skills will be effective in your personal life, our discussion centres primarily on workplace and employment needs.

As you learned earlier, workers are doing more communicating than ever before, largely because of the Internet, team environments, global competition, and an emphasis on customer service. A vital ingredient in every successful workplace is high-quality communication. And three quarters of high-quality communication involves listening.[22]

Listening skills are critical for career success, organization effectiveness, and worker satisfaction.

Listening skills are important for career success, organization effectiveness, and worker satisfaction. Numerous studies and experts report that good listeners make good managers and that good listeners advance more rapidly in their organizations.[23] Listening is especially important in the workplace because we spend so much time doing it. Most workers spend 30 to 45 percent of their communication time listening,[24] whereas executives spend 60 to 70 percent of their communication time listening.[25]

Poor Listening Habits

Although executives and workers devote the bulk of their communication time to listening, research suggests that they are not very good at it. In fact, most of us are poor listeners. Some estimates indicate that only half of the oral messages heard in a day are completely understood.[26] Experts say that we listen at only 25 percent efficiency. In other words, we ignore, forget, distort, or misunderstand 75 percent of everything we hear.

Most of us listen at only 25 percent efficiency.

Poor listening habits may result from several factors. Lack of training is one significant reason. Few schools give as much emphasis to listening as they do to the development of reading, speaking, and writing skills. In addition, our listening skills may be less than perfect because of the large number of competing sounds and stimuli in our lives that interfere with concentration. Finally, we are inefficient listeners because we are able to process speech much faster than others can speak. While most speakers talk at about 125 to 250 words per minute, listeners can think at 450 words per minute.[27] The resulting lag time fosters daydreaming, which clearly reduces listening efficiency.

We are inefficient listeners because of lack of training, competing sounds, slowness of speech, and daydreaming.

Types of Workplace Listening

On the job you can expect to be involved in many types of listening. These include listening to superiors, listening to fellow colleagues and team members, and listening to customers. If you are an entry-level employee, you will probably be most concerned with listening to superiors. But you also must develop skills for listening to colleagues and team members. As you advance in your career and enter the ranks of management, you will need skills for listening to subordinates. Finally, the entire organization must listen to customers to compete in today's service-oriented economy.

Listening to Superiors. On the job one of your most important tasks will be listening to instructions, assignments, and explanations about how to do your work. You will be listening to learn and to comprehend. To focus totally on the speaker, be sure you are not distracted by noisy surroundings or other tasks. Don't take phone calls and don't try to complete another job while listening with one ear. Show your interest by leaning forward and striving for good eye contact.

> Listening to superiors involves hearing instructions, assignments, and explanations of work procedures.

Above all, take notes. Don't rely on your memory. Details are easy to forget. Taking selective notes also conveys to the speaker your seriousness about hearing accurately and completely. Don't interrupt. When the speaker finishes, paraphrase the instructions in your own words. Ask pertinent questions in a nonthreatening manner. And don't be afraid to ask "dumb" questions if it means you won't have to do a job twice. Avoid criticizing or arguing when you are listening to a superior. Your goals should be to hear accurately and to convey an image of competence.

> Good listening techniques include taking notes, not interrupting, and paraphrasing.

Listening to Colleagues and Teammates. Much of your listening will result from interactions with fellow workers and teammates. In these exchanges two kinds of listening are important. *Critical listening* enables you to judge and evaluate what you are hearing. You will be listening to decide whether the speaker's message is fact, fiction, or opinion. You will also be listening to decide whether an argument is based on logic or emotion. Critical listening requires an effort on your part. You must remain objective, particularly when you disagree with what you are hearing. Control your tendency to prejudge. Let the speaker have a chance to complete the message before you evaluate it. *Discriminative listening* is necessary when you must understand and remember. It means you must identify main ideas, understand a logical argument, and recognize the purpose of the message.

> Listening to colleagues and teammates involves critical listening and discriminative listening.

Listening to Customers. As the North American economy becomes increasingly service oriented, the new management mantra has become "customers rule." Many organizations are just learning that listening to customers results in increased sales and profitability, as well as improved customer acquisition and retention. The simple truth is that consumers feel better about companies that value their opinions. Listening is an acknowledgment of caring and is a potent retention tool. Customers want to be cared about. By doing so, companies fulfill a powerful human need.

> Organizations that listen to customers improve sales and profitability.

How can organizations improve their customer listening techniques? Because employees are the eyes and ears of the organization, smart companies begin by hiring employees who genuinely care about customers. Listening organizations also train their employees to listen actively and to ask gentle, probing questions to ensure clear understanding. Employees trained in listening techniques are far more likely to elicit customer feedback and promote goodwill than untrained employees are.

Improving Workplace Listening

Listening on the job is more difficult than listening in college or university classes where experienced professors present well-organized lectures and repeat important points. Workplace listening is more challenging because information is often exchanged casually. It may be disorganized, unclear, and cluttered with extraneous facts. Moreover, your fellow workers are usually friends. Because they are familiar with one another, they may not be as polite and respectful as they are with strangers. Friends tend to interrupt, jump to conclusions, and take each other for granted.

Listening in groups or listening to nonnative speakers further complicates the listening process. In groups, more than one person talks at once, and topics change rapidly. Group members are monitoring both verbal and nonverbal messages to learn what relates to their group roles.

Ten Keys to Building Powerful Listening Skills

Despite the complexities and challenges of workplace listening, good listeners on the job must remember that their goal is to listen carefully and to *understand* what is being said so that they can do their work well. The following recommendations can help you improve your workplace listening effectiveness.

1. **Control external and internal distractions.** Move to an area where you can hear without conflicting noises or conversations. Block out surrounding physical distractions. Internally, try to focus totally on the speaker. If other projects are on your mind, put them on the back burner temporarily. When you are emotionally charged, whether angry or extremely happy, it is a good idea to postpone any serious listening.

2. **Become actively involved.** Show that you are listening closely by leaning forward and maintaining eye contact with the speaker. Don't fidget or try to complete another task at the same time you are listening. Listen to more than the spoken words. How are they said? What implied meaning, reasoning, and feelings do you hear behind the spoken words? Does the speaker's body language (eye contact, posture, movements) support or contradict the main message?

3. **Separate facts from opinions.** Facts are truths known to exist; for example, *PartSource, Mark's Work Wearhouse, and Canadian Tire Financial are all included under Canadian Tire Corporation, Ltd.* is a fact. Opinions are statements of personal judgments or preferences; for example, *Canadian Tire has the best choice of household goods.* Some opinions are easy to recognize because speakers preface them with such statements as *I think, It seems to me,* and *As far as I'm concerned.*[28] Often, however, listeners must evaluate assertions to decide their validity. Good listeners consider whether speakers are credible and speaking within their areas of competence. They do not automatically accept assertions as facts.

4. **Identify important facts.** Speakers on the job often intersperse critical information with casual conversation. Unrelated topics pop up—ball scores, a customer's weird request, a computer glitch, or the boss's extravagant new SUV. Your task is to select what's important and register it mentally. What step is next in your project? Who does what? What is your role?

5. **Avoid interrupting.** While someone else has the floor, do not interrupt with a quick reply or opinion. And don't show nonverbal disagreement, such as negative head shaking, rolling eyes, sarcastic snorting, or audible sighs. Good listeners let speakers have their say. Interruptions are not only impolite, but they also prevent you from hearing the speaker's complete thought. Listeners who interrupt with their opinions sidetrack discussions and cause hard feelings.

6. **Ask clarifying questions.** Good listeners wait for the proper moment and then ask questions that do not attack the speaker. Instead of saying, *But I don't understand how you can say that,* a good listener seeks clarification with questions, such as, *Please help me understand by explaining more about. . . .* Because questions can put you in control of the situation, think about them in advance. Use open questions (those without set answers) to draw out feelings, motivations, ideas, and suggestions. Use closed fact-finding questions to identify key factors in a discussion.[29] Don't ask a question unless you are ready to be quiet and listen to the answer.

7. **Paraphrase to increase understanding.** To make sure you understand a speaker, rephrase and summarize a message in your own words. Be objective and nonjudgmental. Remember, your goal is to understand what the speaker has

You listen better when you control distractions, become actively involved, separate facts from opinion, and identify important facts.

said—not to show how mindless the speaker's words sound when parroted. Remember, too, that other workplace listeners will also benefit from a clear summary of what was said.

8. **Capitalize on lag time.** While you are waiting for a speaker's next idea, use the time to review what the speaker is saying. Separate the central idea, key points, and details. Sometimes you may have to supply the organization. Use lag time to silently rephrase and summarize the speaker's message. Another effective trick for keeping your mind from drifting is to try to guess what a speaker's next point will be. Most important, keep your mind focused on the speaker and his or her ideas—not on all the other work waiting for you.

9. **Take notes to ensure retention.** Do not trust your memory. A wise person once said that he'd rather have a short pencil than a long memory. If you have a hallway conversation with a colleague and don't have a pencil handy, make a mental note of the important items. Then write them down as soon as possible. Even with seemingly easily remembered facts or instructions, jot them down to ease your mind and to be sure you understand them correctly. Two weeks later you will be glad you did. Be sure you have a good place to store notes about various projects, such as file folders, notebooks, or computer files.

10. **Be aware of gender differences.** Men tend to listen for facts, whereas women tend to perceive listening as an opportunity to connect with the other person on a personal level.[30] Men tend to use interrupting behaviour to control conversations, while women generally interrupt to communicate assent, to elaborate on another group member's idea, or to participate in the topic of conversation. Women listeners tend to be attentive, provide steady eye contact, remain stationary, and nod their heads.[31] Male listeners are less attentive, provide sporadic eye contact, and move around. Being aware of these tendencies will make you a more sensitive and knowledgeable listener.

The Checklist box provides tips for improving listening effectiveness.

Checklist

Improving Listening

- **Stop talking.** Accept the role of listener by concentrating on the speaker's words, not on what your response will be.

- **Work hard at listening.** Become actively involved; expect to learn something.

- **Block out competing thoughts.** Concentrate on the message. Don't allow yourself to daydream during lag time.

- **Control the listening environment.** Move to a quiet area where you won't be interrupted by telephone calls or visitors. Check to be certain that listeners can hear speakers.

- **Maintain an open mind.** Know your biases and try to correct for them. Be tolerant of people with disabilities and speakers who may look different from you. Provide verbal and nonverbal feedback. Encourage the speaker with comments, such as *Yes, I see, OK*, and *Uh-huh*, and ask polite questions. Look alert by leaning forward.

- **Paraphrase the speaker's ideas.** Silently repeat the message in your own words, sort out the main points, and identify supporting details. In conversation sum up the main points to confirm what was said.

- **Listen between the lines.** Observe nonverbal cues and interpret the feelings of the speaker: What is really being said?

- **Distinguish between facts and opinions.** Know the difference between factual statements and opinions stated as assertions.

- **Capitalize on lag time.** Use spare moments to organize, review, anticipate, challenge, and weigh the evidence.

- **Use memory devices.** If the information is important, develop acronyms, links, or rhymes to help you remember.

- **Take selective notes.** If you are hearing instructions or important data, record the major points. Then revise your notes immediately or verify them with the speaker.

Communicating Through Nonverbal Messages

LEARNING OBJECTIVE 6

Understand how the functions and forms of nonverbal communication can help you advance your career.

Understanding messages often involves more than merely listening to spoken words. Nonverbal cues also carry powerful meanings. Nonverbal communication includes all unwritten and unspoken messages, both intentional and unintentional. Eye contact, facial expression, body movements, space, time, distance, and appearance—all these nonverbal cues influence the way a message is interpreted, or decoded, by the receiver. Many of the nonverbal messages that we send are used intentionally to accompany spoken words. But people can also communicate nonverbally even when they don't intend to.

Because nonverbal communication is an important tool for you to use and control in the workplace, you need to learn more about its functions and forms.

Functions of Nonverbal Communication

Nonverbal communication helps convey meaning in at least five ways. As you become more aware of the following functions of nonverbal communication, you will be better able to use these silent codes to your advantage in the workplace.

> **Communicators use nonverbal cues to complement and illustrate, to reinforce and accentuate, to replace and substitute, and to control and regulate.**

- **To complement and illustrate.** Nonverbal messages can amplify, modify, or provide details for a verbal message. For example, in describing the size of a cellphone, a speaker holds his fingers 12 cm apart. In pumping up sales reps, the manager jams his fist into the palm of his other hand to indicate the strong effort required.

- **To reinforce and accentuate.** Skilled speakers raise their voices to convey important ideas, but they whisper to suggest secrecy. A grimace forecasts painful news, whereas a big smile intensifies good news. A neat, well-equipped office reinforces a message of professionalism.

- **To replace and substitute.** Many gestures substitute for words: nodding your head for yes, giving a V for victory, making a thumbs-up sign for approval, and shrugging your shoulders for *I don't know* or *I don't care*. In fact, a complex set of gestures totally replaces spoken words in sign language.

- **To control and regulate.** Nonverbal messages are important regulators in conversation. Shifts in eye contact, slight head movements, changes in posture, raising of eyebrows, nodding of the head, and voice inflection—all these cues tell speakers when to continue, to repeat, to elaborate, to hurry up, or to finish.

- **To contradict.** To be sarcastic, a speaker might hold his nose while stating that your new perfume is wonderful. In the workplace, individuals may send contradictory messages with words or actions. The boss, for example, says he wants to promote Kevin, but he fails to submit the necessary recommendation.

In the workplace people may not be aware that they are sending contradictory messages. Researchers have found that when verbal and nonverbal messages contradict each other, listeners tend to believe and act on the nonverbal message.

> **Because nonverbal messages may speak louder than words, effective communicators make sure that their nonverbal cues reinforce their spoken words.**

In one experiment speakers delivered a positive message but averted their eyes as they spoke. Listeners perceived the overall message to be negative. Moreover, listeners thought that gaze aversion suggested nonaffection, superficiality, lack of trust, and non-receptivity.[32] The lesson to be learned here is that effective communicators must be certain that all their nonverbal messages reinforce their spoken words and their professional goals. To make sure that you're on the right track to nonverbal communication competency, let's look more carefully at the specific forms of nonverbal communication.

Forms of Nonverbal Communication

Instead of conveying meaning with words, nonverbal messages carry their meaning in a number of different forms, including facial expressions, body language, and even clothes. Each of us sends and receives thousands of nonverbal messages daily in our business and personal lives. Although the following discussion covers all forms of nonverbal communication, we will be especially concerned with workplace applications. As you learn about the messages sent by eye contact, facial expressions, posture, and gestures, as well as the use of time, space, territory, and appearance, think about how you can use these nonverbal cues positively in your career.

Eye Contact.

The eyes have been called the "windows to the soul." Even if communicators can't look directly into the soul, they consider the eyes to be the most accurate predictor of a speaker's true feelings and attitudes. Most of us cannot look another person straight in the eyes and lie. As a result, we tend to believe people who look directly at us. We have less confidence in and actually distrust those who cannot maintain eye contact. Sustained eye contact suggests trust and admiration; brief eye contact signifies fear or stress. Prolonged eye contact, however, can be intrusive and intimidating.

The eyes are thought to be the most accurate predictor of a speaker's true feelings.

Good eye contact enables the message sender to determine whether a receiver is paying attention, showing respect, responding favourably, or feeling distress. From the receiver's perspective, good eye contact reveals the speaker's sincerity, confidence, and truthfulness. Because eye contact is a learned skill, however, you must be respectful of people who do not maintain it. You must also remember that nonverbal cues, including eye contact, have different meanings in various cultures. Chapter 3 presents more information about the cultural influence of nonverbal cues.

Facial Expression.

The expression on a communicator's face can be almost as revealing of emotion as the eyes. Researchers estimate that the human face can display more than 250,000 expressions.[33] Although a few people can control these expressions and maintain a "poker face" when they want to hide their feelings, most of us display our emotions openly. Raising or lowering the eyebrows, squinting, swallowing nervously, clenching the jaw, and smiling broadly—these voluntary and involuntary facial expressions supplement or entirely replace verbal messages. In the workplace maintaining a pleasant expression with frequent smiles promotes harmony.

Posture and Gestures.

An individual's general posture can convey anything from high status and self-confidence to shyness and submissiveness. Leaning toward a speaker suggests attraction and interest; pulling away or shrinking back denotes fear, distrust, anxiety, or disgust. Similarly, gestures can communicate entire thoughts via simple movements. But remember that these nonverbal cues may have vastly different meanings in different cultures.

Erect posture sends a message of confidence, competence, diligence, and strength.

In the workplace you can make a good impression by controlling your posture and gestures. When speaking, make sure your upper body is aligned with the person to whom you're talking. Erect posture sends a message of confidence, competence, diligence, and strength.

Time.

How we structure and use time tells observers about our personality and attitudes. North Americans generally place a great deal of emphasis on punctuality; however, in other cultures and regions punctuality is viewed differently. In the workplace you can send positive nonverbal messages by being on time for meetings and appointments, staying on task during meetings, and giving ample time to appropriate projects and individuals.

Being on time sends a positive nonverbal message in North American workplaces.

Space.

How we arrange things in the space around us tells something about ourselves and our objectives. Whether the space is a residence room, an office, or a department, people reveal themselves in the design and grouping of furniture within that space. Generally, the more formal the arrangement, the more formal and closed the communication environment.

The way an office is arranged can send nonverbal messages about the openness of its occupant.

Territory.

Each of us has certain areas that we feel are our own territory, whether it is a specific spot or just the space around us. We all maintain zones of privacy in which

FIGURE 2.7 **Four Space Zones for Social Interaction**

Intimate Zone
(1 to 1.5 feet
or 0.3 to 0.5 m)

Personal Zone
(1.5 to 4 feet
or 0.5 to 1.3 m)

Social Zone
(4 to 12 feet
or 1.3 to 3.5 m)

Public Zone
(12 or more feet
or 3.6 m or more)

we feel comfortable. Figure 2.7 categorizes the four zones of social interaction among North Americans, as formulated by anthropologist Edward T. Hall. Notice that we North Americans are a bit standoffish; only intimate friends and family may stand closer than about half a metre. If someone violates that territory, we feel uncomfortable and defensive and may step back to reestablish our space. In the workplace, be aware of the territorial needs of others and don't invade their space.

Your appearance and the appearance of your documents convey nonverbal messages.

Appearance of Business Documents.   The way a letter, memo, or report looks can have either a positive or a negative effect on the receiver. Through their postage, stationery, and printing, envelopes can suggest routine, important, or junk mail. Letters and reports can look neat, professional, well organized, and attractive—or just the opposite. Sloppy, hurriedly written documents convey negative nonverbal messages regarding both the content and the sender. Among the worst offenders are e-mail messages.

Although they seem like conversation, e-mails are business documents that create a permanent record and often a bad impression. Sending an e-mail message full of errors conveys a damaging nonverbal message. It says that the writer doesn't care enough about this message to take the time to make it read well or look good. The receiver immediately doubts the credibility of the sender. How much faith can you put in someone who can't spell, capitalize, or punctuate and won't make the effort to communicate clearly?

In succeeding chapters you will learn how to create documents that send positive nonverbal messages through their appearance, format, organization, readability, and correctness.

Viewers judge a person's status, credibility, personality, and potential on the nonverbal message sent by that person's appearance.

Appearance of People.   The way you look—your clothing, grooming, and posture—telegraphs an instant nonverbal message about you. Based on what they see, viewers make quick judgments about your status, credibility, personality, and potential. Business communicators who look the part are more likely to be successful in working with superiors, colleagues, and customers.

Invest in appropriate, professional-looking clothing and accessories. Remember that quality is more important than quantity. Avoid flashy garments, clunky jewellery, garish makeup, and overpowering colognes. Pay attention to good grooming, including a neat hairstyle, body cleanliness, polished shoes, and clean nails. Project confidence in your posture, both standing and sitting.

One of the latest fashion rages is body art in the form of tattoos. Once seen primarily on bikers, prisoners, and sailors, inked images, such as butterflies, bluebirds, spiders, and angels, increasingly adorn the bodies of those who seek to be glamorous. Think twice, however, before displaying tattoos at work. They may make a person feel distinctive and slightly daring, but they could derail a professional career.

A less risky trend is the movement toward one or more days per week of casual dress at work. Be aware, though, that casual clothes change the image you project and also may affect your work style.

Unit 1: Communication Foundations

FIGURE 2.8 Sending Positive Nonverbal Signals in the Workplace

Eye contact	Maintain direct but not prolonged eye contact.
Facial expression	Express warmth with frequent smiles.
Posture	Convey self-confidence with erect stance.
Gestures	Suggest accessibility with open-palm gestures.
Time	Be on time; use time judiciously.
Space	Maintain neat, functional work areas.
Territory	Use closeness to show warmth and to reduce status differences.
Business documents	Produce careful, neat, professional, well-organized messages.
Appearance	Be well groomed, neat, and appropriately dressed.

In the preceding discussion of nonverbal communication, you learned that each of us gives and responds to thousands of nonverbal messages daily in our personal and work lives. You can harness the power of silent messages by reviewing Figure 2.8 and by studying the tips in the Checklist box.

Developing a Competitive Edge With Professionalism and Business Etiquette Skills

Good manners and a businesslike, professional demeanour are among the soft skills that employers seek in job candidates. Employers are far more likely to hire and promote someone who is courteous and professional than someone who lacks these skills and traits. You can learn how to be courteous, civil, and professional. This section gives you a few pointers.

LEARNING OBJECTIVE 7

Enhance your competitive edge by developing professionalism and business etiquette skills.

Checklist

Techniques for Improving Nonverbal Communication Skills in the Workplace

- **Establish and maintain eye contact.** Remember that in Canada and the United States appropriate eye contact signals interest, attentiveness, strength, and credibility.

- **Use posture to show interest.** Encourage communication interaction by leaning forward, sitting or standing erect, and looking alert.

- **Reduce or eliminate physical barriers.** Move out from behind a desk or lectern; arrange meeting chairs in a circle.

- **Improve your decoding skills.** Watch facial expressions and body language to understand the complete verbal and nonverbal message being communicated.

- **Probe for more information.** When you perceive nonverbal cues that contradict verbal meanings, politely seek additional clues (*I'm not sure I understand, Please tell me more about . . . ,* or *Do you mean that . . .*).

- **Avoid assigning nonverbal meanings out of context.** Make nonverbal assessments only when you understand a situation or a culture.

- **Associate with people from diverse cultures.** Learn about other cultures to widen your knowledge and tolerance of intercultural nonverbal messages.

- **Appreciate the power of appearance.** Remember that the appearance of your business documents, your business space, and yourself send immediate positive or negative messages to others.

- **Observe yourself on videotape.** Ensure that your verbal and nonverbal messages are in sync by taping and evaluating yourself making a presentation.

- **Enlist friends and family.** Ask friends and family members to monitor your conscious and unconscious body movements and gestures to help you become a more effective communicator.

Professionalism Leads to Success

Projecting and maintaining a professional image is key to getting hired and being promoted.

Not everyone who seeks a job is aware of the employer's expectations. Some new hires have no idea that excessive absenteeism or tardiness is grounds for termination. Others are surprised to learn that they are expected to devote their full attention to their duties when on the job. Many employees don't realize that they are sabotaging their careers when they sprinkle their conversation with *like, you know,* and uptalk (making declarative statements sound like questions). Projecting and maintaining a professional image can make a real difference in obtaining the job of your dreams. Once you get that job, you are more likely to be taken seriously and much more likely to be promoted if you look and sound professional. Do not send the wrong message with unintended or unprofessional behaviour. Figure 2.9 reviews six areas you will want to check to be sure you are projecting professionalism.

Gaining an Etiquette Edge

Being courteous and well mannered gives you a competitive edge in the job market.

Etiquette, civility, and goodwill efforts may seem out of place in today's fast-paced, high-tech offices. However, an awareness of courtesy and etiquette can give you a competitive edge in the job market. When two candidates have equal qualifications, the one who appears to be more polished and professional is more likely to be hired and promoted.

FIGURE 2.9 Projecting Professionalism When You Communicate

	Unprofessional	Professional
Speech habits	Speaking in *uptalk*, a singsong speech pattern that has a rising inflection, making sentences sound like questions; using *like* to fill in mindless chatter, substituting *go* for *said*, relying on slang, or letting profanity slip into your conversation.	Recognizing that your credibility can be seriously damaged by sounding uneducated, crude, or adolescent.
E-mail	Writing messages with incomplete sentences, misspelled words, exclamation points, IM slang, and senseless chatting. Sloppy, careless messages send a nonverbal message that you don't care, don't know, or aren't smart enough to know what is correct.	Employers like to see subjects, verbs, and punctuation marks. They may not recognize IM abbreviations. They value conciseness and correct spelling, even in brief e-mail messages.
Internet	Using an unprofessional e-mail address such as *hotbabe@hotmail.com, supasnugglykitty@yahoo.com,* or *buffedguy@aol.com.*	An e-mail address should include your name or a relevant, positive, business-like expression. It should not sound cute or like a chat room nickname.
Voice mail	An outgoing message with strident background music, weird sounds, or a joke message.	An outgoing message that states your name or phone number and provides instructions for leaving a message.
Telephone	Soap operas, thunderous music, or a TV football game playing noisily in the background when you answer the phone.	A quiet background when you answer the telephone, especially if you are expecting a prospective employer's call.
Cellphones and smartphones	Taking or placing calls during business meetings or during conversations with fellow employees; raising your voice (cell yell) or engaging in cell calls when others must reluctantly overhear; using a PDA during meetings.	Turning off phone and message notification, both audible and vibrate, during meetings; using your cellphone only when conversations can be private.
Texting	Sending and receiving text messages during meetings, allowing texting to interrupt face-to-face conversations, or texting when driving.	Sending appropriate business text messages only when necessary (perhaps when a cellphone call would disturb others).

As workloads increase and face-to-face meetings decline, bad manners and incivility are becoming alarmingly common in the North American workplace.[34] Employers, of course, suffer from the resulting drop in productivity and exodus of talent. Employees, too, suffer. They worry about incidents, think about changing jobs, and cut back their efforts on the job. It is not hard to understand why employers are looking for people who are courteous, polite, respectful, and well mannered.

Good manners convey a positive image of an organization. People like to do business with those who show respect and treat others civilly. Most of us also like to work in a pleasant environment. Considering how much time we spend at work, it makes sense that people prefer an agreeable environment to one that is rude and uncivil.

Etiquette is more about attitude than about formal rules of behaviour. That attitude is a desire to show others consideration and respect. It includes a desire to make others feel comfortable. You don't have to become an etiquette nut, but you might need to polish your social competencies a little to be an effective businessperson today. Here are a few simple pointers:

> **Etiquette involves a desire to show others consideration and respect.**

- **Use polite words.** Be generous with words and such phrases as *please, thank you,* and *you're welcome.*

- **Express sincere appreciation and praise.** Tell co-workers how much you appreciate their efforts. Remember that written thank-you notes are even better than saying thanks.

- **Be selective in sharing personal information.** Avoid talking about health concerns, personal relationships, or finances in the office.

- **Don't put people down.** If you have a reputation for criticizing people, your co-workers will begin to wonder what you are saying behind their backs.

- **Respect co-workers' space.** Turn down the ringer on your business phone, minimize the use of speakerphones, and turn your personal cellphone down or off during business hours. Avoid wearing heavy perfumes or bringing strong-smelling food.

- **Rise above others' rudeness.** Don't use profanity or participate in questionable joke telling.

- **Be considerate when sharing space and equipment with others.** Clean up after yourself.

- **Choose the high road in conflict.** Avoid letting discussions degenerate into shouting matches. Keep a calm voice tone and focus on the work rather than on personality differences.

- **Disagree agreeably.** You may not agree with everyone, but you should respect co-workers' opinions.

For more information on business etiquette and workplace manners, visit **www.guffeybrief4e.nelson.com.** You will find tips on networking manners, coping with cubicles, managers' manners, business gifts, dealing with angry customers, and gender-free etiquette.

Summary of Learning Objectives

1 **Explain the importance of professionalism, soft skills, and teamwork in today's workplace.** Employers seek workers who have strong communication, team, listening, nonverbal, and etiquette skills. Team skills are especially important because many organizations are forming teams in today's competitive, fast-paced, global economy. Virtual teams are groups of people who work independently with a shared purpose across space, time, and organization boundaries by using technology. Teams typically go through four stages of development: forming, storming, norming, and performing. Some teams never reach the performing stage; however, when they do, information flows freely, deadlines are met, and production exceeds expectations.

2 **Understand how you can contribute positively to team performance, including resolving workplace conflicts, avoiding groupthink, and reaching group decisions.** You can contribute positively if you abide by team rules, analyze tasks in problem solving, offer ideas, stimulate discussion, listen actively, show interest in others' ideas, praise others, and move the group toward its goal. In resolving conflict, team members should listen, understand the other's point of view, show a concern for the relationship, look for common ground, invent new problem-solving options, and reach an agreement that is fair. Open discussion of conflict prevents *groupthink*, a condition that leads to faulty decisions. Methods for reaching group decisions include majority, consensus, minority, averaging, and authority rule with discussion. Successful teams are small, diverse, and able to agree on their purpose, procedures, and method of conflict resolution. They use good communication techniques, collaborate rather than compete, accept ethical responsibilities, and share leadership.

3 **Discuss effective techniques for planning and participating in face-to-face workplace meetings.** Effective meetings are called only when urgent two-way communication is necessary. Leaders should limit participation to those directly involved. Leaders should start the meeting on time and keep the discussion on track. Conflict should be confronted openly by letting each person present his or her views fully before having the group decide which direction to take. Leaders should summarize what was said, end the meeting on time, and distribute minutes afterward. To participate actively, attendees should arrive early, come prepared, bring a positive attitude, and contribute respectfully. They should wait for others to finish, use calm and pleasant voices, give credit to others, avoid using cellphones and laptops, help summarize the discussion, express views in the meeting (not afterward), and follow up by completing assigned actions.

4 **Describe effective practices and technologies for planning and participating in virtual meetings.** Virtual meetings are gatherings that use technology to connect people who cannot be together physically. Such meetings are increasingly popular because they save travel time, trim costs, and reduce employee fatigue. *Audioconferencing* enables one or more people in a work area to use an enhanced speakerphone to confer with others by telephone. *Videoconferencing* combines video, audio, and communications networking technologies for real-time interaction in telepresence rooms. *Web conferencing* enables participants to stay in their offices and use their computers to present slides, share documents, and converse in real time. During virtual meetings, participants should control background noise, give full attention (avoiding cellphones or e-mail), mention their names before speaking, be precise, use simple language, and project a strong voice.

5 **Explain and implement active listening techniques.** Experts say that we listen at only 25 percent efficiency. While listening to superiors on the job, take selective notes, avoid interrupting, ask pertinent questions, and paraphrase what you hear. When listening to colleagues and teammates, listen critically to recognize facts and listen discriminately to identify main ideas and to understand logical arguments. When listening to customers, defer judgment, pay attention to content rather than form, listen completely, control emotions, give affirming statements, and invite additional comments. Keys to building powerful listening skills include controlling external and internal distractions, becoming actively involved, separating facts from opinions, identifying important facts, refraining from interrupting, asking clarifying questions, paraphrasing, taking advantage of lag time, taking notes to ensure retention, and being aware of gender differences.

6 **Understand how the functions and forms of nonverbal communication can help you advance your career.** Nonverbal communication includes all unwritten and unspoken messages, both intentional and unintentional. Nonverbal communication takes many forms including eye contact, facial expressions, posture, and gestures, as well as the use of time, space, and territory. To improve your nonverbal skills, establish and maintain eye contact, use posture to show interest, reduce or eliminate physical barriers, improve your decoding skills, probe for more information, avoid assigning nonverbal meanings out of context, associate with people from diverse cultures, appreciate the power of appearance, observe yourself on videotape, and enlist friends and family to monitor your conscious and unconscious body movements and gestures.

7 **Enhance your competitive edge by developing professionalism and business etiquette skills.** You are more likely to be hired and promoted if you project professionalism in the workplace. This includes avoiding speech habits that make you sound uneducated, crude, or adolescent. Professionalism also is reflected in careful e-mail messages, a businesslike e-mail address, and good voice mail, cellphone, and telephone manners. To gain a competitive etiquette edge, use polite words, express sincere appreciation and praise, be selective in sharing personal information with work colleagues, avoid criticizing people, respect co-workers' space, rise above others' rudeness, be considerate when sharing space, choose the high road in conflict, and disagree agreeably.

Chapter Review

1. List seven reasons that explain why organizations are forming groups and teams. (Obj. 1)

2. What are virtual teams, and how can misunderstandings among participants be reduced? (Obj. 1)

3. Compare and contrast positive and negative team behaviour. (Obj. 2)

4. What is *groupthink*, and how can it be avoided? (Obj. 2)

5. Why are team decisions based on consensus generally better than decisions reached by majority rule? (Obj. 2)

6. If you are considering organizing a meeting, what should you do before the meeting? (Obj. 3)

7. List five behaviours you consider most important in participating actively in organizational meetings. (Obj. 3)

8. How is videoconferencing different from Web conferencing? (Obj. 4)

9. What techniques can make virtual meetings as effective as face-to-face meetings? (Obj. 4)

10. According to experts, we ignore, forget, distort, or misunderstand 75 percent of everything we hear. Why are we such poor listeners? (Obj. 5)

11. What are ten techniques for improving workplace listening? Be prepared to describe each. (Obj. 5)

12. List five functions of nonverbal communication. Provide an original example of each. (Obj. 6)

13. List ten techniques for improving nonverbal communication skills in the workplace. Be prepared to discuss each. (Obj. 6)

14. Compare and contrast examples of professional and unprofessional behaviour concerning workplace speech habits and e-mail. (Obj. 7)

15. What five specific behaviours do you think would be most important in giving you an etiquette edge in your business career? (Obj. 7)

Critical Thinking

1. As a critical thinker, how would you respond to the statement that research "consistently shows that teams underperform despite all their extra resources."?[35] (Obj. 1)

2. Evaluate the following statement: "Technical proficiency has never been enough for a professional to grow beyond the staff level."[36] Do you agree or disagree, and why? (Obj. 1)

3. Why do executives and managers spend more time listening than do workers? (Obj. 5)

4. What arguments could you give for or against the idea that body language is a science with principles that can be interpreted accurately by specialists? (Obj. 6)

5. **Ethical Issue:** Rochelle is a good member of your team. However, you are disturbed that she is constantly promoting her Arbonne beauty products to other members of the team. She shows catalogues and keeps a supply of samples ready to distribute during lunch or after hours. Her desk smells like a perfume counter. During team meetings, she puts an order form on the table. As a team member, what should you do? What if Rochelle were selling Girl Guide cookies?

Activities

2.1 Soft Skills: Identifying Personal Strengths (Obj. 1)

When hiring workers, employers look for hard skills, which are those we can learn, such as mastery of software applications or accountancy procedures, and soft skills. Soft skills, also known as employability skills, are personal characteristics, strengths, or other assets a person possesses. Studies have divided soft skills into four categories:

- Thinking or cognitive
- Oral and written communication
- Personal qualities and work ethic
- Interpersonal and teamwork

Your Task. Using the preceding categories to guide you, identify your own soft skills, paying attention to those attributes you think a potential employer would value. The Conference Board of Canada provides a list of employability skills that will help you recognize which attributes best describe you. It is available at www.conferenceboard.ca/topics/education/learning-tools/employability-skills.aspx. You will want to weave these words and phrases into cover letters and résumés, which are covered in Chapter 15.

2.2 Reaching Group Decisions: Majority, Consensus, or What? (Obj. 2)

TEAM

Your Task. In small groups decide which decision strategy is best for the following situations:

a. A team of nine employees must decide whether to choose Macs or PCs for their new equipment. They must all use the same computer system.

b. Company employees, numbering around 900, must decide whether to adopt a floating holiday plan proposed by management or stay with the current plan. An accept-or-reject vote is required.

c. The owner of your company is meeting with all managers to decide which departments will be allowed to move into a new facility.

d. Appointed by management, an employee team is charged with making recommendations regarding casual Fridays. Management feels that too many employees are abusing the privilege.

e. A national professional organization with thousands of members must choose the site for its next convention.

2.3 Resolving Workplace Conflicts: Apply a Plan (Obj. 2)

TEAM

Although conflict is a normal part of every workplace, if unresolved, it can create hard feelings and reduce productivity. **Your Task.** Analyze the following scenarios. In teams, discuss each scenario and apply the six-step procedure for dealing with conflict described in this chapter. Choose two scenarios to role-play, with two of your team members taking roles.

a. Team member Ashton is angry. Once again he has been asked to represent the company at an evening charity event because he is not married, has no children, and therefore is available. Fellow team member Andrea declined, saying that she has a family and children and must help them with their homework on school nights. Other team members keep ducking these invitations saying that they have families and cannot be expected to give up their evenings. Ashton has represented the company at three events in the past year, and he believes it is time for Andrea or the others to step up.

b. A company policy manual is posted and updated on the company intranet, an internal Web site. Employees must sign that they have read and understand the manual. A conflict arises when one team member insists that employees should sign electronically. Another team member thinks that a paper form should be signed by employees so that better records may be kept.

c. Two management team members disagree on a new company e-mail policy. One wants to ban personal e-mail totally. The other thinks that an outright ban is impossible to implement. He is more concerned with limiting Internet misuse, including visits to online game, pornography, and shopping sites. The management team members agree that they need an e-mail policy, but they disagree on what to allow and what to prohibit.

d. A manager and his assistant plan to attend a conference together at a resort location. Six weeks before the conference, the company announces a cutback and limits conference support to only one person. The assistant, who has developed a presentation specifically for the conference, feels that he should be the one to attend. Travel arrangements must be made immediately.

e. Customer service rep Jackie comes to work one morning and finds Ayehsa sitting at Workstation 2. Although the customer service reps have no special workstation assigned to them, Jackie has the longest seniority and has always assumed that Workstation 2 was hers. Other workstations were available, but the supervisor told Ayesha to use Workstation 2 that morning because she didn't know that Jackie would be coming in. When Jackie arrives and sees her workstation occupied, she becomes angry and demands that Ayesha vacate "her" station.

2.4 Evaluating Meetings: Effective or Ineffective? (Obj. 3)

A recent poll of senior executives revealed that 45 percent thought that employees could be more productive if meetings were banned one day a week.[37] Now that you have studied how to plan and participate in productive meetings, you should be able to judge whether meetings are successful and why. **Your Task.** Attend a structured meeting of a university, college, social, business, or other organization. Compare the way the meeting is conducted with the suggestions presented in this chapter. Why did the meeting succeed or fail? In a class discussion or in a memo (see Chapter 7) to your instructor, discuss your analysis.

2.5 Virtual Meetings: Improving Distance Meeting Buy-In (Obj. 4)

TEAM

Marina Elliot works at the headquarters for a large organization that works with franchisees in various locations across the nation. Her position requires her to impose organizational objectives and systems on smaller groups that often resist such interference. Marina recently needed to inform regional groups that the home office was instituting a systemwide change to hiring practices. To save costs, she set up a Web conference between her office in Charlottetown and others in Etobicoke, Calgary, and Victoria. Marina set the meeting for 10 a.m. Eastern Standard Time. At the designated date and hour, she found that the Victoria team was not logged on and she had to delay the session. When the Victoria team finally did log on, Marina launched into her presentation. She explained the reasons behind the change in a PowerPoint presentation that contained complex data she had not distributed prior to the conference. Marina heard cellphone ringtones and typing in the background as she spoke. Still, she pushed through her one-hour presentation without eliciting any feedback.

Your Task. In teams, discuss ways Marina might have improved the Web conference.

2.6 Listening: Recognizing Good Habits (Obj. 5)

You've probably never paid much attention to listening. But now that you have studied it, you have become more conscious of both good and bad listening behaviour.

Your Task. For one week focus on the listening behaviour of people around you—at work, at school, and at home. Make a list of five good listening habits that you see and five bad habits. Identify the situation and participants for each item on your list. Who is the best listener you know? What makes that person a good listener? Be prepared to discuss your responses in class, with your team, or in a memo to your instructor.

2.7 Listening: Skills Required in Different Careers (Obj. 5)

TEAM

Do the listening skills and behaviours of individuals differ depending on their careers?

Your Task. Your instructor will divide you into teams and give each team a role to discuss, such as business executive, teacher, physician, police officer, lawyer, accountant, administrative assistant, mentor, or team leader. Create a list of verbal and nonverbal cues that a member of this profession would display to indicate that he or she is listening. Would the cues and behaviour change if the person were trying to listen discriminatively versus critically? How?

2.8 Nonverbal Communication: Recognizing Functions (Obj. 6)

Most of us use nonverbal cues and react to them unconsciously. We seldom think about the functions they serve.

Your Task. To become more aware of the functions of nonverbal communication, keep a log for one week. Observe how nonverbal communication is used by friends, family, instructors, co-workers, managers, politicians, newsmakers, businesses, and others. For each of the five functions of nonverbal communication identified in this chapter, list examples illustrating that function. For example, under "To reinforce and accentuate,"

you might list a friend who whispers a message to you, thus suggesting that it is a secret. Under "To control and regulate," you might list the steady gaze of your instructor who has targeted a student not paying attention. Train yourself to become more observant and begin making notes in your log. How many examples can you name for each of the five functions? Be prepared to submit your list or discuss it in class.

2.9 Nonverbal Communication: Defining Business Casual (Obj. 6)

TEAM
WEB

Although many business organizations are adopting business casual dress, most people cannot define the term. Your boss asks your internship team to use the Web to find out exactly what *business casual* means.

Your Task. Using a good search engine, such as Google, explore the Web for *business casual dress code*. A few Web sites try to define the term and give examples of appropriate clothing. Visit many sites and decide whether they are reliable enough to use as sources of accurate information. Print several relevant pages. Get together with your team and compare notes. Then write a memo to your boss explaining what men and women should and shouldn't wear on business casual days.

2.10 Business Etiquette: Staying Connected During Meetings (Obj. 7)

TEAM

Businesspeople are increasingly caving in to the temptation to use their BlackBerrys and smartphones to check e-mail, Google, Facebook, and Twitter during meetings. Techies say that ignoring real-time text messages in today's hurry-up world risks danger. They are tuned in to what is happening and can respond immediately. Traditionalists say that checking messages and texting during meetings is tasteless and shows poor manners. But times are changing. A third of the workers recently polled by Yahoo HotJobs said they frequently checked e-mail during meetings. They also admitted, however, to being castigated for poor manners for using wireless devices.

Many professionals insist that they use their wireless devices for legitimate purposes, such as surfing the Web for urgent information, meeting deadlines, taking notes, and responding to customers. Yet the practice annoys many observers. One college student sank his chances to land an internship when he whipped out his BlackBerry during an interview to support an answer with an online fact. Unfortunately, he lingered to check an e-mail message from a friend, and watchful recruiters found this dalliance unprofessional. Among high-level professionals, the appearance of a BlackBerry is almost a boast. These professionals seem to be announcing that they are connected, busy, and important, but they will give full attention. The implication, too, is that this meeting had better be essential and efficient because they have more important things to do.[38]

Your Task. Few organizations have established policies on smartphone or cellphone use in meetings. Your team has been asked to develop such a policy. Your boss can't decide whether to ask your team to develop a short policy or a more rigorous one. Unable to make a decision, he asks for two statements: (1) a short statement that treats employees as grownups who can exercise intelligent judgment, and (2) a more complete set of guidelines that spell out exactly what should and should not be done.

Grammar and Mechanics C.L.U.E. Review 2

Verbs

Review Guides 4–10 in Appendix A: Grammar and Mechanics Guide (Competent Language Usage Essentials), beginning on page A-3. On a separate sheet, revise the following sentences to correct any errors in verbs. For each error that you locate, write the guide number that reflects this usage. If a sentence is correct, write C. When finished, compare your responses with the key beginning on page Key-1.

Example: Her identity was **stole** when she charged a restaurant meal.

Revision: Her identity was **stolen** when she charged a restaurant meal. [Guide 4]

1. Our recruiter must chose from among four strong candidates.

2. The use of smartphones and laptops during meetings are prohibited.

3. If I was you, I would finish my degree program.

4. Considerable time and money was spent on communication training for employees.

5. Neither the president nor the operations manager have read the complete report.

6. Disagreement and dissension is normal and should be expected in team interactions.

7. Everything in the meeting minutes and company reports are open to public view.

8. A committee of three employees and two managers are working to establish office priorities.

9. Greg said that he seen the report before it was distributed to management.

10. Each of the office divisions are expected to work together to create common procedures.

Endnotes

1 Microsoft. (2005). Survey finds workers productive only three days per week [press release]. Retrieved August 12, 2011, from http://www.microsoft.com/presspass/press/2005/mar05/03-15threeproductivedayspr.mspx

2 Office Team poll. (2008, June 23). Meetings and productivity [graphic]. *USA Today*, p. 1.

3 O'Toole, J., & Lawler, E. E., III. (2005). *The new American workplace*. New York: Palgrave Macmillan, p. 20.

4 Hoffman, A. (n.d.). IT workers improve your writing skills. Retrieved August 12, 2011, from http://career-advice.monster.ca/career-development/education-training/it-workers-improve-your-writing-skills/article.aspx

5 Ibid.

6 Crash course in managing a virtual team. (2007, September 3). *Management Today*. Retrieved June 3, 2009, from InfoTrac College Edition database.

7 Lipnack, J., & Stamps, J. (2000). *Virtual teams: People working across boundaries with technology* (2nd ed.). New York: Wiley, p. 18.

8 O'Toole, J., & Lawler, E. E., III. (2006, July). *The new American workplace*. New York: Palgrave Macmillan, p. 17.

9 Janis, I. L. (1982). *Groupthink: Psychological studies on policy decisions and fiascoes*. Boston: Houghton Mifflin. See also Miranda, S. M., & Saunders, C. (1995, Summer). Group support systems: An organization development intervention to combat groupthink. *Public Administration Quarterly, 19*, 193–216. Retrieved June 1, 2009, from Business Source Complete database.

10 Amason, A. C., Hochwarter, W. A., Thompson, K. R., & Harrison, A. W. (1995, Autumn). Conflict: An important dimension in successful management teams. *Organizational Dynamics, 24*, 1. Retrieved June 2, 2009, from InfoTrac College Edition database.

11 Katzenbach, J. R., & Smith, D. K. (1994). *Wisdom of teams*. New York: HarperBusiness, p. 45.

12 Turner, F. (2002). An effective employee suggestion program has a multiplier effect. *The CEO Refresher*. Retrieved August 17, 2009, from http://www.refresher.com/archives13/html

13 Microsoft. (2005). Survey finds workers average only three productive days per week [press release]. Retrieved June 8, 2009, from http://www.microsoft.com/presspass/press/2005/mar05/03-15threeproductivedayspr.mspx. See also Heming, H. B. (2006, June 18). Endless meetings: The black holes of the workday. *The New York Times*. Retrieved June 4, 2009, from http://www.nytimes.com

14 Herring, H. B. (2006, June 18). Endless meetings: The black holes of the workday. *The New York Times*. Retrieved June 4, 2009, from http://www.nytimes.com

15 Bruening, J. C. (1996, July). There's good news about meetings. *Managing Office Technology, 41*, 24–25. Retrieved December 4, 2006, from InfoTrac College Edition database.

16 Schabacker, K. (1991, June). A short, snappy guide to meaningful meetings. *Working Women*, 73.

17 These techniques are based on the following sources: Briefings Media Group. (2010). Stop the meeting madness: Make the most of your time together. *Communication Briefings* (Special Report). Retrieved August 12, 2011, from http://www.communicationbriefings.com/reports/Meeting_Madness.pdf; Egan, M. (2006, March 13). Meetings can make or break your career. *Insurance Advocate, 117*, 24.

18 Lohr, S. (2008, July 22). As travel costs rise, more meetings go virtual. *The New York Times*. Retrieved June 4, 2009, from http://www.nytimes.com

19 Yu, R. (2009, June 23). Videoconferencing eyes growth spurt. *USA Today*, p. 3B.

20 Schindler, E. (2008, February 15). Running an effective teleconference or virtual meeting. *CIO*. Retrieved June 5,

2009, from http://www.cio.com. See also Brenowitz, R. S. (2004, May). Virtual meeting etiquette (Article 601). *Innovative Leader.* Retrieved June 5, 2009, from http://www.winstonbrill.com

[21] Schindler, E. (2008, February 15). Running an effective teleconference or virtual meeting. *CIO.* Retrieved June 5, 2009, from http://www.cio.com. See also Brenowitz, R. S. (2004, May). Virtual meeting etiquette (Article 601), *Innovative Leader.* Retrieved June 5, 2009, from http://www.winstonbrill.com

[22] Robbins, H., & Finley, M. (1995). *Why teams don't work.* Princeton, NJ: Peterson's/Pacesetter Books, p. 123.

[23] Pellet, J. (2003, April). Anatomy of a turnaround guru. *Chief Executive,* 41; Mounter, P. (2003). Global internal communication: A model. *Journal of Communication Management, 3,* 265; Feiertag, H. (2002, July 15). Listening skills, enthusiasm top list of salespeople's best traits. *Hotel and Motel Management,* 20; Goby, V. P., & Lewis, J. H. (2000, June). The key role of listening in business: A study of the Singapore insurance industry. *Business Communication Quarterly, 63,* 41–51; Cooper, L. O. (1997, December). Listening competency in the workplace: A model for training. *Business Communication Quarterly, 60,* 75–84; Penley, L. E., Alexander, E. R., Jerigan, I. E., & Henwood, C. I. (1997). Communication abilities of managers: The relationship to performance. *Journal of Management, 17,* 57–76.

[24] Harris, T. W. (1989, June). Listen carefully. *Nation's Business,* p. 78.

[25] Steil, L. K., Barker, L. I., & Watson, K. W. (1983). *Effective listening: Key to your success* Reading, MA: Addison-Wesley; Harris, J. A. (1998, August). Hear what's really being said. *New Zealand Management, 45,* 18.

[26] Nelson, E., & Gypen, J. (1979, September/October). The subordinate's predicament. *Harvard Business Review,* 133.

[27] International Listening Association. (2009). Listening and speech rates. Retrieved June 20, 2009, from http://www.listen.org

[28] Wolvin, A., & Coakley, C. G. (1996). *Listening* (5th ed.). New York: McGraw-Hill, pp. 136–137.

[29] Effective communication. (1994, November). *Training Tomorrow,* pp. 32–33.

[30] Wood, J. T. (2003). *Gendered lives: Communication, gender, and culture* (5th ed.). Belmont, CA: Wadsworth, pp. 119–120; Anderson, K. J., & Leaper, C. (1998, August). Meta-analyses of gender effects on conversational interruption: Who, what, when, where, and how. *Sex Roles: A Journal of Research,* 225; Booth-Butterfield, M. (1984). She hears: What they hear and why. *Personnel Journal, 44,* 39.

[31] Tear, J. (1995, November 20). They just don't understand gender dynamics. *The Wall Street Journal,* p. A12; Wolfe, A. (1994, December 12). She just doesn't understand. *New Republic,* pp. 26–34.

[32] Burgoon, J., Coker, D., & Coker, R. (1986). Communication explanations. *Human Communication Research,* 463–494.

[33] Birdwhistell, R. (1970). *Kinesics and context.* Philadelphia: University of Pennsylvania Press.

[34] Chao, L. (2006, January 17). Not-so-nice costs. *The Wall Street Journal,* p. B1.

[35] Coutu, D., & Beschloss, M. (2009, May). Why teams don't work. *Harvard Business Review, (87)*5, 98–105. Retrieved June 1, 2009, from Business Source Complete database.

[36] Maturo, D. (2007, Winter). Being a technician is not enough: Develop leadership and communication skills. *The Pennsylvania CPA Journal.* Retrieved June 4, 2009, from http://www.picpa.org/Content/cpajournal/2006/winter/3.aspx

[37] Office Team poll. (2008, June 23). Meetings and productivity [graphic]. *USA Today,* p. 1.

[38] Williams, A. (2008, June 24). At meetings, it's mind your BlackBerry or mind your manners. *The New York Times,* pp. A1, A3.

CHAPTER 3

Intercultural Communication

OBJECTIVES

After studying this chapter, you should be able to

1. Understand how three significant trends have increased the importance of intercultural communication.

2. Define *culture*, describe five noteworthy cultural characteristics, and compare and contrast five key dimensions of culture, including high and low context.

3. Explain the effects of ethnocentrism, and show how tolerance and patience help in achieving intercultural proficiency.

4. Apply techniques for improving nonverbal and oral communication in intercultural settings.

5. Identify techniques for improving written messages to intercultural audiences.

6. Explain in what ways workforce diversity provides benefits and poses challenges, and how you can learn to be sensitive to racial and gender issues.

LWA/Getty Images

springboard to discussion

The 2010 Winter Olympics in Vancouver introduced a new patriotism to Canada with the bold and unprecedented Canadian "Own the Podium" campaign. This unique confidence was seen as a defining moment in Canadian sport and created a new perception of Canada on the world stage. The classic Canadian stereotypes of Mounties and mountains, and hockey players and hosers, are part of our national identity; however, should we rethink and redefine Brand Canada?[1] How do you define Canada?

The Increasing Importance of Intercultural Communication

Domestic businesses today sell their products across borders and seek customers in diverse foreign markets. Especially in North America, this movement toward a global economy has swelled to a torrent.

The "global village" predicted many years ago is increasingly a reality. To succeed in this global village, business communicators will want to become more aware of their own culture and how it differs from that of others. In this chapter you will learn basic characteristics and dimensions of culture and how to achieve intercultural proficiency. We will focus on techniques for improving nonverbal, oral, and written messages to intercultural audiences. You will study techniques for capitalizing on workforce diversity at home.

To better compete, many organizations form multinational alliances; however, many expanding companies stumble when they are forced to confront obstacles never before encountered. Significant obstacles involve misunderstandings and contrary views resulting from intercultural differences. You may face such intercultural differences in your current or future jobs. Your employers, fellow workers, or clients could very well be from other countries. You may travel abroad for your employer or on your own. Learning more about the powerful effect that culture has on behaviour will help you reduce friction and misunderstanding in your dealings with people from other cultures. Before examining strategies for helping you surmount intercultural obstacles, let's take a closer look at three significant trends: (1) the globalization of markets, (2) technological advancements, and (3) an intercultural workforce.

Globalization of Markets

Doing business beyond borders is now commonplace. Not only are market borders blurring, but acquisitions, mergers, alliances, and buyouts are obscuring the nationality of many companies.

To be successful in this interdependent global village, North American companies are increasingly finding it necessary to adapt to other cultures. In China, Frito-Lay had to accommodate yin and yang, the Chinese philosophy that nature and life must balance opposing elements. Chinese consider fried foods to be hot and avoid them in summer because two hots don't balance. They prefer cool snacks in summer; therefore, Frito-Lay created "cool lemon" potato chips dotted with green specks and mint. The yellow, lemon-scented chips are delivered in a package showing blue skies and rolling green grass.[2]

Why are North American businesses and those of other countries rushing to expand around the world? What is causing this dash toward globalization of markets and blurring of national identities? Many companies are increasingly looking overseas as domestic markets mature. They can no longer expect double-digit sales growth at home. Another significant factor is the passage of favourable trade agreements. The

LEARNING OBJECTIVE 1

Understand how three significant trends have increased the importance of intercultural communication.

Learning how culture affects behaviour helps you reduce friction and misunderstandings.

National boundaries mean less as businesses expand through acquisitions, mergers, alliances, and buyouts.

North American companies in global markets must adapt to other cultures.

General Agreement on Tariffs and Trade promotes open trade globally, and the North American Free Trade Agreement (NAFTA) expanded free trade among Canada, the United States, and Mexico. NAFTA created the largest and richest free-trade region on earth. In addition, the opening of Eastern Europe and the shift away from communism in Russia further expanded world markets. In Asia, China's admission to the World Trade Organization unlocked its economy and suddenly provided access to a huge population.

Beyond favourable trade agreements, other changes fuel globalization. Parts of the world formerly considered underdeveloped now boast robust middle classes. These consumers crave everything from cola to smartphones to high-definition TVs. What's more, such countries as China and India have become more receptive to foreign investment and free trade. Rules and red tape previously prevented many companies from doing business at home, much less abroad. Of paramount importance in explaining the explosive growth of global markets is the development of new transportation and information technologies.

Technological Advancements

Amazing new transportation and information technologies are major contributors to the development of our global interconnectivity. Supersonic planes now carry goods and passengers to other continents overnight and are so fast and reliable that most of the world is rapidly becoming an open market.

The Internet and the Web are changing the way we live, the way we do business, and the way we communicate. Advancements in communication and transportation have made markets and jobs more accessible. They've also made the world of business more efficient and more globally interdependent. High-speed, high-capacity, and relatively low-cost communications have opened up new global opportunities and made geographic location virtually irrelevant for many activities and services. Workers have access to company records, software programs, and colleagues whether they're working at home, in the office, or at the beach. As discussed in Chapters 1 and 2, technology is making a huge difference in the workplace. Communication technologies streamline business processes and improve access to critical company information. In addition, the Internet permits instantaneous oral and written communication across time zones and continents.

The changing landscape of business clearly demonstrates the need for technology savvy and connectedness around the world. Career success and personal wealth depend on the ability to use technology effectively.

Intercultural Workforce

As world commerce mingles more and more, another trend gives intercultural communication increasing importance: people are on the move. Lured by the prospects of peace, prosperity, education, or a fresh start, people from many cultures are moving to countries promising to fulfill their dreams. For generations the two most popular destinations have been Canada and the United States.

Because of increases in immigration, foreign-born persons are an ever-growing portion of the total Canadian population. Statistics Canada estimates that by 2026 the Canadian population will reach 36 million.[4] In 2001, 13 percent of Canadians identified themselves as belonging to a visible minority group, and by 2017, according to Statistics Canada projections, that number could climb to between 19 and 23 percent, with more than 95 percent of members of visible minorities living in metropolitan areas. As a result, Canada's immigrant population could reach between 7 million and 9.3 million in 2017.[5]

As we seek to accommodate multiethnic neighbourhoods, multinational companies, and an intercultural workforce, we can expect some changes to happen smoothly. Other changes will involve conflict and resentment, especially for people losing their positions of power and privilege. Learning to accommodate and manage intercultural change is an important part of the education of any business communicator.

Toronto Star/GetStock.com

Hockey fans have the option of watching *Hockey Night in Canada* not only in both of Canada's official languages of English and French but also in Punjabi! As a result of positive response, the pilot project became a regular feature of the hockey broadcast. "The community response has been fantastic!" said commentator Parminder Singh, who hosts with Harnarayan Singh. The last official census found that Punjabi is the fourth most spoken language in Canada after English, French, and Chinese. The success of the Punjabi broadcast led the CBC to expand its audience outreach even further, so Hockey Night in Canada is now also being televised in Mandarin.[3]

Understanding Culture

Every country or region within a country has its own common heritage, joint experience, or shared learning. This shared background produces the culture of a region, country, or society. For our purposes, *culture* may be defined as the complex system of values, traits, morals, and customs shared by a society. Culture teaches people how to behave and conditions their reactions. It is a powerful operating force that conditions the way we think and behave. The purpose of this chapter is to broaden your view of culture and help you develop a flexible attitude so that you can avoid frustration when cultural adjustment is necessary.

LEARNING OBJECTIVE **2**

Define culture, describe five noteworthy cultural characteristics, and compare and contrast five key dimensions of culture, including high and low context.

Characteristics of Culture

Culture is shaped by attitudes learned in childhood and later internalized in adulthood. As we enter this current period of globalization and interculturalism, we should expect to make adjustments and adopt new attitudes. Adjustment and accommodation will be easier if we understand some basic characteristics of culture.

> Understanding basic characteristics of culture helps us make adjustments and accommodations.

Culture Is Learned. The rules, values, and attitudes of a culture are not inherent. They are learned and passed down from generation to generation. For example, in many Middle Eastern and some Asian cultures, same-sex people may walk hand in hand in the street, but opposite-sex people may not do so. In Arab cultures conversations are often held in close proximity, sometimes nose to nose. But in Western cultures, if a person stands too close, the other may feel uncomfortable. Cultural rules of behaviour learned from your family and society are conditioned from early childhood.

Cultures Are Inherently Logical. The rules in any culture originated to reinforce that culture's values and beliefs. They act as normative forces. Rules about how close to stand may be linked to values about sexuality, aggression, modesty, and respect. Acknowledging the inherent logic of a culture is extremely important when learning to accept behaviour that differs from our own cultural behaviour.

Culture Is the Basis of Self-Identity and Community. Culture is the basis for how we tell the world who we are and what we believe. People build their identities through cultural overlays to their primary culture. When North Americans make choices in education, career, place of employment, and life partner, they consider certain rules, manners, ceremonies, beliefs, language, and values. These considerations add to their total cultural outlook, and they represent major expressions of a person's self-identity.

> Culture determines our sense of who we are and our sense of community.

Culture Combines the Visible and Invisible. To outsiders, the way we act—those things that we do in daily life and work—are the most visible parts of our culture. In India, for example, people avoid stepping on ants or other insects because they believe in reincarnation and are careful about all forms of life. Such practices are outward symbols of deeper values that are invisible but that pervade everything we think and do.

Culture Is Dynamic. Over time, cultures will change. Changes are caused by advancements in technology and communication, as discussed earlier. Local differences are modified or slowly erased. Change is also caused by such events as migration, natural disasters, and conflicts. One major event in this country was the exodus of people living on farms. When families moved to cities, major changes occurred in the way family members interacted. Attitudes, behaviours, and beliefs change in open societies more quickly than in closed societies.

Dimensions of Culture

The more you know about culture in general and your own culture in particular, the better able you will be to adapt to an intercultural perspective. A typical North American has habits and beliefs similar to those of other members of Western, technologically advanced societies. In our limited space in this book, it is impossible to cover fully the infinite facets of culture. But we can outline some key dimensions of culture and look at them from different views.

So that you will better understand your culture and how it contrasts with other cultures, we will describe five key dimensions of culture: context, individualism, formality, communication style, and time orientation.

Context. Context is probably the most important cultural dimension and also the most difficult to define. It is a concept developed by cultural anthropologist Edward T. Hall. In his model, context refers to the stimuli, environment, or ambience surrounding an event. Communicators in low-context cultures (such as those in North America, Scandinavia, and Germany) depend little on the context of a situation to convey their meaning. They assume that listeners know very little and must be told practically everything. In high-context cultures (such as those in Japan, China, and Arab countries), the listener is already "contexted" and does not need to be given much background information.[6] To identify low- and high-context countries, Hall arranged them on a continuum, as shown in Figure 3.1.

Low-context cultures tend to be logical, analytical, and action oriented. Business communicators stress clearly articulated messages that they consider to be objective, professional, and efficient. High-context cultures are more likely to be intuitive and contemplative. Communicators in high-context cultures pay attention to more than the words spoken. They emphasize interpersonal relationships, nonverbal expression, physical setting, and social setting. In high-context cultures, communication cues are transmitted by posture, voice inflection, gestures, and facial expression. Establishing relationships is an important part of communicating and interacting.

In terms of thinking patterns, low-context communicators tend to use *linear logic*. They proceed from point A to point B to point C and finally arrive at a conclusion. High-context communicators, however, may use *spiral logic*, circling around a topic indirectly and looking at it from many tangential or divergent viewpoints. A conclusion

> Low-context cultures (such as those in North America and Western Europe) depend less on the environment of a situation to convey meaning than do high-context cultures (such as those in Japan, China, and Arab countries). People in low-context cultures tend to be logical, analytical, and action oriented.

FIGURE 3.1 Comparing Low- and High-Context Cultures

Low Context	High Context
Tend to prefer direct verbal interaction	Tend to prefer indirect verbal interaction
Tend to understand meaning at one level only	Tend to understand meanings embedded at many sociocultural levels
Are generally less proficient in reading nonverbal cues	Are generally more proficient in reading nonverbal cues
Value individualism	Value group membership
Rely more on logic	Rely more on context and feeling
Employ linear logic	Employ spiral logic
Say no directly	Talk around point; avoid saying no
Communicate in highly structured messages, provide details, stress literal meanings, give authority to written information	Communicate in simple, sometimes ambiguous, messages; understand visual messages readily

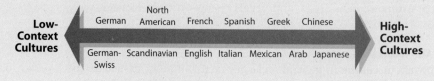

may be implied but not argued directly. For a concise summary of important differences between low- and high-context cultures, see Figure 3.1.

Individualism. An attitude of independence and freedom from control characterizes individualism. Members of low-context cultures, particularly North Americans, tend to value individualism. They believe that initiative and self-assertion result in personal achievement. They believe in individual action and personal responsibility, and they desire a large degree of freedom in their personal lives.

Members of high-context cultures are more collectivist. They emphasize membership in organizations, groups, and teams; they encourage acceptance of group values, duties, and decisions. They typically resist independence because it fosters competition and confrontation instead of consensus.

Many cultures, of course, are quite complex and cannot be characterized as totally individualistic or group oriented. For example, Canadians of European descent are generally quite individualistic, while those with Asian backgrounds may be closer to the group-centred dimension.[7]

Formality. People in some cultures place less emphasis on tradition, ceremony, and social rules than do members of other cultures. North Americans, for example, dress casually and are soon on a first-name basis with others. Their lack of formality is often characterized by directness. In business dealings North Americans come to the point immediately; indirectness, they feel, wastes time, a valuable commodity in North American culture.

This informality and directness may be confusing abroad. In Japan, for example, signing documents and exchanging business cards are important rituals. In Europe first names are never used without invitation. In Arab, South American, and Asian cultures, a feeling of friendship and kinship must be established before business can be transacted.

In Western cultures people are more relaxed about social status and the appearance of power.[8] Deference is not generally paid to individuals merely because of their wealth, position, seniority, or age. In many Asian cultures, however, these characteristics are important and must be respected.

Communication Style. People in low- and high-context cultures tend to communicate differently with words. To North Americans and Germans, words are very important, especially in contracts and negotiations. People in high-context cultures, conversely, place more emphasis on the surrounding context than on the words describing a negotiation. A Greek may see a contract as a formal statement announcing the intention to build a business for the future. The Japanese may treat contracts as statements of intention, and they assume changes will be made as a project develops.[9]

North Americans tend to take words literally, whereas Arabs and South Americans sometimes speak with extravagant or poetic figures of speech that may be misinterpreted if taken literally.[10]

In communication style North Americans value straightforwardness, are suspicious of evasiveness, and distrust people who might have a "hidden agenda" or who "play their cards too close to the chest."[11] North Americans also tend to be uncomfortable with silence and impatient with delays. Some Asian businesspeople have learned that the longer they drag out negotiations, the more concessions impatient North Americans are likely to make.

Western cultures have developed languages that use letters describing the *sounds* of words. But Asian languages are based on pictographic characters representing the *meanings* of words. Asian language characters are much more complex than the Western alphabet; therefore, Asians are said to have a higher competence in the discrimination of visual patterns.

Time Orientation. North Americans consider time a precious commodity to be conserved. They correlate time with productivity, efficiency, and money. Keeping people waiting for business appointments wastes time and is also rude.

In other cultures time may be perceived as an unlimited and never-ending resource to be enjoyed. Basic concepts of time can make international mergers more difficult. *Long term* in Canada means three years; in Japan *long term* is 30 years.[12]

As you can see, high-context cultures differ from low-context cultures in many dimensions. These differences can be significant for companies engaging in international business.

Stereotypes, Prototypes, Prejudices, and Generalizations

Most experts recognize that it is impossible to talk about cultures without using mental categories, representations, and generalizations to describe groups. These categories are sometimes considered stereotypes. Because the term *stereotype* has a negative meaning, intercultural authors Iris Varner and Linda Beamer suggested that we distinguish between stereotype and prototype.

A *stereotype* is an oversimplified behavioural pattern applied uncritically to groups. The term was used originally by printers to describe identical type set in two frames, hence *stereotype*. Stereotypes are fixed and rigid. Although they may be exaggerated and overgeneralized beliefs when applied to groups of people, stereotypes are not always entirely false.[13] Often they contain a grain of truth. When a stereotype develops into a rigid attitude and when it is based on erroneous beliefs or preconceptions, then it should be called a *prejudice*.

Varner and Beamer recommended using the term *prototype* to describe "mental representations based on general characteristics that are not fixed and rigid but rather are open to new definitions."[14] Prototypes, then, are dynamic and change with fresh experience. Prototypes based on objective observations usually have a considerable amount of truth in them. That is why they can be helpful in studying culture. For example, South American businesspeople often talk about their families before getting down to business. This prototype is generally accurate, but it may not universally apply and it may change over time.

Some people object to making any generalizations about cultures. It is wise to remember, however, that whenever we are confronted with something new and unfamiliar, we naturally strive to categorize the data to make sense out of it. In categorizing these new data, we are making generalizations. Significant intellectual discourse is impossible without generalizations. Unfounded generalizations about people and cultures, of course, can lead to bias and prejudice. But for our purposes, when we discuss cultures, it is important to be able to make generalizations and describe cultural prototypes.

The Benefits of Intercultural Proficiency

Being aware of your own culture and how it contrasts with others is an important first step in achieving intercultural proficiency. Another step involves recognizing barriers to intercultural accommodation and striving to overcome them. Some of these barriers occur quite naturally and require a conscious effort to surmount. Probably the most important reasons for becoming interculturally competent are that your personal life will be more satisfying and your work life will be more productive, gratifying, and effective.

Avoiding Ethnocentrism

A person's belief in the superiority of his or her own culture or ethnic group is known as *ethnocentrism*, a natural attitude inherent in all cultures. If you were raised in North America, many of the dimensions of culture described previously probably seem "right" to you.

Ethnocentrism causes us to judge others by our own values. We expect others to react as we would, and they expect us to behave as they would. Misunderstandings naturally result. A North American who wants to set a deadline for completion of negotiations is considered pushy by an Arab. That same Arab, who prefers a handshake to a written contract, is seen as naive and possibly untrustworthy by a North American. These ethnocentric reactions can be reduced through knowledge of other cultures and the development of increased intercultural sensitivity.

Bridging the Gap

Developing cultural competence often involves changing attitudes. Remember that culture is learned. Through exposure to other cultures and through training, such as you are receiving in this course, you can learn new attitudes and behaviours that help bridge gaps between cultures.

Tolerance. One desirable attitude in achieving intercultural proficiency is *tolerance*. Closed-minded people cannot look beyond their own ethnocentrism. But as global markets expand and as our own society becomes increasingly multiethnic, tolerance becomes especially significant. Some job descriptions now include such statements as *Must be able to interact with ethnically diverse personnel.*

To improve tolerance, you will want to practise *empathy*. This means trying to see the world through another's eyes. It means being less judgmental and more eager to seek common ground.

Accepting cultural differences and adapting to them with tolerance and empathy often results in a harmonious compromise.

Saving Face. In business transactions North Americans often assume that economic factors are the primary motivators of people. It is wise to remember, though, that strong cultural influences are also at work. *Saving face,* for example, is important in many parts of the world. *Face* refers to the image a person holds in his or her social network. Positive comments raise a person's social standing, but negative comments lower it.

People in low-context cultures are less concerned with face. High-context cultures, on the other hand, are more concerned with preserving social harmony and saving face. They are indirect and go to great lengths to avoid giving offence by saying *no.* The empathic listener recognizes the language of refusal and pushes no further.

Patience. Being tolerant also involves patience. If a foreigner is struggling to express an idea in English, North Americans must avoid the temptation to finish the sentence and provide the word that they presume is wanted. When we put words into their mouths, our foreign friends often smile and agree out of politeness, but our words may in fact not express their thoughts. Remaining silent is another means of exhibiting tolerance. Instead of filling every lapse in conversation, North Americans, for example, should recognize that in Asian cultures people deliberately use periods of silence for reflection and contemplation.

> Because culture is learned, you can learn new attitudes and behaviours through training.

> Saving face may require indirectness to respect the feelings and dignity of others.

> Tolerance sometimes involves being patient and silent.

Effective Communication in Intercultural Settings

Thus far we have discussed the increasing importance of intercultural proficiency as a result of globalization of markets, increasing migration, and technological advancements. We have described characteristics and dimensions of cultures, and we have talked about avoiding ethnocentrism. Our goal was to motivate you to unlock the opportunities offered by intercultural proficiency. Remember, the key to future business success may very well lie in finding ways to work harmoniously with people from different cultures.

LEARNING OBJECTIVE 4

Apply techniques for improving nonverbal and oral communication in intercultural settings.

Successful Nonverbal Communication in Intercultural Environments

Verbal skills in another culture can generally be mastered if a person studies hard enough. But nonverbal skills are much more difficult to learn. Nonverbal behaviour includes the areas described in Chapter 2, such as eye contact, facial expression, posture, gestures, and the use of time, space, and territory. The messages sent by body language and the way we arrange time and space have always been open to interpretation. Does a raised eyebrow mean that your boss doubts your statement or just that she is seriously considering it? Does that closed door to an office mean that your co-worker is angry or just that he is working on a project that requires concentration? Deciphering nonverbal communication is difficult for people who are culturally similar, and it is even more troublesome when cultures differ.

Understanding nonverbal messages is particularly difficult when cultures differ.

In Western cultures, for example, people perceive silence as a negative trait. Silence suggests rejection, unhappiness, depression, regret, embarrassment, or ignorance. However, the Japanese admire silence and consider it a key to success.

Although nonverbal behaviour is ambiguous within cultures and even more problematic between cultures, it nevertheless conveys meaning. If you've ever had to talk with someone who does not share your language, you probably learned quickly to use gestures to convey basic messages. Because gestures can create very different reactions in different cultures, we must be careful in using and interpreting them.

Gestures can create different reactions in intercultural environments.

As businesspeople increasingly interact with their counterparts from other cultures, they will become more aware of these differences. Some behaviours are easy to warn against, such as touching people from the Middle East with the left hand (because it is considered unclean and is used for personal hygiene). We are also warned not to touch anyone's head (even children) in Thailand, as the head is considered sacred. Numerous lists of cultural dos and don'ts have been compiled. However, learning all the nuances of nonverbal behaviour in other cultures is impossible; such lists are merely the tip of the cultural iceberg.

Although we cannot ever hope to understand fully the nuances of meaning transmitted by nonverbal behaviour in various cultures, we can grow more tolerant, more flexible, and, eventually, more competent. An important part of achieving nonverbal competence is becoming more aware of our own nonverbal behaviours and their meanings. Much of our nonverbal behaviour is learned in early childhood from our families and from society, and it is largely unconscious. Once we become more aware of the meaning of our own gestures, posture, eye contact, and so on, we will become more alert and more sensitive to variations in other cultures. Striving to associate with people from different cultures can further broaden our intercultural competence.

Techniques for Achieving Intercultural Competence

In improving effectiveness and achieving intercultural competence, one expert, M. R. Hammer, suggested that three processes or attitudes are effective. *Descriptiveness* refers to the use of concrete and specific feedback. As you learned in Chapter 1, descriptive feedback is more effective than judgmental feedback. A second attitude is what Hammer called *nonjudgmentalism*. This attitude goes a long way in preventing defensive reactions from communicators. Most important in achieving effective communication is *supportiveness*. This attitude requires us to support others positively with head nods, eye contact, facial expression, and physical proximity.[15]

Descriptiveness, nonjudgmentalism, and supportiveness all help you broaden your intercultural competence.

From a practical standpoint, when interacting with businesspeople in other cultures, it is always wise to follow their lead. If they avoid intense eye contact, don't stare. If no one is putting his or her elbows on a table, don't be the first to do so. Until you are knowledgeable about the meaning of gestures, it is probably a good idea to keep yours to a minimum. Learning the words for *please, yes,* and *thank you* is even better than relying on gestures.[16] Intercultural competence regarding nonverbal behaviour may never be completely attained, but sensitivity, nonjudgmentalism, and tolerance go a long way toward improving interactions.

Keep your gestures to a minimum or follow the lead of native businesspeople.

Successful Oral Communication in Intercultural Environments

Although it is best to speak a foreign language fluently, many of us lack that skill. Fortunately, global business transactions are increasingly conducted in English. English has become the language of technology, the language of Hollywood, and the language to know in global business even for traditionally non-English-speaking countries. English is so dominant in business that when Koreans go to China, English is the language they use to conduct business.[17] However, the level of proficiency may be limited among those for whom English is a second language. North Americans abroad make a big mistake in thinking that people who speak English always understand what is being said. Comprehension can be fairly superficial. The following suggestions are helpful for situations in which one or both communicators is using English as a second language.

- **Learn foreign phrases.** In conversations, even when English is used, foreign nationals appreciate it when you learn greetings and a few phrases in their language. Practise the phrases phonetically so that you will be understood.

- **Use simple English.** Speak in short sentences (fewer than 20 words) with familiar short words. For example, use *old* rather than *obsolete* and *rich* rather than *luxurious* or *sumptuous*. Eliminate puns, sports and military references, slang, and jargon (special business terms). Be especially alert to idiomatic expressions that can't be translated, such as *burn the midnight oil* and *under the weather*.

- **Speak slowly and enunciate clearly.** Avoid fast speech, but don't raise your voice. Overpunctuate with pauses and full stops. Always write numbers for all to see.

- **Observe eye messages.** Be alert to a glazed expression or wandering eyes—these tell you the listener is lost.

- **Encourage accurate feedback.** Ask probing questions and encourage the listener to paraphrase what you say. Do not assume that a yes, a nod, or a smile indicates comprehension.

- **Check frequently for comprehension.** Avoid waiting until you finish a long explanation to request feedback. Instead, make one point at a time, pausing to check for comprehension. Do not proceed to B until A has been grasped.

- **Accept blame.** If a misunderstanding results, graciously accept the blame for not making your meaning clear.

- **Listen without interrupting.** Curb your desire to finish sentences or to fill out ideas for the speaker. Keep in mind that North Americans abroad are often accused of listening too little and talking too much.

- **Smile when appropriate.** Roger Axtell, international behaviour expert, calls the smile the single most understood and most useful form of communication in either personal or business transactions.[18] In some cultures, however, excessive smiling may seem insincere.[19]

- **Follow up in writing.** After conversations or oral negotiations, confirm the results and agreements with follow-up letters. For proposals and contracts, engage a translator to prepare copies in the local language.

Effective Written Messages to Intercultural Audiences

In sending letters and other documents to businesspeople in other cultures, try to adapt your writing style and tone appropriately. For example, in cultures where formality and tradition are important, be scrupulously polite. Don't even think of sharing the latest joke. Humour translates very poorly and can cause misunderstanding and negative reactions. Familiarize yourself with accepted channels of communication. Are letters, e-mail, and faxes common? Would a direct or an indirect organizational pattern be more effective? Forget about trying to cut through red tape. In some cultures red tape is appreciated. The following suggestions, coupled with the earlier guidelines, can help you prepare successful written messages for intercultural audiences.

- **Consider local styles.** Learn how documents are formatted and addressed in the intended reader's country. Decide whether to use your organization's preferred format or to adjust to local styles.

- **Observe titles and rank.** Use last names, titles, and other signals of rank and status. Send messages to higher-status people and avoid sending copies to lower-rank people.

Don't assume that speakers of English as a second language understand everything you say.

Use simple English and avoid puns, sports references, slang, and jargon when communicating with people for whom English is a second language.

To improve communication with those for whom English is a second language, speak slowly, enunciate clearly, observe eye messages, encourage feedback, check for comprehension, accept blame, don't interrupt, remember to smile, and follow up important conversations in writing.

LEARNING OBJECTIVE **5**

Identify techniques for improving written messages to intercultural audiences.

To improve written messages, consider local formats, use short sentences and short paragraphs, avoid ambiguous expressions, strive for clarity, use correct grammar, cite numbers carefully, and accommodate readers in organization, tone, and style.

- **Use short sentences and short paragraphs.** Sentences with fewer than 20 words and paragraphs with fewer than eight lines are most readable.

- **Avoid ambiguous expressions.** Include relative pronouns (*that, which, who*) for clarity in introducing clauses. Stay away from contractions (especially ones like *Here's the problem*). Avoid idioms and figurative clichés (*once in a blue moon*), slang (*my presentation really bombed*), acronyms (*ASAP*, for *as soon as possible*), abbreviations (*DBA*, for *doing business as*), jargon (*input, bottom line*), and sports references (*play ball, slam dunk, ballpark figure*). Use action-specific verbs (*purchase a printer* rather than *get a printer*).

- **Strive for clarity.** Avoid words that have many meanings (the word *light* has 18 different meanings!). If necessary, clarify words that may be confusing. Replace two-word verbs with clear single words (*return* instead of *bring back; delay* instead of *put off; maintain* instead of *keep up*).

- **Use correct grammar.** Be careful of misplaced modifiers, dangling participles, and sentence fragments. Use conventional punctuation.

- **Cite numbers carefully.** For international trade it is a good idea to use the metric system. In citing numbers use numerals (*15*) instead of words (*fifteen*). Always convert dollar amounts into local currency. Avoid using numerals to express the month of the year. In North America, for example, March 5, 2013, might be written as 3/5/13, whereas in Europe the same date might appear as 5.3.13.

- **Accommodate the reader in organization, tone, and style.** Organize your message to appeal to the reader. For example, use the indirect strategy for high-context audiences.

The Checklist box summarizes suggestions for improving communication with intercultural audiences.

Checklist

Improving Intercultural Proficiency and Communication

- **Study your own culture.** Learn about your customs, biases, and views and how they differ from those in other societies. This knowledge can help you better understand, appreciate, and accept the values and behaviour of other cultures.

- **Learn about other cultures.** Education can help you alter cultural misconceptions, reduce fears, and minimize misunderstandings. Knowledge of other cultures opens your eyes and teaches you to expect differences. Such knowledge also enriches your life.

- **Curb ethnocentrism.** Avoid judging others by your personal views. Get over the view that the other cultures are incorrect, defective, or primitive. Try to develop an open mind.

- **Avoid judgmentalism.** Strive to accept other behaviour as different rather than as right or wrong. Try not to be defensive in justifying your culture. Strive for objectivity.

- **Seek common ground.** When cultures clash, look for solutions that respect both cultures. Be flexible in developing compromises.

- **Observe nonverbal cues in your culture.** Become more alert to the meanings of eye contact, facial expression, posture, and gestures and the use of time, space, and territory. How do they differ in other cultures?

- **Use plain English.** Speak and write in short sentences and use simple words and standard English. Eliminate puns, slang, jargon, acronyms, abbreviations, and any words that cannot be easily translated.

- **Encourage accurate feedback.** In conversations, ask probing questions and listen attentively without interrupting. Do not assume that a *yes* or a smile indicates assent or comprehension.

- **Adapt to local preferences.** Shape your writing to reflect the reader's document styles, if appropriate. Express monetary amounts in local currency. Write out months of the year for clarity.

Advantages and Challenges of Workforce Diversity

At the same time as North American businesspeople are interacting with people from around the world, the domestic workforce is becoming more diverse. This diversity has many dimensions—race, ethnicity, age, religion, gender, national origin, physical ability, and countless other qualities. No longer, say the experts, will the workplace be predominantly Anglo oriented or male. By 2017, according to Statistics Canada projections, the number of Canadians belonging to a visible minority group could climb to between 19 and 23 percent of the population.[20] In addition, the Canadian population has been growing older in recent decades, and people over age 65 represent one of the fastest-growing segments of the population.[21] Trends suggest that many of these older people will remain in the workforce. Because of technological advances, more people with disabilities are also joining the workforce.

LEARNING OBJECTIVE 6

Explain in what ways workforce diversity provides benefits and poses challenges, and how you can learn to be sensitive to racial and gender issues.

Dividends of Diversity

As society and the workforce become more diverse, successful interaction and communication among the various identity groups bring distinct challenges and dividends in three areas.

A diverse workforce benefits consumers, work teams, and business organizations.

Consumers. A diverse staff is better able to read trends and respond to the increasingly diverse customer base in local and world markets. Diverse consumers now want specialized goods and services tailored to their needs. Teams made up of people with different experiences are better able to create products that these markets require. Consumers also want to deal with companies that respect their values and reflect themselves.

Work Teams. As you learned in Chapter 2, employees today work in teams. Team members with different backgrounds may come up with more creative and effective problem-solving techniques than homogeneous teams. Chains of command, narrow job descriptions, and hierarchies are gradually becoming things of the past. Today's teams are composed of knowledgeable, diverse individuals who are concerned with sustainability, competence, and ownership within the project, team, and organization.[22]

Business Organizations. Companies that set aside time and resources to cultivate and capitalize on diversity will suffer fewer discrimination lawsuits, fewer union clashes, and less government regulatory action. Most important, though, is the growing realization among organizations that diversity is a critical bottom-line business strategy to improve employee relationships and to increase productivity. Developing a diverse staff that can work together cooperatively is one of the biggest challenges facing business organizations today.

Divisiveness of Diversity

Diversity can be a positive force within organizations. But all too often it can also cause divisiveness, discontent, and clashes. Many of the identity groups, the so-called workforce *disenfranchised*, have legitimate concerns.

Diversity can cause divisiveness, discontent, and clashes.

Women complain of the *glass ceiling*, that invisible barrier of attitudes, prejudices, and "old boy networks" blocking them from reaching important corporate positions. Some women feel that they are the victims of sexual harassment, unequal wages, sexism, and even their style of communication. Men, too, have gender issues. One manager described gender discrimination in his office: "My boss was a woman and was very verbal about the opportunities for women to advance in my company. I have often felt she gave much more attention to the women in the office than the men."[23]

Older employees may feel that organizations favour younger employees. Members of minority groups complain that they are discriminated against in hiring, retention, wages, and promotions. People with disabilities feel that their limitations should not hold them back, and they fear that their potential is often prejudged. Individuals with different religious beliefs may feel uncomfortable working alongside each other.

Some people believe that the glass ceiling is an invisible barrier of attitudes, prejudices, and "old boy networks" that blocks women from reaching important positions.

Tips for Improving Communication Among Diverse Workplace Audiences

Integrating all this diversity into one seamless workforce is a formidable task and a vital one. Harnessed effectively, diversity can enhance productivity and propel a company to success. Mismanaged, it can become a tremendous drain on a company's time and resources. How companies deal with diversity will make all the difference in how they compete in an increasingly global environment. This means that organizations must do more than just pay lip service to these issues. Harmony and acceptance do not happen automatically when people who are dissimilar work together. The following suggestions can help you and your organization find ways to improve communication and interaction.

A diverse workforce may reduce productivity unless trained to value differences.

- **Seek training.** Especially if an organization is experiencing diversity problems, awareness-raising sessions may be helpful. Spend time reading and learning about workforce diversity and how it can benefit organizations. Look on diversity as an opportunity, not a threat. Intercultural communication, team building, and conflict resolution are skills that can be learned in diversity training programs.

- **Understand the value of differences.** Diversity makes an organization innovative and creative. Sameness fosters an absence of critical thinking called groupthink, which you learned about in Chapter 2. Diversity in problem-solving groups encourages independent and creative thinking.

Don't expect all workers to think or act alike.

- **Don't expect conformity.** Gone are the days when businesses could say, "This is our culture. Conform or leave."[24] Paul Fireman, former CEO of Reebok, stressed seeking people who have new and different stories to tell. "And then you have to make real room for them, you have to learn to listen, to listen closely, to their stories. It accomplishes next to nothing to employ those who are different from us if the condition of their employment is that they become the same as us. For it is their differences that enrich us, expand us, provide us the competitive edge."[25]

- **Learn about your cultural self.** Begin to think of yourself as a product of your culture and understand that your culture is just one among many. Try to stand outside and look at yourself. Do you see any reflex reactions and automatic thought patterns that are a result of your upbringing? These may be invisible to you until challenged by difference. Remember, your culture was designed to help you succeed and survive in a certain environment. Be sure to keep what works and yet be ready to adapt as environments change.

- **Make fewer assumptions.** Be careful of seemingly insignificant, innocent workplace assumptions. For example, don't assume that everyone wants to mark the holidays with a Christmas party and a decorated tree. Celebrating only Christian holidays in December and January excludes those who observe Hanukkah, Kwanzaa, and the Lunar New Year. Moreover, in workplace discussions don't assume that everyone is married or wants to be or is even heterosexual, for that matter. For invitations avoid such phrases as *managers and their wives. Spouses* or *partners* is more inclusive. Valuing diversity means making fewer assumptions that everyone is like you or wants to be like you.

In times of conflict, look for areas of agreement and build on similarities.

- **Build on similarities.** Look for areas in which you and others not like you can agree or at least share opinions. Be prepared to consider issues from many perspectives, all of which may be valid. Accept that there is room for different points of view to coexist peacefully. Although you can always find differences, it is much harder to find similarities. Look for common ground in shared experiences, mutual goals, and similar values. Concentrate on your objective even when you may disagree on how to reach it.

Summary of Learning Objectives

1 **Understand how three significant trends have increased the importance of intercultural communication.** Three trends are working together to crystallize the growing need for developing intercultural proficiencies and improved communication techniques. First, the globalization of markets means that you can expect to be doing business with people from around the world. Second, technological advancements in transportation and information are making the world smaller and more intertwined. Third, more and more immigrants from other cultures are settling in North America, thus changing the makeup of the workforce. Successful interaction requires awareness, tolerance, and accommodation.

2 **Define *culture*, describe five noteworthy cultural characteristics, and compare and contrast five key dimensions of culture, including high and low context.** *Culture* is the complex system of values, traits, morals, and customs shared by a society. Significant characteristics of culture include the following: (a) culture is learned, (b) cultures are inherently logical, (c) culture is the basis of self-identity and community, (d) culture combines the visible and invisible, and (e) culture is dynamic. Members of low-context cultures (such as those in North America, Scandinavia, and Germany) depend on words to express meaning, whereas members of high-context cultures (such as those in Japan, China, and Arab countries) rely more on context (social setting; a person's history, status, and position) to communicate meaning. Other key dimensions of culture include individualism, degree of formality, communication style, and time orientation.

3 **Explain the effects of ethnocentrism, and show how tolerance and patience help in achieving intercultural proficiency.** *Ethnocentrism* refers to an individual's feeling that the culture he or she belongs to is superior to all others and holds all truths. To function effectively in a global economy, we must acquire knowledge of other cultures and be willing to change our attitudes. Developing tolerance often involves practising *empathy*, which means trying to see the world through another's eyes. Saving face and promoting social harmony are important in many parts of the world. Moving beyond narrow ethnocentric views often requires tolerance and patience.

4 **Apply techniques for improving nonverbal and oral communication in intercultural settings.** We can minimize nonverbal miscommunication by recognizing that meanings conveyed by eye contact, posture, and gestures are largely culture dependent. Nonverbal messages are also sent by the use of time, space, and territory. Becoming aware of your own nonverbal behaviour and what it conveys is the first step in broadening your intercultural competence. In improving oral messages, you can learn foreign phrases, use simple English, speak slowly and enunciate clearly, observe eye messages, encourage accurate feedback, check for comprehension, accept blame, listen without interrupting, smile, and follow up important conversations in writing.

5 **Identify techniques for improving written messages to intercultural audiences.** To improve written messages, adopt local formats, observe titles and rank, use short sentences and short paragraphs, avoid ambiguous expressions, strive for clarity, use correct grammar, and cite numbers carefully. Also try to accommodate the reader in organization, tone, and style.

6 **Explain in what ways workforce diversity provides benefits and poses challenges, and how you can learn to be sensitive to racial and gender issues.** Having a diverse workforce can benefit consumers, work teams, and business organizations. However, diversity can also cause divisiveness among various identity groups. Business communicators should be aware of and sensitive to differences in the communication techniques of men and women. To promote harmony and communication in diverse workplaces, many organizations develop diversity training programs. As an individual, you must understand and accept the value of differences. Don't expect conformity and do create zero tolerance for bias and prejudice. Learn about your cultural self, make fewer assumptions, and seek common ground when disagreements arise.

Chapter Review

1. Why is intercultural communication increasingly important, and what must business communicators do to succeed? (Obj. 1)

2. Why is geographic location virtually irrelevant for many activities and services today? (Obj. 1)

3. What is culture and how is culture learned? (Obj. 2)

4. Describe five major dimensions of culture. (Obj. 2)

5. Briefly, contrast high- and low-context cultures. (Obj. 2)

6. How do the words *backward*, *advanced*, *primitive*, and *sophisticated* relate to ethnocentrism? (Obj. 3)

7. How is a stereotype different from a prototype? (Obj. 3)

8. Name techniques for bridging the gap between cultures and achieving intercultural proficiency. (Obj. 3)

9. When interacting with people who do not use your language, why is it important to learn the words for *please, yes,* and *thank you* rather than relying on gestures? (Obj. 4)

10. What should you assume about the level of proficiency in nonnative speakers of English? (Obj. 4)

11. Describe five specific ways you can improve oral communication with someone who speaks another language. (Obj. 4)

12. Describe five specific ways you can improve written communication with someone who speaks another language. (Obj. 5)

13. What categories of ambiguous expressions should be avoided because they could confuse readers for whom English is a second language? (Obj. 5)

14. Name three groups that benefit from workforce diversity and explain why. (Obj. 6)

15. Describe six tips for improving communication among diverse workplace audiences. (Obj. 6)

Critical Thinking

1. Queen Elizabeth II once said, "Stereotypes wither when human contacts flourish."[26] What does this statement mean? Have you found this to be accurate in your own experience? (Objs. 1, 3)

2. Because English is becoming the world's business language, why should Canadians bother to learn about other cultures? (Objs. 1, 2, and 6)

3. Cultural expert John Engle complained that his North American students resist references to cultural generalizations. He asserted, "Thoughtful generalizations are the heart of intercultural communication, allowing us to discuss meaningfully the complex web of forces acting upon individuals that we call culture."[27] Do you agree or disagree? Why? (Objs. 2, 3)

4. Some economists and management scholars argue that such statements as "diversity is an economic asset" or "diversity is a new strategic imperative" are unproved and perhaps unprovable assertions. Should social responsibility or market forces determine whether an organization strives to create a diverse workforce? Why? (Obj. 6)

5. **Ethical Issue:** You know that it's not acceptable to make ethnic jokes, least of all in the workplace, but a colleague of yours keeps invoking the worst ethnic and racial stereotypes. How do you respond? Do you remain silent and change the subject, or do you pipe up? What other options do you have in dealing with such a co-worker? Consider whether your answer would change if the offender were your boss. (Obj. 6)

Activities

3.1 Trouble on a Global Scale: Analyzing Intercultural Blunders (Objs. 1–3)

INTERCULTURAL

As business organizations become increasingly global in their structure and marketing, they face communication problems resulting from cultural misunderstandings.

Your Task. Based on what you have learned in this chapter, describe several broad principles that could be applied in helping the individuals involved understand what went wrong in the following events. What suggestions could you make for remedying the problems involved?

a. During a festive dinner for a delegation from Singapore visiting the government of the Czech Republic, the conversation turned to the tasty main course they were eating. One of the Czech hosts explained to the inquiring foreign guests that they were enjoying a Czech specialty, rabbit, known for its light white meat. The Singaporeans' faces showed shock, embarrassment, and irritation. As inconspicuously as possible they put down their silverware. Only later did the Czech delegation learn that a rabbit is a pet in Singapore much like the house cat in European or North American households.[28]

b. An advertising agency manager, new to his post in Japan, gathered his team for an old-fashioned brainstorming session in the boardroom. A big presentation loomed, and he expected creative ideas from his staff. Instead, he was met with silence. What went wrong? How could he coax ideas from his staff?[29]

c. The employees of a large North American pharmaceutical firm became angry over the e-mail messages they received from the firm's employees in Spain. The messages weren't offensive. Generally, these routine messages just explained ongoing projects. What riled the North Americans was this: every Spanish message was copied to the hierarchy within its division. The North Americans could not understand why e-mail messages had to be sent to people who had little or nothing to do with the issues being discussed. But this was accepted practice in Spain.[30]

3.2 Learning to Cope With International Time (Objs. 1–5)

WEB

Assume you are a virtual assistant working from your home. As part of your job, you schedule webcasts, online chats, and tele-conference calls for businesspeople who are conducting business around the world.

Your Task. To broaden your knowledge of time zones, respond to the following:

a. What does the abbreviation UTC indicate? (Use Google and search for UTC definition.)

b. Internationally, time is shown with a 24-hour clock (sometimes called *military time*). What time does 13.00 indicate? (Use Google; search for 24-hour clock.) How is a 12-hour clock different from a 24-hour clock? With which are you most familiar?

c. What are the best business hours for an online chat between an executive in Markham, Ontario, and a vendor in Singapore? Your instructor may select other cities for you to search.

3.3 The World Is Atwitter—Hot New Medium Opens Up Countries and Cultures (Obj. 1)

WEB

You may know the *share* feature in Facebook that lets you update your activities, favourite links, pictures, and whereabouts for your friends to see. Twitter, founded in 2006, started out as a place for such updates and online banter in fewer than 140 characters.

Unlike Facebook, though, Twitter is a personal yet also very public broadcasting medium that lends itself to easy and speedy transmission. It is free and doubly mobile, running on the SMS network for cellphones and on the Internet as well.

Your Task: Go to **www.twitter.com**. You don't need to register to search for and view tweets in your Internet browser, but you may want to open a Twitter account to enjoy the full benefits of the free service. Signing up is quick and intuitive. Execute the onscreen directions and watch the brief instructional video clip, if you like. You will be able to follow not only friends and family but also news, business updates, film reviews, and sports, or receive and share other up-to-the-minute messages.

Get started by viewing *trending topics*. Some may be business related. A few may be international in scope. Use the search box to type any current international or business event to see what twitterers are saying about it. For instance, check out the tweets of CTV's Lisa LaFlamme or those of another newscaster. In the classroom, discuss the usefulness of Twitter as you see it. Is the information you find interesting and trustworthy? You will learn more about Twitter and other highly portable new media in Chapter 7.

3.4 Cross-Cultural Gap at Resort Hotel in Thailand (Objs. 1–4)

INTERCULTURAL　　**TEAM**

The Laguna Beach Resort Hotel in Phuket, Thailand, nestled between a tropical lagoon and the sparkling Andaman Sea, is one of the most beautiful resorts in the world. (You can take a virtual tour by using Google and searching for Laguna Beach Resort Phuket.) When Brett Peel arrived as the director of the hotel's kitchen, he thought he had landed in paradise. On the job only six weeks, he began wondering why his Thai staff would answer *yes* even when they didn't understand what he had said. Other foreign managers discovered that junior staff managers rarely spoke up and never expressed an opinion contrary to those of senior executives. What's more, guests with a complaint thought that Thai employees were not taking them seriously because the Thais smiled at even the worst complaints. Thais also did not seem to understand deadlines or urgent requests.[31]

Your Task. In teams decide how you would respond to the following. If you were the director of this hotel, would you implement a training program for employees? If so, would you train only foreign managers, or would you include local Thai employees as well? What topics should a training program include? Would your goal be to introduce Western ways to the Thais? At least 90 percent of the hotel guests are non-Thai.

3.5 Negotiating Traps (Objs. 2–5)

INTERCULTURAL

Businesspeople often have difficulty reaching agreement on the terms of contracts, proposals, and anything that involves bargaining. They have even more difficulty when the negotiators are from different cultures.

Your Task. Discuss the causes and implications of the following common mistakes made by North Americans in their negotiations with foreigners.

a. Assuming that a final agreement is set in stone

b. Lacking patience and insisting that matters progress more quickly than the pace preferred by the locals

c. Believing that individuals who speak English understand every nuance of your meaning

3.6 Learning About Other Countries (Obj. 4)

INTERCULTURAL

When meeting businesspeople from other countries, you will feel more comfortable if you know the basics of business etiquette and intercultural communication, such as greetings, attire, or dos and don'ts. On the Web, you will find many resources, some more reliable than others.

Your Task. Visit Executive Planet at **www.executiveplanet.com** and the International Business Center's (IBC) site at **www.cyborlink.com**. At Executive Planet, click the region or the individual country link to obtain brief but useful information. The IBC site provides analysis based on renowned Dutch psychologist Geert Hofstede's five dimensions of culture applied to each country. Peruse both Web sites and answer the following questions:

a. How do people greet each other in Australia, India, Japan, Korea, the Netherlands, and Spain?

b. In what countries is it important to keep a certain distance from the person you are greeting?

c. In what countries is a kiss appropriate?

3.7 Calling iPhone or iPod Touch Owners: Pick up a Few Foreign Phrases (Objs. 3, 4)

INTERCULTURAL   **WEB**

If you own an iPhone or an iPod Touch, you are familiar with the App Store. You can download thousands of low-cost or free applications for these devices. Try Oxford Translator for some of the world's most popular languages—Spanish, Chinese, French, Russian, German, and Portuguese. As opposed to the "pro" apps, the trial versions are free.

Your Task. After choosing a language and downloading its free Oxford Translator application to iTunes or directly to your Apple device, try out simple greetings and phrases. Repeat after the audio samples to perfect your pronunciation. After practising, try to apply the expressions you learned in a brief exchange with a visitor or fellow student from your chosen country.

3.8 Examining Cultural Stereotypes (Objs. 1, 3)

INTERCULTURAL   **TEAM**   **WEB**

As you have learned in this chapter, generalizations are necessary as we acquire and categorize new knowledge. As long as we remain open to new experiences, we won't be stymied by rigid, stereotypical perceptions of other cultures. Almost all of us are at some point in our lives subject to stereotyping by others, whether we are immigrants, members of minority groups, women, members of certain professions, North Americans abroad, and so forth. Generally speaking, negative stereotypes sting. However, even positive stereotypes can offend or embarrass because they fail to acknowledge the differences among individuals.

Your Task. Think about a nation or culture about which you have only a hazy idea. Jot down a few key traits that come to mind. For example, you may not know much about the Netherlands and the Dutch people. You can probably think of Gouda cheese, wooden clogs, Heineken beer, tulips, and windmills. Anything else? Then consider a culture with which you are very familiar, whether it is yours or that of a country you visited or studied. In one column, write down a few stereotypical perceptions that are positive. Then, in another column, record negative stereotypes you associate with that culture. Share your notes with your team or the whole class, as the instructor may direct. How do you respond to others' descriptions of your culture? Which stereotypes irk you and why? For a quick fact check and overview at the end of this exercise, Google the *CIA World Factbook* or *BBC News Country Profiles*.

3.9 Drop in Anytime: Ambiguous Expressions Invite New Friends (Obj. 5)

INTERCULTURAL

To end conversations, North Americans often issue casual invitations to new acquaintances and even virtual strangers, such as *Visit me when you come to Montréal,* or *Come on over anytime.* However, nonnative speakers and visitors may misinterpret such casual remarks. They may embarrass their hosts and suffer disappointment by taking the offhand invitation literally and acting on it. Psychologists Cushner and Brislin warn: "Those interacting across cultures would be wise to avoid using expressions that have multiple meanings."[32]

Your Task. Assume you are a businessperson engaged in exporting and importing. As such, you are in constant communication with suppliers and customers around the world. In messages sent abroad or in situations with nonnative speakers of English at home, what kinds of ambiguous expressions should you avoid? In teams or individually, list three to five original examples of idioms, slang, acronyms, sports references, abbreviations, jargon, and two-word verbs. Which phrases or behaviour could be taken literally by a person from a different culture?

3.10 What Makes a "Best" Company for Members of Minority Groups? (Obj. 6)

To determine the winners of the Canada's Best Diversity Employers competition, Mediacorp editors reviewed a short-listed group of employers that had developed noteworthy and interesting diversity initiatives. Each candidate's diversity and inclusiveness programs were reviewed to determine how these efforts compared with those of other employers in their field. The finalists chosen represented the diversity leaders in their industry and region of Canada.[33]

Your Task. Assume you are an individual who believes your organization would be better if it were more diverse. Because of your interest in this area, your boss says he'd like you to give a three- to five-minute informational presentation at the next board meeting. Your assignment is to provide insights on what the leading companies for minority employees are doing. You decide to prepare your comments based on Canada's Best Diversity Employers. You plan to provide examples of each type of effective diversity initiative. Your instructor may ask you to give your presentation to the entire class or to small groups. Visit **www.canadastop100.com/diversity** for a list of organizations.

Grammar and Mechanics C.L.U.E. Review 3

Pronouns

Review Guides 11–18 about pronoun usage in Appendix A: Grammar and Mechanics Guide (Competent Language Usage Essentials), beginning on page A-6. On a separate sheet, revise the following sentences to correct errors in pronouns. For each error that you locate, write the guide number that explains this usage. Some sentences may have two errors. If the sentence is correct, write C. When finished, compare your responses with the key beginning on page Key-1.

Example: Me and **her** are the most senior sales reps in the Northeast Division.

Revision: She and **I** are the most senior sales reps in the Northeast Division. [Guide 12]

1. Direct the visitors to my boss and I; she and I will give them a tour of our facility.

2. Judging by you and I alone, this department will be the most productive one in the company.

3. The team knew that it's project was doomed once the funding was cut.

4. You and me did the work of three; she only did hers and poorly so.

5. The shift manager and I will work overtime tonight, so please direct all calls to him or myself.

6. Each new job candidate must be accompanied to their interview by a staff member.

7. Please deliver the printer supplies to whomever ordered them.

8. Most applications arrived on time, but your's and her's were not received.

9. As we were pulling out of the parking lot, one of our colleagues waved at Peter and me asking us to stop.

10. Whom did you say left messages for Connie and me?

Endnotes

[1] Based on material from Bolton, D. (2010). Are Canadian brands ready for the global podium? *Best Canadian Brands 2010: The Definitive Guide to Canada's Most Valuable Brands.* Toronto: Interbrand, pp. 4–5. Retrieved March 23, 2011, from www.interbrand.com/Libraries/Branding_Studies/Best_Canadian_Brands_2010.sflb.ashx; O'Keefe, E. (2010). Defining brand Canada—with confidence. *Best Canadian Brands 2010: The Definitive Guide to Canada's Most Valuable Brands.* Toronto: Interbrand, pp. 6–9. Retrieved March 23, 2011, from www.interbrand.com/Libraries/Branding_Studies/Best_Canadian_Brands_2010.sflb.ashx

[2] Flannery, R. (2004, May 10). China is a big prize. *Forbes, 173*(10), p. 163. Retrieved July 25, 2009, from ProQuest database.

[3] Canadian Broadcasting Corporation. (n.d.). *Hockey Night In Canada*—in Punjabi! Retrieved May 16, 2009, from http://citiesofmigration.ca/hockey-night-in-canada-in-punjabi/

[4] Zikmund, W. G., et al. (2008). *Effective marketing* (1st Cdn ed.). Toronto: Nelson Education.

[5] Canadian Broadcasting Corporation. (2008, June 10). Immigration in Canada: From 1947 to 2017. Retrieved May 17, 2009, from http://www.cbc.ca/news/background/immigration

[6] Hall, E. T., & Hall, M. R. (1990). *Understanding cultural differences.* Yarmouth, ME: Intercultural Press, pp. 183–184.

[7] Gallois, C., & Callan, V. (1997). *Communication and culture.* New York: Wiley, p. 24.

[8] Ibid, p. 29.

[9] Copeland, L., & Griggs, L. (1985). *Going international.* New York: Penguin, p. 94.

[10] Ibid.

[11] Ibid.

[12] Zikmund, W. G., et al. (2008). *Effective marketing* (1st Cdn ed.). Toronto: Nelson Education.

[13] Chen, G. M., & Starosta, W. J. (1998). *Foundations of intercultural communication.* Boston: Allyn and Bacon, p. 40.

[14] Varner, I., & Beamer, L. (2001). *Intercultural communication in the global workplace.* Boston: McGraw-Hill Irwin, p. 18.

[15] Hammer, M. R. (1993). Quoted in Chen, G. M., & Starosta, W. J. (1998). *Foundations of intercultural communication.* Boston: Allyn and Bacon, p. 247.

[16] Chaney, L. H., & Martin, J. S. (1995). *Intercultural business communication.* Englewood Cliffs, NJ: Prentice Hall Career and Technology, p. 67.

[17] Weber, G. (2004, May). English rules. *Workforce Management,* 47–50; Desai, D. (2008). Globalization and the English skills gap. *Chief Learning Officer, 7*(6), 62–63. Retrieved July 25, 2009, from Business Source Premier (EBSCO) database; Dvorak, P. (2007, November 5). Plain English gets harder in global era. *Wall Street Journal.* Retrieved July 25, 2009, from ProQuest database.

[18] Axtell, R. E. (Ed.). (1990). *Do's and taboos around the world* (2nd ed.) New York: Wiley, p. 71.

[19] Martin, J. S., & Chaney, L. H. (2006). *Global business etiquette.* Westport, CT: Praeger, p. 36.

[20] Canadian Broadcasting Corporation. (2008, June 10). Immigration in Canada: From 1947 to 2017. Retrieved May 22, 2009, from http://www.cbc.ca/news/background/immigration/

[21] Zikmund, W. G., et al. (2008). *Effective marketing* (1st Cdn ed.). Toronto: Nelson Education.

[22] Hammett, C. (2003). Companies win through team building. *Toronto Sun Career Connection.* Retrieved February 12, 2003, from http://www.canoe.ca/CareerConnectionNews/030213_teambuilding.html

[23] Andre, R. (1995, June). Diversity stress as morality stress. *Journal of Business Ethics,* 489–496.

[24] Capowski, G. (1996, June). Managing diversity. *Management Review,* p. 16.

[25] Makower, J. (1995, Winter). Managing diversity in the workplace. *Business and Society Review,* 48–54.

[26] Queen Elizabeth II. (2004, November). Speech during state visit to Germany. Retrieved February 28, 2011, from http://ukingermany.fco.gov.uk/en/about-us/working-with-germany/teachers-schools/

[27] Engle, J. (2007, February 2). Culture's unacknowledged iron grip. *Chronicle of Higher Education,* p. B16).

[28] Špaček, L. (2008). *Nová velká kniha etikety.* Prague: Mladá Fronta, p. 260.

[29] Rothrock, V. (2004, July 16). Culture clash. Retrieved January 23, 2007, from Business Source Premier (EBSCO) database.

[30] Cottrill, K. (2000, November 6). The world according to Hollywood. *Traffic World,* 15.

[31] Thapanachai, S. (2003, October 6). Awareness narrows cross-cultural gap in Thai management training courses. *Bangkok Post.* Retrieved July 21, 2009, from Factiva database.

[32] Brislin, R., & Cushner, K. (1996). *Intercultural interactions: a practical guide.* Thousand Oaks, CA: Sage, p. 292

[33] Mediacorp Canada Inc. (2009.) Canada's best diversity employers: Recognizing the employers that offer Canada's most inclusive workplaces. Retrieved May 31, 2009, from http://www.canadastop100.com/diversity/

UNIT 2

The Writing Process

PhotoAlto/Eric Audras/Getty Images

CHAPTER 4

Planning Business Messages

OBJECTIVES

After studying this chapter, you should be able to

1. Identify four basic principles of business writing, summarize the 3-×-3 writing process, and explain how a writing process helps a writer.

2. Recognize the components of the first phase of the writing process (prewriting), including analyzing your purpose, anticipating the audience, selecting the best channel, and adapting your message to the audience.

3. Effectively apply audience benefits, the "you" view, and conversational but professional language.

4. Effectively employ a positive and courteous tone, bias-free language, simple expression, and vigorous words.

5. Understand how teams approach collaborative writing projects and which collaboration tools support team writing.

6. Summarize the legal and ethical responsibilities of business communicators in the areas of investments, safety, marketing, human resources, and copyright law.

Yuri Arcurs/Shutterstock

Understanding the Writing Process for Business Messages

LEARNING OBJECTIVE 1

Identify four basic principles of business writing, summarize the 3-x-3 writing process, and explain how a writing process helps a writer.

The task of preparing a written business message or a presentation is easier and more efficient if you have a systematic process to follow. This chapter presents a systematic writing process that you can use to approach all business communication, whether it's an e-mail message, a report, an oral presentation, or even an instant message. The 3-x-3 writing process guides you through three phases, making it easy for you to plan, organize, and complete any message. Following the 3-x-3 writing process takes the guesswork out of writing. It tells you what happens in each phase and guides you to effective results.

Starting With the Basics

Business writing differs from other writing you may have done. In preparing high school, university, or college compositions and term papers, you probably focused on discussing your feelings or displaying your knowledge. Your instructors wanted to see your thought processes, and they wanted assurance that you had internalized the subject matter. You may have had to meet a minimum word count. Business writers, however, have different goals. For business messages and oral presentations, your writing should be as follows:

Business writing is purposeful, persuasive, economical, and reader oriented.

- **Purposeful.** You will be writing to solve problems and convey information. You will have a definite purpose to fulfill in each message.

- **Persuasive.** You want your audience to believe and accept your message.

- **Economical.** You will try to present ideas clearly but concisely. Length is not rewarded.

- **Audience oriented.** You will concentrate on looking at a problem from the reader's perspective instead of seeing it from your own.

Business writers seek to express rather than to impress.

These distinctions actually ease the writer's task. You will not be searching your imagination for creative topic ideas. You won't be stretching your ideas to make them appear longer. Writing consultants and businesspeople complain that many post-secondary graduates entering industry have at least an unconscious perception that quantity enhances quality. Delete this notion that longer is better. Conciseness and clarity are prized in business.

The ability to prepare concise, audience-centred, persuasive, and purposeful messages does not come naturally. Very few people, especially beginners, can sit down and compose a terrific letter or report without training. However, following a systematic process, studying model messages, and practising the craft can make nearly anyone a successful business writer or speaker.

Following the 3-x-3 Writing Process

Whether you are preparing an e-mail message, a memo, a letter, or an oral presentation, the process will be easier if you follow a systematic plan. The 3-x-3 writing process breaks the entire task into three phases: prewriting, writing, and revising, as shown in Figure 4.1.

FIGURE 4.1 The 3-x-3 Writing Process

1 Prewriting

Analyze: Decide on your purpose. What do you want the receiver to do or believe? What channel or form is best? Should you deliver your message in writing, orally, electronically, or graphically?

Anticipate: Profile the audience. What does the receiver already know? Will the receiver's response be neutral, positive, or negative? Use the direct method for positive messages; consider using the indirect method for negative or persuasive messages.

Adapt: What techniques can you use to adapt your message to its audience and the audience's anticipated reaction? Include audience benefits and the "you" view, as well as positive, conversational, and courteous language.

2 Writing

Research: Gather data to provide facts. Search company files, previous correspondence, and the Internet. What do you need to know to write this message? How much does the audience already know?

Organize: Group similar facts together. Organize direct messages with the big idea first, followed by an explanation and an action request in the closing. For persuasive or negative messages, use an indirect, problem-solving plan. For short messages, make quick notes. For longer messages, outline your plan and make notes.

Compose: Prepare a first draft, usually writing quickly. Focus on short, clear sentences using the active voice. Link ideas to build paragraph coherence.

3 Revising

Revise: Edit your message to be sure it is clear, conversational, concise, and readable. Revise to eliminate wordy fillers, long lead-ins, redundancies, compound prepositions, wordy noun phrases, and trite business phrases. Develop parallelism and consider using headings and numbered and bulleted lists for quick comprehension.

Proofread: Take the time to read over every message carefully. Look for errors in spelling, grammar, punctuation, names, numbers, and format.

Evaluate: Decide whether this message will achieve your purpose. Have you thought enough about the audience to be sure this message is appropriate and appealing?

Prewriting. The first phase of the writing process prepares you to write and involves *analyzing* the audience and your purpose for writing. Prewriting also involves *anticipating* how your audience will react to your message. In *adapting* your message to the audience, you try to think of the right words and the right tone that will win approval.

Writing. The second phase involves researching, organizing, and then composing the message. *Researching* means gathering the information you need to support your message. This information may come from primary or secondary sources. Once you have collected enough information, you would focus on *organizing* your message. The final step in the second phase of the writing process is actually *composing* the message. Naturally, you will do it at your computer so that you can revise it later.

Revising. The third phase of the writing process involves revising, proofreading, and evaluating your writing. After writing the first draft, you will spend a lot of time *revising* the message for clarity, conciseness, tone, and readability. You will *proofread* carefully to ensure correct spelling, grammar, punctuation, and format. Finally, you will *evaluate* the message to see whether it accomplishes your goal.

Scheduling the Writing Process

Although Figure 4.1 shows three equal phases, the time you spend on each varies depending on the complexity of the message, the purpose, the audience, and your schedule. One expert gives these rough estimates for scheduling a writing project:

- **Prewriting:** 25 percent (thinking and planning)
- **Writing:** 25 percent (organizing and composing)
- **Revising:** 50 percent (45 percent revising, and 5 percent proofreading)

These are rough guides, yet you can see that good writers spend the most time revising. Much depends, of course, on your project, its importance, and your familiarity with it. What is critical to remember, though, is that revising is a major component of the writing process.

> In the writing process, revising takes the most time.

This process may seem a bit complicated for the daily messages and oral presentations that many businesspeople prepare. Does this same process apply to e-mails, memos, and short letters? How do collaborators and modern computer technologies affect the process?

It may appear that you perform one step and progress to the next, always following the same order. Most business writing, however, is not that rigid. Although writers perform the tasks described, the steps may be rearranged, abbreviated, or repeated. Some writers revise every sentence and paragraph as they go. Many find that new ideas occur after they have begun to write, causing them to back up, alter the organization, and rethink their plan. Beginning business writers often follow the writing process closely. With experience, though, you will become like other good writers and presenters who alter, compress, and rearrange the steps as needed.

> **Steps in the writing process may be rearranged, shortened, or repeated.**

Analyzing Your Purpose and Selecting Your Channel

We devote the remainder of this chapter to the first phase of the writing process. You will learn to analyze the purpose for writing, anticipate how your audience will react, select the best channel, and adapt your message to the audience. It is surprising how many people begin writing and discover only as they approach the end of a message what they are trying to accomplish. If you analyze your purpose before you begin, you can avoid backtracking and starting over.

Identifying the Purpose

As you begin to compose a message, ask yourself two important questions: (1) *Why am I sending this message?* and (2) *What do I hope to achieve?* Your responses will determine how you organize and present your information.

Your message may have primary and secondary purposes. For university or college work, your primary purpose may be merely to complete the assignment; secondary purposes might be to make yourself look good and to get a good grade. The primary purposes for sending business messages are typically to inform and to persuade. A secondary purpose is to promote goodwill: you and your organization want to look good in the eyes of your audience.

Most business messages do nothing more than *inform*. They explain procedures, announce meetings, answer questions, and transmit findings. Some business messages, however, are meant to *persuade*. These messages sell products, convince managers, motivate employees, and win over customers. Informative messages are developed differently from persuasive messages.

Selecting the Best Channel

After identifying the purpose of your message, you need to select the most appropriate communication channel. As you learned in Chapter 1, some information is most efficiently and effectively delivered orally. Other messages should be written, and still others are best delivered electronically. A number of channels are available, as summarized in Figure 4.2. Whether to set up a meeting, send a message electronically, or write a report depends on some of the following factors:

- Importance of the message
- Amount and speed of feedback required
- Necessity of a permanent record
- Cost of the channel
- Degree of formality desired
- Confidentiality and sensitivity of the message.

FIGURE 4.2 Choosing Communication Channels

Channel	Best Use
Blog	When one person needs to present digital information easily so that it is available to others.
E-mail	When you need feedback but not immediately. Lack of security makes it problematic for personal, emotional, or private messages.
Face-to-face conversation	When you need a rich, interactive medium. Useful for delivering persuasive, bad news, and personal messages.
Face-to-face group meeting	When group decisions and consensus are important. Inefficient for merely distributing information.
Fax	When your message must cross time zones or international boundaries, when a written record is significant, or when speed is important.
Instant message	When you are online and need a quick response. Useful for determining whether someone is available for a phone conversation.
Letter	When a written record or formality is required, especially with customers, the government, suppliers, or others outside an organization.
Memo	When you want a written record to clearly explain policies, discuss procedures, or collect information within an organization.
Phone call	When you must deliver or gather information quickly, when nonverbal cues are unimportant, and when you cannot meet in person.
Report or proposal	When you are delivering complex data internally or externally.
Voice mail message	When you want to leave important or routine information that the receiver can respond to when convenient.
Videoconference or teleconference	When group consensus and interaction are important but members are geographically dispersed.
Wiki	When digital information must be made available to others. Useful for collaboration because participants can easily add, remove, and edit content.

An interesting theory, called the media richness theory, describes the extent to which a channel or medium recreates or represents all the information available in the original message. A richer medium, such as face-to-face conversation, permits more interactivity and feedback. A leaner medium, such as a report or proposal, presents a flat, one-dimensional message. Richer media enable the sender to provide more verbal and visual cues, and allow the sender to tailor the message to the audience.

Many factors help you decide which of the channels shown in Figure 4.2 is most appropriate for delivering a workplace message.

Switching to Faster Channels

Technology and competition continue to accelerate the pace of business today. As a result, communicators are switching to ever-faster means of exchanging information. In the past business messages within organizations were delivered largely by hard-copy memos. Responses would typically take a couple of days. However, that's too slow for today's communicators. They want answers and action now! Mobile phones, instant messaging, faxes, Web sites, and especially e-mail can deliver that information much faster than can traditional channels of communication.

Within many organizations, hard-copy memos are still written, especially for messages that require persuasion, permanence, or formality. They are also prepared as attachments to e-mail messages. Clearly, however, the channel of choice for corporate communicators today is e-mail. It's fast, inexpensive, and easy. Businesspeople are sending fewer hard-copy interoffice memos and fewer customer letters. Customer service functions can now be served through Web sites or by e-mail.

Many businesses now help customers with live chat. Customers visit the company Web site and chat with representatives by keying their questions and answers back and forth. Customer representatives must have not only good keying skills but also an ability to write conversational and correct responses. One company found that it could

> Mobile phones, instant messaging, faxes, Web sites, and e-mail deliver information within organizations more quickly than traditional hard-copy memos.

not easily convert its telephone customer service people to chat representatives because many lacked the language skills necessary to write clear and correct messages. They were good at talking but not at writing, again making the point that the Internet has increased the need for good writing skills.

Whether your channel choice is live chat, e-mail, a hard-copy memo, or a report, you will be displaying your communication skills and applying the writing process. The best writers spend sufficient time in the prewriting phase.

Anticipating the Audience

A good writer anticipates the audience for a message: What is the reader or listener like? How will that person react to the message? Although you can't always know exactly who the receiver is, you can imagine some of that person's characteristics. Even writers of direct-mail sales letters have a general idea of the audience they want to target. Picturing a typical receiver is important in guiding what you write. By profiling your audience and shaping a message to respond to that profile, you are more likely to achieve your communication goals.

Profiling the Audience

Visualizing your audience is a pivotal step in the writing process. The questions in Figure 4.3 will help you profile your audience. How much time you devote to answering these questions depends greatly on your message and its context. An analytical report that you compose for management or an oral presentation before a big group would, of course, demand considerable audience anticipation. Conversely, an e-mail to a co-worker or a letter to a familiar supplier might require only a few moments of planning. No matter how short your message, though, spend some time thinking about the audience so that you can tailor your words to your readers or listeners. Remember that most receivers will be thinking, *What's in it for me?* or, *What am I supposed to do with this information?*

Responding to the Audience Profile

By profiling your audience before writing, you can identify the appropriate tone, language, and channel.

Profiling your audience helps you make decisions about shaping the message. You will discover what kind of language is appropriate, whether you are free to use specialized technical terms, whether you should explain everything, and so on. You will decide whether your tone should be formal or informal, and you will select the most desirable channel. Imagining whether the receiver is likely to be neutral, positive, or negative will help you determine how to organize your message.

Another result of profiling your audience will be recognizing whether a secondary audience is possible. Analyzing the task and anticipating the audience help you adapt your message so that it will accomplish what you intend.

FIGURE 4.3 Asking the Right Questions to Profile Your Audience

Primary Audience	Secondary Audience
Who is my primary reader or listener?	Who might see or hear this message in addition to the primary audience?
What are my personal and professional relationships with that person?	How do these people differ from the primary audience?
What position does the person hold in the organization?	Do I need to include more background information?
How much does that person know about the subject?	How must I reshape my message to make it understandable and acceptable to others to whom it might be forwarded?
What do I know about that person's education, beliefs, culture, and attitudes?	
Should I expect a neutral, positive, or negative response to my message?	

Writing Process Phase 1: Adapt

After analyzing your purpose and anticipating your audience, you begin to think about how to adapt your message to the task and the audience. Adaptation is the process of creating a message that suits your audience. One important aspect of adaptation is *tone*. Conveyed largely by the words in a message, tone affects how a receiver feels on reading or hearing a message. For example, think how you would react to these statements:

You must return the form by 5 p.m.

Would you please return the form by 5 p.m.

The wording of the first message establishes an aggressive or negative tone—no one likes being told what to do. The second message is worded in a friendlier, more positive manner. Poorly chosen words may sound demeaning, condescending, discourteous, pretentious, or demanding.

Skilled communicators create effective messages by using a number of adaptive techniques, some of which are unconscious. These include developing audience benefits, cultivating a "you" view, sounding conversational but professional, and using positive, courteous expressions. Additional adaptive techniques include using bias-free language and preferring plain language with familiar but vigorous words.

LEARNING OBJECTIVE **3**

Effectively apply audience benefits, the "you" view, and conversational but professional language.

Developing Audience Benefits

A contemporary communication consultant gives this solid advice to his business clients: "Always stress the benefit to the readers of whatever it is you're trying to get them to do. If you can show them how you're going to save them frustration or help them meet their goals, you have the makings of a powerful message."[2]

Adapting your message to the receiver's needs means putting yourself in that person's shoes. It is called empathy. Empathic senders think about how a receiver will decode a message. They try to give something to the receiver, solve the receiver's problems, save the receiver's money, or just understand the feelings and position of that person. Which version of the following messages is more appealing to the receiver?

> **Empathic communicators envision the receiver and focus on benefits to that person.**

> **Empathy means being able to understand another's situation, feelings, and motives.**

Sender Focus

We are proud to announce our new software virus checker that we think is the best on the market!

Our warranty becomes effective only when we receive an owner's registration.

Audience Focus

Now you can be sure that all your computers will be protected with our real-time virus scanning.

Your warranty begins working for you as soon as you return your owner's registration.

Cultivating the "You" View

Notice how many of the previous audience-focused messages included the word *you*. In concentrating on receiver benefits, skilled communicators naturally develop the "you" view. They emphasize second-person pronouns (you, your) instead of first-person pronouns (I/we, us, our). Whether your goal is to inform, persuade, or promote goodwill, the catchiest words you can use are *you* and *your*. Compare the following examples.

> **Effective communicators develop the "you" view in a sincere, not manipulative or critical, tone.**

"I/We" View

We are requiring all employees to respond to the attached survey about health benefits.

I need your account number before I can do anything.

"You" View

Because your ideas count, please complete the attached survey about health benefits.

Would you mind giving me your account number so that I can locate your records and help you solve this problem?

Although you want to focus on the reader, don't overuse or misuse the second-person pronoun *you*. Readers and listeners appreciate genuine interest; however, they resent obvious attempts at manipulation. The authors of some sales messages, for example, are guilty of overkill when they include *you* dozens of times in a direct mail promotion. Furthermore, the word can sometimes create the wrong impression. Consider this statement: *You cannot return merchandise until you receive written approval. You* appears twice, but the reader feels singled out for criticism. In the following version, the message is less personal and more positive: *Customers may return merchandise with written approval.*

Another difficulty in emphasizing the "you" view and de-emphasizing *we/I* is that it may result in overuse of the passive voice. For example, to avoid *We will give you* (active voice), you might write *You will be given* (passive voice). The active voice in writing is generally preferred because it identifies who is doing the acting. You will learn more about active and passive voice in Chapter 5.

In recognizing the value of the "you" attitude, writers do not have to sterilize their writing and avoid any first-person pronouns or words that show their feelings. Skilled communicators are able to convey sincerity, warmth, and enthusiasm by the words they choose. Don't be afraid to use such phrases as *I'm happy* or *We're delighted* if you truly are.

When speaking face to face, communicators show sincerity and warmth with nonverbal cues, such as a smile and pleasant voice tone. In letters, memos, and e-mail messages, however, only expressive words and phrases can show these feelings. These phrases suggest hidden messages that say to readers and customers, *You are important, I hear you*, and *I'm honestly trying to please you.*

Being Conversational but Professional

Most instant messages, e-mail messages, business letters, memos, and reports replace conversation. Thus, they are most effective when they convey an informal, conversational tone instead of a formal, pretentious tone. Workplace messages should not, however, become so casual that they sound unprofessional.

Instant messaging (IM) enables co-workers to have informal, spontaneous conversations. Some companies have accepted IM as a serious workplace tool. With the increasing use of IM and e-mail, however, a major problem has developed. Sloppy, unprofessional expression appears in many workplace messages. You will learn more about the dangers of e-mail in Chapter 7. At this point, though, we are focusing on the tone of the language.

To project a professional image, you must sound educated and mature. Overuse of such expressions as *totally awesome, you know,* and *like,* as well as reliance on needless abbreviations (*BTW* for *by the way*), makes a businessperson sound like a teenager. Professional messages do not include IM abbreviations, slang, sentence fragments, and chitchat. We urge you to strive for a warm, conversational tone that avoids low-level diction. Levels of diction, as shown in Figure 4.4, range from unprofessional to formal.

Your goal is a warm, friendly tone that sounds professional. Although some writers are too casual, others are overly formal. To impress readers, they use big words, long

FIGURE 4.4 Levels of Diction

Unprofessional (low-level diction)	Conversational (mid-level diction)	Formal (high-level diction)
guts	nerve	courage
pecking order	line of command	dominance hierarchy
ticked off	upset	provoked
Sentence example: If we just hang in there, we can snag the contract.	**Sentence example:** If we don't get discouraged, we can win the contract.	**Sentence example:** If the principals persevere, they can secure the contract.

sentences, legal terminology, and third-person constructions. Stay away from such expressions as *the undersigned, the writer,* and *the affected party*. You will sound friendlier with familiar pronouns, such as *I, we,* and *you*. Study the following examples to see how to achieve a professional, yet conversational tone:

Avoid both extremes: sounding too informal and sounding too formal.

Unprofessional

Look, dude, this report is totally bogus. And the figures don't look kosher. Show me some real stats. Got sources?

Improved

Because the figures in this report seem inaccurate, please submit the source statistics.

Overly Formal

Pertaining to your order, we must verify the sizes that your organization requires prior to consignment of your order to our shipper.

Conversational

We will send your order as soon as we confirm the sizes you need.

LEARNING OBJECTIVE 4

Effectively employ a positive and courteous tone, bias-free language, simple expression, and vigorous words.

Expressing Yourself Positively

You can improve the clarity, tone, and effectiveness of a message if you use positive rather than negative language. Positive language generally conveys more information than negative language does. Moreover, positive messages are uplifting and pleasant to read. Positive wording tells what is and what can be done rather than what isn't and what can't be done. For example, *Your order cannot be shipped by January 10* is not nearly as informative as *Your order will be shipped January 20*.

Using positive language also involves avoiding negative words that create ill will. Some words appear to blame or accuse your audience. For example, opening a letter to a customer with *You claim that* suggests that you don't believe the customer. Other loaded words that can get you in trouble are *complaint, criticism, defective, failed, mistake,* and *neglected*. Often the writer is not conscious of the effect of these words. Notice in the following examples how you can revise the negative tone to create a more positive impression.

Negative expressions can be rephrased to sound positive.

Positive language creates goodwill and gives more options to readers.

Negative

This plan definitely cannot succeed if we don't obtain management approval.

Employees cannot park in Lot H until April 1.

Positive

This plan definitely can succeed if we obtain management approval.

Employees may park in Lot H starting April 1.

Being Courteous

Maintaining a courteous tone involves not just guarding against rudeness but also avoiding words that sound demading or preachy. Such expressions as *you should, you must,* and *you have to* cause people to instinctively react with *Oh, yeah?* One remedy is to turn these demands into polite commands that begin with *Please*. . . . Giving reasons for a request also softens the tone.

Even when you feel justified in displaying anger, remember that losing your temper or being sarcastic will seldom accomplish your goals as a business communicator to inform, to persuade, and to create goodwill. When you are irritated, frustrated, or infuriated, keep cool and try to defuse the situation. In dealing with customers in telephone conversations, use polite phrases, such as *I would be happy to assist you with that, Thank you for being so patient,* and *It was a pleasure speaking with you.*

Even when you are justifiably angry, courteous language is the best way to achieve your goals.

Less Courteous

Can't you people get anything right? This is the second time I've written!

You should organize a car pool in this department.

More Courteous and Helpful

Please credit my account for $340. My latest statement shows that the error noted in my letter of May 15 has not yet been corrected.

Organizing a car pool will reduce your transportation costs and help preserve the environment.

Choosing Bias-Free Language

In adapting a message to its audience, be sure your language is sensitive and bias free. Few writers set out to be offensive. Sometimes, though, we all say things that we never thought might be hurtful. The real problem is that we don't think about the words that stereotype groups of people, such as *the boys in the mailroom* or *the girls in the front office*. Be cautious about expressions that might be biased in terms of gender, race, ethnicity, age, and disability. Generally, you can avoid gender-biased language by leaving out the words *man* and *woman*, by using plural nouns and pronouns, or by changing to a gender-free word (*person* or *representative*). Avoid the *his or her* option whenever possible. It's wordy and conspicuous. With a little effort, you can usually find a construction that is graceful, grammatical, and unselfconscious.

Specify age only if it is relevant, and avoid expressions that are demeaning or subjective (such as *spry old codger*). To avoid disability bias, do not refer to an individual's disability unless it is relevant. When necessary, use terms that do not stigmatize people with disabilities. The following examples give you a quick look at a few problem expressions and possible replacements. The real key to bias-free communication, though, lies in your awareness and commitment. Be on the lookout to be sure that your messages do not exclude, stereotype, or offend people.

> Sensitive communicators avoid gender, racial, ethnic, age, and disability biases.

Gender Biased	Improved
female doctor, woman attorney, cleaning woman	doctor, attorney, cleaner
waiter/waitress, authoress, stewardess	server, author, flight attendant
the doctor . . . he	doctors . . . they
the teacher . . . she	teachers . . . they

Racially or Ethnically Biased	Improved
An Indian accountant was hired.	An accountant was hired.
James Lee, a Chinese Canadian man, applied.	James Lee applied.

Age Biased	Improved
The law applied to old people.	The law applied to people over 65.
Sally Kay, 55, was transferred.	Sally Kay was transferred.
a spry old gentleman	a man
a little old lady	a woman

Disability Biased	Improved
afflicted with, suffering from, crippled by	has
defect, disease	condition
confined to a wheelchair	uses a wheelchair

Using Plain Language and Familiar Words

In adapting your message to your audience, whenever possible use plain language and familiar words that you think audience members will recognize. Do not, however, avoid a big word that conveys your idea efficiently and is appropriate for the audience. Your goal is to shun pompous and pretentious language. If you mean *begin*, don't say *commence* or *initiate*. If you mean pay, don't write *compensate*. By substituting everyday, familiar words for unfamiliar ones, as shown here, you help your audience comprehend your ideas quickly.

Unfamiliar	Familiar
materialize	appear
obfuscate	confuse
remuneration	pay, salary
terminate	end

At the same time, be selective in your use of jargon. *Jargon* describes technical or specialized terms within a field. These terms enable insiders to communicate complex ideas briefly, but to outsiders they mean nothing. Human resources professionals, for example, know precisely what's meant by *cafeteria plan* (a benefits option program), but most of us would be thinking about lunch. Use specialized language only when the audience will understand it. In addition, don't forget to consider secondary audiences: Will those potential receivers understand any technical terms used?

Employing Precise, Vigorous Words

Strong verbs and concrete nouns give readers more information and keep them interested. Don't overlook the thesaurus (or the thesaurus program on your computer) for expanding your word choices and vocabulary. Whenever possible, use specific words, as shown here.

> Using familiar but precise language helps receivers understand.

Imprecise, Dull	More Precise
a change in profits	a 25 percent hike in profits
	a 10 percent plunge in profits
to say	to promise, confess, understand
	to allege, assert, assume, judge
to think about	to identify, diagnose, analyze
	to probe, examine, inspect

The Checklist box reviews important elements in the first phase of the 3-x-3 writing process. As you review these tips, remember the three basics of prewriting: analyzing, anticipating, and adapting.

Checklist

Adapting a Message to Its Audience

- **Identify the message purpose.** Ask yourself why you are communicating and what you hope to achieve. Look for primary and secondary purposes.

- **Select the most appropriate form.** Determine whether you need a permanent record or whether the message is too sensitive to put in writing.

- **Profile the audience.** Identify your relationship with the reader and your knowledge about that individual or group. Assess how much the receiver knows about the subject.

- **Focus on audience benefits.** Phrase your statements from the readers' viewpoint, not the writer's. Concentrate on the "you" view (*Your order will arrive, You can enjoy, Your ideas count*).

- **Be conversational but professional.** Strive for a warm, friendly tone that is not overly formal or familiar. Avoid slang and low-level diction.

- **Express ideas positively rather than negatively.** Instead of *Your order can't be shipped before June 1,* say *Your order can be shipped June 1.*

- **Avoid gender and racial bias.** Use bias-free words (*businessperson* instead of *businessman; working hours* instead of *man-hours*). Omit ethnic identification unless the context demands it.

- **Avoid age and disability bias.** Include age only if relevant. Avoid potentially demeaning expressions (*spry old gentleman*) and use terms that do not stigmatize people with disabilities (*he has a disability* instead of *he is a cripple* or *he has a handicap*).

- **Use plain language and familiar words.** Use technical terms and big words only if they are appropriate for the audience (*end* not *terminate, required* not *mandatory*).

- **Employ precise, vigorous words.** Use a thesaurus if necessary to find strong verbs and concrete nouns (*announces* instead of *says, brokerage* instead of *business*).

Writing in Teams

LEARNING OBJECTIVE 5

Understand how teams approach collaborative writing projects and which collaboration tools support team writing.

As you learned in Chapter 2, many of today's workers will work in teams to deliver services, develop products, and complete projects. It is almost assumed that today's progressive organizations will employ teams in some capacity to achieve their objectives. Because much of a team's work involves writing, you can expect to be putting your writing skills to work as part of a team.

When Are Team-Written Documents Necessary?

Collaboration on team-written documents is necessary for projects that (a) are big, (b) have short deadlines, and (c) require the expertise or consensus of many people. Businesspeople sometimes collaborate on short documents, such as memos, letters, information briefs, procedures, and policies. But more often teams work together on big documents and presentations.

Why Are Team Documents Better?

Team-written documents are necessary for big projects that have short deadlines and that require the efforts of many people.

Team-written documents and presentations are standard in most organizations because collaboration has many advantages. Most important, collaboration usually produces a better product because many heads are better than one. In addition, team members and organizations benefit from team processes. Working together helps socialize members. They learn more about the organization's values and procedures. They are able to break down functional barriers, and they improve both formal and informal chains of communication. Additionally, they buy into a project when they are part of its development. Members of effective teams are eager to implement their recommendations.

How Are Team Documents Divided?

With big writing projects, teams may not actually function together for each phase of the writing process. Typically, team members gather at the beginning to brainstorm. They iron out answers to questions about the purpose, audience, content, organization, and design of their document or presentation. They develop procedures for team functioning, as you learned in Chapter 2. Then they often assign segments of the project to individual members.

Teams work together closely in Phase 1 (prewriting) of the writing process. However, members generally work separately in Phase 2 (writing), when they conduct research, organize their findings, and compose a first draft. During Phase 3 (revising) teams may work together to synthesize their drafts and offer suggestions for revision. They might assign one person the task of preparing the final document and assign another the job of proofreading. The revision and evaluation phase might be repeated several times before the final product is ready for presentation.

Teams generally work closely in Phase 1, work separately in Phase 2, and synthesize their drafts in Phase 3.

Which Online Collaboration Tools Support Team Writing?

One of the most frustrating tasks for teams is writing shared documents. Keeping the different versions straight and recognizing who made what comment can be confusing. Fortunately, many online collaboration tools are constantly being developed and improved. They range from simple to complex, inexpensive to expensive, locally installed to remotely hosted, commercial to open source, and large to small. Online collaboration tools are especially necessary when team members are not physically in the same location. But even when members are nearby, they may find it necessary to use online collaboration tools, such as the following:[3]

- **E-mail.** Despite its many drawbacks, e-mail remains a popular tool for online asynchronous (intermittent data transmission) collaboration. However, as projects grow more complex and involve more people who are not working nearby, e-mail becomes a clumsy, ineffective tool, especially for collaborative writing tasks.

- **Mailing lists.** With the right software, mailing lists can be archived online, providing a threaded listing of posts and full-text searching.

- **Discussion boards.** Participants can upload documents to the board instead of sending large files to everyone.

- **Instant messaging.** Because it ensures immediate availability, instant messaging is gaining acceptance. It allows members to clear up minor matters immediately, and it is helpful in initiating a quick group discussion.

- **Blogs and wikis.** A *blog* is a Web site with journal entries usually written by one person with comments added by others. A *wiki* is a Web site that allows multiple users to collaboratively create and edit pages. Wikis are good tools for building a knowledge repository that can be edited by participants. You will learn more about blogs and wikis in Chapter 7.

- **Groupware and portals.** Groupware and portals in the past involved expensive software featuring online discussion areas, document- and file-sharing areas, integrated calendaring, and collaborative authoring tools. More recently, less expensive tools have become available.

In writing shared documents, teams may use e-mail, mailing lists, discussion boards, instant messaging, groupware, portals, blogs, and wikis.

What Tools Work Well for Student Collaboration?

Student groups collaborating on assignments may find several helpful software tools. Google Docs is a free Web-based word processor, spreadsheet, presentation, and form application program that keeps documents current and allows team members to update files from their own computers. Another free collaborative writing tool is Writeboard. Check out either of these free tools by searching Google.

A number of tools accompanying Microsoft Word enable team members to track changes and insert comments while editing one team document. The Plugged In box discusses these tools.

PLUGGED IN

Using Technology to Edit and Revise Collaborative Documents

Collaborative writing and editing projects are challenging. Fortunately, Microsoft Word offers useful tools to help team members edit and share documents electronically. Two simple but useful editing tools are **Text Highlight Color** and **Font Color**. These tools, which are found on the **Home** tab in MS Office 2007, enable reviewers to point out errors and explain problematic passages through the use of contrast. However, some projects require more advanced editing tools, such as **Track Changes** and **Comment**.

Track Changes. To suggest specific editing changes to other team members, **Track Changes** is handy. The revised wording is visible on screen, and deletions show up in callout balloons in the right-hand margin. Suggested revisions offered by various team members are identified and dated. The original writer may accept or reject these changes. In Office 2007 you will find **Track Changes** on the **Review** tab.

Comment. Probably the most useful editing tool is the **Comment** function. This tool allows users to point out problematic passages or errors, ask or answer questions, and share ideas without changing or adding text. When more than one person adds comments, the comments appear in different colours and are identified by the writer's name and a date/time stamp. To use this tool in Word 2007, click **New Comment** from the drop-down **Review** tab. Then type your comment, which can be seen in the Web or print layout view (click **View** and **Print Layout** or **Web Layout**).

Completing a Document. When a document is finished, be sure to accept or reject all changes on the **Review** tab, a step that removes the tracking information.

Adapting to Legal and Ethical Responsibilities

LEARNING OBJECTIVE 6

Summarize the legal and ethical responsibilities of business communicators in the areas of investments, safety, marketing, human resources, and copyright law.

One of your primary responsibilities in writing for an organization or for yourself is to avoid language that may land you in court. Another responsibility is to be ethical. Both these concerns revolve around the use and abuse of language. You can protect yourself and avoid litigation by knowing what's legal and by adapting your language accordingly. Be especially careful when your messages involve investments, safety, marketing, human resources, and copyright law.

Investment Information

Writers describing the sale of stocks or financial services must follow specific laws written to protect investors. Any messages—including e-mails, letters, newsletters, and pamphlets—must be free from misleading information, exaggerations, or half-truths. A software company caused a flurry of lawsuits by withholding information that revealed problems in a new version of one of its most popular programs. Stockholders sued, charging that managers had deliberately concealed the bad news, thus keeping stock prices artificially high. Experienced financial writers know that careless language and even poor timing may provoke litigation.

Safety Information

Writers describing potentially dangerous products worry not only about protecting people from physical harm but also about being sued. Although far fewer product liability cases are filed in Canada than in the United States,[4] litigation arising from these cases is an active area of tort law (tort law involves compensating those who have been injured by the wrongdoing of others).[5] Manufacturers are obligated to warn consumers of any risks in their products. These warnings must do more than suggest danger: they must also clearly tell people how to use the product safely. In writing warnings, concentrate on major points. Omit anything that is not critical. In the work area, describe a potential problem and tell how to solve it. For example, *Lead dust is harmful and gets on your clothes. Change your clothes before leaving work.*

Clearly written safety messages use easy-to-understand words, such as *doctor* instead of *physician, clean* instead of *sanitary,* and *burn* instead of *incinerate.* Technical terms are

Warnings on dangerous products must be written especially clearly.

defined, for example, *Asbestos is a carcinogen (something that causes cancer)*. Effective safety messages also include highlighting techniques, such as headings and bullets. In other chapters you will learn more about these techniques for improving readability.

Marketing Information

Sales and marketing messages are illegal if they falsely advertise prices, performance capability, quality, or other product characteristics. Marketing messages must not deceive the buyer in any way. In Canada the Competition Bureau responds to consumer complaints regarding such issues as false advertising and unfair pricing practices. If enough people complain that a product does not perform as advertised, the bureau may investigate. Additionally, if there are complaints by individuals or companies that a company—or group of companies—is trying to control the price of a product, the bureau may get involved.[6] Sellers of services must also be cautious about the language they use to describe what they will do. Letters, reports, and proposals that describe services to be performed are interpreted as contracts in court. Therefore, language must not promise more than intended. Here are some dangerous words (and recommended alternatives) that have created misunderstandings leading to lawsuits.[7]

Dangerous Word	Court Interpretation	Recommended Alternative
determine	to come to a decision, to decide; to resolve	to evaluate, to assess, to analyze
assure or ensure	to render safe, to make secure, to give confidence, to cause to feel certain	to facilitate, to provide further confidence, to enhance the reliability of

Human Resources Information

The vast number of lawsuits relating to employment makes this a treacherous area for business communicators. In evaluating employees in the workplace, avoid making unsubstantiated negative comments. It is also unwise to assess traits (*she is unreliable*) because doing so requires subjective judgment. Concentrate instead on specific incidents (*in the last month she missed four workdays and was late three times*). Defamation lawsuits have become so common that some companies no longer provide letters of recommendation for former employees. To be safe, give recommendations only when the former employee authorizes the recommendation and when you can say something positive. Stick to job-related information.

Statements in employee handbooks also require careful wording because a court might rule that such statements are "implied contracts." Consider the following handbook remark: "We at Hotstuff, Inc., show our appreciation for hard work and team spirit by rewarding everyone who performs well." This seemingly harmless statement could make it difficult to fire an employee because of the implied employment promise.[8] Companies are warned to avoid promissory phrases in writing job advertisements, application forms, and offer letters. Phrases that suggest permanent employment and guaranteed job security can be interpreted as contracts.[9]

In adapting messages to meet today's litigious business environment, be sensitive to the rights of others and to your own rights. The key elements in this adaptation process are awareness of laws, sensitivity to interpretations, and careful use of language.

Copyright Information

The Canadian *Copyright Act* protects creative endeavours by ensuring that the creators have the sole right to authorize their publication, performance, or reproduction. Copyright applies to all original literary or textual works, dramatic works, musical works, artistic works, and architectural works. The word *copyright* refers to the "right to copy," and a key provision is *fair dealing,* the exception to the exclusive rights of copyright holders. Fair dealing creates a limited number of exceptions, including private study, research, criticism, review, and news reporting. This list is exhaustive, such that fair dealing applies only to those categories of dealings that are specifically mentioned. The law of copyright also applies to the Internet, so most individual works found there are protected: using Internet text or graphics without the permission of the copyright holder, for instance, is an infringement of copyright law.[10]

How to Avoid Copyright Infringement. Whenever you borrow words, charts, graphs, photos, music, or anything created privately, be sure you know what is legal and acceptable. The following guidelines will help:

- **Assume that everything is copyrighted.** In Canada, copyright entitlement legally ends at a certain point: generally, it endures for the lifetime of the creator, the remainder of the calendar year in which the creator dies, and for 50 years after the end of that calendar year.[11]

- **Realize that Internet items are NOT in the "public domain."** Nothing modern is in the "public domain" (free to be used by anyone) unless the owner explicitly says so.

- **Ask for permission.** You are always safe if you obtain permission. Write to the source, identify the material you want to include, and explain where it will be used. Expect to pay for permission.

- **Don't assume that a footnote is all that is needed.** Including a footnote to a source prevents plagiarism but not copyright infringement. Anything copied beyond the boundaries of fair dealing requires permission. You will learn more about citation methods and ways to avoid plagiarism in Chapter 12.

For more information about *copyright law, fair dealing, public domain,* and *acceptable use,* you can search the Web with these keywords.

> Writers can avoid violating copyright law by assuming that everything is copyrighted and not in the public domain.

Summary of Learning Objectives

1 **Identify four basic principles of business writing, summarize the 3-x-3 writing process, and explain how a writing process helps a writer.** Business writing differs from academic writing in that it strives to solve business problems. It is also economical, persuasive, and audience oriented. Phase 1 of the 3-x-3 writing process (prewriting) involves analyzing the message, anticipating the audience, and considering ways to adapt the message to the audience. Phase 2 (writing) involves researching the topic, organizing the material, and composing the message. Phase 3 (revising) includes proofreading and evaluating the message. A writing process helps a writer by providing a systematic plan describing what to do in creating messages.

2 **Recognize the components of the first phase of the writing process (prewriting), including analyzing your purpose, anticipating the audience, selecting the best channel, and adapting your message to the audience.** Communicators must decide why they are delivering a message and what they hope to achieve. Although many messages only inform, some must also persuade. After identifying the purpose of a message, communicators must choose the most appropriate channel. That choice depends on the importance of the message, the amount and speed of feedback required, the need for a permanent record, the cost of the channel, and the degree of formality desired. Communicators should also anticipate the primary and secondary audiences to adapt the message appropriately.

3 **Effectively apply audience benefits, the "you" view, and conversational but professional language.** Skilled communicators strive to emphasize audience benefits in business messages. This involves looking for ways to give something to the receiver, solve the receiver's problems, save the receiver's money, or just understand the feelings and position of that person. Skilled communicators look at a message from the receiver's perspective, applying the "you" view without attempting to manipulate. Effective business messages convey a warm, friendly tone but avoid expressions that may make the writer sound immature or unprofessional.

4 **Effectively employ a positive and courteous tone, bias-free language, simple expression, and vigorous words.** Skilled communicators improve the clarity, tone, and effectiveness of messages by using positive language that tells what can be done rather than what can't be done (*The project will be successful with your support* rather than *The project won't be successful without your support*). A courteous tone means guarding against rudeness and avoiding sounding preachy or demanding. Messages should also avoid language that excludes, stereotypes, or offends people, such as *lady lawyer, spry old gentlemen,* and *confined to a wheelchair*). Messages are improved by strong verbs and concrete nouns rather than imprecise, dull expressions.

5 **Understand how teams approach collaborative writing projects and which collaboration tools support team writing.** Team writing, which is necessary for large projects or when wide expertise is necessary, alters the writing process. Teams often work together in brainstorming and working out their procedures and assignments. Then individual members write their portions of the report or presentation during Phase 2. During Phase 3 (revising) teams may work together to combine their drafts. Teams use online collaboration tools, such as e-mail, mailing lists, discussion boards, instant messaging, blogs, wikis, groupware, and portals.

6 **Summarize the legal and ethical responsibilities of business communicators in the areas of investments, safety, marketing, human resources, and copyright law.** In writing about investments, communicators must avoid misleading information, exaggerations, and half-truths. Safety information, including warnings, must tell people clearly how to use a product safely and motivate them to do so. In addition to being honest, marketing information must not promise more than intended. Communicators in human resources must use careful wording (particularly in employment recommendations and employee handbooks) to avoid potential lawsuits. They must also avoid oral promises that can result in lawsuits. All writers must be mindful of copyright laws. Assume that everything is copyrighted, even items borrowed from the Internet. Know the implications and limitations of *fair dealing*.

Chapter Review

1. Why do you think business writing differs from school essay writing? (Obj. 1)

2. List the three phases of the writing process and summarize what happens in each phase. Which phase requires the most time? (Obj. 1)

3. What six factors are important in selecting an appropriate channel to deliver a message? What makes one channel richer than another? (Obj. 2)

4. How does profiling the audience help a business communicator prepare a message? (Obj. 2)

5. What is meant by *audience benefits*? (Obj. 3)

6. When is the "you" view appropriate, and when is it inappropriate? (Obj. 3)

7. Why is it appropriate to use instant messaging abbreviations (such as *BTW*) and happy faces in messages to friends but inappropriate in business messages? (Obj. 3)

8. What is wrong with using such expressions as *you claim, complaint, criticism, defective, failed, mistake,* and *neglected*? (Obj. 4)

9. What is wrong with the following statement? *Pertaining to the above-referenced infraction, all employees are herewith warned by the undersigned not to install private software on company computers.* (Obj. 4)

10. What is bias-free language? Give original examples. (Obj. 4)

11. Why should business writers strive to use short, familiar, simple words? Does this "dumb down" business messages? (Obj. 4)

12. What is *jargon,* and when is it appropriate for business writing? (Obj. 4)

13. Revise the following expression to show more courtesy: *For the last time, I'm warning all staff members that they must use virus-protection software—or else!* (Obj. 4)

14. What are the advantages and disadvantages of team-written documents? (Obj. 5)

15. What kinds of works are protected by copyright laws? (Obj. 6)

Critical Thinking

1. Why do you think employers prefer messages that are not written like high school, college, or university essays? (Obj. 1)

2. A wise observer once said that bad writing makes smart people look dumb. Do you agree or disagree, and why? (Objs. 1–4)

3. Discuss the following statement: "The English language is a landmine—it is filled with terms that are easily misinterpreted as derogatory and others that are blatantly insulting.... Being fair and objective is not enough; employers must also appear to be so."[12] (Obj. 5)

4. Why do you think that writing in a natural, conversational tone is difficult for many people? (Obj. 3)

5. **Ethical Issue:** Peter Whitney, an employee at Wells Fargo, launched an Internet blog to chat about his life, his friends, and his job. After criticizing some of his co-workers in his blog, he was fired from his job handling mail and the front desk. Whitney said, "There needs to be clearer guidelines. Some people go to a bar and complain about workers. I decided to do it online. Some people say I deserve what happened, but it was really harsh. It was unfair."[13] Do you agree or disagree, and why?

Writing Improvement Exercises

4.1 Audience Benefits and the "You" View (Obj. 3)

Your Task. Revise the following sentences to emphasize the audience's perspective and the "you" view.

a. To prevent us from possibly losing large sums of money in stolen identity schemes, our bank now requires verification of any large cheque presented for immediate payment.

b. So that we may bring our customer records up to date and eliminate the expense of duplicate mailings, we are asking you to complete and return the enclosed card.

c. For just $159 per person, we have arranged a two-night getaway package to Niagara Falls that includes hotel accommodations, Maid of the Mist tickets, and complimentary breakfasts.

d. We find it necessary to request all employees to complete the enclosed questionnaire so that we may develop a master schedule for summer vacations.

e. To enable us to continue our policy of selling name brands at discount prices, we can give store credit but we cannot give cash refunds on returned merchandise.

4.2 Conversational but Professional (Obj. 3)

Your Task. Revise the following statements to make the tone conversational yet professional.

a. BTW, Amy was pretty ticked off because the manager accused her of ripping off office supplies.

b. Hey, Sam! Look, I need you to pound on Lisa so we can drop this budget thingy in her lap.

c. Kindly be informed that your vehicle has been determined to require corrective work.

d. Under separate cover the above-referenced items (printer toner and supplies) are being sent to your Oakville office, as per your telephone conversation of April 1.

e. The undersigned respectfully reminds affected individuals that employees desirous of changing their health plans must do so before December 30.

4.3 Positive and Courteous Expression (Obj. 4)

Your Task. Revise the following statements to make them more positive.

a. In the complaint that you sent in your July 2 letter, you claim that our representative was hostile and refused to help you.

b. Plans for the new health centre cannot move forward without full community support.

c. This is the last time I'm writing to try to get you to record my January 6 payment of $500 to my account. Anyone who can read can see from the attached documents that I've tried to explain this to you before.

d. Although you apparently failed to read the operator's manual, we are sending you a replacement blade for your food processor. Next time read page 18 carefully so that you will know how to attach this blade.

e. Customers are ineligible for the 10 percent discount unless they show their membership cards.

4.4 Bias-Free Language (Obj. 4)

Your Task. Revise the following sentences to reduce gender, racial, ethnic, age, and disability stereotypes.

a. Every employee must wear his photo ID on the job.

b. Media Moguls hired Sheena Love, an Aboriginal Canadian, for the position of project manager.

c. A skilled assistant proofreads her boss's documents and catches any errors he makes.

d. The conference will include special excursions for the wives of executives.

e. Serving on the panel are a lady veterinarian, a female doctor, two businessmen, and a Pakistani CGA.

4.5 Plain Language and Familiar Words (Obj. 4)

Your Task. Revise the following sentences to avoid unfamiliar words.

a. The salary we are offering is commensurate with other managers' remuneration.

b. To expedite ratification of this agreement, we urge you to vote in the affirmative.

c. In a dialogue with the manager, I learned that you plan to terminate our contract.

d. Did the braking problem materialize subsequent to our recall effort?

e. Pursuant to your invitation, we will interrogate our agent.

4.6 Precise, Vigorous Words (Obj. 4)

Your Task. From the choices in parentheses, select the most precise, vigorous words.

a. When replying to e-mail, (*bring in, include, put*) enough of the old message for (*someone, the person, the recipient*) to recognize the original note.

b. For a (*hard, long, complicated*) e-mail message, (*make, create, have*) the note in your word processing program.

c. If an e-mail (*thing, catch, glitch*) interferes while writing, you can easily (*get, have, retrieve*) your message.

d. We plan to (*acknowledge, publicize, applaud*) the work of exemplary employees.

For the following sentences, provide more precise alternatives for the italicized words.

e. In her e-mail memo, she said that she would (a) *change* over-time hours to (b) *fix* the budget.

f. Our new manager (a) *said* that only (b) *the right kind of* applicants should apply.

g. After (a) *reading* the report, I decided it was (b) *bad*.

4.7 Legal Language (Obj. 6)

Your Task. To avoid possible litigation, revise the italicized words in the following sentences taken from proposals.

a. We have *inspected* the environmental project and will send a complete report.

b. Our goal is to *ensure* completion of the project on schedule.

c. We will *determine* the amount of stress for each supporting column.

Activities

Note: All Documents for Analysis may be downloaded from www.guffeybrief4e.nelson.com so that you do not have to rekey the entire message.

4.8 Document for Analysis: Improving the Tone of an E-Mail Message (Objs. 3–5)

TEAM

Your Task. Analyze the following demanding e-mail to be sent by the vice president to all employees. In teams or individually, discuss the tone and writing faults in this message. Your instructor may ask you to revise the message so that it reflects some of the writing techniques you learned in this chapter. How can you make this message more courteous, positive, and precise? Focus on conciseness, familiar words, and developing the "you" view. Consider revising this e-mail as a collaboration project by using Word's Comment feature.

To: All Employees
From: B. A. Cartwright<bacartwright@integrity.com>
Subject: Your Excessive Use of E-Mail!
Cc:
Attached: E-Mail and Internet Policy

Once again I have the decidedly unpleasant task of reminding all employees that you may NOT utilize company computers or the Internet other than for work-related business and essential personal messages. Effective immediately a new policy will be implemented.

Our guys in IT tell me that our bandwidth is now seriously compromised by some of you boys and girls who are using company computers for gaming, blogging, shopping, chatting, and downloading streaming video. Yes, we have given you the right to use e-mail responsibly for essential personal messages. But that does not include checking your

Facebook or MySpace accounts during work hours or downloading your favourite shows or sharing music.

We distributed an e-mail policy a little while ago. We have now found it necessary to amplify and extrapolate that policy to include use of the Internet. If our company does not control its e-mail and Internet use, you will continue to suffer slow downloads. You may also lose the right to use e-mail at all. In the past every employee has had the right to send a personal e-mail occasionally, but he must use that right carefully. We may have to prohibit the personal use of e-mail entirely. Don't make me do this!

You will be expected to study the attached E-Mail and Internet policy and return the signed form with your agreement to adhere to this policy. You must return this form by March 1. No exceptions!

4.9 Channel Selection: Various Business Scenarios (Obj. 2)

Your Task. Using Figure 4.2, suggest the best communication channels for the following messages. Assume that all channels shown are available. Be prepared to explain your choices.

a. As part of a task force to investigate cellphone marketing, you need to establish a central location where each team member can see general information about the task as well as add comments for others to see. Task force members are located throughout the country.

b. As a manager during a company reorganization, you must tell nine workers that their employment is being terminated.

c. You need to know whether Thomas in Reprographics can produce a rush job for you in two days.

d. Members of your product development team need a central location where each one can see general information about the job and add comments for others to see.

e. As assistant to the vice president, you are to investigate the possibility of developing internship programs with several nearby colleges and universities.

4.10 Analyzing Audiences (Obj. 3)

Your Task. Using the questions in Figure 4.3, write a brief analysis of the audience for each of the following communication tasks.

a. You are preparing a cover letter for a job that you saw advertised in a local newspaper. You are confident that your qualifications match the job description.

b. You are about to send an e-mail memo to your district sales manager describing your visit to a new customer who demands special discounts.

c. You are planning to write an e-mail memo to your boss persuading her to allow you to attend a computer class that will require you to leave work early two days a week for ten weeks.

d. You are preparing an unsolicited sales letter to a targeted group of executives promoting part-time ownership in a corporate jet plane.

e. As an administrator at the municipal water department, you must write a letter to water users explaining that the tap water may taste and smell bad, but poses no threats to health.

4.11 Copyright Confusion: Myths and Facts (Obj. 6)

ETHICS

Your Task. You overheard the following statements as a group of students discussed copyright issues.[14] Which of these statements do you think are true and which are false?

a. If it doesn't have a copyright notice, it's not copyrighted.

b. If I don't charge for it, it's not a violation.

c. If I make up my own stories but base them on another work, my new work belongs to me.

d. Copyright violation isn't a crime or anything, is it?

e. It doesn't hurt anybody. In fact, it's free advertising.

Grammar and Mechanics C.L.U.E. Review 4

Adjectives and Adverbs

Review Guides 19–20 about adjectives and adverbs in Appendix A: Grammar and Mechanics Guide (Competent Language Usage Essentials), beginning on page A-9. On a separate sheet, revise the following sentences to correct errors in adjectives and adverbs. For each error that you locate, write the guide number that reflects this usage. Some sentences may have two errors. If a sentence is correct, write C. When finished, compare your responses with the key beginning on page Key-1.

1. Business writers strive to use easy to understand language and familiar words.

2. Louise said she did good in her employment interview.

3. Having prepared for months, we won the contract easy.

4. Collaboration on team written documents is necessary for big projects.

5. Jenna felt badly when her team project was completed.

6. The 3-x-3 writing plan provides step by step instructions for writing messages.

7. Our recently-revised office handbook outlined all recommended document formats.

8. The project ran smooth after Maria organized the team.

9. Locally-installed online collaboration tools are easy-to-use and work well.

10. Well written safety messages include short, familiar words.

Endnotes

1 Like, whatever: Poll results find most annoying English words. (2010, December 15). *Postmedia News*. Retrieved March 3, 2011, from http://www.canada.com/life/Like+whatever+Poll+results+find+most+annoying+English+words/3995521/story

2 Bacon, M. (1988, April). Business writing: One-on-one speaks best to the masses. *Training*, p. 95. See also Effective communication: Remember to pack your writing with reader focus. (2009, March 22). *Sales Insider*. p. 4. Retrieved July 1, 2009, from Business Source Premier database; Danziger, E. (1998, February). Communicate up. *Journal of Accountancy*, p. 67.

3 Based on Fichter, D. (2005, July/August). The many forms of e-collaboration: Blogs, wikis, portals, groupware, discussion boards, and instant messaging. *Online*, pp. 48–50. Retrieved July 15, 2009, from Business Source Complete database.

4 Rindegard, J. (1999, November 22). Use clear writing to show you mean business. *InfoWorld*, 78.

5 Effect of product liability laws on small business: An introduction to international exposure through a comparison of U.S. and Canadian Law. (1998, January 7). *Journal of Small Business Management*, 72.

6 Indepth: Competition bureau. (2004, May 26). *CBC News Online*. Retrieved April 26, 2009, from http://www.cbc.ca/news/background/competitionbureau/

7 Woolever, K. R. (1990, June 2). Corporate language and the law: Avoiding liability in corporate communications. *IEE Transactions on Professional Communication*, 95–98.

8 Ibid.

9 Newark, N. A. (2005). Avoiding an "implied" employment contract or drafting a favorable one: A primer. *FindLaw*. Retrieved January 29, 2007, from http://library.findlaw.com/2005/Mar/2/157726.html. See also Jenner, L. (1994, March). Employment-at-will liability: How protected are you? *HR Focus*, 11.

10 Media Awareness Network. (2009). Canadian Copyright Act—Overview. Retrieved May 6, 2009, from http://www.media-awareness.ca/english/resources/legislation/canadian_law/federal/copyright_act/cdn_copyright_ov.cfm

11 Ibid.

12 Pickens, J. (1985, August). Communication: Terms of equality: A guide to bias-free language. *Personnel Journal*, p. 5.

13 Armour, S. (2005, June 14). Warning: Your clever little blog could get you fired. *USA Today*. Retrieved July 16, 2009, from http://www.usatoday.com/money/workplace/2005-06-14-worker-blogs-usat_x.htm

14 Templeton, B. (2004, October). 10 big myths about copyright explained. Retrieved February 24, 2007, from http://www.templetons.com/brad/copymyths.html

CHAPTER 5

Organizing and Writing Business Messages

OBJECTIVES

After studying this chapter, you should be able to

1. Apply Phase 2 of the 3-x-3 writing process, which begins with formal and informal methods for researching data and generating ideas.

2. Explain how to organize data into lists and alphanumeric or decimal outlines.

3. Compare direct and indirect patterns for organizing ideas.

4. Compose the first draft of a message, avoiding sentence fragments, run-on sentences, and comma splices, and emphasizing important ideas, avoiding misplaced modifiers, and using active and passive voice effectively.

5. Compose effective paragraphs by using three classic paragraph plans and by applying techniques for achieving paragraph coherence.

David Joel/Getty Images

Gathering Information Through Research

Business communicators face daily challenges that require data collection, idea generation, and concept organization. Before they can make decisions and convey those decisions in written messages or presentations, they must gather and organize information. These activities are part of the second phase of the 3-×-3 writing process. You will recall that the 3-×-3 writing process, as reviewed in Figure 5.1, involves three phases. This chapter focuses on the second phase of the process: researching, organizing, and composing.

No smart businessperson would begin writing a message before collecting all the needed information. We call this collection process research, a rather formal-sounding term. For simple documents, though, the procedure can be quite informal. Research is necessary before beginning to write because the information you collect helps shape the message. Discovering significant data after a message is half completed often means starting over and reorganizing. To avoid frustration and inaccurate messages, collect information that answers a primary question:

- What does the receiver need to know about this topic?

LEARNING OBJECTIVE 1

Apply Phase 2 of the 3-×-3 writing process, which begins with formal and informal methods for researching data and generating ideas.

FIGURE 5.1 The 3-×-3 Writing Process

1 Prewriting

Analyze: Decide on the purpose of your message. What do you want the receiver to do or believe? What communication channel is best?

Anticipate: Profile the audience. What does the receiver already know? Will the receiver's response be neutral, positive, or negative?

Adapt: What writing techniques and strategies can you use to adapt your message to its audience? How can you shape the message to achieve your purpose?

2 Writing

Research: Gather background data to provide facts. Search company files, previous correspondence, and the Internet. What do you need to know to write this message?

Organize: Group similar information together. Decide whether to organize your information directly or indirectly. Outline your plan and make notes.

Compose: Prepare a first draft, usually writing quickly. Remember that you will be revising it to improve its readability and impact.

3 Revising

Revise: Edit your message to be sure it is clear, conversational, concise, and readable. Look for ways to highlight important information. Consider bullets, lists, and headings to help the reader understand related points.

Proofread: Read carefully to find and correct errors in spelling, grammar, punctuation, names, numbers, and format.

Evaluate: Will this message achieve your purpose? Have you thought enough about the audience to be sure this message is appropriate and appealing?

When the message involves action, search for answers to secondary questions:

- What is the receiver to do?
- How is the receiver to do it?
- When must the receiver do it?
- What happens if the receiver doesn't do it?

Whenever your communication problem requires more information than you have in your head or at your fingertips, you must conduct research. This research may be formal or informal.

Formal Research Methods

Long reports and complex business problems generally require some use of formal research methods. Let's say you are part of the management team at a major retailer and you want to evaluate several locations for the placement of a new store. Or assume you must write a term paper for a university or college class. Both tasks require more data than you have in your head or at your fingertips. To conduct formal research, you could do the following:

- **Access electronically.** Much information is now available on the Internet, on CDs or DVDs, and in databases that can be accessed by computer. College, university, and public libraries subscribe to retrieval services that permit you to access most periodic literature. You can also find extraordinary amounts of information by searching the Web. You will learn more about using electronic sources in Chapter 11.

- **Search manually.** You will find helpful background and supplementary information through manual searching of resources in public, college, and university libraries. These traditional resources include books and newspaper, magazine, and journal articles. Other manual sources are encyclopaedias, reference books, handbooks, dictionaries, directories, and almanacs.

- **Investigate primary sources.** To develop first-hand, primary information for a project, go directly to the source. In searching for locations for retail stores, you might travel to possible sites and check them out. If you need information about how many shoppers pass by a location or visit a shopping centre, you might conduct a traffic count. To learn more about specific shoppers who might become customers, you could use questionnaires, interviews, or focus groups. Formal research includes scientific sampling methods that enable investigators to make accurate judgments and valid predictions.

- **Conduct scientific experiments.** Another source of primary data is experimentation. Instead of merely asking for the target audience's opinion, scientific researchers present choices with controlled variables. Assume, for example, that your management team wants to know at what price and under what circumstances consumers would purchase jeans from your store rather than a competitor's. Instead of jeans, let us say that management wants to study the time of year and type of weather conditions that motivate consumers to begin purchasing sweaters, jackets, and cold-weather gear. The results of such experimentation would provide valuable data for managerial decision making. Because formal research techniques are particularly necessary for reports, you will study resources and techniques more extensively in Unit 4.

Informal Research Methods

Most routine tasks—such as composing e-mails, memos, letters, informational reports, and oral presentations—require data that you can collect informally. For some projects, though, you rely more on your own ideas instead of—or in addition to—researching existing facts. Here are some techniques for collecting informal data and for generating ideas:

- **Look in the files.** If you are responding to an inquiry, you often can find the answer to that inquiry by investigating the company files or by consulting colleagues.

- **Talk with your boss.** Get information from the individual making the assignment. What does that person know about the topic? What slant should you take? What other sources would he or she suggest?

- **Interview the target audience.** Consider talking with individuals at whom the message is aimed. They can provide clarifying information that tells you what they want to know and how you should shape your remarks. Suggestions for conducting more formal interviews are presented in Chapter 11.

- **Conduct an informal survey.** Gather unscientific but helpful information via questionnaires, telephone surveys, or online surveys. In preparing a memo report predicting the success of a proposed fitness centre, for example, circulate a questionnaire asking for employee reactions.

Informal research may involve looking in the files, talking with your boss, interviewing the audience, and conducting an informal survey.

Generating Ideas by Brainstorming

One popular method for generating ideas is brainstorming. We should point out, however, that some critics argue that brainstorming groups "produce fewer and poorer quality ideas than the same number of individuals working alone." Even brainstorming proponents agree that, when done poorly, it can be a waste of time. But done properly, brainstorming is quite effective in unleashing ideas and creative energy.[2] One recent writer claims that groups can generate more and better ideas when "brainwriting"; that is, silently sharing written ideas in a structured group format.[3] Another group suggests using Twitter to exchange brainstorming ideas quickly.[4] Most business communicators, however, meet face to face to brainstorm, and they follow these suggestions to produce the best ideas:

- Define the problem and create an agenda that outlines the topics to be covered.

- Establish time limits, remembering that short sessions are best.

- Set a quota, such as a minimum of 100 ideas. The goal is quantity, not quality.

- Require every participant to contribute ideas, accept the ideas of others, or improve on ideas.

- Encourage wild, "out-of-the-box" thinking. Allow no one to criticize or evaluate ideas.

- Write ideas on flipcharts or on sheets of paper hung around the room.

- Organize and classify the ideas, retaining the best. Consider using cluster diagrams, discussed shortly.

Collecting Information and Generating Ideas on the Job

Assume that you work in the corporate offices of a major retailer and that you have been given the task of developing a postsecondary recruiting brochure for all stores. You think this is a great idea because your organization has hundreds of stores, and many postsecondary students don't know about the variety of career opportunities and benefits it offers. You know right away that you want the brochure to be colourful, exciting, concise, youthfully oriented, lightweight (because it has to be carried to college and university campuses), and easily updated. Beyond that you realize that you need ideas from others on how to develop this recruiting brochure.

To collect data for this project, you decide to use both formal and informal research methods. You study recruiting brochures from other companies. You talk with postsecondary students about information they would like to see in a brochure. You conduct

FIGURE 5.2 Creating Cluster Diagram to Generate Ideas for Recruiting Brochure

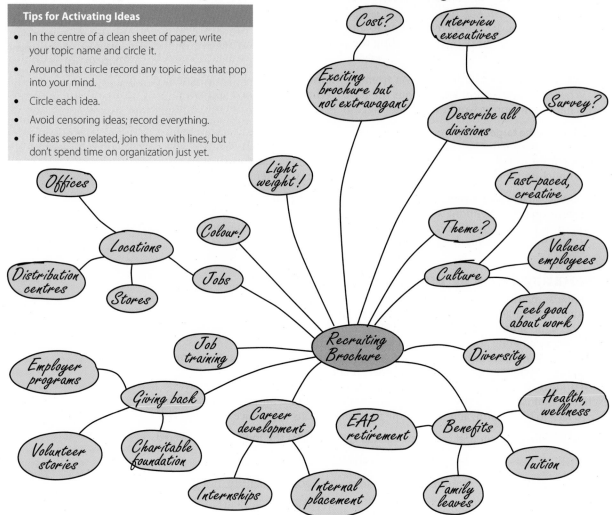

Tips for Activating Ideas

- In the centre of a clean sheet of paper, write your topic name and circle it.
- Around that circle record any topic ideas that pop into your mind.
- Circle each idea.
- Avoid censoring ideas; record everything.
- If ideas seem related, join them with lines, but don't spend time on organization just yet.

To develop ideas for a recruiting brochure, use both formal and informal research.

more formal research among recently hired employees and among division presidents and executives to learn what they think a recruiting brochure should include. Working with an outside consultant, you prepare a questionnaire to use in personal interviews with employees and executives. The interviews include some open-ended questions, such as, *How did you start with the company?* The questionnaire also asks specific questions about career paths, degree or diploma requirements, personality traits desired, and so forth.

Next, you ask five or six fellow employees and team members to help brainstorm ideas for the brochure. In a spirited session, your team comes up with the cluster diagram shown in Figure 5.2. The ideas range from the cost of the brochure to career development programs and your company's appealing location in the Vancouver area.

From the jumble of ideas in the initial cluster diagram, you see that you can organize most of the information into three main categories relating to the brochure—Development, Form, and Content. You eliminate, simplify, and consolidate some ideas and add other new ideas. Then you organize the ideas into subclusters, shown in Figure 5.3. This set of subclusters could form the basis for an outline, which we will talk about shortly. Or you could make another set of subclusters, further outlining the categories.

FIGURE 5.3 Organizing Ideas From Cluster Diagram Into Subclusters

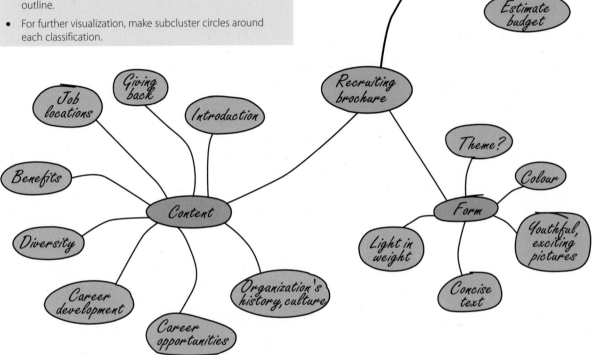

Tips for Organizing Ideas

- Analyze the ideas generated in the original cluster diagram.
- Cross out ideas that are obviously irrelevant; simplify and clarify.
- Add new ideas that seem appropriate.
- Study the ideas for similarities.
- Group similar ideas into classifications (such as Content, Development, and Form).
- If the organization seems clear at this point, prepare an outline.
- For further visualization, make subcluster circles around each classification.

Organizing Ideas

One of the most important tasks in preparing well-organized messages is grouping similar ideas together. These groups of ideas are then sequenced in a way that helps the reader understand relationships and accept the writer's views. Unorganized messages proceed freeform, jumping from one thought to another. They look like the jumbled ideas in our Figure 5.2 cluster diagram. Such messages fail to emphasize important points. Puzzled readers can't see how the pieces fit together, and they become frustrated and irritated. Many communication experts regard poor organization as the greatest failing of business writers. Two simple techniques can help you organize data: the scratch list and the outline.

Using Lists and Outlines to Organize Ideas

In developing simple messages, some writers make a quick scratch list of the topics they want to cover. Writers often jot this scratch list in the margin of the letter or memo to which they are responding (the majority of business messages are written in response to other documents). These writers then compose a message at their computers directly from the scratch list.

LEARNING OBJECTIVE 2

Explain how to organize data into lists and alphanumeric or decimal outlines.

FIGURE 5.4 Two Outlining Formats

Format for Alphanumeric Outline	Format for Decimal Outline
Title: Major Idea, Purpose	Title: Major Idea, Purpose
I. First major component	1.0. First major component
A. First subpoint	1.1. First subpoint
1. Detail, illustration, evidence	1.1.1. Detail, illustration, evidence
2. Detail, illustration, evidence	1.1.2. Detail, illustration, evidence
B. Second subpoint	1.2. Second subpoint
1.	1.2.1.
2.	1.2.2.
II. Second major component	2.0. Second major component
A. First subpoint	2.1. First subpoint
1.	2.1.1.
2.	2.1.2.
B. Second subpoint	2.2. Second subpoint
1.	2.2.1.
2.	2.2.2.
III. Third major component	3.0. Third major component
A.	3.1.
1.	3.1.1.
2.	3.1.2.
B.	3.2.
1.	3.2.1.
2.	3.2.2.
(This method is simple and familiar.)	*(This method relates every item to the overall outline.)*

Tips for Making Outlines

- Define the main topic (purpose of message) in the title.
- Divide the main topic into major components or classifications (preferably three to five). If necessary, combine small components into one larger category.
- Break the components into subpoints.
- Don't put a single item under a major component; if you have only one subpoint, integrate it with the main item above it or reorganize.
- Strive to make each component exclusive (no overlapping).
- Use details, illustrations, and evidence to support subpoints.

Two techniques for organizing data are a scratch list and an outline.

Most writers, though, need to organize their ideas—especially if the project is complex—into a hierarchy, such as an outline. The beauty of preparing an outline is that it gives you a chance to organize your thinking before you get bogged down in word choice and sentence structure. Figure 5.4 shows two outline formats: alphanumeric and decimal. The familiar alphanumeric format uses Roman numerals, letters, and numbers to show major and minor ideas. The decimal format, which takes a little getting used to, has the advantage of showing how every item at every level relates to the whole. Both outlining formats force you to focus on the topic, identify major ideas, and support those ideas with details, illustrations, or evidence.

Probably the hardest part of outlining is grouping ideas into components or categories—ideally three to five. These categories are very important because they will

FIGURE 5.5 Typical Major Components in Business Outlines

Letter or Memo
I. Opening
II. Body
III. Closing

Procedure
I. Step 1
II. Step 2
III. Step 3
IV. Step 4

Informational Report
I. Introduction
II. Facts
III. Summary

Analytical Report
I. Introduction/ problem
II. Facts/findings
III. Conclusions
IV. Recommendations (if requested)

Proposal
I. Introduction
II. Proposed solution
III. Staffing
IV. Schedule, cost
V. Authorization

become the major headings in your report. If you have more than five components, look for ways to combine smaller segments into broader topics. The following example shows how a portion of the recruiting brochure subclusters (see Figure 5.3) can be organized into an alphanumeric outline.[5]

I. Introduction	II. Careers
A. Brief history of our organization	A. Opportunities
1. Founding	1. Internships
2. Milestones	2. Management trainee programs
B. Corporate culture	3. MBA programs
1. Emphasize upbeat attitude	B. Development
2. Value diversity, employees	1. Internal promotion
3. Value social responsibility	2. Job training

Note that each major category is divided into at least two subcategories. These categories are then fleshed out with examples, details, statistics, case histories, and other data. In moving from major point to subpoint, you are progressing from large, abstract concepts to small, concrete ideas. Each subpoint could be further subdivided with more specific illustrations if you desired. You can determine the appropriate amount of detail by considering what your audience (primary and secondary) already knows about the topic and how much persuading you must do.

How you group ideas into components depends on your topic and your channel of communication. Business documents usually contain typical components arranged in traditional patterns, as shown in Figure 5.5.

Thus far, you've seen how to collect information, generate ideas, and prepare an outline. How you order the information in your outline, though, depends on what pattern or strategy you choose.

Organizing Ideas Into Patterns

Two organizational patterns provide plans of action for typical business messages: the direct pattern and the indirect pattern. The primary difference between the two patterns is where the main idea is placed. In the direct pattern, the main idea comes first, followed by details, explanation, or evidence. In the indirect pattern, the main idea follows the details, explanation, and evidence. The pattern you select is determined by how you expect the audience to react to the message, as shown in Figure 5.6.

> Grouping ideas into categories is the hardest part of outlining. Alphanumeric outlines show major and minor ideas; decimal outlines show how ideas relate to one another.

> Every major category in an outline should have at least two subcategories.

LEARNING OBJECTIVE 3
Compare direct and indirect patterns for organizing ideas.

FIGURE 5.6 Audience Response Determines Pattern of Organization

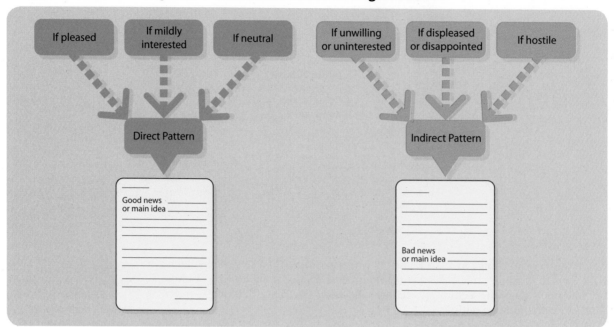

Direct Pattern for Receptive Audiences.

In preparing to write any message, you need to anticipate the audience's reaction to your ideas and frame your message accordingly. When you expect the reader to be pleased, mildly interested, or, at worst, neutral, use the direct pattern. That is, put your main point—the purpose of your message—in the first or second sentence. Dianna Booher, renowned writing consultant, points out that typical readers begin any message by saying, "So what am I supposed to do with this information?" In business writing you have to say, "Reader, here is my point!"[6] As quickly as possible, tell why you are writing. Compare the direct and indirect patterns in the following memo openings. Notice how long it takes to get to the main idea in the indirect opening.

Business messages typically follow either the (a) direct pattern, with the main idea first, or (b) the indirect pattern, with the main idea following explanation and evidence.

Indirect Opening

Our company has been concerned with attracting better-qualified prospective job candidates. For this reason, the Management Council has been gathering information about an internship program for postsecondary students. After considerable investigation, we have voted to begin a pilot program starting next fall.

Direct Opening

The Management Council has voted to begin a college or university internship pilot program next fall.

> **Frontloading saves the reader's time, establishes the proper frame of mind, and prevents frustration.**

Explanations and details should follow the direct opening. What's important is getting to the main idea quickly. This direct method, also called *frontloading*, has at least three advantages:

- **Saves the reader's time.** Many of today's businesspeople can devote only a few moments to each message. Messages that take too long to get to the point may lose their readers along the way.

- **Sets a proper frame of mind.** Learning the purpose upfront helps the reader put the subsequent details and explanations in perspective. Without a clear opening, the reader may be thinking, "Why am I being told this?"

- **Reduces frustration.** Readers forced to struggle through excessive verbiage before reaching the main idea become frustrated. They resent the writer. Poorly organized messages create a negative impression of the writer.

This frontloading technique works best with audiences that are likely to be receptive to or at least not disagree with what you have to say. Typical business messages that follow the direct pattern include routine requests and responses, orders and acknowledgments, nonsensitive memos, e-mail messages, informational reports, and informational oral presentations. All these tasks have one element in common: none has a sensitive subject that will upset the reader. It should be noted, however, that some business communicators prefer to use the direct pattern for nearly all messages.

Indirect Pattern for Unreceptive Audiences.

When you expect the audience to be uninterested, unwilling, displeased, or perhaps even hostile, the indirect pattern is more appropriate. In this pattern you don't reveal the main idea until after you have offered explanation and evidence. This approach works well with three kinds of messages: (1) bad news, (2) ideas that require persuasion, and (3) sensitive news, especially when being transmitted to superiors. The indirect pattern has these benefits:

- **Respects the feelings of the audience.** Bad news is always painful, but the trauma can be lessened when the receiver is prepared for it.

- **Facilitates a fair hearing.** Messages that may upset the reader are more likely to be read when the main idea is delayed. Beginning immediately with a piece of bad news or a persuasive request, for example, may cause the receiver to stop reading or listening.

- **Minimizes a negative reaction.** A reader's overall reaction to a negative message is generally improved if the news is delivered gently.

Typical business messages that could be developed indirectly include letters and memos that refuse requests, deny claims, and disapprove credit. Persuasive requests, sales letters, sensitive messages, and some reports and oral presentations also benefit from the indirect strategy. You will learn more about how to use the indirect pattern in Chapters 9 and 10.

In summary, business messages may be organized directly, with the main idea first, or indirectly, with the main idea delayed. Although these two patterns cover many communication problems, they should be considered neither universal nor inviolate. Every business transaction is distinct. Some messages are mixed: part good news, part bad; part goodwill, part persuasion. In other chapters you will practise applying the direct and indirect patterns in typical situations. Then you will have the skills and confidence to evaluate communication problems and vary these patterns depending on the goals you want to achieve.

Composing the First Draft

Once you've researched your topic, organized the data, and selected a pattern of organization, you're ready to begin composing. Most writers expect to use their computers for composition, but many are unaware of all the ways a computer can help create better written messages, oral presentations, and Web pages. See the Plugged In box to learn how you can take full advantage of your computer.

Even with a computer, some writers have trouble getting started, especially if they haven't completed the preparatory work. Organizing your ideas and working from an outline are very helpful in overcoming writer's block. Composition is also easier if you have a quiet environment in which to concentrate. Businesspeople with messages to compose set aside a time and allow no calls, visitors, or other interruptions. This is a good technique for students as well.

LEARNING OBJECTIVE 4

Compose the first draft of a message, avoiding sentence fragments, run-on sentences, and comma splices, and emphasizing important ideas, avoiding misplaced modifiers, and using active and passive voice effectively.

PLUGGED IN

Seven Ways Computers Can Help You Create Better Written Messages, Oral Presentations, and Web Pages

Although computers can't actually do the writing for you, they provide powerful tools that make the composition process easier and the results more professional. Here are seven ways your computer can help you improve your written documents, oral presentations, and even Web pages.

1. **Fighting writer's block.** Because word processors enable ideas to flow almost effortlessly from your brain to a screen, you can expect fewer delays resulting from writer's block. You can compose rapidly, and you can experiment with structure and phrasing, later retaining and polishing your most promising thoughts.

2. **Collecting information electronically.** As a knowledge worker in an information economy, you must find information quickly. Much of the world's information is now accessible in databases or on the Web. You will learn more about these exciting electronic resources in Unit 4.

3. **Outlining and organizing ideas.** Most word processors include some form of outliner, a feature that enables you to divide a topic into a hierarchical order with main points and subpoints. Your computer keeps track of the levels of ideas automatically so that you can easily add, cut, or rearrange points in the outline.

4. **Improving correctness and precision.** Nearly all word processing programs today provide features that catch and correct spelling and typographical errors. Grammar checkers detect many errors in capitalization, word use (such as *it's, its*), double negatives, verb use, subject–verb agreement, sentence structure, number agreement, number style, and other writing faults. But the errors are merely highlighted—not corrected. You have to do that.

5. **Adding graphics for emphasis.** Your letters, memos, and reports may be improved by the addition of graphs and artwork to clarify and illustrate data. You can import charts, diagrams, and illustrations created in database, spreadsheet, graphics, or draw-and-paint programs. Clip art is available to symbolize or illustrate ideas.

6. **Designing and producing professional-looking documents, presentations, and Web pages.** Most software now includes a large selection of scalable fonts (for different character sizes and styles), italics, boldface, symbols, and styling techniques to aid you in producing consistent formatting and professional-looking results. Presentation software enables you to incorporate showy slide effects, colour, sound, pictures, and even movies into your talks for management or customers. Web document builders also help you design and construct Web pages.

7. **Using collaborative software for team writing.** Special programs with commenting and revision features, described in Chapter 4, allow you to make changes and to identify each team member's editing.

When composing the first draft, some writers prefer to write quickly; others are more deliberate.

As you begin composing, think about what style fits you best. Some experts suggest that you write quickly (*freewriting*). Get your thoughts down now and refine them in later versions. As you take up each idea, imagine that you are talking to the reader. Don't let yourself get bogged down. If you can't think of the right word, insert a substitute or type *find perfect word later*. Freewriting works well for some writers, but others prefer to move more slowly and think through their ideas more deliberately. Whether you are a speedy or a deliberate writer, keep in mind that you are writing the first draft. You will have time later to revise and polish your sentences.

Creating Effective Sentences

In creating your first draft, you will be working at the sentence level of composition. Although you've used sentences all your life, you may be unaware of how they can be shaped and arranged to express your ideas most effectively.

Recognizing Basic Sentence Elements

Sentences must have subjects and verbs and must make sense.

To avoid writing sentence fragments and making punctuation errors, let's review some basic sentence elements. Complete sentences have subjects and verbs and make sense.

SUBJECT   VERB

The manager of Information Technology sent an e-mail to all employees.

Clauses and phrases, the key building blocks of sentences, are related groups of words. Clauses have subjects and verbs; phrases do not.

Clauses have subjects and verbs, but phrases do not.

PHRASE   PHRASE

The manager of Information Technology sent an e-mail to all employees.

PHRASE   PHRASE

By reading carefully, we learned about the latest computer viruses.

CLAUSE   CLAUSE

Because he is experienced, Adam can repair most computer problems.

CLAUSE   CLAUSE

When we have technology problems, we call a technician in our support group.

Clauses may be divided into two groups: independent and dependent. Independent clauses are grammatically complete. Dependent clauses depend for their meaning on independent clauses. In the two preceding examples, the clauses beginning with *Because* and *When* are dependent. Dependent clauses are often introduced by words such as *if, when, because,* and *as.*

Independent clauses may stand alone; dependent clauses cannot stand alone.

INDEPENDENT CLAUSE

Adam solves our technology problems.

DEPENDENT CLAUSE   INDEPENDENT CLAUSE

When employees need help, Adam solves our technology problems.

By learning to distinguish phrases, independent clauses, and dependent clauses, you will be able to punctuate sentences correctly and avoid three basic sentence faults: the fragment, the run-on sentence, and the comma splice.

Avoiding Three Common Sentence Faults

As you craft your sentences, beware of three common traps: fragments, run-on (fused) sentences, and comma-splice sentences. If any of these faults appears in a business message, the writer immediately loses credibility.

Fragments. One of the most serious errors a writer can make is punctuating a fragment as if it were a complete sentence. A fragment is usually a broken-off part of a complex sentence.

Fragment

Because most transactions require a permanent record. Good writing skills are critical.

The recruiter requested a writing sample. Even though the candidate seemed to communicate well.

Revision

Because most transactions require a permanent record, good writing skills are critical.

The recruiter requested a writing sample even though the candidate seemed to communicate well.

Fragments often can be identified by the words that introduce them—such words as *although, as, because, even, except, for example, if, instead of, since, such as, that, which,* and *when.* These words introduce dependent clauses. Make sure such clauses always connect to independent clauses.

Run-On (Fused) Sentences. A sentence with two independent clauses must be joined by a coordinating conjunction (*and, or, nor, but*) or by a semicolon (;) or separated into two sentences. Without a conjunction or a semicolon, a run-on sentence results.

Run-On Sentence	Revision
Most job seekers present a printed résumé some are also using Web sites as electronic portfolios.	Most job seekers present a printed résumé. Some are also using Web sites as electronic portfolios.
One candidate sent an e-mail résumé another sent a traditional résumé.	One candidate sent an e-mail résumé; another sent a traditional résumé.

Comma-Splice Sentences. A comma splice results when a writer joins (splices together) two independent clauses with a comma. Independent clauses may be joined with a coordinating conjunction (*and, or, nor, but*) or a conjunctive adverb (*however, consequently, therefore,* and others). Notice that clauses joined by coordinating conjunctions require only a comma. Clauses joined by a coordinating adverb require a semicolon. Here are three ways to fix a comma splice:

Comma Splice	Possible Revisions
Some employees responded by e-mail, others picked up the telephone.	Some employees responded by e-mail, and others picked up the telephone.
	Some employees responded by e-mail; however, others picked up the telephone.
	Some employees responded by e-mail; others picked up the telephone.

Preferring Short Sentences

Because your goal is to communicate clearly, you should strive for sentences that average 20 words. Some sentences will be shorter; some will be longer. The American Press Institute reports that reader comprehension drops off markedly as sentences become longer.[7] Therefore, in crafting your sentences, think about the relationship between sentence length and comprehension:

> Effective sentences are short and stress important ideas.

Sentence Length	Comprehension Rate
8 words	100 percent
15 words	90 percent
19 words	80 percent
28 words	50 percent

Instead of stringing together clauses with *and, but,* and *however,* break some of those complex sentences into separate segments. Business readers want to grasp ideas immediately. They can do that best when thoughts are separated into short sentences. Conversely, too many monotonous short sentences will sound "grammar schoolish" and may bore or even annoy the reader. Strive for a balance between longer sentences and shorter ones. Your computer probably can point out long sentences and give you an average sentence length.

Emphasizing Important Ideas

You can stress prominent ideas mechanically by underscoring, italicizing, or boldfacing. We will discuss these graphic highlighting devices shortly. You can also emphasize important ideas with five stylistic devices.

> Emphasize an important idea by using vivid words, labelling the main idea, placing the idea first or last in a sentence, or making it the sentence subject.

- **Use vivid words.** Vivid words are emphatic because the reader can picture ideas clearly.

General	Vivid
One business uses personal selling techniques.	Avon uses face-to-face selling techniques.

- **Label the main idea.** If an idea is significant, tell the reader:

Unlabelled	**Labelled**
Explore the possibility of leasing a site, but also hire a consultant.	Explore the possibility of leasing a site; but, *most important,* hire a consultant.

- **Place the important idea first or last in the sentence.** Ideas have less competition from surrounding words when they appear first or last in a sentence. Observe how the date of the meeting can be emphasized:

Unemphatic	**Emphatic**
All production and administrative personnel will meet on May 23, at which time we will announce a new plan of salary incentives.	On May 23 all personnel will meet to learn about salary incentives.

- **Place the important idea in a simple sentence or in an independent clause.** Don't dilute the effect of the idea by making it share the spotlight with other words and clauses.

Unemphatic	**Emphatic**
Although you are the first trainee that we have hired for this program, we have interviewed many candidates and expect to expand the program in the future. (Main idea lost in introductory dependent clause.)	You are the first trainee that we have hired for this program. (Simple sentence contains main idea.)

- **Make sure the important idea is the sentence subject.** You will learn more about active and passive voice shortly, but at this point just focus on making the important idea the subject.

Unemphatic	**Emphatic**
The environmental report was written by Koshi. (de-emphasizes *Koshi;* emphasizes the report.)	Koshi wrote the environmental report. (Emphasizes *Koshi.*)

Managing Active and Passive Voice

In sentences with active-voice verbs, the subject is the doer of the action. In passive-voice sentences, the subject is acted on.

> In active-voice sentences, the subject is the doer; in passive-voice sentences, the subject is acted on.

Passive-Voice Verb	**Active-Voice Verb**
The tax return *was completed* before the April 30 deadline. (The subject, *tax return,* is acted on.)	Marcelo *completed* his tax return before the April 30 deadline. (The subject, *Marcelo,* is the doer of the action.)

In the first sentence, the passive-voice verb emphasizes the tax return. In the second sentence, the active-voice verb emphasizes Marcelo. Active-voice sentences are more direct because they reveal the performer immediately. They are easier to understand and shorter. Most business writing should be in the active voice. Nevertheless, passive-voice is useful in certain instances, such as the following:

- **To emphasize an action or the recipient of the action.** *An investigation was launched.*

- **To de-emphasize negative news.** *Cash refunds cannot be made.*

- **To conceal the doer of an action.** *An error was made in our sales figures.*

How can you tell whether a verb is active or passive? Identify the subject of the sentence and decide whether the subject is doing the acting or is being acted on. For example,

FIGURE 5.7 Using Active and Passive Voice Effectively

Use active voice for directness, vigour, and clarity.

Direct and Clear in Active Voice	Indirect and Less Clear in Passive Voice
The manager completed performance reviews for all employees.	Performance reviews were completed for all employees by the manager.
Evelyn initiated a customer service blog last year.	A customer service blog was initiated last year.
IBM will accept applications after January 1.	Applications will be accepted after January 1 by IBM.

Use passive voice to be tactful or to emphasize the action rather than the doer.

Less Tactful or Effective in Active Voice	More Tactful or Effective in Passive Voice
We cannot grant you credit.	Credit cannot be granted.
The CEO made a huge error in projecting profits.	A huge error was made in projecting profits.
I launched a successful fitness program for our company last year.	A successful fitness program was launched for our company last year.
We are studying the effects of Bill C-198 on our accounting procedures.	The effects of Bill C-198 on our accounting procedures are being studied.

in the sentence *An appointment was made for January 1*, the subject is *appointment*. The subject is being acted on; therefore, the verb (*was made*) is passive. Another clue in identifying passive-voice verbs is that they generally include a *to be* helping verb, such as *is, are, was, were, be, being,* or *been*. Figure 5.7 summarizes effective uses for active and passive voice.

Avoiding Dangling and Misplaced Modifiers

Modifiers must be close to the words they describe or limit.

For clarity, modifiers must be close to the words they describe or limit. A dangling modifier describes or limits a word or words that are missing from the sentence. A misplaced modifier occurs when the word or phrase it describes is not close enough to be clear. To fix a dangling modifier, supply the missing part of the sentence. To remedy a misplaced modifier, move the modifier closer to the word(s) it describes or limits. Introductory verbal phrases are particularly dangerous; be sure to follow them immediately with the words they logically describe or modify.

Dangling Modifier

After working nine hours, the report was finally finished. (Did the report work nine hours? The introductory verbal phrase must be followed by a logical subject.)

Driving along the Cabot Trail, the ocean suddenly came into view. (Is the ocean driving along the Cabot Trail?)

Improved

After working nine hours, we finally finished the report.

As we drove along the Cabot Trail, the ocean suddenly came into view.

A modifier is misplaced when the word or phrase it describes is not close enough to be clear.

Try this trick for detecting and remedying these dangling modifiers. Ask the question *Who?* or *What?* after any introductory phrase. The words immediately following should tell the reader *who* or *what* is performing the action. Try the *who?* test on the previous danglers and on the following misplaced modifiers.

Misplaced Modifier

A wart appeared on my left hand that I want removed. (*Is the left hand to be removed?*)

The busy recruiter interviewed only candidates who had excellent computer skills in the morning. (*Were the candidates skilled only in the morning?*)

Improved

A wart that I want removed appeared on my left hand.

In the morning the busy recruiter interviewed only candidates who had excellent computer skills.

Drafting Meaningful Paragraphs

A paragraph is one or more sentences designated as a separate thought group. To avoid muddled paragraphs, writers should be able to recognize basic paragraph elements, conventional sentence patterns, and ways to organize sentences into one of three classic paragraph patterns. They must also be able to polish their paragraphs by linking sentences and using transitional expressions.

Well-constructed paragraphs discuss only one topic. They reveal the primary idea in a topic sentence that usually, but not always, appears first. Paragraphs may be composed of three kinds of sentences:

- **Topic sentence:** expresses the primary idea of the paragraph

- **Supporting sentence:** illustrates, explains, or strengthens the primary idea

- **Limiting sentence:** opposes the primary idea by suggesting a negative or contrasting thought; may precede or follow the main sentence

These sentences may be arranged in three classic paragraph plans: direct, pivoting, and indirect.

Using the Direct Paragraph Plan to Define, Classify, Illustrate, or Describe

Paragraphs arranged in the direct plan begin with the topic sentence, followed by supporting sentences. Most business messages use this paragraph plan because it clarifies the subject immediately. This plan is useful whenever you must define (a new product or procedure), classify (parts of a whole), illustrate (an idea), or describe (a process). Start with the main sentence, then strengthen and amplify that idea with supporting ideas, as shown here:

Topic Sentence	<u>A social audit is a report on the social performance of a company.</u>
Supporting Sentences	Such an audit may be conducted by the company itself or by outsiders who evaluate the company's efforts to produce safe products, engage in socially responsible activities, and protect the environment. Many companies publish the results of their social audits in their annual reports. Commitment to the environment and social responsibility have been core values for Vancouver City Savings Credit Union (Vancity) since 1993. The company conducts social audits to combine measures of financial return, social responsibility, and environmental performance.[8]

You can alter the direct plan by adding a limiting sentence if necessary. Be sure, though, that you follow with sentences that return to the main idea and support it, as shown here:

Topic Sentence	<u>Flexible work scheduling could immediately increase productivity and enhance employee satisfaction in our entire organization.</u>
Limiting Sentence	<u>Such scheduling, however, is impossible for all employees.</u>
Supporting Sentences	Managers would be required to maintain their regular hours. For many other employees, though, flexible scheduling permits extra time to manage family responsibilities. Feeling less stress, employees are able to focus their attention better at work; hence they become more relaxed and more productive.

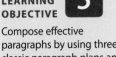

LEARNING OBJECTIVE 5

Compose effective paragraphs by using three classic paragraph plans and by applying techniques for achieving paragraph coherence.

Effective paragraphs focus on one topic, link ideas to build coherence, and use transitional devices to enhance coherence.

The direct paragraph pattern is appropriate when defining, classifying, illustrating, or describing.

Using the Pivoting Paragraph Plan to Compare and Contrast

The pivoting paragraph pattern is appropriate when comparing and contrasting.

Paragraphs arranged in the pivoting plan start with a limiting sentence that offers a contrasting or negative idea before delivering the topic sentence. Notice in the following example how two limiting sentences about drawbacks to foreign service careers open the paragraph; only then do the main and supporting sentences describing rewards in foreign service appear. The pivoting plan is especially useful for comparing and contrasting ideas. In using the pivoting plan, be sure you emphasize the turn in direction with an obvious *but* or *however*.

Limiting Sentences	Foreign service careers are certainly not for everyone. Many representatives are stationed in remote countries where harsh climates, health hazards, security risks, and other discomforts exist.
Topic Sentence	However, careers in the foreign service offer special rewards for the special people who qualify.
Supporting Sentences	Foreign service employees enjoy the pride and satisfaction of representing Canada abroad. They enjoy frequent travel, enriching cultural and social experiences in living abroad, and action-oriented work.

Using the Indirect Paragraph Plan to Explain and Persuade

The indirect paragraph pattern is appropriate when delivering bad news.

Paragraphs arranged in the indirect plan start with the supporting sentences and conclude with the topic sentence. This useful plan enables you to build a rationale, a foundation of reasons, before hitting the audience with a big idea—possibly one that is bad news. It enables you to explain your reasons and then in the final sentence draw a conclusion from them. In the following example, the vice president of a large accounting firm begins by describing the trend toward casual dress and concludes with a recommendation that his firm change its dress code. This indirect plan works well for describing causes followed by an effect.

Supporting Sentences	According to a recent poll, more than half of all white-collar workers are now dressing casually at work. Many high-tech engineers and professional specialists have given up suits and ties, favouring khakis and sweaters instead. In our own business our consultants say they stand out like "sore thumbs" because they are attired in traditional buttoned-down styles, while the businesspeople they visit are usually wearing comfortable, casual clothing.
Topic Sentence	Therefore, I recommend that we establish an optional "business casual" policy allowing consultants to dress casually, if they want, as they perform their duties both in and out of the office.

You will learn more techniques for applying direct and indirect writing strategies when you prepare letters, memos, e-mail messages, reports, and presentations in subsequent chapters.

Building Paragraph Coherence

Coherent paragraphs link ideas by sustaining the main idea, using pronouns, dovetailing sentences, and using transitional expressions.

Paragraphs are coherent when ideas cohere—that is, when one idea leads logically to the next. Well-written paragraphs take the reader through a number of steps. When the author skips from Step 1 to Step 3 and forgets Step 2, the reader is lost. You can use several techniques to keep the reader in step with your ideas.

Sustaining the Key Idea. Repeating a key expression or using a similar one helps sustain a key idea. In the following example, notice that the repetition of *guest* and *VIP* connects ideas.

*Our philosophy holds that every customer is really a **guest**. All new employees to our theme parks are trained to treat **guests** as **VIPs**. These **VIPs** are never told what they can or cannot do.*

Dovetailing Sentences. Sentences are dovetailed when an idea at the end of one connects with an idea at the beginning of the next. Dovetailing of sentences is especially helpful with dense, difficult topics. It is also helpful with ordinary paragraphs, such as the following.

> New hosts and hostesses learn about the theme park and its **facilities**. These **facilities** include telephones, food services, washrooms, and attractions, as well as the location of **offices**. Knowledge of administrative **offices** and the internal workings of the company, such as who's who in administration, ensures that staffers will be able to serve guests fully. Serving guests, of course, is our No. 1 priority.

Dovetailing sentences means connecting ending and beginning ideas.

Using Pronouns. Familiar pronouns, such as *we, they, he, she,* and *it,* help build continuity, as do demonstrative pronouns, such as *this, that, these,* and *those*. These words confirm that something under discussion is still being discussed. However, be careful with such pronouns. They often need a noun with them to make their meaning absolutely clear. In the following example, notice how confusing *this* becomes if the word *training* is omitted.

> All new park employees receive a two-week orientation. They learn that every staffer has a vital role in preparing for the show. This training includes ways to maintain enthusiasm.

Using pronouns strategically helps build coherence and continuity.

Including Transitional Expressions. Transitional expressions are another excellent device for showing connections and achieving paragraph coherence. These words, some of which are shown in Figure 5.8, act as verbal road signs to readers and listeners. Transitional expressions enable the receiver to anticipate what's coming, reduce uncertainty, and speed up comprehension. They signal that a train of thought is moving forward, being developed, possibly detouring, or ending.

As Figure 5.8 shows, transitions can add or strengthen a thought, show time or order, clarify ideas, show cause and effect, contradict thoughts, and contrast ideas. Thus, you must be careful to select the best transition for your purpose. Look back at the examples of direct, pivoting, and indirect paragraphs to see how transitional expressions and other devices build paragraph coherence. Remember that coherence in communication rarely happens spontaneously; it requires effort and skill.

Transitional expressions help readers anticipate what's coming, reduce uncertainty, and speed comprehension.

Composing Short Paragraphs for Readability. Although no rule regulates the length of paragraphs, business writers recognize that short paragraphs are more attractive and readable than longer ones. Paragraphs with eight or fewer lines look inviting. Long, solid chunks of print appear formidable. If a topic can't be covered in eight or fewer printed lines (not sentences), consider breaking it up into smaller segments.

The Checklist box summarizes the key points of composing a first draft.

Paragraphs with eight or fewer printed lines are inviting and readable.

FIGURE 5.8 **Transitional Expressions to Build Coherence**

To Add or Strengthen	To Show Time or Order	To Clarify	To Show Cause and Effect	To Contradict	To Contrast
additionally	after	for example	accordingly	actually	as opposed to
accordingly	before	for instance	as a result	but	at the same time
again	earlier	I mean	consequently	however	in contrast
also	finally	in other words	for this reason	in fact	conversely
besides	first	put another way	hence	instead	on the contrary
indeed	meanwhile	that is	so	rather	on the other hand
likewise	next	this means	therefore	still	similarly

Checklist

Composing Sentences and Paragraphs

For Effective Sentences

- **Control sentence length.** Use longer sentences occasionally but rely primarily on short and medium-length sentences.

- **Emphasize important ideas.** Place main ideas at the beginning of short sentences for emphasis.

- **Apply active- and passive-voice verbs carefully.** Use active-voice verbs (*She sent the e-mail* instead of *The e-mail was sent by her*) most frequently; they immediately identify the doer. Use passive-voice verbs to be tactful, to emphasize an action, or to conceal the performer.

- **Eliminate misplaced modifiers.** Be sure that introductory verbal phrases are followed by the words that can logically be modified. To check the placement of modifiers, ask *Who?* or *What?* after such phrases.

For Meaningful Paragraphs

- **Develop one idea.** Use topic, supporting, and limiting sentences to develop a single idea within each paragraph.

- **Use the direct plan.** Start most paragraphs with the main sentence followed by supporting sentences. This direct plan is useful in defining, classifying, illustrating, and describing.

- **Use the pivoting plan.** To compare and contrast ideas, start with a limiting sentence, then present the main sentence followed by supporting sentences.

- **Use the indirect plan.** To explain reasons or causes first, start with supporting sentences. Build to the conclusion with the main sentence at the end of the paragraph.

- **Build coherence by linking sentences.** Hold ideas together by repeating words, using pronouns, and dovetailing sentences (beginning one sentence with an idea from the end of the previous sentence).

- **Provide road signs with transitional expressions.** Use verbal signals to help the audience know where the idea is going. Such words and phrases as *moreover, accordingly, as a result*, and *thus* function as idea pointers.

- **Limit paragraph length.** Remember that paragraphs with eight or fewer printed lines look inviting. Consider breaking up longer paragraphs if necessary.

Summary of Learning Objectives

1 **Apply Phase 2 of the 3-x-3 writing process, which begins with formal and informal methods for researching data and generating ideas.** The second phase of the writing process includes researching, organizing, and writing. Researching means collecting information by using formal or informal techniques. Formal research for long reports and complex problems may involve searching electronically or manually and conducting interviews, surveys, focus groups, and experiments. Informal research for routine tasks may include looking in company files, talking with your boss, interviewing the target audience, conducting informal surveys, brainstorming for ideas, and creating cluster diagrams.

2 **Explain how to organize data into lists and alphanumeric or decimal outlines.** One method for organizing data in simple messages is to list the main topics to be discussed. Organizing more complex messages usually requires an outline. To prepare an outline, divide the main topic into three to five major components. Break the components into subpoints consisting of details, illustrations, and evidence. For an alphanumeric outline, arrange items using Roman numerals (I, II), capital letters (A, B), and numbers (1, 2). For a decimal outline, show the ordering of ideas with decimals (1, 1.1, 1.1.1).

3 **Compare direct and indirect patterns for organizing ideas.** The direct pattern places the main idea first. This pattern is useful when audiences will be pleased, mildly interested, or neutral. It saves the reader's time, sets the proper frame of mind, and prevents reader frustration. The indirect pattern places the main idea after explanations. This pattern is useful for audiences that will be unwilling, displeased, or hostile. It respects the feelings of the audience, encourages a fair hearing, and minimizes negative reactions.

4 Compose the first draft of a message, avoiding sentence fragments, run-on sentences, and comma splices, and emphasizing important ideas, avoiding misplaced modifiers, and using active and passive voice effectively. Compose the first draft of a message in a quiet environment where you won't be interrupted. Compose quickly but plan to revise. Avoid fragments (breaking off parts of sentences), comma splices (joining two clauses improperly), and run-on sentences (fusing two clauses improperly). Understand the difference between clauses and phrases so that you can write complete sentences. Remember that sentences are most effective when they are short (20 or fewer words). A main idea may be emphasized by making it the sentence subject, placing it first, and removing competing ideas. Effective sentences use active-voice verbs, although passive-voice verbs may be necessary for tact or de-emphasis. Effective sentences avoid dangling and misplaced modifiers.

5 Compose effective paragraphs by using three classic paragraph plans and by applying techniques for achieving paragraph coherence. Typical paragraphs follow one of three plans. Direct paragraphs (topic sentence followed by supporting sentences) are useful to define, classify, illustrate, and describe. Pivoting paragraphs (limiting sentence followed by topic sentence and supporting sentences) are useful to compare and contrast. Indirect paragraphs (supporting sentences followed by topic sentence) build a rationale and foundation of ideas before presenting the main idea. Paragraphs are more coherent when the writer links ideas by (a) sustaining a key thought, (b) using pronouns effectively, (c) dovetailing sentences, and (d) employing transitional expressions.

Chapter Review

1. Compare the first phase of the writing process with the second phase. (Obj. 1)

2. For routine writing tasks, what are some techniques for collecting informal data and generating ideas? (Obj. 1)

3. Name seven specific techniques for a productive group brainstorming session. (Obj. 1)

4. What is the difference between a list and an outline? (Obj. 2)

5. What are the major components in a letter or memo? (Obj. 2)

6. What are the main components of an analytical report? (Obj. 2)

7. Why do many readers prefer the direct method for organizing messages? (Obj. 3)

8. When is the indirect pattern appropriate, and what are the benefits of using it? (Obj. 3)

9. What is the primary difference between the direct and indirect patterns of organization? (Obj. 3)

10. List four techniques for emphasizing important ideas in sentences. (Obj. 4)

11. When should business writers use active-voice sentences? Passive-voice sentences? Give an original example of each. (Obj. 4)

12. What's wrong with this sentence? *After reading it carefully, the proposal doesn't interest us.* (Obj. 4)

13. What is a topic sentence, and where is it usually found (Obj. 5)

14. Describe three paragraph plans. Identify the uses for each. (Obj. 5)

15. What is coherence, and how is it achieved? (Obj. 5)

Critical Thinking

1. Why is cluster diagramming considered an intuitive process, whereas outlining is considered an analytical process? (Obj. 1)

2. Why is audience analysis so important in the selection of the direct or indirect pattern of organization for a business message? (Obj. 3)

3. How are speakers different from writers in the way they emphasize ideas? (Obj. 4)

4. Why are short sentences and short paragraphs appropriate for business communication? (Objs. 4, 5)

5. **Ethical Issue:** Discuss the ethics of the indirect pattern of organization. Is it manipulative to delay the presentation of the main idea in a message?

5.1 Sentence Elements (Obj. 4)

Your Task. Identify the following groups of words by using these abbreviations: independent clause (IC), dependent clause (DC), or phrase(s) (P). For clauses circle the subject.

a. although you want to make a good impression during your interview

b. the interviewer will size you up in about seven seconds

c. during a study conducted by neuroscientists from Vancouver

d. when they examined brain activity

e. MRI results showed significant activity in two brain areas

5.2 Sentence Faults (Obj. 4)

In the following, identify the sentence fault (fragment, run-on, comma splice). Then revise to remedy the fault.

a. Because 90 percent of all business transactions involve written messages. Good writing skills are critical.

b. The recruiter requested a writing sample. Even though the candidate seemed to communicate well orally.

c. Major pop companies considered a new pricing strategy, they tested vending machines that raise prices in hot weather.

d. Thirsty consumers may think that variable pricing is unfair they may also refuse to use the machine.

e. About half of Pizza Giant's 60 outlets make deliveries, the others concentrate on walk-in customers.

5.3 Emphasis (Obj. 4)

For each of the following sentences, circle (1) or (2). Be prepared to justify your choice.

a. Which is more emphatic?

1. Our dress code is good.

2. Our dress code reflects common sense and good taste.

b. Which de-emphasizes the refusal?

1. Although our resources are committed to other projects this year, we hope to be able to contribute to your worthy cause next year.

2. We can't contribute to your charity this year.

c. Which sentence places more emphasis on the date?

1. The deadline is November 30 for health benefit changes.

2. November 30 is the deadline for health benefit changes.

d. Which sentence gives more emphasis to leadership?

1. Jason has many admirable qualities, but most important is his leadership skill.

2. Jason has many admirable qualities, including leadership skill, good judgment, and patience.

e. Which sentence format is more emphatic?

1. We notified three departments: (1) Marketing, (2) Accounting, and (3) Distribution.

2. We notified three departments:

   a. Marketing

   b. Accounting

   c. Distribution

5.4 Active Voice (Obj. 4)

Business writing is more forceful if it uses active-voice verbs.
Passive: Antivirus software was installed by Craig on his computer.
Active: Craig installed antivirus software on his computer.
Your Task. Revise the following sentences so that verbs are in the active voice. Put the emphasis on the doer of the action.

a. Employees were given their cheques at 4 p.m. every Friday by the manager.

b. New spices and cooking techniques were tried by McDonald's to improve its hamburgers.

c. Our new company logo was designed by my boss.

d. The managers with the most productive departments were commended by the CEO.

e. All team members were asked by the leader to brainstorm for 10 minutes.

5.5 Passive Voice (Obj. 4)

Your Task. Revise the following sentences so that they are in the passive voice.

a. The auditor discovered a computational error in the company's tax figures.

b. We cannot ship your order for ten monitors until June 15.

c. Stacy did not submit the accounting statement on time.

d. Our company provides café-style restaurants for employees in corporate buildings.

e. Thieves are stealing corporate and financial information by using data-stealing malware on the Web.

5.6 Dangling and Misplaced Modifiers (Obj. 4)

Your Task. On a separate sheet, revise the following sentences to remedy dangling and misplaced modifiers. Add subjects as needed, but retain the introductory phrases. Write a C if the sentence is correct.

a. By advertising extensively, all the open jobs were filled quickly.

b. To apply for early admission, submit your application by November 1. (Tricky!)

c. After leaving the midtown meeting, Angela's car would not start.

d. The manager's rules were to be observed by all staff members, no matter how silly they seemed.

e. To complete the project on time, a new deadline was established by the team.

5.7 Paragraph Organization and Revision (Obj. 5)

Your Task. The following paragraphs are poorly organized and poorly expressed. Decide what the main idea is in each paragraph. Then revise each paragraph so that it has a topic sentence and is organized directly. Improve the sentence flow, structure, coherence, and correctness by using the techniques described in this chapter and the previous chapter.

a. You should always have your sound and video files ready for your PowerPoint presentation. When you move the presentation to a network folder or send it to someone else, the presentation has no sound. A common problem in PowerPoint involves lost sound and video files. Create a new folder for your presentation, and copy the sound and video files to that folder before you put them in your presentation. Then you will always have your sound files ready for use with your presentation.

b. Current employees may be interested in applying for new positions within the company. The Human Resources Department has a number of jobs available immediately.

The positions are at a high level. Current employees may apply immediately for open positions in production, for some in marketing, and jobs in administrative support are also available. Interested people should come to the Human Resources Department. We have a list showing the open positions, what the qualifications are, and job descriptions are shown. Many of the jobs are now open, but application must be made immediately. That's why we are sending this now. To be hired, an interview must be scheduled within the next two weeks.

Activities

Note: All Documents for Analysis may be downloaded from **www.guffeybrief4e.nelson.com** so that you do not have to rekey the entire message.

5.8 Document for Analysis: Weak E-Mail Message (Objs. 3–5)

TEAM

Your Task. The following e-mail suffers from numerous writing faults such as dangling modifiers, overuse of passive voice, and fragments. Notice that small superscript numbers identify each sentence. Individually or in a group, analyze this message. For each sentence or group of words, identify the following faults: dangling modifier (DM), passive voice (PV), and fragment (FR). Your group should agree on its analysis. Your instructor may ask you to revise the message to remedy its faults.

> To: Jeremy.Gibbons12@aol.com
> From: Andrea Kelly<akelly@bodyfitness.com>
> Subject: Improving Your Experience at Body Fitness Centre
> Cc:
> Bcc:

Dear Mr. Gibbons,
[1]Body Fitness Centre here in Windsor was probably chosen by you because it is one of the top-rated gyms in Southwestern Ontario. [2]Our principal goal has always been making your workouts enjoyable. [3]To continue to provide you with the best equipment and programs, your feedback is needed.

[4]An outstanding program with quality equipment and excellent training programs has been provided by Body Fitness. [5]However, more individual attention could be given by us to our customers if our peak usage time could be extended. [6]You have probably noticed that attendance at the gym increases from 4 p.m. to 8 p.m. [7]We wish it were possible to accommodate all our customers on their favourite equipment during those hours. [8]Although we can't stretch an hour. [9]We would like to make better use of the time between 8 p.m. and 11 p.m. [10]With more members coming later, we would have less crush from 4 p.m. to 8 p.m.

[11]To encourage you to stay later, security cameras for our parking area are being considered by my partner and me. [12]Cameras for some inside facilities may also be added. [13]This matter has been given a lot of thought. [14]Although Body Fitness has never previously had an incident that endangered a member.

[15]Please fill in the attached interactive questionnaire. [16]Which will give us instant feedback about scheduling your workouts.

[17]By completing this questionnaire, your workouts and training sessions can be better planned so that you can enjoy exactly the equipment and trainers you prefer.

Cordially,

5.9 Collaborative Brainstorming (Obj. 1)

TEAM

Brainstorming can be a productive method for generating problem-solving ideas. You can improve your brainstorming skills through practice.

Your Task. In teams of four or five, analyze a problem on your campus, such as the following: unavailable classes, unrealistic degree or diploma requirements, a lack of student intern programs, poor parking facilities, an inadequate registration process, a lack of diversity among students on campus, and so forth. Use brainstorming techniques to generate ideas that clarify the problem and explore its solutions. Each team member should prepare a cluster diagram to record the ideas generated. Either individually or as a team, organize the ideas into an outline with three to five main points and numerous subpoints. Assume that your ideas will become part of a letter to be sent to an appropriate campus official or to your campus newspaper discussing the problem and your solution. Remember, however, your role as a student. Be polite, positive, and constructive—not negative, hostile, or aggressive.

5.10 Individual Brainstorming (Objs. 1, 2)

E-MAIL

Brainstorming techniques can work for individuals and groups. Assume that your boss or department chair wants you to submit a short report analyzing a problem.

Your Task. Analyze a problem that exists where you work or go to school, such as long lines at the copy or fax machines, overuse of express mail services, understaffing during peak customer service hours, poor scheduling of employees, inappropriate cellphone use, an inferior or inflexible benefits package, outdated equipment, or one of the campus problems listed in **Activity 5.9**. Select a problem about which you have some knowledge. Prepare a cluster diagram to develop ideas. Then, organize the ideas into an outline with three to five main points and numerous subpoints. Be polite, positive, and constructive. E-mail the outline to your boss (your instructor). Include an introduction (such as, *Here is the outline you requested regarding . . .*). Include a closing that offers to share your cluster diagram if your boss would like to see it.

5.11 Brainstorming Tips for Productive Sessions (Obj. 1)

Your supervisor, Casandra Morris, has been asked to lead a brainstorming group in an effort to generate new ideas for the company's product line. Although Casandra knows a great deal about the company and its products, she doesn't know much about brainstorming. She asks you to research the topic quickly and give her a concise guide on how to brainstorm. One other thing—Casandra doesn't want to read a lot of articles. She wants you to outline tips for productive brainstorming.

Your Task. Conduct an Internet or database keyword search for brainstorming tips. Locate a number of articles with helpful tips. Prepare an outline that tells how to (a) prepare for a brainstorming session, (b) conduct the session, and (c) follow up after the meeting. Submit your outline in a memo or an e-mail to your supervisor (your instructor).

5.12 Collecting Primary Information: Research Interviewing (Obj. 1)

In your follow-up meeting with Casandra Morris from **Activity 5.11**, she asks you to complete one more task in preparation for the brainstorming session. She needs further insight in defining the problem and creating an agenda for the outline of topics to be covered in the brainstorming session. She asks you to conduct informal interviews of current shoppers.

Your Task. Choose a major retailer, such as Loblaws, The Bay, or Rona. Form five-member class groups. Two members of each group, if possible, should be familiar with the organization you've chosen. Decide who will role-play the interviewer and the two interviewees (those most familiar with organization), and who will act as recorder and group spokesperson. If your group has fewer than five members, some will have to fill more than one role. The interviewer asks both interviewees the same three questions outlined below. The recorder takes notes, and the group spokesperson summarizes the group's research results during the class discussion. Use the following interview questions:

a. During your last two visits to this retailer, were there any products you expected the two stores to carry but couldn't find?

b. Can you think of any seasonal products you would like this retailer to carry? Specifically, identify products for winter, spring, summer, and fall.

c. If you were in charge of this retailer's product lines, what three changes would you make to the existing product lines? What three totally new product lines would you want to create?

As a team or individually, prepare an outline that summarizes the information gathered from the in-class interviews.

5.13 Researching, Brainstorming, and Organizing: Student Loans (Objs. 1–3)

Sarah was all smiles when she graduated and got that degree in her hand. Soon, however, she began to worry about her student loans. A recent Statistics Canada National Graduates Survey reported that 45 percent of graduates with bachelor's degrees left school owing an average of $19,500 to government student loan programs. Additionally, students who also owed money to nongovernment sources (such as credit card issuers) reported an average debt of $32,200. The survey revealed that about one in seven owed more than $25,000, and 24 percent cited difficulty repaying their loans.[9]

Your Task. In teams, collect information about student debt. Who has it? How much debt does an average student carry? How do most students repay their loans? What strategies are proposed for helping students avoid, reduce, and repay educational loans? As a group, discuss your findings. Brainstorm for additional strategies. Then organize your findings into an outline with a title, an introduction, and recommendations for helping current students avoid, reduce, and repay their student loans. Submit your outline to your instructor.

Grammar and Mechanics C.L.U.E. Review 5

Commas

Review Guides 21–26 about commas in Appendix A: Grammar and Mechanics Guide (Competent Language Usage Essentials), beginning on page A-10. On a separate sheet, revise the following sentences to correct errors in comma usage. For each error that you locate, write the guide number and abbreviation that reflects this usage. The more you recognize the reasons, the better you will learn these punctuation guidelines. If a sentence is correct, write *C*. When finished, compare your responses with the key beginning on page Key-1.

Guide 21, CmSer (Comma series)

Guide 22, CmIntr (Comma introductory)

Guide 23, CmConj (Comma conjunction)

Guide 24, CmDate (Comma, dates, addresses, geographic names, etc.)

Guide 25, CmIn (Comma, internal sentence interrupters)

Example: When we use company e-mail we know our messages are monitored.
Revision: When we use company e-mail, we know our messages are monitored. [Guide 22, CmIntr]

1. The 3-x-3 writing process includes prewriting, writing and revising.

2. Before asking others for information see what you can find yourself.

3. Formal research methods include accessing electronically, searching manually and investigating primary sources.

4. If a project is complex consider organizing it by outlining the major points.

5. Careful writers define the main topic and they divide it into three to five components.

6. We decided that Jill Hawkins who is the best writer on the team should prepare the final draft.

7. The company's executives expected new office construction to be finished by September 1, 2013 in Whistler B.C.

8. Grammar checkers by the way often highlight passive voice as a grammar fault.

9. When you must be tactful and avoid naming the doer of an action the passive voice can be helpful.

10. The direct paragraph plan is useful when you want to define a process or when you must describe something such as a product.

Endnotes

[1] English, K. (2011, March 18). 10 facts about list week. *Toronto Star*, p. IN6. Retrieved March 20, 2011, from http://www.thestar.com/opinion/publiceditor/article/955922--english-10-facts-about-list-week

[2] Sutton, R. I. (2006, September 5). The truth about brainstorming. *BusinessWeek*, p. 17. Retrieved January 2, 2010, from InfoTrac College Edition database.

[3] Heslin, P. (2009, March). Better than brainstorming? *Journal of Occupational & Organizational Psychology, 82*(2), 129–145. Retrieved January 4, 2010, from Business Source Complete database.

[4] Harris, A., Finkelstein, D., et al. (2009, July 9). BRW Twitter homepage. *BRW Magazine*, p. 7. Retrieved January 2, 2010, from Business Source Complete database.

[5] Based on information retrieved February 7, 2007, from http://www.gapinc.com

[6] Rindegard, J. (1999, November 22). Use clear writing to show you mean business. *InfoWorld*, p. 78.

[7] Goddard, R. W. (1989, April). Communication: Use language effectively. *Personnel Journal*, 32.

[8] Vancity. (2009). Being accountable. Retrieved June 20, 2009, from https://www.vancity.com/AboutUs/WhoWeAre/CorporateReports/AccountabilityReport/0203AccountabilityReport/FrameworkAndProcess/

[9] McFeat, T. (2004, September 20). Students in debt—the high price of higher education. *CBC News Online*. Retrieved March 16, 2006, from http://www.cbc.ca/news/background/personalfinance.studentdebt.html

CHAPTER 6

Revising Business Messages

OBJECTIVES

After studying this chapter, you should be able to

1. Complete business messages by revising for conciseness, which includes eliminating flabby expressions, long lead-ins, *there is/are* and *it is/was* fillers, redundancies, and empty words.

2. Improve clarity in business messages by keeping the ideas simple, eliminating trite business phrases, dropping clichés and slang, unburying verbs, and controlling exuberance.

3. Enhance readability by understanding document design, including the use of white space, margins, typefaces, fonts, numbered and bulleted lists, and headings.

4. Recognize proofreading problem areas and apply effective techniques to proofread both routine and complex documents.

5. Evaluate a message to judge its success.

Yuri Arcurs/Shutterstock

Good grammar can have an impact not only on getting and keeping a job but also on your social life. Recruiters admit they will discard a résumé with spelling and grammar errors, and a utility company in Canada was fined $2.13 million because a comma was in the wrong place. On the social side, would you respond to a personal ad that was filled with spelling and grammatical errors?[1] What do such errors say about a person?

Applying Phase 3 of the Writing Process

The final phase of the 3-×-3 writing process focuses on revising, proofreading, and evaluating. *Revising* means improving the content and sentence structure of your message. *Proofreading* involves correcting its grammar, spelling, punctuation, format, and mechanics. *Evaluating* is the process of analyzing whether your message achieved its purpose. While at first glance it might not seem obvious that people in certain types of businesses require these kinds of skills, you must realize that even the best ideas are worth little unless they can be communicated effectively to fellow workers and to management. In the communication process, the techniques of revision can often mean the difference between the acceptance or rejection of ideas.

Although the composition process differs for individuals and situations, this final phase should occupy a significant share of the total time you spend on a message. As you learned earlier, some experts recommend devoting about half the total composition time to revising and proofreading.[2]

Rarely is the first or even second version of a message satisfactory. Only amateurs expect writing perfection on the first try. The revision stage is your chance to make sure your message says what you mean. Many professional writers compose the first draft quickly without worrying about language, precision, or correctness. Then they revise and polish extensively. Other writers, however, prefer to revise as they go—particularly for shorter business documents.

Whether you revise immediately or after a break, you'll want to examine your message critically. You should be especially concerned with ways to improve its clarity, conciseness, vigour, and readability.

LEARNING OBJECTIVE 1

Complete business messages by revising for conciseness, which includes eliminating flabby expressions, long lead-ins, *there is/are* and *it is/was* fillers, redundancies, and empty words.

Because few writers can produce a satisfactory copy on the first attempt, revision is an important step in the writing process.

Revising for Conciseness

In business, time is indeed money. Translated into writing, this means that concise messages save reading time and, thus, money. In addition, messages that are written directly and efficiently are easier to read and comprehend. In the revision process, look for shorter ways to say what you mean. Examine every sentence that you write. Could the thought be conveyed in fewer words? Your writing will be more concise if you eliminate flabby expressions, drop unnecessary introductory words, get rid of redundancies, and purge empty words.

Short messages require more effort than long, flabby ones.

Eliminating Flabby Expressions

As you revise, focus on eliminating flabby expressions. This takes conscious effort. Turning out slim sentences and lean messages means that you will strive to "trim the fat." For example, notice the flabbiness in this sentence: *Because of the fact that sales are booming, profits are good.* It could be said more concisely: *Because sales are booming, profits are good.* Many flabby expressions can be shortened to one concise word, as shown here and illustrated in Figure 6.1. Also notice in this figure that you may use different methods for revising printed documents and digital documents.

Flabby	Concise
as a general rule	generally
at a later date	later
at this point in time	now, presently
despite the fact that	although
due to the fact that, inasmuch as, in view of the fact that, because of the fact that	because
feel free to	please
for the period of	for
in addition to the above	also
in all probability	probably
in the event that	if
in the near future	soon
in very few cases	seldom
until such time as	until

Limiting Long Lead-Ins

Long lead-ins delay getting to the meat of the sentence.

Another way to create concise sentences is to delete unnecessary introductory words. Consider this sentence: *I am sending you this e-mail to announce that we have hired a new manager.* A more concise and more direct sentence deletes the long lead-in: *We have hired a new manager.* The meat of the sentence often follows the words *that* or *because*, as shown in the following:

Wordy	Concise
We are sending this announcement to let everyone know that new parking permits will be available January 1.	New parking permits will be available January 1.
I am writing this letter because Professor John Donnellan suggested that your organization was hiring trainees.	Professor John Donnellan suggested that your organization was hiring trainees.

Dropping Unnecessary *there is/are* and *it is/was* Fillers

In many sentences the expressions *there is/are* and *it is/was* function as unnecessary fillers. In addition to taking up space, these fillers delay getting to the point of the sentence. Eliminate them by recasting the sentence. Many—but not all—sentences can be revised so that fillers are unnecessary.

Wordy	Concise
There was an unused computer in the back office.	An unused computer was in the back office.
It was our auditor who discovered the theft.	Our auditor discovered the theft.

Rejecting Redundancies

Redundancies convey the same meaning more than once.

Expressions that repeat meaning or include unnecessary words are redundant. Saying *unexpected surprise* is like saying *surprise surprise* because *unexpected* carries the same meaning as *surprise*. Excessive adjectives, adverbs, and phrases often create redundancies

FIGURE 6.1 **Revising Manually and Digitally**

Revising Digital Documents by Using Strikethrough and Colour

When revising digital documents, you can use simple word processing tools, such as strikethrough and colour. In this example, strikethroughs in red identify passages to be deleted. The strikethrough function is located on the **Font** tab. We used blue to show inserted words, but you may choose any colour you prefer. If you need to add comments, use the MS Word **Comment** feature, shown in Chapter 4, the Plugged In box called Using Technology to Edit and Revise Collaborative Documents, on page 92.

~~This is a short note to let you know that, as~~ As you requested, I ~~made an investigation of~~ investigated several of our competitors' Web sites. Attached ~~hereto~~ is a summary of my findings. ~~of my investigation.~~ I was ~~really~~ most interested in ~~making a comparison of the employment of strategies for~~ comparing marketing strategies as well as ~~the use of~~ navigational graphics ~~used~~ to guide visitors through the sites. ~~In view of the fact that~~ Because we will be revising our own Web site ~~in the near future~~ soon, I was ~~extremely~~ intrigued by the organization, ~~kind of~~ marketing tactics, and navigation at ~~each and~~ every site I visited.

Revising Printed Documents by Using Proofreading Symbols

When revising printed documents, use standard symbols to manually show your revisions.

~~This is a short note to let you know that,~~ as you requested, I ~~made an~~ investigation ~~of~~ [ed] several of our competitors' Web sites. Attached ~~hereto~~ is a summary of my findings. ~~of my investigation.~~ I was ~~really~~ most interested in ~~making a comparison of the employment of~~ [comparing] strategies ~~for~~ [marketing] ~~marketing~~ as well as ~~the use of~~ navigational graphics ~~used~~ to guide visitors through the sites. ~~In view of the fact that~~ [Because] we will be revising our own Web site ~~in the near future,~~ [soon] I was ~~extremely~~ intrigued by the organization, ~~kind of~~ marketing tactics, and navigation at ~~each and~~ every site I visited.

Popular Proofreading Symbols

Delete	ℐ
Capitalize	≡
Insert	∧
Insert comma	⋀
Insert period	⊙
Start paragraph	¶

and wordiness. Redundancies do not add emphasis, as some people think. Instead, they identify a writer as inexperienced. As you revise, look for redundant expressions such as the following:

Redundant	Concise
absolutely essential	essential
adequate enough	adequate
basic fundamentals	fundamentals *or* basics
big in size	big
combined together	combined
exactly identical	identical
each and every	each *or* every
necessary prerequisite	prerequisite
new beginning	beginning
refer back	refer
repeat again	repeat
true facts	facts

Purging Empty Words

Good writers avoid saying what is obvious.

Familiar phrases roll off the tongue easily, but many contain expendable parts. Be alert to these empty words and phrases: *case, degree, the fact that, factor, instance, nature,* and *quality*. Notice how much better the following sentences sound when we remove all the empty words:

> ~~In the case of~~ Maclean's, ~~the magazine~~ improved its readability.

> Because of ~~the degree of~~ active participation by our sales reps, profits soared.

> We are aware ~~of the fact~~ that many managers need assistance.

> She chose a career in a field that was analytical ~~in nature~~. [OR: She chose a career in an analytical field.]

> Student writing in that class is excellent ~~in quality~~.

Also avoid saying the obvious. In the following examples, notice how many unnecessary words we can omit through revision:

> ~~When it arrived,~~ I cashed your cheque immediately. (Announcing the cheque's arrival is unnecessary. That fact is assumed in its cashing.)

> ~~We need printer cartridges; therefore,~~ please send me two dozen laser cartridges. (The first clause is obvious.)

Finally, look carefully at clauses beginning with *that, which,* and *who*. They can often be shortened without loss of clarity. Search for such phrases as *it appears that*. These phrases often can be reduced to a single adjective or adverb, such as *apparently*.

>   *successful*
> Changing the name of a ^ company ~~that is successful~~ is always risky.

> All employees ~~who are among those~~ completing the course will be reimbursed.

> *final*
> Our ^ proposal, ~~which was~~ slightly altered ~~in its final form,~~ won approval.

>   *weekly*
> We plan to schedule ^ meetings ~~on a weekly basis~~.

Revising for Clarity

A major revision task involves assessing the clarity of your message. A clear message is one that is immediately understood. Employees, customers, and investors increasingly want to be addressed in a clear and genuine way. Fuzzy and bombastic writing alienates these stakeholders.[3] Business writers appreciate clear messages that are immediately understandable. Techniques that improve clarity include applying the KISS formula (keep it short and simple), eliminating trite business phrases, and avoiding clichés and slang.

Keep It Short and Simple

To achieve clarity, resist the urge to show off or be fancy. Remember that your goal is not to impress a reader. Instead, the goal of business writing is to *express*, not *impress*. One way to achieve clear writing is to apply the familiar KISS formula. Use active-voice sentences that avoid indirect, pompous language.

Wordy and Unclear	Improved
Employees have not been made sufficiently aware of the potentially adverse consequences regarding the use of these perilous chemicals.	Warn your employees about these dangerous chemicals.
In regard to the matter of obtaining optimal results, it is essential that employees be given the implements that are necessary for jobs to be completed satisfactorily.	To get the best results, give employees the tools they need to do the job.

Eliminating Trite Business Phrases

To sound "businesslike," many writers repeat the same stale expressions that other writers have used over the years. Your writing will sound fresher and more vigorous if you eliminate these trite phrases or find more original ways to convey the idea.

Trite Phrase	Improved
as per your request	as you request
pursuant to your request	at your request
enclosed please find	enclosed is
every effort will be made	we'll try
in accordance with your wishes	as you wish
in receipt of	have received
please do not hesitate to	please
under separate cover	separately
with reference to	about

Dropping Clichés and Slang

Clichés are expressions that have become exhausted by overuse. Many cannot be explained, especially to those who are new to our culture. Clichés lack not only freshness but also clarity. Instead of repeating clichés, such as the following, try to find another way to say what you mean.

below the belt	last but not least
better than new	make a bundle
beyond a shadow of a doubt	pass with flying colours
easier said than done	quick as a flash
exception to the rule	shoot from the hip
fill the bill	stand your ground
first and foremost	think outside the box
good to go	true to form

Slang is composed of informal words with arbitrary and extravagantly changed meanings. Slang words quickly go out of fashion because they are no longer appealing when everyone begins to understand them. If you want to sound professional, avoid such expressions as *snarky, lousy, blowing the budget, bombed,* and *getting burned.*

Unburying Verbs

Buried verbs are those that are needlessly converted to wordy noun expressions. This happens when such verbs as *acquire, establish,* and *develop* are made into nouns, such as *acquisition, establishment,* and *development.* Such nouns often end in *-tion, -ment,* and *-ance.* Using these nouns increases sentence length, drains verb strength, slows the reader, and muddies the thought. Notice how you can make your writing cleaner and more forceful by avoiding wordy verb-to-noun conversions:

Buried Verbs	Unburied Verbs
conduct a discussion of	discuss
create a reduction in	reduce
engage in the preparation of	prepare
give consideration to	consider
make an assumption of	assume
make a discovery of	discover
perform an analysis of	analyze
reach a conclusion that	conclude
take action on	act

Controlling Exuberance

Occasionally we show our exuberance with such words as *very, definitely, quite, completely, extremely, really, actually,* and *totally.* These intensifiers can emphasize and strengthen your meaning. Overuse, however, sounds unbusinesslike. Control your enthusiasm and guard against excessive use.

Excessive Exuberance	Businesslike
We *totally* agree that we *actually* did not *really* give his proposal a *very* fair trial.	We agree that we did not give his proposal a fair trial.
The manufacturer was *extremely* upset to learn that its printers were *definitely* being counterfeited.	The manufacturer was upset to learn that its printers were being counterfeited.

Designing Documents for Readability

Well-designed documents improve your messages in two important ways. First, they enhance readability and comprehension. Second, they make readers think you are a well-organized and intelligent person. In the revision process, you have a chance to adjust formatting and make other changes so that readers grasp your main points quickly. Significant design techniques to improve readability include the appropriate use of white space, margins, typefaces, numbered and bulleted lists, and headings for visual impact.

Employing White Space

Empty space on a page is called *white space*. A page crammed full of text or graphics appears busy, cluttered, and unreadable. To increase white space, use headings, bulleted or numbered lists, and effective margins. As discussed earlier, short sentences (20 or fewer words) and short paragraphs (eight or fewer printed lines) improve readability and comprehension. As you revise, think about shortening long sentences. Consider breaking up long paragraphs into shorter chunks. Be sure, however, that each part of the divided paragraph has a topic sentence.

Understanding Margins and Text Alignment

Margins determine the white space on the left, right, top, and bottom of a block of type. They define the reading area and provide important visual relief. Business letters and memos usually have side margins of 2.5 to 3 cm.

Your word processing program probably offers four forms of margin alignment: (1) lines align only at the left, (2) lines align only at the right, (3) lines align at both left and right (*justified*), and (4) lines are centred. Nearly all text in Western cultures is aligned at the left and reads from left to right. The right margin may be *justified* or *ragged right*. The text in books, magazines, and other long works is often justified on the left and right for a formal appearance. However, justified text may require more attention to word spacing and hyphenation to avoid awkward empty spaces or "rivers" of spaces running through a document. When right margins are "ragged"—that is, without alignment or justification—they provide more white space and improve readability. Therefore, you are best served by using left-justified text and ragged-right margins without justification. Centred text is appropriate for headings but not for complete messages.

Choosing Appropriate Typefaces

Business writers today may choose from a number of typefaces on their word processors. A typeface defines the shape of text characters. As shown in Figure 6.2, a wide range of typefaces is available. Some are decorative and useful for special purposes. For most business messages, however, you should choose from *serif* or *sans serif* categories.

FIGURE 6.2 Typefaces With Different Personalities for Different Purposes

All-Purpose Sans Serif	Traditional Serif	Happy, Creative Script/Funny	Assertive, Bold Modern Display	Plain Monospaced
Arial	Century	*Brush Script*	**Britannic Bold**	Courier
Calibri	Garamond	Comic Sans	**Broadway**	Letter Gothic
Helvetica	Georgia	*Gigi*	**Elephant**	Monaco
Tahoma	Goudy	*Jokerman*	**Impact**	Prestige Elite
Univers	Palatino	Lucinda	Bauhaus 93	
Verdana	Times New Roman	Kristen	**SHOWCARD**	

Serif typefaces have small features at the ends of strokes. The most common serif typeface is Times New Roman. Other popular serif typefaces are Century, Georgia, and Palatino. Serif typefaces suggest tradition, maturity, and formality. They are frequently used for body text in business messages and longer documents. Because books, newspapers, and magazines favour serif typefaces, readers are familiar with them.

Sans serif typefaces include Arial, Calibri, Gothic, Tahoma, Helvetica, and Univers. These clean characters are widely used for headings, signs, and material that does not require continuous reading. Web designers often prefer sans serif typefaces for simple, pure pages. For longer documents, however, sans serif typefaces may seem colder and less accessible than familiar serif typefaces.

For less formal messages or special decorative effects, you might choose one of the happy fonts, such as Comic Sans, or a bold typeface, such as Impact. You can simulate handwriting with a script typeface. Despite the wonderful possibilities available on your word processor, don't get carried away with fancy typefaces. All-purpose sans serif and traditional serif typefaces are most appropriate for your business messages. Generally, use no more than two typefaces within one document.

Capitalizing on Type Fonts and Size

Font refers to a specific style (such as *italic*) within a typeface family (such as Times New Roman). Most typeface families offer various fonts, such as ALL CAPITALIZATION, SMALL CAPS, **boldface**, *italic*, and underline, as well as fancier fonts, such as outline and shadow.

Font styles are a mechanical means of adding emphasis to your words. All caps, small caps, and bold are useful for headings, subheadings, and single words or short phrases in the text. ALL CAPS, HOWEVER, SHOULD NEVER BE USED FOR LONG STRETCHES OF TEXT BECAUSE ALL THE LETTERS ARE THE SAME HEIGHT, MAKING IT DIFFICULT FOR READERS TO DIFFERENTIATE WORDS. In addition, excessive use of all caps feels like shouting and irritates readers. Boldface, italics, and underlining are effective for calling attention to important points and terms. Be cautious, however, when using fancy or an excessive number of font styles. Don't use them if they will confuse, annoy, or delay readers.

During the revision process, think about type size. Readers are generally most comfortable with 10- to 12-point type for body text. Smaller type enables you to fit more words into a space. Tiny type, however, makes text look dense and unappealing. Slightly larger type makes material more readable. Overly large type (14 points or more), looks amateurish and out of place for body text in business messages. Larger type, however, is appropriate for headings.

Numbering and Bulleting Lists for Quick Comprehension

One of the best ways to ensure rapid comprehension of ideas is through the use of numbered or bulleted lists. Lists provide high "skim value." This means that readers can browse quickly and grasp main ideas. By breaking up complex information into smaller chunks, lists improve readability, understanding, and retention. They also force the writer to organize ideas and write efficiently.

In the revision process, look for ideas that could be converted to lists and follow these techniques to make your lists look professional:

- **Numbered lists:** Use for items that represent a sequence or reflect a numbering system.

- **Bulleted lists:** Use to highlight items that don't necessarily show a chronology.

- **Capitalization:** Capitalize the first word of each line.

- **Punctuation:** Add end punctuation only if the listed items are complete sentences.

- **Parallelism:** Make all the lines consistent; for example, start each with a verb.

Font refers to a specific style within a typeface family.

Numbered and bulleted lists improve readability by making important ideas stand out.

In the following examples, notice that the list on the left presents a sequence of steps with numbers. The bulleted list does not show a sequence of ideas; therefore, bullets are appropriate. Also notice the parallelism in each example. In the numbered list, each item begins with a verb. In the bulleted list, each item follows an adjective-noun sequence. Business readers appreciate lists because they focus attention. Be careful, however, not to use so many that your messages look like grocery lists.

<table>
<tr><td>Numbered List</td><td>Bulleted List</td></tr>
<tr><td>Our recruiters follow these steps when hiring applicants:</td><td>To attract upscale customers, we feature the following:</td></tr>
<tr><td>1. Examine the application.</td><td>• Quality fashions</td></tr>
<tr><td>2. Interview the applicant.</td><td>• Personalized service</td></tr>
<tr><td>3. Check the applicant's references.</td><td>• A generous return policy</td></tr>
</table>

Adding Headings for Visual Impact

Headings are an effective tool for highlighting information and improving readability. They encourage the writer to group similar material together. Headings help the reader to separate major ideas from details. They enable a busy reader to skim familiar or less important information. They also provide a quick preview or review. Headings appear most often in reports, which you will study in greater detail in Chapters 9 and 10. However, main headings, subheadings, and category headings can also improve readability in e-mails, memos, and letters. In the following example, they are used with bullets to summarize categories:

> **Headings help writers to organize information and enable readers to absorb important ideas.**

Category Headings
Our company focuses on the following areas in the employment process:

- **Attracting applicants.** We advertise for qualified applicants, and we also encourage current employees to recommend good people.

- **Interviewing applicants.** Our specialized interviews include simulated customer encounters and scrutiny by supervisors.

- **Checking references.** We investigate every applicant thoroughly. We contact former employers and all listed references.

In Figure 6.3 the writer was able to convert a dense, unappealing e-mail message into an easier-to-read version by applying document design. Notice that the all-caps font in the first paragraph makes its meaning difficult to decipher. Justified margins and lack of white space further reduce readability. In the revised version, the writer changed the all-caps font to upper case and lowercase and also used ragged-right margins to enhance visual appeal. One of the best document design techniques in this message is the use of headings and bullets to help the reader see chunks of information in similar groups. All these improvements are made in the revision process. You can make any message more readable by applying the document design techniques presented here.

Proofreading

Once you have the message in its final form, it's time to proofread. Don't proofread earlier because you may waste time checking items that eventually are changed or omitted. Important messages—such as those you send to management or to customers or turn in to instructors for grades—deserve careful revision and proofreading. When you finish a first draft, plan for a cooling-off period. Put the document aside and return to it after a break, preferably after 24 hours or longer. Proofreading is especially difficult because most of us read what we thought we wrote. That's why it's important to look for specific problem areas.

LEARNING OBJECTIVE 4

Recognize proofreading problem areas and apply effective techniques to proofread both routine and complex documents.

FIGURE 6.3 Using Document Design to Improve E-Mail Readability

Draft

Hi, folks.

GOOD NEWS! YOU MAY NOW SCHEDULE TELECONFERENCES BECAUSE WE HAVE HIRED INTERCALL TO BE OUR WEB CONFERENCING PROVIDER! ← Reduces readability with all-caps font and justified margins

To get started, please call or write Sarah at ext. 246 to establish your personal calling code. Do this before August 1. We have also arranged a practice session, and if you would like to participate to gain practice, ask Sarah for details. ← Puts action items in wrong place

For those of you unfamiliar with running a Web conference, here are a few guidelines. Before your Web conference, establish an agenda. You can e-mail the package to all attendees, or you can upload it to a central distribution point, such as our intranet or wiki. During your conference you should greet participants as their names pop up or a chime announces their arrival. It's a good idea to be prepared with a slide presentation that everyone will see on their computer screens. However, you will also want to encourage participants to interact on the virtual whiteboard by drawing or writing comments. It is important that everyone state his or her name before speaking. Finally, I've seen a lot of conferences ruined by ringing cellphones or inattentive people who are multitasking during the meeting and not paying attention. ← Groups too much information without white space; fails to organize for quick comprehension

← Does not end with action request and details

Trent

Revision

Message Transfer Special Tools Window Help

Send

To: Managers, Supervisors E-Mail List
From: Trent Glover <trent.glover@worldwide.com>
Subject: Introducing Web Conferencing Service
Cc:
Attached:

Uses upper- and lowercase fonts and left-aligned and ragged-right margins throughout for easy reading

Hi, folks.

Good news! You may now schedule teleconference meetings because we have hired InterCall to be our Web conferencing provider. For those of you unfamiliar with running a Web conference, here are a few guidelines.

Before Your Web Conference

Improves readability with side headings and ample white space

- Establish an agenda covering all the topics to be discussed.
- Gather all the relevant files and documents in one package to be distributed to all participants.
- E-mail the package to all attendees, or upload it to a central distribution point, such as our intranet or wiki.

During Your Web Conference

- Greet participants as their names pop up or a chime announces their arrival.
- Be prepared with a slide presentation that all participants will see on their computer screens.

Groups information into chunks, and bullets items for quick "skim value"

- Encourage participants to interact on the virtual whiteboard by drawing or writing comments.
- Be sure everyone states his or her name before speaking.
- Encourage participants to turn off cellphones and PDAs and give their full attention to the meeting.

Getting Started

Puts action item at end of message and uses boldface to emphasize important date

Please call Sarah at ext. 246 or write to her at *sarah.wu@worldwide.com* to establish your personal calling code before **August 1**. If you would like to participate in a practice session, ask Sarah for details.

Trent Glover
Computer Information Systems
E-Mail: trent.glover@worldwide.com
Office: (905) 692-4430
Cell: (289) 359-3391

What to Watch for in Proofreading

Careful proofreaders check for problems in the following areas.

Proofreading before a document is completed is generally a waste of time.

- **Spelling.** Now is the time to consult the dictionary. Is *recommend* spelled with one or two *c*'s? Do you mean *affect* or *effect*? Use your computer spell checker, but don't rely on it totally.

- **Grammar.** Locate sentence subjects; do their verbs agree with them? Do pronouns agree with their antecedents? Review the grammar and mechanics principles in Appendix A if necessary. Use your computer's grammar checker, but be suspicious, as explained in the Plugged In box.

- **Punctuation.** Make sure that introductory clauses are followed by commas. In compound sentences put commas before coordinating conjunctions (*and, or, but, nor*). Double-check your use of semicolons and colons.

- **Names and numbers.** Compare all names and numbers with their sources because inaccuracies are not always visible. Especially verify the spelling of the names of individuals receiving the message. Most of us immediately dislike someone who misspells our name.

- **Format.** Be sure that your document looks balanced on the page. If you indent paragraphs, be certain that all are indented.

How to Proofread Routine Documents

Most routine documents require a light proofreading. If you read on screen, use the down arrow to reveal one line at a time. This focuses your attention at the bottom of the screen. A safer proofreading method, however, is reading from a printed copy.

Routine documents require a light proofreading.

PLUGGED IN

Using Spell Checkers and Grammar or Style Checkers Wisely

Spell-checking and grammar-checking software are two useful tools that can save you from many embarrassing errors. They can also greatly enhance your revision techniques—if you know how to use them wisely.

Spell Checking

Although some writers dismiss spell checkers as an annoyance, most of us are happy to have our typos, repeated words, and misspelled words detected. If you are using Microsoft Word 2007, you need to set relevant options. (Click the **MS Office** button, choose **Word Options,** select **Proofing,** and check **Flag repeated words, Check spelling as you type,** and **Use contextual spelling.**) When you see a wavy line under a word, you know that the highlighted word may be faulty. Right-click for a list of suggested replacements and other actions. Word 2007 can even detect the misuse of words in context. For example, it usually knows whether *they're, their,* and *there* are being used correctly and may automatically correct errors.

Spell checkers are indeed wonderful, but they are far from perfect. When you mistype a word, the spell checker may not be sure what you meant and the suggested replacements may be way off target. What's more, a spell checker cannot know when you type *form* that you meant *from.* Lesson: Don't rely totally on spell checkers to find all typos and spelling errors.

Grammar and Style Checking

Like spell checkers, today's grammar and style checkers are amazingly sophisticated. Microsoft Word marks faults in capitalization, possessives, plurals, punctuation, subject–verb agreement, and gender-specific words, as well as misused words, double negatives, fragments, wordiness, and many other problems.

How does a grammar checker work? Say you typed the sentence *The office and its equipment is for sale.* You would see a wavy line appear under *is.* If you right-click on it, a box identifies the subject–verb agreement error and suggests the verb *are* as a correction. When you click **Change,** the error is corrected. Be sure to set your grammar and style options (**MS Office** button →**Word Options** → **Proofing** → **When correcting spelling and grammar in Word** → **Settings**). However, before you decide that a grammar checker will solve all your writing problems, think again. Even Word's highly developed software misses plenty of errors, and it also mismarks some correct expressions.

Regardless of which method you use, look for typos and misspellings. Search for easily confused words, such as *to* for *too* and *then* for *than*. Read for missing words and inconsistencies. For handwritten or printed messages, use standard proofreading marks, shown on the inside front cover of this book, to indicate changes. For digital documents and collaborative projects, use the simple word processing tools shown in Figure 6.1

How to Proofread Complex Documents

Most proofreaders use standard marks to indicate revisions.

Long, complex, or important documents demand more careful proofreading. Apply the previous suggestions but also add the following techniques:

- Print a copy, preferably double-spaced, and set it aside for at least a day. You will be more alert after a breather.

- Allow adequate time to proofread carefully. A common excuse for sloppy proofreading is lack of time.

- Be prepared to find errors. Psychologically, we don't expect to find errors, and we don't want to find them. You can overcome this obstacle by anticipating errors and congratulating, not criticizing, yourself each time you find one.

- Read the message at least twice—once for word meanings and once for grammar and mechanics. For very long documents (book chapters and long articles or reports), read a third time to verify consistency in formatting.

- Reduce your reading speed. Concentrate on individual words rather than ideas.

- For documents that must be perfect, enlist a proofreading buddy. Have someone read the message aloud. Spell names and difficult words, note capitalization, and read punctuation.

- Use standard proofreading marks shown on the inside front cover to indicate changes.

Many of us struggle with proofreading our own writing because we are seeing the same information over and over. We tend to see what we expect to see as our eyes race over the words without looking at each one carefully. We tend to know what is coming next and glide over it. To change the appearance of what you are reading, you might print it on a different-coloured paper or change the font. If you are proofing on screen, enlarge the page view or change the background colour of the screen.

How to Proofread and Revise PDF Files

"Soft proofing" involves using Adobe Acrobat markup tools.

As documents are increasingly sent as PDF (portable document format) files, business writers are learning to proof without a pen. "Soft proofing" involves using Adobe Acrobat markup tools. The advantages of soft proofing include enabling collaborators in distant locales to proof each other's work electronically and saving days of time in sending hard-copy proofs back and forth. Corrections and edits can be transferred electronically among authors, editors, proofreaders, and typesetters—and then on to the printer without pen ever touching paper. The disadvantages of soft proofing include tired eyes, especially if you are working on long documents, and the fear of losing your work because of a computer crash.

Adobe Acrobat Pro and Standard provide a rich array of tools that can make markup and work flow fairly intuitive. You can insert, replace, highlight, delete, or underline material, as well as add notes, all with an insertion point that looks like that used in traditional proofreading, as shown in Figure 6.4. Adobe Acrobat enables you to add comments easily, but the markup tools require practice to use effectively. You can even make your own proofreading marks by using the **Create Custom Stamp** feature.

FIGURE 6.4 **Proofreading and Marking PDF Files**

You may proofread and edit PDF files by using Adobe Acrobat software that allows you to insert, replace, highlight, delete, and underline material as well as add notes.

Evaluating

LEARNING OBJECTIVE **5**

Evaluate a message to judge its success.

As part of applying finishing touches, take a moment to evaluate your writing. Remember that everything you write, whether for yourself for someone else, takes the place of a personal appearance. If you were meeting in person, you would be certain to dress appropriately and professionally. The same standard applies to your writing. Evaluate what you have written to be certain that it attracts the reader's attention. Is it polished and clear enough to convince the reader that you are worth listening to? How successful will this message be? Does it say what you want it to? Will it achieve your purpose? How will you know whether it succeeds?

As you learned in Chapter 1, the best way to judge the success of your communication is through feedback. For this reason you should encourage the receiver to respond to your message. This feedback will tell you how to modify future efforts to improve your communication technique.

Your instructor will also be evaluating some of your writing. Although any criticism is painful, try not to be defensive. Look on these comments as valuable advice tailored to your specific writing weaknesses—and strengths. Many businesses today spend thousands of dollars bringing in communication consultants to improve employee writing skills. You are getting the same training in this course. Take advantage of this chance—one of the few you may have—to improve your skills. The best way to improve your skills, of course, is through instruction, practice, and evaluation.

Checklist

Proofreading, Revising, and Evaluating

- **Eliminate flabby expressions.** Strive to reduce wordy phrases to single words (*as a general rule* becomes *generally*; *at this point in time* becomes *now*).

- **Avoid opening fillers and long lead-ins.** Revise sentences so that they don't start with fillers (*there is, there are, it is, it was*) and long lead-ins (*this is to inform you that*).

- **Shun redundancies.** Eliminate words that repeat meanings, such as *refer back*. Watch for repetitious adjectives, adverbs, and phrases.

- **Tighten your writing.** Check phrases that include *case, degree, the fact that, factor,* and other words and phrases that unnecessarily increase wordiness. Avoid saying the obvious.

- **Keep the message simple.** Express ideas directly. Don't show off or use fancy language.

- **Avoid trite business phrases.** Keep your writing fresh, direct, and contemporary by skipping such expressions as *enclosed please find* and *pursuant to your request*.

- **Don't use clichés or slang.** Avoid expressions that are overused and unclear (*below the belt, shoot from the hip*).

Don't use slang, which is not only unprofessional but also often unclear to a wide audience.

- **Unbury verbs.** Keep your writing vigorous by not converting verbs to nouns (*analyze* not *make an analysis of*).

- **Control exuberance.** Avoid overusing intensifiers, such as *really, very, definitely, quite, completely, extremely, actually,* and *totally*.

- **Improve readability through document design.** Use bullets, lists, headings, capital letters, underlining, boldface, italics, and blank space to spotlight ideas and organization.

- **Proofread for correctness.** Check spelling, grammar, and punctuation. Compare names and numbers with their sources. Double-check the format to be sure you have been consistent.

- **Evaluate your final product.** Will your message achieve its purpose? Could it be improved? How will you know whether it is successful?

The task of revising, proofreading, and evaluating, summarized in the Checklist box, is hard work. It demands objectivity and a willingness to cut, cut, cut. Though painful, the process is also gratifying. It's a great feeling when you realize your finished message is clear, concise, and effective.

Summary of Learning Objectives

1 Complete business messages by revising for conciseness, which includes eliminating flabby expressions, long lead-ins, *there is/are* and *it is/was* fillers, redundancies, and empty words. Concise messages make their points by using the least number of words. Revising for conciseness involves eliminating flabby expressions (*as a general rule, at a later date, at this point in time*). Concise writing also excludes opening fillers (*there is, there are*), redundancies (*basic essentials*), and empty words (*in the case of, the fact that*).

2 Improve clarity in business messages by keeping the ideas simple, eliminating trite business phrases, dropping clichés and slang, unburying verbs, and controlling exuberance. To be sure your messages are clear, apply the KISS formula: keep it short and simple. Avoid foggy, indirect, and pompous language. Do not include trite business phrases (*as per your request, enclosed please find, pursuant to your request*), clichés (*better than new, beyond a shadow of a doubt, easier said than done*), and slang (*snarky, lousy, bombed*). Also avoid burying verbs (*to conduct an investigation* rather than *to conduct, to perform an analysis* rather than *to analyze*). Noun conversion lengthens sentences, saps the force of the verb, and muddies the message. Finally, do not overuse intensifiers that show exuberance (*totally, actually, very, definitely*). These words can emphasize and strengthen meaning, but overusing them makes your messages sound unbusinesslike.

Get more practice at **www.guffeybrief4e.nelson.com**

3 Enhance readability by understanding document design, including the use of white space, margins, typefaces, fonts, numbered and bulleted lists, and headings. Well-designed messages enhance readability and comprehension. The most readable messages have ample white space, appropriate side margins, and ragged-right (not justified) margins. Serif typefaces (fonts with small features at the ends of strokes, such as Times New Roman, Century, and Palatino) are most used for body text. Sans serif typefaces (clean fonts without small features, such as Arial, Helvetica, and Tahoma) are often used for headings and signs. Numbered and bulleted lists provide high "skim value" in messages. Headings add visual impact and aid readability in business messages as well as in reports.

4 Recognize proofreading problem areas and apply effective techniques to proofread both routine and complex documents. Proofreaders must be especially alert to spelling, grammar, punctuation, names, numbers, and document format. Routine documents may be proofread immediately after completion. They may be read line by line on the computer screen or, better yet, from a printed draft copy. More complex documents, however, should be proofread after a breather. To do a good job, you must read from a printed copy, allow adequate time, reduce your reading speed, and read the document at least three times—for word meanings, for grammar and mechanics, and for formatting.

5 Evaluate a message to judge its success. Encourage feedback from the receiver so that you can determine whether your communication achieved its goal. Try to welcome any advice from your instructor on how to improve your writing skills. Both techniques help you evaluate the success of a message.

Chapter Review

1. How is proofreading different from revising? (Objs. 1, 4)
2. Why should business writers strive for conciseness? (Obj. 1)
3. What's wrong with such expressions such as *due to the fact that* and *in view of the fact that*? (Obj. 1)
4. What is a redundancy? Give an example. Why should writers avoid redundancies? (Obj. 1)
5. Why should a writer avoid this opening? *I am sending this e-mail because we have just hired a new manager, and I would like to introduce her.* (Obj. 1)
6. Why should writers avoid opening a sentence with *There is* or *There are*? (Obj. 1)
7. What is a buried verb? Give an original example. Why should they be avoided? (Obj. 2)
8. Why would a good writer avoid this sentence? *When it arrived, I read your message and am now replying.* (Obj. 2)

9. What are five document design techniques that business writers can use to enhance readability? (Obj. 3)
10. How can writers increase white space to improve readability? (Obj. 3)
11. What is the difference between serif and sans serif typefaces? What is the preferred use for each? (Obj. 3)
12. What are five specific items to check in proofreading? Be ready to discuss methods you find useful in spotting these errors. (Obj. 4)
13. In proofreading, why is it difficult to find your own errors? How can you overcome this barrier? (Obj. 4)
14. List four or more effective techniques for proofreading complex documents. (Obj. 4)
15. How can you overcome defensiveness when your writing is criticized constructively? (Obj. 5)

Critical Thinking

1. Is the revision and proofreading process different for short and long documents? Can you skip revising if your message is brief? (Objs. 1, 4)
2. Would you agree or disagree with the following statement by the Right Honourable Beverley McLachlin, P.C., Chief Justice of Canada, regarding alarmingly low literacy rates in Canada? *If we cannot understand our rights, we have no rights.*[4] (Objs. 1–5)
3. Because business writing should have high "skim value," why not write everything in bulleted lists? (Obj. 3)

4. Conciseness is valued in business. However, can messages be too short? (Obj. 1)
5. **Ethical Issue:** What advice would you give in this ethical dilemma? Becky is serving as interim editor of the company newsletter. She receives an article written by the company president describing, in abstract and pompous language, the company's goals for the coming year. Becky thinks the article will need considerable revising to make it readable. Attached to the president's article are complimentary comments by two of the company vice presidents. What action should Becky take?

Writing Improvement Exercises

6.1 Flabby Expressions (Obj. 1)

Your Task. Revise the following sentences to eliminate flabby expressions.

a. Despite the fact that we lost the contract, we must at this time move forward.

b. We cannot fill the order until such time as payment is received for previous shipments.

c. As a general rule, we would not accept the return; however, we will in all probability make an exception in this case.

6.2 Long Lead-Ins (Obj. 1)

Your Task. Revise the following to eliminate long lead-ins.

a. This message is to let you know that I received your e-mail and its attachments.

b. I am writing this letter to inform you that your home-owner's coverage expires soon.

c. This is to warn everyone that the loss of laptops endangers company security.

6.3 There is/are and It is/was Fillers (Obj. 1)

Your Task. Revise the following to avoid unnecessary *there is/are* and *it is/was* fillers.

a. There are many businesses that are implementing strict e-mail policies.

b. It is the CEO who must approve the plan.

c. The manager says that there are many employees who did not return the health surveys.

6.4 Redundancies (Obj. 1)

Your Task. Revise the following to avoid redundancies.

a. Because the proposals are exactly identical, we need not check each and every item.

b. All requests for iPods and BlackBerrys were combined together in our proposal.

c. Our supervisor requested that team members return back to the office.

6.5 Empty Word (Obj. 1)

Your Task. Revise the following to eliminate empty words and saying the obvious.

a. He scheduled the meeting for 11 a.m. in the morning.

b. Because of the surprising degree of response, the company expanded its free gift program.

c. Are you aware of the fact that our budget has a deficit in the amount of approximately $100,000?

6.6 Trite Business Phrases (Obj. 2)

Your Task. Revise the following sentences to eliminate trite business phrases.

a. Thank you in advance for considering our plea for community support.

b. Pursuant to your request, we are sending the original copies under separate cover.

c. Enclosed please find a cheque in the amount of $700.

6.7 Clichés, Slang, and Wordiness (Obj. 2)

Your Task. Revise the following sentences to avoid confusing slang, clichés, and wordiness.

a. Although our last presentation bombed, we think that beyond the shadow of a doubt our new presentation will fly.

b. Our team must be willing to think outside the box in coming up with marketing ideas that pop.

c. True to form, our competitor has made a snarky claim that we think is way below the belt.

6.8 Buried Verbs (Obj. 2)

Your Task. Revise the following to unbury the verbs.

a. Ms. Nelson gave an appraisal of the home's value.

b. Web-based customer service causes a reduction in overall costs.

c. The board of directors will give consideration to the contract at its next meeting.

6.9 Lists, Bullets, and Headings (Obj. 3)

a. Use the information in the following dense paragraph to compose a concise, easy-to-read bulleted vertical list with an introductory statement.

Here at SecurityPlus we specialize in preemployment background reports, which we describe in the following. Among our preemployment background reports are ones that include professional reference interviews, criminal reports, driving records, employment verification, and credit information.

b. Create an introduction and a list from the following wordy paragraph.

A high-powered MBA program costs hundreds of dollars an hour. Our program covers the same information. That information includes how to start a business. You will also learn information about writing a business plan and understanding taxes. In addition, our MBA program covers how to go about writing a marketing feasibility study. Another topic that students cover in our program is employment benefits plans and licensing requirements.

c. From the following wordy paragraph, create a concise bulleted list with category headings.

This is to inform you that our on-site GuruGeek computer technicians can provide you with fast, affordable solutions to residential and also to small business clients. Our most popular offerings include antivirus security. This service involves having our GuruGeek protect your computer against viruses, worms, and spyware and help you avoid e-mail attacks, identity theft, and malicious hacker programs. Our wireless networking service enables you to share Internet access through a single wireless router so that many computer users use one network at the same time. They are all using the same network. Another popular service is data backup and recovery. Our technicians focus on helping small businesses and home users protect their data without making an investment of a lot of time and energy.

Activities

Note: All Documents for Analysis may be downloaded from **www.guffeybrief4e.nelson.com** so that you do not have to rekey the entire message.

6.10 Document for Analysis: Poorly Written E-Mail Message (Objs. 1–5)

Your Task. Study the following message. In teams or in class discussion, list five specific weaknesses. If your instructor directs, revise to remedy flabby expressions, long lead-ins, there is/are fillers, trite business expressions, clichés, slang, buried verbs, lack of parallelism, and general wordiness. Look for ways to improve readability with bulleted or numbered points.

To:	Marcy Love<marcy.love@sokia.com>
From:	Shelton Matthews<shelton.matthews@sokia.com>
Subject:	Improving Presentation Techniques
Cc:	

Marcy,

I am writing this message because, pursuant to your request, I attended a seminar about the use of PowerPoint in business presentations. You suggested that there might be tips that I would learn that we could share with other staff members, many of whom make presentations that almost always include PowerPoint. The speaker, Gary Dixon, made some very good points on the subject of PowerPoint. There were several points of an important nature that are useful in avoiding what he called a "PowerPoint slumber party." Our staff members should give consideration to the following:

Create first the message, not the slide. Only after preparing the entire script should you think about how to make an illustration of it.

You should prepare slides with short lines. Your slides should have only four to six words per line. Short lines act as an encouragement to people to listen to you and not read the slide.

Don't put each and every thing on the slide. If you put too much on the slide, your audience will be reading Item C while you are still talking about Item A. As a last and final point, she suggested that presenters think in terms of headlines. What is the main point? What does it mean to the audience?

Please let me know whether you want me to elaborate and expand on these presentation techniques subsequent to the next staff meeting.

Shelton

6.11 Document for Analysis: Poorly Written Response Letter (Objs. 1–5)

Your Task. Study the following message. In teams or in class discussion, list five specific weaknesses. If your instructor directs, revise to remedy flabby expressions, long lead-ins, there is/are fillers, trite business expressions, clichés, slang, buried verbs, lack of parallelism, and general wordiness. Look for ways to improve readability with bulleted or numbered points.

Current date

Mr. Anthony Burciaga
Lakeview Systems, Inc.
4122 Lakeview Drive
Ajax, ON L1S 7L8

Dear Mr. Burciaga

We have received your request for information. As per your request, the undersigned is transmitting to you the attached documents with regard to the improvement of security in your business. To ensure the improvement of your after-hours security, you should initially make a decision with regard to exactly what you contemplate must have protection. You are, in all probability, apprehensive not only about your electronic equipment and paraphernalia but also about your company records, information, and data.

Because of the fact that we feel you will want to obtain protection for both your equipment and data, we will make suggestions for taking a number of judicious steps to inhibit crime. First and foremost, we make a recommendation that you install defensive lighting. A consultant for lighting, currently on our staff, can design both outside and inside lighting, which brings me to my second point. Exhibit security signs, because of the fact that nonprofessional thieves are often as not deterred by posted signs on windows and doors.

As my last and final recommendation, you should install space alarms, which are sensors that look down over the areas that are to receive protection, and activate bells or additional lights, thus scaring off intruders.

After reading the materials that are attached, please call me to initiate a verbal discussion regarding protection of your business.

Sincerely,

Grammar and Mechanics C.L.U.E. Review 6

Semicolons, Colons

Review Guides 27–30 about semicolons and colons in Appendix A, Grammar and Mechanics Guide, beginning on page A-13. On a separate sheet, revise the following sentences to correct errors in semicolon and colon usage. Do not start new sentences. For each error that you locate, write the guide number that reflects this usage. The more you recognize the reasons, the better you will learn these punctuation guidelines. If a sentence is correct, write *C*. When finished, compare your responses with the key beginning on page Key-1.

Example: Companies find it difficult to name new products consequently they often hire specialists.
Revision: Companies find it difficult to name new products; consequently they often hire specialists. [Guide 27]

1. Successful product names may appear to have been named by magic, however the naming process is methodical and deliberate.

2. Choosing the right name and tagline is critical consequently companies are eager to hire specialists.

3. Naming is a costly endeavour, fees may range up to $70,000 for a global name.

4. Expanding markets are in Paris France Beijing China and Dubai City United Arab Emirates.

5. As she was about to name a fashion product, Rachel Hermes said "If I am launching a new fashion label, the task becomes very difficult. I have to find a name that communicates the creative style that the brand is to embody."

6. For a new unisex perfume, Hermes considered the following names Declaration, Serenity, and Earth.

7. Naming is not a problem for small companies however it is a big problem for global brands.

8. Hermes started with a thorough competitive analysis it included quantifying the tone and strength of competing names.

9. Attending the naming sessions were James Harper, marketing director, Reva Cruz, product manager, and Cheryl Chang, vice president.

10. Distribution of goods has become global therefore names have to be registered in many countries.

Endnotes

[1] M. Forgarty (Grammar Girl). (2009, June 9). Does grammar really matter? Retrieved April 11, 2011, from http://grammar.quickanddirtytips.com/does-grammar-matter.aspx

[2] Elbow, P. (1998). *Writing with power: Techniques for mastering the writing process.* Oxford: Oxford University Press, p. 30.

[3] van Roon, I. (2006, May 23). Quoted in Sorry, no more excuses for bad business writing. *PR Newswire.* Retrieved January 4, 2010, from InfoTrac College Edition database.

[4] McLachlin, B. (2002, February 2). Preserving public confidence in the courts and the legal profession. Distinguished visitor's lecture, University of Manitoba, Winnipeg, MB. Quoted in Council of Canadian Administrative Tribunals. (2005.) *Literacy and access to administrative justice in Canada: a guide for the promotion of plain language.* Ottawa: Author. Retrieved August 31, 2011, from http://www.ccat-ctac.org/en/pdfs/literacy/Literacyandjustice.pdf

Fuse/Getty Images

CHAPTER 7

Electronic Messages and Digital Media

OBJECTIVES

After studying this chapter, you should be able to

1. Describe the role digital media play in the changing world of business in contrast to traditional paper-based messages.

2. Meet professional e-mail standards for usage, structure, and format, and follow the rules of 'netiquette' and other best practices.

3. Explain how business professionals communicate by instant messaging and texting.

4. Identify professional uses of podcasts, blogs, and wikis, and describe prudent policies to protect authors of electronic content.

5. Understand business uses of social and professional networking sites, as well as RSS feeds and social bookmarking.

Comstock/Getty

How Organizations Exchange Messages and Information

LEARNING OBJECTIVE 1

Describe the role digital media play in the changing world of business in contrast to traditional paper-based messages.

Although today's workplaces are still far from paperless, increasingly information is exchanged electronically and on the go. Social media sites, such as Twitter, have highlighted the appetite of many people today for instant status updates and the immediate sharing of information. The Web itself has evolved from a mere repository of passively consumed information to Web 2.0—a dynamic, interactive environment. Users are empowered, active participants who create content, review products, and edit and share information.

Ever more data are stored on and accessed from remote networks, not individual computers. This storing and accessing of data and software applications in remote network closters, or "clouds," is called *cloud computing* (see the Plugged In box for more information on cloud computing). Mobile communication and cloud computing are the two prevailing technological trends today. In many businesses, desktop computers are fast becoming obsolete with the advent of ever smaller laptops, netbooks, smartphones, personal digital assistants (PDAs), and other compact mobile devices. Furthermore, virtual private networks (VPN) offer secure access to company information from any location in the world that provides an Internet connection.

Today's workforce must stay connected at all times. Knowledge and information workers are expected to remain tethered to their jobs wherever they are, even on the weekends or on vacation. The technological revolution of the last 25 years has resulted in amazing productivity gains. However, technological advances have also made 50-hour workweeks without overtime pay a reality for those "i-workers" lucky enough to snag or keep a promising position in a tough economy.

Electronic communication is the lifeblood of a functioning organization today, especially with more employees than ever before telecommuting. Fewer layers of management after downsizing and the flattening of corporate hierarchies have meant that more rank-and-file staff members are now empowered to make decisions and tend to work in cross-functional teams. These significant changes would not be possible without a speedy yet accurate exchange of information. In this fast-paced workplace, you will be expected to collect, evaluate, and exchange information in clearly written messages, whether electronic or paper based.

You may already be sharing digitally with your friends and family, but chances are that you need to understand how businesses transmit information electronically and how they use new technology. This chapter explores professional electronic communication, specifically e-mail, corporate blogs, instant messaging, and text messaging. You will also learn about business uses of podcasts, wikis, and social networking sites. You will read about best practices in composing e-mails and interacting through other electronic media. Knowing how to prepare an effective message and understanding business technology can save you time, reduce stress, and build your image as a professional.

Communicating With Paper-Based Messages

Although the business world is quickly switching to electronic communication channels, paper-based documents still have definite functions.

PLUGGED IN

Cloud Computing

For businesses, cloud computing might as well mean "cloud nine." Companies are increasingly relying on cloud-based computer systems that can be accessed by mobile phones and PCs anytime and anywhere. Google is spearheading efforts to enable future consumers to use inexpensive gadgets to manage their files and media in huge data centres on the Internet. If you use Flickr, Gmail, or Facebook, to name a few, you are already participating in cloud computing. Your photos and other data are stored in a remote location, and you can access them by using your PC, laptop, netbook, smartphone, or PDA.

The Lure and Lucre of the Cloud. Companies are lured to cloud computing by the promise of greater efficiency and higher profit. In Canada, IBM recently invested $42 million in the IBM Compute Cloud Centre, created to help Canadian organizations reduce costs, increase efficiencies, and access new technologies, such as analytics and mobile computing, while keeping data secure and resident within Canadian borders in accordance with Canadian privacy law.[2] "This is an innovation investment in Canada that will help Canadian businesses capture the promise of new computing models to drive productivity and increase competitiveness," said Bruce Ross, president, IBM Canada. The IBM Compute Cloud Centre will help Canadian companies grow their social and business applications.[3]

Vast Opportunities and Risks. The shift from storing information on isolated machines to information sharing in digital and social networks is seen by some as the largest growth opportunity since the Internet boom. The market for cloud products and services will likely soar. However, skeptics warn that caution about the risks of convenience is in order. For one thing, once the information leaves our computing device for the cloud, we don't know who may intercept it. In addition to data security, networks must be reliable so that users can access them anytime.

> **Paper-based documents remain the best channel when a permanent record is necessary.**

Business Letters. Writers prepare business letters on letterhead stationery. This is the best channel when a permanent record is necessary, when confidentiality is important, when sensitivity and formality are essential, and when you need to make a persuasive, well-considered presentation.

Interoffice Memos. Paper-based interoffice memos were once the chief form of internal communication. Today, employees use memos primarily to convey confidential information, emphasize ideas, introduce lengthy documents, or lend importance to a message. Memos are especially appropriate for explaining organizational procedures or policies that become permanent guidelines. In Chapter 8 you will learn more about positive letters, memos, and e-mail messages that follow the direct pattern of organization.

Communicating With Electronic Messages

A number of electronic communication channels enable businesspeople to exchange information rapidly and efficiently. All these new electronic channels showcase your writing skills.

> **Electronic messages enable communicators to exchange information rapidly and efficiently.**

Electronic Mail. In most businesses today, e-mail is the communication channel of choice. It has been hailed as one of the greatest productivity tools of our time.[4] Users can send messages to single addressees or broadcast them to multiple recipients. When a message arrives in the inbox, the recipient may read, print, forward, store, or delete it. E-mail is most appropriate for short messages. It is inappropriate for sensitive, confidential, or lengthy documents. Increasingly, e-mail is written on laptops, netbooks, and smart devices, such as the BlackBerry, Palm, and iPhone. The smaller screen poses its own challenges, yet even short mobile messages need to be correct and professional. You will learn more about safe e-mail practices later in the chapter.

Instant Messaging. More interactive and immediate than e-mail, instant messaging (IM) involves the exchange of text messages in real time between two or more people logged into an IM service. IM creates a form of private chat room so that individuals can carry on conversations similar to telephone calls. IM is especially useful for back-and-forth online conversations, such as a customer communicating with a tech support person to solve a problem. Like e-mail, instant messaging creates a permanent text record and must be used carefully.

Text Messaging. Sending really short messages (160 or fewer characters) from mobile phones and other wireless devices is called *text messaging* or *texting*. This method uses short message service (SMS) and is available on most mobile phones and PDAs. SMS gateways connect mobile phones with instant message services, the Web, desktop computers, and even landline telephones. Busy communicators use text messaging for short person-to-person inquiries and responses that keep them in touch while away from the office.

Podcasts. A *podcast* is a digital media file that is distributed over the Internet and downloaded on portable media players and personal computers. Podcasts, also called *netcasts* or *webcasts*, are distinguished by their ability to be syndicated, subscribed to, or downloaded automatically when new content is added. In business, podcasts are useful for improving customer relations, marketing, training, product launches, and viral marketing (creating online buzz about new products).

Blogs. A *blog* is a Web site with journal entries (posts) usually written by one person with comments added by others. It may combine text, images, and links to other blogs or Web pages. Businesses use blogs to keep customers and employees informed and to receive feedback. Company news can be posted, updated, and categorized for easy cross-referencing. Blogs may be a useful tool for marketing and promotion and for showing a company's personal side. Twitter is often referred to as a microblogging site, but it also functions as a social networking site.

Wikis. A *wiki* is a public or private Web site that enables multiple users to collaboratively create, post, edit, and access information. A wiki serves as a central location where shared documents can be viewed and revised by a large or dispersed team. Unlike a standard Web site, a wiki is linked to a database that records all changes, thus allowing the viewing of previous versions. The best-known wiki is the online encyclopaedia Wikipedia.[5] Because a wiki can be used to manage and organize meeting notes, team agendas, and company calendars, it is a valuable project management tool.

Social Networking. Over the past few years, social networking has become one of the most popular uses of the Internet. Also called *social online communities,* social networking sites, such as Facebook, LinkedIn, and Google+, allow participants with various interests to connect and collaborate. Businesses have recognized e-commerce opportunities and use social media to reach out to customers and the public. Most of the sites are now targeting professionals, who are welcome to establish business contacts, network, post their career credentials, apply for jobs, and seek advice.

Preparing and Composing Professional E-Mail Messages

E-mail has replaced paper memos for many messages inside organizations and for some letters to external audiences. However, as Chapter 8 explains, paper-based documents still have their proper functions. Because they are committed to paper, hard-copy messages tend to carry more weight and are taken more seriously in certain situations. They are considered more formal than electronic communication. Moreover, even if e-mail writers have access to sophisticated HTML mail, the recipient may receive only plain text messages. Poor layout and little visual appeal may result when elaborate formatting disappears on the receiver's end. The e-mail message may also be difficult to print. This is why business communicators often deliver electronic copies of memos or letters as

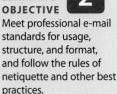

LEARNING OBJECTIVE 2
Meet professional e-mail standards for usage, structure, and format, and follow the rules of netiquette and other best practices.

attachments accompanied by a brief e-mail cover message. PDF documents in particular guarantee that the reader receives a message that looks exactly as the writer intended it.

Early e-mail users were encouraged to ignore stylistic and grammatical considerations. They thought that "words on the fly" required little editing or proofing. Correspondents used emoticons (such as sideways happy faces) to express their emotions. Some e-mail today is still very informal, but as this communication channel continues to mature, messages are becoming more proper and more professional.

Today it is estimated that more than 210 billion e-mails are sent each day worldwide.[6] E-mail is twice as likely as the telephone to be used to communicate at work.[7] E-mail growth has slowed recently, and rival services are booming. Twitter and Facebook, for example, offer faster, always-on connectedness. However, e-mail in the workplace is here to stay.

Because e-mail is a standard form of communication within organizations, it will likely be your most common business communication channel. E-mails perform critical tasks, such as informing employees, giving directions, outlining procedures, requesting data, supplying responses, and confirming decisions.

Analyzing the Components of E-Mail Messages

Much like hard-copy memos, routine e-mails generally contain four parts: (1) an informative subject line that summarizes the message; (2) an opening that reveals the main idea immediately; (3) a body that explains and justifies the main idea; and (4) a closing that presents action information, summarizes the message, or offers a closing thought. Remember that routine messages deliver good news or standard information.

Subject Line.
In e-mail messages an informative subject line is essential. It summarizes the central idea, thus providing quick identification for reading and filing. Busy readers glance at a subject line and decide when and whether to read the message. Those without subject lines are often automatically deleted.

What does it take to get your message read? For one thing, stay away from meaningless or dangerous words. A sure way to get your message deleted or ignored is to use a one-word heading, such as *Issue, Problem, Important,* or *Help.* Including the word *Free* is dangerous because it may trigger spam filters. Try to make your subject line "talk" by including a verb. Explain the purpose of the message and how it relates to the reader (*Need You to Showcase Two Items at Our Next Trade Show* rather than *Trade Show*). Finally, update your subject line to reflect the current message (*Staff Meeting Rescheduled for May 12* rather than *Re: Re: Staff Meeting*). Remember that a subject line is usually written in an abbreviated style, often without articles (*a, an, the*). It need not be a complete sentence, and it does not end with a period.

Opening.
Most e-mails cover nonsensitive information that can be handled in a straightforward manner. Begin by frontloading; that is, reveal the main idea immediately. Even though the purpose of the e-mail is summarized in the subject line, that purpose should be restated—and amplified—in the first sentence. As you learned in Chapters 5 and 6, busy readers want to know immediately why they are reading a message. Notice how the following indirect opener can be improved by frontloading.

Indirect Opening	Direct Opening
For the past six months, the Human Resources Development Department has been considering changes to our employees' benefits plan.	Please review the following proposal regarding employees' benefits and let me know by May 20 if you approve these changes.

Body.
The body provides more information about the reason for writing. It explains and discusses the subject logically. Good e-mails generally discuss only one topic. Limiting the topic helps the receiver act on the subject and file it appropriately. A writer

who describes a computer printer problem and also requests permission to attend a conference runs a 50 percent failure risk. The reader may respond to the printer problem but delay responding to or forget about the conference request.

Design your data for easy comprehension by using numbered lists, headings, tables, and other document design techniques introduced in Chapter 6. Compare the following versions of the same message. Notice how the graphic devices of bullets, columns, headings, and white space make the main points easier to comprehend.

Hard-to-Read Paragraph Version

Effective immediately are the following air travel guidelines. Between now and December 31, only account executives may take company-approved trips. These individuals will be allowed to take a maximum of two trips, and they are to travel economy or budget class only.

Improved Version

Effective immediately are the following air travel guidelines:

- Who may travel: Account executives only
- How many trips: A maximum of two trips
- By when: Between now and December 31
- Air class: Economy or budget class only

Closing. Generally conclude an e-mail with (a) action information, dates, or deadlines; (b) a summary of the message; or (c) a closing thought. Here again the value of thinking through the message before actually writing it becomes apparent. The closing is where readers look for deadlines and action language. An effective e-mail closing might be, *Please submit your report by June 15 so that we can have your data before our July planning session.*

In more detailed messages, a summary of main points may be an appropriate closing. If no action request is made and a closing summary is unnecessary, you might end with a simple concluding thought (*I'm glad to answer your questions* or *This sounds like a useful project*). You needn't close messages to co-workers with goodwill statements, such as those found in letters to customers or clients. However, some closing thought is often necessary to prevent a feeling of abruptness. Closings can show gratitude or encourage feedback with such remarks as *I sincerely appreciate your help* or *What are your ideas on this proposal?* Other closings look forward to what's next, such as, *How would you like to proceed?* Avoid closing with overused expressions, such as *Please let me know if I may be of further assistance.* This ending sounds mechanical and insincere.

> Three features typically appearing in the closing of a message are (1) action information, dates, or deadlines; (2) a summary of the message; or (3) a closing thought.

Applying E-Mail Formats

Although e-mail is still a fairly new communication channel, people are beginning to agree on specific formatting and usage conventions. The following suggestions identify current formatting standards. Always check with your organization, however, to observe its practices.

> E-mails generally contain these components: guide words, greeting, body, and complimentary closing and signature block.

Guide Words. Following the guide word *To*, some writers insert just the recipient's electronic address, such as *william.harding@schilling-vogt.com*. Other writers prefer to include the receiver's full name plus the electronic address, as shown in Figure 7.1. By including full names in the *To* and *From* slots, both receivers and senders are better able to identify the message. The order of *Date, To, From, Subject*, and other guide words varies depending on your e-mail program and whether you are sending or receiving the message.

FIGURE 7.1 Formatting an E-Mail Message

1 Prewriting

Analyze: The purpose of this e-mail is to solicit feedback regarding a casual-dress policy.

Anticipate: The message is going to a subordinate who is busy but probably eager to be consulted in this policy matter.

Adapt: Use a direct approach beginning with the most important question. Strive for a positive, professional tone rather than an autocratic, authoritative tone.

2 Writing

Research: Collect secondary information about dress-down days in other organizations. Collect primary information by talking with company managers.

Organize: Begin with the main idea followed by a brief explanation and questions. Conclude with an end date and a reason.

Compose: Prepare the first draft, remembering that the receiver is busy and appreciates brevity.

3 Revising

Revise: Rewrite questions to ensure that they are parallel and readable.

Proofread: Decide whether to hyphenate *casual-dress policy* and *dress-down days*. Be sure commas follow introductory clauses. Check question marks.

Evaluate: Does this memo encourage participatory management? Will the receiver be able to answer the questions and respond easily?

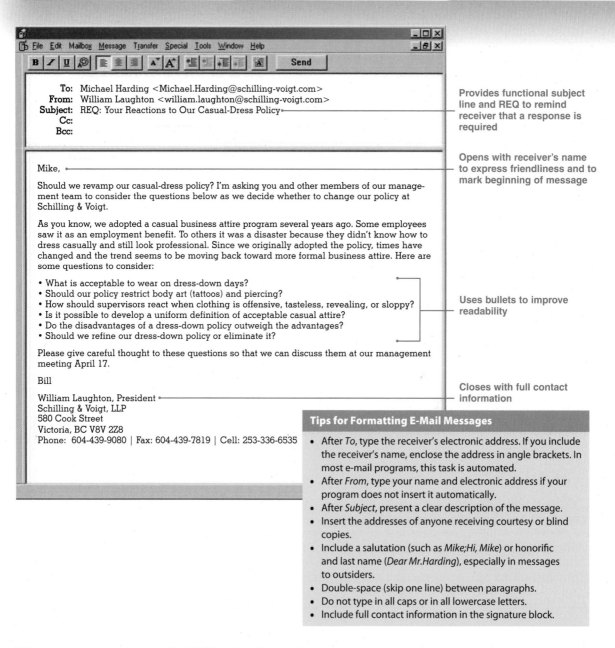

File   Edit   Mailbox   Message   Transfer   Special   Tools   Window   Help

To: Michael Harding <Michael.Harding@schilling-voigt.com>
From: William Laughton <william.laughton@schilling-voigt.com>
Subject: REQ: Your Reactions to Our Casual-Dress Policy
Cc:
Bcc:

Provides functional subject line and REQ to remind receiver that a response is required

Mike,

Opens with receiver's name to express friendliness and to mark beginning of message

Should we revamp our casual-dress policy? I'm asking you and other members of our management team to consider the questions below as we decide whether to change our policy at Schilling & Voigt.

As you know, we adopted a casual business attire program several years ago. Some employees saw it as an employment benefit. To others it was a disaster because they didn't know how to dress casually and still look professional. Since we originally adopted the policy, times have changed and the trend seems to be moving back toward more formal business attire. Here are some questions to consider:

- What is acceptable to wear on dress-down days?
- Should our policy restrict body art (tattoos) and piercing?
- How should supervisors react when clothing is offensive, tasteless, revealing, or sloppy?
- Is it possible to develop a uniform definition of acceptable casual attire?
- Do the disadvantages of a dress-down policy outweigh the advantages?
- Should we refine our dress-down policy or eliminate it?

Uses bullets to improve readability

Please give careful thought to these questions so that we can discuss them at our management meeting April 17.

Bill

William Laughton, President
Schilling & Voigt, LLP
580 Cook Street
Victoria, BC V8V 2Z8
Phone: 604-439-9080 | Fax: 604-439-7819 | Cell: 253-336-6535

Closes with full contact information

Tips for Formatting E-Mail Messages

- After *To*, type the receiver's electronic address. If you include the receiver's name, enclose the address in angle brackets. In most e-mail programs, this task is automated.
- After *From*, type your name and electronic address if your program does not insert it automatically.
- After *Subject*, present a clear description of the message.
- Insert the addresses of anyone receiving courtesy or blind copies.
- Include a salutation (such as *Mike;Hi, Mike*) or honorific and last name (*Dear Mr.Harding*), especially in messages to outsiders.
- Double-space (skip one line) between paragraphs.
- Do not type in all caps or in all lowercase letters.
- Include full contact information in the signature block.

Most e-mail programs automatically add the current date after *Date*. On the *Cc* line (which stands for *carbon copy* or *courtesy copy*), you can type the e-mail address of anyone who is to receive a copy of the message. Remember, though, to send copies only to those people directly involved with the message. Most e-mail programs also include a line for *Bcc* (*blind carbon copy*). This sends a copy without the addressee's knowledge. Many considerate writers today use *Bcc* for the names and addresses of a list of receivers, a technique that avoids revealing the addresses to the entire group. On the subject line, identify the subject of the message. Be sure to include enough information to be clear and compelling.

Greeting. Begin your message with a friendly greeting, such as the following:

Hi, Greg,	Thank you, Haley,
Greetings, Amy,	Dear Mr. Cotter:
Leslie,	Dear Leslie:

In addition to being friendly, a greeting provides a visual cue marking the beginning of the message. Many messages are transmitted or forwarded with such long headers that finding the beginning of the message can be difficult. A greeting helps, as shown in Figure 7.1.

Body. When typing the body of an e-mail message, use standard caps and lowercase characters—never all upper-case or all lowercase characters. Cover just one topic, and try to keep the total message under three screens in length. To assist you, many e-mail programs have basic text-editing features, such as cut, copy, paste, and word-wrap.

Complimentary Closing and Signature Block. In closing your message, you may elect to sign off with a complimentary closing, such as *Cheers, All the best*, or *Many thanks*. Such a closing is optional. However, providing your name is mandatory. It is also smart to include full contact information as part of your signature block. Some writers prepare a number of "signatures" in their e-mail programs, depending on what information they want to reveal. They can choose a complete signature with all their contact information, or they can use a brief version. See Figure 7.1 for an example of a complete signature.

Composing Professional E-Mail Messages

Wise business communicators are aware of the importance and the dangers of e-mail as a communication channel. They know that their messages can travel, intentionally or unintentionally, long distances. A quickly drafted e-mail may end up in the boss's inbox or be forwarded to an enemy. Making matters worse, computers never forget. Even erased messages can remain on multiple servers that are backed up by companies or Internet service providers. Increasingly, e-mail has turned into the "smoking gun" uncovered by prosecutors to prove indelicate or even illegal intentions.

Writers simply forget that their e-mail messages are permanent and searchable and can be forwarded as easily to a thousand people as to just one.[8] One observer noted that e-mail is like an electronic truth serum.[9] Writers blurt out thoughts without thinking. For these reasons, e-mail and other electronic communication channels pose a number of dangers, to both employees and employers. Best practices for using electronic media in general are discussed at the end of the chapter.

Despite its dangers and limitations, e-mail has become a mainstream channel of communication. That's why it's important to take the time to organize your thoughts, compose carefully, and be concerned with correct grammar and punctuation. Understanding netiquette and proper tone is also important if you wish to be perceived as a professional. The pointers in Figure 7.2 will help you get off to a good start in using e-mail smartly and safely.

Chapter 7: Electronic Messages and Digital Media

FIGURE 7.2 Using E-Mail Safely and Smartly

Tips	E-Mail Best Practices Explained
Try composing offline.	Especially for important messages, use your word processing program to write offline. Then upload your message to your e-mail. This avoids "self-destructing" (losing all your writing through some glitch or pressing the wrong key) when working online.
Get the address right.	If you omit one character or misread the character *l* for the number 1, your message bounces. Solution: Use your electronic address book for people you write to frequently. Double-check every address that you key in manually. Don't accidentally reply to a group of receivers when you intend to answer only one.
Avoid misleading subject lines.	Make sure your subject line is relevant and helpful. Generic tags, such as *Hi!* and *Important*, may cause your message to be deleted before it is opened.
Apply the top-of-screen test.	When readers open your message and look at the first screen, will they see what is most significant? Your subject line and first paragraph should convey your purpose. Frontload the message.
Be concise.	Omit unnecessary information. Remember that monitors are small and typefaces are often difficult to read. Organize your ideas tightly.
Don't send anything you wouldn't want published.	E-mail creates a permanent record that does not go away even when deleted. Every message is a corporate communication that can be used against you or your employer. Don't write anything that you wouldn't want your boss, your family, or a judge to read.
Don't use e-mail to avoid contact.	E-mail is inappropriate for breaking bad news or for resolving arguments. For example, it's improper to fire a person by e-mail. It is also a poor channel for clashing with supervisors, subordinates, or others. Before risking hurt feelings, call or pay the person a visit.
Care about correctness.	People are still judged by their writing, whether electronic or paper based. Sloppy e-mail messages (with missing apostrophes, haphazard spelling, and jumbled writing) make readers work too hard. They resent not only the message but also the writer.
Care about tone.	Your words and writing style affect the reader. Avoid sounding curt, negative, or domineering.
Resist humour and sarcasm.	Without the nonverbal cues conveyed by your face and your voice, humour and sarcasm can easily be misunderstood.
Limit any tendency to send blanket copies.	Send copies only to people who really need to see a message. Don't document every business decision and action with an electronic paper trail.
Never send spam.	Sending unsolicited advertisements (spam) either by fax or by e-mail wastes valuable time and electronic resources.
Use capital letters only for emphasis.	Avoid writing entire messages in all caps, which is like SHOUTING.
Don't forward without permission, and beware of long threads.	Obtain approval before forwarding a message. Beware of forwarding e-mail consisting of a long thread (string) of messages. Some content at the beginning of the thread may be inappropriate for the third receiver. Leaving sensitive information in the thread can lead to serious trouble.
Use attachments sparingly.	Because attachments may carry viruses, some receivers won't open them. Consider including short attachments within an e-mail message. If you must send a longer attachment, announce it.
Scan all messages in your inbox before replying to each individually.	Because subsequent messages often affect the way you respond, skim all messages first (especially all those from the same individual). Respond immediately to messages that can be answered in two minutes or less.
Print only when necessary.	Read and answer most messages online without saving or printing. Use folders to archive messages on special topics. Print only those messages that are complex, controversial, or involve significant decisions and follow-up.
Acknowledge receipt.	If you can't reply immediately, tell when you can (*Will respond Friday*).
Don't automatically return the sender's message.	When replying, cut and paste the relevant parts. Avoid irritating your recipients by returning the entire thread (sequence of messages) on a topic.
Revise the subject line if the topic changes.	When replying or continuing an e-mail exchange, revise the subject line as the topic changes.
Provide a clear, complete first sentence.	Avoid fuzzy replies, such as *That's fine with me* or *Sounds good!* Busy respondents forget what was said in earlier messages, so be sure to fill in the context and your perspective when responding.

(Continued)

FIGURE 7.2 **(Continued)**

Tips	E-Mail Best Practices Explained
Never respond when you are angry.	Calm down before shooting off a response to an upsetting message. You will come up with different and better options after thinking about what was said. If possible, iron out differences in person.
Don't use company computers for personal matters.	Unless your company specifically allows it, never use your employer's computers for personal messages, personal shopping, or entertainment.
Assume that all e-mail is monitored.	Employers legally have the right to monitor e-mail, and many do.
Design your messages effectively.	When a message requires several screens, help the reader with headings, bulleted lists, side headings, and perhaps an introductory summary that describes what will follow. Although these techniques lengthen a message, they shorten reading time.
Consider cultural differences.	Be clear and precise in your language. Remember that figurative clichés (*pull up stakes, playing second fiddle,*) sports references (*hit a home run, play by the rules*), and slang (*cool, stoked*) may confuse nonnative speakers of English.
Double-check before hitting the Send button.	Avoid the necessity of sending a second message, which makes you look careless. Use spell check and reread for fluency before sending. Verify important facts and the spelling of names.

Sometimes taken lightly, e-mail messages, like other business documents, should be written carefully. Once they leave the author's hands, they are essentially published. They can't be retrieved, corrected, or revised. Review the Checklist box for tips for writing typical e-mail messages that will accomplish what you intend.

Checklist

Professional E-Mail

Subject Line

- **Summarize the central idea.** Express concisely what the message is about and how it relates to the reader.

- **Include labels if appropriate.** Labels, such as *FYI* (for your information) and *REQ* (required), help receivers recognize how to respond.

- **Avoid empty or dangerous words.** Don't write one-word subject lines, such as *Help*, *Problem*, or *Free*.

Opening

- **State the purpose for writing.** Include the same information that is in the subject line, but expand it.

- **Highlight questions.** If you are requesting information, begin with the most important question, use a polite command (*Please answer the following questions about ...*), or introduce your request courteously.

- **Supply information directly.** If responding to a request, give the reader the requested information immediately in the opening. Explain later.

Body

- **Explain details.** Arrange information logically. For detailed topics develop separate coherent paragraphs.

- **Enhance readability.** Use short sentences, short paragraphs, and parallel construction for similar ideas.

- **Apply document design.** If appropriate, provide bulleted or numbered lists, columns, tables, or other graphic devices to improve readability and comprehension.

- **Be cautious.** Remember that e-mail messages often travel far beyond their intended audiences.

Closing

- **Request action.** If appropriate, state specifically what you want the reader to do. Include a deadline, with reasons, if possible.

- **Provide a goodwill statement or a closing thought.** When communicating outside of the company or with management, include a positive goodwill statement, such as *Our team enjoyed working on the feasibility report, and we look forward to your feedback*. If no action request is necessary, end with a closing thought.

- **Avoid cliché endings.** Use fresh remarks rather than overused expressions such as *If you have additional questions, please do not hesitate to call* or *Thank you for your cooperation*.

Using Instant Messaging and Texting Professionally

LEARNING OBJECTIVE **3**

Explain how business professionals communicate by instant messaging and texting.

Making their way from teen bedrooms to office boardrooms, instant messaging (IM) and text messaging have become permanent and powerful communication tools. IM enables you to use the Internet to communicate in real time in a private chat room with one or more individuals. It is like live e-mail or a text telephone call. More and more workers are using it as a speedy communication channel to exchange short messages.

Text messaging, or texting, is another popular means for exchanging brief messages in real time. Usually delivered by smartphone, texting requires a short message service (SMS) supplied by a cell phone service provider. Increasingly, both IM and text messages are sent by computer or handheld device.

> Instant messaging (IM) and texting have become permanent and powerful communication tools in the workplace.

How Instant Messaging and Texting Work

To send an instant message, you might use a public IM service, called a client, such as Google Talk or Microsoft's Windows Live Messenger. These are public IM services. Once the client is installed, you enter your name and password to log on. The software checks whether any of the users in your contact list are currently logged on. If the server finds any of your contacts, it sends a message to your computer. If the person you want to contact is online, you can click that person's name and a window opens into which you can enter text. You type a message, such as that shown in Figure 7.3, and click Send. Because your client has the Internet address and port number for the computer of the person you addressed, your message is sent directly to the client on that person's computer.

FIGURE 7.3 Instant Message for Brief, Fast Communication

> Figure 7.3 shows a brief IM exchange between a supervisor and a subordinate. Both are using a computer-based IM program. Texting is a convenient tool that enables team members to locate quick information and answers in solving immediate problems even when they are apart.

```
Ryan Mlodzik - Conversation                              _ □ X

File   Edit   View   Actions   Help

To:  Ryan Mlodzik <mlodzik@armour.com>          Start Camera  ⩔
                                                Start Talking  ⩔
Camille Montano says:                           I Want To . .  ⩔
   Hi, Ryan, are you free for a quick question?
                                                • Invite Someone to
Ryan Mlodzik says:                                this Conversation
   Sure thing. What have you got?               🖼 Send a File or Photo
                                                ✉ Send E-mail
Camille Montano says:                           • Ask for Remote
   I just finished my meeting with the folks at Zymak Enterprises,    Assistance
   and they've agreed to terms we discussed yesterday, but they    • Start Application
   want 45-day terms instead of 30.               Sharing
                                                • Start Whiteboard
Ryan Mlodzik says:
   Did they agree to a 2-year or 3-year contract?

Camille Montano says:
   3-year.

Ryan Mlodzik says:
   OK, let's go with it. I approve the 45-day adjustment. Good
   work!

🌐 Block   A Font   ☺ ▾ Emoticons

[                                               ]    Send

Last message received on 8/4/14 at 1:26 PM.
```

Typically, IM communication is exchanged between two computers that are linked by servers. However, new applications allow people to use IM not only on their computers but also on their handheld devices, such as the popular iPhone. Many smartphones work on a 3G cellphone network where they consume minutes, but they may also be able to access free Wi-Fi where available.

Texting, on the other hand, usually requires a smartphone or PDA, and users are charged for the service, often by choosing a flat rate for a certain number of text or media messages per month. Voice-over-Internet providers, such as Skype, also offer texting. For a small fee, Skype subscribers can send text messages to SMS-enabled cellphones in North America and send IM messages both domestically and internationally. Again, Skype and many other formerly computer-based applications are now available on mobile devices and are making communication on the go more convenient than ever before.

Pros and Cons of Instant Messaging and Texting

In today's fast-paced world, instant messaging (IM) offers numerous benefits. Its major attraction is real-time communication with colleagues anywhere in the world—as long as a cellphone signal or a Wi-Fi connection is available. IM is a convenient alternative to the telephone and may eventually even replace e-mail. Because IM allows people to share information immediately and make decisions quickly, its impact on business communication has been dramatic. Group online chat capabilities allow co-workers on far-flung project teams to communicate instantly. Skype is but one of many providers.

Texting by SMS is rapidly spreading around the world within individual markets and regions, but incompatible wireless standards have prevented the reach of SMS across continents. Like IM, texting can be a low-cost substitute for voice calls, delivering a message between private mobile phone users quietly and discreetly. SMS is particularly popular in Europe, New Zealand, Australia, and Asia.[10] Using bulk text messages, companies around the world provide news alerts, financial information, and advertising to customers.

The immediacy of instant and text messaging has created many fans. A user knows right away whether a message was delivered. Messaging avoids phone tag and eliminates the downtime associated with personal telephone conversations. Another benefit includes "presence functionality." Co-workers can locate each other online, thus avoiding having to hunt for someone who is out of the office. Many people consider instant messaging and texting to be productivity boosters because they enable users to get answers quickly and allow multitasking.

Despite its popularity among workers, some organizations forbid employees to use instant and text messaging for a number of reasons. Employers consider instant messaging yet another distraction in addition to the telephone, e-mail, and the Web. Organizations also fear that privileged information and company records will be revealed through public instant messaging systems, which hackers can easily penetrate.

Companies also worry about *phishing* (fraudulent) schemes, viruses, malware (malicious software programs), and *spim* (IM spam). Like e-mail, instant and text messages are subject to discovery (disclosure); that is, they can become evidence in lawsuits. Moreover, companies fear instant messaging and texting because the services necessitate that businesses track and store messaging conversations to comply with legal requirements. This task may be overwhelming. Finally, IM and texting have been implicated in traffic accidents and inappropriate uses, such as the notorious *sexting*.

Best Practices for Instant Messaging and Texting

Instant messaging and texting can definitely save time and simplify communication with co-workers and customers. Before using IM or text messaging on the job, however, be sure you have permission. Do not use public systems without checking with your supervisor. If your organization does allow IM or texting, you can use it efficiently and professionally by following these best practice guidelines:

- Learn about your organization's IM policies. Are you allowed to use instant and text messaging? With whom may you exchange messages?

- Don't text or IM while driving a car. Pull over if you must read or send a message.

Useful guidelines for writers of instant messages include learning about organizational policies, organizing contact lists, and keeping personal messaging to a minimum (if allowed at all).

- Make yourself unavailable when you need to complete a project or meet a deadline.

- Organize your contact lists to separate business contacts from family and friends.

- Keep your messages simple and to the point. Avoid unnecessary chitchat, and know when to say goodbye.

- Don't use IM or text messages to send confidential or sensitive information.

- Be aware that instant or text messages can be saved. As with e-mail, don't say anything that would damage your reputation or that of your organization.

- If personal messaging is allowed, keep it to a minimum. Your organization may prefer that personal chats be done during breaks or the lunch hour.

- Show patience by not blasting multiple messages to co-workers if a response is not immediate.

- Keep your presence status up-to-date so that people trying to reach you don't waste their time.

- Beware of jargon, slang, and abbreviations, which, although they may reduce keystrokes, may be confusing and appear unprofessional.

- Respect your receivers by using good grammar and proper spelling and by proofreading carefully.

Using Podcasts or Webcasts, Blogs, and Wikis for Business

LEARNING OBJECTIVE 4

Identify professional uses of podcasts, blogs, and wikis, and describe prudent policies to protect authors of electronic content.

Like Twitter, podcasts, blogs, and wikis are part of the new user-centred virtual environment called Web 2.0. Far from being passive consumers, today's Internet users have the power to create Web content; interact with businesses and each other; review products, self-publish, or blog; contribute to wikis; or tag and share images and other files. Individuals wield enormous power because they can potentially reach huge audiences, which may have a viral effect.

The democratization of the Web means that in the online world, Internet users can bypass gatekeepers who filter content in the traditional print and visual media. Hence, even extreme views often reach audiences of thousands or even millions. The dangers are obvious. Fact checking often falls by the wayside, buzz may become more important than truth, and a single keystroke can make or destroy a reputation. This section addresses prudent business uses of podcasts, blogs, and wikis because you are likely to encounter these and other electronic communication tools on the job.

Business Podcasts or Webcasts

Although the terms *podcast* and *podcasting* have caught on, they are somewhat misleading. The words *broadcasting* and *iPod* combined to create the word *podcast*; however, audio and video files can be played on any number of devices, not just Apple's iPod. *Webcasting* for audio and *vcasting* for video content would be more accurate, but most people simply refer to them as podcasting. Podcasts can extend from short clips of a few minutes to 30-minute or longer digital files. Naturally, large video files consume a lot of memory, so they tend to be streamed on a Web site rather than downloaded.

Podcasts can be used in education to allow students to access instructors' lectures, sporting events, and other events.

How Organizations Use Podcasts.
Like blogging, podcasting has experienced large growth and has spread among various user groups online. Major news organizations and media outlets, such as CBC and CTV, podcast radio shows (e.g., CBC Radio/Radio-Canada) and TV shows. Podcasts are also used in education. Students can access instructors' lectures, interviews, sporting events, and other content. Unlike streaming

video that users can view only with an active Internet connection, podcasts encoded as MP3 files can be downloaded to a computer, a smartphone, or an MP3 player to be enjoyed on the go, often without subsequent Web access.

Delivering and Accessing Podcasts. Businesses have embraced podcasting for sending audio and video messages that do not require a live presence yet offer a friendly human face. Because they can broadcast repetitive information that does not require interaction, podcasts can replace costlier live teleconferences. IBM is training its sales force with podcasts that are available anytime. Real estate agents create podcasts to enable buyers to take virtual walking tours of available properties at their leisure. HR policies can also be presented in the form of podcasts for unlimited viewing on demand or when convenient. Marketing pitches also lend themselves to podcasting.

Podcasts are featured on media Web sites and company portals or shared on social networking sites and blogs. They can usually be streamed or downloaded as media files. Really simple syndication (RSS) allows the distribution of current information published in podcasts, blogs, video files, and news items. Users can select RSS feeds from various sources and personalize the information they want to receive. GreenTalk Radio, shown in Figure 7.4, is just one example of a Web site that provides podcasts on many topics, such as green living and environmental stewardship. Frequently, business podcasts include short commercial segments. Nonprofit organizations may play public-service announcements to raise money. Interestingly, this ease of access has not produced multitudes of independent podcasters; the medium is still dominated by professional news organizations, such as National Public Radio.

FIGURE 7.4 GreenTalk Radio Podcasts

In his audio podcasts, host Sean Daily examines eco-friendly lifestyles and dispenses tips on becoming greener.

Courtesy of Personal Life Media

Creating a Podcast. Producing a simple podcast does not require sophisticated equipment. With inexpensive recording, editing, and publishing software, such as the popular Propaganda, ePodcast Creator, Audacity, or Gabcast, users can inform customers, mix their own music, or host interviews. In fact, any digital recorder can be used to create a quality primitive podcast, especially if the material is scripted and well rehearsed. If you are considering creating your own podcast, here are a few tips:

- **Decide whether to record one podcast or a series.** You can create a one-time podcast for a specific purpose or a series of podcasts on a related subject. Make sure you have enough material to sustain a steady flow of information.

- **Download software.** The program Audacity is available for free; other popular recording and editing software programs are relatively inexpensive.

- **Obtain hardware.** Depending on the sound quality you desire, you may need a sophisticated microphone and other audio equipment. The recording room must be properly shielded against noise, echo, and other interference. Many universities and some libraries provide language labs that feature recording booths.

- **Organize the message.** Make sure your broadcast has a beginning, middle, and end. Build in some redundancy. Tell the listeners what you will tell them, then tell them, and finally, tell them what you've told them. This principle, known to effective PowerPoint users, also applies to podcasting. Previews, summaries, and transitions are important to help your audience follow the message.

- **Choose an extemporaneous or scripted delivery.** Think about how you will deliver the information, whether speaking freely or using a manuscript. Extemporaneous delivery means that you prepare but you use only brief notes. It usually sounds more spontaneous and natural than reading from a script, but it can also lead to redundancy, repetition, and flubbed lines. Reading from a script, if done skillfully, can sound natural and warm. However, in the wrong hands, reading can come across as mechanical and amateurish.

- **Prepare and practice.** Before recording, do a few practice runs. Editing audio or video is difficult and time-consuming. Try to get your recording right so that you won't have to edit much.

- **Publish and distribute your message.** If you post the podcast to a blog, you can introduce it and solicit your audience's feedback. Consider distributing your podcast by an RSS feed.

Professional Blogs

A blog is a Web site with journal entries on any imaginable topic usually written by one person, although some blogs feature multiple commentators. Typically, readers leave feedback. Businesses use blogs to keep customers and employees informed and to interact with them. The biggest advantage of business blogs is that they have the potential to reach a far-flung, vast audience. Marketing firms and their clients are looking closely at blogs because blogs can produce unbiased consumer feedback faster and more cheaply than such staples of consumer research as focus groups and surveys. Employees and executives at such companies as Google, Sun Microsystems, IBM, and Hewlett-Packard maintain blogs. They use blogs to communicate internally with employees and externally with clients.

As an online diary or journal, a blog allows visitors to leave public comments. By 2007, writers had posted 70 million blogs, up nearly 30 percent in one year.[11] However, only about half of these blogs are active, meaning that posts were published in the three months before the report. Although blogs may still be underused, they do represent an amazing new information stream if used wisely.

How Companies Use Blogs

The potential applications of blogs in business are vast. Like other Web 2.0 phenomena, corporate blogs usually invite feedback and help build communities. Specifically, companies use blogs for public relations, customer relations, crisis communication, market research, viral marketing, internal communication, and recruiting.

Public Relations, Customer Relations, and Crisis Communication. One of the prominent uses of blogs is to provide up-to-date company information to the press and the public. Blogs can be written by executives or by rank-and-file employees. Jonathan Schwartz, president and CEO of Sun Microsystems, is an occasional blogger. General Electric's Global research blog addresses industry insiders and the interested public. Ask a Blueshirt, a site authored by Best Buy employees, offers tips and other types of customer support.

A company blog is a natural forum for late-breaking news, especially when disaster strikes. Business bloggers can address rumours and combat misinformation. Although a blog cannot replace other communication channels in an emergency, it should be part of the overall effort to soothe the public's emotional reaction with a human voice of reason.

Market Research and Viral Marketing. Because most blogs invite feedback, they can be invaluable sources of opinion from customers and industry experts. In addition to monitoring visitor comments on their corporate blogs, many companies now have appointed employees who scrutinize the blogosphere for buzz and positive or negative postings about their organization and products.

The term *viral marketing* refers to the rapid spread of messages online, much like infectious diseases that pass from person to person. Marketers realize the potential of getting the word out about their products and services in the blogosphere, where their messages are often cross-referenced and linked by interested bloggers. Viral messages must be unexpected and elicit an emotional response, much like BMW's hip series of short films by popular directors starring Clive Owen.

Online Communities. Like Twitter, which has a loyal core following, company blogs can attract a devoted community of participants who want to keep informed about company events, product updates, and other news. In turn, those enthusiasts can contribute new ideas. Similar to Dell's Ideastorm, Starbucks' blog Ideas In Action solicits product and service ideas from customers.

Internal Communication and Recruiting. Blogs can be used to keep virtual teams on track and share updates on the road. Members in remote locations can stay in touch by smartphone and other devices, exchanging text, images, sound, and video clips. In many companies, blogs have replaced hard-copy publications in offering late-breaking news or tidbits of interest to employees. They may feature profiles of high-performing workers, information about benefits, and so forth.

Blogs mirror the company culture and present an invaluable opportunity for job candidates to size up a potential employer and the people working there.

Tips for Creating a Professional Blog

Blogging has grown up as a commercial activity and now offers sound business opportunities. Some bloggers make a living, although most remain unknowns in the boundless thickets of information on the Internet. To even have a shot at competing with established blog sites, consider the following guidelines if you would like to start a successful business blog:

- **Identify your audience.** As with any type of communication, you must know your audience in order to decide what to write to get people to read your blog. Does your blog stand out? What makes you interesting and unique?

> Tips for crafting effective professional blogs include identifying the audience, crafting the message, and attracting search engines by choosing the right keywords.

- **Find a home for your blog.** You can use software that will let you attach a blog function to your Web site. Alternatively, you can join a blog hosting site that will provide a link on your Web site to attract visitors. You can usually find templates and other options to help build traffic to your site, especially if you use trackers that identify recent posts and popular message threads. Visit **www.businessblogconsulting.com** to learn more about blog publishing. Windows Live Spaces at **http://home.spaces.live.com** will help you set up a blog effortlessly and quickly.

- **Craft your message.** Blog about topics that showcase your expertise and insights. Offer a fresh, unique perspective on subjects your audience cares about. Your writing should be intriguing and sincere. Experts suggest that authors get to know the blogosphere in their industry and comment on what other bloggers are writing about. Stick with what you know.

- **Make "blogrolling" work for you.** Your goal is to attract repeat visitors to your blog. One way to achieve this objective is to increase traffic between blogs. "Blogrolling" means that you provide links to other sites or blogs on the Web that you find valuable and that are related to your business or industry. Respond to other bloggers' postings and link to them.

- **Attract search engines by choosing the right keywords.** In headlines and text, emphasize potential search terms that may draw traffic to your site. Focus on one topic and use a variety of synonyms to propel your blog to the top of search engine listings. An import company doing business with China would want to stress the keywords *import* and *China,* as well as *trade, Asia,* and so forth, in addition to more industry-specific terms, such as *toys.*

- **Blog often.** Provide fresh content regularly. Stay current. Stale information puts visitors off. Post short, concise messages, but do so often.

- **Monitor the traffic to your site.** If necessary, vary your subjects to attract interest. If traffic slows down, experiment with new themes while staying with your core business and expertise. Also, evaluate the effectiveness of your publishing platform. Some blog publishing sites are more valuable than others in increasing your blog's visibility to search engines.

- **Seek permission.** If you are employed, explore your company's blogging policy. Even if neither a policy nor a prohibition against blogging exists, avoid writing about your employer, coworkers, customers, and events at the office, however veiled your references may be. The Internet is abuzz with stories about bloggers who got fired for online indiscretions.

- **Stay away from inappropriate topics.** Whether you are a rank-and-file employee or a freelance blogger, remember not to write anything you wouldn't want your family, friends, and the public at large to read. Blogs are not private journal entries; therefore, don't entrust to them any risqué, politically extreme, or private information.

Wikis and Collaboration

Wikis employ easy-to-use collaborative software to allow users to create and edit documents.

At least as important to business as blogs are new communication tools, such as wikis and social networking sites. A wiki is a Web site that employs easy-to-use collaborative software to allow users to create documents that can be edited by tapping into the same technology that runs the well-known online encyclopaedia Wikipedia. Large companies, such as British Telecom, encourage their employees to team up to author software, launch branding campaigns, and map cellphone stations. Most projects are facilitated with the help of wikis, a tool that's especially valuable across vast geographic distances and multiple time zones.[12]

How Businesses Use Wikis. Far from being just a tool for geeks, wikis are used beyond information technology departments. Figure 7.5 illustrates how to create a wiki

FIGURE 7.5 Creating a Wiki With Google Sites and Google Docs

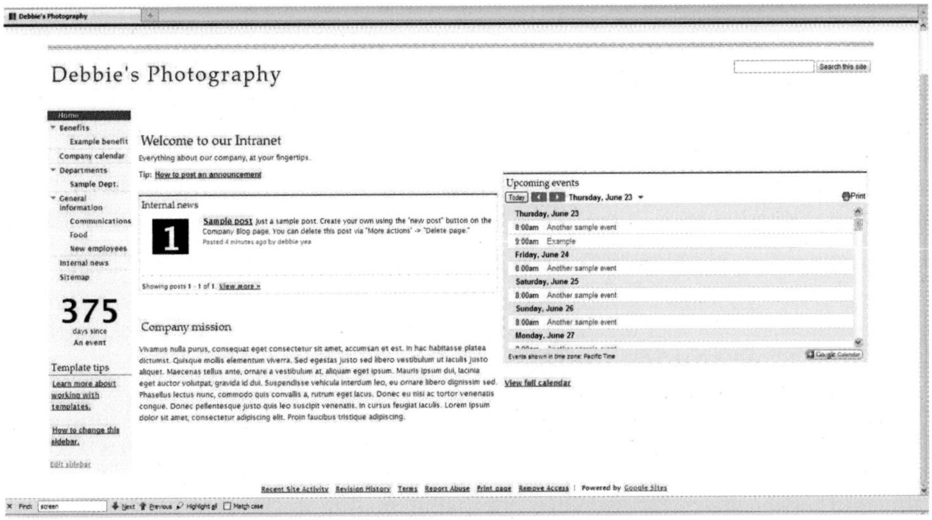

This screen shot shows a template created in Google Sites, a simple, template-driven wiki and document editor. Google Sites and the user-friendly document editing and revision tool Google Docs allow users to create, edit, share, and manage documents online in real time. Unlike in typical wikis, here multiple editors can modify files simultaneously.

with Google Sites and Google Docs. The five main uses range from providing a shared internal knowledge base to storing templates for business documents:

- **The global wiki.** For companies with a global reach, a wiki is an ideal tool for information sharing between headquarters and satellite offices. Team members can easily edit their work and provide input to the home office and each other.

- **The wiki knowledge base.** Teams or departments use wikis to collect and disseminate information to large audiences, creating a database for knowledge management. For example, an IT department may compile frequently asked questions that help users resolve the most common problems themselves. Human resources managers may update employee policies, make announcements, and convey information about benefits.

- **Wikis for meetings.** Wikis can facilitate feedback before and after meetings or serve as repositories of meeting minutes. In fact, wikis may replace some meetings, yet still keep a project on track. An often-cited example of a huge global wiki meeting is IBM's famous massive online discussion and brainstorming session that involved more than 100,000 participants from more than 160 countries.

- **Project management with wikis.** Wikis offer a highly interactive environment ideal for projects by enabling information to be centralized for easy access and user input. All participants have the same information available and can share ideas freely, more freely than in traditional face-to-face meetings. Instead of a top-down information flow, wikis empower employees and foster a team environment in which ideas can thrive.

- **Documentation and wikis.** Wikis can help to document projects large and small, as well as technical and nontechnical. Wikis may also provide templates for reports.

How to Be a Valuable Wiki Contributor. Whether you want to contribute to a wiki on the Web or at work, try to be an effective participant. As with most electronic communication, abide by the conventions of polite society and follow the commonsense rules explained here.

First, show respect and watch out for improper or ambiguous language. Don't attack or otherwise severely criticize another contributor. Don't be a "troll," an annoying individual who posts irrelevant, controversial, or provocative comments online that may anger fellow users and disrupt a discussion. Because expression online allows for little subtlety, give some thought to how your words could be interpreted. Members of online communities can form deep bonds and strongly dislike contributors they consider vicious or mean.

Pay attention to correct grammar and spelling, and verify your facts. Every comment you contribute is essentially published on the Web and available to any reader. If the content appears on the company intranet, it is for the whole company to see. Don't be sloppy; it could cause you to suffer embarrassment or worse. Wikipedia, a wiki that is trying to marry credibility with its desire for openness, recently tightened the rules. Errors introduced by cyber attacks and innocent errors alike are often perpetuated by people who blindly trust wiki content.

Follow the guidelines for contributors, and give credit where credit is due. Read the rules to make sure your work fits into the group effort in style, content, and format. As a newbie, ask for help if necessary. Leave your ego behind. Contributors to a wiki are part of a team, not individual authors who can reasonably expect recognition or maintain control over their writing. When borrowing, be sure to cite your sources to avoid plagiarism.

Negotiating Social and Professional Networking Sites

Far from being only entertaining leisure sites, social networking sites, such as Facebook and Twitter are used by businesses for similar reasons and in much the same way as podcasts, blogs, and wikis. Social networking sites enable businesses to connect with customers and employees, share company news, and exchange ideas. Social online communities for professional audiences (e.g., LinkedIn) help recruiters find talent and encounter potential employees before hiring them.

Tapping Into Social Networks

Business interest in social networking sites is not surprising if we consider that 73 percent of millennials, also called Generation Y, regularly socialize and chat online. An average of 55 percent of all consumers between 14 and 75 regularly visit social online communities. All groups spend between 11 and 19 hours a week on the Internet solely for entertainment.[13] Not surprisingly, then, businesses are trying to catch on and tap the vast potential of social networking.

How Businesses Use Social Networks. Some firms use social online communities for brainstorming and teamwork. They provide the collaboration tools and watch what happens. British Telecom (BT) has about 11,000 employees on Facebook in addition to offering its own internal social network. A British Telecom IT executive says that his company can observe online relationships to see how information travels and decision making occurs. The company is able to identify teams that form spontaneously and naturally and then assigns targeted projects to them. Idea generators are easy to spot. The BT executive considers these contributors invaluable, suggesting that "a new class of supercommunicators has emerged."[14] The key to all the new media is that they thrive in a highly mobile and interactive Web 2.0 environment.

Other companies harness the power of online communities to boost their brand image or to provide a forum for collaboration. McDonald's has a strong presence on Facebook, boasting nearly 1.5 million "fans." The fast-food chain also maintains a private networking site, StationM, for its 650,000 hourly employees in 15,000 locations across Canada and the United States.[15] Insurer MetLife has launched connect. MetLife, an online social network collaboration tool. Resembling Facebook, this internal

FIGURE 7.6 Big Companies Rule on Facebook: Netflix

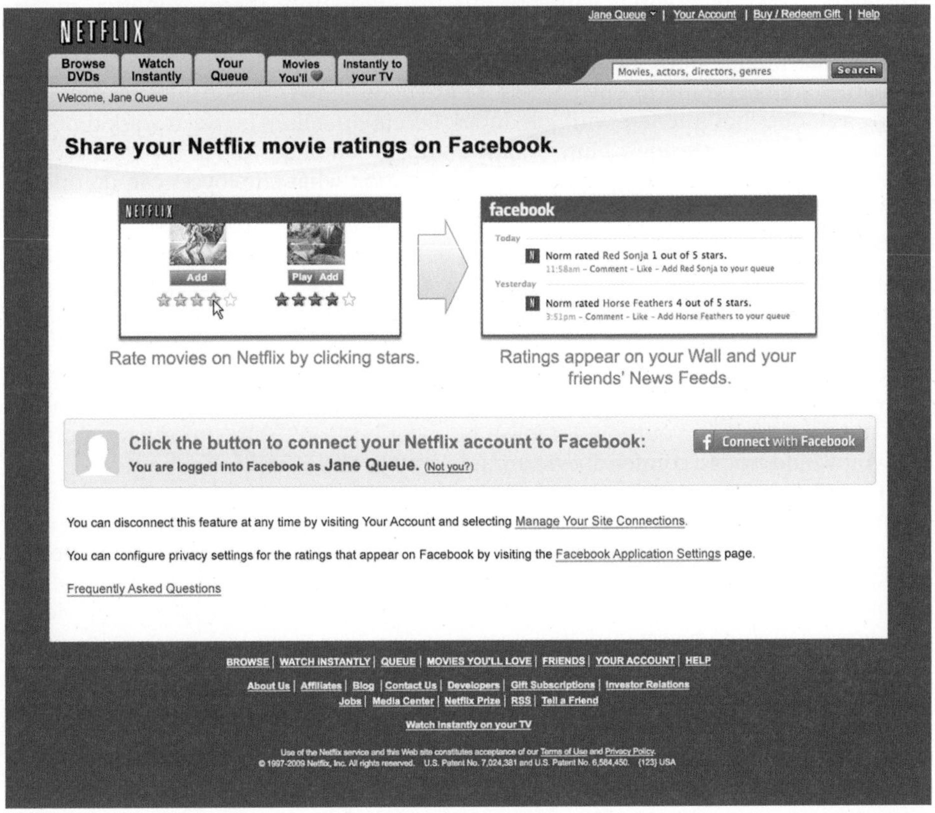

Facebook recently reached 750 million users. The site allows registered users to create individual home pages and to choose from more than 200 groups based on their interests. Large corporations seem to thrive on Facebook. *Slate* magazine ranked Coca-Cola "first among companies with the best Facebook presences." Newer companies, such as online film rental service Netflix, may draw 100,000 fans, as opposed to Coca-Cola's whopping 5,300,000 fans.

networking tool sits safely behind the corporate firewall.[16] Best Buy has created its own social network, Blue Shirt Nation, with currently more than 20,000 participants, most of them sales associates. IBM's in-house social network, Beehive, has 30,000 employees on it. Managers notice avid networkers who create buzz and promote the brand. The drawback is that quieter employees may be overlooked.[17] Figure 7.6 shows how one organization takes advantage of social media.

Potential Risks of Social Networks for Businesses. Online social networks hold great promise for businesses while also presenting some risk. Most managers want plugged-in employees with strong tech skills. They like to imagine their workers as brand ambassadors. They fantasize about their products becoming overnight sensations thanks to viral marketing. However, they also fret about incurring productivity losses, compromising trade secrets, attracting the wrath of huge Internet audiences, and facing embarrassment over inappropriate and damaging employee posts.[18]

Businesses take different approaches to the "dark side" of social networking. Some, such as Zappos.com, take a hands-off approach to employee online activity. Others, such as IBM, have drafted detailed policies to cover all forms of self-expression online. Some of IBM's guidelines include people being honest about their identity, accepting personal responsibility for published posts, and hitting Send only after careful thought. The technology giant asks its workers to avoid any controversies outside their professional role. The company wants workers to "add value" as they are building their social reputations, not dwell on trivia.[19] Finally, Enterprise Rent-A-Car and other organizations block some or all social sites.

Younger workers in particular are often stunned when their employers block access to Facebook, Gmail, and other popular Web destinations. The key is to strike a balance between allowing employees access to the Web and protecting security and ensuring productivity. Consultant Gary Rudman sees parallels to old-fashioned chatting around

> Unwise use of social networking sites can result in lost productivity, compromised trade secrets, and the wrath of huge Internet audiences.

the water cooler or making personal phone calls, grudgingly accepted as they were by managers: "These two worlds will continue to collide until there's a mutual understanding that performance, not Internet usage, is what really matters."[20]

Personal mobile devices make monitoring during work time tougher, and some companies are beginning to open access. Kraft Foods allows "reasonable" personal use as long as it does not interfere with job duties. Because the lines between work time and personal time are increasingly blurry, many companies hesitate to ban the Internet outright on the job. Some allow partial access by limiting what employees can do online. They may disable file sharing to protect sensitive information.

Tips for Using Social Networking Sites and Keeping Your Job.
Experts agree that, as with any public online activity, users of social networking sites would do well to exercise caution. Privacy is a myth, and sensitive information should not be shared lightly, least of all risqué photographs. Furthermore, refusing friend requests or unfriending individuals could jeopardize professional relationships. Consider the following tip by career counsellor Julie Powell if you like to visit social networking sites and want to keep your job: Establish boundaries. Don't share information online that you would not be comfortable sharing openly in the office.[21]

The advice to think twice before posting online applies to most communication channels used on the job. Facebook expert and blogger Nick O'Neill cautions account holders never to assume that the content they post on a social networking site is protected unless they have activated the privacy option. Many users leave their pages open and risk trouble with their employers by assuming that online comments are hidden from view.[22] Even privacy settings, however, do not guarantee complete protection from prying eyes.

Among the many risks in the cyber world are inappropriate photographs and making friends online. Tags make pictures searchable so that an embarrassing incident in college or university may resurface years later. Another potential minefield, says consultant Rachel Weingarten, is rejecting friend requests from some colleagues while accepting such offers from others.[23]

Harnessing the Potential of Professional Networking Sites

Business networking sites can serve as a source for referrals and recommendations.

Experts agree that connecting online offers professional opportunities by expanding the traditional Rolodex. They see social networking online as a natural extension of work.[24] Small businesses may view such sites as forums for sharing slideshow presentations and other office documents. Artists may feature their work. Medical doctors can discuss surgical techniques with peers.

As we have seen, the lines between social and professional networking are increasingly blurry. However, among business-oriented Web sites where users can post job openings, résumés, and career profiles, LinkedIn is the most popular networking tool, at least in North America. Xing is attracting large professional audiences in Europe. A great value of such business networking sites is that they can serve as a source for referrals and recommendations. Job seekers can also browse jobs posted by a company with a LinkedIn presence, such as Adobe Systems, shown in Figure 7.7.

Increasingly, companies are using social media—mostly LinkedIn—as a recruiting tool. Experts recommend that job seekers keep their profiles "clean"—that is, free of risqué photos, profanity, and negative comments. Instead, job candidates are encouraged to highlight awards, professional goals, and accomplishments. Although professional networking sites cannot replace face-to-face interviews, they allow hiring managers to form first impressions before inviting job hunters or to vet interviewees being considered for an open position.

The advantages that social and professional networking sites offer recruiters and applicants are plain. In the right hands, the sites are inexpensive, simple, and fast ways to advertise current business opportunities and to connect. However, as innovative as this new type of job search seems to be, the basics remain the same. Candidates need to craft their profiles with the same care they use when putting together their traditional résumés and cover letters. The job hunter's public appearance online must always be professional, and the profile should be up-to-date. You will learn more about job searching online in Chapter 15.

FIGURE 7.7 Adobe Systems Jobs on LinkedIn

Multimedia and creativity software company Adobe Systems uses the professional networking site LinkedIn to post job openings in its global branch offices.

© Courtesy of LinkedIn Corporation

Sharing Information Through RSS Feeds and Social Bookmarking

You may wonder how businesspeople navigate the vast resources available on the Internet. Seeking information on the Web that is relevant to you and your business can be time consuming and sometimes tedious, especially if it means browsing many Web sites for updates. Really Simple Syndication, RSS for short, is a time-saver, allowing users to monitor many news sources in one convenient spot. Likewise, social bookmarking helps busy professionals stay informed about topics of interest and negotiate the vast information jungle of the Web.

Really simple syndication (RSS) allows users to monitor many news sources in one convenient spot.

Really Simple Syndication. RSS, a fast and easy way to search and manage information, is a data file format capable of transmitting changing Web content. News organizations, bloggers, and other online information providers syndicate (i.e., publish and distribute) their content to subscribers. RSS documents are called feeds or channels, and they can be read most efficiently with a Web-based feed reader (also known as an aggregator), an easy-to-use software application. Feeds help alert subscribers to up-to-the-minute blog entries, news items, videos, and podcasts from various sources.

How does RSS work? Each time a syndicated Web site is updated, a summary of the new information travels by RSS feed to the site's subscribers. Users can read RSS feeds within their Internet browsers and in e-mail programs, such as MS Outlook, but local files are likely to become very large. This is why many subscribers prefer stand-alone cloud reader programs online that automatically receive updates from the subscribers' favourite Web sites. Some of the popular news aggregators are Google Reader, Bloglines, SharpReader, NetNewsWire, and Straw. Web-based feed readers also work well with mobile devices, helping busy executives keep up with customized news feeds on the go.

Content providers have a vital interest in providing RSS feeds. For one thing, feeds increase traffic to syndicated Web sites because they can be indexed in search engines and tagged to appear in feed lists, making them easier to find. This helps content providers stay ahead of the vast competition in cyberspace. A number of software applications automatically create RSS feeds—Mambo or Drupal are just two among many free, open-source programs available.

Social Bookmarking. In the battle for "eyeballs" on the Internet, social bookmarking is another critical component. Business Web sites, blogs, and other online content gain an edge if readers link to them and, thus, share content with other online users. Digg, Del.icio.us, Reddit, StumbleUpon, and Squidoo are just a few of the many

FIGURE 7.8 Social Bookmarking Sites

Bloggers and other online content providers don't need to list dozens of buttons so that users can spread content on the Internet. Just one *Share* widget allows visitors to choose which social service they want to use for sharing or bookmarking.

© Courtesy of Amit Agarwal (labnol.org)

Social bookmarking helps users search, organize, manage, and store bookmarks on the Web with the help of metadata.

fast-growing social bookmarking and content aggregator (collector) Web sites. Social bookmarking helps users search, organize, manage, and store bookmarks on the Web with the help of metadata—that is, information tags or keywords.

Many Web sites, blogs, and other content providers on the Internet offer various widgets or icons of social bookmarking sites to enable content sharing. Web publishers hope readers will link their information to social bookmarking sites and alert others to the information. Figure 7.8 shows common configurations of bookmarking icons that Web designers insert into Web pages to allow visitors to share content.

Typical search engines favour Web resources generating the most traffic. *High-traffic* Web sites are those that rack up the most hits and are indexed and bookmarked the most. As a result, they receive a high ranking and pop up topmost in keyword searches. Social bookmarking sites are aggregators, which means that they compile and list current, popular news items that will most likely appeal to their readers.

Perhaps you can see now how RSS feeds and social bookmarking sites could help you stay abreast of breaking news from many sources and save you valuable time. Whether you want to grab a broadcast from CBC.ca or check the most recent sports scores, look for the square orange RSS feed icon on your favorite Web sites or a rectangular button with the letters RSS or XML. On most high-traffic Web sites, you will also see *Share* links, or widgets, that will take you to social bookmarking sites.

Best Practices for Using Electronic Media Smartly, Safely, and Professionally

As advances in computer technology continue to change the way we work and play, Internet use on and off the job has become a danger zone for employees and employers. Misuse costs employers millions of dollars in lost productivity and litigation, and it can cost employees their jobs. Companies struggle with fair Internet use policies knowing that more than half of their employees with Web access shop online from the office.[25]

Recreational activities, as well as unintentional but careless miscues, can gobble up precious network resources and waste valuable work time. Even more important is concern over lawsuits and network security. Companies must maintain a workplace free of harassment. If employees download pornography, transmit sexually explicit jokes, or use inappropriate screen savers, the work environment can become "poisoned" and employers may be sued. Furthermore, security problems arise when employees open phishing e-mail or fall for malware when browsing the Web.

The Checklist box highlights some employee dos and don'ts that you should abide by to keep out of trouble on the job.

> Guidelines for the effective and professional use of electronic media include knowing and following workplace policies, treating all online speech as public, and avoiding questionable content, personal documents, and file sharing.

Checklist

Using Electronic Media Professionally: Dos and Don'ts

Dos: Know Workplace Policies and Avoid Private Use of Media at Work

- **Learn your company's rules.** One employee knew that her employer restricted personal use of work computers, but she believed it focused on Web surfing, not e-mail. She was stunned when her agency fired her after finding 418 personal e-mail messages on her PC.[26] Companies have been slow to adapt Internet policies to advances, such as IM, texting, and tweeting. Being informed is your best protection.

- **Avoid or minimize sending personal e-mail, IM messages, or texts from work.** Even if your company allows personal use during lunch or after hours, keep it to a minimum. Better yet, wait to use your home computer to access your personal e-mail and social networking sites.

- **Separate work and personal data.** Keep information that could embarrass you or expose you to legal liability on your personal storage devices or hard drives, never on your office computer.

Dos: Treat All Online Speech as Public and Protect Your Computer

- **Be careful when blogging, tweeting, or posting on social networking sites.** A Canadian blogger lost his job for an entry that read, "Getting to blog for three hours while being paid: priceless."[27]

- **Keep your virus and malicious software protection current.** Always download the newest definitions and updates to your operating system, browser, antivirus program, and antispyware.

- **Pick strong passwords and vary them.** Use a combination of letters, numbers, and symbols. Select a different password for each Web service, and never use your Web passwords as PIN codes on credit or debit cards. Change your passwords every few months.

- **Keep sensitive information private.** Monitor the privacy settings on social networking sites, but don't trust the "private" areas on Facebook, Flickr, and other services that provide public access to most material they store.

Don'ts: Avoid Questionable Content, Personal Documents, and File Sharing

- **Don't send, download, print, or exhibit pornography, sexually explicit jokes, or inappropriate screen savers.** Anything that might "poison" the work environment is prohibited.

- **Don't open attachments sent by e-mail.** Attachments with executable files or video files may carry viruses, spyware, or other malware (malicious programs).

- **Don't download free software and utilities to company machines.** Employees can unwittingly introduce viruses, phishing schemes, and other cyber "bugs."

- **Don't store your music library and photos on a company machine (or server), and don't watch streaming videos.** Capturing precious company bandwidth for personal use is a sure way to be shown the door.

- **Don't share files and avoid file-sharing services.** At work, clarify whether you may use Google Docs and other services that offer optional file sharing. As with any free cloud-based application, exercise caution. Security breaches are always possible. Stay away from LimeWire, and other distributors of pirated files. File-sharing services and downloads can subject you to breaches by third parties.

Summary of Learning Objectives

1 **Describe the role digital media play in the changing world of business in contrast to traditional paper-based messages.** The exchange of information in organizations today is increasingly electronic and mobile, although office workers still send paper-based messages when they need a permanent record, want to maintain confidentiality, or need to convey formal, long, and important messages. E-mail is still the lifeblood of businesses today, but instant messaging is gaining popularity. Likewise, phone-based SMS services enable cellular customers to send each other short text messages, images, and videos. Businesses have embraced podcasts, blogs, wikis, and social networking to help them communicate with employees, customers, and clients. The use of all digital media requires professionalism and caution because it creates permanent records.

2 **Meet professional e-mail standards for usage, structure, and format, and follow the rules of 'netiquette' and other best practices.** Direct (nonsensitive) e-mails begin with a subject line that summarizes the central idea. The opening repeats that idea and amplifies it. The body explains and provides more information. The closing includes (a) action information, dates, and deadlines; (b) a summary; or (c) a closing thought. E-mail messages should be formatted with a meaningful subject line, a greeting, a single-spaced body that is typed with a combination of upper-case and lowercase letters, and a closing "signature" that includes contact information. Careful e-mail users write concisely and don't send anything they wouldn't want published. They care about correctness, resist humour, never send spam, use identifying labels when appropriate, and use attachments sparingly. They don't access company computers for personal use unless specifically allowed to do so, and they realize that e-mail may be monitored. They strive to improve readability through design and consider cultural differences.

3 **Explain how business professionals communicate by instant messaging and texting.** Both instant messaging (IM) and text messaging have become increasingly relevant for business in communicating with customers, employees, and suppliers. IM participants must share the same software to conduct private chats in real time. Texting generally requires a smartphone-delivered SMS service from a wireless company. Text and IM messages can be delivered by a computer or a handheld device. To keep IM and texts professional, know your company's policies, separate personal from business contacts, stay away from personal messaging at work, make yourself unavailable when you need to concentrate, wait until receiving a reply before shooting off multiple messages, avoid sending confidential information, and use correct grammar and spelling.

4 **Identify professional uses of podcasts, blogs, and wikis, and describe prudent policies to protect authors of electronic content.** Business podcasts are digital audio or video files ranging from short clips to long media files. Any applications that do not require a human presence (e.g., certain training videos) lend themselves to podcast recordings that users can stream or download on demand. Creating simple podcasts requires only inexpensive or free recording software and low-cost equipment. Blogs help businesses to keep customers, employees, and suppliers informed and receive feedback. Online communities can form around a blog. Companies employ blogs for public relations and crisis communication, market research and viral marketing, internal communication, and recruiting. Before blogging, seek permission and know company policies. Avoid sensitive or inappropriate topics. Wikis enable far-flung team members to share information and build a knowledge base, and can be used to replace meetings, manage projects, and document projects large and small. When contributing to a wiki, don't post irrelevant or annoying content, check your facts and your grammar, follow guidelines for contributors, and give credit where appropriate.

5 **Understand business uses of social and professional networking sites, as well as RSS feeds and social bookmarking.** Facebook and Twitter allow firms to share company news; exchange ideas; and connect with customers, employees, other stakeholders, and the public at large. Tech companies in particular harness the power of

NEL

social networking for teamwork and brainstorming. Other companies boost their brand recognition and provide a forum for collaboration by participating in established social networks or by creating their own in-house communities. The downsides of social media participation are productivity losses, fallout from inappropriate employee posts, leaking of trade secrets, and angry Internet users. Keep safe by sharing only information that you would openly discuss in the office. Be sure to activate your privacy options. Don't post questionable photographs. Professional networking sites, such as LinkedIn, help companies and job seekers to connect. The virtual network is a logical extension of face-to-face networking, and members need to conduct themselves professionally in both. Really Simple Syndication (RSS) and social bookmarking allow users to navigate the huge resources on the Internet. RSS feeds are time-savers because they allow businesspeople to monitor many news sources in one convenient online location. Social bookmarking sites, such as Digg, Del.icio.us, and Reddit, can help you search, organize, share, and store bookmarks on the Web.

Chapter Review

1. What is Web 2.0, and how has it changed the way users engage with information? (Obj. 1)

2. Name and describe the two prevailing technological trends today. (Obj. 1)

3. List and concisely describe at least six electronic communication channels used most commonly by businesspeople today. (Obj. 1)

4. List and briefly describe the four parts of typical e-mails. (Obj. 2)

5. Suggest ten pointers that you could give to a first-time e-mail user. (Obj. 2)

6. How can you use instant messaging and texting safely on the job? (Obj. 3)

7. Name five reasons some organizations forbid employees to use instant and text messaging. (Obj. 3)

8. How can you show professionalism and respect for your receivers in writing business IM messages and texts? (Obj. 3)

9. Describe the process of creating a simple podcast. (Obj. 4)

10. Explain why companies use blogs. (Obj. 4)

11. What is a wiki, and what are its advantages to businesses? (Obj. 4)

12. Name a few of the potential risks that social networking sites may pose to business. (Obj. 5)

13. What do employment and hiring experts recommend to young job seekers who want to connect with companies on LinkedIn and other professional networking sites? (Obj. 5)

14. What is Really Simple Syndication (RSS), and why is it helpful? (Obj. 5)

15. Explain the role of social bookmarking sites, such as Digg, Del.icio.us, Reddit, StumbleUpon, and Squidoo. (Obj. 5)

Critical Thinking

1. How could IM be useful in your career field? Does IM produce a permanent record? Do you think that common abbreviations, such as *lol* and *imho,* and all-lowercase writing are acceptable in text messages for business? Will the use of shorthand abbreviations and creative spelling negatively affect writing skills? (Obj. 3)

2. Tweeting, texting, and quick e-mailing all may foster sloppy messages. Author Mark Garvey argues, "In business, in education, in the arts, in any writing that takes place outside the linguistic cul-de-sac of our close friends and relatives, writers are expected to reach for certain standards of clarity, concision and care."[28] What does Garvey mean? Do you agree? (Objs. 2, 3)

3. Why are lawyers and technology experts warning companies to store, organize, and manage computer data, including e-mails and instant messages, with sharper diligence? (Obj. 2)

4. Discuss the ramifications of the following statement: *Once an e-mail, instant message, text, or any other document leaves your hands, you have essentially published it.* (Obj. 2)

5. **Ethical Issue:** What Internet behaviour could get employees fired? Do employees deserve broad Internet access on the job—if they are responsible? Should employers block access to Web sites? If so, what kind? (Objs. 2, 3, 4, and 5)

Activities

Note: All Documents for Analysis may be downloaded from **www.guffeybrief4e.nelson.com** so that you do not have to rekey the entire message.

7.1 Document for Analysis: Jumbled E-Mail Message (Obj. 2)

Your Task. Analyze the following poorly written e-mail. List its weaknesses. Consider redundancies, wordiness, poor organization, weak subject line, and lack of contact information. If your instructor directs, revise it.

> To: Greta Targa<greta.targa@gamma.com>
> From: Jim Morales<jim.morales@gamma.com>
> Subject: HELP!
> Cc:
> Bcc:

As you already know, we have been working hard to plan the Gamma Fall Training Conference. It will be held in Mississauga. Here are the speakers I have lined up for training sessions. I'm thinking that on Tuesday, November 12, we will have Nicole Gold. Her scheduled topic is "Using E-Mail and IM Effectively." Anthony Mills said he could speak to our group on November 13 (Wednesday). "Leading Groups and Teams" is the topic for Mills. Here are their e-mail addresses: tony.mills@sunbelt.net. and n.gold@etc.com.

You can help us make this one of the best training sessions ever. I need you to send each of these people an e-mail and confirm the dates and topics. Because of the fact that we must print the program soon (by September 1), I will need this done as soon as possible. Don't hesitate to call if you have any questions.

Jim

7.2 Document for Analysis: Poorly Organized E-Mail (Obj. 2)

Your Task. Analyze the following poorly written and poorly organized e-mail. List its specific weaknesses. Would bulleted headings improve readability? If your instructor directs, revise it.

> To: Mitchell Moraga<mitchell.moraga@media.com>
> From: Eleanor Hutchinson<ehutchinson@media.com>
> Subject: My Report
> Cc:
> Bcc:

Mitchell,

This is in response to your request that I attend the Workplace Issues and tell you about it. As you know, I attended the Workplace Issues conference on November 3, as you suggested. The topic was how to prevent workplace violence, and I found it very fascinating. Although we have been fortunate to avoid serious incidents at our company, it's better to be safe than sorry. Because I was the representative from our company and you asked for a report, here it is. Kit Adkins was the presenter, and she made suggestions in three categories, which I will summarize here.

Ms. Atkins cautioned organizations to prescreen job applicants. As a matter of fact, wise companies do not offer employment until after a candidate's background has been checked. Just the mention of a background check is enough to make some candidates withdraw. These candidates, of course, are the ones with something to hide.

A second suggestion was that companies should prepare a good employee handbook that outlines what employees should do when they suspect potential workplace violence. This handbook should include a way for informers to be anonymous.

A third recommendation had to do with recognizing red-flag behaviour. This involves having companies train managers to recognize signs of potential workplace violence. What are some of the red flags? One sign is an increasing number of arguments (most of them petty) with co-workers. Another sign is extreme changes in behaviour or statements indicating depression over family or financial problems. Another sign is bullying or harassing behaviour.

I think that the best recommendation is prescreening job candidates. This is because it is most feasible. If you want me to do more research on prescreening techniques, do not hesitate to let me know. Let me know by November 18 if you want me to make a report at our management meeting, which is scheduled for December 3.

Ellie

7.3 Document for Analysis: Instant Messaging at Local Auto Dealer (Obj. 3)

Read the following log of a live IM chat between a customer service representative and a visitor to a Markham car dealership's Web site.

Your Task. In class discuss how Alex could have made this interaction with a customer more effective. Is his IM chat with Mr. Rhee professional, polite, and respectful? If your instructor directs, rewrite Alex's responses to Mr. Rhee's queries.

Service rep: Hey, I'm Alex. How's it goin? Welcome to Harkin BMW of Markham!

Customer: ??

Service rep: Im supposed to provid live assistance. What can I do you for?

Customer: I want buy car.

Service rep: May I have your name fist?

Customer: Jin Bae Rhee

Service rep: Whoa! Is that a dude's name? Okay. What kind? New inventory or preowned?

Customer: BMW. 2013 model. for family, for business.

Service rep: New, then, huh? Where are you from?

Customer: What car you have?

Service rep: We got some that will knock your socks off.

Customer: I want green car, low mileage, less gasoline burn.

Service rep: My man, if you can't afford the gas on these puppies, you shouldn't buy a Beemer, you know what I mean? Or ya want green colour?

Customer: ?

Service rep: Okeydoke, we got a full lineup. Which series, 3, 5, 6, or 7? Or an X3 or X5? A Z4 convertible?

Customer: 760 sedan?

Service rep: Nope. We got just two 550i, one for $68,695 and one for 71,020

Customer: Eureopean delivery?

Service rep: Oh, I know zip about that. Let me find someone who does. Can I have your phone number and e-mail?

Customer: i prefer not get a phone call yet... but 299-484-9807 is phone numer and jrhee@techtrade.com email

Service rep: Awsome. Well give you a jingle back or shoot you an e-mail pronto! Bye.

7.4 Choosing a Holiday Plan (Obj. 2)

E-MAIL

In the past your company offered all employees 11 holidays, starting with New Year's Day in January and proceeding through Christmas Day the following December. Other companies offer similar holiday schedules. In addition, your company has given all employees one floating holiday. That day was determined by a company-wide vote. As a result, all employees had the same day off. Now, however, management is considering a new plan that involves a floating holiday that each employee may choose. Selections, however, would be subject to staffing needs within individual departments. If two people wanted the same day, the employee with the most seniority would have the day off.

Your Task. As a member of the Human Resources staff, write an e-mail to employees asking them to choose between continuing the current company-wide uniform floating holiday or instituting a new plan for an individual floating holiday. Be sure to establish an end date.

7.5 Reaching Consensus About Business Attire (Obj. 2)

E-MAIL

TEAM

Casual dress in professional offices has been coming under attack. Your boss, Michael Harding, received the e-mail shown in Figure 7.1. He thinks it would be a good assignment for his group of management trainees to help him respond to that message. He asks your team to research answers to the first five questions in CEO William Laughton's message. He doesn't expect you to answer the final question, but any information you can supply to the first questions would help him shape a response.

Schilling & Voigt is a public accounting firm with a staff of 120 CGAs, bookkeepers, managers, and support personnel. Located in downtown Victoria, B.C., the plush offices on Water Street overlook Waterfront Park and the ocean. The firm performs general accounting and audit services, as well as tax planning and preparation. Accountants visit clients in the field and also entertain them in the downtown office.

Your Task. Decide whether the entire team will research each question in Figure 7.1 or whether team members will be assigned certain questions. Collect information, discuss it, and reach consensus on what you will report to Mr. Harding. As a team write a concise one-page response. Your goal is to inform, not persuade. Remember that you represent management, not students or employees.

7.6 Twitter: Learning to Write Superefficient Tweets (Objs. 1, 4 and 5)

Twitter forces its users to practise extreme conciseness. Some music reviewers have risen to the challenge and reviewed whole albums in no more than 140 characters. National Public Radio put Stephen Thompson, one of its music editors, to the test. "I approach Twitter as a science," Thompson says.[29] He sees well-designed tweets as online equivalents of haiku, a highly structured type of Japanese poetry. Thompson believes that tweets should be properly punctuated, be written in complete sentences, and of course, not exceed the 140-character limit. His rules also exclude abbreviations.

Here are two samples of Thompson's mini reviews: "Mos Def is a hip-hop renaissance man on smart songs that look to the whole world and its conflicts. Slick Rick's guest spot is a nice touch." The second one reads: "The Phenomenal Handclap Band: Chugging, timeless, jammy throwback from eight shaggy Brooklyn hipsters. Starts slowly, gets hypnotically fun."[30]

Your Task. As an intern in Stephen Thompson's office, review your favourite album in 140 characters or fewer, following your boss's rules. After you have warmed up, your instructor may direct you to other concise writing tasks. Send a tweet to your instructor, if appropriate, or practise writing Twitter posts in MS Word. The best tweets could be shared with the class.

7.7 Podcast, Twitter, Texting: Analyzing a Podcast (Obj. 4)

E-MAIL

Browsing the podcasts at iTunes, you stumble across the Quick and Dirty Tips series, specifically Money Girl, who dispenses financial advice. You sign up for the free podcasts that cover a variety of business topics. You also visit the Web site at **www.quickanddirtytips.com.**

Your Task. Pick a QDNow.com podcast that interests you. Listen to it or obtain a transcript on the Web site and study it for its structure. Is it direct or indirect? Informative or persuasive? At your instructor's request, write an e-mail that discusses the podcast you analyzed. Alternatively, if your instructor allows, you could also send a very concise summary of the podcast by text message from your cellphone or an ultrashort tweet (140 characters or fewer) to your instructor.

7.8 Creating a Twitter Group (Obj. 4)

WEB

Tweetworks.com is designed to make microblogging useful for private individuals and businesses. The site is based on the premise that people like to talk with other like-minded people. Users come together in communities around specific topics (politics, sports, art, business, and so on). Tweetworks invites members to talk about the big news stories of the day, bounce ideas off other participants online, or just join the conversation—all in fewer than 140 characters. Your instructor may choose to create a public or private group for the class. Within this Tweetworks group for your course, you may be asked to complete short assignments in the form of tweets. Posts in a private group are not shared with other general users, yet they should be relevant to the class content and professional.

Your Task. Use your Twitter username and password to log on at **www.tweetworks.com/groups.** Sign into and follow the group designated by your instructor. Your instructor may ask you to comment on a topic he or she assigns or may encourage you to enter into a freewheeling discussion with other members of your class online. Your instructor may act as a group moderator evaluating the frequency and quality of your contributions.

7.9 Social Networking: Building an Online Community on Facebook (Obj. 5)

WEB

TEAM

Chances are you already have a Facebook profile and communicate with friends and family. You may be a fan of a celebrity or a business. Now you can also become a fan of your business communication class if your instructor decides to create a course page on Facebook. The main purpose of such a social networking site for a class is to exchange links and interesting stories relevant to the material being learned. Intriguing tidbits and business news might also be posted on the wall to be shared by all signed-up fans. Everybody, even students who are quiet in class, could contribute. However, before you can become a fan of your business communication class, it needs to be created online.

Your Task. If you posted a profile on Facebook, all you need to do is search for the title of the newly created business communication Facebook page and become a fan. If you don't have an account yet, begin by signing up at **www.facebook.com**. On-screen prompts will make it easy for you to build a profile.

7.10 Social Networking: Preparing a Professional LinkedIn Profile (Obj. 5)

TEAM

Virtual networking on a professional networking site, such as LinkedIn, is an extension of seeking face-to-face contacts—the most effective way to find a job to date. Consider creating a credible, appealing presence on LinkedIn to make yourself attractive to potential business connections and hiring managers. Your LinkedIn site should serve purely to build your career and professional reputation.

Your Task. Go to **www.linkedin.com** and sign up for a free account. Follow the on-screen directions to create a profile, add a professional-looking photograph, and upload a polished résumé. You will be prompted to invite contacts from your e-mail address books. If your instructor directs, form teams and critique each other's profiles. Link to those profiles of your peers that have been prepared most diligently and strike you as having the best eye appeal.

Grammar and Mechanics C.L.U.E. Review 7

Apostrophes and Other Punctuation

Review Guides 31–38 about apostrophes and other punctuation in Appendix A, Grammar and Mechanics Guide, beginning on page A-14. On a separate sheet or on your computer, revise the following sentences to correct errors in the use of apostrophes and other punctuation. For each error that you locate, write the guide number that reflects this usage. The more you recognize the reasons, the better you will learn these punctuation guidelines. If a sentence is correct, write *C*. When you finish, check your answers on page Key-2.

Example: We needed the boss signature before we could mail the report.

Revision: We needed the **boss's** signature before we could mail the report. [Guide 32]

1. Facebook users accounts will be suspended if the members don't abide by the sites policies.

2. James performance review was outstanding again.

3. Would you please give me directions to your downtown headquarters

4. The shipping supervisor resented Barbara being late almost every morning.

5. Is it true that the CEO decided to write a weekly blog

6. You must replace the ink cartridge see page 8 in the manual, before printing.

7. Justin wondered whether all sales managers databases needed to be updated.

8. (Direct quotation) Health care costs said the CEO will increase substantially this year.

9. In just two months time, we expect to interview five candidates for the opening.

10. The meeting starts at 10 a.m. sharp, doesn't it

Endnotes

[1] Internet 2010 in numbers. (2011). Retrieved March 16, 2011, from http://royal.pingdom.com/2011/01/12/internet-2010-in-numbers

[2] Gallon, A. (2011, March 21). How can cloud computing help reduce IT costs? *Business Review Canada*. Retrieved April 23, 2011 from http:// www.businessreviewcanada.ca/sectors/data-centers/how-can-cloud-computing-help-reduce-it-costs

[3] Smith, R. (2011, February 1). IBM Compute Cloud Centre storms into Canada, *Business Review Canada*. Retrieved April 23, 2011 from http://www.businessreviewcanada.ca/sectors/data-centers/ibm-compute-cloud-centre-storms-canada

[4] Sandberg, J. (2006, September 26). Employees forsake dreaded email for the beloved phone. *The Wall Street Journal*, p. B1.

[5] Wikipedia. (2009, October 24). *Wikipedia, the free encyclopedia*. Retrieved February 24, 2010, from http://en.wikipedia.org/wiki/Wikipedia

[6] Tschabitscher, H. (2009). How many emails are sent every day? *About.com: Email*. Retrieved January 29, 2010, from http://email.about.com/od/emailtrivia/f/emails_per_day.htm

7 Maney, K. (2003, July 24). How the big names tame e-mail. *USA Today*, p. 2A.

8 Goldsmith, M. (2007, May 16). Understanding the perils of e-mail. *BusinessWeek*. Retrieved January 20, 2010, from http://www.businessweek.com/careers/content/may2007/ca20070516_392697.htm?chan=rss_topEmailedStories_ssi_5

9 Sanati, C. (2008, June 20). Dealbook extra: E-crimination. *The New York Times*, p. C6. Retrieved January 29, 2010, from LexisNexis Academic database; Goldsmith, M. (2007, May 17). Understanding the perils of e-mail. *BusinessWeek Online*, p. 31. Retrieved January 19, 2010, from Academic Search Premier database.

10 Living the fast, young life in Asia. (2008, April). *Change Agent*. Retrieved January 24, 2010, from http://www.synovate.com/changeagent/index.php/site/full_story/living_the_fast_living_young_in_asia/

11 Beutler, W. (2007, April 10). Yes, but how many blogs are there really? *Blog, P. I.* Retrieved January 6, 2010, from http://www.blogpi.net/yes-but-how-many-blogs-are-there-really

12 Ibid.

13 Deloitte Development. (2008). Reality check: State of the media democracy survey. Retrieved January 3, 2010, from http://www.deloitte.com/us/realitycheck

14 Baker, S., & Green, H. (2008, June 2). Beyond blogs: What business needs to know. *BusinessWeek Online*. Retrieved January 6, 2010, from http://www.businessweek.com/magazine/content/08_22/b4086044617865.htm?chan=search

15 Taking cues from Facebook. (2009, March 31a). *About McDonald's*. Retrieved January 14, 2010, from http://www.aboutmcdonalds.com/mcd/students/did_you_know/taking_cues_from_facebook.html

16 Conlin, M., & MacMillan, D. (2009, June 1). Managing the tweets. *BusinessWeek*, p. 21.

17 Baker, S., & Green, H. (2008, June 2). Beyond blogs. *BusinessWeek*, pp. 46, 48.

18 Conlin, M., & MacMillan, D. (2009, June 1). Managing the tweets. *BusinessWeek*, p. 20.

19 Ibid., pp. 20–21.

20 Ibid.

21 Villano, M. (2009, April 26). The online divide between work and play. *The New York Times*. Retrieved February 14, 2010, from http://www.nytimes.com

22 Ibid.

23 Ibid.

24 Ibid.

25 Klein, K. E. (2009, December 1). Putting a fair Internet use policy in place. *BusinessWeek.com*. Retrieved January 28, 2010, from http://www.businessweek.com/smallbiz/content/dec2009/sb2009121_245449.htm

26 Zetter, K. (2006, October). Employers crack down on personal net use: Misusing e-mail or browsing the wrong sites can cost you your job. *PC World*, p. 26. Retrieved January 28, 2010, from Factiva database.

27 Breaton, S. (2007, January/February). Blogging: Priceless? *CA Magazine*, p. 13. Retrieved January 28, 2010, from Business Source Premier (EBSCO) database.

28 Garvey, M. (2009, October 31). Fifth years of simplicity as style. *The Wall Street Journal*, p. A19.

29 Greene, D. (Host). (2009, July 2). Twitter music reviews: Criticism as haiku. *Morning Edition*. Washington, DC: National Public Radio. Retrieved January 31, 2010, from http://www.npr.org/templates/story/story.php?storyId=106178234

30 Ibid.

CHAPTER 8

Positive Messages

OBJECTIVES

After studying this chapter, you should be able to

1. Apply the 3-x-3 writing process to creating successful positive messages, including e-mails, interoffice memos, and business letters.

2. Understand the appropriate use of e-mails, interoffice memos, and business letters.

3. Compose direct messages that make requests and respond to inquiries.

4. Write messages that clearly explain step-by-step instructions.

5. Prepare messages that make direct claims.

6. Create adjustment messages that regain the confidence of customers and promote further business.

7. Write special messages that convey kindness and goodwill.

Yuri Arcurs/Shutterstock

springboard to discussion

Successful Positive Messages Start With the Writing Process

Business and professional organizations thrive on information that is exchanged externally and internally. In most organizations, external messages go to customers, vendors, other businesses, and the government. Internal messages travel upward to superiors, downward to employees, and horizontally among workers. Most of those messages are positive, straightforward communications that conduct everyday business and convey goodwill.

In this book we divide business messages into three content areas: (1) *positive* messages communicating straightforward requests, replies, and goodwill, covered in this chapter; (2) *negative* messages delivering refusals and bad news, covered in Chapter 9; and (3) *persuasive* messages, including sales pitches, covered in Chapter 10. Most of these business messages are exchanged in the form of e-mails, memos, or letters. As you study how to prepare positive, negative, and persuasive messages, you will also be learning which channel is appropriate for the message and situation you face. Should you send an e-mail or a memo? If the message is going outside the organization, should it be a letter?

This chapter focuses on routine, positive messages. These will make up the bulk of your messages. Although such messages may be short and straightforward, they benefit from attention to the composition process. Taking the time to think through what you want to achieve and how the audience will react makes writing much easier.[3] Here is a quick review of the 3-×-3 writing process to help you think through its application to positive messages.

Phase I: Analysis, Anticipation, and Adaptation

In Phase I, prewriting, you will need to spend a few moments analyzing your task. Too often, people start a message without enough preparation. Veteran message writers understand the problem. They know that if they're having problems writing a message it's usually because they haven't thought carefully about what they want to say.

In the letter shown in Figure 8.1, the writer responds to a request from a potential customer asking about special rates for seniors. Before writing the letter, the writer considered the receiver and tried to find a way to personalize what could have been a form letter. Although the writer could have simply referred the reader to the company's Web site, she chose to provide the information in writing.

As you prepare a message, ask yourself these important questions:

- **Do I really need to write this e-mail, memo, or letter?** A phone call or a quick visit to a nearby co-worker might solve the problem—and save the time and expense of a written message. Conversely, some written messages are needed to provide a permanent record or to show a well-conceived plan.

- **Why am I writing?** Know why you are writing and what you hope to achieve. This will help you recognize what the important points are and where to place them.

- **How will the reader react?** Visualize the reader and the effect your message will have. In preparing written messages, imagine that you are sitting and talking with

LEARNING OBJECTIVE 1

Apply the 3-x-3 writing process to creating successful positive messages, including e-mails, interoffice memos, and business letters.

> Before beginning a message, ask yourself why you are writing and how the reader will react.

FIGURE 8.1 VIA Rail's Response to Customer Inquiry

1 Prewriting

Analyze: The purpose of this letter is to build goodwill and promote VIA Rail services.
Anticipate: The reader is mature, interested in travelling, and eager to hear from VIA Rail. She will appreciate personalized comments.
Adapt: Use short sentences, positive and respectful thoughts, and plenty of references to the reader's interests in train travel and visiting family.

2 Writing

Research: Reread the customer's letter. Decide what information to include.
Organize: Open directly with a positive response. Refer to your Web site. Find ways to make the reader feel a special connection with Via Rail.
Compose: Write the first draft quickly. Realize that revision will improve it.

3 Revising

Revise: Revise the message, striving for a warm tone. Use the receiver's name. Edit long paragraphs and add bulleted items.
Proofread: Check the address of the receiver. Decide how to cite information from your Web site and how to punctuate quotations.
Evaluate: Consider how you would feel if you received this letter.

January 18, 2014

Ms. Jennifer Ball
1401 Churchville Lane
Sarnia, ON N7T 7W6

Dear Ms. Ball:

We're delighted to hear of your interest in travelling by VIA Rail this summer and to send you the information you request. *(Opens directly with response to reader's request)*

A family wedding is always an exciting event, but expenses can certainly add up. One way that you can definitely control your costs is by booking your travel on VIA Rail. For example, right now you can travel from Windsor to Toronto for as little as $59 one-way, economy class. To book your trip, simply visit your local travel agent, call 1 888 VIA-RAIL (1 888 842-7245), or visit us online at www.viarail.ca. *(Personalizes reply and builds goodwill with reference to reader's request and upcoming travels)*

VIA Rail extends many exciting offers to our travellers who are 60 and over. We invite you to visit our Seniors VIA E-letter (available at www.viarail.ca/en/via-e-letters-offer-you/) to find out more about

- Ideas for Canadian destinations
- Useful travel tips
- Special offers
- Exclusive contests

(Itemizes and explains information available to reader)

In addition, Ms. Ball, we've enclosed the most recent issue of our VIA destinations magazine, which is published six times a year and will give you even more details about different Canadian destinations. *(Uses receiver's name to make letter sound conversational and personal)*

Enjoy your trip to Toronto for your grandson's wedding. We hope that you'll continue to choose VIA Rail for all your travel needs. *(Ties in cordial closing with more references to reader's future travel plans)*

Sincerely,

Francis Daly
Customer Service Representative
VIA Rail

Enclosure

---

your reader. Avoid speaking bluntly, failing to explain, or ignoring your reader's needs. Consider ways to shape the message to benefit the reader. Also remember that with e-mails, your message may very well be forwarded to someone else.

- **What channel should I use?** It's tempting to use e-mail for much of your correspondence. However, a phone call or face-to-face visit is a better channel choice if you need to (a) convey enthusiasm, warmth, or another emotion;

(b) supply a context; or (c) smooth over disagreements. A business letter is better when the matter requires (a) a permanent record, (b) confidentiality, or (c) formality.

- **How can I save my reader's time?** Think of ways that you can make your message easier to comprehend at a glance. Use bullets, lists, headings, and white space to improve readability. Notice in the letter in Figure 8.1 that the writer used bullets to highlight the enclosures.

Phase 2: Research, Organization, and Composition

In Phase 2, writing, you will first want to check the files, gather documentation, and prepare your message. Make a list of the points you want to cover. For short messages jot down notes on the document you are answering or make a scratch list at your computer.

For longer documents that require formal research, use a cluster diagram or the outlining techniques discussed in Chapter 5. As you compose your message, avoid amassing huge blocks of text. No one wants to read endless lines of type. Instead, group related information into paragraphs, preferably short ones. Paragraphs separated by white space look inviting. Be sure that each paragraph includes a topic sentence backed up by details and evidence. If you bury your main point in the middle of a paragraph, the reader may miss it. Also plan for revision, because excellence is rarely achieved on the first effort.

> **In Phase 2 of the writing process, gather information, make notes or prepare an outline, and compose the first draft.**

Phase 3: Revision, Proofreading, and Evaluation

Phase 3, revising, involves putting the final touches on your message. Careful and caring writers ask themselves the following questions:

- **Is the message clear?** Viewed from the receiver's perspective, are the ideas clear? Did you use plain language? If the message is passed on to others, will they need further explanation? Consider having a colleague critique your message if it is an important one.

- **Is the message correct?** Are the sentences complete and punctuated properly? Did you overlook any typos or misspelled words? Remember to use your spell checker and grammar checker to proofread your message before sending it.

- **Did I plan for feedback?** How will you know whether this message is successful? You can improve feedback by asking questions (such as, *Are you comfortable with these suggestions?* or, *What do you think?*). Remember to make it easy for the receiver to respond.

- **Will this message achieve its purpose?** The last step in the 3-×-3 writing process is evaluating the product. Before a message leaves your desk, ask yourself: "How would I feel if I were receiving it?"

Watching the Writing Process in Action

To see how the writing process can improve an internal message, look at Figure 8.2. It shows the first draft and revision of an e-mail that Jeff Fritsch, senior marketing manager, wrote to his boss, Sara Watts. Although it contained solid information, the first draft was so wordy and dense that the main points were lost.

In the revision stage, Jeff realized that he needed to reorganize his message into an opening, body, and closing. He desperately needed to improve the readability. In studying what he had written, he recognized that he was talking about two main problems. He discovered that he could present a three-part solution. These ideas didn't occur to him until he had written the first draft. Only in the revision stage was he able to see that he was talking about two separate problems and a three-part solution. The revision process can help you think through a problem and clarify a solution.

As he revised, Jeff was more aware of the subject line, opening, body, and closing. He used an informative subject line and opened directly by explaining why he was

FIGURE 8.2 Applying the Writing Process to an E-Mail

1 Prewriting

Analyze: The purpose of this memo is to describe database problems and recommend solutions.

Anticipate: The audience is the writer's boss, who is familiar with the topic and who appreciates brevity.

Adapt: Because the reader requested this message, the direct pattern is most appropriate.

2 Writing

Research: Gather data documenting the customer database and how to use Access software.

Organize: Announce recommendations and summarize problems. In the body, list the three actions for solving the problem. In the closing, describe reader benefits, provide a deadline, and specify the next action.

Compose: Prepare the first draft.

3 Revising

Revise: Highlight the two main problems and the three recommendations. Use asterisks, caps, and headings to improve readability. Make the bulleted ideas parallel.

Proofread: Double-check to see whether *database* is one word or two. Use spell checker.

Evaluate: Does this e-mail supply concise information the boss wants in an easy-to-read format?

DRAFT

To: Sara Watts <swatts@morris.com>
From: Jeff Fritsch <jfritsch@morris.com>
Subject: Problems

This is in response to your recent inquiry about our customer database. Your message of February 18 said that you wanted to know how to deal with the database problems.

I can tell you that the biggest problem is that it contains a lot of outdated information, including customers who haven't purchased anything in five or more years. Another problem is that the old database is not compatible with the new Access software that is being used by our mailing service, and this makes it difficult to merge files. I think I can solve both problems, however, by starting a new database. This would be the place where we put the names of all new customers. And we would have it keyed by using Access software. The problem with outdated information could be solved by finding out if the customers in our old database want to continue receiving our newsletter and product announcements. Finally, we would rekey the names of all active customers in the new database.

Jeff

Uses meaningless subject line
Fails to reveal purpose quickly
Buries two problems and three-part solution in huge paragraph
Forgets to conclude with next action and end date

REVISION

File Edit Mailbox Message Transfer Special Tools Window Help

B *I* U ... | Send

To: Sara Watts <swatts@morris.com>
From: Jeffrey Fritsch <jfritsch@morris.com>
Subject: Improving Our Customer Database

Sara,

As you requested, I am submitting my recommendations for improving our customer database. The database has two major problems. First, it contains many names of individuals who have not made purchases in five or more years. Second, the format is not compatible with the new Access software used by our mailing service.

The following three procedures, however, should solve both problems:

- **Start a new database.** Effective immediately enter the names of all new customers in a new database by using Access software.
- **Determine the status of customers in our old database.** Send out a mailing asking whether recipients want to continue receiving our newsletter and product announcements.
- **Rekey or scan the names of active customers.** Enter the names of all responding customers in our new database so that we have only one active database.

These changes will enable you, as team leader, to request mailings that go only to active customers. Please let me know by February 25 whether you think these recommendations are workable. If so, I will investigate costs.

All the best,

Jeff

Jeffrey Fritsch
Senior Technician
Information Technology
Mail: jfritsch@morris.com
Phone: (902) 480-3920
Fax: (902) 480-2981

Informative subject line summarizes purpose
Opening states purpose concisely and highlights two problems
Body organizes main points for readability
Closing includes key benefit, deadline, and next action
Signature block provides full contact information

writing. His opening outlined the two main problems so that his reader understood the background of the following recommendations. In the body of the message, Jeff identified three corrective actions, and he highlighted them for improved readability. Notice that he listed his three recommendations by using numbers with boldface headings, and he started each item with an action verb. Jeff closed his message with a deadline and a reference to the next action to be taken.

Positive Messages: E-Mails, Memos, and Letters

In the workplace positive messages may take the form of e-mails, memos, and letters. When you need information from a team member in another office, you might send an e-mail. If you must explain to employees a new procedure for ordering supplies, you would probably write an interoffice memo. When you respond to a customer asking about your products, you would most likely prepare a letter.

Comparing E-Mails and Memos

Most internal messages will be exchanged as e-mails or interoffice memos. E-mail is most appropriate for short messages, such as sharing "need to know" facts, setting up appointments, distributing documents, giving updates, requesting information, getting answers to specific questions, and documenting conversations when a paper trail is needed. You probably have already written many e-mails to your friends. However, professional e-mails sent on the job are quite different from notes to friends. The purpose of business e-mails is to get work done rather than interact socially with people.[4] In Chapter 7 you learned about formatting of e-mail, and you studied best practices for using e-mail effectively and safely in the workplace. In this chapter we discuss composing e-mails, interoffice memos, and business letters. You may be thinking, *What are memos? Haven't memos been eclipsed by e-mail?*

E-mail messages are most appropriate for short, work-related messages.

Although e-mail is very popular, printed hard-copy memos still serve vital functions in the workplace. They remain useful for important internal messages that require a permanent record or formality. For example, organizations use memos to deliver instructions, official policies, short reports, long internal documents, and important announcements. The formatting of memos makes them easy to read and understand, especially when compared with e-mails that have long threads of comments by many receivers. The sender and receiver of memos are always recognizable. The guide words in memos immediately tell you what you want to know—who wrote the message, who was the intended receiver, the date it was sent, and what it is about.

Printed hard-copy memos are useful for important internal messages that require a permanent record or formality.

Preparing Interoffice Memos

The formatting of interoffice memos has much in common with e-mails, which you studied in Chapter 7. Like e-mails, interoffice memos begin with guide words, such as *Date, To, From,* and *Subject.* Some organizations have preprinted memo letterhead paper with the name of the organization at the top. In addition to guide words, these forms may include other identifying headings, such as *File Number, Floor, Extension, Location,* and *Distribution.* Because of the difficulty of aligning computer printers with preprinted forms, business writers may use default templates available on their word processors (sometimes called *wizards*). Writers can customize these templates with their organization's name.

Interoffice memos begin with guide words, such as Date, To, From, and Subject.

If you are preparing a memo on plain paper, set 2.5 to 3.0 cm top, bottom, and side margins. Provide a heading that includes the name of the company and the word *Memo* or *Memorandum.* Begin the guide words a triple space (two blank lines) below the last line of the heading. Key in bold the guide words: Date:, To:, From:, and Subject: at the left margin. The guide words may appear in all caps or with only

FIGURE 8.3 Interoffice Memo That Responds to a Request

Aligns all heading words with those following SUBJECT

Leaves side margins of 3.2 cm

Omits a closing and signature

↓ 3.8 cm

MEMORANDUM

↓ 2 blank lines

DATE: November 11, 2014
↓ 1 blank line
TO: Stephanie Sato, President, Hollywood Audience Services
↓ 1 blank line
FROM: Sundance Richardson, Special Events Manager *SR*
↓ 1 blank line
SUBJECT: Improving Web Site Information

↓ 1 or 2 blank lines

In response to your request for ideas to improve our Web site, I am submitting the following suggestions. Because interest in our audience member, seat-filler, and usher services is growing constantly, we must use our Web site more strategically. Here are three suggestions.

First, our Web site should explain our purpose. We specialize in providing customized and responsive audiences for studio productions and award shows. The Web site should distinguish between audience members and seat-fillers. Audience members have a seat for the entire taping of a TV show. Seat-fillers sit in the empty seats of celebrity presenters or performers so that the front section does not look empty to the home audience.

Second, I suggest that our Web designer include a listing such as the following so that readers recognize the events and services we provide:

Event	Audience Members Provided Last Year	Seat-Fillers and Ushers Provided Last Year
Stratford	26	8
Shaw Festival	14	8
Juno Awards	15	11
Gemini Awards	16	8
Canadian Country Music Awards	29	10
Selected TV shows	285	28

Third, our Web site should provide answers to commonly asked questions, such as the following:

- Do audience members or seat-fillers have to pay to attend the event?
- How often do seat-fillers have to move around?
- Will seat-fillers be on television?

Our Web site can be more informative and boost our business if we implement some of these ideas. Are you free to talk about these suggestions at 10 a.m. on Monday, November 19?

Includes initials after printed name and title

Provides ragged line endings — not justified

Uses headings, columns, bold, and white space to highlight information

Tips for Formatting Hard-Copy Memos

- On plain paper, type MEMORANDUM 3.8 cm from the top. Leave two blank lines after this heading.
- Set one tab to align entries evenly after Subject.
- Leave one or two blank lines after the subject line.
- Single-space all but the shortest memos. Double-space between paragraphs.
- Use 3.2-cm side margins.
- For a two-page memo, use a second-page heading with the addressee's name, page number, and date.
- Handwrite your initials after your typed name.
- Place bulleted or numbered lists flush left or indent them 1.25 cm.

the initial letter capitalized. Triple-space (two blank lines) after the last line of the heading. Do not justify the right margins. As discussed in the document design section of Chapter 6, ragged-right margins in printed messages make them easier to read. Single-space the message, and double-space between paragraphs, as shown in Figure 8.3.

Preparing Memos as E-Mail Attachments

E-mail has become increasingly important for exchanging internal messages. However, it is inappropriate for long documents or for items that require formality or permanence. For such messages, writers may prepare the information in standard memo format and send it as an attachment to a cover e-mail.

In preparing e-mail attachments, be sure to include identifying information. Because the cover e-mail may become separated from the attachment, the attachment must be fully identified. Preparing the e-mail attachment as a memo provides a handy format that identifies the date, sender, receiver, and subject.

Understanding Business Letters

Thus far we have discussed positive messages that circulate inside an organization. Now let's talk about positive messages that are delivered outside an organization. One important channel for external communication is business letters. Even with the new media available today, a business letter remains one of the most powerful and effective ways to get your message across.

Knowing When to Send a Letter

You will know when to send a business letter by the situation and by the preference of your organization. Although you may be tempted to dash off an e-mail, think twice before descending into digital mode. This section discusses reasons business letters are still indispensable.

The situation and the preference of your organization will determine if a business letter should be sent.

Business letters are necessary when the situation calls for a permanent record. For example, when a company enters into an agreement with another company, business letters introduce the agreement and record decisions and points of understanding. Although telephone conversations and e-mails may be exchanged, important details are generally recorded in business letters that are kept in company files. Business letters deliver contracts, explain terms, exchange ideas, negotiate agreements, answer vendor questions, and maintain customer relations.

Business letters are confidential. Carefree use of e-mail was once a sign of sophistication. Today, however, communicators know how dangerous it is to entrust confidential and sensitive information to digital channels.

Business letters presented on company stationery carry a sense of formality and importance not possible with e-mail. They look important. They carry a nonverbal message that the writer considered the message so significant and the receiver so prestigious that the writer cared enough to write a real message. Business letters deliver more information than e-mail because they are written on stationery that usually is printed with company information, such as logos, addresses, titles, and contact details.

Finally, business letters deliver persuasive, well-considered messages. When a business communicator must be persuasive and can't do it in person, a business letter is more effective than other communication channels. Letters can persuade people to change their actions, adopt new beliefs, make donations, contribute their time, and try new products. Direct-mail letters remain a powerful tool to promote services and products, boost online and retail traffic, and solicit contributions. Business letters represent deliberate communication. They give you a chance to think through what you want to say, organize your thoughts, and write a well-considered argument. You will learn more about writing persuasive and sales messages in Chapter 10.

Using Correct Form in Business Letters

A business letter conveys silent messages beyond those contained in its printed words. The letter's appearance and format reflect the writer's carefulness and experience. A short letter bunched at the top of a sheet of paper, for example, looks as though it were prepared in a hurry or by an amateur.

A letter's appearance and format reflect the writer's carefulness and experience.

For your letters to make a good impression, you need to select an appropriate format. The block style shown in Figure 8.4 is a popular format. In this style the parts of a letter—dateline, inside address, body, and so on—are set flush left on the page. The

FIGURE 8.4 Formatting a Direct Request Business Letter in Block Style

Letterhead —————→ **CYPRESS ASSOCIATES, INC.**
9524 Stratham Drive
Edmonton, AB T6C 4E2

WEB: cypress@grid.com
PHONE: (403) 329-4330
FAX: (403) 329-4259

Dateline —————→ September 12, 2014

Inside address —————→ Ms. Bridget Rosales, Manager
Meeting and Events Department
The Venetian Resort Hotel Casino
3355 Las Vegas Boulevard South
Las Vegas, NV 89109

Salutation —————→ Dear Ms. Rosales:

Can The Venetian Resort Hotel Casino provide meeting rooms and accommodations for about 250 Paragon Enterprise Solutions sales representatives from
March 20 through March 24?

Your hotel received strong recommendations because of its excellent resort
and conference facilities. Our spring sales conference is scheduled for next
March, and I am collecting information for our planning committee. Please
answer these additional questions regarding The Venetian:

Body —————→
- Does the hotel have (a) a banquet room that can seat 250 plus (b) four smaller
  meeting rooms each to accommodate a maximum of 75?

- What computer facilities are available for electronic presentations?

- What is the nearest airport, and do you provide transportation to and from it?

- Do you have a special room rates for groups at that time of the year?

Answers to these questions and any other information you can provide will help
us decide which conference facility to choose. Your response before September 18
would be most appreciated since our planning committee meets September 25.

Complimentary
close —————→ Sincerely yours,

Richard M. Mahar

Author's name and
identification —————→ Richard M. Mahar, Associate
Corporate Travel Department

Reference initials —————→ RMM:gdr

Tips for Formatting Letters

- Start the date 5 cm from the top or 1 blank line below the
  letterhead.
- For block style, begin all lines at the left margin.
- Leave side margins of 2.5 to 4 cm depending on the length
  of the letter and the font size.
- Single-space the body and double-space between paragraphs.
- Use left, not right, justification.
- Place the title of the receiver wherever it best balances the
  inside address.
- Place the title of the author wherever it best balances the
  closing lines.

letter is arranged on the page so that it is centred and framed by white space. Most letters have margins of 2.5 to 4 cm.

In preparing business letters, be sure to use ragged-right margins; that is, don't allow
your computer to justify the right margin and make all lines end evenly. Unjustified
margins improve readability, say experts, by providing visual stops and by making it
easier to tell where the next line begins. Although book publishers use justified right
margins, as you see on this page, your letters should use ragged-right margins. Study
Figure 8.4 for more tips on making your letters look professional.

Routine Request and Response Messages

Most of your business messages will involve routine requests and responses to requests, which are organized directly. Requests and replies may take the form of e-mails, memos, or letters. You might, for example, need to request information from a hotel as you plan a company conference. You might be answering an inquiry from a customer about your services or products. These kinds of routine requests and replies follow a similar pattern.

LEARNING OBJECTIVE 3

Compose direct messages that make requests and respond to inquiries.

Creating Request Messages

When you write messages that request information or action and you think your request will be received positively, start with the main idea first. The most emphatic positions in a message are the opening and closing. Readers tend to look at them first. You should capitalize on this tendency by putting the most significant statement first. The first sentence of an information request is usually a question or a polite command. It should not be an explanation or justification, unless resistance to the request is expected. When the information or action requested is likely to be forthcoming, immediately tell the reader what you want.

A letter inquiring about hotel accommodations, shown in Figure 8.4, begins immediately with the most important idea: Can the hotel provide meeting rooms and accommodations for 250 people? Instead of opening with an explanation of who the writer is or why the writer happens to be writing this message, the letter begins directly.

If several questions must be asked, you have two choices. You can ask the most important question first, as shown in Figure 8.4, or you can begin with a summary statement, such as *Please answer the following questions about providing meeting rooms and accommodations for 250 people from March 20 through March 24.* Avoid beginning with *Will you please. . . .* Although such a statement sounds like a question, it is actually a disguised command. Because you expect an action rather than a reply, you should punctuate this polite command with a period instead of a question mark. To avoid having to choose between a period and a question mark, just omit *Will you* and start with *Please answer.*

Providing Details. The body of a message that requests information or action provides necessary details. Remember that the quality of the information obtained from a request depends on the clarity of the inquiry. If you analyze your needs, organize your ideas, and frame your request logically, you are likely to receive a meaningful answer that doesn't require a follow-up message. Whenever possible, focus on benefits to the reader (*To ensure that you receive the exact sweater you want, send us your colour choice*). To improve readability, itemize appropriate information in bulleted or numbered lists. Notice that the questions in Figure 8.4 are bulleted, and they are parallel. That is, they use the same balanced construction.

> Wherever possible, focus on reader benefits.

Closing With Appreciation and an Action Request. In the closing, tell the reader courteously what is to be done. If a date is important, set an end date to take action and explain why. Some careless writers end request messages simply with *Thank you*, forcing the reader to review the contents to determine what is expected and when. You can save the reader time by spelling out the action to be taken. Avoid other overused endings such as *Thank you for your cooperation* (trite), *Thank you in advance for . . .* (trite and presumptuous), and *If you have any questions, do not hesitate to call me* (suggests that you didn't make yourself clear).

Showing appreciation is always appropriate, but try to do so in a fresh and efficient manner. For example, you could hook your thanks to the end date (*Thanks for returning the questionnaire before May 5, when we will begin tabulation*). You might connect your appreciation to a statement developing reader benefits (*We are grateful for the information you will provide because it will help us serve you better*). You could briefly describe how the information will help you (*I appreciate this information, which will enable me to ...*). When possible, make it easy for the reader to comply with your request (*Note your answers on this sheet and return it in the postage-paid envelope* or *Here is my e-mail address so that you can reach me quickly*).

> Show your appreciation in a fresh and efficient manner by hooking your thanks to the end date.

Responding to Requests

Often, your messages will respond directly and favourably to requests for information or action. A customer wants information about a product, a supplier asks to arrange a meeting, an employee inquires about a procedure, or a manager requests your input on a marketing campaign. In complying with such requests, you will want to apply the same direct strategy you used in making requests.

The opening of a customer response letter might contain an optional subject line, as shown in Figure 8.5. A subject line helps the reader recognize the topic immediately. Usually appearing two lines below the salutation, the subject line refers in abbreviated form to previous correspondence or summarizes the message (*Subject: Your July 12 Inquiry About WorkZone Software*). Knowledgeable business communicators use a subject line to refer to earlier correspondence so that in the first sentence, the most emphatic spot in a letter, they are free to emphasize the main idea.

In the first sentence of a direct response letter, deliver the information the reader wants. Avoid wordy, drawn-out openings, such as *I have before me your letter of August 5, in which you request information about. . . .* More forceful and more efficient is an opener that answers the inquiry (*Here is the information you wanted about . . .*). When agreeing to a request for action, announce the good news promptly (*Yes, I will be happy to speak to your business communication class on the topic of . . .*).

In the body of your response, supply explanations and additional information. Because a letter written on company stationery is considered a legally binding contract, be sure to check facts and figures carefully. If a policy or procedure needs authorization, seek approval from a supervisor or executive before writing the letter.

When customers or prospective customers inquire about products or services, your response should do more than merely supply answers. Try to promote your organization and products. Be sure to present the promotional material with attention to the "you" view and to reader benefits (*You can use our standardized tests to free you from time-consuming employment screening*).

In concluding a response message, refer to the information provided or to its use. (*The enclosed list summarizes our recommendations. We wish you all the best in redesigning your Web site.*) If further action is required, describe the procedure and help the reader with specifics (*The Small Business Administration publishes a number of helpful booklets. Its Web address is . . .*). Avoid signing off with clichés (*If I may be of further assistance, don't hesitate to . . .*).

The Checklist box reviews the direct strategy for information or action requests and replies to such messages.

An optional subject line can help the reader recognize the topic immediately.

Try to promote your organization and products while answering the customer's request.

Checklist

Writing Direct Requests and Reponses

Requesting Information or Action

- **Open by stating the main idea.** To elicit information, ask a question or issue a polite command (*Please answer the following questions . . .*).

- **Explain and justify the request.** In the body arrange questions or information logically in parallel, balanced form. Clarify and substantiate your request.

- **Request action in the closing.** Close a request by summarizing exactly what is to be done, including dates or deadlines. Express appreciation. Avoid clichés (*Thank you for your cooperation, Thanking you in advance*).

Responding to Requests

- **Open directly.** Immediately deliver the information the receiver wants. Avoid wordy, drawn-out openings (*I have before me your request of August 5*). When agreeing to a request, announce the good news immediately.

- **Supply additional information.** In the body, provide explanations and expand initial statements. For customer letters, promote products and the organization.

- **Conclude with a cordial statement.** Refer to the information provided or its use. If further action is required, describe the procedures and give specifics. Avoid clichés (*If you have questions, please do not hesitate to let me know*).

FIGURE 8.5 Customer Response Letter

1 Prewriting

Analyze: The purpose of this letter is to provide helpful information and to promote company products.

Anticipate: The reader is the intelligent owner of a small business who needs help with personnel administration.

Adapt: Because the reader requested this data, he will be receptive to the letter. Use the direct pattern.

2 Writing

Research: Gather facts to answer the business owner's questions. Consult brochures and pamphlets.

Organize: Prepare a scratch outline. Plan for a fast, direct opening. Use numbered answers to the business owner's three questions.

Compose: Write the first draft on a computer. Strive for short sentences and paragraphs.

3 Revising

Revise: Eliminate jargon and wordiness. Look for ways to explain how the product fits the reader's needs. Revise for "you" view.

Proofread: Double-check the form of numbers (*July 12, page 6, 8 to 5 PST*).

Evaluate: Does this letter answer the customer's questions and encourage an order?

KELOWNA SOFTWARE, INC.

777 Raymer Road
Kelowna, BC V1W 1H7
(250) 784-2219
www.kelownasoft.com

July 16, 2014

Mr. Jeffrey M. White
Director, Human Resources
White-Rather Enterprises
220 Telford Court
Leduc, AB T9E 5M6

Dear Mr. White:

Subject: Your July 12 Inquiry About WorkZone Software

Yes, we do offer personnel record-keeping software specially designed for small businesses like yours. Here are answers to your three questions about this software:

1. Our WorkZone software provides standard employee forms so that you are always in compliance with current government regulations.

2. You receive an interviewer's guide for structured employee interviews, as well as a scripted format for checking references by telephone.

3. Yes, you can update your employees' records easily without the need for additional software, hardware, or training.

Our WorkZone software was specially designed to provide you with expert forms for interviewing, verifying references, recording attendance, evaluating performance, and tracking the status of your employees. We even provide you with step-by-step instructions and suggested procedures. You can treat your employees as if you had a professional human resources specialist on your staff.

On page 6 of the enclosed pamphlet, you can read about our WorkZone software. To receive a preview copy or to ask questions about its use, just call 1-800-354-5500. Our specialists are eager to help you weekdays from 8 to 5, PST. If you prefer, visit our Web site to receive more information or to place an order.

Sincerely,

Linda DeLorme

Linda DeLorme
Senior Marketing Representative

Enclosure

Annotations (left):
- Puts most important information first
- Lists answers to sender's questions in order asked
- Helps reader find information by citing pages

Annotations (right):
- Identifies previous correspondence and subject
- Emphasizes "you" view
- Links sales promotion to reader benefits
- Makes it easy to respond

Instruction Messages

LEARNING OBJECTIVE

Write messages that clearly explain step-by-step instructions.

Instruction messages describe how to complete a task. You may be asked to write instructions about how to repair a paper jam in the photocopier, order supplies, file a grievance, or hire new employees. Instructions are different from policies and official procedures, which establish rules of conduct to be followed within an organization. We are most concerned with creating messages that clearly explain how to complete a task.

Like requests and responses, instruction messages follow a straightforward, direct approach. Before writing instructions for a process, be sure you understand the process completely. Practise doing it yourself. A message that delivers instructions should open with an explanation of why the procedure or set of instructions is necessary.

Dividing Instructions Into Steps

> When writing instructions, use plain language and familiar words to describe the process.

The body of an instruction message should use plain language and familiar words to describe the process. Your messages explaining instructions will be most readable if you follow these guidelines:

- Divide the instructions into steps.

- List the steps in the order in which they are to be carried out.

- Arrange the items vertically with bullets or numbers.

- Begin each step with an action verb using the imperative (command) mood rather than the indicative mood.

Indicative Mood	Imperative Mood
The contract should be sent immediately.	Send the contract immediately.
The first step involves loading the software.	Load the software first.
A survey of employees is necessary to learn what options they prefer.	Survey employees to learn the options they prefer.

In the closing of a message issuing instructions, consider connecting following the instructions with benefits to the organization or individual.

If you are asked to prepare a list of instructions that is not part of a message, include a title such as *How to Clear Paper Jams*. Include an opening paragraph explaining why the instructions are needed.

Revising a Message Delivering Instructions

Figure 8.6 shows the first draft of an interoffice memo written by Troy Bell. His memo was meant to announce a new method for employees to follow in advertising open positions. However, the tone was negative, the explanation of the problem rambled, and the new method was unclear. Notice, too, that Troy's first draft told readers what they *shouldn't* do (*Do not submit advertisements for new employees directly to an Internet job bank or a newspaper*). It is more helpful to tell readers what they *should* do. Finally, Troy's first memo closed with a threat instead of showing readers how this new practice will help them.

In the revision Troy improved the tone considerably. The subject line contains a *please*, which is always pleasant to see even if the writer is giving an order. The subject line also includes a verb and specifies the purpose of the memo. Instead of expressing his ideas with negative words and threats, Troy revised his message to explain objectively and concisely what went wrong.

> Numbered steps and action verbs improve the clarity of instructions.

Troy realized that his original explanation of the new procedure was vague and unclear. To clarify the instructions, he itemized and numbered the steps. Each step begins with an action verb in the imperative (command) mood (*Write, Bring, Let,* and *Pick up*). It is sometimes difficult to force all the steps in a list into this kind of command

FIGURE 8.6 Interoffice Memo Delivering Instructions

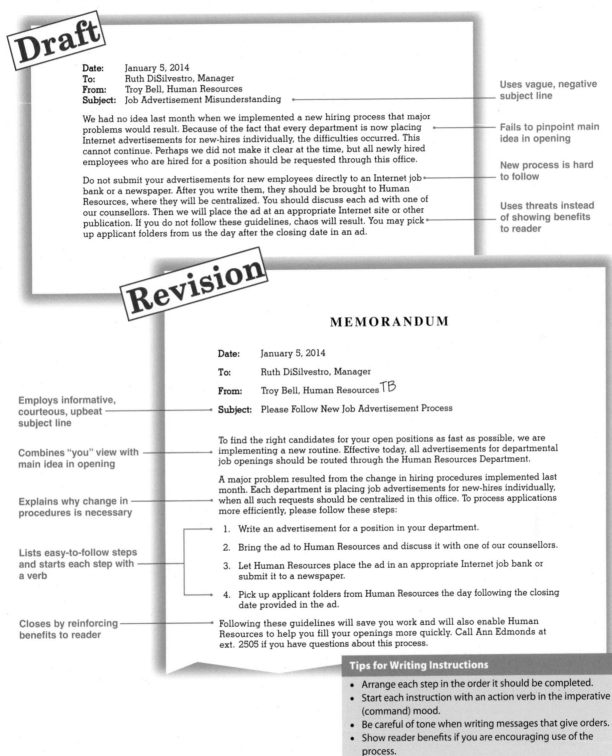

Draft

Date: January 5, 2014
To: Ruth DiSilvestro, Manager
From: Troy Bell, Human Resources
Subject: Job Advertisement Misunderstanding   •——— Uses vague, negative subject line

We had no idea last month when we implemented a new hiring process that major problems would result. Because of the fact that every department is now placing Internet advertisements for new-hires individually, the difficulties occurred. This cannot continue. Perhaps we did not make it clear at the time, but all newly hired employees who are hired for a position should be requested through this office.   •——— Fails to pinpoint main idea in opening

Do not submit your advertisements for new employees directly to an Internet job bank or a newspaper. After you write them, they should be brought to Human Resources, where they will be centralized. You should discuss each ad with one of our counsellors. Then we will place the ad at an appropriate Internet site or other publication. If you do not follow these guidelines, chaos will result. You may pick up applicant folders from us the day after the closing date in an ad.   •——— New process is hard to follow

•——— Uses threats instead of showing benefits to reader

Revision

MEMORANDUM

Date: January 5, 2014

To: Ruth DiSilvestro, Manager

From: Troy Bell, Human Resources TB

Subject: Please Follow New Job Advertisement Process

Employs informative, courteous, upbeat subject line

To find the right candidates for your open positions as fast as possible, we are implementing a new routine. Effective today, all advertisements for departmental job openings should be routed through the Human Resources Department.

Combines "you" view with main idea in opening

A major problem resulted from the change in hiring procedures implemented last month. Each department is placing job advertisements for new-hires individually, when all such requests should be centralized in this office. To process applications more efficiently, please follow these steps:

Explains why change in procedures is necessary

Lists easy-to-follow steps and starts each step with a verb

1. Write an advertisement for a position in your department.

2. Bring the ad to Human Resources and discuss it with one of our counsellors.

3. Let Human Resources place the ad in an appropriate Internet job bank or submit it to a newspaper.

4. Pick up applicant folders from Human Resources the day following the closing date provided in the ad.

Closes by reinforcing benefits to reader

Following these guidelines will save you work and will also enable Human Resources to help you fill your openings more quickly. Call Ann Edmonds at ext. 2505 if you have questions about this process.

Tips for Writing Instructions

- Arrange each step in the order it should be completed.
- Start each instruction with an action verb in the imperative (command) mood.
- Be careful of tone when writing messages that give orders.
- Show reader benefits if you are encouraging use of the process.

language. Troy struggled, but by trying different wording, he finally found verbs that worked.

Why should you go to so much trouble to make lists and achieve parallelism? Because readers can comprehend what you have said much more quickly. Parallel language also makes you look professional and efficient.

In writing messages that deliver instructions, be careful of tone. Today's managers and team leaders seek employee participation and cooperation. These goals can't be achieved, though, if the writer sounds like a dictator or an autocrat. Avoid making accusations and fixing blame. Rather, explain changes, give reasons, and suggest benefits to the reader. Assume that employees want to contribute to the success of the organization and to their own achievement. Notice in the Figure 8.6 revision that Troy tells readers that they will save time and have their open positions filled more quickly if they follow the new method.

Learning More About Writing Instructions

The writing of instructions is so important that we have developed a special bonus online supplement called *How to Write Instructions*. It provides more examples and information. This online supplement at **www.guffeybrief4e.nelson.com** extends your textbook with in-depth material including links to real businesses showing you examples of well-written instructions.

Direct Claims

LEARNING OBJECTIVE 5

Prepare messages that make direct claims.

In business, things can and do go wrong—promised shipments are late, warrantied goods fail, or service is disappointing. When you as a customer must write to identify or correct a wrong, the letter is called a *claim*. Straightforward claims are those to which you expect the receiver to agree readily. Even these claims, however, often require a letter. Your first action may be a telephone call or an e-mail to submit your claim, but you may not be satisfied with the result. Claims written as letters are taken more seriously than telephone calls or e-mails, and letters also establish a record of what happened. Straightforward claims use a direct approach. Claims that require a persuasive response are presented in Chapter 10.

Opening a Claim With a Clear Statement

Claims written as letters are taken more seriously than telephone calls or e-mails.

When you, as a customer, have a legitimate claim, you can expect a positive response from a company. Smart businesses want to hear from their customers. They know that retaining a customer is far less costly than recruiting a new customer.

Open your claim with a compliment, point of agreement, statement of the problem, brief review of action you have taken to resolve the problem, or clear statement of the action you want. You might expect a replacement, a refund, a new product, a credit to your account, a correction of a billing error, free repairs, a free inspection, or the cancellation of an order. When the remedy is obvious, state it immediately (*Please send us 25 Sanyo digital travel alarm clocks to replace the Sanyo analog travel alarm clocks sent in error with our order shipped January 4*). When the remedy is less obvious, you might ask for a change in policy or procedure or simply for an explanation (*Because three of our employees with confirmed reservations were refused rooms September 16 in your hotel, would you please clarify your policy regarding reservations and late arrivals*).

Explaining and Justifying a Claim

In the body of a claim letter, explain the problem and justify your request. Provide the necessary details so that the difficulty can be corrected without further correspondence. Avoid becoming angry or trying to assign blame. Although you may be upset, bear in mind that the person reading your letter is seldom responsible for the problem. Instead, state the facts logically, objectively, and unemotionally; let the reader decide on the causes. Include copies of all pertinent documents, such as invoices, sales slips, catalogue descriptions, and repair records. Be sure to send copies and *not* your originals, which could be lost. When service is involved, cite the names of individuals you spoke to and the dates of the calls. Assume that a company honestly wants to satisfy its customers—because most do. When an alternative remedy exists, spell it out (*If you are unable to send 25 Sanyo digital travel alarm clocks immediately, please credit our account now and notify us when they become available*).

Concluding a Claim With an Action Request

End a claim with a courteous statement that promotes goodwill and summarizes your action request. If appropriate, include an end date (*We realize that mistakes in ordering and shipping sometimes occur. Because we've enjoyed your prompt service in the past, we hope that you will be able to send us the Sanyo digital travel alarm clocks by January 15*). Finally, in making claims, act promptly. Delaying claims makes them appear less important. Delayed claims are also more difficult to verify. By taking the time to put your claim in writing, you indicate your seriousness. A written claim starts a record of the problem, should later action be necessary. Be sure to keep a copy of your message.

Claims submitted promptly are taken more seriously than delayed ones.

When Keith Krahnke received a statement showing a charge for a three-year service warranty that he did not purchase, he was furious. He called the store but failed to get satisfaction. Then he decided to write. You can see the first draft of his direct claim letter in Figure 8.7. This draft gave him a chance to vent his anger, but it accomplished little else. The tone was belligerent, and it assumed that the company intentionally mischarged him. Furthermore, it failed to tell the reader how to remedy the problem. The revision, also shown in Figure 8.7, tempered the tone, described the problem objectively, and provided facts and figures. Most important, it specified exactly what Keith wanted to be done.

Notice in Figure 8.7 that Keith used the personal business letter style, which is appropriate for you to use in writing personal messages. Your return address, but not your name, appears above the date.

Adjustments

Even the best-run and best-loved businesses occasionally receive claims from consumers. When a company receives a claim and decides to respond favourably, the message is called an *adjustment*. Most businesses make adjustments promptly: they replace merchandise, refund money, extend discounts, send coupons, and repair goods. Businesses make favourable adjustments to legitimate claims for two reasons. First, consumers are protected by contractual and tort law for recovery of damages. Second, and more obviously, most organizations genuinely want to satisfy their customers and retain their business.

LEARNING OBJECTIVE **6**

Create adjustment messages that regain the confidence of customers and promote further business.

In responding to customer claims, you must first decide whether to grant the claim. Unless the claim is obviously fraudulent or excessive, you will probably grant it. When you say yes, your adjustment message will be good news to the reader. Deliver that good news by using the direct strategy. When your response is no, the indirect strategy might be more appropriate. Chapter 9 discusses the indirect strategy for conveying negative news. You have three goals in adjustment letters:

Businesses make favourable adjustments to legitimate claims because they genuinely want to satisfy their customers.

- Rectifying the wrong, if one exists

- Regaining the confidence of the customer

- Promoting further business

Revealing Good News Up Front in an Adjustment Message

Instead of beginning with a review of what went wrong, present the good news immediately. When Amy Hopkins responded to the claim of customer Sound Systems, Inc. about a missing shipment, her first draft, shown at the top of Figure 8.8, was angry. No wonder. Sound Systems, Inc. had apparently provided the wrong

Begin the adjustment letter with the good news.

FIGURE 8.7 **Direct Claim Letter**

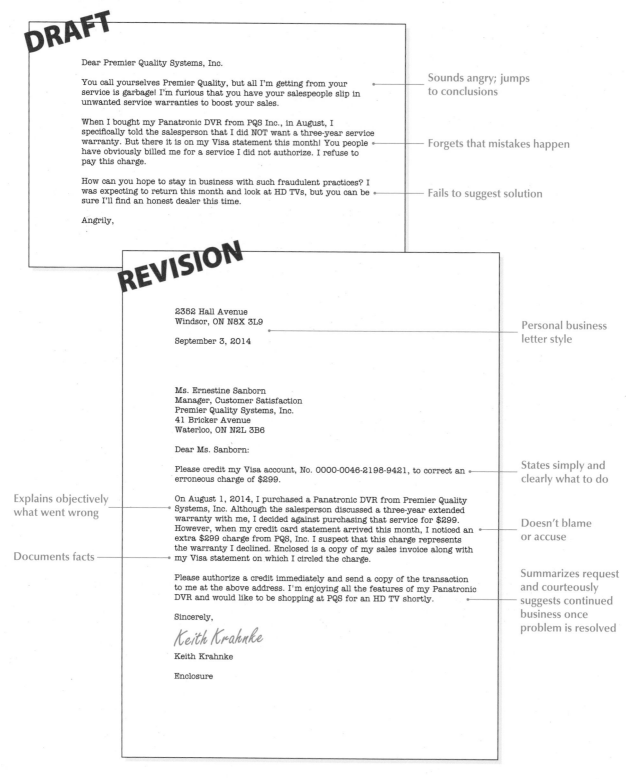

DRAFT

Dear Premier Quality Systems, Inc.

You call yourselves Premier Quality, but all I'm getting from your service is garbage! I'm furious that you have your salespeople slip in unwanted service warranties to boost your sales. — *Sounds angry; jumps to conclusions*

When I bought my Panatronic DVR from PQS Inc., in August, I specifically told the salesperson that I did NOT want a three-year service warranty. But there it is on my Visa statement this month! You people have obviously billed me for a service I did not authorize. I refuse to pay this charge. — *Forgets that mistakes happen*

How can you hope to stay in business with such fraudulent practices? I was expecting to return this month and look at HD TVs, but you can be sure I'll find an honest dealer this time. — *Fails to suggest solution*

Angrily,

REVISION

2352 Hall Avenue
Windsor, ON N8X 3L9

September 3, 2014 — *Personal business letter style*

Ms. Ernestine Sanborn
Manager, Customer Satisfaction
Premier Quality Systems, Inc.
41 Bricker Avenue
Waterloo, ON N2L 3B6

Dear Ms. Sanborn:

Please credit my Visa account, No. 0000-0046-2198-9421, to correct an erroneous charge of $299. — *States simply and clearly what to do*

On August 1, 2014, I purchased a Panatronic DVR from Premier Quality Systems, Inc. Although the salesperson discussed a three-year extended warranty with me, I decided against purchasing that service for $299. However, when my credit card statement arrived this month, I noticed an extra $299 charge from PQS, Inc. I suspect that this charge represents the warranty I declined. Enclosed is a copy of my sales invoice along with my Visa statement on which I circled the charge. — *Explains objectively what went wrong* / *Documents facts* / *Doesn't blame or accuse*

Please authorize a credit immediately and send a copy of the transaction to me at the above address. I'm enjoying all the features of my Panatronic DVR and would like to be shopping at PQS for an HD TV shortly. — *Summarizes request and courteously suggests continued business once problem is resolved*

Sincerely,

Keith Krahnke

Keith Krahnke

Enclosure

FIGURE 8.8 Customer Adjustment Letter

DRAFT

Fails to reveal good news immediately and blames customer

Creates ugly tone with negative words and sarcasm

Sounds grudging and reluctant in granting claim

Gentlemen:

In response to your recent complaint about a missing shipment, it's very difficult to deliver merchandise when we have been given an erroneous address.

Our investigators looked into your problem shipment and determined that it was sent immediately after we received the order. According to the shipper's records, it was delivered to the warehouse address given on your stationery: 3590 University Avenue, Toronto, ON M1Z 2K3. Unfortunately, no one at that address would accept delivery, so the shipment was returned to us. I see from your current stationery that your company has a new address. With the proper address, we probably could have delivered this shipment.

Although we feel that it is entirely appropriate to charge you shipping and restocking fees, as is our standard practice on returned goods, in this instance we will waive those fees. We hope this second shipment finally catches up with you at your current address.

Sincerely,

Amy Hopkins

REVISION

Ew ELECTRONIC WAREHOUSE

601 Scottsdale Road
Guelph, ON N16 3E7

Phone: (519) 876-8201
Fax: (519) 876-8345
Web: www.ewarehouse.com

February 21, 2014

Mr. Jeremy Garber, CEO
Sound Systems, Inc.
1432 Front Street
Toronto, ON M6V 2J8

Dear Mr. Garber:

Uses customer's name in salutation

Subject: Your February 14 Letter About Your Purchase Order

You should receive by February 25 a second shipment of the speakers, DVDs, headphones, and other electronic equipment that you ordered January 20.

Announces good news immediately

The first shipment of this order was delivered January 28 to 3590 University Avenue, Toronto, ON M1Z 2K3. When no one at that address would accept the shipment, it was returned to us. Now that I have your letter, I see that the order should have been sent to 1432 Front Street, Toronto, ON M6V 2J8. When an order is undeliverable, we usually try to verify the shipping address by telephoning the customer. Somehow the return of this shipment was not caught by our normally painstaking shipping clerks. You can be sure that I will investigate shipping and return procedures with our clerks immediately to see whether we can improve existing methods.

Regains confidence of customer by explaining what happened and by suggesting plans for improvement

Your respect is important to us, Mr. Garber. Although our rock-bottom discount prices have enabled us to build a volume business, we don't want to be so large that we lose touch with valued customers like you. Over the years our customers' respect has made us successful, and we hope that the prompt delivery of this shipment will retain yours. Please call me at (519) 876-8201, ext. 450, if I can serve you personally.

Closes confidently with genuine appeal for customer's respect

Sincerely,

Amy Hopkins

Amy Hopkins
Distribution Manager

c: David Cole
   Shipping Department

shipping address, and the goods were returned. Once Amy and her company decided to send a second shipment and comply with the customer's claim, however, she had to give up the anger. Her goal was to regain the goodwill and the business of this customer. The improved version of her letter announces that a new shipment will arrive shortly.

If you decide to comply with a customer's claim, let the receiver know immediately. Don't begin your letter with a negative statement (*We are very sorry to hear that you are having trouble with your dishwasher*). This approach reminds the reader of the problem and may rekindle the heated emotions or unhappy feelings experienced when the claim was written. Instead, focus on the good news. The following openings for various letters illustrate how to begin a message with good news:

- You will be receiving shortly a new slim Nokia cellphone to replace the one that shattered when dropped recently.

- Please take your portable Admiral microwave oven to A-1 Appliance Service, 200 Orange Street, Saskatoon, where it will be repaired at no cost to you.

- The enclosed cheque for $325 demonstrates our desire to satisfy our customers and earn their confidence.

In announcing that you will make an adjustment, be sure to do so without a grudging tone—even if you have reservations about whether the claim is legitimate. Once you decide to comply with the customer's request, do so happily. Avoid half-hearted or reluctant responses (*Although the Admiral microwave oven works well when used properly, we have decided to allow you to take yours to A-1 Appliance Service for repair at our expense*).

Explaining Compliance in the Body of an Adjustment Message

In responding to claims, most organizations sincerely want to correct a wrong. They want to do more than just make the customer happy. They want to stand behind their products and services; they want to do what is right.

In the body of the letter, explain why you are complying with the claim.

In the body of the letter, explain how you are complying with the claim. In all but the most routine claims, you should seek to regain the confidence of the customer. You might reasonably expect that a customer who has experienced difficulty with a product, with delivery, with billing, or with service has lost faith in your organization. Rebuilding that faith is important for future business.

How to rebuild lost confidence depends on the situation and the claim. If procedures need to be revised, explain what changes will be made. If a product has defective parts, tell how the product is being improved. If service is faulty, describe genuine efforts to improve it. Notice in Figure 8.8 that the writer promises to investigate shipping procedures to see whether improvements might prevent future mishaps.

Sometimes the problem is not with the product but with the way it is being used. In other instances customers misunderstand warranties or inadvertently cause delivery and billing mix-ups by supplying incorrect information. Remember that rational and sincere explanations will do much to regain the confidence of unhappy customers.

In your explanation avoid emphasizing negative words, such as *trouble, regret, misunderstanding, fault, defective, error, inconvenience,* and *unfortunately*. Keep your message positive and upbeat.

Deciding Whether to Apologize

While attorneys generally discourage apologies, both judges and juries tend to look favourably on them.

Whether to apologize is a debatable issue. Attorneys generally discourage apologies, fearing that they admit responsibility and will trigger lawsuits. However, both judges and juries tend to look on apologies favourably. Some Canadian provinces have passed an *Apology Act*, "which makes it easier for people to say sorry for their actions without worry that their words will be used against them in a civil suit." Supporters of this law believe it will lead to fewer court cases over damages by allowing those who want only an apology getting what they want without going to court.[5]

Some business writing experts advise against apologies, contending that they are counterproductive and merely remind the customer of the unpleasantness related to the claim. If, however, apologizing seems natural, do so.

People like to hear apologies. It raises their self-esteem, shows the humility of the writer, and acts as a form of "psychological compensation."[6] Don't, however, fall back on the familiar phrase *I'm sorry for any inconvenience we may have caused*. It sounds mechanical and insincere. Instead, try something like this: *We understand the frustration our delay has caused you, We're sorry you didn't receive better service*, or *You're right to be disappointed*. If you feel that an apology is appropriate, do it early and briefly. You will learn more about delivering effective apologies in Chapter 9 when we discuss negative messages.

The primary focus of an adjustment message is on how you are complying with the request, how the problem occurred, and how you are working to prevent its recurrence.

Using Sensitive Language in Adjustment Messages

The language of adjustment messages must be particularly sensitive, because customers are already upset. Here are some don'ts:

To regain the confidence of your reader, consider including resale information.

- Don't use negative words (*trouble, regret, misunderstanding, fault, error, inconvenience, you claim*).

- Don't blame customers—even when they may be at fault.

- Don't blame individuals or departments within your organization; it's unprofessional.

- Don't make unrealistic promises; you can't guarantee that the situation will never recur.

To regain the confidence of your reader, consider including resale information. Describe a product's features and any special applications that might appeal to the reader. Promote a new product if it seems appropriate.

Showing Confidence in the Closing

End positively by expressing confidence that the problem has been resolved and that continued business relations will result. You might mention the product in a favourable light, suggest a new product, express your appreciation for the customer's business, or anticipate future business. It's often appropriate to refer to the desire to be of service and to satisfy customers. Notice how the following closings illustrate a positive, confident tone:

End positively by expressing confidence that the problem has been resolved.

> You were most helpful in informing us of this situation and permitting us to correct it. We appreciate your thoughtfulness in writing to us.

> Thanks for writing. Your satisfaction is important to us. We hope that this refund cheque convinces you that service to our customers is our No. 1 priority. Our goals are to earn your confidence and continue to justify that confidence with quality products and excellent service.

> Your Asus Netbook will come in handy whether you are connecting with friends, surfing the net, listening to music, watching movies, or playing games. What's more, you can add an HDTV tuner and built-in GPS for a little more. Take a look at the enclosed booklet detailing the big savings for essential technology on a budget. We value your business and look forward to your future orders.

Although the direct strategy works for many requests and replies, it obviously won't work for every situation. With more practice and experience, you will be able to alter the pattern and apply the writing process to other communication problems. See the Checklist box on page 194 for a summary of what to do when you must write claim and adjustment messages.

Checklist

Direct Claim and Adjustment Messages

Messages That Make Claims

- **Begin directly with the purpose.** Present a clear statement of the problem or the action requested, such as a refund, a replacement, credit, an explanation, or the correction of an error. Consider adding a compliment if you have been pleased in other respects.

- **Explain objectively.** In the body tell the specifics of the claim. Consider reminding the receiver of ethical and legal responsibilities, fairness, and a desire for return business. Provide copies of necessary documents.

- **Conclude by requesting action.** Include an end date, if important. Add a pleasant, forward-looking statement. Keep a copy of the letter.

Messages That Make Adjustments

- **Open with approval.** Comply with the customer's claim immediately. Avoid sounding grudging or reluctant.

- **In the body, win back the customer's confidence.** Explain the cause of the problem, or describe your ongoing efforts to avoid such difficulties. Focus on your efforts to satisfy customers. Apologize if you feel that you should, but do so early and briefly. Avoid negative words, accusations, and unrealistic promises. Consider including resale and sales promotion information.

- **Close positively.** Express appreciation to the customer for writing, extend thanks for past business, anticipate continued patronage, refer to your desire to be of service, or mention a new product if it seems appropriate.

Goodwill Messages

LEARNING OBJECTIVE 7

Write special messages that convey kindness and goodwill.

Many communicators are intimidated when they must write goodwill messages expressing thanks, recognition, and sympathy. Finding the right words to express feelings is often more difficult than writing ordinary business documents. That is why writers tend to procrastinate when it comes to goodwill messages. Sending a ready-made card or picking up the telephone is easier than writing a message. Remember, though, that the personal sentiments of the sender are always more expressive and more meaningful to readers than are printed cards or oral messages. Taking the time to write gives more importance to our well-wishing. Personal notes also provide a record that can be reread, savoured, and treasured.

In expressing thanks, recognition, or sympathy, you should always do so promptly. These messages are easier to write when the situation is fresh in your mind. They also mean more to the recipient. Don't forget that a prompt thank-you note carries the hidden message that you care and that you consider the event to be important. The best goodwill messages—whether thanks, congratulations, praise, or sympathy—concentrate on the five Ss. Goodwill messages should be the following:

- **Selfless.** Be sure to focus the message solely on the receiver, not the sender. Don't talk about yourself; avoid such comments as *I remember when I ....*

- **Specific.** Personalize the message by mentioning specific incidents or characteristics of the receiver. Telling a colleague *Great speech* is much less effective than *Great story about McDonald's marketing in Moscow*. Take care to verify names and other facts.

- **Sincere.** Let your words show genuine feelings. Rehearse in your mind how you would express the message to the receiver orally. Then transform that conversational language to your written message. Avoid pretentious, formal, or flowery language (*It gives me great pleasure to extend felicitations on the occasion of your firm's twentieth anniversary*).

- **Spontaneous.** Keep the message fresh and enthusiastic. Avoid canned phrases (*Congratulations on your promotion, Good luck in the future*). Strive for directness and naturalness, not creative brilliance.

- **Short.** Although goodwill messages can be as long as needed, try to accomplish your purpose in only a few sentences. What is most important is remembering an individual. Such caring does not require documentation or wordiness. Individuals and business organizations often use special note cards or stationery for brief messages.

Expressing Thanks

When someone has done you a favour or when an action merits praise, you need to extend thanks or show appreciation. Letters of appreciation may be written to customers for their orders, to hosts and hostesses for their hospitality, to individuals for kindnesses performed, and especially to customers who complain. After all, complainers are actually providing you with "free consulting reports from the field." Complainers who feel that they were listened to often become the greatest promoters of an organization.[7]

Written notes that show appreciation and express thanks are significant to their receivers. In expressing thanks, you generally write a short note on special notepaper or heavy card stock. The following messages provide models for expressing thanks for a gift, for a favour, and for hospitality.

To Express Thanks for a Gift. When expressing thanks, tell what the gift means to you. Use sincere, simple statements.

> *Thanks, Laura, to you and the other members of the department for honouring me with the elegant Waterford crystal vase at the party celebrating my twentieth anniversary with the company. The height and shape of the vase are perfect to hold roses and other bouquets from my garden. Each time I fill it, I'll remember your thoughtfulness in choosing this lovely gift for me.*

> Identify the gift, tell why you appreciate it, and explain how you will use it.

To Send Thanks for a Favour. In showing appreciation for a favour, explain the importance of the gesture to you.

> *I sincerely appreciate your filling in for me last week when I was too ill to attend the planning committee meeting for the spring exhibition.*

> *Without your participation much of my preparatory work would have been lost. Knowing that competent and generous individuals like you are part of our team, Mark, is a great comfort. Moreover, counting you as a friend is my very good fortune. I'm grateful to you.*

> Tell what the favour means using sincere, simple statements.

To Extend Thanks for Hospitality. When you have been a guest, send a note that compliments the fine food, charming surroundings, warm hospitality, excellent host and hostess, and good company.

> *Jeffrey and I want you to know how much we enjoyed the dinner party for our department that you hosted Saturday evening. Your charming home and warm hospitality, along with the lovely dinner and sinfully delicious chocolate dessert, combined to create a truly memorable evening. Most of all, though, we appreciate your kindness in cultivating togetherness in our department. Thanks, Jamila, for being such a special person.*

> Compliment the fine food, charming surroundings, warm hospitality, excellent host and hostess, and good company.

Responding to Goodwill Messages

Should you respond when you receive a congratulatory note or a written pat on the back? By all means! These messages are attempts to connect personally; they are efforts to reach out, to form professional or personal bonds. Failing to respond to notes of congratulations and most other goodwill messages is like failing to say *You're welcome* when someone says *Thank you.* Responding to such messages is simply the right thing to do. Do avoid, though, minimizing your achievements with comments that suggest you don't really deserve the praise or that the sender is exaggerating your good qualities.

> Take the time to respond to any goodwill message you may receive.

To Answer a Congratulatory Note. In responding to congratulations, keep it short and simple.

> *Thanks for your kind words regarding my award, and thanks, too, for sending me the newspaper clipping. I truly appreciate your thoughtfulness and warm wishes.*

To Respond to a Pat on the Back. When acknowledging a pat-on-the-back note, use simple words in conveying your appreciation.

> *Your note about my work made me feel good. I'm grateful for your thoughtfulness.*

Conveying Sympathy

Most of us can bear misfortune and grief more easily when we know that others care. Notes expressing sympathy, though, are probably more difficult to write than any other kind of message. Commercial "In sympathy" cards make the task easier—but they are far less meaningful. Grieving friends want to know what you think—not what Hallmark's card writers think. To help you get started, you can always glance through cards expressing sympathy. They will supply ideas about the kinds of thoughts you might wish to convey in your own words. In writing a sympathy note, (a) refer to the death or misfortune sensitively, using words that show you understand what a crushing blow it is; (b) in the case of a death, praise the deceased in a personal way; (c) offer assistance without going into excessive detail; and (d) end on a reassuring, forward-looking note. Sympathy messages may be typed, although handwriting seems more personal. In either case, use notepaper or personal stationery.

> **Sympathy notes should refer to the misfortune sensitively and offer assistance.**

To Express Condolences. Mention the loss tactfully, recognize good qualities of the deceased, assure the receiver of your concern, offer assistance, and conclude on a reassuring note.

We are deeply saddened, Gayle, to learn of the death of your husband. Anwar's kind nature and friendly spirit endeared him to all who knew him. He will be missed.

Although words seem empty in expressing our grief, we want you to know that your friends at QuadCom extend their profound sympathy to you. If we may help you or lighten your load in any way, you have but to call.

We know that the treasured memories of your many happy years together, along with the support of your family and many friends, will provide strength and comfort in the months ahead.

The Checklist box summarizes the key points to remember when writing goodwill messages.

Checklist

Goodwill Messages

General Guidelines: The Five Ss

- **Be selfless.** Discuss the receiver, not the sender.
- **Be specific.** Instead of generic statements (*You did a good job*), include special details (*Your marketing strategy to target key customers proved to be outstanding*).
- **Be sincere.** Show your honest feelings with conversational, unpretentious language (*We are all very proud of your award*).
- **Be spontaneous.** Strive to make the message natural, fresh, and direct. Avoid canned phrases (*If I may be of service, please do not hesitate...*).
- **Keep the message short.** Remember that, although they may be as long as needed, most goodwill messages are fairly short.

Giving Thanks

- **Cover three points in gift thank-yous.** (1) Identify the gift, (2) tell why you appreciate it, and (3) explain how you will use it.
- **Be sincere in sending thanks for a favour.** Tell what the favour means to you. Avoid superlatives and gushiness. Maintain credibility with sincere, simple statements.

- **Offer praise in expressing thanks for hospitality.** Compliment, as appropriate, the (a) fine food, (b) charming surroundings, (c) warm hospitality, (d) excellent host and hostess, and (e) good company.

Responding to Goodwill Messages

- **Respond to congratulations.** Send a brief note expressing your appreciation. Tell how good the message made you feel.
- **Accept praise gracefully.** Don't make belittling comments (*I'm not really all that good!*) to reduce awkwardness or embarrassment.

Extending Sympathy

- **Refer to the loss or tragedy directly but sensitively.** In the first sentence, mention the loss and your personal reaction.
- **For deaths, praise the deceased.** Describe positive personal characteristics (*Howard was a forceful but caring leader*).
- **Offer assistance.** Suggest your availability, especially if you can do something specific.
- **End on a reassuring, positive note.** Perhaps refer to the strength the receiver finds in friends, family, colleagues, or religion.

Summary of Learning Objectives

1 **Apply the 3-×-3 writing process to creating successful positive messages, including e-mails, interoffice memos, and business letters.** Positive messages—whether e-mails, interoffice memos, or business letters—can be straightforward and direct because they carry nonsensitive, routine information. In applying Phase 1 of the writing process for positive messages, you should determine your purpose, visualize the audience, and anticipate the reaction of the reader to your message. In Phase 2 you should collect information, make an outline of the points to cover, and write the first draft. In Phase 3 you should revise for clarity, proofread for correctness, and look for ways to promote "skim value." Finally, you should decide whether the message accomplishes its goal.

2 **Understand the appropriate use of e-mails, interoffice memos, and business letters.** E-mail is appropriate for short, informal messages. Interoffice memos are appropriate for internal messages that are important, lengthy, or formal. Like e-mails, interoffice memos follow a standard form with the guide words *Date, To, From,* and *Subject.* Memos that serve as attachments to e-mails must be properly identified. Business letters are necessary when a permanent record is required; when confidentiality is critical; when formality and sensitivity are essential; and when a persuasive, well-considered presentation is important. Business letters written on company stationery often use block style with all lines starting at the left margin.

3 **Compose direct messages that make requests and respond to inquiries.** In direct messages requesting information or action, the opening immediately states the purpose of the message, perhaps asking a question. The body explains and justifies the request. If many questions are asked, they should be expressed in parallel form and balanced grammatically. The closing tells the reader courteously what to do and shows appreciation. In a message that replies directly and complies with a request, a subject line may identify previous correspondence, and the opening immediately delivers the good news. The body explains and provides additional information. The closing is cordial and personalized. If action is necessary, the ending tells the reader how to proceed and gives helpful details.

4 **Write messages that clearly explain step-by-step instructions.** When writing messages that explain instructions, you should (a) divide the instructions into steps, (b) list each step in the order in which it is to be carried out, (c) arrange the items vertically with bullets or numbers, and (d) begin each step with an action verb using the imperative (command) mood rather than the indicative mood (e.g., *Open the paper drawer, load the paper, and push the Start button*). Messages that give instructions should not sound dictatorial. When changing existing procedures, avoid making accusations and assigning blame. Explain changes, give reasons, and suggest benefits to the reader.

5 **Prepare messages that make direct claims.** When a customer writes to identify a wrong and request a correction, the message is called a *claim.* A direct claim is one to which the receiver is expected to readily agree. A well-written claim begins by describing the problem clearly or telling what action is to be taken. The body of the claim explains and justifies the request without anger or emotion. The closing summarizes the request or action to be taken. It includes an end date, if appropriate, and courteously looks forward to continued business if the problem is resolved. Copies of relevant documents should be enclosed.

6 **Create adjustment messages that regain the confidence of customers and promote further business.** When a company grants a customer's claim, it is called an *adjustment.* An adjustment message has three goals: (1) rectifying the wrong, if one exists; (2) regaining the confidence of the customer; and (3) promoting further business. The opening immediately grants the claim without sounding grudging. To regain the confidence of the customer, the body may explain what went wrong and how the problem will be rectified. However, the writer may strive to avoid accepting responsibility for any problems. The closing expresses appreciation, extends thanks for past business, refers to a desire to be of service, and may mention a new product. If an apology is offered, it should be presented early and briefly.

7 Write special messages that convey kindness and goodwill. Messages that deliver thanks, praise, or sympathy should be selfless, specific, sincere, spontaneous, and short. Gift thank-yous should identify the gift, tell why you appreciate it, and explain how you will use it. Favour thank-yous should tell, without gushing, what the favour means to you. Expressions of sympathy should mention the loss tactfully; recognize good qualities in the deceased (in the case of a death); offer assistance; and conclude on a positive, reassuring note.

Chapter Review

1. Into what three content categories can most business messages be organized? What group will make up the bulk of your messages? (Obj. 1)

2. How can you save the reader's time and make your business message easy to comprehend at a glance? (Obj. 1)

3. What kinds of messages are sent as interoffice memos? (Obj. 2)

4. When is it important to send a business letter rather than an e-mail? (Obj. 2)

5. What are the most emphatic positions in a message, and what goes there? (Obj. 3)

6. What should you include in the closing of a request message? (Obj. 3)

7. How should instructions be written? Give a brief original example. (Obj. 4)

8. What is the imperative mood, and why is it important to use it in writing instructions? (Obj. 4)

9. What is a claim? When should it be straightforward? (Obj. 5)

10. Why should a direct claim be made by letter rather than by e-mail or a telephone call? (Obj. 5)

11. What is an adjustment message? (Obj. 6)

12. What are a writer's three goals in writing adjustment messages? (Obj. 6)

13. Name four things to avoid in adjustment letters. (Obj. 6)

14. What are five characteristics of goodwill messages? (Obj. 7)

15. What are four groups of people to whom business communicators might write letters of appreciation? (Obj. 7)

Critical Thinking

1. Are the writing skills that are required for sending business e-mails and text messages different from those required for writing interoffice memos and business letters? Explain. (Objs. 1, 2)

2. An article in a professional magazine carried this headline: "Is Letter Writing Dead?"[8] How would you respond to such a question? (Obj. 1)

3. In promoting the value of letter writing, a well-known columnist recently wrote, "To trust confidential information to e-mail is to be a rube."[9] What did he mean? Do you agree? (Obj. 1)

4. Why is it important to regain the confidence of a customer in an adjustment letter? How can it be done? (Obj. 6)

5. **Ethical Issue:** Assume that you have drafted a letter to a customer in which you apologize for the way the customer's account was fouled up by the Accounting Department. You show the letter to your boss, and she instructs you to remove the apology. It admits responsibility, she says, and the company cannot allow itself to be held liable. You are not a lawyer, but you can't see the harm in a simple apology. What should you do? Refer to the section "Tools for Doing the Right Thing" in Chapter 1 to review the five questions you might ask yourself in trying to do the right thing.

Writing Improvement Exercises

8.1 Direct Openings (Objs. 1–7)

Your Task. Revise the following openings so that they are more direct. Add information if necessary.

a. Alliance Associates has undertaken a management initiative to pursue an internship program. I have been appointed as the liaison person to conduct research regarding our proposed program. We are fully aware of the benefits of a strong internship program, and our management team is eager to take advantage of some of these benefits. We would be deeply appreciative if you would be kind enough to help us out with answers to a number of specific questions.

b. My name is Justin Wilmot, and I am assistant to the manager of Information Services & Technology at Meredian, Inc. Our company wants to improve its integration of human resources and payroll functions. I understand that you have a software product called HRFocus that might do this, and I need to ask you some questions about it.

c. Your letter of March 4 has been referred to me. Pursuant to your inquiry, I have researched your question in regard to whether or not we offer our European-style patio umbrella in colours. This unique umbrella is one of our most popular items. Its 3-metre canopy protects you when the sun is directly overhead, but it also swivels and tilts to virtually any angle for continuous sun protection all day long. It comes in two colours: cream and forest green.

8.2 Writing Instructions (Obj. 4)

Revise each of the following wordy, dense paragraphs into a set of concise instructions. Include an introductory statement.

a. Orders may be placed at our Web site by following certain steps. Here they are. As a visitor to our site, you should first look over everything and find the items you want from our catalogue. Then your shopping cart is important. You will add items to your shopping cart. When you are finished adding things to your shopping cart, the next step is to proceed to checkout. But wait! Have you created a new account? After creating a new account, we next need to know what shipping address to ship your items to. We will also need to have you choose a shipping method. Then you will be expected to provide payment information. Finally, you are nearly done! Payment information must be provided, and then you are ready to review your order and submit it.

b. If you want to make a YouTube video, here are some important tips for those who have not done it before. First, you will need to obtain a video recording device, such as a cellphone, webcam, or camcorder. Another thing you will have to do is make a decision on whether or not to make a video blog, comedy skit, how-to video, or a video that is about travel. Remember that your video must be 10 minutes or less for traditional YouTube membership accounts. You will want to create a video with good light quality, and that usually means daytime recording. Finally, be sure to use computer editing software to change or delete anything.

Activities

Note: All Documents for Analysis may be downloaded from **www.guffeybrief4e.nelson.com** so that you do not have to rekey the entire message.

8.3. Document for Analysis: Direct Request (Obj. 3)

Your Task. Analyze the following poorly written message. List at least five weaknesses. If your instructor directs, revise the message by using the suggestions you learned in this and previous chapters.

To:	Cansoft Manager List
From:	Stella Soto<stella.soto@Cansoft.com>
Subject:	E-Mail Problems
Cc:	
Bcc:	

Dear Managers,

As Cansoft vice president, I am troubled by a big problem. I am writing this note to ask for your help and advice to address an urgent problem—the problem of excessive e-mail. If you will do me the favour of answering the questions below, I'm sure your ideas will assist us in the development of a plan that should benefit your staff, yourself, and our organization will be improved. Your replies in writing to these questions (preferably by May 5) will help me prepare for our supervisory committee meeting on May 10.

Although e-mail is a great productivity tool, I'm afraid that its use is becoming extremely excessive. For our organization it is actually cutting into work time. Did you know that one study found that the average office worker is spending two hours a day on e-mail? In our organization we may be spending even more than this. It's exceedingly difficult to get any work done because of writing and answering an extraordinary number of e-mails coming in each and every day. Excessive e-mail is sapping the organization's strength and productivity. I would like to have your answers to some questions before the above referenced dates to help us focus on the problem.

Can you give a ballpark figure for how many e-mails you receive and answer on a personal basis each day? Think about how many hours the staff members in your department spend on e-mail each day. Approximately how many hours would you estimate? Do you have any ideas about how we can make a reduction in the volume of e-mails being sent and received within our own organization? Do you think that e-mail is being used by our employees in an excessive manner?

I'm wondering what you think about an e-mail-free day once a week. How about Fridays? I appreciate your suggestions and advice in developing a solution to the problem of controlling e-mail and making an improvement in productivity.

Stella Soto
Vice President, Operations

8.4 Document for Analysis: Direct Claim (Obj. 5)

Your Task. Analyze the following poorly written letter and list at least five weaknesses. If your instructor directs, revise it by using the suggestions you learned in this chapter.

Current date
Mr. Orion Murillo
Manager, Customer Response Centre
Eastern Atlantic Car Rentals
35 Mactaquac Road
Fredericton, New Brunswick E3E 1L2

Dear Manager Orion Murillo:

I am writing this letter to inform you that you can't have it both ways. Either you provide customers with cars with full gas tanks or you don't. And if you don't, you shouldn't charge them when they return with empty tanks!

In view of the fact that I picked up a car in Fredericton on June 23 with an empty tank, I had to fill it immediately. Then I drove it until June 26. When I returned the car to Wolfville, as previously planned, I naturally let the tank go nearly empty, since that is the way I received the car in Fredericton. But your attendant in Wolfville charged me to fill the tank—$49.43 (premium gasoline at premium prices)! Although I explained to her that I had received it with an empty tank, she kept telling me that company policy required that she charge for a fill-up. My total bill came to $426.50, which, you must agree, is a lot of money for a rental period of only three days. I have the signed rental agreement and a receipt showing that I paid the full amount and that it included $49.43 for a gas fill-up when I returned the car. Any correspondence should be directed to the undersigned at Impact Group, 900 St. Charles Street East, Longueuil, Montréal, QC J4H 3Y2.

Inasmuch as my company is a new customer and inasmuch as we had hoped to use your agency for our future car rentals because of your competitive rates, I trust that you will give this matter your prompt attention.

Your unhappy customer,

8.5 Document for Analysis: Instructions (Obj. 4)

Your Task. Analyze the following first draft of an e-mail describing a new process for reporting equipment repairs. The message is addressed to one employee, but it will also be sent to others. List at least five weaknesses. If your instructor directs, revise the message.

To:	Sam Oliver<sam.oliver@stcc.edu>
From:	Alexandra Tutson<alex.tutson@stcc.edu>
Cc:	
Subject:	Repairs

This message is to let you know that we have recently instituted a new process for all equipment repairs. Effective immediately, we are no longer using the "Equipment Repair Form" that we formerly used. We want to move everyone to an online database system. This new process will help us repair your equipment faster and keep track of it better. You will find the new procedure at http://www.BigWebDesk.net. That's where you log in. You should indicate the kind of repair you need. It may be for AudioVisual, Mac, PC, or Printer. Then you should begin the process of data entry for your specific problem by selecting Create New Ticket. The new ticket should be printed and attached securely to the equipment. Should you have questions or trouble, just call Sylvia at Extension 255. You can also write to her at *sylvia.freeman@stcc.edu*. The warehouse truck driver will pick up and deliver your equipment as we have always done in the past.

Alexandra Tutson, Manager
Operations and Facilities
alex.tutson@stcc.edu
(705) 355-3200, Ext. 230

8.6 Direct Request: Seeking a New Look for the Company Web Site (Obj. 3)

E-MAIL

You are part of the newly formed committee on Web site redesign. Its function is to look into the possible redesign of your company Web site. Some managers think that the site is looking a bit dated. The committee delegates you to ask Cole Prewarski, Web master and manager, some questions. The committee wonders whether he has done any usability tests on the current site. The committee wants to know how much a total site redesign might cost.

It also would like to know about the cost of a partial redesign. Someone wanted to know whether animation, sound, or video could be added and wondered if Cole would recommend doing so. Someone else thought that the timing of a redesign might be important. The committee asks you to add other questions to your memo. Invite Cole to a meeting April 6. Assume that he knows about the committee.

Your Task. Write an e-mail to Cole Prewarski (*cprewarski@global.net*) requesting answers to several questions and inviting him to a meeting.

8.7 Direct Response Memo: Luxury Hotels Embrace Signature Scents (Obj. 3)

WEB

Hotel chains are constantly seeking new ways to make guests want to return. Comfy beds and smiling clerks are not enough. Many hotels are now developing signature scents to waft through lobbies, restaurants, meeting rooms, and pool areas.

As an assistant to Michelle Long, CEO of a small hotel chain, you received an interesting assignment. Ms. Long recently visited the Westin Grand in Vancouver, B.C, and was impressed not only with its atmosphere but also with its custom fragrance. You discovered that Westin Hotels & Resorts uses a custom designed white tea aroma, which is also available to customers to enjoy at home in the form of candles, potpourri, and room diffusers. She asks you to conduct research online to discover what hotels are using fragrances and what scents are associated with each property. Her goal is to decide whether this trend is something her small hotel chain might follow.

In your research you discovered that Omni Hotels engage hidden machines to spray a lemongrass and green tea scent into the lobby. Omni also uses a coconut fragrance, for a tropical effect, near the pool. Apparently finding that scents are appealing, Omni plans to extend its fragrances to its meeting spaces. It is considering citrus, which is supposed to enhance energy. In Paris the fashionable Hotel Costes treats guests to an exclusive custom scent with notes of lavender, bay tree, coriander, white pepper, rose, incense, woods, and musk. Luxury properties are embracing signature fragrances to create an emotional connection to their hotels.

Your research also reveals a Web site complaining that hotels are contributing to the "sick building syndrome" by masking chemical smells with fragrances. Proponents of fragrance-free hotels recommend striving for fresh, not perfumed, air.

Your Task. Conduct additional Web research so that you can report on at least five hotels and their signature scents. Address a concise interoffice memo (or an e-mail if your instructor directs) to CEO Michelle Long. Decide whether to mention the argument for fragrance-free hotels. In addition, think about how you can make your findings most readable.

8.8 Instruction E-Mail or Memo: New Process for Purchase Requests (Obj. 4)

E-MAIL

Along with your parents, brothers, and sisters, you own a share of a growing family business with 55 employees. As the head of the Purchasing Department, you realize that the business must keep better track of purchases. Some employees use the company purchasing order forms, but others submit sloppy e-mails or handwritten notes that are barely legible. What's worse, you are not sure whether the requested purchase has been authorized by the budget manager. You talk to the family management council, and they urge you to establish a standard procedure for submitting purchase requests.

Because the business has a good Web site, you decide that purchase requests must now be downloaded from the company intranet (http://www.lynch.com/intranet). To provide the fastest service, employees should fill out the new purchase request form. This may be done manually or digitally. Employees must include complete information for each requested purchase: date, quantities, catalogue numbers, complete descriptions, complete vendor mailing address and contact information, delivery requirements, and shipping methods (usually f.o.b.). The Purchasing Department should be sent the original, and a copy should be kept by the requesting employee. An important step in the new procedure is approval by the budget manager on the request form. That is, employees should talk to the budget manager and get her approval before submitting the purchase request. You think this new procedure will solve many problems for you and for employees.

Your Task. As Purchasing Department manager, write an e-mail or a hard-copy memo (as your instructor directs) to all employees informing them of the new procedure.

8.9 Instruction E-Mail or Memo: Describing a Workplace Procedure (Obj. 4)

E-MAIL

At your job or organization, assume that a new employee has joined the staff and the boss has asked you to write out a set of instructions for some task. It could be sending faxes, printing copies, answering the phone, setting up appointments, scheduling conferences, training employees, greeting customers, closing a cash register, opening the office, closing the office, or any other task that has at least five steps.

Your Task. Prepare an e-mail or memo to your manager, Josh Washington, in response to his request for a set of instructions for the task.

8.10 Direct Claim: Protesting Unexpected Charges (Obj. 5)

As vice president of Breaktime Preferred Travel, you are upset with Premier Promos. Premier is a catalogue company that provides imprinted promotional products for companies. Your travel service was looking for something special to offer in promoting its cruise ship travel packages. Premier offered free samples of its promotional merchandise, under its "No Surprise" policy.

You thought, *What can we lose?* So on January 11, you placed a telephone order for a number of samples. These included an insulated lunch sack, a portable power strip in a zippered case, a square-ended barrel bag with fanny pack, a deluxe canvas attaché case, and two colours of garment-dyed sweatshirts. All items were supposed to be free. You did think it odd that you were asked for your company's MasterCard number, but Premier promised to bill you only if you kept the samples.

When the items arrived, you were not pleased, and you returned them all on January 21 (you have a postal receipt showing the return). But your February credit card statement showed a charge of $258.20 for the sample items. You called Premier in February and spoke to Virginia, who assured you that a credit would be made on your next statement. However, your March statement showed no credit. You called again and received a similar promise. It's now April and no credit has been made. You realize that this situation is now too complicated for another telephone call, and you decide to write and demand action.

Your Task. Write a claim letter that documents the problem and states the action that you want taken. Add any information you feel is necessary. Address your letter to Ms. Arletta Sandusky, Customer Services, Premier Promos, 240 Ninth Street South, Langley, BC V2Y 2R1.

8.11 Adjustment: Backing Up "No Surprise" Offer (Obj. 6)

Premier Promos prides itself on its "No Surprise" offer. This means that anything ordered from its catalogue of promotional products may be returned for a full refund within two weeks of purchase. The claim from Breaktime Preferred Travel (see Activity 8.10) describes an order placed January 11 and returned January 21. As assistant to the Customer Services manager, you check the return files and see that items were received January 25. You speak with service agent Virginia, who agrees with you—the credit of $258.20 should have been granted to Breaktime Preferred Travel. She reminds you that a new system for handling returns was implemented in February. Perhaps the Breaktime return slipped through the cracks. Regardless of the reason, you decide to tell accounting to issue the credit immediately.

Your Task. In an adjustment letter, try to regain the confidence and the business of Breaktime Preferred Travel, 1101 Bloor

Street East, Oshawa, ON L1H 7K6. Include a sample imprinted travel mug in a gift box and a Coleman 8-quart jug cooler. You know that you are the most reliable source for the lowest-priced imprinted promotional products in the field, and this travel agency should be able to find something suitable in your catalogue. Address your letter to Leticia Vascellaro, and sign it with your name.

8.12 Thanks for a Favour: Got the Job! (Obj. 7)

Congratulations! You completed your degree or diploma and got a terrific job in your field. One of your instructors was especially helpful to you when you were a student. This instructor also wrote an effective letter of recommendation that was instrumental in helping you obtain your job.

Your Task. Write a letter thanking your instructor.

Grammar and Mechanics C.L.U.E. Review 8

Capitalization

Review Guides 39–46 about capitalization in Appendix A: Grammar and Mechanics Guide (Competent Language Usage Essentials), beginning on page A-16. On a separate sheet, revise the following sentences to correct capitalization errors. For each error that you locate, write the guide number that reflects this usage. Sentences may have more than one error. If a sentence is correct, write C. When finished, compare your responses with the key beginning on page Key-1.

Example: Neither the President nor the Operations Manager would comment on the Company rumour that it would close its midwest factory.

Revision: Neither the **president** nor the **operations manager** would comment on the **company** rumour that it would close its **Midwest** factory. [Guides 41, 43]

1. Once the Management Team and the Union members finally agreed, mayor knox signed the Agreement.

2. All westjet airlines passengers must exit the Plane at gate 14 when they reach pearson international airport.

3. The vice president of the united states urged members of the european union to continue to seek peace in the middle east.

4. My Uncle, who lives in the west, has Skippy Peanut Butter and coca-cola for Breakfast.

5. Our Marketing Manager and Director of Sales thought that the Company should purchase BlackBerry Smartphones for all Sales Reps.

6. Personal Tax Rates for japanese citizens are low by International standards, according to professor yamaguchi at osaka university.

7. Jinhee Kim, who heads our customer communication division, has a Master's Degree in social psychology from the university of calgary.

8. Please consult figure 4.5 in chapter 4 to obtain statistics Canada population figures for the pacific northwest.

9. Last Fall did you see the article titled "The global consequences of using crops for fuel"?

10. Toby plans to take courses in Marketing, Business Law, and English in the Spring.

Endnotes

[1] Goar, C. (2011, February 1). A smarter post office might thrive. *Toronto Star*. Retrieved April 15, 2011, from http://www.thestar.com/opinion/editorialopinion/article/931800-goar-a-smarter-post-office-might-thrive

[2] Goar, C. (2011, February 2). Canada Post struggles to deliver in digital age. *Toronto Star*. Retrieved April 15, 2011, from http://www.thestar.com/opinion/editorialopinion/article/930194--goar-canada-post-struggles-to-deliver-in-digital-age

[3] Messmer, M. (2001, January). Enhancing your writing skills. *Strategic Finance*, pp. 8–10. Retrieved January 15, 2010, from Business Source Complete database.

[4] Zhu, Y., & White, C. (2009, September). Practitioners' views about the use of business email within organizational settings: Implications for developing student generic competence. *Business Communication Quarterly, 72*(3), 292.

[5] Laidlaw, S. (2009, April 27). Saying "sorry" is a way back to grace. *Toronto Star*, pp. E1, E6.

[6] Davidow, M. (2003, February). Organizational responses to customer complaints: What works and what doesn't.

Journal of Service Research, 5(3), 225. Retrieved February 2, 2010, from Business Source Premier database; Blackburn-Brockman, E., & Belanger, K. (1993, June). You-attitude and positive emphasis: Testing received wisdom in business communication. *Bulletin of the Association for Business Communication*, 1–5; Mascolini, M. (1994, June). Another look at teaching the external negative message. *Bulletin of the Association for Business Communication*, 46.

[7] Liao, H. (2007, March). Do it right this time: The role of employee service recovery performance in customer-perceived justice and customer loyalty after service failures. *Journal of Applied Psychology, 92*(2), 475. Retrieved June 3, 2007, from Business Source Premier (EBSCO) database; Gilbert, P. (1996, December). Two words that can help a business thrive. *The Wall Street Journal*, p. A12.

[8] Caddell, M. H. (2003, November/December). Is letter writing dead? OfficePro, 22.

[9] Fallows, J. (2005, June 12). Enough keyword searches. Just answer my question. *The New York Times*, p. BU3.

Get more practice at **www.guffeybrief4e.nelson.com**

CHAPTER 9

Negative Messages

OBJECTIVES

After studying this chapter, you should be able to

1. Describe the goals and strategies of business communicators in conveying negative news effectively, including applying the writing process and avoiding legal liability.

2. Decide whether to use the direct or indirect strategy in conveying negative news.

3. Analyze the components of effective negative messages, including opening with a buffer, apologizing, conveying empathy, presenting the reasons, cushioning the bad news, and closing pleasantly.

4. Describe and apply effective techniques for refusing typical requests.

5. Explain and apply effective techniques for handling bad news with customers.

6. Understand and apply effective techniques for delivering bad news within organizations.

© i love images/Alamy

Apologies are an important part of Western society. People not only value an apology but also expect one when they feel wronged. Apologies provide an opportunity to validate the hurt of another person; however, a defensive apology, such as "I am sorry, but . . ." negates any positive effect.[1] How can you tell when an apology is sincere? When do you expect an apology?

Conveying Negative News Effectively

LEARNING OBJECTIVE 1

Describe the goals and strategies of business communicators in conveying negative news effectively, including applying the writing process and avoiding legal liability.

Bad things happen in all businesses. At major airlines, for example, storms cancel or delay flights, baggage is misplaced, and air traffic interrupts schedules. In other businesses, goods are not delivered, products fail to perform as expected, service is poor, billing gets fouled up, or customers are misunderstood. You may have to write messages ending business relationships, declining proposals, announcing price increases, refusing requests for donations, terminating employees, turning down invitations, or responding to unhappy customers. You might have to apologize for mistakes in orders, errors in pricing, the rudeness of employees, overlooked appointments, substandard service, pricing errors, faulty accounting, defective products, or jumbled instructions. As a company employee, you may even have to respond to complaints voiced to the world on Twitter, Facebook, or complaint Web sites.

The sad truth is that everyone occasionally must deliver bad news in business. Because bad news disappoints, irritates, and sometimes angers the receiver, such messages must be written carefully. The bad feelings associated with disappointing news can generally be reduced if the receiver (a) knows the reasons for the rejection, (b) feels that the news was revealed sensitively, and (c) believes the matter was treated seriously and fairly.

In this chapter you will learn when to use the direct strategy and when to use the indirect strategy to deliver bad news. You will study the goals of business communicators in working with bad news and learn techniques for achieving those goals.

Establishing Goals in Communicating Negative News

Delivering negative news is not the happiest communication task you may have, but it can be gratifying if you do it effectively. As a business communicator working with bad news, you will have many goals, the most important of which are these:

When working with bad news, explain clearly and completely, project a professional image, and maintain friendly relations.

- **Explaining clearly and completely.** Your message should be clear so that the receiver understands and, we hope, accepts the bad news. The receiver should not have to call or write to clarify the message.

- **Projecting a professional image.** You will strive to project a professional and positive image of you and your organization. Even when irate customers use a threatening tone or overstate their claims, you must use polite language, control your emotions, and respond with clear explanations of why a negative message was necessary.

- **Conveying empathy and sensitivity.** Bad news is better accepted if it is delivered sensitively. Use language that respects the receiver and attempts to reduce bad feelings. Accepting blame, when appropriate, and apologizing go far in smoothing over negative messages. But avoid creating legal liability or responsibility for you or your organization.

- **Being fair.** Show that the situation or decision was fair, impartial, and rational. Receivers are far more likely to accept negative news if they feel they were treated fairly.

- **Maintaining friendly relations.** Make an effort to include statements that show your desire to continue pleasant relations with the receiver. As you learned in Chapter 8 in writing adjustment messages, one of your goals is to regain the confidence of customers.

These are ambitious goals, and we are not always successful in achieving them all. However, many senders have found the strategies and techniques you are about to learn helpful in conveying disappointing news sensitively and safely. With experience, you will be able to vary these strategies and adapt them to your organization's specific communication tasks.

Applying the 3-x-3 Writing Process

Thinking through the entire writing process is especially important in bad-news messages because the way bad news is revealed often determines how it is accepted. Certain techniques can help you deliver bad news sensitively, beginning with the familiar 3-x-3 writing process.

The 3-x-3 process is especially helpful in crafting bad-news messages.

Analysis, Anticipation, and Adaptation.

In Phase 1 (prewriting), you need to analyze the bad news and anticipate its effect on the receiver. When you have bad news to convey, one of your first considerations is how that message will affect its receiver. If the disappointment will be mild, announce it directly. If the bad news is serious or personal, consider techniques to reduce the pain. For example, prepare the reader, give reasons for the negative news, possibly offer alternatives, and seek the goodwill of the receiver.

Choose words that show you respect the reader as a responsible, valuable person. Select the best channel to deliver the bad news. In many negative situations, you will be dealing with a customer. If your goal is retaining the goodwill of a customer, a letter on company stationery will be more impressive than an e-mail.

Research, Organization, and Composition.

In Phase 2 (writing), you will gather information and brainstorm for ideas. Jot down all the reasons you have that explain the bad news. If four or five reasons prompted your negative decision, concentrate on the strongest and safest ones. Avoid presenting any weak reasons; readers may seize on them to reject the entire message. Include ample explanation of the negative situation, and avoid fixing blame. In composing any negative message, conduct research if necessary to help you explain what went wrong and why a decision or action is necessary.

Revision, Proofreading, and Evaluation.

In Phase 3 (revising), you will read over your message carefully to ensure that it says what you intend. Check your wording to be sure you are concise without being brusque. If you find that you have overused certain words, click on your word processing thesaurus to find synonyms. Read your sentences to see if they sound like conversation and flow smoothly. This is the time to edit and improve coherence and tone. In bad-news messages, the tone is especially important. Readers are more likely to accept negative messages if the tone is friendly and respectful. Even when the bad news can't be changed, its effect can be reduced somewhat by the way it is presented.

In the last phase of the writing process, proofread to make sure your verbs agree with their subjects, your sentences are properly punctuated, and all words are spelled correctly. Pay attention to common mistakes (*its/it's; than/then; their/there*). If your word processing program checks grammar, be sure to investigate those squiggly underscores. Finally, evaluate your message. Is it too blunt? Too subtle? Have you delivered the bad news clearly but professionally?

Avoiding Legal Liability in Conveying Negative News

Before we examine the components of a negative message, let's look more closely at how you can avoid exposing yourself and your employer to legal liability in writing negative messages. Although we can't always anticipate the consequences of our words, we should be alert to three causes of legal difficulties: (1) abusive language, (2) careless language, and (3) the good-guy syndrome.

Abusive Language.

Calling people names (such as *deadbeat*, *crook*, or *quack*) can get you into trouble. *Defamation* is the legal term for any false statement that harms an individual's reputation. When the abusive language is written, it is called *libel*; when spoken, it is *slander*.

To be actionable (likely to result in a lawsuit), abusive language must be (a) false, (b) damaging to the person's good name, and (c) "published"—that is, written or spoken within the presence of others. Therefore, if you were alone with Jane Doe and accused her of accepting bribes and selling company secrets to competitors, she couldn't sue because the defamation wasn't published. Her reputation was not damaged. However, if anyone heard the words or if they were written, you might be legally liable.

In a new wrinkle, you may now be prosecuted if you transmit a harassing or libellous message by e-mail or post it on social networking sites, such as Facebook and Twitter.[2] Such electronic transmissions are considered to be published. Moreover, a company may incur liability for messages sent through its computer system by employees. That's why many companies are increasing their monitoring of both outgoing and internal messages. Instant messaging adds another danger for companies. Whether your message is in print or electronic, avoid making unproven charges or letting your emotions prompt abusive language.

Careless Language.

As the marketplace becomes increasingly litigious, we must be certain that our words communicate only what we intend. Take the case of a factory worker injured on the job. His lawyer subpoenaed company documents and discovered a seemingly harmless letter sent to a group regarding a plant tour. These words appeared in the letter: "Although we are honoured at your interest in our company, we cannot give your group a tour of the plant operations as it would be too noisy and dangerous." The court found in favour of the worker, inferring from the letter that working conditions were indeed hazardous.[3] The letter writer did not intend to convey the impression of dangerous working conditions, but the court accepted that interpretation.

The Good-Guy Syndrome.

Most of us hate to have to reveal bad news—that is, to be the bad guy. To make ourselves look better, to make the receiver feel better, and to maintain good relations, we are tempted to make statements that are legally dangerous.

Business communicators must be aware that they act as agents of their organizations. Their words, decisions, and opinions are assumed to represent those of the organization. If you want to communicate your personal feelings or opinions, use your home computer or write on plain paper (rather than company letterhead) and sign your name without title or affiliation. Second, volunteering extra information can lead to trouble. Therefore, avoid supplying data that could be misused, and avoid making promises that can't be fulfilled. Don't admit or imply responsibility for conditions that caused damage or injury. As mentioned in Chapter 8, even apologies (*We're sorry that a faulty bottle cap caused damage to your carpet*) may suggest liability.

Language becomes legally actionable if it is false, damaging to someone's good name, and published.

Careful writers ensure that their words communicate only what they intend.

In an effort to make the receiver feel better, some writers may be tempted to make legally dangerous statements.

Examining Negative News Strategies

LEARNING OBJECTIVE 2

Decide whether to use the direct or indirect strategy in conveying negative news.

You have at your disposal two basic strategies for delivering negative news: direct and indirect. Which approach is best suited for your particular message? One of the first steps you will take before delivering negative news is analyzing how your receiver will react to this news. In earlier chapters we discussed applying the direct strategy to positive messages. We suggested using the indirect strategy when the audience might be unwilling, uninterested, displeased, disappointed, or hostile. In this chapter we expand on that advice and suggest additional considerations that help you decide which strategy to use.

When to Use the Direct Strategy

Many bad-news messages are organized indirectly, beginning with a buffer and reasons. However, the direct strategy, with the bad news first, may be more effective in such situations as the following:

- **When the bad news is not damaging.** If the bad news is insignificant (such as a small increase in cost) and doesn't personally affect the receiver, then the direct strategy certainly makes sense.

- **When the receiver may overlook the bad news.** Changes in service, new policy requirements, legal announcements—these critical messages may require boldness to ensure attention.

- **When the organization or receiver prefers directness.** Some companies and individuals expect all internal messages and announcements—even bad news— to be straightforward and presented without frills.

- **When firmness is necessary.** Messages that must demonstrate determination and strength should not use delaying techniques. For example, the last in a series of collection letters that seek payment of overdue accounts may require a direct opener.

Notice in Figure 9.1 that a small rate increase for a newspaper subscription is announced directly because it is unlikely to upset or irritate the receiver. However, many companies prefer to announce even small rate increases more indirectly. They usually want to explain why the increase is necessary before announcing it. Let's now explore when and how to use the indirect strategy in delivering negative news.

When to Use the Indirect Strategy

Many communicators prefer to use the indirect strategy to present negative news. Whereas good news can be revealed quickly, bad news may be easier to accept when broken gradually. Here are instances when the indirect strategy works well:

- **When the bad news is personally upsetting.** If the negative news involves the receiver personally, such as a layoff notice, the indirect strategy makes sense. Telling an employee that he or she no longer has a job is probably best done in person and by starting indirectly and giving reasons first. When a company has made a mistake that inconveniences or disadvantages a customer, the indirect strategy makes sense.

- **When the bad news will provoke a hostile reaction.** When your message will irritate or infuriate the recipient, the indirect method may be best. It begins with a buffer and reasons, thus encouraging the reader to finish reading or hearing the message. A blunt announcement may make the receiver stop reading.

  > Use the indirect strategy when the bad news is personally upsetting or if it will provoke a hostile reaction.

- **When the bad news threatens the customer relationship.** If the negative message may damage a customer relationship, the indirect strategy may help salvage the customer bond. Beginning slowly and presenting reasons that explain what happened can be more helpful than directly announcing bad news or failing to adequately explain the reasons.

- **When the bad news is unexpected.** Readers who are totally surprised by bad news tend to have a more negative reaction than those who expected the bad news. If

FIGURE 9.1 **Announcing Bad News Directly**

Uses direct
strategy
because this
small rate
increase is
unlikely to
upset receiver

Mentions specific
improvements
and how these
changes benefit
the receiver

The Calgary Times

The Calgary Times
404 17th Street West
Calgary, AB T2E 3P5

KAREN R. McDonald
Senior Vice President
Circulation

February 3, 2014

Dear Home Delivery Customer:

Effective February 5, *The Calgary Times* will increase the price of home delivery—the first time we have raised rates in the past five years.

The increase, averaging 8 cents a day for the daily paper and 25 cents for the Sunday paper, reflects higher costs of producing and distributing the paper, including increased newsprint prices and improvements to better serve our customers nationwide.

Since our last rate increase, *The Calgary Times* has introduced a number of significant changes to the paper, including later deadlines for news and enhanced news coverage, with such new sections as "Circuits." In addition, as many of our readers across the country know, we have made extensive efforts to build our national delivery network—so that more readers can benefit from the convenience of home delivery, wherever they live.

We truly value your readership and remain dedicated to meeting the highest journalistic and customer service standards on behalf of our readers in the months and years ahead.

Sincerely,

Karen R. McDonald

Karen R. McDonald
Vice President, Circulation

P.S. If you are currently receiving *The Calgary Times* at a special introductory rate, the new rates will take effect at the end of your introductory period.

Explains why
rate increase is
necessary and
breaks increase
into small
segments to
reduce impact

Ends on pleasant
note with positive
forward look

a company suddenly closes an office or a plant and employees had no inkling of the closure, that bad news would be better received if it were revealed cautiously with reasons first.

Whether to use the direct or indirect strategy depends largely on the situation, the reaction you expect from the audience, and your goals. The direct method saves time and is preferred by some who consider it to be more professional and even more ethical than the indirect method. Others think that revealing bad news slowly and indirectly shows sensitivity to the receiver. By preparing the receiver, you tend to soften the impact. As you can see in Figure 9.2, the major differences between the two strategies depend on whether you start with a buffer and how early you explain the reasons for the negative news.

FIGURE 9.2 **Comparing the Direct and Indirect Strategies for Negative Messages**

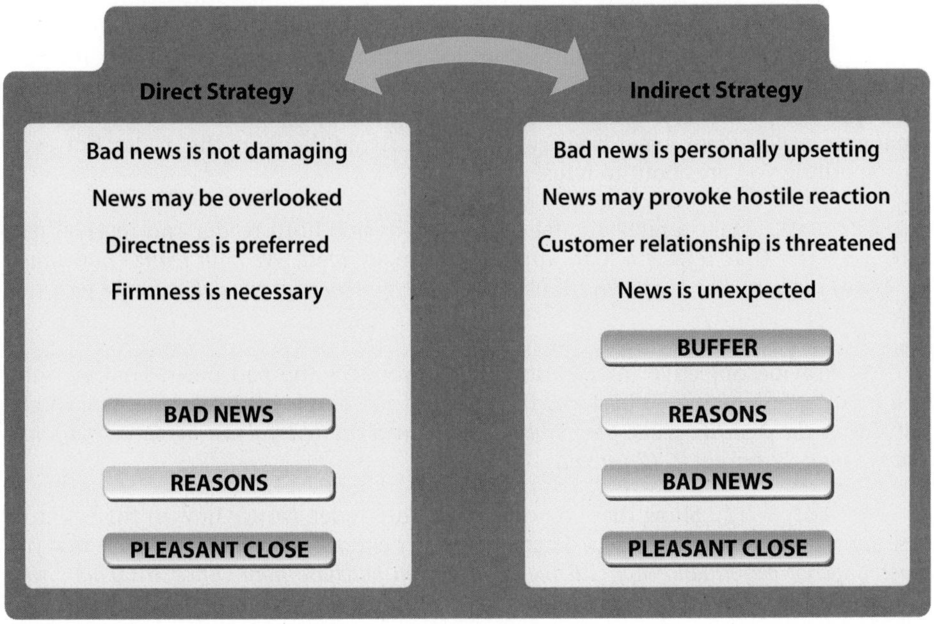

Direct Strategy ⟷ **Indirect Strategy**

Direct Strategy	Indirect Strategy
Bad news is not damaging	Bad news is personally upsetting
News may be overlooked	News may provoke hostile reaction
Directness is preferred	Customer relationship is threatened
Firmness is necessary	News is unexpected
	BUFFER
BAD NEWS	REASONS
REASONS	BAD NEWS
PLEASANT CLOSE	PLEASANT CLOSE

Analyzing the Components of Effective Negative Messages

Even though it may be impossible to make the receiver happy when delivering negative news, you can reduce bad feelings and resentment by structuring your message sensitively. Most negative messages contain some or all of these parts: buffer, reasons, bad news, and closing. This section also discusses apologies and how to convey empathy in delivering bad news.

Buffer to Open Indirect Messages

If you decide to use the indirect strategy, your message might begin with a buffer. A buffer is a device to reduce shock or pain. To buffer the pain of bad news, begin with a neutral but meaningful statement that makes the reader continue reading. The buffer should be relevant and concise and provide a natural transition to the explanation that follows. The individual situation, of course, will help determine what you should put in the buffer. Avoid trite buffers, such as *Thank you for your letter.*

It should be noted that not all business communication authors agree that buffers actually increase the effectiveness of negative messages. However, in many cultures softening bad news is appreciated. Following are various buffer possibilities.

Best News. Start with the part of the message that represents the best news. For example, a message to workers announced new health plan rules limiting prescriptions to a 34-day supply and increasing co-payments. With home delivery, however, employees could save up to $24 on each prescription. To emphasize the good news, you might write, *You can now achieve significant savings and avoid trips to the drugstore by having your prescription drugs delivered to your home.*[4]

Compliment. Praise the receiver's accomplishments, organization, or efforts, but do so with honesty and sincerity. For instance, in a letter declining an invitation to speak,

LEARNING OBJECTIVE 3

Analyze the components of effective negative messages, including opening with a buffer, apologizing, conveying empathy, presenting the reasons, cushioning the bad news, and closing pleasantly.

Buffer the opening of a bad-news message by beginning with the best news, a compliment, or appreciation.

you could write, *The Thalians have my sincere admiration for their fundraising projects on behalf of hungry children. I am honoured that you asked me to speak Friday, November 5.*

Appreciation. Convey thanks for doing business, for sending something, for showing confidence in your organization, for expressing feelings, or simply for providing feedback. Suppose you had to draft a letter that refuses employment. You could say, *I appreciated learning about the hospitality management program at Niagara College and about your qualifications in our interview last Friday.* Avoid thanking the reader, however, for something you are about to refuse.

Agreement. Make a relevant statement with which both reader and receiver can agree. A letter that rejects a loan application might read, *We both realize how much the export business has been affected by the relative weakness of the dollar in the past two years.*

Facts. Provide objective information that introduces the bad news. For example, in a memo announcing cutbacks in the hours of the employees' cafeteria, you might say, *During the past five years, the number of employees eating breakfast in our cafeteria has dropped from 32 percent to 12 percent.*

Understanding. Show that you care about the reader. Notice how in this letter to customers announcing a product defect, the writer expresses concern: *We know that you expect superior performance from all the products you purchase from OfficeCity. That's why we're writing personally about the Omega printer cartridges you recently ordered.*

Apologizing

Apologies to customers are important if you or your company erred.

You learned about making apologies in adjustment messages discussed in Chapter 8. We expand that discussion here because apologies are often part of negative-news messages. The truth is that sincere apologies work. Peter Post, great-grandson of famed etiquette expert Emily Post and director of the Emily Post Institute, said that North Americans love apologies. They will forgive almost anything if presented with a sincere apology.[5] An apology is defined as an "admission of blameworthiness and regret for an undesirable event."[6] Apologies to customers are especially important if you or your company erred. They cost nothing, and they go a long way in soothing hard feelings. Here are some tips on how to apologize effectively in business messages:

- **Apologize sincerely.** People dislike apologies that sound hollow (*We regret that you were inconvenienced* or *We regret that you are disturbed*). Focusing on your regret does not convey sincerity. Explaining what you will do to prevent recurrence of the problem projects sincerity in an apology.

- **Accept responsibility.** One CEO was criticized for the following weak apology: *"I want our customers to know how much I personally regret any difficulties you may experience as a result of the unauthorized intrusion into our computer systems."* Apology experts faulted this apology because it did not acknowledge responsibility.[7]

- **Use good judgment.** Don't admit blame if it might prompt a lawsuit.

Consider these poor and improved apologies:

Poor apology: *We regret that you are unhappy with the price of ice cream purchased at one of our scoop shops.*

Improved apology: *We are genuinely sorry that you were disappointed in the price of ice cream recently purchased at one of our scoop shops. Your opinion is important to us, and we appreciate your giving us the opportunity to look into the problem you describe.*

Poor apology: *We apologize if anyone was affected.*

Improved apology: *I apologize for the frustration our delay caused you. As soon as I received your message, I began looking into the cause of the delay and realized that our delivery tracking system must be improved.*

Conveying Empathy

One of the hardest things to do in negative messages is to convey sympathy and empathy. As discussed in Chapter 3, *empathy* is the ability to understand and enter into the feelings of another. When a listeriosis outbreak at Maple Leaf Foods caused illness and even death, CEO Michael McCain publicly apologized. He said, "Tragically, our products have been linked to illness and loss of life. To those people who are ill, and to the families who have lost loved ones, I offer my deepest and sincerest sympathies. Words cannot begin to express our sadness for their pain."[8] McCain put himself into the shoes of his customers and tried to experience their pain. Here are other examples of ways to express empathy in written messages:

- In writing to an unhappy customer: *We did not intentionally delay the shipment, and we sincerely regret the disappointment and frustration you must have suffered.*

- In laying off employees: *It is with great regret that we must take this step. Rest assured that I will be more than happy to write letters of recommendation for anyone who asks.*

- In responding to a complaint: *I am deeply saddened that our service failure disrupted your sale, and we will do everything in our power to. . . .*

- In showing genuine feelings: *You have every right to be disappointed. I am truly sorry that. . . .*

Empathy is the ability to understand and enter into the feelings of another.

Presenting the Reasons

The most important part of a negative message is the section devoted to reasons. Without sound reasons for denying a request, refusing a claim, or revealing other bad news, a message will fail, no matter how cleverly it is organized or written. For example, if you must deny a customer's request, as part of your planning before writing, you analyzed the request and decided to refuse it for specific reasons. Where do you place your reasons? In the indirect strategy, explain your reasons before disclosing the bad news. In the direct strategy, the reasons appear immediately after the disclosure of the bad news. Providing an explanation reduces feelings of ill will and improves the chances that readers will accept the bad news.

The most important part of a bad-news letter is the section devoted to reasons.

Explaining Clearly. If the reasons are not confidential and if they will not create legal liability, you can be specific: *Growers supplied us with a limited number of patio roses, and our demand this year was twice that of last year.* In responding to a billing error, explain what happened: *After you informed us of an error on your January bill, we investigated the matter and admit the mistake was ours. Until our new automated system is fully online, we are still subject to the frailties of human error. Rest assured that your account has been credited as you will see on your next bill.* In refusing a speaking engagement, tell why the date is impossible: *On January 17 we have a board of directors meeting that I must attend.* Don't, however, make unrealistic or dangerous statements in an effort to be the "good guy."

Citing Reader or Other Benefits, if Plausible. Readers are more open to bad news if in some way, even indirectly, it may help them. In refusing a customer's request for free hemming of skirts and slacks, one clothing company wrote: "We tested our ability to hem skirts a few months ago. This process proved to be very time-consuming. We have decided not to offer this service because the additional cost would have increased the selling price of our skirts substantially, and we did not want to impose that cost on all our customers."[9] Readers also accept bad news more readily if they recognize that someone or something else benefits, such as other workers or the environment: *Although we would like to consider your application, we prefer to fill managerial positions from within.* Avoid trying to show reader benefits, though, if they appear insincere: *To improve our service to you, we are increasing our brokerage fees.*

Explaining Company Policy.

Readers resent blanket policy statements prohibiting something: *Company policy prevents us from making cash refunds* or *Contract bids may be accepted from local companies only* or *Company policy requires us to promote from within*. Instead of hiding behind company policy, gently explain why the policy makes sense: *We prefer to promote from within because it rewards the loyalty of our employees. In addition, we have found that people familiar with our organization make the quickest contribution to our team effort.* By offering explanations, you demonstrate that you care about readers and are treating them as important individuals.

Choosing Positive Words.

Because the words you use can affect a reader's response, choose carefully. Remember that the objective of the indirect strategy is holding the reader's attention until you have had a chance to explain the reasons justifying the bad news. To keep the reader in a receptive mood, avoid expressions with punitive, demoralizing, or otherwise negative connotations. Stay away from such words as *cannot, claim, denied, error, failure, fault, impossible, mistaken, misunderstand, never, regret, rejected, unable, unwilling, unfortunately,* and *violate*.

Showing That the Matter Was Treated Seriously and Fairly.

In explaining reasons, demonstrate to the reader that you take the matter seriously, have investigated carefully, and are making an unbiased decision. Receivers are more accepting of disappointing news when they feel that their requests have been heard and that they have been treated fairly. In cancelling funding for a program, board members provided this explanation: *As you know, the publication of* Rural Artist *was funded by a renewable annual grant from the Alberta Foundation for the Arts. Recent cutbacks in provincially sponsored arts programs have left us with few funds. Because our grant has been discontinued, we have no alternative but to cease publication of* Rural Artist. *You have my assurance that the board has searched long and hard for some other viable funding, but every avenue of recourse has been closed before us. Accordingly, June's issue will be our last.*

Cushioning the Bad News

Although you can't prevent the disappointment that bad news brings, you can reduce the pain somewhat by breaking the news sensitively. Be especially considerate when the reader will suffer personally from the bad news. A number of thoughtful techniques can cushion the blow.

Positioning the Bad News Strategically.

Instead of spotlighting it, sandwich the bad news between other sentences, perhaps among your reasons. Don't let the refusal begin or end a paragraph; the reader's eye will linger on these high-visibility spots. Another technique that reduces shock is putting a painful idea in a subordinate clause: *Although another candidate was hired, we appreciate your interest in our organization and wish you every success in your job search.* Subordinate clauses often begin with such words as *although, as, because, if,* and *since*.

Using the Passive Voice.

Passive-voice verbs enable you to depersonalize an action. Whereas the active voice focuses attention on a person (*We don't give cash refunds*), the passive voice highlights the action (*Cash refunds are not given because . . .*). Use the passive voice for the bad news. In some instances you can combine passive-voice verbs and a subordinate clause: *Although franchise scoop shop owners cannot be required to lower their ice cream prices, we are happy to pass along your comments for their consideration.*

Accentuating the Positive.

As you learned earlier, messages are far more effective when you describe what you can do instead of what you can't do. Rather than *We will no longer allow credit card purchases,* try a more positive appeal: *We are now selling gasoline at discount cash prices.*

Implying the Refusal.

It is sometimes possible to avoid a direct statement of refusal. Often, your reasons and explanations leave no doubt that a request has been denied. Explicit refusals may be unnecessary and at times cruel. In this refusal to contribute to a charity, for example, the writer never actually says *no: Because we will soon be moving into new offices in Glendale, all our funds are earmarked for relocation costs. We hope that next year we will be able to support your worthwhile charity.* The danger of an implied refusal, of course, is that it is so subtle that the reader misses it. Be certain that you make the bad news clear, thus preventing the need for further correspondence.

Suggesting a Compromise or an Alternative. A refusal is not as depressing—for the sender or the receiver—if a suitable compromise, substitute, or alternative is available. In denying permission to a group of students to visit a historical private residence, for instance, this writer softens the bad news by proposing an alternative: *Although private tours of the grounds are not given, we do open the house and its gardens for one charitable event in the fall.* You can further reduce the impact of the bad news by refusing to dwell on it. Present it briefly (or imply it) and move on to your closing.

Closing Pleasantly

After explaining the bad news sensitively, close the message with a pleasant statement that promotes goodwill. The closing should be personalized and may include a forward look, an alternative, good wishes, freebies, an off-the-subject remark, or resale information. *Resale* refers to mentioning a product or service favourably to reinforce the customer's choice. For example, *you chose our best-selling model.*

Forward Look. Anticipate future relations or business. A letter that refuses a contract proposal might read: *Thanks for your bid. We look forward to working with your talented staff when future projects demand your special expertise.*

Alternative Follow-Up. If an alternative exists, end your letter with follow-through advice. For example, in a letter rejecting a customer's demand for replacement of landscaping plants, you might say: *I will be happy to give you a free inspection and consultation. Please call 613-746-8112 to arrange a date for my visit.* In a message to a prospective homebuyer: *Although the lot you saw last week is now sold, we do have two excellent view lots available at a slightly higher price.* In reacting to an Internet misprint: *Please note that our Web site contained an unfortunate misprint offering $850-per-night Bora Bora bungalows at $85. Although we cannot honour that rate, we are offering a special half-price rate of $425 to those who responded.*

Good Wishes. A letter rejecting a job candidate might read: *We appreciate your interest in our company, and we extend to you our best wishes in your search to find the perfect match between your skills and the job requirements.*

Freebies. When customers complain—primarily about food products or small consumer items—companies often send coupons, samples, or gifts to restore confidence and to promote future business. In response to a customer's complaint about a frozen dinner, you could write: *Your loyalty and your concern about our frozen entrées are genuinely appreciated. Because we want you to continue enjoying our healthful and convenient dinners, we are enclosing a coupon that you can take to your local market to select your next Green Valley entrée.*

Resale or Sales Promotion. When the bad news is not devastating or personal, references to resale information or promotion may be appropriate: *The computer workstations you ordered are unusually popular because of their stain-, heat-, and scratch-resistant finishes. To help you locate hard-to-find accessories for these workstations, we invite you to visit our Web site where our online catalogue provides a huge selection of surge suppressors, multiple outlet strips, security devices, and PC tool kits.*

Avoid endings that sound canned, insincere, inappropriate, or self-serving. Don't invite further correspondence (*If you have any questions, do not hesitate ...*), and don't refer to the bad news. Figure 9.3 reviews suggestions for delivering bad news sensitively.

> Close the bad-news message with a pleasant statement that creates goodwill.

FIGURE 9.3 **Delivering Bad News Sensitively**

Buffer	Reasons	Bad News	Closing
• Best news • Compliment • Appreciation • Agreement • Facts • Understanding • Apology	• Cautious explanation • Reader or other benefits • Company policy explanation • Positive words • Evidence that matter was considered fairly and seriously	• Embedded placement • Passive voice • Implied refusal • Compromise • Alternative	• Forward look • Information about alternative • Good wishes • Freebies • Resale • Sales promotion

Refusing Typical Requests

LEARNING OBJECTIVE 4

Describe and apply effective techniques for refusing typical requests.

As you move forward in your career and become a professional or a representative of an organization, you may receive requests for favours or contributions. You may also be invited to speak or give presentations. When you must refuse typical requests, you will first think about how the receiver will react to your refusal and decide whether to use the direct or the indirect strategy. If you have any doubt, use the indirect strategy.

Rejecting Requests for Favours, Money, Information, and Action

> The reasons-before-refusal plan works well when turning down requests for favours, money, information, and action.

Requests for favours, money, information, and action may come from charities, friends, or business partners. Many are from people representing commendable causes, and you may wish you could comply. However, resources are usually limited. In a letter from Forest Financial Services, shown in Figure 9.4, the company must refuse a request for a donation to a charity. Following the indirect strategy, the letter begins with a buffer acknowledging the request. It also praises the good works of the charity and uses those words as a transition to the second paragraph. In the second paragraph, the writer explains why the company cannot donate. Notice that the writer reveals the refusal without actually stating it (*Because of sales declines and organizational downsizing, we are forced to take a much harder look at funding requests that we receive this year*). This gentle refusal makes it unnecessary to be blunter in stating the denial.

In some donation refusal letters, the reasons may not be fully explained: *Although we can't provide financial support at this time, we all unanimously agree that the World Wildlife Federation contributes a valuable service through its conservation efforts.* The emphasis is on the foundation's good deeds rather than on an explanation for the refusal. In the letter shown in Figure 9.4, the writer felt a connection to the charity. Thus, he wanted to give a fuller explanation. If you were required to write frequent refusals, you might prepare a form letter, changing a few variables as needed.

Declining Invitations

> In declining an invitation, explain your reasons and make a special effort to soften the refusal.

When you must decline an invitation to speak or make a presentation, you generally try to provide a response that says more than *I can't* or *I don't want to*. Unless the reasons are confidential or business secrets, try to explain them. Because responses to invitations are often taken personally, make a special effort to soften the refusal. In the letter shown in Figure 9.5, an accountant must say no to the invitation from a friend's son to speak before the young man's college business club. This refusal starts with conviviality and compliments.

FIGURE 9.4 Refusing Donation Request

1 Prewriting

Analyze: The purpose of this letter is to reject the request for a monetary donation without causing bad feelings.

Anticipate: The reader is proud of her organization and the good work it pursues.

Adapt: The writer should strive to cushion the bad news and explain why it is necessary.

2 Writing

Research: Collect information about the receiver's organization as well as reasons for the refusal.

Organize: Use the indirect strategy. Begin with complimentary comments, present reasons, reveal the bad news gently, and close pleasantly.

Compose: Write the message and consider keeping a copy to serve as a form letter.

3 Revising

Revise: Be sure that the tone of the message is positive and that it suggests that the matter was taken seriously.

Proofread: Check the receiver's name and address to be sure they are accurate. Check the letter's format.

Evaluate: Will this message retain goodwill of the receiver despite its news?

FOREST FINANCIAL SERVICES
3410 Willow Grove Boulevard
London, ON N5Z 2Z7
519.593.4400
www.forestfinancial.com

November 14, 2014

Ms. Rachel Brown, Chair
Oxford-Wellington County Chapter
National Reye's Syndrome Foundation
RR #2
Kerwood, ON N0M 2B0

Dear Ms. Brown:

We appreciate your letter describing the good work your Oxford-Wellington County chapter of the National Reye's Syndrome Foundation is doing in preventing and treating this serious condition. Your organization is to be commended for its significant achievements resulting from the efforts of dedicated members.

Supporting the good work of your organization and others, although unrelated to our business, is a luxury we have enjoyed in past years. Because of sales declines and organizational downsizing, we're forced to take a much harder look at funding requests that we receive this year. We feel that we must focus our charitable contributions on areas that relate directly to our business.

We're hopeful that the worst days are behind us and that we'll be able to renew our support for worthwhile projects like yours next year.

Sincerely,

Paul Rosenberg

Paul Rosenberg
Vice President

Annotations (left):
- Opens with praise and compliments
- Transitions with repetition of key idea (*good work*)
- Reveals refusal without actually stating it

Annotations (right):
- Doesn't say *yes* or *no*
- Explains sales decline and cutback in gifts
- Closes graciously with forward look

FIGURE 9.5 Declining an Invitation

Opens cordially with praise

Focuses attention on alternative

GALLAGHER, BRACIO, CASAGRANDE, L.L.P.
Certified General Accountants
942 Lafayette Boulevard
Montreal, QC H3E 1H6
(514) 435-9800

E-mail: cga@gbcllp.com   www.gbcllp.com

April 16, 2014

Mr. Tyler Simpson
21607 Lacombe Avenue
Montreal, QC H5B 2G6

Dear Tyler:

News of your leadership position in your campus student association fills me with delight and pride. Your father must be proud also of your educational and extracurricular achievements.

You honour me by asking me to speak to your group in the spring about codes of ethics in the accounting field. Because our firm has not yet adopted such a code, we have been investigating the codes developed by other accounting firms. I am decidedly not an expert in this area, but I have met others who are. Although your invitation must be declined, I would like to recommend Dr. Carolyn S. Marshall, who is a member of the ethics subcommittee of the Institute of Internal Auditors. Dr. Marshall is a professor who often addresses groups on the subject of ethics in accounting. I spoke with her about your club, and she indicated that she would be happy to consider your invitation.

It's good to learn that you are guiding your organization toward such constructive and timely program topics. Please call Dr. Marshall at (514) 389-2210 if you would like to arrange for her to address your club.

Sincerely,

Joan F. Gallagher

Joan F. Gallagher, CGA

JFG:mhr

Reduces impact of refusal by placing it in subordinate clause

Ends positively with compliments and offer of assistance

The writer then explains why she cannot accept. The refusal is embedded in a long paragraph and de-emphasized in a subordinate clause (*Although your invitation must be declined*). The reader naturally concentrates on the main clause that follows (*I would like to recommend . . .*). If no alternative is available, focus on something positive about the situation (*Although I'm not an expert, I commend your organization for selecting this topic*). Overall, the tone of this refusal is warm, upbeat, and positive.

Handling Bad News With Customers

LEARNING OBJECTIVE 5

Explain and apply effective techniques for handling bad news with customers.

Businesses must occasionally respond to disappointed customers. In some instances disappointed customers are turning to the Internet to air their grievances. Complaints about products and services now appear on such sites as Complaints.com and iRipoff. com, as well as on Facebook and Twitter. See the Plugged In box for tips on how companies are responding to negative messages appearing in these emerging communication channels.

PLUGGED IN

Managing Negative News on Facebook, Twitter, and Other Web Sites

Today's consumers eagerly embrace the idea of delivering their complaints to social networking sites rather than telling friends or calling customer service departments. Why rely on word of mouth or send a letter to a company about poor service or a defective product when you can shout your grievance to the entire world? Internet sites, such as Complaints.com, Ripoff Report, and smartcanucks.ca, encourage consumers to quickly share complaints about stores, products, and services that fall short of their standards. Twitter and Facebook are also favourite sites for consumers to make public their ire.

Why are online complaints so popular?
Complaint sites are gaining momentum for many reasons. Consumers may receive faster responses to tweets than to customer service calls. Airing gripes in public also helps other consumers avoid the same problems and may improve the complainer's leverage in solving a problem. In addition, sending a 140-word tweet is much easier and more satisfying than writing a complaint letter to a customer service department or navigating endless telephone menus to reach an agent.

How can business organizations manage negative news on social networking sites and blogs?
- **Recognize social networks as an emerging communication channel.** Instead of fearing social networks as a disruptive force, smart companies greet these channels as exciting opportunities to look into the true mind-set of customers.
- **Become proactive.** Company blogs and active Web sites with community forums help companies listen to their customers and to spread the word about their own good deeds. Home Depot's site describing its foundation, workshops, and careers now outranks Home DepotSucks.com, which used to rank No. 1 for searches on the keywords *home depot*.
- **Join the fun.** Wise companies have joined such sites as Twitter, Facebook, Flickr, YouTube, and LinkedIn so they can see how these sites function and benefit from site interaction.
- **Monitor comments.** Many companies employ tech-savvy staff members to monitor comments and respond immediately whenever possible. In 2009, Rogers Communications hired Keith McArthur as the company's senior director of social media. He works with a team of social-media specialists to help make sure that people have more good experiences than bad ones.[10]

Whether companies deal with unhappy customers in cyberspace or up close and personal, they face the same challenges. Maintaining market share and preserving goodwill require sensitive and skillful communication. In Chapter 8 you learned to use the direct strategy in granting claims and making adjustments—because these were essentially good-news messages. But in some situations, you have little good news to share. Sometimes your company is at fault, in which case an apology is generally in order. Other times the problem is with orders you can't fill, claims you must refuse, or credit you must deny. Messages with bad news for customers generally follow the same pattern as other negative messages. Customer messages, though, differ in one major way: they usually include resale information or sales promotions.

Damage Control: Dealing With Disappointed Customers

All companies occasionally disappoint their customers. Merchandise is not delivered on time, a product fails to perform as expected, service is deficient, charges are erroneous, or customers are misunderstood. All businesses offering products or services must sometimes deal with troublesome situations that cause unhappiness to customers. Whenever possible, these problems should be dealt with immediately and personally. Most business professionals strive to control the damage and resolve such problems in the following manner:[11]

- Call the individual involved.
- Describe the problem and apologize.

> When a customer problem arises and your company is at fault, deal with the issue immediately and personally.

- Explain why the problem occurred, what you are doing to resolve it, and how you will prevent it from happening again.

- Follow up with a message that documents the phone call and promotes goodwill.

Dealing with problems immediately is very important in resolving conflict and retaining goodwill. Written correspondence is generally too slow for problems that demand immediate attention. But written messages are important (a) when personal contact is impossible, (b) to establish a record of the incident, (c) to formally confirm follow-up procedures, and (d) to promote good relations.

A bad-news follow-up letter is shown in Figure 9.6. Consultant Catherine Martinez found herself in the embarrassing position of explaining why she had given out the name of her client to a salesperson. The client, Alliance Resource International, had hired her firm, Paragon Consulting Associates, to help find an appropriate service for outsourcing its payroll functions. Without realizing it, Catherine had mentioned to a potential vendor (Payroll Services, Inc.) that her client was considering hiring an outside service to handle its payroll. An overeager salesperson from Payroll Services immediately called on Alliance, thus angering the client. The client had hired the consultant to avoid this very kind of intrusion. Alliance did not want to be hounded by vendors selling their payroll services.

When she learned of the problem, the first thing consultant Catherine Martinez did was call her client to explain and apologize. She was careful to control her voice and rate of speaking. A low-pitched, deliberate pace gives the impression that you are thinking clearly, logically, and reasonably—not emotionally and certainly not irrationally. However, she also followed up with the letter shown in Figure 9.6. The letter not only confirms the telephone conversation but also adds the right touch of formality. It sends the nonverbal message that the writer takes the matter seriously and that it is important enough to warrant a written letter.

Many consumer problems are handled with letters, written either by consumers as complaints or by companies in response. However, as noted, social networking sites on the Internet are an emerging channel for delivering complaints and negative messages.

> **Follow-up messages are important when personal contact is impossible, to establish a record of the incident, and to formally confirm follow-up procedures.**

Handling Problems With Orders

Not all customer orders can be filled as received. Suppliers may be able to send only part of an order or none at all. Substitutions may be necessary, or the delivery date may be delayed. Suppliers may suspect that all or part of the order is a mistake; the customer may actually want something else. In writing to customers about problem orders, it is generally wise to use the direct strategy if the message has some good-news elements. However, when the message is disappointing, the indirect strategy may be more appropriate.

Let's say you represent Live and Learn Toys, a large toy manufacturer, and you are scrambling for business in a slow year. A big customer, Child Land, calls in August and asks you to hold a block of your best-selling toy, the Space Station. Like most vendors, you require a deposit on large orders. September rolls around, and you still haven't received any money from Child Land. You must now write a tactful letter asking for the deposit—or else you will release the toy to other buyers. The problem, of course, is delivering the bad news without losing the customer's order and goodwill. Another challenge is making sure the reader understands the bad news. An effective letter might begin with a positive statement that also reveals the facts:

> **Follow the direct strategy when your company can't fill an order.**

You were smart to reserve a block of 500 Space Stations, which we have been holding for you since August. As the holidays approach, the demand for all our learning toys, including the Space Station, is rapidly increasing.

Next, the letter should explain why the payment is needed and what will happen if it is not received:

Toy stores from St. John's to Victoria are asking us to ship these Space Stations. One reason the Space Station is moving out of our warehouses so quickly is its assortment of gizmos that

FIGURE 9.6 **Bad-News Follow-Up Message**

PARAGON CONSULTING ASSOCIATES

942 Lascelles Blvd.   Voice: (416) 259-0971
Toronto, ON M4P 2BA   Web: www.paragonassociates.com

May 7, 2014

Mr. Eric Nasserizad
Director, Administrative Operations
Alliance Resources International
4208 Collins Avenue
Toronto, ON M3H 1A5

Dear Mr. Nasserizad:

You have every right to expect complete confidentiality in your transactions ●――――― Opens with agreement and apology
with an independent consultant. As I explained in yesterday's telephone call,
I am very distressed that you were called by a salesperson from Payroll
Services, Inc. This should not have happened, and I apologize to you again for
inadvertently mentioning your company's name in a conversation with a
potential vendor, Payroll Services, Inc.

All clients of Paragon Consulting are assured that their dealings with our
firm are held in the strictest confidence. Because your company's payroll ●――――― Explains what caused the problem and how it was resolved
needs are so individual and because you have so many contract workers, I
was forced to explain how your employees differed from those of other
companies. Revealing your company name was my error, and I take full
responsibility for the lapse. I can assure you that it will not happen again. I ●――――― Takes responsibility and promises to prevent recurrence
have informed Payroll Services that it had no authorization to call you
directly and its actions have forced me to reconsider using its services for
my future clients.

A number of other payroll services offer outstanding programs. I'm sure we
can find the perfect partner to enable you to outsource your payroll
responsibilities, thus allowing your company to focus its financial and human ●――――― Closes with forward look
resources on its core business. I look forward to our next appointment when
you may choose from a number of excellent payroll outsourcing firms.

Sincerely,

PARAGON CONSULTING ASSOCIATES

Catherine Martinez

Catherine Martinez
Partner

Tips for Resolving Problems and Following Up
• Whenever possible, call or see the individual involved.
• Describe the problem and apologize.
• Explain why the problem occurred.
• Take responsibility, if appropriate.
• Explain what you are doing to resolve the problem.
• Explain how it will not happen again.
• Follow up with a letter that documents the personal contact.
• Look forward to positive future relations.

*children love, including a land rover vehicle, a shuttle craft, a hovercraft, astronauts, and even
a robotic arm. As soon as we receive your deposit of $4,000, we will have this popular item on
its way to your stores. Without a deposit by September 20, though, we must release this block to
other retailers.*

The closing makes it easy to respond and motivates action:

*Use the enclosed envelope to send us your cheque immediately. You can begin showing this
fascinating Live and Learn toy in your stores by November 1.*

Introduce the concept of audience benefits into messages announcing rate increases and price hikes.

Announcing Rate Increases and Price Hikes

Informing customers and clients of rate increases or price hikes can be like handling a live grenade. These messages necessarily cause consumers to recoil. With skill, however, you can help your customers understand why the rate or price increase is necessary.

The important steps in these negative messages are explaining the reasons and hooking the increase to benefits. For example, a price increase might be necessitated by higher material costs, rising taxes, escalating insurance, driver pay increase—all reasons you cannot control. You might cite changing industry trends or technology innovations as causes of increased costs.

In developing audience benefits and building goodwill, think about how the increase will add new value or better features, make use more efficient, or make customers' lives easier. Whenever possible, give advance warning of rate increases—for example: *Because you are an important customer to us, I wanted to inform you about this right away. Our energy costs have almost doubled over the last year, forcing us to put through a 10 percent price increase effective July 1. You order these items regularly, so I thought I'd better check with you to see if it would make sense to reorder now to save you money and prevent last-minute surprises.*

In today's digital environment, rate and price increases may be announced online, as shown in Figure 9.7. DVD City had to increase the charge for access to Blu-ray movies. In its blog it explained how Blu-ray discs are not only superior to DVDs but also more expensive. To provide its customers with a comprehensive library of Blu-ray movies, DVD City has to raise its rates. Notice that the rate increase is tied to benefits to customers.

FIGURE 9.7 Blog Announcing Price Increase With Audience Benefits

Explains expansion of Blu-ray DVD movie collection and describes how costly these films are, thus justifying a price increase

Connects increase in cost to bigger library and wider choice of best movies for customers

Provides name and number for more information

DVD CITY

DVD CITY Blog

Wednesday, June 16, 2014

Price Update for Access to Blu-ray Movies

Hi, Rocko Raider here, VP of Marketing, with a message for our valued members who have added Blu-ray access to their accounts.

Blu-ray represents a huge leap forward in the DVD viewing experience, with greatly enhanced HD video and audio quality as well as advanced interactivity and networking features. The number of titles available for us to purchase on Blu-ray has increased significantly. Our Blu-ray selection has grown more than 70 percent in just 6 months to more than 2300 titles. Blu-ray adoption among our members has also grown–it's now close to 10 percent. As we buy more, you are able to choose from a rapidly expanding selection of Blu-ray titles. And, as you've probably heard, Blu-ray discs are substantially more expensive than standard definition DVDs–often as much as 30 percent more.

Because DVD CITY is committed to providing an extensive library of high quality Blu-ray films for our members who choose to add Blu-ray access, we need to adjust Blu-ray pricing. As a result, the monthly charge for Blu-ray access is increasing for most plans and will now vary by plan.

This change will take effect on your next billing date. You will receive an e-mail from us letting you know the monthly charge for your plan. For more information, call Betsy at 1-800-556-2002.

LINKS

DVD CITY Community Forums

Facebook DVD CITY Page

DVD CITY Home Page

------> RSS Feed Page

------> Top Releases This Week

ABOUT THE DVD CITY BLOG

Thanks for visiting the official DVD CITY Blog! We bloggers are members of the DVD CITY team and are all certifiably rabid movie fans. We want to make this an exciting forum for us to talk about what we are doing and for you to tell us what you think.

Denying Claims

Customers occasionally want something they are not entitled to or that you can't grant. They may misunderstand warranties or make unreasonable demands. Because these customers are often unhappy with a product or service, they are emotionally involved. Letters that say no to emotionally involved receivers will probably be your most challenging communication task.

Fortunately, the reasons-before-refusal plan helps you be empathic and artful in breaking bad news. Obviously, in denial letters you will need to adopt the proper tone. Don't blame customers, even if they are at fault. Avoid *you* statements that sound preachy (*You would have known that cash refunds are impossible if you had read your contract*). Use neutral, objective language to explain why the claim must be refused. Consider offering resale information to rebuild the customer's confidence in your products or organization. In Figure 9.8 the writer denies a customer's claim for the difference between the price the customer paid for speakers and the price he saw advertised locally (which would have resulted in a cash refund of $100). Although the catalogue service does

FIGURE 9.8 Denying a Claim

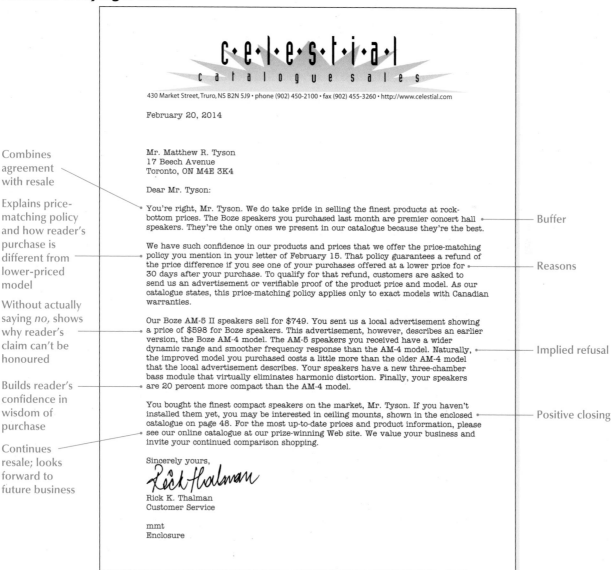

Combines agreement with resale

Explains price-matching policy and how reader's purchase is different from lower-priced model

Without actually saying *no*, shows why reader's claim can't be honoured

Builds reader's confidence in wisdom of purchase

Continues resale; looks forward to future business

c·e·l·e·s·t·i·a·l
catalogue sales

430 Market Street, Truro, NS B2N 5J9 • phone (902) 450-2100 • fax (902) 455-3260 • http://www.celestial.com

February 20, 2014

Mr. Matthew R. Tyson
17 Beech Avenue
Toronto, ON M4E 3K4

Dear Mr. Tyson:

You're right, Mr. Tyson. We do take pride in selling the finest products at rock-bottom prices. The Boze speakers you purchased last month are premier concert hall speakers. They're the only ones we present in our catalogue because they're the best. — Buffer

We have such confidence in our products and prices that we offer the price-matching policy you mention in your letter of February 15. That policy guarantees a refund of the price difference if you see one of your purchases offered at a lower price for 30 days after your purchase. To qualify for that refund, customers are asked to send us an advertisement or verifiable proof of the product price and model. As our catalogue states, this price-matching policy applies only to exact models with Canadian warranties. — Reasons

Our Boze AM-5 II speakers sell for $749. You sent us a local advertisement showing a price of $598 for Boze speakers. This advertisement, however, describes an earlier version, the Boze AM-4 model. The AM-5 speakers you received have a wider dynamic range and smoother frequency response than the AM-4 model. Naturally, the improved model you purchased costs a little more than the older AM-4 model that the local advertisement describes. Your speakers have a new three-chamber bass module that virtually eliminates harmonic distortion. Finally, your speakers are 20 percent more compact than the AM-4 model. — Implied refusal

You bought the finest compact speakers on the market, Mr. Tyson. If you haven't installed them yet, you may be interested in ceiling mounts, shown in the enclosed catalogue on page 48. For the most up-to-date prices and product information, please see our online catalogue at our prize-winning Web site. We value your business and invite your continued comparison shopping. — Positive closing

Sincerely yours,

Rick Thalman

Rick K. Thalman
Customer Service

mmt
Enclosure

match any advertised lower price, the price-matching policy applies *only* to the same models. This claim must be rejected because the advertisement the customer submitted showed a different, older speaker model.

The letter to Matthew Tyson opens with a buffer that agrees with a statement in the customer's letter. It repeats the key idea of product confidence as a transition to the second paragraph. Next comes an explanation of the price-matching policy. The writer does not assume that the customer is trying to pull a fast one. Nor does he suggest that the customer is a dummy who didn't read or understand the price-matching policy. The safest path is a neutral explanation of the policy along with precise distinctions between the customer's speakers and the older ones. The writer also gets a chance to resell the customer's speakers and demonstrate what a quality product they are. By the end of the third paragraph, it is evident to the reader that his claim is unjustified.

Refusing Credit

As much as companies want business, they can extend credit only when payment is likely to follow. Credit applications, from individuals or from businesses, are generally approved or disapproved based on the applicant's credit history. This record is supplied by a credit-reporting agency, such as Northern Credit Bureau, Equifax, or TransUnion. After reviewing the applicant's record, a credit manager applies the organization's guidelines and approves or disapproves the application.

If you must write a letter to a customer denying credit, you have four goals in conveying the refusal:

- Avoiding language that causes hard feelings

- Retaining the customer on a cash basis

- Preparing for possible future credit without raising false expectations

- Avoiding disclosures that could cause a lawsuit

Because credit applicants are likely to continue to do business with an organization even if they are denied credit, you will want to do everything possible to encourage that patronage. Thus, keep the refusal respectful, sensitive, and upbeat. A letter to a customer denying her credit application might begin as follows:

> *We genuinely appreciate your application of January 12 for a Fashion Express credit account.*

To avoid possible litigation, many companies offer no explanation of the reasons for a credit refusal. Instead, they provide the name of the credit-reporting agency and suggest that inquiries be directed to it. In the following example, notice the use of passive voice (*credit cannot be extended*) and a long sentence to de-emphasize the bad news:

> *After we received a report of your current credit record from Equifax, it was apparent that credit cannot be extended at this time. To learn more about your record, you may call an Equifax credit counsellor at (982) 356-0922.*

The cordial closing looks forward to the possibility of a future reapplication:

> *Thanks, Ms. Love, for the confidence you have shown in Fashion Express. We invite you to continue shopping at our stores, and we look forward to your reapplication in the future.*

Some businesses do provide reasons explaining credit denials (*Credit cannot be granted because your firm's current and long-term credit obligations are nearly twice as great as your firm's total assets*). They may also provide alternatives, such as deferred billing or cash discounts. When the letter denies a credit application that accompanies an order, the message may contain resale information. The writer tries to convert the order from credit to cash. For example, if a big order cannot be filled on a credit basis, perhaps part of the order could be filled on a cash basis.

Whatever form the bad-news message takes, it is a good idea to have the message reviewed by legal counsel because of the litigation land mines awaiting unwary communicators in this area.

In refusing credit to a customer, avoid language that causes hard feelings and avoid disclosures that could result in a lawsuit.

Delivering Bad News Within Organizations

A tactful tone and a reasons-first approach help preserve friendly relations with customers. These same techniques are useful when delivering bad news within organizations. Interpersonal bad news might involve telling the boss that something went wrong or confronting an employee about poor performance. Organizational bad news might involve declining profits, lost contracts, harmful lawsuits, public relations controversies, and changes in policy. Whether you use a direct or an indirect strategy in delivering that news depends primarily on the anticipated reaction of the audience. Generally, bad news is better received when reasons are given first. Within organizations, you may find yourself giving bad news in person or in writing.

LEARNING OBJECTIVE 6
Understand and apply effective techniques for delivering bad news within organizations.

Giving Bad News Personally

Whether you are an employee or a supervisor, you may have the unhappy responsibility of delivering bad news. First, decide whether the negative information is newsworthy. For example, trivial, noncriminal mistakes or one-time bad behaviours are best left alone. However, fraudulent travel claims, consistent hostile behaviour, or failing projects must be reported.[12] For example, you might have to tell the boss that the team's computer crashed, losing all its important files. As a team leader or supervisor, you might be required to confront an underperforming employee. If you know that the news will upset the receiver, the reasons-first strategy is most effective. When the bad news involves one person or a small group nearby, you should generally deliver that news in person. Here are pointers on how to do so tactfully, professionally, and safely:[13]

- **Gather all the information.** Cool down and have all the facts before marching in on the boss or confronting someone. Remember that every story has two sides.

- **Prepare and rehearse.** Outline what you plan to say so that you are confident, coherent, and dispassionate.

- **Explain: past, present, future.** If you are telling the boss about a problem, such as the computer crash, explain what caused the crash, the current situation, and how and when you plan to fix it.

- **Consider taking a partner.** If you fear a "shoot the messenger" reaction, especially from your boss, bring a colleague with you. Each person should have a consistent and credible part in the presentation. If possible, take advantage of your organization's internal resources. To lend credibility to your view, call on auditors, inspectors, or human resources experts.

- **Think about timing.** Don't deliver bad news when someone is already stressed or grumpy. Experts also advise against giving bad news on Friday afternoon when people have the weekend to dwell on it.

- **Be patient with the reaction.** Give the receiver time to vent, think, recover, and act wisely.

> When delivering bad news in person, strive to be tactful, professional, and safe.

Refusing Internal Requests

Occasionally, managers must refuse requests from employees. In Figure 9.9 you see the first draft and revision of a message responding to a request from a key specialist, Mark Stevenson. He wants permission to attend a conference. However, he can't attend the conference because the timing is bad; he must be present at budget planning meetings scheduled for the same two weeks. Normally, this matter would be discussed in person. However, Mark has been travelling among branch offices, and he hasn't been in the office recently.

FIGURE 9.9 Refusing an Internal Request

DRAFT

DATE: July 2, 2014

TO: Mark Stevenson
         Manager, Telecommunications

FROM: Ann Wells-Freed   A W-F
         VP, Management Information Systems

SUBJECT: Conference Request

We can't allow you to attend the conference in September, Mark. Perhaps • ——— Announces the bad news
you didn't know that budget-planning meetings are scheduled for that month.   too quickly and painfully

Your expertise is needed here to help keep our telecommunications network
on schedule. Without you, the entire system—which is shaky at best—might • ——— Gives reasons but includes
fall apart. I'm sorry to have to refuse your request to attend the conference.   a dangerous statement
I know this is small thanks for the fine work you have done for us. Please
accept our humble apologies.

In the spring I'm sure your work schedule will be lighter, and we can release • ——— Makes a promise that might
you to attend a conference at that time.   be difficult to keep

REVISION

DATE: July 2, 2014

TO: Mark Stevenson
         Manager, Telecommunications

FROM: Ann Wells-Freed   A W-F
         VP, Management Information Systems

SUBJECT: Request to Attend September Conference

Transition: The Management Council and I are extremely pleased with the leadership you • ——— Buffer: Includes
Uses date to   have provided in setting up live video transmission to our regional offices.   sincere praise
move smoothly   Because of your genuine professional commitment, Mark, I can understand
from buffer   your desire to attend the conference of the Telecommunication Specialists of
to reasons   North America September 23 to 28 in Calgary.

Bad news: •— The last two weeks in September have been set aside for budget planning. As • ——— Reasons: Tells
Implies   you and I know, we have only scratched the surface of our teleconferencing   why refusal
refusal   •— projects for the next five years. Since you are the specialist and we rely heavily   is necessary
                             on your expertise, we need you here for those planning sessions.

Closing: •— If you are able to attend a similar conference in the spring and if our workloads
Contains   permit, we will try to send you then. You are a valuable player, Mark, and I am
realistic   grateful you are on our MIS team.
alternative

The vice president's first inclination was to send a quick e-mail, as shown in Figure 9.9 draft, and "tell it like it is." However, she realized that this message was going to hurt and that it had possible danger areas. Moreover, the message misses a chance to give Mark positive feedback. An improved version of the e-mail starts with a buffer that delivers honest praise (*extremely pleased with the leadership you have provided* and *your genuine professional commitment*). The buffer also includes the date of the meeting, used strategically to connect the reasons that follow. You will recall from Chapter 5 that repetition of a key idea is an effective transitional device to provide smooth flow between components of a message.

The middle paragraph provides reasons for the refusal. Notice that they focus on positive elements: Mark is the specialist; the company relies on his expertise; and everyone will benefit if he passes up the conference. In this section it becomes obvious that the request will be refused. The writer is not forced to say, *No, you may not attend.* Although the refusal is implied, the reader gets the message.

The closing suggests a qualified alternative (*if our workloads permit, we will try to send you then*). It also ends positively with gratitude for Mark's contributions to the organization and with another compliment (*you're a valuable player*). The improved version focuses on explanations and praise rather than on refusals and apologies. The success of this message depends on attention to the entire writing process, not just on using a buffer or scattering a few compliments throughout.

> Organizations can retain employee morale when communicating bad news by focusing on explanations and praise rather than refusals and apologies.

Delivering Bad News to Groups

Many of the same techniques used to deliver bad news personally are useful when organizations face a crisis or must deliver bad news to groups. Smart organizations involved in a crisis prefer to communicate the news openly to employees and stockholders. A crisis might involve serious performance problems, a major relocation, massive layoffs, a management shakeup, or public controversy. Instead of letting rumours distort the truth, managers explain the organization's side of the story honestly and early. Morale can be destroyed when employees learn of major events affecting their jobs through the grapevine or from news accounts—rather than from management.

When bad news must be delivered to employees, management may want to deliver the news personally. With large groups, however, this is generally impossible. Instead, organizations deliver bad news through hard-copy memos, which are formal and create a permanent record. Today's organizations are also experimenting with other delivery channels, such as e-mail, videos, Webcasts, and voice mail.

> Bad news to groups of employees should be delivered through hard-copy memos or other delivery channels, such as e-mail, videos, Webcasts, and voice mail.

The draft of the memo shown in Figure 9.10 announces a substantial increase in the cost of employee extended health care benefits. However, the memo suffers from many problems. It announces jolting news bluntly in the first sentence. Worse, it offers little or no explanation for the steep increase in costs. It also sounds insincere (*We did everything possible ...*) and arbitrary. In a final miscue, the writer fails to give credit to the company for absorbing previous health cost increases.

The revision of this bad-news memo uses the indirect strategy and improves the tone considerably. Notice that it opens with a relevant, upbeat buffer regarding extended health care—but says nothing about increasing costs. For a smooth transition, the second paragraph begins with a key idea from the opening (*comprehensive package*). The reasons section discusses rising costs with explanations and figures. The bad news (*you will be paying $70 a month*) is clearly presented but embedded within the paragraph. Throughout, the writer strives to show the fairness of the company's position. The ending, which does not refer to the bad news, emphasizes how much the company is paying and what a wise investment it is.

Notice that the entire memo demonstrates a kinder, gentler approach than that shown in the first draft. Of prime importance in breaking bad news to employees is providing clear, convincing reasons that explain the decision. This message could have been sent by e-mail, but a memo is more formal, more permanent, and more appropriate for bad news. This channel choice, however, may change as e-mail increasingly gains acceptance.

Chapter 9: Negative Messages

FIGURE 9.10 Announcing Bad News to Employees

1 Prewriting

Analyze: The purpose of this memo is to tell employees that they must share with the company the increasing costs of health care.

Anticipate: The audience will be employees who are unaware of health care costs and, most likely, reluctant to pay more.

Adapt: Because the readers will probably be unhappy and resentful, use the indirect pattern.

2 Writing

Research: Collect facts and statistics that document health care costs.

Organize: Begin with a buffer describing the company's commitment to health benefits. Provide an explanation of health care costs. Announce the bad news. In the closing, focus on the company's major share of the cost.

Compose: Draft the first version with the expectation to revise.

3 Revising

Revise: Remove negativity (*unfortunately, we can't, we were forced, inadvisable*). Explain the increase with specifics.

Proofread: Use quotation marks around *defensive* to show its special sense. Spell out *percent* after 200.

Evaluate: Is there any other way to help readers accept this bad news?

DRAFT

Beginning January 1 your monthly payment for extended health care benefits will be increased to $70 (up from $53 last year).

Every year health care costs go up. Although we considered dropping other benefits, Northern decided that the best plan was to keep the present comprehensive package. Unfortunately, we can't do that unless we pass along some of the extra cost to you. Last year the company was forced to absorb the total increase in extended health care premiums. However, such a plan this year is inadvisable.

We did everything possible to avoid the sharp increase in costs to you this year. A rate schedule describing the increases in payments for your family and dependents is enclosed.

Hits readers with bad news without any preparation

Offers no explanation

Fails to take credit for absorbing previous increases

REVISION

DATE: October 2, 2014

TO: Fellow Employees

FROM: Lawrence R. Romero, President

SUBJECT: Maintaining Quality Extended Health Care

Begins with positive buffer

Extended health care programs have always been an important part of our commitment to employees at Northern, Inc. We're proud that our total benefits package continues to rank among the best in the country.

Offers reasons costs are rising

Such a comprehensive package does not come cheaply. In the last decade health care costs alone have risen more than 200 percent. We're told that several factors fuel the cost spiral: inflation, technology improvements, increased cost of outpatient services, and "defensive" medicine practised by doctors to prevent lawsuits.

Reveals bad news clearly but embeds it in paragraph

Just two years ago our monthly health care cost for each employee was $106. It rose to $115 last year. We were able to absorb that jump without increasing your contribution. But this year's hike to $140 forces us to ask you to share the increase. To maintain your current health care benefits, you will be paying $70 a month. The enclosed rate schedule describes the costs for families and dependents.

Ends positively by stressing the company's major share of the costs

Northern continues to pay half of your extended health care program ($70 each month). We think it's a wise investment.

Enclosure

Saying No to Job Applicants

Being refused a job is one of life's major rejections. Tactless letters intensify the blow (*Unfortunately, you were not among the candidates selected for . . .*).

You can reduce the receiver's disappointment somewhat by using the indirect strategy—with one important variation. In the reasons section, it is wise to be vague in explaining why the candidate was not selected. First, giving concrete reasons may be painful to the receiver (*Your grade point average of 2.7 was low compared with the GPAs of other candidates*). Second, and more important, providing extra information may prove unwise in a lawsuit. Hiring and firing decisions generate considerable litigation today. To avoid charges of discrimination or wrongful actions, legal advisers warn organizations to keep employment rejection letters general, simple, and short.

The job refusal letter shown in Figure 9.11 is tactful but intentionally vague. It implies that the applicant's qualifications don't match those needed for the position, but the letter doesn't reveal anything specific. The writer could have included this alternative closing: *We wish you every success in finding a position that exactly fits your qualifications.*

The Checklist box on p. 228 summarizes tips on how to communicate negative news inside and outside your organization.

> When saying no to job applicants, reduce the receiver's disappointment by using the indirect strategy.

FIGURE 9.11 **Saying No to Job Candidate**

Xeradyne Telecom

1919 Saskatchewan Drive   Regina SK S4P 4H2
800.445.9800   www.xeradynetelecom.com

June 7, 2014

Ms. Tracee Porter
1717 Victoria Avenue
Regina, SK S4P 0P9

Dear Ms. Porter:

Doesn't indicate good or bad news → Thanks for letting us review your résumé submitted for our advertised management trainee opening. ← *Shows appreciation*

To prevent possible lawsuits, gives no explanation → We received a number of impressive résumés for this opening. Although another candidate was selected, your interest in our organization is appreciated. So that you may continue your search for a position at another organization, I am writing to you immediately. ← *Places bad news in dependent clause*

With your credentials I am certain you will find a suitable position because you have a great deal to offer. Please accept my best wishes for the future. ← *Ends with best wishes*

Sincerely,

XERADYNE TELECOM

Leonora M. Kirby

Leonora M. Kirby
Director, Human Resources

Checklist

Conveying Negative News

Prewrite

- Decide whether to use the direct or indirect strategy. If the bad news is minor and will not upset the receiver, open directly. If the message is personally damaging and will upset the receiver, consider techniques to reduce its pain.
- Think through the reasons for the bad news.
- Remember that your primary goal is to make the receiver understand and accept the bad news and maintain a positive image of you and your organization.

Plan the Opening

- In the indirect strategy, start with a buffer. Pay a compliment to the reader, show appreciation for something done, or mention some mutual understanding. Avoid raising false hopes or thanking the reader for something you will refuse.
- In the direct strategy, begin with a straightforward statement of the bad news.

Provide Reasons in the Body

- Except in credit and job refusals, explain the reasons for the negative message.
- In customer mishaps, clarify what went wrong, what you are doing to resolve the problem, and how you will prevent it from happening again.

- Use objective, nonjudgmental, and nondiscriminatory language.
- Avoid negativity (e.g., such words as *unfortunately, unwilling,* and *impossible*) and potentially damaging statements.
- Show how your decision is fair and perhaps benefits the reader or others, if possible.

Soften the Bad News

- Reduce the impact of bad news by using (a) a subordinate clause, (b) the passive voice, (c) a long sentence, or (d) a long paragraph.
- Consider implying the refusal, but be certain it is clear.
- Suggest an alternative, such as a lower price, a different product, a longer payment period, or a substitute. Provide help in implementing an alternative.
- Offset disappointment by offering gifts, a reduced price, benefits, tokens of appreciation, or something appropriate.

Close Pleasantly

- Supply more information about an alternative, look forward to future relations, or offer good wishes and compliments.
- Maintain a bright, personal tone. Avoid referring to the refusal.

Summary of Learning Objectives

1 **Describe the goals and strategies of business communicators in conveying negative news effectively, including applying the writing process and avoiding legal liability.** All businesses occasionally deal with problems. Good communicators have many goals in delivering bad news: explaining clearly and completely, projecting a professional image, conveying empathy and sensitivity, being fair, and maintaining friendly relations. Applying the 3-×-3 writing process helps you prepare, compose, and revise your message so that it accomplishes your purpose. Careful communicators avoid careless and abusive language, which is actionable when it is false, damages a person's reputation, and is "published" (spoken within the presence of others or written). Messages written on company stationery represent that company and can be legally binding.

2 **Decide whether to use the direct or indirect strategy in conveying negative news.** The indirect strategy involves beginning with a buffer and delaying the bad news until reasons have been presented. The direct strategy reveals the main idea immediately. The direct strategy is preferable when the bad news is not damaging, when the receiver may overlook the bad news, when the organization policy suggests directness, when the receiver prefers directness, and when firmness is necessary. The indirect strategy works

Get more practice at **www.guffeybrief4e.nelson.com**

well when the bad news is personally upsetting, provokes a hostile reaction, threatens the customer relationship, and is unexpected.

3 **Analyze the components of effective negative messages, including opening with a buffer, apologizing, conveying empathy, presenting the reasons, cushioning the bad news, and closing pleasantly.** If you use the indirect strategy for a negative message, begin with a buffer, such as a compliment, appreciation, a point of agreement, objective information, understanding, or some part of the message that represents good news. Then explain the reasons that necessitate the bad news, trying to cite benefits to the reader or others. If you use the direct strategy, begin directly with the bad news, followed by the reasons. When apologizing, do so sincerely, accept responsibility, and use good judgment. Throughout a negative message, strive to cushion the bad news by positioning it strategically, using the passive voice, accentuating the positive, choosing positive words, and suggesting a compromise or alternative. Close pleasantly with a forward-looking goodwill statement.

4 **Describe and apply effective techniques for refusing typical requests.** Typical requests ask for favours, money, information, action, and other items. When the answer will be disappointing, use the reasons-before-refusal pattern. Open with a buffer; provide reasons; announce the refusal sensitively; suggest possible alternatives; and end with a positive, forward-looking comment.

5 **Explain and apply effective techniques for handling bad news with customers.** When a company disappoints its customers, most organizations (a) call the individual involved, (b) describe the problem and apologize (when the company is to blame), (c) explain why the problem occurred and what is being done to prevent its recurrence, and (d) follow up with a message that documents the phone call and promotes goodwill. Some organizations also offer gifts or benefits to offset customers' disappointment and to reestablish the business relationship. In announcing rate increases and price hikes, tie the increase to customer benefits. In denying claims, begin indirectly, provide reasons for the refusal, and close pleasantly, looking forward to future business. When appropriate, resell a product or service. When refusing credit, avoid language that causes hard feelings, strive to retain the customer on a cash basis, prepare for possible future credit, and avoid disclosures that could cause a lawsuit.

6 **Understand and apply effective techniques for delivering bad news within organizations.** When delivering bad news personally to a superior, gather all the information, prepare and rehearse, explain what happened and how the problem will be repaired, consider taking a colleague with you, think about timing, and be patient with the reaction. In delivering bad news to groups of employees, use the indirect strategy but be sure to provide clear, convincing reasons that explain the decision. In refusing job applicants, however, keep letters short, general, and tactful.

Chapter Review

1. When delivering bad news, how can a communicator reduce the bad feelings of the receiver? (Obj. 1)

2. What is the most important part of Phase 1 of the writing process for negative messages? (Obj. 1)

3. When should you use the direct strategy in delivering bad news? (Obj. 2)

4. When should you use the indirect strategy in delivering bad news? (Obj. 2)

5. What are the major differences between the direct and indirect strategies in delivering bad news? (Obj. 2)

6. What is a buffer? Name five or more techniques to buffer the opening of a bad-news message. (Obj. 3)

7. What is an apology? When should an apology be offered to customers? (Obj. 3)

8. Name four or more techniques that cushion the delivery of bad news. (Obj. 3)

9. What are some typical requests that big and small businesses must refuse? (Obj. 4)

10. Identify a process used by a majority of business professionals in resolving problems with disappointed customers. (Obj. 5)

11. If you must deny the claim of a customer who is clearly at fault, should you respond by putting the blame squarely on the customer? (Obj. 5)

12. What is an effective technique for announcing rate increases and price hikes? (Obj. 5)

13. List four goals a writer seeks to achieve in writing messages that deny credit to prospective customers. (Obj. 5)

14. How can a subordinate tactfully, professionally, and safely deliver upsetting news personally to a superior? (Obj. 6)

15. What are some channels that large organizations may use when delivering bad news to employees? (Obj. 6)

Critical Thinking

1. Communication author Dana Bristol-Smith likens delivering bad news to removing a Band-Aid—you can do it slowly or quickly. She thinks that quickly is better, particularly when companies must give bad news to employees.[14] Do you agree or disagree? (Objs. 1–6)

2. Respected industry analyst Gartner Research issued a report naming social networking as one of the top ten disruptive influences shaping information technology in the next five years.[15] Should organizations fear Web sites where consumers post negative messages about products and services? What actions can companies take in response to this disruptive influence? (Objs. 1–5)

3. Consider times when you have been aware that others were using the indirect strategy in writing or speaking to you. How did you react? (Obj. 2)

4. When a major airline reported that a laptop containing the names, salary information, and social insurance numbers of thousands of employees had been stolen from an employee's car, the CEO wrote this e-mail to employees: "I've received many e-mails over the past 24 hours from employees expressing disappointment, frustration, and downright anger about yesterday's announcement of personal information belonging to thousands of employees and retirees being on a stolen computer. I'm just as disappointed as you are about it. I know that many of us feel that this data loss amounts to a betrayal of the trust we place in the company to safeguard our personal information. I certainly do." Critics have faulted this apology for its timing and content. Do you agree?

5. **Ethical Issue:** You work for a large corporation with headquarters in a small town. Recently you received shoddy repair work and a huge bill from a local garage. Your car's transmission has the same problems that it did before you took it in for repair. You know that a complaint letter written on your corporation's stationery would be much more authoritative than one written on plain stationery. Should you use corporate stationery? (Obj. 1)

Writing Improvement Exercises

9.1 Organizational Strategies (Objs. 1–5)

Your Task: Identify which organizational strategy you would use for the following messages: direct or indirect.

a. A letter from a credit card company announcing a small increase in rates.

b. An e-mail from a manager refusing an employee's request for funds and time off to attend a professional seminar.

c. A letter refusing a request by a charitable organization to use your office equipment on the weekend.

d. An announcement to employees that a financial specialist has cancelled a scheduled lunchtime talk and cannot reschedule.

e. A letter to bank customers revealing that its central computer system had been hacked, revealing customer addresses, dates of birth, account numbers, and the value of investments.

9.2 Employing Passive-Voice Verbs (Obj. 3)

Your Task. Revise the following sentences to present the bad news with passive-voice verbs.

a. We cannot offer free shipping after January 1.

b. Our retail stores will no longer be accepting credit cards for purchases under $5.

c. Because management now requires more stringent security, we are postponing indefinitely requests for company tours.

d. Your car rental insurance coverage does not cover large SUVs.

e. Company policy prevents us from offering extended health and dental benefits until employees have been on the job for 12 months.

9.3 Subordinating Bad News (Obj. 3)

Your Task. Revise the following sentences to position the bad news in a subordinate clause. (**Hint:** Consider beginning the clause with *Although*.) Use passive-voice verbs for the bad news.

a. We regret that we cannot replace the cabinet hinge you need. The manufacturer no longer offers it. A new hinge should work for you, and we are sending it to you.

b. Provincial law does not allow smoking within nine metres of a public building. But the university has set aside 16 outdoor smoking areas.

c. We now offer all of our catalogue choices at our Web site, which is always current. Unfortunately, we no longer print or mail a complete catalogue.

d. We are sorry to report that we are unable to ship your complete order at this point in time. However, we are able to send two corner workstations now, and you should receive them within five days.

e. We appreciate your interest in our organization, but we are unable to extend an employment offer to you at this time.

9.4 Implying Bad News (Obj. 3)

Your Task. Revise the following statements to *imply* the bad news. If possible, use passive-voice verbs and subordinate clauses to further de-emphasize the bad news.

a. Unfortunately, we find it impossible to contribute to your excellent and worthwhile fund-raising campaign this year. At present all the funds of my organization are needed to lease equipment and offices for our new branch in Hamilton. We hope to be able to support this commendable endeavour in the future.

b. We cannot ship our fresh fruit baskets c.o.d. Your order was not accompanied by payment, so we are not shipping it. We have it ready, though, and will rush it to its destination as soon as you call us with your credit card number.

c. Because of the holiday period, all our billboard space was used this month. Therefore, we are sorry to say that we could not give your charitable group free display space. However, next month, after the holidays, we hope to display your message as we promised.

Activities

NOTE: All Documents for Analysis may be downloaded from www.guffeybrief4e.nelson.com so that you do not have to rekey the entire message.

9.5 Document for Analysis: Wedding Request Refusal (Objs. 1–4)

Your Task. Analyze the following poorly written request refusal. List its weaknesses. If your instructor directs, revise it using the suggestions you learned in this chapter.

Current date
Ms. Sonya Capretta
5911 Minoru Avenue
Richmond, BC V6X 4X7

Dear Ms. Capretta:

We regret to inform you that the wedding date you request in your letter of February 2 at the Sun Valley Inn is unavailable. Unfortunately, we are fully booked for all of the Saturdays in June, as you probably already suspected.

June is our busiest month, and smart brides make their reservations many months—even years—in advance. That's because the Sun Valley Inn is the ideal romantic getaway for weddings. With unparalleled cuisine and service, along with panoramic Sun Valley and mountain views, our Inn offers unique, intimate ambiance in a breathtaking location for your special event.

We apologize if we have caused you any inconvenience. However, if you could change your wedding date to the middle of the week, we would try to accommodate your party. We do have a few midweek spots open in June, but even those dates are rapidly filling up. With 45 Mediterranean-style rooms and suites, each with its own sunny private terrace, the Sun Valley Inn is the perfect location for you and your partner to begin your married lives. Afternoon ceremonies typically begin at 11 a.m., while golden sunsets at the Sun Valley Inn offer a romantic prelude of the evening to come. Evening ceremonies usually begin at 6 p.m. I'm available if you want to arrange something.
Sincerely,

9.6 Document for Analysis: Refusing a Job Applicant (Objs. 1, 2, and 6)

Your Task. Analyze the following letter. List its weaknesses. If your instructor directs, revise it.

Current date
Mr. Kent W. Bradshaw
2050 Copeland Drive
Toronto, ON M4E 1H3

Dear Mr. Bradshaw:

Mrs. Lujan and I wish to thank you for the pleasure of allowing us to interview you last Thursday. We were totally delighted to learn about your superb academic record, and we also appreciated your attentiveness in listening to our description of the operations of Zumerix Technologies.

Unfortunately, we had many well-qualified applicants who were interested in the advertised position of human resources assistant. As you may have guessed, we were particularly eager to find an individual who is a member of a minority group to could help us fill our diversity goals. Although you did not fit one of our goal areas, we enjoyed talking with you. We hired a female graduate from Ryerson University who had most of the qualities we sought.

We realize that the job market is difficult at this time, and you have our heartfelt wishes for good luck in finding precisely what you are looking for.
Sincerely,

9.7 Claim Denial: Sorry—Smokers Must Pay (Objs. 1–4)

Recently the Century Park Hotel embarked on a two-year plan to provide enhanced value and improved product quality to its guests. It always strives to exceed guest expectations. As part of this effort, Century Park has been refurbishing many rooms with updated finishes. The new carpet, paint, upholstery, and draperies, however, absorb the heavy odour of cigarette smoke. To protect the hotel's investment, Century Park enforces a strict non-smoking policy for its non-smoking rooms.

Century Park makes sure that guests know about its policy regarding smoking in non-smoking rooms. It posts a notice in each non-smoking room, and it gives guests a handout from the manager detailing its policy and the consequences for smoking in non-smoking rooms. The handout clearly says, "Should a guest opt to disregard our non-smoking policy, we will process a fee of $150 to the guest's account." For those guests who prefer to smoke, a smoking accommodation can be provided.

On May 10 Wilson M. Wong was a guest in the hotel. He stayed in a room clearly marked "Non-smoking." After he left, the room cleaners reported that the room smelled of smoke. According to hotel policy, a charge of $150 was processed to Mr. Wong's credit card. Mr. Wong has written to demand that the $150 charge be removed. He doesn't deny that he smoked in the room. He just thinks that he should not have to pay.

Your Task. As hotel manager, deny Mr. Wong's claim. You would certainly like to see Mr. Wong return as a Century Park guest, but you cannot budge on your smoking policy. Address your response to Mr. Wilson M. Wong, 634 Middletowne Road, Pickering, ON L9H 7L2.

9.8 Bad News to Customers: Rate Increase of Your Choice (Objs. 1-3, 5)

Select a product or service that you now use. It could be your newspaper, Internet service provider, local water or electricity company, propane or natural gas supplier, cell or landline provider, car insurance company, or some other product or service you regularly use. Assume that the provider must raise its rates, and you are the employee who must notify customers. Should you use a letter, e-mail, company Web site, or blog? Decide whether you should use the direct or indirect strategy. Gather as much information as you can about the product or service. What, if anything, justifies the increase? What benefits can be cited?

Your Task. Prepare a rate increase announcement. Submit it along with a memo explaining your rationale for the strategy you chose.

9.9 Damage Control for Disappointed Customers: Costly SUV Upgrade to a Ford Excursion (Obj. 4)

Steven Clark, a consultant from Calgary, Alberta, was surprised when he picked up his rental car from Budget on a family visit over the Easter weekend. He had reserved a full-size car, but the rental agent told him he could upgrade to a Ford Excursion for an additional $25 a day. "She told me it was easy to drive," Mr. Clark reported. "But when I saw it, I realized it was huge—like a tank. You could fit a full-size bed inside."

On his trip Mr. Clark managed to scratch the paint and damage the rear-door step. He didn't worry, though, because he thought the damage would be covered since he had charged the rental on his American Express card. He knew that the company offered backup car rental insurance coverage. To his dismay, he discovered that its car rental coverage excluded large SUVs. "I just assumed they'd cover it," he confessed. He wrote to Budget to complain about not being warned that certain credit cards may not cover damage to large SUVs or luxury cars. Budget agents always encourage renters to sign up for Budget's own "risk product." But they don't feel that it is their responsibility to study the policies of customers' insurance carriers and explain what may or may not be covered. Moreover, they try to move customers into their rental cars as quickly as possible and avoid lengthy discussions of insurance coverage. Customers who do not purchase insurance are at risk. Mr. Clark does not make any claim against Budget, but he is upset about being "pitched" to upgrade to the larger SUV, which he didn't really want.[16]

Your Task. As a member of the communication staff at Budget, respond to Mr. Clark's complaint. Budget obviously is not going to pay for the SUV repairs, but it does want to salvage his goodwill and future business. Offer him a coupon worth two days' free rental of any full-size sedan. Write to Steven Clark, 5300 Park Ridge, Apt. 4A, Calgary, AB T2P 2M6.

9.10 Bad News to Employees: Company Games Are Not Date Nights (Objs. 1-3, 6)

E-MAIL

As director of Human Resources at Weyerman Paper Company, you received an unusual request. Several employees asked that their spouses or friends be allowed to participate in Weyerman's intramural sports teams. Although the teams play only once a week during the season, these employees claim that they can't afford more time away from friends and family. More than 100 employees currently participate in the eight co-ed volleyball, softball, and tennis teams, which are open to company employees only. The teams were designed to improve employee friendships and to give employees a regular occasion to have fun together.

If nonemployees were to participate, you fear that employee interaction would be limited. Although some team members might have fun if spouses or friends were included, you are not so sure all employees would enjoy it. You are not interested in turning intramural sports into "date night." Furthermore, the company would have to create additional teams if many nonemployees joined, and you don't want the administrative or equipment costs of more teams. Adding teams also would require changes to team rosters and game schedules. This could create a problem for some employees. You do understand the need for social time with friends and families, but guests are welcome as spectators at all intramural games. Also, the company already sponsors a family holiday party and an annual company picnic.

Your Task. Write an e-mail or hard-copy memo to the staff denying the request of several employees to include nonemployees on Weyerman's intramural sports teams.

Grammar and Mechanics C.L.U.E. Review 9

Confusing Words and Frequently Misspelled Words

Review the lists of confusing words and frequently misspelled words in Appendix A, Grammar and Mechanics Guide, beginning on page A-22. On a separate sheet, revise the following sentences to correct word usage errors. Sentences may have more than one error. If a sentence is correct, write *C*. When finished, compare your responses with the key beginning on page Key-1.
Example: Have you allready sent the reccomendation?
Revision: Have you **already** sent the **recommendation?**

1. Included in her bad-news message was a complement and valuable advise.

2. His principle reason for declining the invitation was his busy calander.

3. In her damage-control message, the manager made a conscience effort to regain the customer's confidence.

4. In your every day business affairs, you must show patients even when irritated.

5. Before you procede with the report, please check those embarassing statistics.

6. Although we will look into this matter farther, I am not suprised at your report.

7. The judge declared that the comments of there attorneys were irrevelant to the case at hand.

8. Because the property was to difficult to apprise, its value was unrecorded.

9. Meredith hoped to illicit advice from her counsellor, but she was disapointed.

10. The manager reccommended that we switch to an annual maintinance schedule.

Endnotes

[1] De Giorgio, L. (2011, February 1). Study means never having to say "I'm sorry." *Toronto Star.* A1, A4.

[2] Greenwald, J. (2009, June 1). Layoffs may spark defamation suits. *Business Insurance.* Retrieved January 13, 2009, from Business Source Complete database.

[3] McCord, E. A. (1991, April). The business writer, the law, and routine business communication: A legal and rhetorical analysis. *Journal of Business and Technical Communication,* 183.

[4] Shuit, D. P. (2003, September). Do it right or risk getting burned. *Workforce Management,* p. 80.

[5] Brodkin, J. (2007, March 19). Corporate apologies don't mean much. *Networkworld, 24*(11), p. 8. Retrieved January 4, 2010, from Business Source Complete database.

[6] Schweitzer, M. (2006, December). Wise negotiators know when to say "I'm sorry." *Negotiation,* 4. Retrieved January 4, 2010, from Business Source Complete database.

[7] Brodkin, J. (2007, March 19). Rating apologies. *Networkworld, 24*(11), p. 14. Retrieved January 3, 2010, from Business Source Complete database.

[8] Maple Leaf Foods. (2008, August 23). Maple Leaf CEO Michael H. McCain responds to determination of link to plant [press release]. Retrieved July 14, 2009, from http://newswire.ca/en/releases/archive/August2008/23/c6402.html

[9] Letters to Lands' End. (1991, February). *1991 Lands' End Catalog.* Dodgeville, WI: Lands' End, p. 100.

[10] Timm, J. (2010, May 10). Brands we trust: Branding by the masses. *Canadian Business.* Retrieved March 14, 2011, from http://www.CanadianBusiness.com

[11] Mowatt, J. (2002, February). Breaking bad news to customers. *Agency Sales,* 30; Dorn, E. M. (1999, March). Case method instruction in the business writing classroom. *Business Communication Quarterly, 62*(1), 51–52.

[12] Browning, M. (2003, November 24). Work dilemma: Delivering bad news a good way. *Government Computer News,* p. 41; Mowatt, J. (2002, February). Breaking bad news to customers. *Agency Sales,* p. 30.

[13] Ensall, S. (2007, January 30). Delivering bad news. *Personnel Today,* p. 31. Retrieved January 5, 2010, from Business Source Premier database; Lewis, B. (1999, September 13). To be an effective leader, you need to perfect the art of delivering bad news. *InfoWorld,* p. 124.

[14] Bristol-Smith, D. (2003, November). Quoted in Need to deliver bad news? How & why to tell it like it is. *HR Focus,* p. 3. Retrieved January 5, 2010, from InfoTrac College Edition database.

[15] Gartner Newsroom. (n.d.). Gartner identifies top ten disruptive technologies for 2008–2012 [press release]. Retrieved January 5, 2010, from http://www.gartner.com/it/page.jsp?id=681107

[16] Based on SUV surprise. (2004, June 15). *The Wall Street Journal,* p. W7.

CHAPTER 10

Persuasive and Sales Messages

OBJECTIVES

After studying this chapter, you should be able to

1. Define the concept of persuasion, identify effective and ineffective persuasive techniques, and apply the 3-×-3 writing process to persuasive messages.

2. Explain the four major elements in successful persuasive messages and how to blend those elements into effective and ethical business messages.

3. Write persuasive messages that request favours and actions, make claims, and deliver complaints.

4. Write persuasive messages within organizations.

5. Write effective and ethical direct-mail and e-mail sales messages.

6. Understand basic patterns and techniques in developing persuasive media releases.

© OJO Images/SuperStock

With 94 percent of Canadians belonging to some type of loyalty program, we are second only to the Brits, but researchers have found that not all programs fit all consumers. Successful companies realize that problem, so they target the rewards to the specific needs of the consumer. Personalization is key in making loyalty programs successful. "It's all about knowing our customers and rewarding them in a way we know they will appreciate," says Lisa Gibson of Shoppers Drug Mart.[1] To what loyalty programs do you belong? How is the program successful or unsuccessful in meeting your needs?

Understanding Persuasion and How to Use It Effectively and Ethically

Convincing others that your point of view is the right one is a critical business communication skill. However, many of us do it poorly or unconsciously.[2] You have already studied techniques for writing routine request messages that required subtle forms of persuasion. This chapter focuses on messages that require deliberate and skilled persuasion. You will learn what persuasion is and how to apply it effectively when you write requests for favours and actions, make claims, and prepare sales messages. This is one of the most important chapters in the book because much of your success in business depends on how skilled you are at persuading people to believe, accept, and act on what you are saying.

LEARNING OBJECTIVE 1

Define the concept of persuasion, identify effective and ineffective persuasive techniques, and apply the 3-x-3 writing process to persuasive messages.

What Is Persuasion?

Persuasion is defined as the ability to use argument or discussion to influence an individual's beliefs or actions. Parents use persuasion to cajole their kids into doing their homework. A team member uses persuasion to convince her technology-averse manager that instant messaging is an excellent tool to keep all team members informed about a project. You might want to persuade your boss to allow you to work at home part of the time. In Figure 10.1 Stacy McPherson, general manager of Oak Park Town Centre, uses persuasion in a memo to the mall owner and president. She wants to convince him to restrict the access of unchaperoned teenagers on weekends and evenings.

Some people think that persuasion involves coercion or trickery. They think that they can achieve what they seek only if they twist an arm or deceive someone. Such negative tactics are ineffective and unethical. What's more, these tactics don't truly represent persuasion. To persuade is to present information enabling others to see the benefits of what you are offering, without browbeating or tricking them into agreement.

Successful persuasion depends largely on the reasonableness of your request, your credibility, and your ability to make the request attractive to the receiver. Many techniques can help you be effective in getting your ideas accepted by your fellow workers, superiors, and clients.

Persuasion is the ability to use argument or discussion to change beliefs or actions.

Effective Persuasion Techniques

When you want your ideas to prevail, spend some time thinking about how to present them. Listeners and readers will be more inclined to accept what you are offering if you focus on the following important strategies, which are outlined here and further discussed with illustrations throughout the chapter.

● **Establish credibility.** To be persuasive, you must engender trust. People must believe that you are telling the truth, are experienced, and know what you are talking about. If you lack credentials or experience, use testimonials, expert opinion, and research to support your position.

FIGURE 10.1 Persuasive Action Request

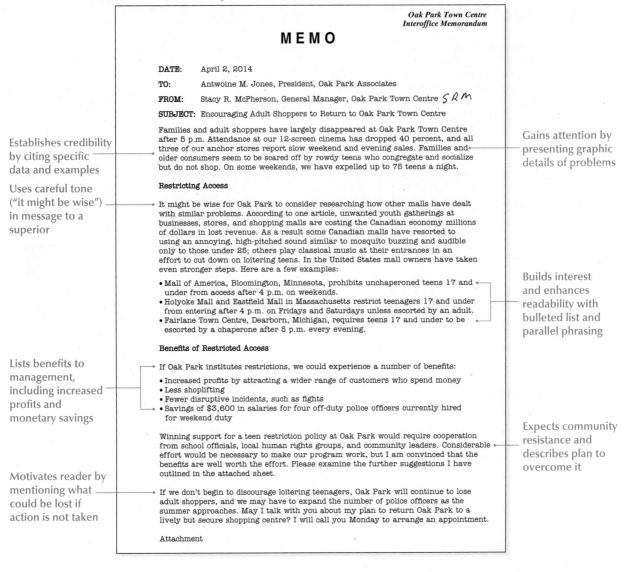

Establishes credibility by citing specific data and examples

Uses careful tone ("it might be wise") in message to a superior

Lists benefits to management, including increased profits and monetary savings

Motivates reader by mentioning what could be lost if action is not taken

Oak Park Town Centre
Interoffice Memorandum

MEMO

DATE: April 2, 2014

TO: Antwoine M. Jones, President, Oak Park Associates

FROM: Stacy R. McPherson, General Manager, Oak Park Town Centre *SRM*

SUBJECT: Encouraging Adult Shoppers to Return to Oak Park Town Centre

Families and adult shoppers have largely disappeared at Oak Park Town Centre after 5 p.m. Attendance at our 12-screen cinema has dropped 40 percent, and all three of our anchor stores report slow weekend and evening sales. Families and older consumers seem to be scared off by rowdy teens who congregate and socialize but do not shop. On some weekends, we have expelled up to 75 teens a night.

Restricting Access

It might be wise for Oak Park to consider researching how other malls have dealt with similar problems. According to one article, unwanted youth gatherings at businesses, stores, and shopping malls are costing the Canadian economy millions of dollars in lost revenue. As a result some Canadian malls have resorted to using an annoying, high-pitched sound similar to mosquito buzzing and audible only to those under 25; others play classical music at their entrances in an effort to cut down on loitering teens. In the United States mall owners have taken even stronger steps. Here are a few examples:

- Mall of America, Bloomington, Minnesota, prohibits unchaperoned teens 17 and under from access after 4 p.m. on weekends.
- Holyoke Mall and Eastfield Mall in Massachusetts restrict teenagers 17 and under from entering after 4 p.m. on Fridays and Saturdays unless escorted by an adult.
- Fairlane Town Centre, Dearborn, Michigan, requires teens 17 and under to be escorted by a chaperone after 5 p.m. every evening.

Benefits of Restricted Access

If Oak Park institutes restrictions, we could experience a number of benefits:

- Increased profits by attracting a wider range of customers who spend money
- Less shoplifting
- Fewer disruptive incidents, such as fights
- Savings of $3,600 in salaries for four off-duty police officers currently hired for weekend duty

Winning support for a teen restriction policy at Oak Park would require cooperation from school officials, local human rights groups, and community leaders. Considerable effort would be necessary to make our program work, but I am convinced that the benefits are well worth the effort. Please examine the further suggestions I have outlined in the attached sheet.

If we don't begin to discourage loitering teenagers, Oak Park will continue to lose adult shoppers, and we may have to expand the number of police officers as the summer approaches. May I talk with you about my plan to return Oak Park to a lively but secure shopping centre? I will call you Monday to arrange an appointment.

Attachment

Gains attention by presenting graphic details of problems

Builds interest and enhances readability with bulleted list and parallel phrasing

Expects community resistance and describes plan to overcome it

---

- **Make a reasonable, precise request.** Persuasion is most effective if your request is realistic, doable, and attainable. Don't ask for $100,000 worth of equipment when your department's budget is $5,000. Also, be clear about your objective. Precise requests are more effective than vague ones.

- **Tie facts to benefits.** Line up solid information to support your view. Use statistics, printed resources, examples, and analogies to help people understand. Remember, however, that information alone rarely changes attitudes. Marketers have pumped huge sums into failed advertising and public relations campaigns that provided facts alone. More important is converting those facts into benefits for the audience, as Stacy did in Figure 10.1.

- **Recognize the power of loss.** Describing the benefits of your proposal is a powerful motivator. Another powerful motivator is the thought of what the other person will lose if he or she doesn't agree. The threat of losing something we already possess—such as time, money, competitive advantage, profits, reputation— seems to be more likely to motivate people than the idea of gaining that very same thing.[3]

- **Expect and overcome resistance.** When proposing ideas, be prepared for resistance. This may arise in the form of conflicting beliefs, negative attitudes, apathy, skepticism, and opposing loyalties. Recognize any weakness in your proposal and be prepared to counter with well-reasoned arguments and facts. In Figure 10.1 Stacy realized that her proposal to restrict the access of unchaperoned teenagers would require acceptance and cooperation from community groups.

- **Share solutions and compromise.** The process of persuasion may involve being flexible and working out a solution that is acceptable to all concerned. Sharing a solution requires listening to people and developing a new position that incorporates their input. When others' views become part of a solution, they gain a sense of ownership; they buy in and are more eager to implement the solution.

The Importance of Tone

Tone is particularly important in persuasion today because the workplace has changed. Gone are the days when managers could simply demand compliance. Today's managers and team leaders strive to generate cooperation and buy-in instead of using intimidation, threats, and punishment to gain compliance.[4] Team members no longer accept command-and-control, top-down, unquestioned authority.[5] How can persuaders improve the tone of their requests?

> The tone of effective persuasive business requests invites cooperation; it avoids intimidation, lecturing, and excessive authoritarianism.

- **Avoid sounding preachy or parental.** People don't want to be lectured or instructed in a demeaning manner. No one likes to be treated like a child.

- **Don't pull rank.** Effective persuasion doesn't result from status or authority. People want to be recognized as individuals of worth. Pulling rank may secure compliance but not buy-in.

- **Avoid making threats.** People may comply when threatened, but their compliance may disappear over time. For example, many drivers follow the speed limit only when a patrol car is near. Threats also may result in retaliation, reduced productivity, and low morale.

- **Soften your words when persuading upward.** When you must persuade someone who has more clout than you, use such words as *suggest* and *recommend*. Craft sentences that begin with *It might be a good idea to. . . .* Make suggestions without threatening authority.

- **Be enthusiastic, positive, and likable.** Convey your passion for an idea through your body language, voice, and words. When you enthusiastically request something to be done, people feel more confident that they can do it. Use sincere compliments and praise. Describe what a positive impact others have had. Offer to reciprocate, if you are asking a favour.

Applying the 3-×-3 Writing Process to Persuasive Messages

Persuasion means changing people's views, and that's often a difficult task. Pulling it off demands planning and perception. The 3-×-3 writing process provides you with a helpful structure for laying a foundation for persuasion. Of particular importance here are (a) analyzing the purpose, (b) adapting to the audience, (c) collecting information, and (d) organizing the message.

Analyzing the Purpose: Knowing What You Want to Achieve. The
purpose of a persuasive message is to convert the receiver to your ideas or to motivate action. A message without a clear purpose is doomed. Not only must you know what your purpose is and what response you want, but you must also know these things when you start writing your message or planning a presentation. Too often, inexperienced writers reach the end of the first draft of a message before discovering exactly what they want the receiver to do. Then they must start over, giving the request a

> Persuasive messages require a careful analysis of the purpose for writing.

different spin or emphasis. Because your purpose establishes the strategy of the message, determine it first.

Let's say you must convince Rachel, your department manager, that you could be more productive if you could work from home. Before approaching Rachel, know exactly what you want. How much time do you want to work at home? Full time? Part time? On special projects? Do you want Rachel to merely talk about it with you? Do you want her to set a time when you could start? Should you suggest a trial period? By identifying your purpose up front, you can shape the message to point toward it. This planning effort saves considerable rewriting time and produces the most successful persuasive messages.

Adapting to the Audience by Finding Ways to Make Your Message Heard.
While you are considering the purpose of a persuasive message, you also need to concentrate on the receiver. How can you adapt your request to that individual so that your message is heard? A persuasive message is equally futile unless it meets the needs of its audience. In a broad sense, you will be seeking to show how your request helps the receiver achieve some of life's major goals or fulfills key needs: money, power, comfort, confidence, importance, friends, peace of mind, and recognition, to name a few.

On a more practical level, you want to show how your request solves a problem, achieves a personal or work objective, or just makes life easier for your audience. In your request for a flexible work schedule, you could appeal to Rachel's expressed concern for increasing productivity. Your goal is to make the boss look good by granting your request. To adapt your request to the receiver, consider these questions that receivers will very likely be asking themselves:

Why should I?

What's in it for me?

What's in it for you?

Who cares?

Adapting to your audience means being ready to answer these questions. It means learning about audience members and analyzing why they might resist your proposal. It means searching for ways to connect your purpose with their needs. If completed before you begin writing, such analysis goes a long way toward overcoming resistance and achieving your goal.

Researching and Organizing Persuasive Data.
Once you have analyzed the audience and considered how to adapt your message to its needs, you are ready to collect data and organize it. You might brainstorm and prepare cluster diagrams to provide a rough outline of ideas. For your request for a flexible work schedule, you might gather information describing how other comparable companies have developed telecommuting programs and how effective they are. You could work out a possible schedule outlining when you would be working at home and when you would be in the office for meetings and face-to-face discussions. You are certain you could complete more work at home, but how can you prove it in your request? To overcome resistance, you might describe your work-at-home office, equipment, and procedures. You could also explain your plan for staying in touch with and being responsive to inquiries and requests.

The next step in a persuasive message is organizing your data into a logical sequence. If you are asking for something that you know will be approved, little persuasion is required. Thus, you would make a direct request, as you studied in Chapter 8. But when you expect resistance or when you need to educate the receiver, the indirect strategy often works better. The following four-part indirect strategy works well for many persuasive requests:

1. Gain attention

2. Build interest

3. Reduce resistance

4. Motivate action

Blending Four Major Elements in Successful Persuasive Messages

Although the indirect strategy appears to contain separate steps, successful persuasive messages actually blend the four steps into a seamless whole. Also, the sequence of the elements may change depending on the situation and the emphasis. Regardless of where they are placed, the key elements in persuasive requests are (a) gaining your audience's attention, (b) building interest by convincing your audience that your proposal is worthy, (c) reducing resistance, and (d) motivating action.

Gaining Attention in Persuasive Messages

To grab attention, the opening statement in a persuasive request should be brief, relevant, and engaging. When only mild persuasion is necessary, the opener can be low key and factual. If, however, your request is substantial and you anticipate strong resistance, provide a thoughtful, provocative opening. Following are some examples.

- **Problem description.** In a recommendation to hire temporary employees: *Last month legal division staff members were forced to work 120 overtime hours, costing us $6,000 and causing considerable employee unhappiness.* With this opener you have presented a capsule of the problem your proposal will help solve.

- **Unexpected statement.** In a memo to encourage employees to attend an optional sensitivity seminar: *Men and women draw the line at decidedly different places in identifying what behaviour constitutes sexual harassment.* Note how this opener gets readers thinking immediately.

- **Reader benefit.** In a letter promoting Clear Card, a service that helps employees make credit card purchases without paying interest: *The average employee carries nearly $13,000 in revolving debt and pays $2,800 in interest and late fees. The Clear Card charges zero percent interest. You can't beat it!* Employers immediately see this offer as a benefit it can offer employees.

- **Compliment.** In a letter inviting a business executive to speak: *Because our members admire your success and value your managerial expertise, they want you to be our speaker.* In offering praise or compliments, however, be careful to avoid obvious flattery.

- **Related facts.** In a message to company executives who are considering restricting cellphone use by employee drivers: *A recent study revealed that employers pay an average of $16,500 each time an employee is in a traffic accident.* This relevant fact sets the scene for the interest-building section that follows.

- **Stimulating question.** In a plea for funds to support environmental causes: *What do golden tortoise beetles, bark spiders, flounders, and Arctic foxes have in common?* Readers will be curious to find the answer to this intriguing question. [They all change colour depending on their surroundings.]

> Successful openers to persuasive requests are brief, relevant, and engaging.

Building Interest in Persuasive Messages

After capturing attention, a persuasive request must retain that attention and convince the audience that the request is reasonable. To justify your request, be prepared to invest in a few paragraphs of explanation. Persuasive requests are likely to be longer than direct requests because the audience must be convinced rather than

> The body of a persuasive request may require several paragraphs to build interest and reduce resistance.

simply instructed. You can build interest and conviction through the use of the following:

- Facts, statistics
- Expert opinion
- Direct benefits
- Examples
- Specific details
- Indirect benefits

Showing how your request can benefit the audience directly or indirectly is a key factor in persuasion. If you were asking alumni to contribute money to a college or university foundation, for example, you might promote *direct benefits,* such as listing the donor's name in the alumni magazine or sending a sweatshirt with the school logo. Another direct benefit is a tax write-off for the contribution. An *indirect benefit* might be feeling good about helping the college or university and knowing that students will benefit from the gift. Nearly all charities rely in large part on indirect benefits to promote their causes.

Reducing Resistance in Persuasive Requests

One of the biggest mistakes in persuasive requests is the failure to anticipate and offset audience resistance. How will the receiver object to your request? In brainstorming for clues, try *What if?* scenarios. Let's say you are trying to convince management that the employees' cafeteria should switch from paper and plastic plates and cups to ceramic. What if managers say the change is too expensive? What if they argue that they are careful recyclers of paper and plastic? What if they contend that ceramic dishes would increase cafeteria labour and energy costs tremendously? What if they protest that ceramic is less hygienic? For each of these *What if?* scenarios, you need a counterargument.

Unless you anticipate resistance, you give the receiver an easy opportunity to dismiss your request. Countering this resistance is important, but you must do it with finesse (*Although ceramic dishes cost more at first, they actually save money over time*). You can minimize objections by presenting your counterarguments in sentences that emphasize benefits: *Ceramic dishes may require a little more effort in cleaning, but they bring warmth and graciousness to meals. Most important, they help save the environment by requiring fewer resources and eliminating waste.* However, don't spend too much time on counterarguments, thus making them overly important. Finally, avoid bringing up objections that may never have occurred to the receiver in the first place.

Another factor that reduces resistance is credibility. Receivers are less resistant if your request is reasonable and if you are believable. When the receiver does not know you, you may have to establish your expertise, refer to your credentials, or demonstrate your competence. Even when you are known, you may have to establish your knowledge in a given area. If you are asking your manager for a new laptop computer, you might have to establish your credibility by showing your manager articles about the latest laptops. You could point out that a laptop would enable you to work away from the office while staying in touch by e-mail. Some charities establish their credibility by displaying on their stationery the names of famous people who serve on their boards. The credibility of speakers making presentations is usually outlined by someone who introduces them.

Motivating Action in Persuasive Messages

After gaining attention, building interest, and reducing resistance, you will want to inspire the receiver to act. This is where your planning pays dividends. Knowing exactly what action you favour before you start to write enables you to point your arguments toward this important final paragraph. Here you will make your recommendation as specifically and confidently as possible—without seeming pushy. A proposal from one manager to another might conclude with, *So that we can begin*

FIGURE 10.2 Four-Part Plan for Persuasive Messages

Gaining Attention	Building Interest	Reducing Resistance	Motivating Action
Summary of problem	Facts, figures	Anticipate objections	Describe specific request
Unexpected statement	Expert opinion	Offer counterarguments	Sound confident
Reader benefit	Examples	Employ *What if?* scenarios	Make action easy to take
Compliment	Specific details	Establish credibility	Offer incentive
Related fact	Direct benefits	Demonstrate competence	Don't provide excuses
Stimulating question	Indirect benefits	Show value of proposal	Repeat main benefit

using the employment assessment tests by May 1, please send a return e-mail immediately. In making a request, don't sound apologetic (*I'm sorry to have to ask you this, but . . .*), and don't supply excuses (*If you can spare the time . . .*). Compare the following closings for a persuasive memo recommending training seminars in communication skills.

Too General

We are certain we can develop a series of training sessions that will improve the communication skills of your employees.

Too Timid

If you agree that our training proposal has merit, perhaps we could begin the series in June.

Too Pushy

Because we are convinced that you will want to begin improving the skills of your employees immediately, we have scheduled your series to begin in June.

Effective

You will see decided improvement in the communication skills of your employees. Please call me at 800-439-2201 by May 1 to give your approval so that training sessions may start in June, as we discussed.

Note how the last opening suggests a specific and easy-to-follow action. It also provides a deadline and a reason for that date. Figure 10.2 summarizes a four-part plan for overcoming resistance and crafting successful persuasive messages.

Being Persuasive and Ethical

Business communicators may be tempted to make their persuasion even more forceful by fudging on the facts, exaggerating a point, omitting something crucial, or providing deceptive emphasis. A persuader is effective only when he or she is believable. If receivers suspect that they are being manipulated or misled or if they find any part of the argument untruthful, the total argument fails. Persuaders can also fall into traps of logic without even being aware of it.

Persuasion becomes unethical when facts are distorted, overlooked, or manipulated with an intent to deceive. Of course, persuaders naturally want to put forth their strongest case. But that argument must be based on truth, objectivity, and fairness.

In prompting ethical and truthful persuasion, two factors act as powerful motivators. The first is the desire to preserve your reputation and credibility. Once lost, a good name or reputation is difficult to regain. An equally important force prompting ethical behaviour, though, is your opinion of yourself. The president of a major retailer tells a story of a supersaleswoman at his store. She vastly outsold her colleagues on

> Ethical business communicators maintain credibility and respect by being honest, fair, and objective.

virtually every shift she worked. The executive went to her store one day to watch and realized that the saleswoman would push anything on customers. It didn't matter whether items matched or the clothes looked good. She was fired. "Our customers are our friends," explained the president. "It's never about the quick sale."[6] He was more concerned with preserving the store's reputation and his own self-image than making money.

Requesting Favours and Actions, Making Claims, and Delivering Complaints

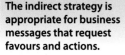

Many of your persuasive messages will be requests for favours or actions. For example, you may ask a businessperson to make a presentation to your club. You might ask a company to encourage its employees to participate in a charity drive. Another form of persuasion involves claims or complaints. All these messages require skill in persuasion. Convincing someone to change a belief or to perform an action when that person is reluctant requires planning and skill—and sometimes a little luck. A written, rather than face-to-face, request may require more preparation but can be more effective. Persuasion is often more precise and controlled when you can think through your purpose and prepare a thoughtful message in writing. The indirect strategy gives you an effective structure.

Preparing Persuasive Requests for Favours and Actions

Persuading someone to do something that largely benefits you may not be the easiest task. Fortunately, many individuals and companies are willing to grant requests for time, money, information, cooperation, and special privileges. They grant these favours for a variety of reasons. They may just happen to be interested in your project, or they may see goodwill potential for themselves. Professionals sometimes feel obligated to contribute their time or expertise to "pay their dues." Often, though, businesses and individuals comply because they see that others will benefit from the request.

Figure 10.3 shows a persuasive favour request from Cynde Ferris. Her research firm seeks to persuade other companies to complete a questionnaire revealing salary data. To most organizations, salary information is strictly confidential. What can she do to convince strangers to part with such private information?

To gain attention, she begins her persuasive favour request by posing two short questions that spotlight the need for salary information. To build interest and establish trust, she mentions that Anderson Research Institute has been collecting business data for a quarter century and has received awards from professional organizations. Developing credibility is especially important when persuading strangers to do something. Making a reasonable request tied to benefits is also important. Cynde does this by emphasizing the need for current salary information.

To reduce resistance, Cynde promises confidentiality and explains that the questionnaire takes but a few moments to complete. She offers free salary data as a direct benefit. The data may help the receiver learn how its salary scale compares with others in its industry. But Cynde doesn't count on this offer as the only motivator. As an indirect benefit, she appeals to the professionalism of the receiver. She's hoping that the receiver will recognize the value of providing salary data to the entire profession. To motivate action, Cynde closes with a deadline and reminds the reader that her company need not be in the dark about comparative salaries within its industry.

This favour request incorporates many of the techniques that are effective in persuasion: establishing credibility, making a reasonable and precise request, tying facts to benefits, and overcoming resistance.

FIGURE 10.3 Persuasive Favour Request

1 Prewriting

Analyze: The purpose of this letter is to persuade the reader to complete and return a questionnaire.

Anticipate: Although the reader is busy, she may respond to appeals to her professionalism and to her need for salary data in her own business.

Adapt: Because the reader may be uninterested at first and require persuasion, use the indirect pattern.

2 Writing

Research: Study the receiver's business and find ways to relate this request to company success.

Organize: Gain attention by opening with relevant questions. Build interest by showing how the reader's compliance will help her company and others. Reduce resistance by promising confidentiality and offering free data.

Compose: Prepare a first draft with the intention to revise.

3 Revising

Revise: Revise to show direct and indirect benefits more clearly. Make sure the message is as concise as possible.

Proofread: In the first sentence, spell out "percent" rather than using the symbol. Check the use of all question marks. Start all lines at the left for a block-style letter.

Evaluate: Will this letter convince the reader to complete and return the questionnaire?

A R A I
Anderson Research Associates, Inc.

1624 Fennell Street
Ottawa, ON K9J 6P7
PH   613-349-2219
FAX   613-349-8967
www.andersonresearch.com

October 15, 2014

Ms. Susan Riverston
Assistant Vice President
Five Star Finance Consultants
2469 Langton Avenue
Thornhill, ON L3J 3M8

Dear Ms. Riverston:

Has your company ever lost a valued employee to another organization that offered 20 percent more in salary for the same position? Have you ever added a unique job title but had no idea what compensation the position demanded?

To remain competitive in hiring and to retain qualified workers, companies rely on survey data showing current salaries. Anderson Research Associates has been collecting business data for a quarter century and has been honoured by professional associations for its accurate data. We need your help in collecting salary data for today's workers. Information from the enclosed questionnaire will supply companies like yours with such data.

Your information, of course, will be treated confidentially. The questionnaire takes but a few moments to complete, and it can provide substantial dividends for professional organizations that need comparative salary data.

To show our gratitude for your participation, we will send you comprehensive salary surveys for your industry and your metropolitan area. Not only will you find basic salaries, but you will also learn about bonus and incentive plans, special pay differentials, expense reimbursements, perquisites, such as a company car and credit card, and special payments, such as beeper pay.

Comparative salary data are impossible to provide without the support of professionals like you. Please complete the questionnaire and return it in the prepaid envelope before November 1, our fall deadline. You will be better informed about how much your employees earn compared with others in your industry.

Sincerely yours,

Cynde Ferris

Cynde Ferris
Director, Survey Research

Enclosures

Callout annotations (left):
- Poses two short questions related to the reader
- Presents reader benefit tied to request explanation; establishes credibility
- Anticipates and counters resistance to confidentiality and time/effort objections
- Offers free salary data as a direct benefit
- Provides deadline and a final benefit to prompt action

Callout annotations (right):
- Gains attention
- Builds interest
- Reduces resistance
- Motivates action

Writing Persuasive Claims

When making a claim or delivering a complaint, use the direct strategy if your request is justified and will be granted.

Persuasive claims typically involve damaged products, mistaken billing, inaccurate shipments, warranty problems, limited return policies, insurance mix-ups, faulty merchandise, and so on. Generally, the direct strategy is best for requesting straight-forward adjustments (see Chapter 8). When you feel your request is justified and will be granted, the direct strategy is most efficient. But if a past request has been refused or ignored, or if you anticipate reluctance, then the indirect strategy is appropriate.

Developing a Logical Persuasive Argument. Strive for logical development in a claim letter. You might open with sincere praise, an objective statement of the problem, a point of agreement, or a quick review of what you have done to resolve the problem. Then you can explain precisely what happened or why your claim is legitimate. Don't provide a blow-by-blow chronology of details; just hit the highlights. Be sure to enclose copies of relevant invoices, shipping orders, warranties, and payments. Close with a clear statement of what you want done: a refund, replacement, credit to your account, or other action. Be sure to think through the possibilities and make your request reasonable.

Appeal to the receiver's sense of responsibility and pride in the company's good name.

Using a Moderate Tone. The tone of your message is important. Don't suggest that the receiver intentionally deceived you or intentionally created the problem. Rather, appeal to the receiver's sense of responsibility and pride in the company's good name. Calmly express your disappointment in view of your high expectations of the product and of the company. Communicating your feelings without rancour is often your strongest appeal.

Composing Effective Complaints

Effective claim and complaint letters make reasonable claims backed by solid evidence.

As their name suggests, complaints deliver bad news. Some complaint messages just vent anger. However, if the goal is to change something (and why bother to write except to motivate change?), then persuasion is necessary. Effective claim messages make a reasonable and valid request, present a logical case with clear facts, and adopt a moderate tone. Anger and emotion are not effective persuaders.

Marilyn Easter's letter, shown in Figure 10.4, follows the persuasive pattern as she seeks credit for two VoIP (voice over Internet protocol) systems. Actually, she was quite upset because her company was counting on these new Internet systems to reduce its phone bills. Instead, the handsets produced so much static that incoming and outgoing calls were all but impossible to hear. What's more, she was frustrated that the Return Merchandise Authorization form she filled out at the company's Web site seemed to sink into a dark hole in cyberspace. She had reason to be angry! But she resolved to use a moderate tone in writing her complaint letter.

Notice that her tone is objective, rational, and unemotional. She begins with a compliment and explains why her company needs a VoIP system. She provides identifying data and justifies her claim by explaining that installation instructions were carefully followed. Claim messages are particularly effective when writers express their personal disappointment and feelings. Marilyn explains her strong disappointment in view of the promotional statement assuring a clear signal. She would like to have been more forceful, but she knew that a calm, unemotional tone would be more effective. She wondered whether she should say that she was really ticked off that she had spent hours researching the product. The new system took additional hours to install and troubleshoot. After all that work, she couldn't use it because of the static. Nevertheless, she stuck to the plan of using a positive opening, a well-documented claim, and a request for specific action in the closing.

The Checklist box on page 246 summarizes key points for requesting favours and actions, making claims, and delivering complaints.

FIGURE 10.4 **Claim (Complaint) Letter**

ARTE INTERNATIONAL FURNISHINGS

141 Rue Champlain, Gatineau, QC J8T 3H9 (819) 690 3500

February 16, 2014

Customer Service
ZTech Electronics
57 Emilie Simard Avenue
Edmundston, NB E3V 3N9

Dear ZTech Customer Service Representative:

Your VoIP Expandable Telephone System came highly recommended and seemed to be the answer to increasingly expensive telephone service. Here at Arte International Furnishings we were looking for a way to reduce our local and long-distance telephone charges. The VoIP system was particularly attractive to us because it offered Internet phone service with unlimited calling within Canada and to the United States. Our business in fine furnishings and unique objets d'art requires us to make and receive national and international calls.

On February 8 we purchased two VoIP systems (SGU #IP7402-2) for our main office here in Gatineau and for our showroom. Each system came with two cordless handsets and charging docks. Although we followed all the installation instructions, we discovered that an irritating static sound interfered with every incoming and outgoing telephone call.

This static is surprising and disappointing because the product description promised the following: "You will experience excellent signal clarity with Frequency Hopping Digital Spread Spectrum (FHDSS) transmission and a frequency of 5.8 GHz. Ninety-five channel auto-search ensures a clear signal."

On February 10 we filled out a Return Merchandise Authorization form at your Web site. However, we are frustrated that we have had no response. We're confident that a manufacturer with your reputation for reliable products and superior customer service will want to resolve this matter quickly.

Please authorize return of these two systems and credit our account for $377.24, which represents the original cost plus taxes and shipping. Enclosed is a copy of the invoice with our credit card number.

Sincerely,

Marilyn Easter

Marilyn Easter
President

Enclosure

Annotations (right margin):

- Begins with compliment; keeps tone objective, rational, and unemotional
- Provides identifying data and justifies claim
- Explains why claim is valid and suggests responsibility of receiver
- Expresses disappointment and appeals to receiver's reputation and customer service
- Tells what action to take

Tips for Making Complaints

- Begin with a compliment, point of agreement, statement of the problem, or brief review of action you have taken to resolve the problem.
- Provide identifying data.
- Prove that your claim is valid; explain why the receiver is responsible.
- Enclose document copies supporting your claim.
- Appeal to the receiver's fairness, ethical and legal responsibilities, and desire for customer satisfaction.
- Describe your feelings and your disappointment.
- Avoid sounding angry, emotional, or irrational.
- Close by stating exactly what you want done.

Checklist

Requesting Favours and Actions, Making Claims, Delivering Complaints

Prewrite

- Determine your purpose. Know exactly what you are requesting.
- Anticipate the reaction of your audience. Remember that the receiver is thinking, *Why should I? What's in it for me? What's in it for you? Who cares?*

Gain Attention

- Use the indirect strategy rather than blurting out the request immediately.
- Begin with a problem description, unexpected statement, compliment, praise, related facts, stimulating question, or reader benefit to grab attention.

Build Interest

- Develop interest by using facts, statistics, examples, testimonials, and specific details.
- Establish your credibility, if necessary, by explaining your background and expertise. Use testimonials, expert opinion, or research if necessary.

- Support your request by tying facts to direct benefits (increased profits, more efficient operations, better customer relations, saving money, a returned favour) or indirect benefits (improving the community, giving back to the profession, helping the environment).
- In claims and complaints, be objective but prove the validity of your request.

Reduce Resistance

- Anticipate objections to your request and provide counterarguments.
- Suggest what might be lost if the request is not granted, but don't make it sound like a threat.
- In claims and complaints, use a moderate, unemotional tone.

Motivate Action

- Make a precise request that spells out exactly what you want done. Add a deadline date if necessary.
- Repeat a benefit, provide additional details, or offer an incentive. Express appreciation.

Writing Persuasive Messages Within Organizations

LEARNING OBJECTIVE 4

Write persuasive messages within organizations.

As discussed in Chapter 1, messages within organizations move in one of three ways: downward, upward, or horizontally. The strategies and tone employed in these messages depend on the organizational position of the sender and that of the receiver. Let's say you want to persuade your boss to handle orders differently on the company's Web site. Your message would follow the indirect strategy. But the tone and content of your message would be different from that of the boss sending a similar persuasive message on the same topic. In this section we focus on messages flowing downward and upward within organizations. Horizontal messages travelling between co-workers are similar to those discussed earlier in requesting favours and actions.

Persuading Employees: Messages Flowing Downward

Persuasive requests flowing downward may ask employees to participate in capacities outside their typical work roles.

Instructions or directives moving downward from superiors to subordinates usually require little persuasion. Employees expect to be directed in how to perform their jobs. These messages (such as information about procedures, equipment, or customer service) use the direct strategy, with the purpose immediately stated. However, employees are sometimes asked to volunteer for projects. For example, some organizations ask employees to join programs to stop smoking, lose weight, or start exercising. Organizations may ask employees to participate in capacities outside their work roles—such as spending their free time volunteering for charity projects. In such cases, the four-part indirect strategy provides a helpful structure.

Messages flowing downward require attention to tone. Warm words and a conversational tone convey a caring attitude. Persuasive requests coming from a trusted superior are more likely to be accepted than requests from a dictatorial executive who relies on threats and punishments to secure compliance. Managers should avoid sounding preachy or parental. Employees don't want to be treated as children. Because the words *should* and *must* sometimes convey a negative tone, be careful in using them.

Figure 10.5 shows a memo from Jessica Jeffers, director of Human Resources at a large bank. Her goal is to persuade employees to participate in a fundraising and community service event that her bank sponsors. In addition to volunteering their services for a day, employees also have to pay $20 to register! You can see that this will be no small persuasion task for Jessica.

Jessica decides to follow the four-part indirect strategy beginning with gaining attention. Notice that she strives to capture attention by describing specific benefits of

FIGURE 10.5 Persuasive Organizational Message Flowing Downward

MEMO

DATE: September 13, 2014

TO: All First Bank Staff Members

FROM: Jessica M. Jeffers, Human Resources ꓹMꓹ

SUBJECT: Serving Our Community and Having Fun for Charity, November 5

Captures attention by describing indirect benefits of volunteering in the community

Every day volunteers make our community a better place to live and work. They feed the homeless, provide companionship to seniors, build low-income housing, restore the natural environment, tutor at-risk children, read to children in shelters, participate in disaster relief efforts, and even care for homeless pets! These and other volunteer opportunities will be available on Helping Hands Day, a fundraising event that we at First Bank endorse with immense pride.

Gains attention

Develops interest with examples and survey results

In partnership with United Way, we at First Bank are joining in this day of change for our community. You can be part of the change as 2,500 hands come together to paint, plant, create murals, and clean neighbourhoods and beaches. Last year during Helping Hands a First Bank team removed graffiti and repainted the wall at a community park. Afterward, a survey showed that 86 percent of the volunteers thought the experience was worthwhile and that their efforts made a difference.

Builds interest

Reduces resistance by emphasizing both direct and indirect benefits

To participate, each volunteer pays a registration fee of $20. You may wonder why you should pay to volunteer. Helping Hands Day is our only corporate fundraising event, and it supports year-round free services and programs for our entire community. For your $20, you receive breakfast and an event T-shirt. Best of all, you share in making your community a better place to live and work.

Reduces resistance

Makes it easy to comply with request

To provide the best registration process possible, we have created a special registration Web site. Just click on Helping Hands on our company intranet before October 19.

Prompts action by providing deadline and incentive

You can make a huge difference to your community by volunteering for Helping Hands Day, November 4. Join the fun and your First Bank colleagues in showing our community that we value volunteerism that achieves community goals. For every employee who volunteers before October 19, First Bank will contribute $20 to United Way. Sign up now and name the team members you will work with.

Motivates action

volunteering. She explains ways that volunteers make their community a better place to live and work. Feeding the homeless, providing companionship to seniors, building low-income housing, restoring the natural environment—all these examples of selfless giving not only gain attention but also suggest indirect benefits to the reader.

Successful internal persuasive messages build interest by emphasizing benefits and overcoming resistance.

The second paragraph of this persuasive message builds interest by listing examples of what volunteers have accomplished during previous fundraising events. Volunteers can expect to join 2,500 other "hands" who paint, plant, create murals, and clean neighbourhoods and beaches. To build further interest, the letter includes the results of a survey showing that a vast majority of volunteers thought the experience was worthwhile and that their efforts made a difference. People are more inclined to agree to do something if they know that others have done it in the past and found it beneficial.

To reduce resistance, the third paragraph explains why the $20 fee makes sense. Jessica skillfully combines both direct benefits (free breakfast and an event T-shirt) with indirect benefits (sharing in making the community a better place to live and work).

Good persuasive requests close by making it easy to comply and by finding some way to motivate action. In complying with the request in this message, all the reader has to do is go to the bank's intranet and request a registration form. To motivate action in the closing, Jessica saved a strong indirect benefit. The bank will chip in $20 for every employee who volunteers before the deadline. Readers can see that their participation reaches beyond their individual contribution. Although readers don't benefit directly from the company's contribution to United Way, they can see that others will benefit. This significant indirect benefit along with the direct benefits of having fun and joining colleagues in a community activity combine for a strong persuasive message.

Persuading the Boss: Messages Flowing Upward

When selling an idea to management, writers often are successful if they make a strong case for saving money.

Another form of persuasion within organizations centres on suggestions made by subordinates. Convincing management to adopt a procedure or invest in a product or new equipment requires skillful communication. Managers are just as resistant to change as others are. Providing evidence is critical when subordinates submit recommendations to their bosses. Be ready to back up your request with facts, figures, and evidence. When selling an idea to management, strive to make a strong dollars-and-cents case.[7] A request that emphasizes how the proposal saves money or benefits the business is more persuasive than one that simply announces a good deal or tells how a plan works.

In describing an idea to your boss, state it confidently and fairly. Don't undermine your suggestions with such statements as *This may sound crazy* or *I know we tried this once before but*. . . . Show that you have thought through the suggestion by describing the risks involved and the potential benefits. You may wonder whether you should even mention the downside of a suggestion. Most bosses will be relieved and impressed to know that you have considered the risks and the benefits of a proposal.[8] Two-sided arguments are generally more persuasive because they make you sound credible and fair. Presenting only one side of a proposal reduces its effectiveness because such a proposal seems biased, subjective, and flawed. You can make a stronger argument by acknowledging and neutralizing opposing points of view.

Persuasive messages travelling upward require a special sensitivity to tone. When asking superiors to change views or take action, use such words as *suggest* and *recommend* rather than *you must* and *we should*. Avoid sounding pushy or argumentative. Strive for a conversational, yet professional, tone that conveys warmth, competence, and confidence.

When Marketing Manager Monique Hartung wanted her boss to authorize the purchase of a multifunction colour laser copier, she knew she had to be persuasive. Her memo, shown in Figure 10.6, illustrates an effective approach. First, she researched prices, features, and the maintenance of colour laser copiers. These machines often serve as copiers, faxes, scanners, and printers and can cost several thousand dollars.

FIGURE 10.6 Persuasive E-Mail and Memo Flowing Upward

To: Samuel Neesen <samuel.neesen@smartmachinetools.com>
From: Monique Hartung <monique.hartung@smartmachinetools.com>
Subject: Saving Time and Money on Copying and Printing
Cc:
Attached: Refurbished Color Copiers.docx (10KB)

Serves as cover e-mail to introduce attached memo in MS Word

Opens with catchy subject line

Sam,

Attached is a brief document that details our potential savings from purchasing a refurbished colour laser copier. After doing some research, I discovered that these sophisticated machines aren't as expensive as one might think.

Please look at my calculations and let me know what you suggest that we to do improve our in-house production of print matter and reduce both time and cost for external copying.

Does not reveal recommendation but leaves request for action to the attached memo

Monique

Monique Hartung
Marketing Assistant * Smart Machine Tools, Inc.
211 Main St. * Hague, SK S0K 1X0
(306) 225-4585 office / (306) 225-3229 fax
Monique.Hartung@smartmachinetools.com

Provides an electronic signature with contact information

↓ 1 inch

MEMORANDUM

↓ 2 blank lines

Date: April 8, 2014

↓ 1 blank line

To: Samuel Neesen, Vice President

↓ 1 blank line

From: Monique Hartung, Marketing M.H.

↓ 1 blank line

Subject: Saving Time and Money on Copying

↓ 1 or 2 blank lines

Describes topic without revealing request

Summarizes problem

We are losing money on our current copy services and wasting the time of employees as well. Because our aging Canon copier is in use constantly and can't handle our growing printing volume, we find it increasingly necessary to send major jobs out to Copy Quick. Moreover, whenever we need colour copies, we can't handle the work ourselves. Take a look at how much we spend each month for outside copy service:

Uses headings and columns for easy comprehension

Copy Costs: Outside Service

10,000 B&W copies/month made at Copy Quick	$ 700.00
1,000 color copies/month, $0.25 per copy (avg.)	250.00
Salary costs for assistants to make 32 trips	480.00
Total	$1,430.00

To save time and money, I have been considering alternatives. Large-capacity colour laser copiers with multiple features (copy, e-mail, fax, LAN fax, print, scan) are expensive. However, reconditioned copiers with all the features we need are available at attractive prices. From Copy City we can get a fully remanufactured Xerox copier that is guaranteed and provides further savings because solid-colour ink sticks cost a fraction of laser toner cartridges. We could copy and print in colour for roughly the same as black and white. After we make an initial payment of $300, our monthly costs would look like this:

Proves credibility of request with facts and figures

Copy Costs: Remanufactured Copier

Paper supplies for 11,000 copies	$160.00
Ink sticks and copy supplies	100.00
Labour of assistants to make copies	150.00
Monthly financing charge for copier (purchase price of $3,105 – $300 amortized at 10% with 36 payments)	93.74
Total	$503.74

Highlights most important benefit

Provides more benefits

As you can see, a remanufactured Xerox 8860MFP copier saves us more than $900 per month. For a limited time Copy City is offering a free 15-day trial offer, a free copier stand (a $250 value), free starter supplies, and free delivery and installation. We have office space available, and my staff is eager to add a second machine.

Counters possible resistance

Makes it easy to grant approval

Please call me at ext. 630 if you have questions. This copier is such a good opportunity that I have prepared a purchase requisition authorizing the agreement with Copy City. With your approval before May 1, we could have our machine by May 10 and start saving time and more than $900 every month. Fast action will also help us take advantage of Copy City's free start-up incentives.

Repeats main benefit with motivation to act quickly

Monique found an outstanding deal offered by a local office supplier. Because she knew that her boss, Samuel Neesen, favoured "cold, hard facts," she listed current monthly costs for copying at Copy Quick to increase her chances of gaining approval. Finally, she calculated the amortization of the purchase price and monthly costs of running the new colour copier.

Persuasive messages often are longer than direct messages because providing a case requires evidence.

Notice that Monique's memo isn't short. A successful persuasive message will typically take more space than a direct message because proving a case requires evidence. In the end, Monique chose to send her memo as an e-mail attachment accompanied by a polite short e-mail because she wanted to keep the document format in MS Word intact. She also felt that the message was too long to paste into her e-mail program. Monique's persuasive memo and her e-mail include subject lines that announce the purpose of the message without disclosing the actual request. By delaying the request until she has had a chance to describe the problem and discuss a solution, Monique prevented the reader's premature rejection.

The strength of this persuasive document, though, is in the clear presentation of comparison figures showing how much money the company can save by purchasing a remanufactured copier. Buying a copier that uses low-cost solid ink instead of expensive laser cartridges is another argument in this machine's favour. Although the organization pattern is not obvious, the memo begins with an attention-getter (a frank description of the problem), builds interest (with easy-to-read facts and figures), provides benefits, and reduces resistance. Notice that the conclusion tells what action is to be taken, makes it easy to respond, and repeats the main benefit to motivate action.

The Checklist box provides a summary of the key points for writing persuasive messages within organizations.

Checklist

Writing Persuasive Messages Within Organizations

Prewrite

- Know your purpose and be able to state it precisely and concisely. What do you want the receiver to do? Make sure your request is doable and attainable.

- Profile the audience. Play *What if?* scenarios to anticipate how the receiver will react to your request. What direct or indirect benefits can you cite?

Gain Attention

- Make the reader aware of a problem, use a startling statement, provide a significant fact related to the request, describe possible benefits, ask a stimulating question, or offer compliments and praise.

- Establish your credibility, but don't pull rank.

Build Interest

- Use facts, statistics, examples, and specific details to build a solid foundation for your request.

- Strive for a personal but professional tone. Be enthusiastic and positive.

- Soften your words when persuading upward. Suggest benefits to the reader.

Reduce Resistance

- Recognize any weakness in your proposal and suggest well-reasoned counterarguments and facts.

- In requests flowing upward, consider making a strong dollars-and-cents appeal for requests involving budgets.

- In requests flowing downward, avoid sounding preachy, parental, or overly authoritarian.

Motivate Action

- State a specific request including a deadline if appropriate. Suggest ways to make it effortless and painless for the receiver to respond.

- Repeat a major benefit that appeals to the reader.

- Include an incentive or a reason to act, and express appreciation if appropriate.

Planning and Composing Effective Direct-Mail and E-Mail Sales Messages

Sales messages use persuasion to promote specific products and services. In our coverage we are most concerned with sales messages delivered by mail or by e-mail. Many of the concepts you will learn about sales persuasion, however, can be applied to online, wireless, TV, print, radio, and other media. The best sales messages, whether delivered by direct mail or by e-mail, have much in common. In this section we look at how to apply the 3-×-3 writing process to sales messages. We also present techniques developed by experts to draft effective sales messages, both in print and online.

Applying the 3-×-3 Writing Process to Sales Messages

Marketing professionals analyze and perfect every aspect of a sales message to encourage consumers to read and act on the message. Like the experts, you will want to pay close attention to the preparatory steps of analysis and adaptation before writing the actual message.

Analyzing the Product and Purpose for Writing. Before sitting down to write a sales message promoting a product, you must study the item carefully. What can you learn about its design, construction, raw materials, and manufacturing process? What can you learn about its ease of use, efficiency, durability, and applications? Be sure to consider warranties, service, price, premiums, exclusivity, and special appeals. At the same time, evaluate the competition so that you can compare your product's strengths against the competitor's weaknesses.

Now you are ready to identify your central selling points. One online retailer's central selling point for one marketing campaign was economical custom clothing. The company used a testimonial from a real customer who said that the $49 custom dress shirts he bought were better than the $120 shirts he previously purchased from custom shops.[9] Analyzing your product and studying the competition help you determine what to emphasize in your sales letter. Equally important is determining the specific purpose of your letter. Do you want the reader to call for a free video and brochure? Listen to a podcast at your Web site? Fill out an order form? Send a credit card authorization? Before you write the first word of your message, know what response you want and what central selling points you will emphasize to achieve that purpose.

Adapting a Sales Message to Its Audience. Blanket mailings sent "cold" to occupants generally produce low responses—typically less than 2 percent. That means that 98 percent of the receivers usually toss direct-mail sales letters right into the trash. But the response rate can be increased dramatically by targeting the audience through selected database mailing lists. These lists can be purchased or compiled. By directing your message to a selected group, you can make certain assumptions about the receivers. Let's say you are selling fitness equipment. A good mailing list might come from subscribers to fitness or exercise magazines. You would expect similar interests, needs, and demographics (age, income, and other characteristics). With this knowledge you can adapt the sales letter to a specific audience.

Crafting Direct-Mail Sales Letters

Sales letters are usually part of direct-mail marketing campaigns. These letters are a powerful means to make sales, generate leads, boost retail traffic, solicit donations, and direct consumers to Web sites. Direct mail allows a personalized, tangible, three-dimensional message that is less invasive than telephone solicitations and less reviled than unsolicited e-mail.

Professionals who specialize in traditional direct-mail services have made it a science. They analyze a market, develop an effective mailing list, study the product, prepare a sophisticated campaign aimed at a target audience, and motivate the reader to act. You have probably received many direct-mail packages, often called junk mail.

These packages typically contain a sales letter, a brochure, a price list, illustrations of the product, testimonials, and other persuasive appeals.

We are most concerned here with the sales letter: its strategy, organization, and evidence. Because sales letters are generally written by specialists, you may never write one on the job. Why, then, learn how to write a sales letter? In many ways, every letter we create is a form of sales letter. We sell our ideas, our organizations, and ourselves. Learning the techniques of sales writing will help you be more successful in any communication that requires persuasion and promotion. What's more, you will recognize sales strategies that enable you to become a more perceptive consumer of ideas, products, and services.

The primary goal in writing a sales message is to get someone to devote a few moments of attention to it.

Your primary goal in writing a sales message is to get someone to devote a few moments of attention to it. You may be promoting a product, a service, an idea, or yourself. In each case the most effective messages will (a) gain attention, (b) build interest, (c) reduce resistance, and (d) motivate action. This is the same recipe we studied earlier, but the ingredients are different.

Gaining Attention in Sales Messages. One of the most critical elements of a sales message is its opening paragraph. This opener should be short (one to five lines), honest, relevant, and stimulating. Marketing pros have found that eye-catching typographical arrangements or provocative messages, such as the following, can hook a reader's attention:

Effective sales message openers include an offer, a promise, a question, or a quotation.

- **Offer:** *A free trip to Hawaii is just the beginning!*

- **Promise:** *Now you can raise your sales income by 50 percent or even more with the proven techniques found in. . . .*

- **Question:** *Do you yearn for an honest, fulfilling relationship?*

- **Quotation or proverb:** *Necessity is the mother of invention.*

- **Fact:** *The Greenland Inuit ate more fat than anyone in the world. And yet . . . they had virtually no heart disease.*

- **Product feature:** *Volvo's snazzy new convertible ensures your safety with a roll bar that pops out when the car tips 40 degrees to the side.*

- **Testimonial:** *My name is Sheldon Schulman. I am a practising medical doctor. I am also a multimillionaire. I didn't make my millions by practising medicine, though. I made them by investing in my spare time.*

- **Startling statement:** *Let the poor and hungry feed themselves! For just $100 they can.*

- **Personalized action setting:** *It's 4:30 p.m. and you've got to make a decision. You need everybody's opinion, no matter where they are. Before you pick up your phone to call them one at a time, pick up this card: WebEx Teleconference Services.*

Other openings calculated to capture attention might include a solution to a problem, an anecdote, a personalized statement that uses the receiver's name, or a relevant current event.

Building Interest With Rational and Emotional Appeals. In this phase of your sales message, you should describe clearly the product or service. In simple language emphasize the central selling points that you identified during your prewriting analysis. Those selling points can be developed by using rational or emotional appeals.

Rational appeals reflect reason and intellect. Emotional appeals reflect status, ego, and sensual feelings.

Rational appeals are associated with reason and intellect. They translate selling points into references to making or saving money, increasing efficiency, or making the best use of resources. In general, rational appeals are appropriate when a product is expensive, long-lasting, or important to health, security, and financial success. Emotional appeals relate to status, ego, and sensual feelings. Appealing to the emotions is sometimes effective when a product is inexpensive, short-lived, or nonessential. Many clever sales messages, however, combine emotional and rational strategies for a dual appeal. Consider these examples:

Rational Appeal

You can buy the things you need and want, pay household bills, and pay off higher-cost loans and credit cards—as soon as you are approved and your Credit-Line account is opened.

Emotional Appeal

Leave the urban bustle behind and escape to sun-soaked Bermuda! To recharge your batteries with an injection of sun and surf, all you need are your bathing suit, a little sunscreen, and your Credit-Line card.

Dual Appeal

New Credit-Line cardholders are immediately eligible for a $200 travel certificate and additional discounts at fun-filled resorts. Save up to 40 percent while lying on a beach in picturesque, sun-soaked Bermuda, the year-round resort island.

A physical description of your product is not enough, however. Your job is to translate those cold facts into warm feelings and reader benefits. Let's say a sales message promotes a hand cream made with aloe and cocoa butter extracts, along with vitamin A. Those facts become this: *Nature's hand helpers—including soothing aloe and cocoa extracts, along with firming vitamin A—form invisible gloves that protect your sensitive skin against the hardships of work, harsh detergents, and constant environmental assaults.*

Reducing Resistance and Building Desire. Marketing specialists use a number of techniques to overcome resistance and build desire. When price is an obstacle, consider these suggestions:

- Delay mentioning price until after you've created a desire for the product.

- Show the price in small units, such as the price per issue of a magazine.

- Demonstrate how the reader saves money—for instance, by subscribing for two or three years.

- Compare your prices with those of a competitor.

In addition, you need to anticipate other objections and questions the receiver may have. When possible, translate these objections into selling points (*If you are worried about training your staff members on the new software, remember that our offer includes $1,000 worth of on-site one-on-one instruction*). Other techniques to overcome resistance and prove the credibility of the product include the following:

- **Testimonials:** *"I never stopped eating, yet I lost 48 kilograms."—Tina Rivers, Woodstock, Ontario*

- **Names of satisfied users (with permission, of course):** *Enclosed is a partial list of private pilots who enthusiastically subscribe to our service.*

- **Money-back guarantee or warranty:** *We offer the longest warranties in the business—all parts and service on-site for five years!*

- **Free trial or sample:** *We are so confident that you will like our new accounting program that we want you to try it absolutely free.*

- **Performance tests, polls, or awards:** *Our TP-3000 was named Best Web Phone, and Etown.com voted it Smartphone of the Year.*

Motivating Action at the Conclusion of a Sales Message. All the effort put into a sales message goes to waste if the reader fails to act. To make it easy for readers to act, you can provide a reply card, a stamped and preaddressed envelope, a toll-free telephone number, an easy-to-scan Web site, or a promise of a follow-up call. Because readers often need an extra push, consider including additional motivators, such as the following:

- **Offer a gift:** *You will receive a free cellphone with the purchase of any new car.*

- **Promise an incentive:** *With every new, paid subscription, we will plant a tree in one of Canada's National Forests.*

- **Limit the offer:** *Only the first 100 customers receive free travel mugs.*

- **Set a deadline:** *You must act before June 1 to get these low prices.*

- **Guarantee satisfaction:** *We will return your full payment if you are not entirely satisfied—no questions asked.*

Techniques for motivating action include offering a gift or an incentive, limiting an offer, and guaranteeing satisfaction.

The final paragraph of the sales letter encourages action. This is where you tell readers what you want them to do and give them reasons for doing it. Most sales letters also include postscripts because they make irresistible reading. Even readers who might skim over or bypass paragraphs are drawn to a P.S. Therefore, use a postscript to reveal your strongest motivator, to add a special inducement for a quick response, or to reemphasize a central selling point. Although you want to be persuasive in sales letters, you must guard against overstepping legal and ethical boundaries. Information contained in sales letters has landed some writers in difficulty. See the accompanying Ethical Insights box to learn how to stay out of trouble.

Putting Together All the Parts of a Sales Message. Sales letters are a preferred marketing medium because they can be personalized, directed to target audiences, and filled with a more complete message than other advertising media. But direct mail is expensive. That's why crafting and assembling all the parts of a sales message are so critical.

Figure 10.7 shows a sales letter addressed to a target group of small-business owners. To sell the new magazine *Small Business Monthly*, the letter incorporates all four components of an effective persuasive message. Notice that the personalized action-setting opener places the reader in a familiar situation (getting into an elevator) and draws an analogy between failing to reach the top floor and failing to achieve a

ETHICAL INSIGHTS

What's Legal and What's Not in Sales Letters

In promoting products and writing sales letters, be careful with the words you choose and the claims you make. How far can you go in praising and selling your product?

- **Puffery.** Avoid making claims of unproven superiority or related to specific product attributes (puffery) unless these claims are accurate and can be substantiated by solid evidence.[10]

- **Proving your claims.** If you write that three out of four dentists recommend your toothpaste, you'd better have competent and reliable scientific evidence to support the claim. Such a claim goes beyond puffery and requires proof.

- **Celebrities.** Although only a few Canadian suits have been filed against "appropriation of personality," the unauthorized use of a celebrity's name, likeness, or nickname is not

permitted in sales messages.[11] It is always best to seek permission before using any reference to a celebrity.

- **Misleading statements.** You cannot tell people that they are winners or finalists in a sweepstake unless they actually are. Canada's *Competition Act* specifically prohibits deceptive prize notices. Doing so may result in civil or criminal action against you and your organization.[12]

- **Unwanted merchandise.** If you enclose unsolicited merchandise with a letter, don't expect the receiver to be required to pay for it or return it. According to Canada's Office of Consumer Affairs, recipients are under no obligation to accept or pay for merchandise they did not order. Furthermore, they may opt to return the merchandise at your expense.[13]

FIGURE 10.7 Sales Letter

① Prewriting

Analyze: The purpose of this letter is to persuade the reader to return the reply card and subscribe to *Small Business Monthly*.

Anticipate: The targeted audience consists of small-business owners. The central selling point is providing practical business data that will help their business grow.

Adapt: Because readers will be reluctant, use the indirect pattern.

② Writing

Research: Gather facts to promote your product, including testimonials.

Organize: Gain attention by opening with a personalized action picture. Build interest with an analogy and a description of magazine features. Use a testimonial to reduce resistance. Motivate action with a free booklet and an easy-reply card.

Compose: Prepare a first draft for pilot study.

③ Revising

Revise: Use short paragraphs and short sentences. Replace *malfunction* with *glitch*.

Proofread: Indent long quotations on the left and right sides. Italicize or underscore titles of publications. Hyphenate *hard-headed* and *first-of-its-kind*.

Evaluate: Monitor the response rate to this letter to assess its effectiveness.

---

small business monthly
160 Duncan Mills Road Toronto, ON M3B 1Z5

April 16, 2014

Mr. James Wehrley
1608 Montlieu Avenue
Listowel, ON N4W 3A2

Dear Mr. Wehrley:

(Puts reader into action setting) *(Gains attention)*
You walk into the elevator and push the button for the top floor. The elevator glides upward. You step back and relax.

But the elevator never reaches the top. A glitch in its electronics prevents it from processing the information it needs to take you to your destination.

(Suggests analogy) *(Builds interest)*
Do you see a similarity between your growing company and this elevator? You're aiming for the top, but a lack of information halts your progress. Now you can put your company into gear and propel it toward success with a new publication—*Small Business Monthly*.

(Emphasizes central selling point)
This first-of-its-kind magazine brings you marketing tips, hard-headed business pointers, opportunities, and inspiration. This is the kind of current information you need today to be where you want to be tomorrow. One executive wrote:

(Uses testimonial for credibility) *(Reduces resistance)*
> As president of a small manufacturing company, I read several top business publications, but I get my "bread and butter" from *Small Business Monthly*. I'm not interested in a lot of "pie in the sky" and theory. I find practical problems and how to solve them in *SBM*.
> —Mitchell M. Perry, Oshawa, Ontario

Mr. Perry's words are the best recommendation I can offer you to try *SBM*. In less time than you might spend on an average business lunch, you learn the latest in management, operations, finance, taxes, business law, compensation, and advertising.

(Repeats central sales pitch in last sentence) *(Motivates action)*
To evaluate *Small Business Monthly* without cost or obligation, let me send you a free issue. Just initial and return the enclosed card to start receiving a wealth of practical information that could keep your company travelling upward to its goal.

Cordially,

Cheryl Owings

Cheryl Owings
Vice President, Circulation

(Spotlights free offer in P.S. to prompt immediate reply)
P.S. Act before May 15 and I'll send you our valuable booklet *Managing for Success*, revealing more than 100 secrets for helping small businesses grow.

business goal. The writer develops a rational central selling point (a magazine that provides valuable information for a growing small business) and repeats this selling point in all the components of the letter. Notice, too, how a testimonial from a small-business executive lends support to the sales message and how the closing pushes for action. Because the price of the magazine is not a selling feature, price is mentioned only on the reply card. This sales letter saves its strongest motivator—a free booklet—for the high-impact P.S. line.

Writing Successful E-Mail Sales Messages

E-mail marketing can attract new customers, keep existing ones, encourage future sales, and cut costs in half the time it takes to print and distribute a traditional message.

To make the best use of limited advertising dollars while reaching a great number of potential customers, many businesses are turning to the Internet and to e-mail marketing campaigns in particular. Much like traditional direct mail, e-mail marketing can attract new customers, keep existing ones, encourage future sales, cross-sell, and cut costs. However, e-marketers can create and send a promotion in half the time it takes to print and distribute a traditional message. As consumers feel more comfortable and secure with online purchases, e-marketing has become more popular.

Selling by E-Mail. If you will be writing online sales messages for your organization, try using the following techniques gleaned from the best-performing e-mails. Although much e-marketing dazzles receivers with colourful graphics, we focus on the words involved in persuasive sales messages.

The first rule of e-marketing is to communicate only with those who have given permission.

The first rule of e-marketing is to communicate only with those who have given permission. By sending messages only to "opt-in" folks, you greatly increase your "open rate"—those e-mails that will be opened. E-mail users detest spam. However, receivers are surprisingly receptive to offers tailored specifically for them. Remember that today's customer is somebody—not just anybody. Here are a few guidelines that will help you create effective e-mail sales messages:

- **Craft a catchy subject line.** Offer discounts or premiums: *Spring Sale: Buy now and save 20 percent!* Promise solutions to everyday work-related problems. Highlight hot new industry topics. Invite readers to scan a top-ten list of items such as issues, trends, or people.

- **Keep the main information "above the fold."** E-mails should be top heavy. Primary points should appear early in the message so that they capture the reader's attention.

- **Make the message short, conversational, and focused.** Because on-screen text is taxing to read, be brief. Focus on one or two central selling points only.

- **Convey urgency.** Top-performing e-mails state an offer deadline or demonstrate why the state of the industry demands action on the reader's part. Good messages also tie the product to relevant current events.

- **Sprinkle testimonials throughout the copy.** Consumers' own words are the best sales copy. These comments can serve as callouts or be integrated into the copy.

- **Provide a means for opting out.** It's polite and a good business tactic to include a statement that tells receivers how to be removed from the sender's mailing database.

Whether you actually write sales message on the job or merely receive them, you will better understand their organization and appeals by reviewing this chapter and the tips in the Checklist box.

Checklist

Preparing Persuasive Direct-Mail and E-Mail Sales Messages

Prewrite

- Analyze your product or service. What makes it special? What central selling points should you emphasize? How does it compare with the competition?

- Profile your audience. How will this product or service benefit this audience?

- Decide what you want the audience to do at the end of your message.

- For e-mails, send only to those who have opted in.

Gain Attention

- Describe a product feature, present a testimonial, make a startling statement, or show the reader in an action setting.

- Offer something valuable, promise the reader a result, or pose a stimulating question.

- Suggest a solution to a problem, offer a relevant anecdote, use the receiver's name, or mention a meaningful current event.

Build Interest

- Describe the product or service in terms of what it does for the reader. Connect cold facts with warm feelings and needs.

- Use rational appeals if the product or service is expensive, long lasting, or important to health, security, and financial success. Use emotional appeals to suggest status, ego, or sensual feelings.

- Explain how the product or service can save or make money, reduce effort, improve health, produce pleasure, or boost status.

Reduce Resistance

- Counter anticipated reluctance with testimonials, money-back guarantees, attractive warranties, trial offers, or free samples.

- Build credibility with results of performance tests, polls, or awards.

- If price is not a selling feature, describe it in small units (*only 99 cents an issue*), show it as savings, or tell how it compares favourably with that of the competition.

Motivate Action

- Close by repeating a central selling point and describing an easy-to-take action.

- Prompt the reader to act immediately with a gift, incentive, limited offer, deadline, or guarantee of satisfaction.

- Put the strongest motivator in a postscript.

- In e-mails, include an opportunity to opt out.

Developing Persuasive Media Releases

Media (news) releases announce information about your company to the media: new products, new managers, new facilities, sponsorships, participation in community projects, awards given or received, joint ventures, donations, or seminars and demonstrations. Naturally, you hope that this news will be published and provide good publicity for your company. But this kind of largely self-serving information is not always appealing to magazine and newspaper editors or to TV producers. To get them to read beyond the first sentence, try these suggestions:

- Open with an attention-getting lead or a summary of the important facts.

- Include answers to the five *W*s and one *H* (*who, what, when, where, why*, and *how*) in the article—but not all in the first sentence!

- Appeal to the audience of the target media. Emphasize reader benefits written in the style of the focus publication or newscast.

- Present the most important information early, followed by supporting information. Don't put your best ideas last because they may be chopped off or ignored.

- Make the release visually appealing. Limit the text to one or two double-spaced pages with attractive formatting.

- Look and sound credible—no typos, no imaginative spelling or punctuation, no factual errors.

LEARNING OBJECTIVE 6
Understand basic patterns and techniques in developing persuasive media releases.

Effective media releases feature an attention-getting opener, place key information upfront, appeal to the target audience, and maintain visual interest.

FIGURE 10.8 Media Releases Must Appeal to Readers

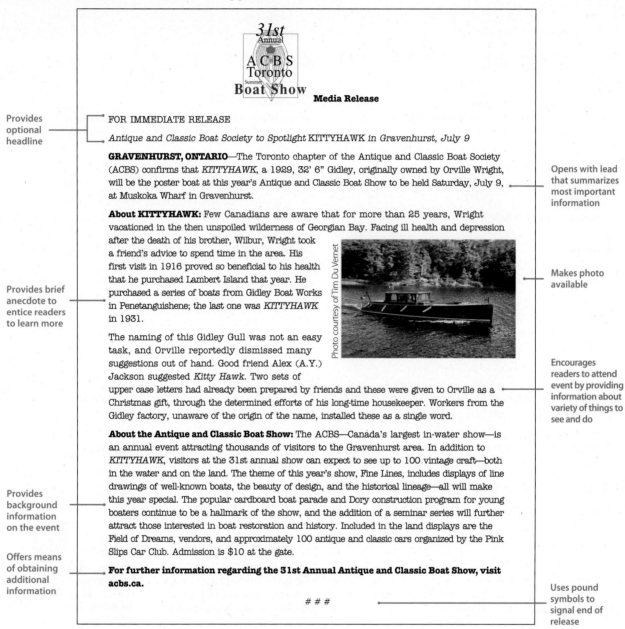

Provides optional headline

Provides brief anecdote to entice readers to learn more

Provides background information on the event

Offers means of obtaining additional information

Opens with lead that summarizes most important information

Makes photo available

Encourages readers to attend event by providing information about variety of things to see and do

Uses pound symbols to signal end of release

31st Annual ACBS Toronto Summer Boat Show

Media Release

FOR IMMEDIATE RELEASE

Antique and Classic Boat Society to Spotlight KITTYHAWK in Gravenhurst, July 9

GRAVENHURST, ONTARIO—The Toronto chapter of the Antique and Classic Boat Society (ACBS) confirms that *KITTYHAWK*, a 1929, 32' 6" Gidley, originally owned by Orville Wright, will be the poster boat at this year's Antique and Classic Boat Show to be held Saturday, July 9, at Muskoka Wharf in Gravenhurst.

About KITTYHAWK: Few Canadians are aware that for more than 25 years, Wright vacationed in the then unspoiled wilderness of Georgian Bay. Facing ill health and depression after the death of his brother, Wilbur, Wright took a friend's advice to spend time in the area. His first visit in 1916 proved so beneficial to his health that he purchased Lambert Island that year. He purchased a series of boats from Gidley Boat Works in Penetanguishene; the last one was *KITTYHAWK* in 1931.

The naming of this Gidley Gull was not an easy task, and Orville reportedly dismissed many suggestions out of hand. Good friend Alex (A.Y.) Jackson suggested *Kitty Hawk*. Two sets of upper case letters had already been prepared by friends and these were given to Orville as a Christmas gift, through the determined efforts of his long-time housekeeper. Workers from the Gidley factory, unaware of the origin of the name, installed these as a single word.

Photo courtesy of Tim Du Vernet

About the Antique and Classic Boat Show: The ACBS—Canada's largest in-water show—is an annual event attracting thousands of visitors to the Gravenhurst area. In addition to *KITTYHAWK*, visitors at the 31st annual show can expect to see up to 100 vintage craft—both in the water and on the land. The theme of this year's show, Fine Lines, includes displays of line drawings of well-known boats, the beauty of design, and the historical lineage—all will make this year special. The popular cardboard boat parade and Dory construction program for young boaters continue to be a hallmark of the show, and the addition of a seminar series will further attract those interested in boat restoration and history. Included in the land displays are the Field of Dreams, vendors, and approximately 100 antique and classic cars organized by the Pink Slips Car Club. Admission is $10 at the gate.

For further information regarding the 31st Annual Antique and Classic Boat Show, visit acbs.ca.

\# \# \#

Used with permission of the Antique and Classic Boat Society – Toronto Chapter.

The most important ingredient of a media release, of course, is *news*. Articles that merely plug products end up in the circular file. The media release in Figure 10.8 announced the Toronto chapter of the Antique and Classic Boat Society's (ACBS) 31st annual boat show in Gravenhurst, Ontario.

Figure 10.8 illustrates many good techniques for creating effective media releases. The ACBS announcement provided a headline, interesting photo, information about the boat show, and basic background to the *KITTYHAWK* story. The best media releases focus on information that appeals to a targeted audience. To attract boat lovers and history buffs, this media release provides a brief anecdote with a promise of a one-of-a-kind experience.

Newspapers and magazines are more likely to publish a media release that is informative, interesting, and helpful. The Web sites of many companies today provide readily available press information, including releases and photos.

Summary of Learning Objectives

1 **Define the concept of persuasion, identify effective and ineffective persuasive techniques, and apply the 3-x-3 writing process to persuasive messages.** Persuasion may be defined as the ability to use argument or discussion to influence an individual's beliefs or actions. Effective persuasive techniques include establishing credibility, making a reasonable and precise request, tying facts to benefits, recognizing the power of loss, expecting and overcoming resistance, sharing solutions, and compromising. Persuasion is more effective if you avoid sounding preachy or parental, don't pull rank, soften the tone when persuading upward, sound enthusiastic, and present a positive and likeable image. The first step in the writing process for a persuasive message is deciding what you want the receiver to do or think. The second step involves thinking of ways to adapt the message to the audience. The writer must collect information and organize it into an appropriate strategy. An indirect strategy is best if the audience might resist the request.

2 **Explain the four major elements in successful persuasive messages and how to blend those elements into effective and ethical business messages.** The most effective persuasive messages include four major elements: gaining attention, building interest, reducing resistance, and motivating action. Writers gain attention by opening with a problem, an unexpected statement, a reader benefit, a compliment, a related fact, a stimulating question, or a similar device. They build interest with facts, expert opinions, examples, details, and direct and indirect reader benefits. They reduce resistance by anticipating objections and presenting counterarguments. They conclude by motivating a specific action and making it easy for the reader to respond. Skilled communicators avoid distortion, exaggeration, and deception when making persuasive arguments.

3 **Write persuasive messages that request favours and actions, make claims, and deliver complaints.** In asking for favours and actions, writers must know exactly what they are requesting and anticipate the receiver's reaction. The opening may begin indirectly with a problem description, an unexpected statement, a compliment, praise, related facts, a stimulating question, or a reader benefit. Interest is built with facts, statistics, examples, testimonials, and details. Claims and complaints require an objective, unemotional tone and proof of the validity of the request. Resistance can be reduced by anticipating objections and providing counterarguments. Action is motivated by stating exactly what is to be done and by when. Add a deadline date if necessary and express appreciation.

4 **Write persuasive messages within organizations.** Before writing a persuasive business message, writers should profile the audience, know exactly what the receiver is to do or believe, and anticipate resistance. To gain attention, the writer might make the receiver aware of a problem, use a startling statement, provide a significant fact related to the request, describe possible benefits, ask a stimulating question, or offer compliments and praise. Facts, statistics, examples, and specific details build a foundation for the request. Receivers are interested in direct benefits, such as how agreeing to the request will help them solve problems or improve their work and career. Recognizing weaknesses in the proposal and offering well-reasoned counterarguments are effective ways to reduce resistance. In messages flowing downward, avoid sounding preachy or overly authoritarian. In messages flowing upward, consider making a strong dollars-and-cents appeal for requests involving budgets. Persuasive messages should end with a specific request and a deadline if appropriate.

5 **Write effective and ethical direct-mail and e-mail sales messages.** Careful analysis of the product or service is necessary before you compose a sales message. Effective sales messages usually begin with an attention-getting statement that is short, honest, relevant, and stimulating. Simple language describing appropriate appeals builds interest. Testimonials, a money-back guarantee, a free trial, or some other device can reduce resistance. A gift, an incentive, a deadline, or another device can motivate action. E-marketing messages should be sent only to opt-in receivers. Writers of effective e-mails begin with a catchy subject line, keep the main information "above the fold," make the message short and focused, convey urgency, sprinkle testimonials throughout, and provide a means for opting out.

6 Understand basic patterns and techniques in developing persuasive media releases. Media releases usually open with an attention-getting lead or summary of the important facts. They attempt to answer the questions *who, what, when, where, why*, and *how*. They are written carefully to appeal to the audience of the target media. The best media releases present the most important information early, are visually appealing, and look and sound credible.

Chapter Review

1. What is persuasion? (Obj. 1)
2. List six general techniques that are effective in persuasion. (Obj. 1)
3. What four questions are receivers of persuasive messages likely to be asking themselves? (Obj. 2)
4. What are the four parts of successful persuasive messages? (Obj. 2)
5. List six ways to gain attention in a persuasive message. (Obj. 2)
6. List effective tools for building interest in a persuasive request. (Obj. 2)
7. Why is a written favour request or action request often more effective than a face-to-face request? (Obj.3)
8. Name five of more examples of typical situations requiring persuasive claim messages. (Obj. 3)
9. How can you reduce resistance in requesting favours, making claims, and delivering complaints? (Obj. 3)
10. When is persuasion necessary in business messages flowing downward in an organization? (Obj. 4)
11. When might persuasion be necessary in messages flowing upward? (Obj. 4)
12. Before composing a letter to sell a product, what should the writer do? (Obj. 5)
13. Name eight or more ways to attract attention in the opening of a sales message. (Obj. 5)
14. How can a writer motivate action in a sales letter? (Obj. 5)
15. List five or more topics that an organization might feature in a media release. (Obj. 6)

Critical Thinking

1. The word *persuasion* turns some people off. What negative connotations can it have? (Obj. 1)
2. What are some of the underlying motivations that prompt individuals to agree to requests that do not directly benefit themselves or their organizations? (Obj. 2)
3. Why is it important to know your needs and have documentation when you make requests of superiors? (Obj. 4)
4. How are direct-mail sales messages and e-mail sales messages similar, and how are they different? (Obj. 5)
5. **Ethical Issue:** Identify and discuss sales messages that you consider unethical.

Activities

Note: All Documents for Analysis may be downloaded from **www.guffeybrief4e.nelson.com** so that you do not have to rekey the entire message.

10.1 Document for Analysis: Weak Favour Request (Obj. 3)

Your Task. Analyze the following poorly written invitation. List its weaknesses. If your instructor directs, revise the letter. Add appropriate information if needed.

Current date
Mr. Nelson J. Daugherty
Operations Manager
Maple Leaf Hotels and Restaurants
249 Redmond Avenue
Calgary, AB T3B 6W7

Dear Mr. Daugherty:

Although you are a busy hospitality professional, we would like you to make a presentation to the Edmonton chapter of the Canadian Restaurant Alliance. I was asked to write you since I am program chair.

I heard that you made a good presentation at your local chapter recently. I think you gave a talk called "Avoiding the Seven Cardinal Sins in Food Service" or something like that. Whatever it was, I'm sure we would like to hear the same or a similar presentation. All restaurant operators are interested in doing what we can to avoid potential problems involving discrimination, safety at work, how we hire people, etc. As you well know, operating a fast-paced restaurant is frustrating—even on a good day. We are all in a gigantic rush from opening the door early in the morning to shutting it again after the last customer has gone.

It's a rat race and easy to fall into the trap with food service faults that push a big operation into trouble.

Enclosed please find a list of questions that our members listed. We would like you to talk about 45 minutes. Our June 10 meeting will be at the Red Sage restaurant in Edmonton and dinner begins at 7 p.m.

How can we get you to come to Edmonton? We can offer you an honorarium of $200, and we would pay for your travel expenses. You can expect a large crowd of restaurateurs who are known for hooting and hollering when they hear good stuff! As you can see, we are a rather informal group. Hope you can join us!

Sincerely,

10.2 Document for Analysis: Weak Persuasive Memo Flowing Upward (Obj. 4)

Your Task. Analyze the following memo, which suffers from many writing faults. List its weaknesses. If your instructor directs, revise the letter.

Date: Current
To: Candace Daly, Vice President, Marketing
From: Robert Forsythe, Exhibit Manager
Subject: Trade Booth

Trade shows are a great way for us to meet customers and sell our Life Fitness equipment. But instead of expanding our visits to these trade shows, we continue to cut back the number that we attend. And we send fewer staff members. I know that you've been asking us to find ways to reduce costs, but perhaps we are not going about it right.

With increased airfares and hotel charges, my staff has tried to find ways to live within our very tight budget. Yet we are being asked to find other ways to reduce our costs. I'm currently thinking ahead to the big Toronto trade show coming up in September.

One area where we could make a change is in the gift that we give away. In the past we have presented booth visitors with a nine-colour T-shirt that is silk screened and gorgeous. But it comes at a cost of $15 for each and every one of these beauties from a top-name designer. To save money, I suggest that we try a $4 T-shirt made in China, which is reasonably presentable. It's got our name on it, and, after all, folks just use these shirts for workouts. Who cares if it is a fancy silk-screened T-shirt or a functional Chinese one that has "Life Fitness" plastered on the chest? Since we give away 2,000 T-shirts at our largest show, we could save big bucks by dumping the designer shirt. But we have to act quickly. I've enclosed a cheap one for you to see.
Let me know what you think.

10.3 Document for Analysis: Poor Claim Letter (Obj. 3)

Your Task. Analyze the following poorly written claim letter. List its weaknesses. If your instructor directs, revise it.

Current date
Mr. Morgan Monroe
Modern Office Systems
82 Peter Street
Perth, ON K7H 1S2

Dear Sir:

Recently my company purchased four of your Matrix 500 photocopiers, and we've had nothing but trouble ever since.

Our salesperson, Sheila Feldman, assured us that the Matrix 500 could easily handle our volume of 3,000 copies a day. This seemed strange since the sales brochure said that the Matrix 500 was meant for 500 copies a day. But we believed Ms. Feldman. Big mistake! Our four Matrix copiers are down constantly; we can't go on like this. Because they are still under warranty, they eventually get repaired. But we are losing considerable business in downtime.

Because your Ms. Feldman has been less than helpful, I telephoned the district manager, Marko Santillan. I suggested that we trade in our Matrix 500 copiers (which we got for $2,500 each) on two Matrix 800 models (at $13,500 each). However, Mr. Santillan said he would have to charge 50 percent depreciation on our Matrix 500 copiers. What a rip-off! I think that 20 percent depreciation is more reasonable since we've had the machines only three months. Mr. Santillan said he would get back to me, and I haven't heard from him since.

Now I'm forced to write to your headquarters because I have no faith in either Ms. Feldman or Mr. Santillan, and I need to see some action on these machines. If you understood anything about business, you would see what a sweet deal I'm offering you. I'm willing to stick with your company and purchase your most expensive model—but I can't take such a steep loss on the Matrix 500 copiers. These copiers are relatively new; you should be able to sell them with no trouble. And think of all the money you will save by not having your repair technicians making constant trips to service our underpowered Matrix 500 copiers! Please let me hear from you immediately.

Sincerely yours,

10.4 Persuasive Favour or Action Request: Borrowing Suits for Interviews (Obj. 3)

You saw an interesting article describing the Suitable Suits program, which offers a closet filled with 21 crisp black suits that students can borrow for job interviews. Students make an appointment with the office and agree to dry clean the suits before returning them. This particular program was paid for with a grant from a prominent financial firm.[14] You think that a Suitable Suits program is worth exploring with your dean.
Your Task. Write a persuasive letter requesting an appointment with your dean to discuss a Suitable Suits program at your school. You don't have all the answers and you are not sure how such a program would operate, but you think the idea is worth discussing. Can you convince the dean to see you?

10.5 Persuasive Claim: Botched Print Job (Obj. 3)

As president of Holiday Travel, you delivered a very complex print job to the Jiffy Printers in the same office complex. It took almost 15 minutes to explain the particulars of this job to the printer. When you left, you wondered whether all of the instructions would be followed precisely. You even brought in your own special paper, which added to the cost of printing. When you got the job back (a total of 1,500 sheets of paper) and returned to your office, you discovered a host of problems. One of the pages had 300 copies made on cheap 20-pound paper. This means that the printer must have run out of your special paper and substituted some thing else for one of the runs. The printer also made copies of your original photos and graphics, so that all the final prints were run from second-generation prints, which reduced the quality of the graphics enormously. What's more, many of the sheets were poorly or improperly cut. In short, the job was unacceptable.

Because you were desperate to complete the job, you allowed the print shop to repeat the job using its paper supply. When you inquired about the cost, the counter person, Don, was noncommittal. He said you would have to talk to the owner, who worked in a different shop. The repeat print job turned out fairly well, and you paid the full price of $782. But you are unhappy, and Don sensed that Jiffy Printers would not see Holiday Travel again as a customer. He encouraged you to write to the owner and ask for an adjustment.

Your Task. Write a claim letter to Mr. Howard Moscatelli, Jiffy Printers, Highway 1 and Yellowquill Trail, Portage La Prairie, MB R1N 3C3. What is a reasonable claim to make? Do you simply want to register your unhappiness, or do you want a refund? Supply any needed information.

10.6 Persuasive Organizational Message Flowing Upward: Training Telecommuters (Obj. 4)

James Lush arose from bed in his Dartmouth home and looked outside to see a heavy snowstorm creating a fairyland of white. But he felt none of the giddiness that usually accompanies a potential snow day. Such days were a gift from heaven when schools closed, businesses shut down, and the world ground to a halt. As an on-and-off telecommuter for many years, he knew that snow days were a thing of the past. These days work for James Lush and more than 1.5 million other Canadian employees is no farther than their home office.[15]

More and more employees are becoming telecommuters. They want to work at home, where they feel they can be more productive and avoid the hassle of driving to work. Some need to telecommute only temporarily while they take care of family obligations, births, illnesses, or personal problems. Others are highly skilled individuals who can do their work at home as easily as in the office. Businesses definitely see advantages to telecommuting. They don't have to supply office space for workers. What's more, as businesses continue to flatten management structures, bosses no longer have time to micromanage employees. Increasingly, they are leaving workers to their own devices.

But the results have not been totally satisfactory. For one thing, in-house workers may resent those who work at home. More important are problems of structure and feedback. Telecommuters don't always have the best work habits, and lack of communication is a major issue. Unless the telecommuter is expert at coordinating projects and leaving instructions, productivity can fizzle. Appreciating the freedom but recognizing that they need guidance, employees are saying, "Push me, but don't leave me out there all alone!"

As human resources manager at your company, you already have 83 employees who are either full- or part-time telecommuters. With increasing numbers asking to work in remote locations, you decide that workers and their managers must receive training on how to do it effectively. You are considering hiring a consultant to train your prospective telecommuters and their managers. Another possibility is developing an in-house training program.

Your Task. As human resources manager, you must convince Victor Mortensen, vice president, that your company needs a training program for all individuals who are currently telecommuting or who plan to do so. Their managers should also receive training. You decide to ask your staff of four to help you gather information. Using the Web, you and your team read several articles on what such training should include. Now you must decide what action you want the vice president to take. Meet with you to discuss a training program? Commit to a budget item for future training? Hire a consultant or agency to come in and conduct training programs? Individually or as a team, write a convincing message that describes the problem, suggests what the training should include, and asks for action by a specific date. Add any reasonable details necessary to build your case.

10.7 Persuasive Organizational Message Flowing Downward: Curbing Profanity on the Job (Obj. 4)

E-MAIL
WEB

As sales manager for a large irrigation parts manufacturer, you are concerned about the use of profanity by your sales associates. Some defend profanity, claiming that it helps them fit in. Your female sales reps have said that it helps relax listeners, drives home a point, and makes them "one of the boys." You have done some research, however, and learned that courts have ruled that profanity can constitute sexual harassment—whether in person or in print. In addition to causing legal problems, profanity on the job projects a negative image of the individual and of the company. Although foul language is heard increasingly on TV and in the movies, you think it is a bad habit and you want to see it curbed on the job.

Your Task. Use the Web or databases to locate articles related to the use of profanity and strategies employed by organizations for dealing with it. One good resource is www.cusscontrol.com. In small groups or in class, discuss the place of formal and informal language in communication. Prepare a list of reasons people curse and reasons not to do so. Your instructor may ask you to interview employers to learn their reactions to the issue of workplace profanity. As sales manager at Rain City, compose a persuasive e-mail or memo to your sales staff that will encourage them to curb their use of profanity.[16]

10.8 Sales Letter: Weighing In at Work (Obj. 5)

WEB

Obesity in this country is swelling to unprecedented levels with rapidly increasing numbers of adults and children overweight. In addition to the risks to individuals, obesity costs Canada an astounding $1.6 billion in direct health care costs in addition to $2.7 billion in indirect costs, including lost productivity, disability, and reduced quality of life.[17] Companies across the country are launching or improving programs to help employees lose weight and develop more balanced, healthy lifestyles.

As a sales representative for Global Fitness, a leading fitness operator, you are convinced that your fitness equipment and programs are instrumental in helping people lose weight. With regular exercise at an on-site fitness centre, employees lose weight and improve overall health.

As employee health improves, absenteeism is reduced, and overall productivity increases. What's more, employees love working out before or after work. They make the routine part of their workday, and they often have work buddies who share their fitness regimen.

Although many companies resist spending money to save money, fitness centres need not be large or expensive to be effective. Studies show that moderately sized centres coupled with motivational and training programs yield the greatest success. For just $30,000 Global Fitness will provide exercise equipment, including treadmills, elliptical trainers, exercise bikes, multigyms, and weight machines. Their fitness experts will design a fitness room, set up the equipment, and create appropriate programs. Best of all, the one-time cost is usually offset by cost savings within one year of centre installation. For additional fees Global can provide fitness consultants for employee fitness assessments. Global specialists will also train employees on the proper use of the equipment and clean and manage the facility—for an extra charge, of course.

Your Task. Use the Web to update your obesity statistics. Then prepare a sales letter addressed to Holly Hadden, Director, Human Resources, Financial One, Inc., 3939 West Highland Blvd., Fredericton, NB E3A 8T4. Ask for an appointment to meet with her. Send a brochure detailing the products and services that Global Fitness provides. As an incentive, offer a free fitness assessment for all employees if Financial One installs a fitness facility by December 1.

10.9 Sales Letter: Promoting Your Product or Service (Obj. 5)

Identify a situation in your current job or a previous one in which a sales letter is or was needed. Using suggestions from this chapter, write an appropriate sales letter that promotes a product or service. Use actual names, information, and examples. If you have no work experience, imagine a business you would like to start: word processing, pet grooming, car detailing, tutoring, specialty knitting, balloon decorating, delivery service, child care, gardening, lawn care, or something else. Write a letter selling your product or service to be distributed to your prospective customers. Be sure to tell them how to respond.

10.10 Media release: This Is New! (Obj. 6)

Your Task. For a company where you now work or an organization you belong to, identify a product or service that could be publicized. Consider writing a media release announcing a new course at your college or university, a new president, new equipment, or a campaign to raise funds. The media release is intended for your local newspaper.

Grammar and Mechanics C.L.U.E. Review 10

Number Use

Review Guides 47–50 about number usage in Appendix A, Grammar and Mechanics Guide, beginning on page A-19. On a separate sheet, revise the following sentences to correct number usage errors. For each error that you locate, write the guide number that reflects this usage. Sentences may have more than one error. If a sentence is correct, write C. When finished, compare your responses with the key beginning on page Key-1.
Example: 13 candidates submitted applications for the position.
Revision: Thirteen candidates submitted applications for the position. [Guide 47]

1. Susan showed me 5 different customer messages with the same 2 complaints.

2. 28 employees indicated they would change their extended health benefits.

3. Did Mike request three hundred dollars to attend the 1-day seminar?

4. Most deliveries arrive before 10:00 o'clock a.m.

5. Personal income tax returns must be mailed by April 30th.

6. We earned 2.5% dividends on our three thousand dollar investment.

7. Our company applied for a one hundred thousand dollar loan at six%.

8. Average attendance at Major League Baseball games totalled 80,000,000 in the United States and Canada.

9. I bought the item on eBay for one dollar and fifty cents and sold it for fifteen dollars.

10. That store offers a thirty-day customer satisfaction return policy.

Endnotes

[1] Androich, A., & and Laird, K. (2011, March 28). Secrets of Canada's top loyalty programs. *Marketing.* pp. 19–24.

[2] Hamilton, C. (2005). *Communicating for results* (7th ed.). Mason, OH: Wadsworth/Thomson, p. 334.

[3] Cialdini, R. B. (1993). *Influence: The power of persuasion.* New York: Quill, William Morrow, p. 238.

[4] Fracaro, K. E. (2004, August). Managing by persuasion. *Contract Management, 44*(8), 4. Retrieved January 29, 2010, from InfoTrac College Edition database

[5] Conde, C. (2010, January 17). Structure? The flatter the better. *The New York Times,* p. BU2.

[6] Newman, R. (2006, September 25). Lessons from the rule breakers. *U.S. News & World Report,* Executive Edition, p. 4. Retrieved January 30, 2010, from InfoTrac College Edition database.

[7] Pollock, T. (2003, June). How to sell an idea. *Supervision,* p. 15. Retrieved January 29, 2010, from InfoTrac College Edition database.

8 Communicating with the boss. (2006, May). *Communication Briefings*, p. 8.

9 Friesen, P. (2003, October). Customer testimonials. *Target Marketing*, p. 137.

10 Healy, M. & Bonner, P. (2006). Does it matter whether the best is really the best? Advertising claims in Canada. Retrieved July 22, 2009, from http://ogilvyrenault.com/files/advertisingclaims12Jul06.pdf

11 Muirhead, L. (1999, September 21). Appropriation of personality: Canada's position. Retrieved July 22, 2009, from http://www.osler.com/resources.aspx?id=8438

12 Competition Act: Misleading advertising and deceptive marketing practices. (2009). Retrieved from http://canadabusiness.ca

13 *Canadian consumer handbook 2008–2009*. (2009). Retrieved July 22, 2009 from http://www.ic.gc.ca

14 Suited for employment. (2005, July 15). *Chronicle of Higher Education*, p. A8.

15 Akyeampong, E. (2007, June 2). Working at home: An update. *Perspectives*. Retrieved July 9, 2009, from http://www.ivc.ca/studies/canada

16 Based on DuFrene, D. D., & Lehman, C. M. (2002, March). Persuasive appeal for clean language. *Business Communication Quarterly, 65*(1), 48–55.

17 Healthy weights for healthy kids. (2007, March). Report of the standing committee on health, House of Commons, Canada. Retrieved July 9, 2009, from http://www.ccfn.ca/pdfs/healthyweightsforhealthykids.pdf

UNIT 4

Reports, Proposals, and Presentations

Chapter 11
Report and Research Basics

Chapter 12
Informal Business Reports

Chapter 13
Proposals, Business Plans, and Formal Business Reports

Chapter 14
Business Presentations

Abel Mitja Varela/Getty Images

CHAPTER 11

Report and Research Basics

OBJECTIVES

After studying this chapter, you should be able to

1. Describe basic features of business reports, including functions, strategies (indirect or direct), writing style, and formats.

2. Apply the 3-×-3 writing process to business reports to create well-organized documents that show a firm grasp of audience and purpose.

3. Find, evaluate, and use print and electronic secondary sources.

4. Understand how to generate and use primary data while avoiding researcher bias.

5. Comprehend fast-changing communication technology: the Web, electronic databases, and other resources for business writers and researchers.

6. Recognize the purposes and techniques of documentation in business reports, and avoid plagiarism.

7. Create meaningful and interesting graphics; display numeric information in the appropriate graphic form; and skillfully generate, use, and convert data to visual aids.

© Purestock/Alamy

Understanding Report Essentials

Reports are indispensable in business. The larger the organization, the more vital the exchange and flow of information becomes. Employees report their activities vertically to supervisors. At the same time, the various divisions of a business communicate horizontally with each other through reports. Occasionally, reports are generated for outside organizations or government agencies. In North America, a low-context culture, our values and attitudes seem to prompt us to write reports. We analyze problems, gather and study the facts, and then assess the alternatives. We pride ourselves on being practical and logical as we apply scientific procedures. When we must persuade a client that our services can add value, we generally write a report outlining our case.

Management decisions in many organizations are based on information submitted in the form of reports. Reports help us understand and study systematically the challenges that we encounter in business before we can outline the steps toward solving them. Business solutions are unthinkable without a thorough examination of the problems that prompted them.

This chapter examines the functions, strategies, writing style, and formats of typical business reports. It also introduces the report-writing process and discusses methods of collecting, documenting, and illustrating data.

Business reports range from informal bulleted lists and half-page trip reports to formal 200-page financial forecasts. Reports may be presented orally in front of a group or electronically on a computer screen. Some reports appear as words on paper in the form of memos and letters. Others are primarily numerical data, such as tax reports or profit-and-loss statements. Increasingly, reports are delivered and presented digitally, for instance, as PDF (portable digital format) documents or as electronic slide decks. These files can then be e-mailed, distributed on the company intranet, or posted on the Internet. Hyperlinks tie together content within the document, between associated files, and with Web site sources. Such linking adds depth and flexibility to traditional linear texts.

Some reports provide information only; others analyze and make recommendations. Although reports vary greatly in length, content, form, and formality level, they all have one or more of the following purposes: *to convey information, answer questions, and solve problems*.

LEARNING OBJECTIVE 1

Describe basic features of business reports, including functions, strategies (indirect or direct), writing style, and formats.

Effective business reports answer questions and solve problems systematically.

Report Functions

In terms of what they do, most reports fit into two broad categories: informational reports and analytical reports.

Informational Reports. Reports that present data without analysis or recommendations are primarily informational. For such reports, writers collect and organize facts, but they do not analyze the facts for readers. A trip report describing an employee's visit to a trade show, for example, presents information. Weekly bulleted status reports

Informational reports present data without comment or recommendations. Analytical reports provide analysis, conclusions, and, if requested, recommendations.

distributed by e-mail to a team record the activities of each group member and are shared with supervisors. Other reports that present information without analysis involve routine operations, compliance with regulations, and company policies and procedures.

Analytical Reports. Reports that provide data, analyses, and conclusions are analytical. If requested, writers also supply recommendations. Analytical reports may intend to persuade readers to act or change their beliefs. For example, if you were writing a feasibility report that compares several potential locations for a fast-food restaurant, you might conclude by recommending one site after discussing several criteria. Your report, an analysis of alternatives and a recommendation, attempts to persuade readers to accept that site.

To distinguish among findings, conclusions, and recommendations, consider the example of an audit report. The auditor compiles facts and figures—the findings of the report—to meet the purpose or objective of the audit. Drawing inferences from the findings, the auditor arrives at conclusions. With the audit objectives in mind, the auditor may then propose corrective steps or actions—the recommendations.

Organizational Strategies

Like other business messages, reports may be organized directly or indirectly. The reader's expectations and the content of a report determine its pattern of development, as illustrated in Figure 11.1. In long reports, such as corporate annual reports, some parts may be developed directly, whereas other parts are arranged indirectly.

Direct Strategy. When the purpose for writing is presented close to the beginning, the organizational pattern is direct. Informational reports, such as the letter report shown in Figure 11.2, are usually arranged directly. They open with an introduction, which is followed by the facts and a summary. In Figure 11.2 the writer explains a legal services plan by using a letter report. The report begins with an introduction. The facts, divided into three subtopics and identified by descriptive headings, follow. The report ends with a summary and a complimentary close.

Analytical reports may also be organized directly, especially when readers are supportive of or familiar with the topic. Many busy executives prefer this pattern because it gives them the results of the report immediately. They don't have to spend time wading

FIGURE 11.1 **Audience Analysis and Report Organization**

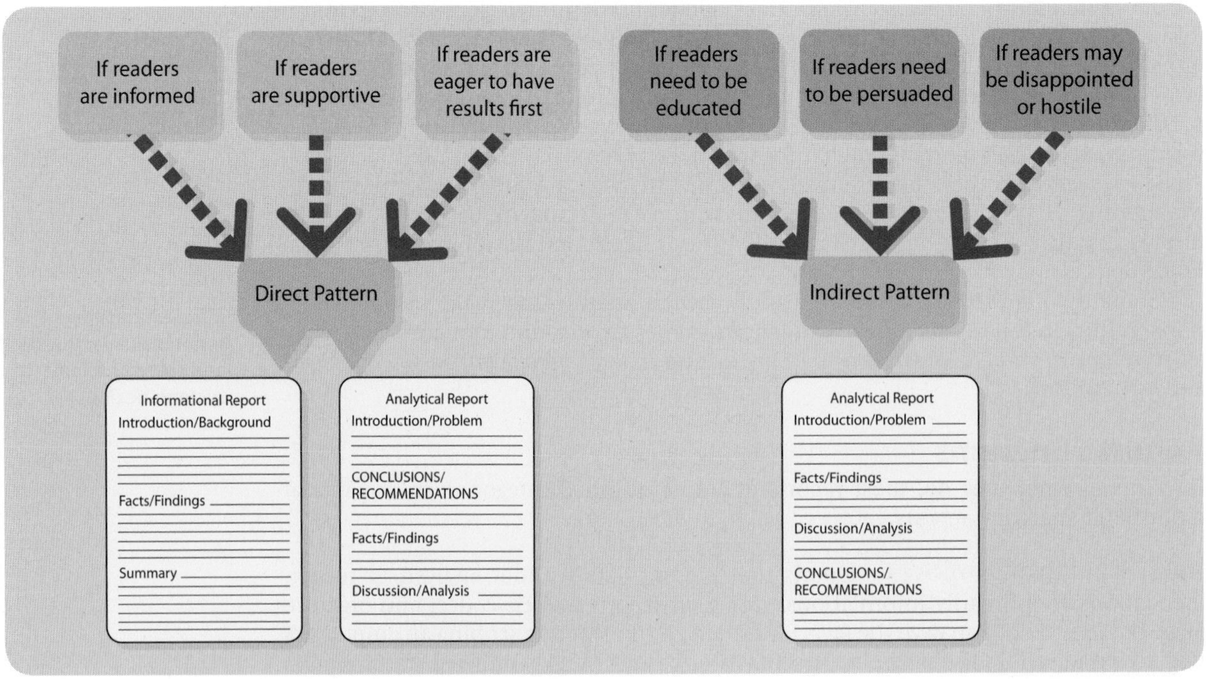

FIGURE 11.2 Informational Report—Letter Format

Centre for Consumers of Legal Services
P.O. Box 260
Kitchener, ON N2K 2Y5

(519) 248- 8931
www. cclegalservices.com

> Uses letterhead stationery for an informal report addressed to an outsider

September 7, 2014

Ms. Lisa Burgess, Secretary
Westwood Homeowners
3902 Westwood Drive
Guelph, ON N1H 6Y7

Dear Ms. Burgess:

As executive director of the Centre for Consumers of Legal Services, I'm pleased to send you this information describing how your homeowners' association can sponsor a legal services plan for its members. After an introduction with background data, this report will discuss three steps necessary for your group to start its plan.

Introduction

> Presents introduction and facts without analysis or recommendations

A legal services plan promotes preventive law by letting members talk to lawyers whenever problems arise. Prompt legal advice often avoids or prevents expensive litigation. Because groups can supply a flow of business to the plan's lawyers, groups can negotiate free consultation, follow-up, and discounts.

Two kinds of plans are commonly available. The first, a free plan, offers free legal consultation along with discounts for services when the participating groups are sufficiently large to generate business for the plan's lawyers. These plans actually act as a substitute for advertising for the lawyers. The second common type is the prepaid plan. Prepaid plans provide more benefits, but members must pay annual fees, usually of $500 or more a year. More than 30 million people are covered by legal services plans today, and a majority belong to free plans.

Since you inquired about a free plan for your homeowners' association, the following information describes how to set up such a program.

Determine the Benefits Your Group Needs

> Arranges facts of report into sections with descriptive headings

The first step in establishing a free legal services plan is to meet with the members of your group to decide what benefits they want. Typical benefits include the following:

Free consultation. Members may consult a participating lawyer—by phone or in the lawyer's office—to discuss any matter. The number of consultations is unlimited, provided each is about a separate matter. Consultations are generally limited to 30 minutes, but they include substantive analysis and advice.

> Emphasizes benefits in paragraph headings with boldface type

Free document review. Important papers—such as leases, insurance policies, and installment sales contracts—may be reviewed with legal counsel. Members may ask questions and receive an explanation of terms.

Tips for Letter Reports
- Use letter format for short informal reports sent to outsiders.
- Organize the facts section into logical divisions identified by consistent headings.
- Single-space the body.
- Double-space between paragraphs.
- Leave two blank lines above each side heading.
- Create side margins of 2.5 to 3 cm.
- Add a second-page heading, if necessary, consisting of the addressee's name, the date, and the page number.

(Continued)

through the facts, findings, discussion, and analyses to get to the two items they are most interested in—the conclusions and recommendations. Figure 11.3 illustrates such an arrangement. This analytical memo report describes environmental hazards of a property that a realtor has just listed. The realtor is familiar with the investigation and eager to find out the recommendations. Therefore, the memo is organized directly. You should be aware, though, that unless readers are familiar with the topic, they may find the direct pattern confusing. Many readers prefer the indirect pattern because it seems logical and mirrors the way they solve problems.

FIGURE 11.2 **(continued)**

Ms. Lisa Burgess   Page 2   September 7, 2014

Identifies second and succeeding pages with headings

Discount on additional services. For more complex matters, participating lawyers will charge members 75 percent of the lawyer's normal fee. However, some organizations choose to charge a flat fee for commonly needed services.

Select the Lawyers for Your Plan

Groups with geographically concentrated memberships have an advantage in forming legal plans. These groups can limit the number of participating lawyers and yet provide adequate service. Generally, smaller panels of lawyers are advantageous.

Assemble a list of candidates, inviting them to apply. The best way to compare prices is to have candidates submit their fees. Your group can then compare fee schedules and select the lowest bidder, if price is important. Arrange to interview lawyers in their offices.

After selecting a lawyer or a panel, sign a contract. The contract should include the reason for the plan, what the lawyer agrees to do, what the group agrees to do, how each side can end the contract, and the signatures of both parties. You may also want to include references to malpractice insurance, assurance that the group will not interfere with the lawyer–client relationship, an evaluation form, a grievance procedure, and responsibility for government filings.

Uses parallel side headings for consistency and readability

Publicize the Plan to Your Members

Members won't use a plan if they don't know about it, and a plan will not be successful if it is unused. Publicity must be vocal and ongoing. Announce it in newsletters, meetings, bulletin boards, and flyers.

Persistence is the key. All too frequently, leaders of an organization assume that a single announcement is all that's needed. They expect members to see the value of the plan and remember that it's available. Most organization members, though, are not as involved as the leadership. Therefore, it takes more publicity than the leadership usually expects to reach and maintain the desired level of awareness.

Summary

A successful free legal services plan involves designing a program, choosing the lawyers, and publicizing the plan. To learn more about these steps or to order a $35 how-to manual, call me at (519) 355-9901.

Sincerely,

Richard M. Ramos

Richard M. Ramos, Esq.
Executive Director
pas

Includes complimentary close and signature

Indirect Strategy. The organizational strategy is indirect when the conclusions and recommendations, if requested, appear at the end of the report. Such reports usually begin with an introduction or a description of the problem, followed by facts and interpretations from the writer. They end with conclusions and recommendations. This pattern is helpful when readers are unfamiliar with the problem. This pattern is also useful when readers must be persuaded or when they may be disappointed in or hostile toward the report's findings. The writer is more likely to retain the reader's interest by first explaining, justifying, and analyzing the facts and then making recommendations. This pattern also seems most rational to readers because it follows the normal thought process: problem, alternatives (facts), solution.

> The indirect strategy works best for analytical reports that convey bad news or seek to persuade.

Writing Style

Like other business messages, reports can range from informal to formal, depending on their purpose, audience, and setting. Research reports from consultants to their clients tend to be rather formal. Such reports must project objectivity, authority, and

FIGURE 11.3 **Analytical Report—Memo Format**

Applies memo format for short, informal internal report

Atlantic Environmental, Inc.

Interoffice Memo

DATE: March 7, 2014

TO: Kermit Fox, President

FROM: Cynthia M. Rashid, Environmental Engineer   *CMR*

SUBJECT: Investigation of Mountain Park Commercial Site

For Laurentian Realty, Inc., I've completed a preliminary investigation of its Mountain Park property listing. The following recommendations are based on my physical inspection of the site, official records, and interviews with officials and persons knowledgeable about the site.

Uses first paragraph as introduction

Presents recommendations first (direct pattern) because reader is supportive and familiar with topic

Recommendations

To reduce its potential environmental liability, Laurentian Realty should take the following steps in regard to its Mountain Park listing:

- Conduct an immediate asbestos survey at the site, including inspection of ceiling insulation material, floor tiles, and insulation around a gas-fired heater vent pipe at 2539 Mountain View Drive.

- Prepare an environmental audit of the generators of hazardous waste currently operating at the site, including Mountain Technology.

- Obtain lids for the dumpsters situated in the parking areas and ensure that the lids are kept closed.

Combines findings and analyses in short report

Findings and Analyses

My preliminary assessment of the site and its immediate vicinity revealed rooms with damaged floor tiles on the first and second floors of 2539 Mountain View Drive. Apparently, in recent remodelling efforts, these tiles had been cracked and broken. Examination of the ceiling and attic revealed further possible contamination from asbestos. The insulation for the hot-water tank was in poor condition.

Located on the property is Mountain Technology, a possible hazardous waste generator. Although I could not examine its interior, this company has the potential for producing hazardous material contamination.

In the parking area large dumpsters collect trash and debris from several businesses. These dumpsters were uncovered, thus posing a risk to the general public.

In view of the construction date of the structures on this property, asbestos-containing building materials might be present. Moreover, this property is located in an industrial part of the city, further prompting my recommendation for a thorough investigation. Laurentian Realty can act immediately to eliminate one environmental concern: covering the dumpsters in the parking area.

Tips for Memo Reports

- Use memo format for most short (ten or fewer pages) informal reports within an organization.
- Leave side margins of 2.5 to 3 cm.
- Sign your initials on the From line.
- Use an informal, conversational style.
- For direct analytical reports, put recommendations first.
- For indirect analytical reports, put recommendations last.

impartiality. But a report to your boss describing a trip to a conference would probably be informal.

An office worker once called a grammar hotline service with this problem: "We've just sent a report to our headquarters, and it was returned with this comment, 'Put it in the third person.' What do they mean?" The hotline experts explained that management apparently wanted a more formal writing style, using third-person constructions (*the company* or *the researcher* instead of *we* and *I*). Figure 11.4, which compares

Reports can be formal or informal depending on the purpose, audience, and setting.

FIGURE 11.4 Report-Writing Styles

	Formal Writing Style	Informal Writing Style
Use	Theses	Short, routine reports
	Research studies	Reports for a familiar audience
	Controversial or complex reports (especially for outsiders)	Noncontroversial reports
		Most reports for company insiders
Effect	Impression of objectivity, accuracy, professionalism, fairness	Feeling of warmth, personal involvement, closeness
	Distance created between writer and reader	
Characteristics	Absence of first-person pronouns; use of third person (*the researcher, the writer*)	Use of first-person pronouns (*I, we, me, my, us, our*)
	Absence of contractions (*can't, don't*)	Use of contractions
	Use of passive-voice verbs (*the study was conducted*)	Emphasis on active-voice verbs (*I conducted the study*)
	Complex sentences; long words	Shorter sentences; familiar words
	Absence of humour and figures of speech	Occasional use of humour, metaphors
	Reduced use of colourful adjectives and adverbs	Occasional use of colourful speech
	Elimination of "editorializing" (author's opinions, perceptions)	Acceptance of author's opinions and ideas

characteristics of formal and informal report-writing styles, can help you decide which writing style is appropriate for your reports. Note that, increasingly, formal reports are written with contractions and in the active voice. Today, report writers try to avoid awkward third-person references to themselves as *the researchers* or *the authors* because it sounds stilted and outdated.

Report Formats

The format of a report depends on its length, topic, audience, and purpose. After considering these elements, you will probably choose from among the following formats.

> A report's format depends on its length, audience, topic, and purpose.

Letter Format. Use letter format for short informal reports (usually eight or fewer pages) addressed outside an organization. Prepared on office stationery, a letter report contains a date, inside address, salutation, and complimentary close, as shown in Figure 11.2. Although they may carry information similar to that found in correspondence, letter reports usually are longer and show more careful organization than most letters. They also include headings.

Memo and E-Mail Formats. For short informal reports that stay within organizations, the memo format is appropriate. Memo reports begin with essential background information, using standard headings: *Date, To, From*, and *Subject*, as shown in Figure 11.3. Like letter reports, memo reports differ from regular memos in length, use of headings, and deliberate organization. Today, memo reports are rarely distributed in hard copy; rather, they are attached to e-mails or, if short, contained in the body of e-mails.

Manuscript Format. For longer, more formal reports, use the manuscript format. These reports are usually printed on plain paper instead of letterhead stationery or memo forms. They begin with a title followed by systematically displayed headings and subheadings. You will see examples of proposals and formal reports that use the manuscript format in Chapter 13.

Preprinted Forms. Prepared forms are often used for repetitive data, such as monthly sales reports, performance appraisals, merchandise inventories, and personnel and financial reports. Standardized headings on these forms save time for the writer. Preprinted forms also make similar information easy to locate and ensure that all necessary information is provided.

Digital Format. Digital media allow writers to produce and distribute reports in electronic form, not in hard copy. With Adobe Acrobat any report can be converted into a PDF document that retains its format and cannot be changed. In addition, today's communicators can use such programs as Microsoft's PowerPoint or Apple's Keynote to create electronic presentations in the form of slides. Because the purpose of such presentations is to concisely display the contents of reports, they are often not intended for verbal delivery. Rather, these text-heavy reports are often posted online or e-mailed. When printed out, the stacks of hard-copy slides resemble decks of playing cards, which is why they are called slide decks. Digital delivery has also changed Microsoft Word documents. This popular program lets users hyperlink multimedia content within the document or with associated text or media files. Thus, such digital documents create a nonlinear reading experience similar to that of browsing Web pages.

Applying the 3-×-3 Writing Process to Reports

Because business reports are systematic attempts to answer questions and solve problems, the best reports are developed methodically. In earlier chapters the 3-×-3 writing process was helpful in guiding short projects, such as e-mails, memos, and letters. That same process is even more necessary in helping you prepare longer projects, such as reports and proposals. After all, an extensive project poses a greater organizational challenge than a short one and, therefore, requires a rigorous structure to help readers grasp the message. Let's channel the writing process into seven specific steps:

LEARNING OBJECTIVE 2

Apply the 3-×-3 writing process to business reports to create well-organized documents that show a firm grasp of audience and purpose.

- **Step 1:** Analyze the problem and purpose.

- **Step 2:** Anticipate the audience and issues.

- **Step 3:** Prepare a work plan.

- **Step 4:** Implement your research strategy.

- **Step 5:** Organize, analyze, interpret, and illustrate the data.

- **Step 6:** Compose the first draft.

- **Step 7:** Revise, proofread, and evaluate.

The best reports grow out of a seven-step process beginning with analysis and ending with proofreading and evaluation.

How much time you spend on each step depends on your report task. A short informational report on a familiar topic might require a brief work plan, little research, and no data analysis. A complex analytical report, however, might demand a comprehensive work plan, extensive research, and careful data analysis. In this section we consider the first three steps in the process—analyzing the problem and purpose, anticipating the audience and issues, and preparing a work plan.

To illustrate the planning stages of a report, we will watch Diane Cameau develop a report she's preparing for her boss, Mike Rivers, at Mycon Pharmaceutical Laboratories. Mike asked Diane to investigate the problem of transportation for sales representatives. Currently, some Mycon reps visit customers (mostly doctors and hospitals) by using company-leased cars. A few reps drive their own cars, receiving reimbursements for use. In three months Mycon's leasing agreement for 14 cars expires, and Mike is considering a major change. Diane's task is to investigate the choices and report her findings to Mike.

Analyzing the Problem and Purpose

Before beginning a report, identify the problem to be solved in a clear statement.

The first step in writing a report is understanding the problem or assignment clearly. For complex reports prepare a written problem statement to clarify the task. In analyzing her report task, Diane had many questions: *Is the problem that Mycon is spending too much money on leased cars? Does Mycon want to invest in owning a fleet of cars? Is Mike unhappy with the paperwork involved in reimbursing sales reps when they use their own cars? Does he suspect that reps are submitting inflated mileage figures?* Before starting research for the report, Diane talked with Mike to define the problem. She learned several dimensions of the situation and wrote the following statement to clarify the problem—both for herself and for Mike.

> *Problem statement: The leases on all company cars will be expiring in three months. Mycon must decide whether to renew them or develop a new policy regarding transportation for sales reps. Expenses and paperwork for employee-owned cars seem excessive.*

Diane further defined the problem by writing a specific question that she would try to answer in her report:

> *Problem question: What plan should Mycon follow in providing transportation for its sales reps?*

Now Diane was ready to concentrate on the purpose of the report. Again, she had questions: *Exactly what did Mike expect? Did he want a comparison of costs for buying and leasing cars? Should she conduct research to pinpoint exact reimbursement costs when employees drive their own cars? Did he want her to do all the legwork, present her findings in a report, and let him make a decision? Or did he want her to evaluate the choices and recommend a course of action?* After talking with Mike, Diane was ready to write a simple purpose statement for this assignment.

A simple purpose statement defines the focus of a report.

> *Simple statement of purpose: To recommend a plan that provides sales reps with cars to be used in their calls.*

Preparing a written purpose statement is a good idea because it defines the focus of a report and provides a standard that keeps the project on target. In writing useful purpose statements, choose action verbs telling what you intend to do: *analyze, choose, investigate, compare, justify, evaluate, explain, establish, determine,* and so on. Notice that Diane's statement begins with the action verb *recommend*.

Some reports require only a simple statement of purpose: *to investigate expanded teller hours, to select a manager from among four candidates,* or *to describe the position of accounts supervisor.* Many assignments, though, demand additional focus to guide the project. An expanded statement of purpose considers three additional factors: scope, significance, and limitations.

Setting boundaries on a project determines its scope.

Scope and Limitations.
What issues or elements will be investigated? The scope statement prepares the audience by clearly defining which problem or problems will be analyzed and solved. To determine the scope, Diane brainstormed with Mike and others to pin down her task. She learned that Mycon currently had enough capital to consider purchasing a fleet of cars outright. Mike also told her that employee satisfaction was almost as important as cost-effectiveness. Moreover, he disclosed his suspicion that employee-owned cars were costing Mycon more than leased cars. Diane had many issues to sort out in setting the boundaries of her report.

What conditions affect the generalizability and utility of a report's findings? As part of the scope statement, the limitations further narrow the subject by focusing on constraints or exclusions. For this report Diane realized that her conclusions and recommendations might apply only to reps in her Edmonton sales district. Her findings would probably not be reliable for reps in Kapuskasing, Windsor, and Brandon. Another limitation for Diane was time. She had to complete the report in four weeks, thus restricting the thoroughness of her research.

Significance.
Why is the topic worth investigating at this time? Some topics, after initial examination, turn out to be less important than originally thought. Others

involve problems that cannot be solved, making a study useless. For Diane and Mike, the problem had significance because Mycon's leasing agreement would expire shortly and decisions had to be made about a new policy for transportation of sales reps.

Diane decided to expand her statement of purpose to define the scope, describe the limitations of the report, and explain the significance of the problem.

> *Expanded statement of purpose: The purpose of this report is to recommend a plan that provides sales reps with cars to be used in their calls. The report will compare costs for three plans: outright ownership, leasing, and compensation for employee-owned cars. It will also measure employee reaction to each plan. The report is significant because Mycon's current leasing agreement expires April 1 and an improved plan could reduce costs and paperwork. The study is limited to costs for sales reps in the Edmonton area.*

An expanded purpose statement considers scope, significance, and limitations.

After expanding her statement of purpose, Diane checked it with Mike Rivers to be sure she was on target.

Anticipating the Audience and Issues

After defining the purpose of a report, a writer must think carefully about who will read it. Concentrating solely on a primary reader is a major mistake. Although one individual may have solicited the report, others within the organization may eventually read it, including upper management and people in other departments. A report to an outside client may first be read by someone who is familiar with the problem and then be distributed to others less familiar with the topic. Moreover, candid statements to one audience may be offensive to another audience. Diane could make a major blunder, for instance, if she mentioned Mike's suspicion that sales reps were padding their mileage statements. If the report were made public—as it probably would be to explain a new policy—the sales reps could feel insulted that their integrity was questioned.

Report writers must take into account both primary and secondary readers.

As Diane considered her primary and secondary readers, she asked herself these questions:

- *What do my readers need to know about this topic?*
- *What do they already know?*
- *What is their educational level?*
- *How will they react to this information?*
- *Which sources will they trust?*
- *How can I make this information readable, believable, and memorable?*

Answers to these questions help writers determine how much background material to include, how much detail to add, whether to include jargon, what method of organization and presentation to follow, and what tone to use.

In the planning stages, a report writer must also break the major investigative problem into subproblems. This process, sometimes called factoring, identifies issues to be investigated or possible solutions to the main problem. In this case Mycon must figure out the best way to transport sales reps. Each possible "solution" or issue that Diane considers becomes a factor or subproblem to be investigated. Diane came up with three tentative solutions to provide transportation to sales reps: (1) purchase cars outright, (2) lease cars, or (3) compensate employees for using their own cars. These three factors form the outline of Diane's study.

Major report problems should be broken down into subproblems—or factored—to highlight possible solutions.

Diane continued to factor these main points into the following subproblems for investigation:

What plan should Mycon use to transport its sales reps?

I. Should Mycon purchase cars outright?

   A. How much capital would be required?

   B. How much would it cost to insure, operate, and maintain company-owned cars?

   C. Do employees prefer using company-owned cars?

II. Should Mycon lease cars?

    A. What is the best lease price available?

    B. How much would it cost to insure, operate, and maintain leased cars?

    C. Do employees prefer using leased cars?

III. Should Mycon compensate employees for using their own cars?

    A. How much has it cost in the past to compensate employees who used their own cars?

    B. How much paperwork is involved in reporting expenses?

    C. Do employees prefer being compensated for using their own cars?

Each subproblem would probably be further factored into additional subproblems. These issues may be phrased as questions, as Diane's are, or as statements. In factoring a complex problem, prepare an outline showing the initial problem and its breakdown into subproblems. Make sure your divisions are consistent (don't mix issues), exclusive (don't overlap categories), and complete (don't skip significant issues).

Preparing a Work Plan

After analyzing the problem, anticipating the audience, and factoring the problem, you're ready to prepare a work plan. A good work plan includes the following:

- Statement of the problem (based on key background and contextual information)

- Statement of the purpose including scope, limitations, and significance

- Research strategy, including a description of potential sources and methods of collecting data

- Tentative outline that factors the problem into manageable chunks

- Work schedule

Preparing a plan encourages you to evaluate your resources, set priorities, outline a course of action, and establish a time schedule. Having a plan keeps you on schedule and provides management with a means of measuring your progress.

A work plan outlines the resources, priorities, stages, and schedule of a project.

A work plan gives a complete picture of a project. Because the usefulness and quality of any report rest primarily on its data, you will want to develop a clear research strategy that includes allocating plenty of time to locate sources of information. For first-hand information you might interview people, prepare a survey, or even conduct a scientific experiment. For secondary information you will probably search printed materials, such as books and magazines, in addition to electronic materials on the Internet. Your work plan describes how you expect to generate or collect data. Because data collection is a major part of report writing, the next section of this chapter treats the topic more fully.

Figure 11.5 shows a complete work plan for a proposal to be presented to Lee Jeans. This work plan is particularly useful because it outlines the issues to be investigated. Notice that considerable thought and discussion and even some preliminary research are necessary to be able to develop a useful work plan.

Although this tentative outline guides investigation, it does not determine the content or order of the final report. You may, for example, study five possible solutions to a problem. If two prove to be useless, your report may discuss only the three winners. Moreover, you will organize the report to accomplish your goal and satisfy the audience. Remember that a busy executive who is familiar with a topic may prefer to read the conclusions and recommendations before a discussion of the findings. If someone authorizes the report, be sure to review the work plan with that individual (your manager, client, or professor, for example) before proceeding with the project.

FIGURE 11.5 **Work Plan for a Formal Report**

Defines purpose, scope, limits, and significance of report

Describes primary and secondary data

Factors problem into manageable chunks

Estimates time needed to complete report tasks

Statement of Problem

Many women between the ages of 18 and 34 have trouble finding jeans that fit. Lee Jeans hopes to remedy that situation with its One True Fit line. We want to demonstrate to Lee that we can create a word-of-mouth campaign that will help it reach its target audience.

Statement of Purpose

The purpose of this report is to secure an advertising contract from Lee Jeans. We will examine published accounts about the jeans industry and Lee Jeans in particular. In addition, we will examine published results of Lee's current marketing strategy. We will conduct focus groups of women in our company to generate campaign strategies for our pilot study of 100 BzzAgents. The report will persuade Lee Jeans that word-of-mouth advertising is an effective strategy to reach women in this demographic group and that BzzAgent is the right company to hire. The report is significant because an advertising contract with Lee Jeans would help our company grow significantly in size and stature.

Research Strategy (Sources and Methods of Data Collection)

We will gather information about Lee Jeans and the product line by examining published marketing data and conducting focus group surveys of our employees. In addition, we will gather data about the added value of word-of-mouth advertising by examining published accounts and interpreting data from previous marketing campaigns, particularly those with similar age groups. Finally, we will conduct a pilot study of 100 BzzAgents in the target demographic.

Tentative Outline

I. How effectively has Lee Jeans marketed to the target population (women, ages 18–34)?
    A. Historically, who has typically bought Lee Jeans products? How often? Where?
    B. How effective are the current marketing strategies for the One True Fit line?
II. Is this product a good fit for our marketing strategy and our company?
    A. What do our staff members and our sample survey of BzzAgents say about this product?
    B. How well does our pool of BzzAgents correspond to the target demography in terms of age and geographic distribution?
III. Why should Lee Jeans engage BzzAgent to advertise its One True Fit line?
    A. What are the benefits of word of mouth in general and for this demographic in particular?
    B. What previous campaigns have we engaged in that demonstrate our company's credibility?
    C. What are our marketing strategies, and how well did they work in the pilot study?

Work Schedule

Investigate Lee Jeans and the One True Fit line's current marketing strategy	July 15–25
Test product using focus groups	July 15–22
Create campaign materials for BzzAgents	July 18–31
Run a pilot test with a selected pool of 100 BzzAgents	August 1–21
Evaluate and interpret findings	August 22–25
Compose draft of report	August 26–28
Revise draft	August 28–30
Submit final report	September 1

Tips for Preparing a Work Plan

- Start early; allow plenty of time for brainstorming and preliminary research.
- Describe the problem motivating the report.
- Write a purpose statement that includes the report's scope, significance, and limitations.
- Describe the research strategy, including data collection sources and methods.
- Divide the major problem into subproblems stated as questions to be answered.
- Develop a realistic work schedule citing dates for completion of major tasks.
- Review the work plan with the person who authorized the report.

LEARNING OBJECTIVE

Find, evaluate, and use print and electronic secondary sources.

One of the most important steps in the process of writing a report is that of gathering information (research). Because a report is only as good as its foundation—the questions you ask and the data you gather to answer those questions—the remainder of this chapter describes the fundamental work of finding, documenting, and illustrating data.

As you analyze a report's purpose and audience and prepare your research strategy, you will identify and assess the data you need to support your argument or explain your topic. As you do, you will answer questions about your objectives and audience: *Will the audience need a lot of background or contextual information? Will your readers value or trust statistics, case studies, or expert opinions? Will they want to see data from interviews or surveys? Will summaries of focus groups be useful? Should you rely on organizational data?* Figure 11.6 lists five forms of data and provides questions to guide you in making your research accurate and productive.

Data fall into two broad categories: primary and secondary. Primary data result from first-hand experience and observation. Secondary data come from reading what others have experienced and observed. Secondary data are easier and cheaper to develop than primary data, which might involve interviewing large groups or sending out questionnaires.

We are going to discuss secondary data first because that is where nearly every research project should begin. Often something has already been written about your topic. Reviewing secondary sources can save time and effort and prevent you from "reinventing the wheel." Most secondary material is available either in print or electronically.

Primary data come from first-hand experience and observation; secondary data come from reading.

Print Resources

Print sources are still the most visible part of libraries.

Although we're seeing a steady movement away from print to electronic data, print sources are still the most visible part of most libraries. Furthermore, much information is available only in print.

FIGURE 11.6 Gathering and Selecting Report Data

Form of Data	Questions to Ask
Background or historical	How much do my readers know about the problem?
	Has this topic or issue been investigated before?
	Are those sources current, relevant, and credible?
	Will I need to add to the available data?
Statistical	What or who is the source?
	How recent are the data?
	How were the figures derived?
	Will these data be useful in this form?
Expert opinion	Who are the experts?
	What are their biases?
	Are their opinions in print?
	Are they available for an interview?
	Do we have in-house experts?
Individual or group opinion	Whose opinion(s) would the readers value?
	Have surveys or interviews been conducted on this topic?
	If not, do questionnaires or surveys exist that I can modify and use?
	Would focus groups provide useful information?
Organizational	What are the proper channels for obtaining in-house data?
	Are permissions required?
	How can I learn about public and private companies?

If you are an infrequent library user, begin your research by talking with a reference librarian about your project. These librarians won't do your research for you, but they will steer you in the right direction. And they are very accommodating. Many librarians help you understand their computer, cataloguing, and retrieval systems by providing advice, brochures, handouts, and workshops.

Books. Although quickly outdated, books provide excellent historical, in-depth data. Books can be located through print or online listings.

- **Card catalogues.** A few small public or high school libraries still maintain card catalogues with all books indexed on 3-×-5 cards alphabetized by author, title, and subject.

- **Online catalogues.** Most libraries today have computerized their card catalogues. Some systems are fully automated, thus allowing users to learn not only whether a book is located in the library but also whether it is currently available. Moreover, online catalogues can help you trace and retrieve items from other area libraries if your college or university doesn't own them.

Periodicals. Magazines, pamphlets, and journals are called periodicals because of their recurrent, or periodic, publication. Journals are compilations of scholarly articles. Articles in journals and other periodicals will be extremely useful because they are concise, limited in scope, and current and can supplement information in books.

> Books provide historical, in-depth data; periodicals focus on up to date information.

- **Print indexes.** Most college and university libraries now offer online access to *The Readers' Guide to Periodical Literature*. You may still find print copies of this valuable index of general-interest magazine article titles in small libraries. It includes such magazines as *Time, Newsweek, Maclean's,* and *The Canadian Forum*. However, business writers today rely almost totally on electronic indexes and databases.

- **Electronic indexes.** Online indexes are stored in digital databases. Most libraries now provide such databases to help you locate references, abstracts, and full-text articles from magazines, journals, and newspapers, such as *The Globe and Mail*. When using Web-based online indexes, follow the on-screen instructions or ask for assistance from a librarian. Beginning with a subject search is helpful because it generally turns up more relevant citations than keyword searches—especially when searching for names of people or companies. Once you locate usable references, either print a copy of your findings, save them to a portable flash memory device, or send them to your e-mail address.

> Exploration of secondary sources includes searching both electronic and print periodicals.

Electronic Databases

As a writer of business reports today, you will probably begin your secondary research with electronic resources. Online databases have become the staple of secondary research. Most writers turn to them first because they are fast and easy to use. This means that you can conduct detailed searches without ever leaving your office, home, or residence room.

> Most researchers begin by looking in electronic databases.

A database is a collection of information stored electronically so that it is accessible by computer and is digitally searchable. Databases provide both bibliographic (titles of documents and brief abstracts) and full-text documents. Most researchers prefer full-text documents because they are convenient. Various databases contain a rich array of magazine, newspaper, and journal articles, as well as newsletters, business reports, company profiles, government data, reviews, and directories. The four databases most useful to business writers for general searches are ABI/INFORM (ProQuest), Factiva (Dow Jones), LexisNexis Academic, and Academic Search Elite (EBSCO). Your college or university library and many businesses probably subscribe to these expensive resources and perhaps to other, more specialized commercial databases. Figure 11.7 shows the ABI/INFORM search menu.

> Commercial databases offer articles, reports, and other full text information online.

FIGURE 11.7 ABI/INFORM

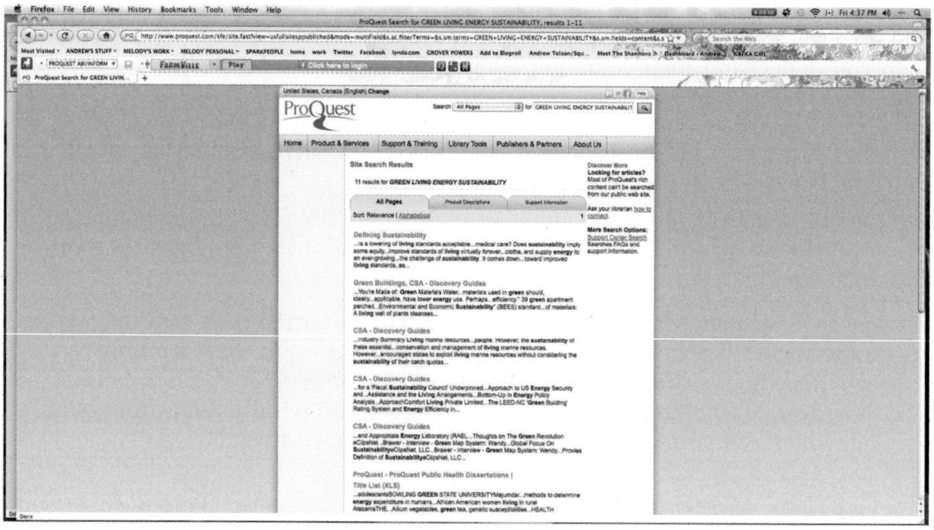

Developing a search strategy and narrowing your search can save time. As you develop your strategy, think about the time frame for your search, the language of publication, and the types of materials you will need. Most databases enable you to focus a search easily. For example, if you were researching the financial crisis that occurred recently and wanted to look at articles published in a specific year, most search tools would enable you to limit your search to that period. All databases and search engines allow you to refine your search and increase the precision of your hits. In addition, for research in international business, don't limit yourself to English-language articles only; some Web sites, most notably AltaVista's Babel Fish, offer rough but free translations. What's more, many organizations overseas present their Web content in multiple languages.

Electronic resources may take time to master. Therefore, before wasting time and retrieving a lot of useless material, talk to a librarian. School and public libraries, as well as some employers, offer free access to several commercial databases, sparing you the high cost of individual subscriptions.

Gathering Information From Primary Sources

LEARNING OBJECTIVE 4

Understand how to generate and use primary data while avoiding researcher bias.

Up to this point, we have been talking about secondary data. You should begin nearly every business report assignment by evaluating the available secondary data. However, you will probably need primary data to give a complete picture. Business reports that solve specific current problems typically rely on primary, first-hand data. Providing answers to business problems often means generating primary data through surveys, interviews, observation, or experimentation.

Surveys

Surveys yield efficient and economical primary data for reports.

Surveys collect data from groups of people. When developing new products, for example, companies often survey consumers to learn their needs. The advantages of surveys are that they gather data economically and efficiently. Mailed surveys reach big groups nearby or at great distances. Moreover, people responding to mailed surveys have time to consider their answers, thus improving the accuracy of the data.

Mailed or e-mailed surveys, of course, have disadvantages. Most of us rank them with junk mail, so response rates may be no higher than 5 percent. Furthermore, those who do respond may not represent an accurate sample of the overall population, thus invalidating generalizations from the group. A final problem with surveys has to do with truthfulness. Some respondents exaggerate their incomes or distort other facts, thus causing the results to be unreliable. Nevertheless, surveys may be the best way to generate data for business and student reports. In preparing print or electronic surveys, consider these pointers:

- **Select the survey population carefully.** Many surveys question a small group of people (a sample) and project the findings to a larger population. To be able to generalize from a survey, you need to make the sample as large as possible. In addition, you need to determine whether the sample is like the larger population. For important surveys you will want to consult books on or experts in sampling techniques.

- **Explain why the survey is necessary.** In a cover letter or an opening paragraph, describe the need for the survey. Suggest how someone or something other than you will benefit. If appropriate, offer to send recipients a copy of the findings.

- **Consider incentives.** If the survey is long, persuasive techniques may be necessary. Response rates can be increased by offering money (such as a loonie), coupons, gift certificates, free books, or other gifts.

- **Limit the number of questions.** Resist the temptation to ask for too much. Request only information you will use. Don't, for example, include demographic questions (income, gender, age, and so forth) unless the information is necessary to evaluate responses.

- **Use questions that produce quantifiable answers.** Check-off, multiple-choice, yes–no, and scale (or rank-order) questions, illustrated in Figure 11.8, provide quantifiable data that are easily tabulated. Responses to open-ended questions (*What should the bookstore do about plastic bags?*) reveal interesting but difficult-to-quantify, perceptions.[2] To obtain workable data, give interviewees a list of possible responses, as shown in items 5 through 8 of Figure 11.8. For scale and multiple-choice questions, try to present all the possible answer choices. To be safe, add an "Other" or "Don't know" category in case the choices seem insufficient to the respondent. Many surveys use scale questions because they capture degrees of feelings. Typical scale headings are *agree strongly, agree somewhat, neutral, disagree somewhat,* and *disagree strongly.*

- **Avoid leading or ambiguous questions.** The wording of a question can dramatically affect responses to it.[3] When respondents were asked, "Are we spending too much, too little, or about the right amount on *assistance to the poor*?" [emphasis added], 13 percent responded "too much." When the same respondents were asked, "Are we spending too much, too little, or about the right amount on *welfare*?"[emphasis added], 44 percent responded "too much." Because words have different meanings for different people, you must strive to use objective language and pilot-test your questions with typical respondents. Stay away from questions that suggest an answer (*Don't you agree that the salaries of CEOs are obscenely high?*). Instead, ask neutral questions (*Do CEOs earn too much, too little, or about the right amount?*). Also avoid queries that really ask two or more things (*Should the salaries of CEOs be reduced or regulated by government legislation?*). Instead, break them into separate questions (*Should the salaries of CEOs be reduced by government legislation? Should the salaries of CEOs be regulated by government legislation?*).

- **Make it easy for respondents to return the survey.** Researchers often provide stamped, return-addressed envelopes or business-reply envelopes. Low-cost Web survey software, such as SurveyMonkey and Zoomerang, help users develop simple, template-driven questions and allow survey takers conveniently to follow a link to take the survey.

- **Conduct a pilot study.** Try the questionnaire with a small group so that you can remedy any problems. For example, in the survey shown in Figure 11.8, a pilot study revealed that female students generally favoured cloth book bags and

> Effective surveys target appropriate samples and ask a limited number of specific questions.

FIGURE 11.8 Preparing a Survey

① Prewriting

Analyze: The purpose is to help the bookstore decide whether it should replace plastic bags with cloth bags for customer purchases.

Anticipate: The audience will be busy students who will be initially uninterested.

Adapt: Because students will be unwilling to participate, the survey must be short and simple. Its purpose must be significant and clear.

② Writing

Research: Ask students how they would react to cloth bags. Use their answers to form question response choices.

Organize: Open by explaining the survey's purpose and importance. In the body, ask clear questions that produce quantifiable answers. Conclude with appreciation and instructions.

Compose: Write the first draft of the questionnaire.

③ Revising

Revise: Try out the questionnaire with a small, representative group. Revise unclear questions.

Proofread: Read for correctness. Be sure that answer choices do not overlap and that they are complete. Provide "other" category if appropriate (as in No. 9).

Evaluate: Is the survey clear, attractive, and easy to complete?

East Shore College Bookstore
STUDENT SURVEY

Explains need for survey (use cover letter for longer surveys)

The East Shore College Bookstore wants to do its part in protecting the environment. Each year we give out 25,000 plastic bags for students to carry off their purchases. We are considering changing from plastic to cloth bags or some other alternative, but we need your views.

Please place checks below to indicate your responses.

Uses groupings that do not overlap (not 9 to 15 and 15 or more)

1. How many credits are you presently carrying?
   ___ 15 or more credits
   ___ 9 to 14 credits
   ___ 8 or fewer credits

   ___ Male
   ___ Female

2. How many times have you visited the bookstore this semester?
   ___ 0 times   ___ 1 time   ___ 2 times   ___ 3 times   ___ 4 or more times

3. Indicate your concern for the environment.
   ___ Very concerned   ___ Concerned   ___ Unconcerned

4. To protect the environment, would you be willing to change to another type of bag when buying books?
   ___ Yes
   ___ No

Indicate your feeling about the following alternatives.

	Agree	Undecided	Disagree
For major purchases the bookstore should			
5. Continue to provide plastic bags.			
6. Provide no bags; encourage students to bring their own bags.	___	___	___
7. Provide no bags; offer cloth bags at reduced price (about $3).	___	___	___
8. Give a cloth bag with each major purchase, the cost to be included in registration fees.	___	___	___
9. Consider another alternative, such as			

Uses scale questions to channel responses into quantifiable alternatives, as opposed to open-ended questions

Allows respondent to add an answer in case choices provided seem insufficient

_____

Please return the completed survey form to your instructor or to the survey box at the East Shore College Bookstore exit. Your opinion counts.

Tells how to return survey form

Thanks for your help!

were willing to pay for them. Male students opposed purchasing cloth bags. By adding a gender category, researchers could verify this finding. The pilot study also revealed the need to ensure an appropriate representation of male and female students in the survey.

Interviews

Some of the best report information, particularly on topics about which little has been written, comes from individuals. These individuals are usually experts or veterans in their fields. Consider both in-house and outside experts for business reports. Tapping these sources will call for in-person, telephone, or online interviews. To elicit the most useful data, try these techniques:

- **Locate an expert.** Ask managers and individuals whom they consider to be most knowledgeable in their areas. Check membership lists of professional organizations and consult articles about the topic or related topics. Most people enjoy being experts or at least recommending them. You could also post an inquiry to an Internet newsgroup. An easy way to search newsgroups in a topic area is through the *Browse all groups* category indexed by the popular search tool Google.

- **Prepare for the interview.** Learn about the individual you are interviewing, and make sure you can pronounce his or her name. Research the background and terminology of the topic. Let's say you are interviewing a corporate communication expert about producing an in-house newsletter. You ought to be familiar with such terms as *font* and such software as QuarkXPress and Adobe InDesign. In addition, be prepared by making a list of questions that pinpoint your focus on the topic. Ask the interviewee if you may record the talk.

- **Maintain a professional attitude.** Call before the interview to confirm the arrangements and then arrive on time. Be prepared to take notes if your recorder fails (and remember to ask permission beforehand if you want to record). Use your body language to convey respect.

- **Make your questions objective and friendly.** Adopt a courteous and respectful attitude. Don't get into a debating match with the interviewee. Remember that you are there to listen, not to talk! Use open-ended rather than yes–no questions to draw experts out.

- **Watch the time.** Tell interviewees in advance how much time you expect to need for the interview. Don't overstay your appointment. If your subject rambles, gently try to draw him or her back to the topic; otherwise, you may run out of time before asking all your questions.

- **End graciously.** Conclude the interview with a general question, such as, *Is there anything you would like to add?* Express your appreciation and ask permission to telephone later if you need to verify points.

Observation and Experimentation

Some kinds of primary data can be obtained only through first-hand observation and investigation. If you determine that the questions you have require observational data, then you need to plan the observations carefully. Most important is deciding what or whom you're observing and how often those observations are necessary to provide reliable data. For example, if you want to learn more about an organization's telephone customer service, you probably need to conduct an observation (along with interviews and perhaps even surveys). You will want to answer such questions as, *How long does a typical caller wait before a customer service rep answers the call?* and *Is the service consistent?* Recording observations for 60-minute periods at different times throughout a week will give you a better picture than just observing for an hour on a Friday before a holiday.

> Interviews with experts yield useful report data, especially when little has been written about a topic.

> Some of the best report data come from first-hand observation and investigation.

When you observe, plan ahead. Arrive early enough to introduce yourself and set up whatever equipment you think is necessary. Make sure that you've received permissions beforehand, particularly if you are recording. In addition, take notes, not only of the events or actions but also of the settings. Changes in environment often have an effect on actions.

Experimentation produces data suggesting causes and effects. Informal experimentation might be as simple as a pretest and posttest in a postsecondary course. Did students expand their knowledge as a result of the course? More formal experimentation is undertaken by scientists and professional researchers who control variables to test their effects. Assume, for example, that the Cadbury Chocolate Company wants to test the hypothesis (which is a tentative assumption) that chocolate lifts people out of the doldrums. An experiment testing the hypothesis would separate sad individuals into two groups: those who ate chocolate (the experimental group) and those who did not (the control group). What effect did chocolate have? Such experiments are not done haphazardly, however. Valid experiments require sophisticated research designs and careful attention to matching the experimental and control groups.

The World Wide Web

If you are like most adults today, you probably use the Web for entertainment and work every day. You stay in touch with your friends by instant messaging and e-mail, not to mention text and picture messages you exchange by using increasingly more capable smartphones. Chances are you have a personal page on a social-networking site, such as Facebook, and perhaps you play one of the countless free online games. You have probably looked up directions on MapQuest and may have bid on or sold items on eBay. You are likely to download ring tones for your cellphone, and perhaps you obtain your favourite music from iTunes, not some illegal file-sharing site. Your generation is much more likely to follow the news online than in the daily paper or even on TV. In short, you rely on the Internet daily for information and entertainment. You are part of a vast virtual community that, in turn, consists of many smaller communities all over the world. The Web and the Internet as a whole are referred to as a "global village" for a reason.

Understanding the Dynamic Complexity of the Web. The Web is an amazing resource. It started as a fast but exclusive network linking scientists, academics, military people, and other "tech heads." In the beginning information travelled purely in text form. Today the Web is interactive, mobile, and user-friendly, with multimedia content ranging from digital sound files to vivid images and video files. Most important for report writers, the Web is considered an ever-expanding democratic medium where anyone can be a publisher and consume most of its boundless content free of charge. Armed with camera phones, average citizens post their videos on the hugely popular site YouTube and act as virtual reporters. Interest groups of all stripes gather in Usenet communities or newsgroups (digital bulletin boards and discussion forums). They exchange news, opinions, and other information.

- **Virtual communities.** The so-called Web 2.0 has fostered interactive environments that have resulted in the emergence of virtual communities that encourage teamwork among strangers all over Canada and globally. One such democratic, free-access tool is the wiki. This group communication software enables users to create and change Web pages. The best known perhaps is Wikipedia, a free online reference that can be edited even by a layperson. Behind company firewalls, many wikis help technical experts and other specialists to collaborate.

- **Information mobility.** Digital content on the Web has also become more mobile in recent years. Thanks to browser-enabled smartphones and wireless personal digital assistants (PDAs), businesspeople can surf Web pages and write e-mail on the go with devices that fit into their pockets. Similarly, users can listen to podcasts, digital recordings of radio programs, and other audio files on demand. Podcasts are distributed for downloading to a computer; a smartphone, such as the iPhone or BlackBerry; or an MP3 audio player, such as the iPod.

Information on the Web grows and changes constantly and is available on the go with handheld devices.

As we saw in Chapter 7, the fastest-growing sector of the Internet is social networking sites. Social networking is a boon, but it also presents risks. On the one hand, online social media and a growing variety of prominent blogs, sometimes labelled the blogosphere, have empowered citizens to get their voices heard and to voice discontent. Online social media, such as Twitter and blogs, allow users to comment on any imaginable topic or event and post their views instantly. Companies have recognized the potential of the new media to reach vast audiences. Corporate blogs and social networks are growing as companies begin to understand their marketing potential.

However, the dark side of the power in the hands of "netizens" is that rumours and savage, no-holds-barred attacks can go viral, which means they travel around the globe overnight, ruining reputations and tarnishing carefully honed brands. Therefore, more and more businesses engage in damage control after online threats surface. In short, the Web is an invaluable resource, but report writers must approach it with caution and sound judgment.

With more than 79 percent of Canadians using the Internet[4] and literally trillions of pages of information available on the World Wide Web, odds are that if you have a question, an answer exists online. To a business researcher, the Web offers a wide range of organizational and commercial information. You can expect to find such items as product and service facts, public relations material, mission statements, staff directories, press releases, current company news, government information, selected article reprints, collaborative scientific project reports, and employment information.

Although a wealth of information is available on the Web, finding exactly what you need can be frustrating and time consuming. The constantly changing contents of the Web and its lack of organization make it more problematic for research than commercial databases, such as LexisNexis. Moreover, Web content is uneven and often the quality is questionable. The problem of gathering information is complicated by the fact that the total number of Web sites recently surpassed 200 million, growing at the rate of about 4 million new domain addresses each month.[5]

To succeed in your search for information and answers, you need to understand the search tools available to you. You also need to understand how to evaluate the information you find.

Identifying Search Tools. Finding what you are looking for on the Web is hopeless without powerful, specialized search tools, such as Google, Yahoo, MSN, AOL, and Ask.com. These search tools can be divided into two types: subject (or Web) directories and search engines. In addition, some search engines specialize in *metasearching*. This means they combine several powerful search engines into one (e.g., Dogpile). See Figure 11.9 for an overview of useful Web search tools. Large search sites, such as Yahoo and Google Directory, are actually search engines and subject directories combined. Subject directories fall into two categories: commercial ones (e.g., Yahoo, About.com, and others) and academic ones (e.g., InfoMine). Organized into subject categories, these human-compiled directories contain a collection of links to Internet resources submitted by site creators or evaluators.

Search engines differ in the way they trawl the vast amount of data on the Web. Google uses automated software "spiders" that crawl through the Web at regular intervals to collect and index the information from each location visited. Yippy by Vivísimo not only examines several search engines but also groups results into topics called clusters. Some search tools (e.g., Ask.com) use natural language–processing technology to enable you to ask questions to gather information. Both search engines and subject directories will help you find specific information. Figure 11.10 shows the *Canadian Business Directory*, a search engine and subject directory in one. This resource indexes any imaginable business topic and is very useful to business communicators.

Search engines, such as Google, used to boast about the numbers of items they had indexed, but they stopped after hitting the 1 trillion milestone of unique links, recognizing that the number of individual Web pages is potentially infinite.[6] No single

FIGURE 11.9 Web Search Tools for Business Writers

Business Databases (Subscription based, commercial)	Features
ABI/INFORM Complete (ProQuest)	Best database for reliable, scholarly sources; recommended first stop for business students
LexisNexis Academic	Database of over 5,000 newspapers, magazines, etc.; very current; forces users to limit their search to fewer than 1,000 hits
Factiva	Stores over 5,000 periodicals; very current; best with a narrow search subject or to add results to other searches (unlimited results)
JSTOR	Scholarly articles; best for historical, not current, information
Search Engines (open-access business information)	
Business.com http://www.business.com	Search engine and subject directory/portal in one; features all business-related subjects
CEO Express http://www.ceoexpress.com	Human-selected directories of subjects relevant to business executives and researchers
Google Scholar http://scholar.google.com	Scholarly articles in various disciplines, including business, administration, finance, and economics
Search Engines (general)	
Google http://www.google.com http://www.google.ca 🍁	Relevance ranking; most popular search site or portal (65 percent of Web searches); advanced search options and subject directories
Yahoo http://www.yahoo.com http://ca.yahoo.com 🍁	Search engine and directory; popular free e-mail site; relevance ranking; ranks second after Google with 16 percent of Web searches
Bing http://www.bing.com/	Microsoft's latest search engine indexing 200 million Web sites; MSN/Bing is in third place with nearly 11 percent of Web searches
All the Web http://www.alltheweb.com	Advanced search option; searches for audio and video files
Ask http://www.ask.com	Plain English (natural language) questions
Metasearch Engines (results from several search sites)	
Vivísimo/Yippy http://vivisimo.com http://yippy.com	Metasearch function clusters results into categories; offers advanced search options and help
InfoSpace http://search.infospace.com http://www.dogpile.com	Metasearch technology; searches Google, Yahoo, Bing, Ask, and more; owns other metasearch engines (e.g., Dogpile, WebCrawler, MetaCrawler)
Search http://www.search.com	Searches Google, Ask, LookSmart, and dozens of other leading search engines
Subject Directories or Portals	
About http://www.about.com	Directory that organizes content from over 2 million sites with commentary from 750 "guides" (chosen experts on 70,000+ topics)
Ipl2 http://www.ipl.org/	Award-winning public service organization and learning/teaching environment maintained by librarians of several universities

No search engine or directory indexes all Web pages.

search engine or directory can come close to indexing all the pages on the Internet. However, if you try a multiple-search site, such as Dogpile, you can save much time because its metasearch technology compares the results of at least seven major search engines, eliminates duplicates, and then ranks the best hits.[7] To help you search for data effectively, consider using the search tools listed in Figure 11.9.

FIGURE 11.10 Canadian Business Directory

The *Canadian Business Directory* indexes any imaginable business topic and is very useful to business communicators.

Applying Internet Search Strategies and Techniques. To conduct a thorough search for the information you need, build a (re)search strategy by understanding the tools available.

Web research is often time consuming and frustrating unless you know special search techniques.

- **Use two or three search tools.** Begin by conducting a topic search. Use a subject directory, such as Yahoo, About, or Open Directory Project. Once you have narrowed your topic, switch to a search engine or metasearch engine.

- **Know your search tool.** When connecting to a search site for the first time, always read the description of its service, including its FAQs (frequently asked questions), Help, and How to Search sections. Often there are special features (e.g., News, Images, Video, Books, and other categories on Google) that can speed up the search process.

- **Understand case sensitivity.** Generally, use lowercase for your searches, unless you are searching for a term that is usually written in upper case and lowercase, such as a person's name.

- **Use nouns as search words and six to eight words in a query.** The right keywords—and more of them—can narrow the search effectively.

- **Combine keywords into phrases.** Phrases, marked by the use of quotation marks (e.g., "business ethics"), will limit results to specific matches.

- **Omit articles and prepositions.** Known as "stop words," articles and prepositions do not add value to a search. Instead of *request for proposal*, use *proposal request*.

- **Use wildcards.** Most search engines support wild cards, such as asterisks. For example, the search term *cent** will retrieve *cents*, while *cent*** will retrieve both *center* and *centre*.

- **Learn basic Boolean search strategies.** You can save yourself a lot of time and frustration by narrowing your search with the following Boolean operators:

  AND Identifies only documents containing all of the specified words: **employee AND productivity AND morale**

  OR Identifies documents containing at least one of the specified words: **employee OR productivity OR morale**

  NOT Excludes documents containing the specified word: **employee productivity NOT morale**

  NEAR Finds documents containing target words or phrases within a specified distance, for instance, within ten words: **employee NEAR productivity**

- **Bookmark the best.** To keep track of your favourite Internet sites, save them as bookmarks or favourites.

- **Keep trying.** If a search produces no results, check your spelling. If you are using Boolean operators, check the syntax of your queries. Try synonyms and variations on words. Try to be less specific in your search term. If your search produces too many hits, try to be more specific. Use the Advanced feature of your search engine to narrow your search. Think of words that uniquely identify what you're looking for. Use as many relevant keywords as possible.

- **Repeat your search a week later.** For the best results, return to your search a couple of days or a week later. The same keywords will probably produce additional results. That's because millions of new pages are being added to the Web every day. The ranking of hits can also change depending on how often a link is accessed by Internet users.

Remember, subject directories and search engines vary in their contents, features, selectivity, accuracy, and retrieval technologies. Only through clever cyber searching can you uncover the jewels hidden in the Internet.

Evaluating Web Sources. Many of us using the Web have a tendency to assume that any information turned up by a search engine has somehow been evaluated as part of a valid selection process. Wrong! The truth is that the Internet is rampant with unreliable sites that reside side by side with reputable sites. Anyone with a computer and an Internet connection can publish anything on the Web. Unlike library-based research, information at many sites has not undergone the editing or scrutiny of scholarly publication procedures. The information we read in journals and most reputable magazines is reviewed, authenticated, and evaluated. That's why we have learned to trust these sources as valid and authoritative.

Information on the Web is much less reliable than data from traditional sources. Wikis, blogs, and discussion forum entries are a case in point. Although they turn up in many Internet searches, they are mostly useless because they are short-lived. They change constantly and may disappear fast, so your source can't be verified. Many don't provide any references or reveal sources that are either obscure or suspect. Academic researchers prefer lasting, scholarly sources. Many professors will not allow you to cite from Wikipedia, for example, because this collaborative tool and online reference can be edited by any contributor and is considered to be unreliable. Moreover, citing from an encyclopaedia shows poor research skills. Some Web sites exist to propagandize; others want to sell you something. To use the Web meaningfully, you must scrutinize

Search engines vary in their ability to retrieve data. Learn about their advanced features and then practise using them.

what you find and check who authored and published it. Here are specific questions to ask as you examine a site:

- **Currency.** What is the date of the Web page? When was it last updated? Is some of the information obviously out-of-date? If the information is time sensitive and the site has not been updated recently, the site is probably not reliable.

- **Authority.** Who publishes or sponsors this Web page? What makes the presenter an authority? Is information about the author or creator available? Is a contact address available for the presenter? Learn to be skeptical about data and assertions from individuals and organizations whose credentials are not verifiable.

- **Content.** Is the purpose of the page to entertain, inform, convince, or sell? How would you classify this page (e.g., news, personal, advocacy, reference)? Who is the intended audience, based on content, tone, and style? Can you judge the overall value of the content compared with the other resources on this topic? Web presenters with a slanted point of view cannot be counted on for objective data. Be particularly cautious with blogs. They often abound with grandstanding and ranting but lack factual information. Read them side by side with reputable news sources.

- **Accuracy.** Do the facts that are presented seem reliable to you? Do you find errors in spelling, grammar, or usage? Do you see any evidence of bias? Are footnotes provided? If you find numerous errors and if facts are not referenced, you should be alert that the data may be questionable.

Evaluate the currency, authority, content, and accuracy of Web sites carefully.

Documenting Data

In writing business and other reports, you will often build on the ideas and words of others. In Western culture, whenever you "borrow" the ideas of others, you must give credit to your information sources. This is called documentation.

LEARNING OBJECTIVE 6

Recognize the purposes and techniques of documentation in business reports, and avoid plagiarism.

Recognizing the Purposes of Documentation

As a careful writer, you should take pains to properly document report data for the following reasons:

- **To strengthen your argument.** Including good data from reputable sources will convince readers of your credibility and the logic of your reasoning.

- **To protect yourself against charges of plagiarism.** Acknowledging your sources keeps you honest. Plagiarism, which is illegal and unethical, is the act of using others' ideas without proper documentation.

- **To instruct the reader.** Citing references enables readers to pursue a topic further and make use of the information themselves.

Documenting data lends credibility, protects the writer from charges of plagiarism, and aids the reader.

Distinguishing Between Academic Documentation and Business Practices

In the academic world, documentation is critical. Especially in the humanities and sciences, students are taught to cite sources by using quotation marks, parenthetical citations, footnotes, and bibliographies. Academic term papers require full documentation to demonstrate that a student has become familiar with respected sources and can cite them properly in developing an argument. Giving credit to the author is extremely important. Students who plagiarize risk a failing grade in a class and even expulsion from school.

In the business world, however, documentation and authorship are sometimes viewed differently. Business communicators on the job may find that much of what is written does not follow the standards they learned in school. In many instances, individual authorship is unimportant. For example, employees may write for the signature of their bosses. The writer receives no credit. Similarly, team projects turn out documents for which none of the team members receives individual credit. Internal business reports, which often include chunks of information from previous reports, also fail to acknowledge sources or give credit. Even information from outside sources may lack proper documentation. Yet, if facts are questioned, business writers must be able to produce their source materials.

Although both internal and external business reports are not as heavily documented as school assignments or term papers, business communication students are well advised to learn proper documentation methods. In the workplace, stealing the ideas of others and passing them off as your own can be corrosive to the business because it leads to resentment and worse.

Plagiarism of words or ideas is a serious charge and can lead to loss of a job. Famous historians, several high-level journalists, and a Canadian prime minister[8] suffered serious consequences for copying from unnamed sources. Your instructor may use a commercial plagiarism detection service, such as Turnitin.com, which can cross-reference much of the information on the Web, looking for documents with similar phrasing. The result, an "originality report," will provide the instructor with a clear idea of whether you've been accurate and honest. You can avoid charges of plagiarism and add clarity to your work by knowing what to document and by developing good research habits.

Learning What to Document

When you write reports, especially in college or university, you are continually dealing with other people's ideas. You are expected to conduct research, synthesize ideas, and build on the work of others. But you are also expected to give proper credit for borrowed material. To avoid plagiarism, you must give credit whenever you use the following:[9]

- Another person's ideas, opinions, examples, or theory

- Any facts, statistics, graphs, and drawings that are not common knowledge

- Quotations of another person's actual spoken or written words

- Paraphrases of another person's spoken or written words

Information that is common knowledge requires no documentation. For example, the statement *The Globe and Mail is a popular business newspaper* would require no citation. Statements that are not common knowledge, however, must be documented. For example, *Five of the nation's top 15 cities are located in the Golden Horseshoe area in Ontario on the densely populated shores of the Great Lakes*[10] would require a citation because most people do not know this fact. Cite sources for proprietary information, such as statistics organized and reported by a newspaper or magazine. You probably know to use citations to document direct quotations, but you must also cite ideas that you summarize in your own words.

Developing Good Research Habits

Report writers who are gathering information have two methods available for recording the information they find. The time-honoured manual method of note taking works well because information is recorded on separate cards, which can then be arranged in the order needed to develop a thesis or an argument. Today, though, writers rely heavily on electronic researching. Traditional note-taking methods may seem antiquated and laborious in comparison. Let's explore both methods.

Manual Note Taking. To make sure you know whose ideas you are using, train yourself to take excellent notes. If possible, know what you intend to find before you begin your research so that you won't waste time on unnecessary notes. Here are some pointers on taking good notes:

- Record all major ideas from various sources on separate note cards.

- Include all publication information (author, date, title, and so forth) along with precise quotations.

- Consider using one card colour for direct quotes and a different colour for your paraphrases and summaries.

- Put the original source material aside when you are summarizing or paraphrasing.

Electronic Note Taking. Instead of recording facts on note cards, wise researchers today take advantage of electronic tools, as noted in the Plugged In box. Be careful, though, not to cut and paste your way into plagiarism. Here are some pointers on taking good electronic notes:

- Begin your research by setting up a folder on your hard drive. On the go, you can use a storage device, such as a USB flash drive, CD-RW, or computer disk to carry your data.

- Create subfolders for major sections, such as introduction, body, and closing.

- When you find facts on the Web or in electronic databases, highlight the material you want to record, copy it, and paste it into a document in an appropriate folder.

- Be sure to include all publication data.

- As discussed in the section on managing research data, consider archiving on a memory stick those Web pages or articles used in your research in case the data must be verified.

> Set up a folder for electronic notes but be careful not to cut and paste excessively in writing reports.

PLUGGED IN

Staying on Top of Research Data

In collecting electronic search results, you can easily lose track of Web sites and articles you quoted. To document Web data that may change and to manage your electronic sources, you need a specific plan for saving the information. At the very least, you will want to create a *working bibliography* or a list of *references* in which you record the URL of each electronic source and its access date. Here are techniques that can help you build your bibliography and manage your electronic data like a pro:

- **Saving sources to disk or portable flash memory device** has advantages, including being able to open the document in a browser even if you don't have access to the Internet. More important, saving sources to disk or memory stick ensures that you will have access to information that may or may not be available later. Using either the **File** and **Save As** or the **File** and **Save Page As** menu command in your browser, you will be able to store the information permanently. Saving images and other kinds of media can be accomplished with your mouse by either right-clicking or command clicking on the item, followed by choosing a command, such as **Save Picture As** or **Save Image As**, from a pop-up window.

- **Copying and pasting information** you find on the Web into word processing documents is an easy way to save and store it. Remember to also copy and paste the URL into the file, as well and record the URL in your working bibliography. If you invest in Adobe's PDF Converter, you can save a Web

page or an MS Word document in the portable document format simply by choosing the **Print** command and selecting Adobe PDF in the **Printer** window of the **Print** menu. The URL, access date, and time stamp will be automatically saved on the document. You can keep your PDF documents as electronic files or print out paper copies later.

- **Printing pages** is a handy way to gather and store information. Doing so enables you to have copies of important data that you can annotate or highlight. Make sure the URL prints with the document (usually on the bottom of the page). If not, write it on the page.

- **Bookmarking favourites** is an option within browsers to enable users to record and store the URLs for important sources. The key to using this option is learning to create folders with names that are relevant and to use names for bookmarks that make sense and are not redundant. If no name is provided, the browser will default to the URL.

- **E-mailing documents, URLs, or messages to yourself** is another useful strategy. Many databases and online magazines permit you to e-mail information and sometimes the entire article to your account. If you combine the copy-and-paste function with e-mail, you can send yourself nearly any information you find on the Web.

Practising the Fine Art of Paraphrasing

In writing reports and using the ideas of others, you will probably rely heavily on paraphrasing, which means restating an original passage in your own words and in your own style. To do a good job of paraphrasing, follow these steps:

1. Read the original material intently to comprehend its full meaning.

2. Write your own version without looking at the original.

3. Avoid repeating the grammatical structure of the original and merely replacing words with synonyms.

4. Reread the original to be sure you covered the main points but did not borrow specific language.

To better understand the difference between plagiarizing and paraphrasing, study the following passages. Notice that the writer of the plagiarized version uses the same grammatical construction as the source and often merely replaces words with synonyms. Even the acceptable version, however, requires a reference to the source author.

Source

While the BlackBerry has become standard armor(sic) for executives, a few maverick leaders are taking action to reduce e-mail use. . . . The concern, say academics and management thinkers, is misinterpreted messages, as well as the degree to which e-mail has become a substitute for the nuanced conversations that are critical in the workplace.[11]

Plagiarized Version

Although smartphones are standard among business executives, some pioneering bosses are acting to lower e-mail usage. Business professors and management experts are concerned that messages are misinterpreted and that e-mail substitutes for nuances in conversations that are crucial on the job (Brady, 2006).

Acceptable Paraphrase

E-mail on the go may be the rage in business. However, some executives are rethinking its use, as communication experts warn that e-mail triggers misunderstandings. These specialists believe that e-mail should not replace the more subtle face-to-face interaction needed on the job (Brady, 2006).

Knowing When and How to Quote

On occasion you will want to use the exact words of a source. But beware of overusing quotations. Documents that contain pages of spliced-together quotations suggest that writers have few ideas of their own. Wise writers and speakers use direct quotations for three purposes only:

- To provide objective background data and establish the severity of a problem as seen by experts

- To repeat identical phrasing because of its precision, clarity, or aptness

- To duplicate exact wording before criticizing

When you must use a long quotation, try to summarize and introduce it in your own words. Readers want to know the gist of a quotation before they tackle it. For example, to introduce a quotation discussing the shrinking staffs of large companies, you could precede it with your words: *In predicting employment trends, Charles Waller believes the corporation of the future will depend on a small core of full-time employees.* To introduce quotations or paraphrases, use wording such as the following:

According to Waller, . . .

Waller argues that . . .

In his recent study, Waller reported . . .

Paraphrasing involves putting an original passage into your own words.

The plagiarized version uses the same sentence structure as the original and makes few changes other than replacing some words.

The acceptable paraphrase presents ideas from a different perspective and uses a different sentence structure than the original.

Use quotations only to cite experts, to repeat memorable phrasing, or to reproduce exact wording before criticizing.

Use quotation marks to enclose exact quotations, as shown in the following: *"The current image," says Charles Waller, "of a big glass-and-steel corporate headquarters on landscaped grounds directing a worldwide army of tens of thousands of employees may soon be a thing of the past" (2006, p. 51).*

Using Citation Formats

You can direct readers to your sources with parenthetical notes inserted into the text and with bibliographies. The most common citation formats are those presented by the Modern Language Association (MLA) and the American Psychological Association (APA). Learn more about how to use these formats in Appendix B.

Creating Effective Visual Aids

After collecting and interpreting information, you need to consider how best to present it. If your report contains complex data and numbers, you may want to consider using graphics, such as tables and charts. These graphics clarify data, create visual interest, and make numerical data meaningful. By simplifying complex ideas and emphasizing key data, well-constructed graphics make key information easier to remember. However, the same data can be shown in many forms, such as in a chart, table, or graph. That's why you need to recognize how to match the appropriate graphic with your objective and incorporate it into your report.

LEARNING OBJECTIVE **7**

Create meaningful and interesting graphics; display numeric information in the appropriate graphic form; and skillfully generate, use, and convert data to visual aids.

Matching Graphics and Objectives

In developing the best graphics, you must decide what data you want to highlight and which graphics are most appropriate to your objectives. Tables? Bar charts? Pie charts? Line charts? Surface charts? Flowcharts? Organization charts? Pictures? Figure 11.11 summarizes appropriate uses for each type of graphic. The following text discusses each visual in more detail.

Tables. Probably the most frequently used graphic in reports is the table. Because a table presents quantitative or verbal information in systematic columns and rows, it can clarify large quantities of data in small spaces. The disadvantage is that tables do not readily display trends. You may have made rough tables to help you organize the raw data collected from questionnaires or interviews. In preparing tables for your readers or listeners, though, you will need to pay more attention to clarity and emphasis. Here are tips for making good tables, such as the one in Figure 11.12:

Tables permit the systematic presentation of large amounts of data, whereas charts and graphs enhance visual comparisons.

- Place titles and labels at the top of the table.

- Arrange items in a logical order (alphabetical, chronological, geographical, highest to lowest), depending on what you need to emphasize.

- Provide clear headings for the rows and columns.

- Identify the units in which figures are given (percentages, dollars, units per worker hour, and so forth) in the table title, in the column or row heading (with the first item in a column), or in a note at the bottom.

- Use *N/A (not available)* for missing data.

- Make long tables easier to read by shading alternate lines or by leaving a blank line after groups of five.

- Place tables as close as possible to the place where they are mentioned in the text.

FIGURE 11.11 Matching Graphics to Objectives

Graphic		Objective
Table	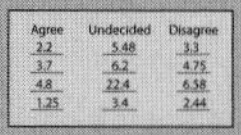	To show exact figures and values
Bar chart		To compare one item with others
Line chart	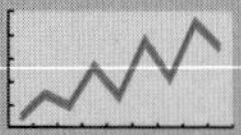	To demonstrate changes in quantitative data over time
Pie chart		To visualize a whole unit and the proportions of its components
Flowchart	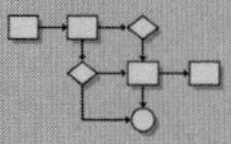	To display a process or procedure
Organization chart	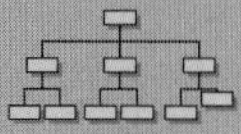	To define a hierarchy of elements
Photograph, map, illustration		To create authenticity, to spotlight a location, and to show an item in use

FIGURE 11.12 Table Summarizing Precise Data

Figure 1 AET ENTERTAINMENT COMPANY Income by Division (in millions of dollars)				
	Theme Parks	Motion Pictures	DVDs & Blu-rays	Total
2009	$15.8	$39.3	$11.2	$66.3
2010	18.1	17.5	15.3	50.9
2011	23.8	21.1	22.7	67.6
2012	32.2	22.0	24.3	78.5
2013 (projected)	35.1	21.0	26.1	82.2

Selecting the appropriate graphic depends on the purpose that it serves.

Figure 11.11 shows how various graphics are effective in serving different purposes. Tables are especially suitable for illustrating exact figures in systematic rows and columns. The table in Figure 11.12 is particularly useful because it presents data about the AET Entertainment Company over several years, making it easy to compare several divisions. Figures 11.13 through 11.16 highlight some of the data shown in the AET Entertainment Company table, illustrating vertical, horizontal, grouped, and segmented bar charts, each of which achieves a different effect.

Bar Charts. Although they lack the precision of tables, bar charts enable you to make emphatic visual comparisons by using horizontal or vertical bars of varying lengths. Bar charts are useful to compare related items, illustrate changes in data over time, and show segments as a part of the whole. Note how the varied bar charts present information in differing ways.

FIGURE 11.13 Vertical Bar Chart

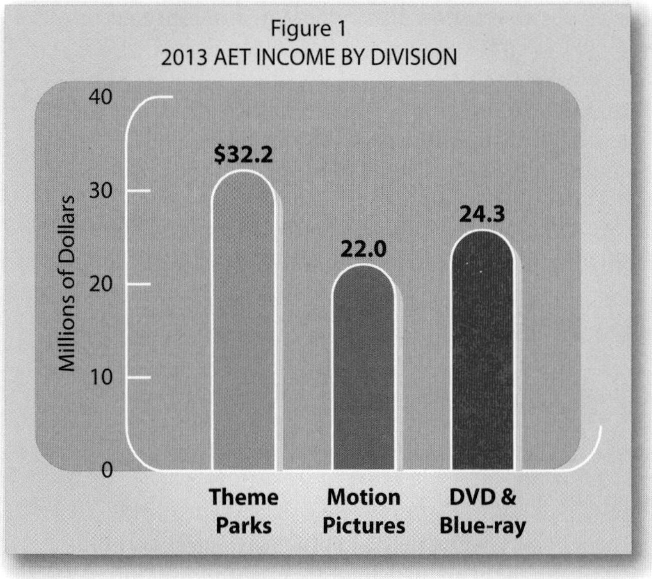

Figure 1
2013 AET INCOME BY DIVISION

$32.2 — Theme Parks
22.0 — Motion Pictures
24.3 — DVD & Blue-ray

(Millions of Dollars, 0–40)

FIGURE 11.14 Horizontal Bar Chart

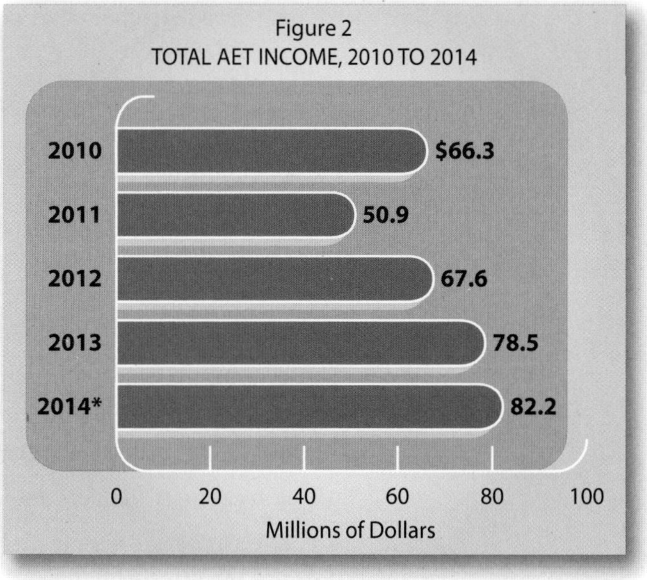

Figure 2
TOTAL AET INCOME, 2010 TO 2014

2010 — $66.3
2011 — 50.9
2012 — 67.6
2013 — 78.5
2014* — 82.2

Millions of Dollars (0–100)

FIGURE 11.15 Grouped Bar Chart

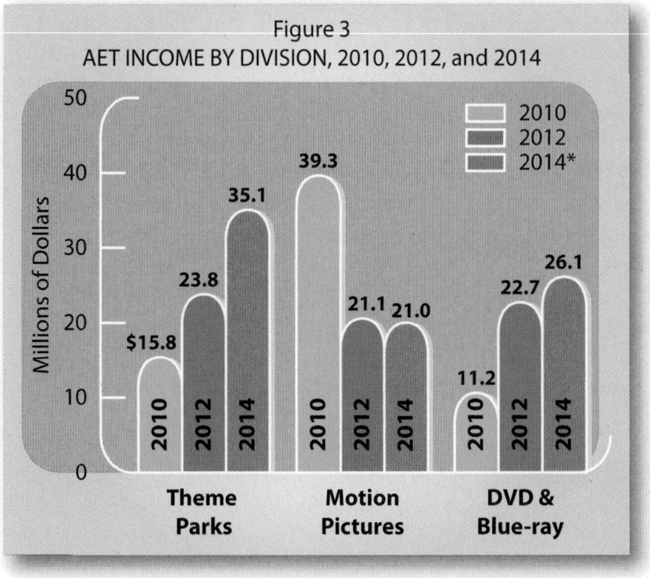

Figure 3
AET INCOME BY DIVISION, 2010, 2012, and 2014

Legend: 2010, 2012, 2014*

Theme Parks: $15.8 (2010), 23.8 (2012), 35.1 (2014)
Motion Pictures: 39.3 (2010), 21.1 (2012), 21.0 (2014)
DVD & Blue-ray: 11.2 (2010), 22.7 (2012), 26.1 (2014)

(Millions of Dollars, 0–50)

FIGURE 11.16 Segmented 100% Bar Chart

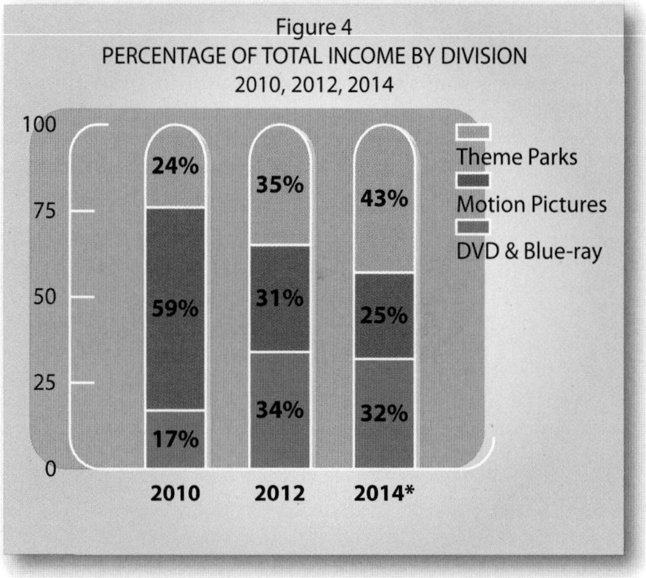

Figure 4
PERCENTAGE OF TOTAL INCOME BY DIVISION
2010, 2012, 2014

Legend: Theme Parks, Motion Pictures, DVD & Blue-ray

2010: 24% (Theme Parks), 59% (Motion Pictures), 17% (DVD & Blue-ray)
2012: 35% (Theme Parks), 31% (Motion Pictures), 34% (DVD & Blue-ray)
2014*: 43% (Theme Parks), 25% (Motion Pictures), 32% (DVD & Blue-ray)

(Percentage, 0–100)

Many techniques for constructing tables also hold true for bar charts. Here are a few additional tips:

- Keep the length and width of each bar and segment proportional.

- Include a total figure in the middle of the bar or at its end if the figure helps the reader and does not clutter the chart.

- Start dollar or percentage amounts at zero.

- Place the first bar at some distance (usually half the amount of space between bars) from the y-axis.

- Avoid showing too much information, which produces clutter and confusion.
- Place each bar chart as close as possible to the place where it is mentioned in the text.

Line charts illustrate trends and changes in data over time.

Line Charts. The major advantage of line charts is that they show changes over time, thus indicating trends. The vertical axis is typically the dependent variable, and the horizontal axis is the independent one. Simple line charts (Figure 11.17) show just one variable. Multiple line charts compare items, such as two or more data sets, by using the same variable (Figure 11.18). Segmented line charts (Figure 11.19), also called surface charts, illustrate how the components of a whole change over time. To prepare a line chart, remember these tips:

- Begin with a grid divided into squares.
- Arrange the time component (usually years) horizontally across the bottom; arrange values for the other variable vertically.
- Draw small dots at the intersections to indicate each value at a given year.
- Connect the dots and add colour if desired.
- To prepare a segmented (surface) chart, plot the first value (say, DVD and Blu-ray disc income) across the bottom; add the next item (say, motion picture income) to the first figures for every increment; for the third item (say, theme park income), add its value to the total for the first two items. The top line indicates the total of the three values.

Pie charts are most useful in showing the proportion of parts to a whole.

Pie Charts. Pie, or circle, charts enable readers to see a whole and the proportion of its components, or wedges. Although less flexible than bar or line charts, pie charts are useful in showing percentages, as Figure 11.20 illustrates. They are very effective for lay or nonexpert audiences. Notice that a wedge can be "exploded" or popped out for special emphasis, as seen in Figure 11.20. MS Excel and other spreadsheet programs provide a selection of three-dimensional pie charts. For the most effective pie charts, follow these suggestions:

- Make the biggest wedge appear first. Computer spreadsheet programs correctly assign the biggest wedge first (beginning at the 12 o'clock position) and arrange

FIGURE 11.17 Simple Line Chart

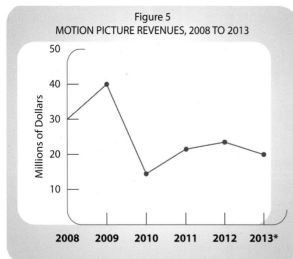

Figure 5
MOTION PICTURE REVENUES, 2008 TO 2013

FIGURE 11.18 Multiple Line Chart

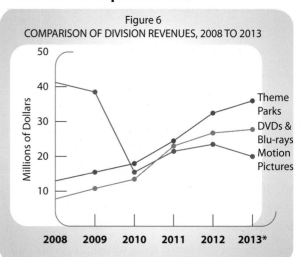

Figure 6
COMPARISON OF DIVISION REVENUES, 2008 TO 2013

FIGURE 11.19 Segmented Line (Surface) Chart

FIGURE 11.20 Pie Chart

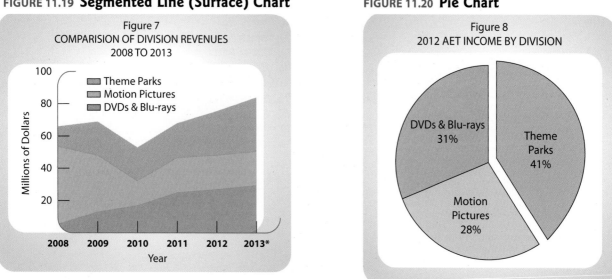

the others in order of decreasing size as long as you list the data representing each wedge on the spreadsheet in descending order.

- Include, if possible, the actual percentage or absolute value for each wedge.
- Use four to six segments for best results; if necessary, group small portions into a wedge called *Other*.
- Draw radii from the centre.
- Distinguish wedges with colour, shading, or cross-hatching.
- Keep all the labels horizontal.

Flowcharts. Procedures are simplified and clarified by diagramming them in a flow-chart, as shown in Figure 11.21. Whether you need to describe the procedure for handling a customer's purchase, highlight steps in solving a problem, or display a problem with a process, flowcharts help the reader visualize the process. Traditional flowcharts use the following symbols:

- Ovals to designate the beginning and end of a process
- Diamonds to designate decision points
- Rectangles to represent major activities or steps

Organization Charts. Many large organizations are so complex that they need charts to show the chain of command, from the boss down to the line managers and employees. Organization charts provide such information as who reports to whom, how many subordinates work for each manager (the span of control), and what channels of official communication exist. These charts may illustrate a company's structure, for example, by function, customer, or product. They may also be organized by the work being performed in each job or by the hierarchy of decision making.

> Organization charts show the line of command and thus the flow of official communication from management to employees.

Photographs, Maps, and Illustrations. Some business reports include photographs, maps, and illustrations to serve specific purposes. Photos, for example, add authenticity and provide a visual record. An environmental engineer may use photos to document hazardous waste sites. Maps enable report writers to depict activities or

FIGURE 11.21 Flowchart

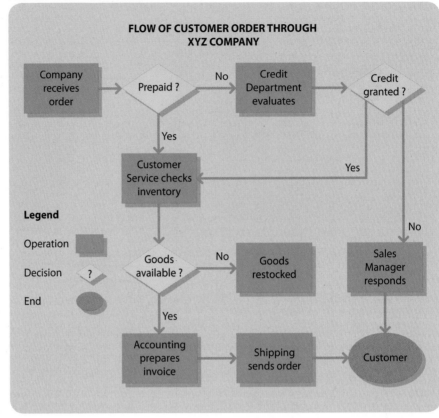

FLOW OF CUSTOMER ORDER THROUGH XYZ COMPANY

Legend

Operation

Decision ?

End

---

concentrations geographically, such as dots indicating sales reps in provinces and territories across the country. Illustrations and diagrams are useful in indicating how an object looks or operates. A drawing showing the parts of a printer with labels describing their functions, for example, is more instructive than a photograph or verbal description. With today's computer technology, photographs, maps, and illustrations can be scanned directly into business reports, or they can be accessed through hyperlinks within an electronically delivered document.

Incorporating Graphics in Reports

Used appropriately, graphics make reports more interesting and easier to understand. In putting graphics into your reports, follow these suggestions for best effects:

- **Evaluate the audience.** Consider the reader, the content, your schedule, and your budget. Graphics take time and can be costly to print in colour, so think carefully before deciding how many graphics to use. Six charts in an internal report to an executive may seem like overkill, but in a long technical report to outsiders, six may be too few.

- **Use restraint.** Don't overuse colour or decorations. Although colour can effectively distinguish bars or segments in charts, too much colour can be distracting and confusing. Remember, too, that colours themselves sometimes convey meaning: reds suggest deficits or negative values, blues suggest calmness and authority, and yellow may suggest warning.

- **Be accurate and ethical.** Double-check all graphics for accuracy of figures and calculations. Be certain that your visuals aren't misleading—either accidentally or intentionally. Manipulation of a chart scale can make trends look steeper and more dramatic than they really are. Moreover, be sure to cite sources when you use someone else's facts. The Ethical Insights box discusses in more detail how to make ethical charts and graphs.

- **Introduce a graphic meaningfully.** Refer to every graphic in the text and place the graphic close to the point where it is mentioned. Most important, though, help the reader understand the significance of the graphic. You can do this by telling the reader what to look for or by summarizing the main point of the graphic. Don't assume the reader will automatically draw the same conclusions you reached from a set of data. Instead of *The findings are shown in Figure 3*, tell the reader what to look for: *Two thirds of the responding employees, as shown in Figure 3, favour a flextime schedule.* The best introductions for graphics interpret them for readers.

- **Choose an appropriate caption or title style.** Like reports, graphics may use "talking" titles or generic, descriptive titles. Talking titles are more persuasive; they tell the reader what to think. Descriptive titles describe the facts more objectively.

> Graphics should be introduced by statements that help readers interpret them.

Talking Title
Average Annual Health Care Costs per Worker Rise Steeply as Workers Grow Older

Descriptive Title
Average Annual Health Care Costs per Worker as Shown by Age Groups

ETHICAL INSIGHTS

Making Ethical Charts and Graphics

Business communicators must present graphical data in the same ethical, honest manner required for all other messages. Remember that the information shown in your charts and graphics will be used to inform others or help them make decisions. If this information is not represented accurately, the reader will be incorrectly informed; any decisions based on the data are likely to be faulty. And mistakes in interpreting such information may have serious and long-lasting consequences.

Chart data can be distorted in many ways. Figure 1 shows advertising expenses displayed on an appropriate scale. Figure 2 shows the same information, but the horizontal scale, from 2008 to 2013, has been lengthened. Notice that the data have not changed, but the increases and decreases are smoothed out, so changes in expenses appear to be slight. In Figure 3 the vertical scale is taller and the horizontal scale is shortened,

resulting in what appear to be sharp increases and decreases in expenses.

To avoid misrepresenting data, keep the following pointers in mind when designing your graphics:

- Use an appropriate type of chart or graphic for the message you want to convey.

- Design the chart so that it focuses on the appropriate information.

- Include all relevant or important data; don't arbitrarily leave out necessary information.

- Don't hide critical information by including too much data in one graphic.

- Use appropriate scales with equal intervals for the data you present.

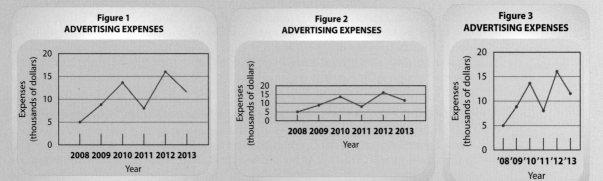

Summary of Learning Objectives

1 **Describe basic features of business reports, including functions, strategies (indirect or direct), writing style, and formats.** Business reports generally function either as informational reports (without analysis or recommendations) or as analytical reports (with analysis, conclusions, and possibly recommendations). Reports organized directly present the purpose and conclusions immediately. This strategy is appropriate when the audience is supportive and familiar with the topic. Reports organized indirectly provide the conclusions and recommendations last. This strategy is helpful when the audience is unfamiliar with the problem or may be disappointed or hostile. Reports written in a formal style use third-person constructions (*the researcher* instead of *I*), avoid contractions (*do not* instead of *don't*), and may include passive-voice verbs (*the findings were analyzed*). Reports written informally use first-person constructions, contractions, shorter sentences, familiar words, and active-voice verbs. Reports may be formatted as letters, memos, e-mails, manuscripts, prepared forms, or electronic slides.

2 **Apply the 3-×-3 writing process to business reports to create well-organized documents that show a firm grasp of audience and purpose.** Report writers begin by analyzing a problem and writing a problem statement, which may include the scope, significance, and limitations of the project. Writers then analyze the audience and define major issues. They prepare a work plan, including a tentative outline and work schedule. They collect, organize, interpret, and illustrate their data. Then they compose the first draft. Finally, they revise (often many times), proofread, and evaluate.

3 **Find, evaluate, and use print and electronic secondary sources.** Secondary data may be located by searching for books, periodicals, and newspapers through print or electronic indexes. Writers can look for information by using electronic databases, such as ABI/INFORM and LexisNexis. They may also find information on the Internet, but searching for it requires a knowledge of search tools and techniques. Popular search tools include Google, Yahoo, and Bing. Once found, however, information obtained on the Internet should be scrutinized for currency, authority, content, and accuracy.

4 **Understand how to generate and use primary data while avoiding researcher bias.** Researchers generate firsthand, primary data through surveys (in-person, print, and online), interviews, observation, and experimentation. Surveys are most economical and efficient for gathering information from large groups of people. Interviews are useful when working with experts in a field. First-hand observation can produce rich data, but they must be objective. Experimentation produces data that suggest causes and effects. Valid experiments require sophisticated research designs and careful attention to matching the experimental and control groups.

5 **Comprehend fast-changing communication technology: the Web, electronic databases, and other resources for business writers and researchers.** The World Wide Web is used every day by individuals and organizations for business and pleasure. A vast resource, the Web offers a wealth of varied and often uneven secondary data. It is a complex network of information from private citizens, businesses, and other institutions that form a global virtual community. At the same time, these users also announce and advertise their local presence. Business communicators must be aware that information online changes rapidly and is not considered as lasting as scholarly sources. Making the most of Web sites means being a critical consumer of the information retrieved and understanding the function of Web search tools. Honest researchers keep track of the retrieved data and incorporate them ethically into their documents.

6 **Recognize the purposes and techniques of documentation in business reports, and avoid plagiarism.** Documentation means giving credit to information sources. Careful writers document data to strengthen an argument, protect against charges of plagiarism, and instruct readers. Although documentation is less strict in business reports than in academic reports, business writers should learn proper techniques to be able to verify their sources and to avoid charges of plagiarism. Report writers should document others' ideas, facts that are not common knowledge, quotations, and paraphrases. Good note taking, either manual or electronic, enables writers to give accurate credit to sources. Paraphrasing involves putting another's ideas into your own words. Quotations may be used to provide objective background data, to repeat memorable phrasing, and to duplicate exact wording before criticizing.

7 **Create meaningful and interesting graphics; display numeric information in the appropriate graphic form; and skillfully generate, use, and convert data to visual aids.** Good graphics improve reports by clarifying, simplifying, and emphasizing data. Tables organize precise data into rows and columns. Bar and line charts enable data to be compared visually. Line charts are especially helpful in showing changes over time. Pie charts show a whole and the proportion of its components. Organization charts, pictures, maps, and illustrations serve specific purposes. In choosing or crafting graphics, effective communicators evaluate their audience, purpose, topic, and budget to determine the number and kind of graphics. They write "talking" titles (telling readers what to think about the graphic) or descriptive titles (summarizing the topic objectively). Finally, they work carefully to avoid distorting visual aids.

Chapter Review

1. What are the main purposes of business reports? (Obj. 1)
2. Describe the writing style of typical business reports. (Obj. 1)
3. Name five common report formats. (Obj. 1)
4. List the seven steps in the report-writing process. (Obj. 2)
5. What is a statement of purpose, and what function does it serve? (Obj. 2)
6. Compare primary data and secondary data. Give an original example of each. (Obj. 3, 4)
7. Name at least two of the top four business databases and identify their chief strengths. (Objs. 3, 5)
8. List four major sources of primary information. (Obj. 4)
9. How can you ensure that your survey will be effective and appeal to as many respondents as possible? (Obj. 4)

10. Why are your professors likely to discourage your use of Wikipedia, blogs, and many other sources found on the Web as sources in your reports? (Obj. 5)
11. Can any single search engine index all Web pages? How can you optimize your search of Web sources? (Obj. 5)
12. Describe what documentation is and why it is necessary in reports. (Obj. 6)
13. In what way is documentation of sources different in colleges and universities than in business? (Obj. 6)
14. Briefly compare the advantages and disadvantages of illustrating data with charts (bar and line) versus tables. (Obj. 7)
15. Name five techniques you can use to ensure that visual aids do not distort graphic information. (Obj. 7)

Critical Thinking

1. Why do businesses spend so much time producing reports, both informational and analytical? Why do they compose long reports when no one seems to have time to read them?
2. Why must report writers anticipate their audiences and issues? (Obj. 2)
3. Is information obtained on the Web as reliable as information obtained from journals, newspapers, and magazines? (Obj. 3)
4. Some people say that business reports never contain footnotes. If you were writing your first report for a business

and you did considerable research, what would you do about documenting your sources? (Obj. 6)

5. **Ethical Issue:** Your sales team has experienced a sharp decline of revenue after the departure of the two top sellers, and you dread the sales meeting at headquarters where the latest numbers will be crunched and compared with past performance. Your presentation partner suggests that you stretch the timeline of your graphic to make the drop in sales revenue look less steep. Should you go along?

Activities

11.1 Report Functions, Writing Styles, and Formats (Obj. 1)

Your Task. For the following reports, (a) name the report's primary function (informational or analytical), (b) recommend a direct or an indirect pattern of development, and (c) select a report format (memo, letter, or manuscript).

a. A feasibility report in the leisure industry put together by consultants who compare the potential of a future theme park at two different sites

b. A report submitted by a sales rep to her manager describing her attendance at a marathon prerace exhibition, including the reactions of runners to a new low-carbohydrate energy drink

c. A recommendation report from a special review team (composed of members of the board of directors and staff) to the executive director of a major nonprofit organization to outline the necessary computer and phone system upgrades for the organization's headquarters building

d. A progress report from a location manager to a Toronto production company describing safety, fire, and environmental precautions taken for the shooting of a stunt involving blowing up a power boat in Toronto Harbour

e. A report prepared by an outside consultant examining whether a sports franchise should refurbish its stadium or look to relocate to another city

11.2 Data Forms and Questions (Obj. 3)

Your Task. In conducting research for the following reports, name at least one form of data you will need and questions you should ask to determine whether that set of data is appropriate (see Figure 11.6).

a. A report on business attire in banking that you must submit to your company's executives who want to issue a formal professional dress code on the job

b. A report by the Concerned Children's Advertisers (CCA) investigating the nutritional value of products advertised on afternoon and Saturday television for kids[12]

c. A report examining the effectiveness of ethics codes in Canadian businesses

11.3 Problem, Purpose, and Scope Statements (Obj. 2)

Your Task. The following situations require reports. For each situation write (a) a concise problem question, (b) a simple statement of purpose, and (c) a scope statement.

a. Last winter a severe ice storm damaged more than 50 percent of the maple trees lining the main street in the small town of Somerset. The local university's experts believe that more than 70 percent of the damaged trees will die in the next two years and that this variety is not the best one for providing shade (one of the major reasons for planting them ten years ago).

b. The B.C. provincial government announced new restrictions on Friday to limit trans fats, which have been linked to a higher incidence of heart disease and other health problems, in all food prepared and served in B.C. restaurants, cafeterias, bakeries, delis, schools, and healthcare and educational institutions. The rules, which take effect September 30, will make B.C. the first province in Canada to regulate the use of trans fats. The Thin Crust Bakery worries that it may have to change its production process and rewrite all its package labels. Thin Crust doesn't know whether to hire a laboratory or a consultant for this project.

c. Customers placing telephone orders for outdoor gear with REI typically order only one or two items. The company wonders whether it can train telephone service reps to motivate customers to increase the number of items ordered per call.

11.4 Plagiarism, Paraphrasing, and Citing Sources (Obj. 6)

One of the biggest problems for student writers is paraphrasing secondary sources correctly to avoid plagiarism.

Your Task. For each of the following, read the original passage. Analyze the paraphrased version. List the weaknesses in relation to what you have learned about plagiarism and the use of references. Then write an improved version.

a. **Original Passage**

The collapse in the cost of computing has made cellular communication economically viable. Worldwide, one in two new phone subscriptions is cellular. The digital revolution in telephony is most advanced in poorer countries because they have been able to skip the outdated technological step of relying on land lines.

Paraphrased Passage

The drop in computing costs now makes cellular communication affordable around the world. In fact, one out of every two new phones is cellular. The digital revolution in cellular telephones is developing faster in poorer countries because they could skip the outdated technological process of using land lines (Henderson 44).

b. **Original Passage**

Search site Yahoo kept world news prominent on its front page because users feel secure knowing that it is easily accessible, even if they don't often click it. Conspicuous placement also went to entertainment, which draws heavy traffic from people seeking a diversion at work. By contrast, seemingly work-related content such as finance gets ample use in the evening when people pay bills and manage personal portfolios.[13]

Paraphrased Passage

Search giant Yahoo kept news prominent on its portal since its customers feel good knowing it is there, even though they don't read it much. Such noticeable placement was also used for entertainment news that attracts heavy traffic from users searching for a distraction at work. As opposed to that, what may seem work related, such as finance, is much visited at night when people pay their bills and manage their portfolios.

11.5 Factoring and Outlining a Problem (Obj. 2)

Japan Airlines (JAL) has asked your company, Connections International, to prepare a proposal for a training school for tour operators. JAL wants to know whether Victoria would be a good spot for its school. Victoria interests JAL but only if nearby entertainment facilities can be used for tour training. JAL also needs an advisory committee consisting, if possible, of representatives of the travel community and perhaps executives of other major airlines. The real problem is how to motivate these people to cooperate with JAL.

You think that Camosun College's Hospitality and Tourism program in Victoria might offer training seminars, guest speakers, and other resources for tour operators. You wonder whether the Royal British Columbia Museum would also be willing to cooperate with the proposed school. And you remember that Craigdarroch Castle is nearby and might make a good tour training spot. Before JAL will settle on Victoria as its choice, it wants to know whether access to air travel is adequate. JAL's management team is also concerned about available school building space. Moreover, JAL wants to know whether city officials in Victoria would be receptive to this tour training school proposal.

Your Task. To guide your thinking and research, factor this problem into an outline with several areas to investigate. Further divide the problem into subproblems, phrasing each entry as a question. For example, *Should the JAL tour training program be located in Victoria?* (See the work plan model in Figure 11.5.)

11.6 Using Secondary Sources (Obj. 3)

Secondary sources can provide quite different information depending on your mode of inquiry.

Your Task. Pick a business-related subject you want to know more about and run it through a search engine, such as Google. Compare your results with Dogpile, a metasearch site. Write a short memo or e-mail message to your instructor explaining the differences in the search results. In your message, describe what you have learned about the advantages and disadvantages of each search tool.

11.7 Creating an Online Survey With SurveyMonkey or Zoomerang (Obj. 4)

Your Campus Business Club (CBC) is abuzz about a Sodexo study that surveyed North American postsecondary students about their favourite comfort foods. Food service provider Sodexo tracks flavour trends, holds taste test focus groups with students, and consults with top-notch chefs to identify students' favourite cafeteria foods. The current top three items are apricot-glazed turkey, meatloaf with frizzle-dried onions, and pho, a wholesome Vietnamese beef and rice noodle soup. You read the Sodexo press release and decide to use this quotation in your report:

"Comfort food is trendy for students because familiar favourites can alleviate stress linked to studying and being away from home," said Tom Post, Sodexo president of campus services. "The biggest change we're seeing is that students are expanding the category of feel-good foods to include comfort world cuisine, such as a Mexican stew or a Vietnamese noodle soup, and they are more open to vegetarian dishes with a flair."[14]

CBC wants to advocate for a new small student-run restaurant in the campus food court. Your club colleagues have chosen you to create an online survey to poll fellow students, staff, and faculty about their preferences. You hope to generate data that will support the feasibility of the eatery.

The two main providers of online survey software, SurveyMonkey and Zoomerang, make creating questionnaires fast, fun, and easy. Depending on their research needs and the survey features they desire, businesses subscribe to the two survey creation services for fees ranging from $17 to $20 (SurveyMonkey) or $20 to $150 (Zoomerang) per month. As long as you sign up for the free no-frills basic plans, you can create brief online questionnaires and e-mail the links to your targeted respondents. The programs analyze and display the results for you—at no charge.

Your Task. In pairs or teams of three, design a questionnaire to survey students on your campus about comfort food options in the campus cafeteria. Visit **www.surveymonkey.com** or **www.zoomerang.com**, and sign up for the basic plan. You may also want to view the Sodexo Web site at **www.sodexo.ca**.

After creating the online survey, e-mail the survey link to as many members of the campus community as possible. Interpret the results. As a team, write a memo to the campus food services advocating for the top-scoring national or regional comfort food type.

Your instructor may ask you to complete this activity as a report or proposal assignment after you study Chapter 12. If so, write a feasibility report or proposal for the campus food services and support your advocacy with the survey results.

11.8 Finding Secondary Data: The Future of Tech (Objs. 3, 5, and 6)

Are you a member of the "thumb generation"? Can you work the keyboard of your cellphone or personal digital assistant faster than most people can speak? The term "thumb generation" was coined in South Korea and Japan and is applied to young people under 25 who furiously use their handheld devices to text message, e-mail, and complete other electronic functions at lightning speed.

More technological innovations are coming that are likely to transform our lives. WiMAX is a new wireless supertechnology that will cover entire cities at cable speeds. New-Field Communication (NFC) takes the Bluetooth technology a step further to connect cellphones and other devices. NFC is touted for its boundless commercial applications enabling North Americans soon to complete many sales transactions by cellphone, as is already customary in Korea, Japan, and Finland. These and other trends are described in a *BusinessWeek* article titled "Upward Mobility,"[15] which your boss pulled out of his files to show you. However, you know that you can find more current discussions of future national and global technology trends online.

Your Task. You are one of several marketing interns at MarketNet Global, a worldwide e-commerce specialist. Your busy boss, Rick Rivera, wants to know more about the cutting-edge trends described in a newspaper article he saw. He is particularly interested in learning whether they might be successfully used in selling and marketing. Individually or as a team, research one or several of these high-tech concepts. Chances are you will not find scholarly articles on these subjects because peer-reviewed publications take years to complete. Instead, rely on the Web and on electronic databases to find up-to-date information. If you use search engines, you will retrieve many forum and discussion board contributions as well. Examine them critically for authority and validity. In teams or individually, write an informative memo to Rick Rivera, complete with a short list of references in MLA or APA documentation style. Explain what each new trend is. Your instructor may ask you to complete this activity as a report assignment after you study Chapter 12. You could use your research to write a short informational memo report describing to Rick Rivera what your sources suggest the new trends may mean for the future of business, specifically e-commerce and online marketing.

11.9 Selecting Graphics (Obj. 7)

Your Task. Identify the best graphics form to illustrate the following data.

a. Figures comparing the costs of cable, DSL, and satellite Internet service in ten major Canadian metropolitan areas for the past ten years (for a parliamentary investigation)

b. Figures showing the process of delivering electricity to a metropolitan area

c. Data showing areas in Canada most likely to have earthquakes

d. Data showing the academic, administrative, and operation divisions of a college, from the president to department chairs and division managers

e. Percentages showing the causes of forest fires (lightning, 73 percent; arson, 5 percent; campfires, 9 percent; and so on) in the Rocky Mountains

11.10 Avoiding Huge Credit Card Debt for Postsecondary Students (Objs. 3, 5, and 6)

> WEB

> CONSUMER

Recent college and university graduates face an astounding amount of debt, with the total accumulated debt now exceeding $13 billion, according to the Canada Student Loans Program. This translates into an average of more than $20,000 per graduate across the country.[16] Part of this debt is due to increasing numbers of easy-to-obtain, high-interest credit cards. Because they can't buy cars, rent homes, or purchase insurance, graduates with big credit debt see a bleak future for themselves.

A local newspaper plans to run a self-help story about credit cards for postsecondary students. The editor asks you, a young part-time reporter, to prepare a memo with information that could be turned into an article. The article would be targeted to parents of students who are about to leave for college or university. What can parents do to help students avoid sinking deeply into credit card debt?

Your Task. Using ABI/INFORM, Factiva, or LexisNexis and the Web, locate basic information about student credit card options. In a memo discuss shared credit cards and other options. Your goal is to be informative, not to reach conclusions or make recommendations. Use one or more of the techniques discussed in this chapter to track your sources. Address your memo to Barbara Hagler, Editor.

Grammar and Mechanics C.L.U.E. Review 11

Total Review

The first ten chapters reviewed specific guides from Appendix A: Grammar and Mechanics Guide (Competent Language Usage Essentials). The remaining exercises are total reviews, covering all the grammar and mechanics guides and confusing words and frequently misspelled words.

Each of the following sentences has a total of **three** errors in grammar, punctuation, capitalization, usage, or spelling. On a separate sheet, write a correct version. Avoid adding new phrases, starting new sentences, or rewriting in your own words. When finished, compare your responses with the key beginning on page Key-1.

Example: To succede as a knowledge worker in todays digital work-place you need highly developed communication skills.
Revision: To **succeed** as a knowledge worker in **today's** digital **workplace**, you need highly developed communication skills.

1. The recruiter cited studys showing that mangers leave, when they lose autonomy.

2. As they are working more than forty hours a week without overtime pay, most proffesionals today wonder weather their jobs can survive the recession.

3. One organization paid three thousand dollars each for twelve employees to attend a one week workshop in communication training.

4. My company spend five hundred dollars on ink cartridges every month, but the cost doesn't worry my partner and I because our printed materials look sharp and professional.

5. If you find a open document on a colleague's computer screen its inappropriate to peek.

6. Todays workers should brush up their marketable skills otherwise they may not find another job after being laid off.

7. On June 1st our company President revealed a four million dollar drop in profits, which was bad news for everyone.

8. Most of us prefer to be let down gently, when we are being refused something, that is why the reasons before refusal pattern is effective.

9. Between you and I, if we where to share a ride each morning we would save a lot of money.

10. Despite the recent economic downturn our President and CEO gave an optimistic assessment of the companys outlook.

Endnotes

[1] City Librarian. (2010, May 10). 2009 annual performance measures and strategic plan update. Retrieved September 8, 2011, from http://www.torontopubliclibrary.ca/content/about-the-library/pdfs/board/meetings/2010/may10/17.pdf; Government of Nova Scotia. (n.d.). Use of public libraries in hard economic times. Retrieved April 13, 2011, fromhttp://www.library.ns.ca/content/use-public-libraries-hard-economic-times

[2] Brennan, M., & Holdershaw, J. (1999). The effect of question tone and form on responses to open-ended questions: Further data. *Marketing Bulletin*, 57–64.

[3] Goldsmith, B. (2002, June). The awesome power of asking the right questions. *OfficeSolutions*, 52; Bracey, G. W. (2001, November). Research-question authority. *Phi Delta Kappan*, 191.

[4] Miniwatts Marketing Group. (2011, July 12). Canada: Internet usage, broadband and telecommunications reports. Retrieved September 8, 2011, from http://www.internetworldstats.com/am/ca.htm

[5] Lenhart, A. (2009, October 8). The democratization of online social networks. Pew Internet & American Life Project, slide 4. Retrieved January 22, 2010, from http://www.pewinternet.org/Presentations/2009/41--The-Democratization-of-Online-Social-Networks.aspx

[6] Netcraft, Ltd. (n.d.) January 2010 Web server survey. Retrieved January 22, 2010, from http://news.netcraft.com/archives/web_server_survey.html

[7] Little, L. (2006, March 7). Using a multiple search. *The Wall Street Journal*, p. D1. Retrieved November 23, 2006, from Factiva database.

[8] Canada PM faces plagiarism claim. (2008, October 1). *BBC News*. Retrieved July 9, 2009, from http://news.bbc.co.uk/2/hi/americas/7645593.stm

[9] Writing Tutorial Services, Indiana University. (2004, 27 April). Plagiarism: What it is and how to recognize and avoid it. Retrieved November 5, 2006, from http://www.indiana.edu/~wts/pamphlets/plagiarism.shtml

[10] Bonoguore, T. (2009, March 31). Canadian census sees cities surging. *The Globe and Mail*. Retrieved June 1, 2009, from http://www.theglobeandmail.com/news/national/article745946.ece

[11] Brady, D. (2006, December 4). *!#?@ the e-mail. Can we talk? *BusinessWeek*, p. 109.

[12] Children's food and beverage advertising initiative: Kellogg Canada Inc. commitment. (2008). Retrieved July 29, 2009, from http://www.adstandards.com/en/childrensinitiative/Kellogg_E.pdf

[13] Hibbard, J. (2006, October 9). How Yahoo! gave itself a face-lift. *BusinessWeek*, p. 77.

[14] 2010 college food trends: Students crave global, national and regional comfort food with a twist. (2009, December 14). *SodexoUSA.com*. Retrieved February 5, 2010, from http://www.sodexousa.com/usen/newsroom/press/press09/2010collegefoodtrends.asp

[15] Edwards, C., & Ihlwan, M. (2006, December 4). Upward mobility. *BusinessWeek*, pp. 68–82.

[16] Financial Consumer Agency of Canada. (2009, April 12). Credit cards and you: Getting the most from your credit card. Retrieved July 31, 2009, from http://www.fcac-acfc.gc.ca/eng/publications/creditcardsyou/gettingthemost/default.asp; McFeat, T. (2006, September 12). Buy now, pay later: Canadians in debt. *CBCNews Online*. Retrieved July 31, 2009, from http://www.cbc.ca/news/background/personalfinance/debt.html; Shmuel, J. (2009, January 21). Student debt exceed $13-billion in Canada. *FP Posted*. Retrieved July 31, 2009, from http://www.cbc.ca/ news/background/personalfinance/debt.html

CHAPTER 12

Informal Business Reports

OBJECTIVES

After studying this chapter, you should be able to

1. Tabulate information, use statistical techniques, and create decision matrices to sort and interpret business report data skillfully and accurately.

2. Draw meaningful conclusions and make practical report recommendations after sound and valid analysis.

3. Organize report data logically and provide cues to aid comprehension.

4. Write short informational reports that describe routine tasks.

5. Compose short analytical reports that solve business problems.

© Fancy/Alamy

springboard to discussion

Social media provides an excellent opportunity for companies to tap into customers' needs and wants. Successful companies are capturing the information from Facebook and Twitter, which are packed with instant feedback about people's likes and dislikes. Proactive companies are listening; for example,

Scene, the rewards program created by Cineplex and Scotiabank, enhanced their program based on feedback posted on Facebook.[1] How can the use of social media help companies research trends and perceptions? Why are these platforms valuable tools in meeting customer needs?

Interpreting Data

Organizations need information to stay abreast of what is happening inside and outside their firms. Much of the information that allows decision makers to run their organizations efficiently comes to them in the form of reports. This chapter focuses on interpreting and organizing data, drawing conclusions, providing reader cues, and writing informal business reports.

Collecting information is effortless today, given the easy access to electronic databases, the Web, and other sources of digitized information. However, making sense of the massive amounts of data you may collect is much harder. You may feel overwhelmed as you look at a jumble of digital files, printouts, note cards, copies of articles, interview notes, questionnaire results, and statistics. It is a little like being a contractor who allowed suppliers to dump all the building materials for a new house in a monstrous pile. Like the contractor, you must sort the jumble of raw material into meaningful, usable groups. Unprocessed data become meaningful information through skillful and accurate sorting, analysis, combination, and recombination. You will be examining each item to see what it means by itself and what it means when connected with other data. You are looking for meanings, relationships, and answers to the research questions posed in your work plan.

LEARNING OBJECTIVE 1

Tabulate information, use statistical techniques, and create decision matrices to sort and interpret business report data skillfully and accurately.

> **Interpreting data means sorting, analyzing, combining, and recombining to yield meaningful information.**

Tabulating and Analyzing Responses

If you have collected considerable numerical and other information, you must tabulate and analyze it. Fortunately, several tabulating and statistical techniques can help you create order from the chaos. These techniques simplify, summarize, and classify large amounts of data into meaningful terms. From the condensed data, you are more likely to be able to draw valid conclusions and make reasoned recommendations. The most helpful summarizing techniques include tables, statistical concepts (mean, median, and mode), correlations, grids, and decision matrices.

Tables. Numerical data from questionnaires or interviews are usually summarized and simplified in tables. Using systematic columns and rows, tables make quantitative information easier to comprehend. After assembling your data, you will want to prepare preliminary tables to enable you to see what the information means. Here is a table summarizing the response to one question from a campus survey about student parking:

> **Numerical data must be tabulated and analyzed statistically to bring order out of chaos.**

Question: Should student fees be increased to build parking lots?

	Number	Percentage	
Strongly agree	76	11.5	} To simplify the table, combine these items.
Agree	255	38.5	
No opinion	22	3.3	
Disagree	107	16.1	} To simplify the table, combine these items.
Strongly disagree	203	30.6	
Total	**663**	**100.0**	

Notice that this preliminary table includes a total number of responses and a percentage for each response. (To calculate a percentage, divide the number for each response by the total number of responses times 100.) To simplify the data and provide a broad overview, you can join categories. For example, combining *Strongly agree* (11.5 percent) and *Agree* (38.5 percent) reveals that 50 percent of the respondents supported the proposal to finance new parking lots with increased student fees.

Sometimes data become more meaningful when cross-tabulated. This process allows analysis of two or more variables together. By breaking down our student survey data into male and female responses, shown in the following table, we make an interesting discovery.

Question: Should student fees be increased to build parking lots?

	Total		Male		Female	
	Number	Percentage	Number	Percentage	Number	Percentage
Strongly agree	76	11.5	8	2.2	68	22.0
Agree	255	38.5	54	15.3	201	65.0
No opinion	22	3.3	12	3.4	10	3.2
Disagree	107	16.1	89	25.1	18	5.8
Strongly disagree	203	30.6	191	54.0	12	4.0
Total	**663**	**100.0**	**354**	**100.0**	**309**	**100.0**

Although 50 percent of all student respondents supported the proposal, among females the approval rating was much stronger. Notice that 87 percent of female respondents (combining 22 percent *Strongly agree* and 65 percent *Agree*) endorsed the proposal to increase fees for new parking lots. But among male students, only 17 percent agreed with the proposal. You naturally wonder why such a disparity exists. *Are female students more unhappy than male students with the current parking situation? If so, why? Is safety a reason? Are male students more concerned with increased fees than female students are?*

By cross-tabulating the findings, you sometimes uncover data that may help answer your problem question or that may prompt you to explore other possibilities. Do not, however, undertake cross-tabulation unless it serves more than mere curiosity. Tables also help you compare multiple data collected from questionnaires and surveys. Figure 12.1 shows, in raw form, responses to several survey items. To convert these data into a more usable form, you need to calculate percentages for each item. Then you can arrange the responses in some rational sequence, such as largest percentage to smallest.

Once the data are displayed in a table, you can more easily draw conclusions. As Figure 12.1 shows, North Shore College students apparently are not interested in public transportation or shuttle buses from satellite lots. They want to park on campus, with restricted visitor parking, and only half are willing to pay for new parking lots.

> Three statistical concepts—mean, median, and mode—help you describe data.

The Three Ms: Mean, Median, Mode. Tables help you organize data, and the three Ms help you describe it. These statistical terms—mean, median, and mode—are all occasionally used loosely to mean "average." To be safe, though, you should learn to apply these statistical terms precisely. When people say *average,* they usually intend to indicate the *mean,* or arithmetic average. Let's say that you are studying the estimated starting salaries of graduates from various disciplines:

> A range of starting salaries becomes more meaningful when one can see a mode, median, and mean.

Education	$ 41,000	*Mode (number occurring most frequently)*
Sociology	41,000	
Humanities	41,000	
Biology	45,000	
Health sciences	50,000	*Median (middle point in continuum)*
Business	56,000	*Mean (arithmetic average)*
Engineering	60,000	
Law	65,000	
Medicine	105,000	

FIGURE 12.1 **Converting Survey Data Into Finished Tables**

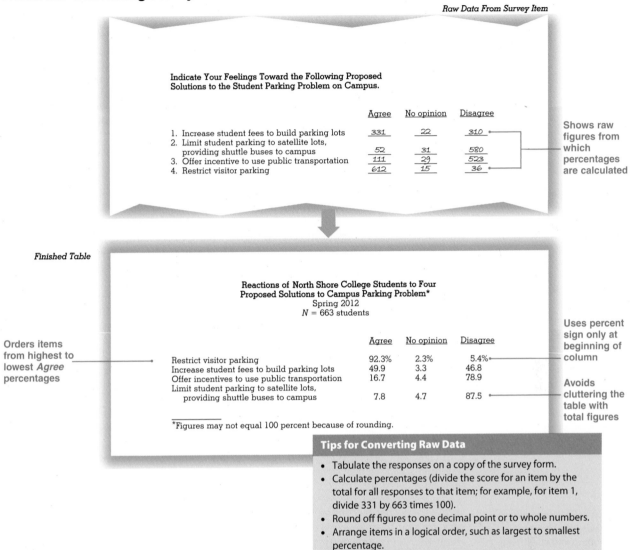

Raw Data From Survey Item

Indicate Your Feelings Toward the Following Proposed Solutions to the Student Parking Problem on Campus.

	Agree	No opinion	Disagree
1. Increase student fees to build parking lots	331	22	310
2. Limit student parking to satellite lots, providing shuttle buses to campus	52	31	580
3. Offer incentive to use public transportation	111	29	523
4. Restrict visitor parking	612	15	36

Shows raw figures from which percentages are calculated

Finished Table

Reactions of North Shore College Students to Four Proposed Solutions to Campus Parking Problem*
Spring 2012
N = 663 students

	Agree	No opinion	Disagree
Restrict visitor parking	92.3%	2.3%	5.4%
Increase student fees to build parking lots	49.9	3.3	46.8
Offer incentives to use public transportation	16.7	4.4	78.9
Limit student parking to satellite lots, providing shuttle buses to campus	7.8	4.7	87.5

*Figures may not equal 100 percent because of rounding.

Orders items from highest to lowest *Agree* percentages

Uses percent sign only at beginning of column

Avoids cluttering the table with total figures

Tips for Converting Raw Data

- Tabulate the responses on a copy of the survey form.
- Calculate percentages (divide the score for an item by the total for all responses to that item; for example, for item 1, divide 331 by 663 times 100).
- Round off figures to one decimal point or to whole numbers.
- Arrange items in a logical order, such as largest to smallest percentage.
- Prepare a table with a title that tells such things as who, what, when, where, and why.
- Include the total number of respondents.

To find the mean, you add up all the salaries and divide by the total number of items ($504,000 ÷ 9 = $56,000). Therefore, the mean salary is $56,000. Means are very useful to indicate central tendencies of numbers, but they have one major flaw: extremes at either end cause distortion. Notice that the $105,000 figure makes the mean salary of $56,000 deceptively high. It does not represent a valid average for the group. Because means can be misleading, you should use them only when extreme numbers do not distort the result.

The median represents the midpoint in a group of numbers arranged from lowest to highest (or vice versa). In our list of salaries, the median is $50,000 (health sciences). In other words, half the salaries are above this point, and half are below it. The median is useful when extreme numbers may warp the mean. Although salaries for medicine distort the mean, the median, at $50,000, is still a representative number.

The mean is the arithmetic average; the median is the midpoint in a group of numbers; the mode is the most frequently occurring number.

The mode is the value that occurs most frequently. In our list $41,000 (for education, sociology, and the humanities) is the mode because it occurs three times. The mode has the advantage of being easily determined—just a quick glance at a list of arranged values reveals it. Although mode is infrequently used by researchers, knowing the mode is useful in some situations. To remember the meaning of mode, think about fashion; the most frequent response, the mode, is the most fashionable.

Mean, median, and mode numbers are especially helpful when the range of values is also known. Range represents the span between the highest and lowest values. To calculate the range, you simply subtract the lowest number from the highest. In starting salaries for graduates, the range is $64,000 ($105,000–$41,000). Knowing the range enables readers to put mean and median numbers into perspective. This knowledge also prompts researchers to wonder why such a range exists, thus stimulating hunches and further investigation to solve problems.

Correlations between variables suggest possible relationships that will explain research findings.

Correlations. In tabulating and analyzing data, you may see relationships among two or more variables that help explain the findings. If your data for graduates' starting salaries also included years of education, you would doubtless notice that graduates with more years of education received higher salaries. For example, beginning teachers, with four to five years of education, earn less than beginning physicians, who have completed nine or more years of education. Thus, a correlation may exist between years of education and starting salary.

Intuition suggests correlations that may or may not prove to be accurate. Is there a relationship between studying and good grades? Between new office computers and increased productivity? If a correlation seems to exist, can we say that one event caused the other? Does studying cause good grades? Does more schooling guarantee increased salary? Although one event may not be said to cause another, the business researcher who sees a correlation begins to ask why and how the two variables are related. In this way, apparent correlations stimulate investigation and present possible solutions to be explored.

In reporting correlations, you should avoid suggesting that a cause-and-effect relationship exists when none can be proved. Only sophisticated research methods can statistically prove cause and effect. Instead, present a correlation as a possible relationship (*The data suggest that beginning salaries are related to years of education*). Cautious statements followed by explanations gain you credibility and allow readers to make their own decisions.

Grids permit analysis of raw verbal data by grouping and classifying.

Grids. Another technique for analyzing raw data—especially verbal data—is the grid. Let's say you have been asked by the CEO to collect opinions from all vice presidents about the CEO's four-point plan to build cash reserves. The grid shown in Figure 12.2 enables you to summarize the vice presidents' reactions to each point. Notice how this complex verbal information is transformed into concise, manageable data; readers can

FIGURE 12.2 Grid to Analyze Complex Verbal Data About Building Cash Reserves

	Point 1	Point 2	Point 3	Point 4	Overall Reaction
Vice President 1	Disapproves. "Too little, too late."	Strongly supports. "Best of all points."	Mixed opinion. "Must wait and see market."	Indifferent.	Optimistic but "hates to delay expansion for six months."
Vice President 2	Disapproves. "Creates credit trap."	Approves.	Strongly disapproves.	Approves. "Must improve receivable collections."	Mixed support. "Good self-defence plan."
Vice President 3	Strongly disapproves.	Approves. "Key to entire plan."	Indifferent.	Approves but with "caveats."	"Will work only with sale of unproductive fixed assets."
Vice President 4	Disapproves. "Too risky now."	Strongly supports. "Start immediately."	Approves "but may damage image."	Approves. "Benefits far outweigh costs."	Supports plan. Suggests focus on Pacific Rim markets.

see immediately which points are supported and which are opposed. Imagine how long you could have struggled to comprehend the meaning of this verbal information before plotting it on a grid.

Arranging data in a grid also works for such projects as feasibility studies and yardstick reports that compare many variables. Assume you must recommend a new printer to your manager. To see how four models compare, you could lay out a grid with the names of printer models across the top. Down the left side, you would list such significant variables as price, warranty, service, capacity, compatibility, and specifications. As you fill in the variables for each model, you can see quickly which model has the lowest price, longest warranty, and so forth. *Consumer Reports* often uses grids to show information.

In addition, grids help classify employment data. For example, suppose your boss asks you to recommend one individual from among many job candidates. You could arrange a grid with names across the top and distinguishing characteristics—experience, skills, education, and other employment interests—down the left side. Summarizing each candidate's points offers a helpful tool for drawing conclusions and writing a report.

Decision Matrices. A decision matrix is a special grid that helps managers make the best choice among complex options. Designed to eliminate bias and poor judgment, decision matrices are helpful in many fields. Assume you need to choose the most appropriate laptop computer for your sales representatives. You are most interested in weight, battery life, price, and hard drive size. You want to compare these features in four laptop models. Figure 12.3 shows a simple decision matrix to help you make the choice. In this case, the most important criteria were weight, battery, price, and hard drive size. In Table 1, you evaluate each of these features on a scale of 1 to 5. Because the Dell Inspiron has a good price, you give it a score of 4. However, its weight is less desirable, and you give it a score of 2.

After you have evaluated all of the laptop models in Table 1, you assign relative weights to each feature. You decide to assign a factor of 5 to weight and to unit price because these two aspects are of average importance. However, your field sales reps want laptops with batteries that last. Therefore, battery life is twice as important; you assign it a factor of 10. You assign a factor of 7 to the size of the hard drive because this option is slightly more important than price but somewhat less important than battery life. Then you multiply the scores in Table 1 with the weights and total them, as shown in Table 2. According to the weighted matrix and the rating system used, the Dell Inspiron should be purchased for the sales reps because it received the highest score of 95 points, closely followed by the Acer Aspire with 91 points.

Drawing Conclusions and Making Recommendations

The most widely read portions of a report are the sections devoted to conclusions and recommendations. Knowledgeable readers go straight to the conclusions to see what the report writer thinks the data mean. Because conclusions summarize and explain the findings, they represent the heart of a report.

LEARNING OBJECTIVE 2

Draw meaningful conclusions and make practical report recommendations after sound and valid analysis.

Your value in an organization rises considerably if you can draw conclusions that analyze information logically and show how the data answer questions and solve problems. To tap into a potential $1 billion market for cellular phones in developing countries, Finnish mobile-phone manufacturer Nokia researched the needs of its customers. It created handsets that can withstand the tough living conditions and harsh weather in India and Africa. To reach customers, the company sent vans into rural India. Kai Oistamo, executive vice president and general manager for mobile phones, said, "You have to understand where people live, what the shopping patterns are. You have to work with local means to reach people—even bicycles or rickshaws."[2] Doing research and drawing logical conclusions from data are crucial to business success.

FIGURE 12.3 Decision Matrix Used to Choose a Laptop for Sales Reps

Unweighted Decision Matrix—Table 1

Features	Weight	Battery Life	Price	Hard Drive	Total
Laptop Options					
Dell Inspiron i1464-4382OBK: 2.13 GHz, Intel Core i3 330M, 2.2 kg, 3:20 hrs, $699, 500 GB	3	2	5	5	
Apple MacBook Pro: 2.26 GHz, Intel Core 2 Duo P7550, 2 kg, 4:44 hrs, $1200, 160 GB	4	3	1	1	
Acer Aspire Timeline AS4810TZ-4120: 1.3 GHz, Intel Dual-Core SU4100, 2.3 kg, 9:10 hrs, $830, 320 GB	2	5	2	3	
HP Pavilion dv4-2153cl: 2.13 GHz, Intel Core i3 330M, 2.4 kg, 3:13 hrs, $780, 320 GB	2	2	3	3	

Weighted Decision Matrix—Table 2

Features	Weight	Battery Life	Price	Hard Drive	Total
Laptop Options Weights:	5	10	5	7	
Dell Inspiron i1464-4382OBK: 2.13 GHz, Intel Core i3 330M, 2.2 kg, 3:20 hrs, $699, 500 GB	15	20	25	35	95
Apple MacBook Pro: 2.26 GHz, Intel Core 2 Duo P7550, 2 kg, 4:44 hrs, $1200, 160 GB	20	30	5	7	62
Acer Aspire Timeline AS4810TZ-4120: 1.3 GHz, Intel Dual-Core SU4100, 2.3 kg, 9:10 hrs, $830, 320 GB	10	50	10	21	91
HP Pavilion dv4-2153cl: 2.13 GHz, Intel Core i3 330M, 2.4 kg, 3:13 hrs, $780, 320 GB	10	20	15	21	66

Tips for Creating a Decision Matrix

- **Select the most important criteria.** For a laptop computer, the criteria were weight, battery life, price, and size of hard drive.

- **Create a matrix.** List each laptop model (Dell, Apple, and others) down the left side. Place the features across the top of the columns.

- **Evaluate the criteria.** Use a scale of 1 (lowest) to 5 (highest). Rate each feature for each option, as shown in Table 1.

- **Assign relative weights.** Decide how important each feature is and give it a weight.

- **Multiply the scores.** For each feature in Table 1, multiply by the weights in Table 2 and write the score in the box.

- **Total the scores.** The total reveals the best choice.

Analyzing Data to Arrive at Conclusions

Conclusions summarize and explain the findings in a report.

Any set of data can produce a variety of meaningful conclusions. Always bear in mind, though, that the audience for a report wants to know how these data relate to the problem being studied. What do the findings mean in terms of solving the original report problem?

For example, the Marriott Corporation recognized a serious problem among its employees. Conflicting home and work requirements seemed to be causing excessive employee turnover and decreased productivity. To learn the extent of the problem and to consider solutions, Marriott surveyed its staff. It learned, among other things, that nearly 35 percent of its employees had children under age 12, and 15 percent had children under age five. Other findings, shown in Figure 12.4, indicated that one third of its staff with young children took time off because of child-care difficulties. Moreover, many current employees left previous jobs because of work and family conflicts. The survey also showed that managers did not consider child-care or family problems to be appropriate topics for discussion at work.

A sample of possible conclusions that could be drawn from these findings is shown in Figure 12.4. Notice that each conclusion relates to the initial report problem. Although only a few possible findings and conclusions are shown here, you can see that the conclusions try to explain the causes for the home–work conflict among employees. Many report writers would expand the conclusion section by explaining each item and

FIGURE 12.4 **Report Conclusions and Recommendations**

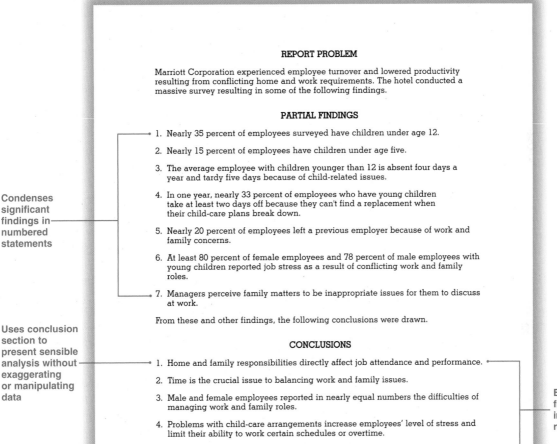

REPORT PROBLEM

Marriott Corporation experienced employee turnover and lowered productivity resulting from conflicting home and work requirements. The hotel conducted a massive survey resulting in some of the following findings.

PARTIAL FINDINGS

Condenses significant findings in numbered statements

1. Nearly 35 percent of employees surveyed have children under age 12.
2. Nearly 15 percent of employees have children under age five.
3. The average employee with children younger than 12 is absent four days a year and tardy five days because of child-related issues.
4. In one year, nearly 33 percent of employees who have young children take at least two days off because they can't find a replacement when their child-care plans break down.
5. Nearly 20 percent of employees left a previous employer because of work and family concerns.
6. At least 80 percent of female employees and 78 percent of male employees with young children reported job stress as a result of conflicting work and family roles.
7. Managers perceive family matters to be inappropriate issues for them to discuss at work.

From these and other findings, the following conclusions were drawn.

CONCLUSIONS

Uses conclusion section to present sensible analysis without exaggerating or manipulating data

1. Home and family responsibilities directly affect job attendance and performance.
2. Time is the crucial issue to balancing work and family issues.
3. Male and female employees reported in nearly equal numbers the difficulties of managing work and family roles.
4. Problems with child-care arrangements increase employees' level of stress and limit their ability to work certain schedules or overtime.
5. A manager supportive of family and personal concerns is central to a good work environment.

Explains what findings mean in terms of report problem

Tips for Writing Conclusions

- Interpret and summarize the findings; tell what they mean.
- Relate the conclusions to the report problem.
- Limit the conclusions to the data presented; do not introduce new material.
- Number the conclusions and present them in parallel form.
- Be objective; avoid exaggerating or manipulating the data.
- Use consistent criteria in evaluating options.

FIGURE 12.4 (*continued*)

RECOMMENDATIONS

Arranges actions to solve problems from most important to least important

1. Provide managers with training in working with personal and family matters.
2. Institute a flextime policy that allows employees to adapt their work schedules to home responsibilities.
3. Investigate opening a pilot child development centre for preschool children of employees at company headquarters.
4. Develop a child-care resource program to provide parents with professional help in locating affordable child care.
5. Offer a child-care discount program to help parents pay for services.
6. Authorize weekly payroll deductions, using tax-free dollars, to pay for child care.
7. Publish a quarterly employee newsletter devoted to family and child-care issues.

Tips for Writing Recommendations

- Make specific suggestions for actions to solve the report problem.
- Prepare practical recommendations that will be agreeable to the audience.
- Avoid conditional words such as *maybe* and *perhaps*.
- Present each suggestion separately as a command beginning with a verb.
- Number the recommendations for improved readability.
- If requested, describe how the recommendations may be implemented.
- When possible, arrange the recommendations in an announced order, such as most important to least important.

citing supporting evidence. Even for simplified conclusions, such as those shown in Figure 12.4, you will want to itemize each item separately and use parallel construction (balanced sentence structure).

Although your goal is to remain objective, drawing conclusions naturally involves a degree of subjectivity. Your goals, background, and frame of reference all colour the inferences you make. All writers interpret findings from their own perspectives, but they should not manipulate them to achieve a preconceived purpose.

Effective report conclusions are objective and bias free.

You can make your report conclusions more objective if you use consistent evaluation criteria. Let's say you are comparing computers for an office equipment purchase. If you evaluate each by the same criteria (such as price, specifications, service, and warranty), your conclusions are more likely to be bias free.

You also need to avoid the temptation to sensationalize or exaggerate your findings or conclusions. Be careful of words such as *many, most,* and *all.* Instead of *many of the respondents felt . . .,* you might more accurately write *some of the respondents. . . .* Examine your motives before drawing conclusions. Do not let preconceptions or wishful thinking colour your reasoning.

Preparing Report Recommendations

Conclusions explain a problem; recommendations offer specific suggestions for solving the problem.

Conclusions explain what the problem is, whereas recommendations tell how to solve it. Typically, readers prefer specific, practical recommendations. They want to know exactly how to implement the suggestions. The specificity of your recommendations depends on your authorization. What are you commissioned to do, and what does the reader expect? In the planning stages of your report project, you anticipate what the reader wants in the report. Your intuition and your knowledge of the audience indicate how far your recommendations should be developed.

In the recommendations section of the Marriott employee survey, shown in Figure 12.4, many of the recommendations are summarized. In the actual report, each recommendation could have been backed up with specifics and ideas for implementing them. For example, the child-care resource recommendation would be explained: it provides parents with names of agencies and professionals who specialize in locating child care across the country.

A good report provides practical recommendations that are agreeable to the audience. In the Marriott survey, for example, report researchers knew that the company wanted to help employees cope with conflicts between family and work obligations. Hence, the report's conclusions and recommendations focused on ways to resolve the conflict. If Marriott's goal had been merely to save money by reducing employee absenteeism, the recommendations would have been quite different.

The best recommendations offer practical suggestions that are feasible and agreeable to the audience.

If possible, make each recommendation a command. Note in Figure 12.4 that each recommendation begins with a verb. This structure sounds forceful and confident and helps the reader comprehend the information quickly. Avoid such words as *maybe* and *perhaps*; they suggest conditional statements that reduce the strength of recommendations.

Experienced writers may combine recommendations and conclusions. In short reports writers may omit conclusions and move straight to recommendations. An important point about recommendations is that they include practical suggestions for solving the report problem. Furthermore, they are always the result of prior logical analysis.

Moving From Findings to Recommendations

Recommendations evolve from interpretation of the findings and conclusions. Consider the following examples from the Marriott survey:

Finding

Managers perceive family matters to be inappropriate issues to discuss at work.

Conclusion

Managers are neither willing nor trained to discuss family matters that may cause employees to miss work.

Recommendation

Provide managers with training in recognizing and working with personal and family matters that affect work.

Finding

Within a one-year period, nearly 33 percent of employees who have young children take at least two days off because they can't find a replacement when their child-care plans break down.

Conclusion

Problems with child-care arrangements increase employees' level of stress and limit their ability to work certain schedules or overtime.

Recommendation

Develop a child-care resource program to provide parents with professional help in locating affordable child care.

Organizing Data

After collecting sets of data, interpreting them, drawing conclusions, and thinking about the recommendations, you are ready to organize the parts of the report into a logical framework. Poorly organized reports lead to frustration. Readers will not understand, remember, or be persuaded. Wise writers know that reports rarely "just organize themselves." Instead, organization must be imposed on the data, and cues must be provided so the reader can follow the writer's logic.

LEARNING OBJECTIVE 3

Organize report data logically and provide cues to aid comprehension.

FIGURE 12.5 Organizational Patterns for Informational and Analytical Reports

	Analytical Reports	
Informational Reports	**Direct Strategy**	**Indirect Strategy**
I. Introduction/background	I. Introduction/problem	I. Introduction/problem
II. Facts/findings	II. Conclusions/recommendations	II. Facts/findings
III. Summary/conclusion	III. Facts/findings	III. Discussion/analysis
	IV. Discussion/analysis	IV. Conclusions/recommendations

The direct strategy is appropriate for informed or receptive readers; the indirect strategy is appropriate when educating or persuading.

Informational reports, as you learned in Chapter 11, generally present data without interpretation. As shown in Figure 12.5, informational reports typically consist of three parts: (1) introduction/background, (2) facts/findings, and (3) summary/concluding remarks. Analytical reports, which generally analyze data and draw conclusions, typically contain four parts: (1) introduction/problem, (2) facts/findings, (3) discussion/analysis, and (4) conclusions/recommendations. However, the parts in analytical reports do not always follow the same sequence. For readers who know about the project, are supportive, or are eager to learn the results quickly, the direct method is appropriate. Conclusions and recommendations, if requested, appear up front. For readers who must be educated or persuaded, the indirect method works better. Conclusions/recommendations appear last, after the findings have been presented and analyzed.

Although every report is different, the overall organizational patterns described here typically hold true. The real challenge, though, lies in (a) organizing the facts/findings and discussion/analysis sections and (b) providing reader cues.

Ordering Information Logically

Organization by time, component, importance, criteria, or convention helps readers comprehend data.

Whether you are writing informational or analytical reports, the data you have collected must be structured coherently. Five common organizational methods are by time, component, importance, criteria, or convention. Regardless of the method you choose, be sure that it helps the reader understand the data. Reader comprehension, not writer convenience, should govern organization. Additional examples of organizational principles can be found in Chapter 14.

Time. Ordering data by time means establishing a chronology of events. Agendas, minutes of meetings, progress reports, and procedures are usually organized by time. For example, a report describing an eight-week training program would most likely be organized by weeks. A plan for step-by-step improvement of customer service would be organized by steps. A monthly trip report submitted by a sales rep might describe customers visited Week 1, Week 2, and so on. Beware of overusing chronologies (time) as an organizing method for reports, however. Although this method is easy and often mirrors the way data are collected, chronologies—like the sales rep's trip report—tend to be boring, repetitious, and lacking in emphasis. Readers cannot always pick out what is important.

Component. Especially for informational reports, data may be organized by components, such as location, geography, division, product, or part. For instance, a report detailing company expansion might divide the plan into West Coast, East Coast, and Central expansion. The report could also be organized by divisions: personal products, consumer electronics, and household goods. A report comparing profits among makers of athletic shoes might group the data by company: Nike, Reebok, Adidas, and so forth. Organization by components works best when the classifications already exist.

Importance. Organization by importance involves beginning with the most important item and proceeding to the least important—or vice versa. For example, a report discussing the reasons for declining product sales would present the most important reason first followed by less important ones. The Marriott report describing work–family conflicts might begin by discussing child care, if the writer considered it the most

Organizing by level of importance saves the time of busy readers and increases the odds that key information will be retained.

important issue. Using importance to structure findings involves a value judgment. The writer must decide what is most important, always keeping in mind the readers' priorities and expectations. Busy readers appreciate seeing important points first; they may skim or skip other points. Conversely, building to a climax by moving from least important to most important enables the writer to focus attention at the end. Thus, the reader is more likely to remember the most important item. Of course, the writer also risks losing the attention of the reader along the way.

Criteria. Establishing criteria by which to judge helps writers treat topics consistently. Let's say your report compares health plans A, B, and C. For each plan you examine the same standards: Criterion 1, cost per employee; Criterion 2, amount of deductible; and Criterion 3, patient benefits. The resulting data could then be organized either by plans or by criteria:

By Plan	By Criteria
Plan A	Criterion 1
Criterion 1	Plan A
Criterion 2	Plan B
Criterion 3	Plan C
Plan B	Criterion 2
Criterion 1	Plan A
Criterion 2	Plan B
Criterion 3	Plan C
Plan C	Criterion 3
Criterion 1	Plan A
Criterion 2	Plan B
Criterion 3	Plan C

> To evaluate choices or plans fairly, apply the same criteria to each.

Although you might favour organizing the data by plans (because that is the way you collected the data), the better way is by criteria. When you discuss patient benefits, for example, you would examine all three plans' benefits together. Organizing a report around criteria helps readers make comparisons instead of forcing them to search through the report for similar data.

Convention. Many operational and recurring reports are structured according to convention. That is, they follow a prescribed plan that everyone understands. For example, an automotive parts manufacturer might ask all sales reps to prepare a weekly report with these headings: *Competitive observations* (competitors' price changes, discounts, new products, product problems, distributor changes, product promotions), *Product problems* (quality, performance, needs), and *Customer service problems* (delivery, mailings, correspondence). Management gets exactly the information it needs in an easy-to-read form.

> Organizing by convention simplifies the organizational task and yields easy-to-follow information.

Like operating reports, proposals are often organized conventionally. They might use such groupings as background, problem, proposed solution, staffing, schedule, costs, and authorization. As you might expect, reports following these conventional, prescribed structures greatly simplify the task of organization. Proposals and long reports are presented in Chapter 13.

Providing Reader Cues

When you finish organizing a report, you probably see a neat outline in your mind: major points, supported by subpoints and details. Readers, however, do not know the material as well as you do; they cannot see your outline. To guide them through the data, you need to provide the equivalent of a map and road signs. For both formal and informal reports, such devices as introductions, transitions, and headings prevent readers from getting lost.

Introduction. One of the best ways to point a reader in the right direction is to provide a report introduction that does three things:

- Tells the purpose of the report
- Describes the significance of the topic
- Previews the main points and the order in which they will be developed

The following paragraph includes all three elements in introducing a report on computer security:

> *This report examines the security of our current computer operations and presents suggestions for improving security. Lax computer security could mean loss of information, loss of business, and damage to our equipment and systems. Because many former employees released during recent downsizing efforts know our systems, major changes must be made. To improve security, I will present three recommendations: (1) begin using smart cards that limit access to our computer system, (2) alter sign-on and log-off procedures, (3) move central computer operations to a more secure area.*

This opener tells the purpose (examining computer security), describes its significance (loss of information and business, damage to equipment and systems), and outlines how the report is organized (three recommendations). Good openers in effect set up a contract with the reader. The writer promises to cover certain topics in a specified order. Readers expect the writer to fulfill the contract. They want the topics to be developed as promised—using the same wording and presented in the order mentioned. For example, if in your introduction you state that you will discuss the use of *smart cards,* do not change the heading for that section to *access cards.* Remember that the introduction provides a map to a report; switching the names on the map will ensure that readers get lost. To maintain consistency, delay writing the introduction until after you have completed the report. Long, complex reports may require introductions for each section.

Transitions. Such expressions as *on the contrary, at the same time,* and *however* show relationships and help reveal the logical flow of ideas in a report. These transitional expressions enable writers to tell readers where ideas are headed and how they relate. Notice how abrupt the following two sentences sound without a transition: *The Microsoft Zune player offers several technological advances that exceed the capabilities of Apple's iPod devices. The Zune [however] is locked into a clunky online music store that isn't likely to win many fans.*

The following transitional expressions (see Chapter 5 for a complete list) enable you to show readers how you are developing your ideas.

- **To present additional thoughts:** *additionally, again, also, moreover, furthermore*
- **To suggest cause and effect:** *accordingly, as a result, consequently, therefore*
- **To contrast ideas:** *at the same time, but, however, on the contrary, though, yet*
- **To show time and order:** *after, before, first, finally, now, previously, then, to conclude*
- **To clarify points:** *for example, for instance, in other words, that is, thus*

In using these expressions, recognize that they do not have to sit at the head of a sentence. Listen to the rhythm of the sentence and place the expression where a natural pause occurs. If you are unsure about the placement of a transitional expression, position it at the beginning of the sentence. Used appropriately, transitional expressions serve readers as guides; misused or overused, they can be as distracting and frustrating as too many road signs on a highway.

Headings. Good headings are another structural cue that assists readers in comprehending the organization of a report. They highlight major ideas, allowing busy readers to see the big picture at a glance. Moreover, headings provide resting points for the mind and for the eye, breaking up large chunks of text into manageable and inviting segments.

Report writers may use functional or talking headings. Functional headings (for example, *Background, Findings, Personnel,* and *Production Costs*) describe functions or general topics. They show the outline of a report but provide little insight for readers.

Functional headings are useful for routine reports. They are also appropriate for sensitive topics that might provoke emotional reactions. By keeping the headings general, experienced writers hope to minimize reader opposition or response to controversial subjects. Talking headings (for example, *Lack of Space and Cost Compound Campus Parking Problem* or *Survey Shows Support for Parking Fees*) provide more information and interest. Unless carefully written, however, talking headings can fail to reveal the organization of a report. With some planning, though, headings can be both functional and talking, such as *Parking Recommendations: Shuttle and New Structures*.

The best strategy for creating helpful talking headings is to write a few paragraphs first and then generate talking headings that sum up the major point of each paragraph. To create the most effective headings, follow a few basic guidelines:

● **Use appropriate heading levels.** The position and format of a heading indicate its level of importance and relationship to other points. Figure 12.6 illustrates and discusses a commonly used heading format for business reports. For an overview of alphanumeric and decimal outlines, see Chapter 5.

> **Headings should be brief, parallel, and ordered in a logical hierarchy.**

FIGURE 12.6 Levels of Headings in Reports

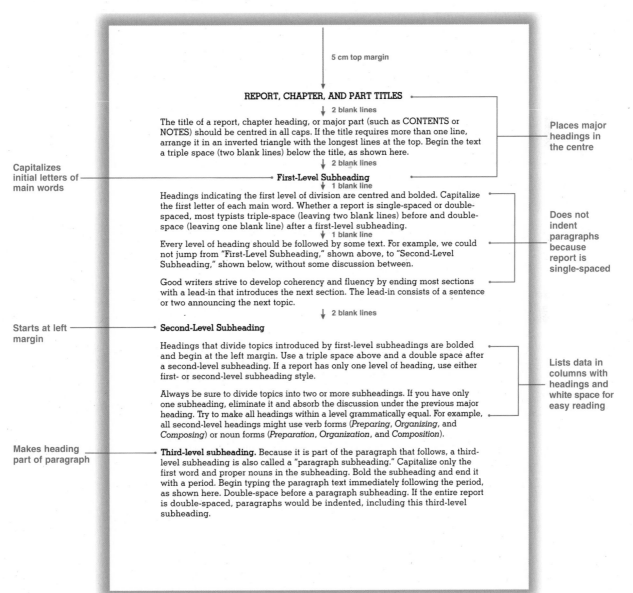

- **Capitalize and underline carefully.** Most writers use all capital letters (without underlines) for main titles, such as the report, chapter, and unit titles. For first- and second-level headings, they capitalize only the first letter of main words. For additional emphasis, they use a bold font, as shown in Figure 12.6.

- **Try to balance headings within levels.** Although it may not always be possible, attempt to create headings that are grammatically similar at a given level. For example, *Developing Product Teams* and *Presenting Plan to Management* are balanced, but *Development of Product Teams* and *Presenting Plan to Management* are not.

- **For short reports use first-level or first- and second-level headings.** Many business reports contain only one or two levels of headings. For such reports use first-level headings (centred, bolded) and second-level headings (flush left, bolded). See Figure 12.6.

- **Include at least one heading per report page.** Headings increase the readability and attractiveness of report pages. Use at least one per page to break up blocks of text.

- **Keep headings short but clear.** One-word headings are emphatic but not always clear. For example, the heading *Budget* does not adequately describe numbers for a summer project involving student interns for an oil company in Alberta. Try to keep your headings brief (no more than eight words) but make sure they are understandable. Experiment with headings that concisely tell who, what, when, where, and why.

Writing Short Informational Reports

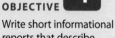

LEARNING OBJECTIVE 4

Write short informational reports that describe routine tasks.

Informational reports provide data on periodic and situational activities for readers who do not need to be persuaded.

Now that we have covered the basics of gathering, interpreting, and organizing data, we are ready to put it all together into short informational or analytical reports. Informational reports often describe periodic, recurring activities (such as monthly sales or weekly customer calls) and situational, nonrecurring events (such as trips, conferences, and progress on special projects). What they have in common is delivering information to readers who do not have to be persuaded. Informational report readers usually are neutral or receptive.

You can expect to write many informational reports as an entry-level or middle-management employee. Because these reports generally deliver nonsensitive data and thus will not upset the reader, they are organized directly. Often they need little background material or introductory comments because readers are familiar with the topics. Although they are generally conversational and informal, informational reports should not be so casual that the reader struggles to find the important points. Main points must be immediately visible. Headings, lists, bulleted items, and other graphic highlighting, as well as clear organization, enable readers to grasp major ideas immediately. The lessons that you have learned about conciseness, clarity, courtesy, and effective writing in general throughout earlier chapters apply to report writing as well. After all, competent reports can boost your visibility in the company and promote your advancement. The Career Coach box on page 321 provides additional pointers on design features and techniques that can improve your reports.

Summaries

A summary compresses the main points from a book, a report, an article, a Web site, a meeting, or a convention. A summary saves time because it can reduce a report or an article by 85 to 95 percent. Employees are sometimes asked to write summaries that condense technical reports, periodical articles, or books so that their staffs or superiors may grasp the main ideas quickly. Students may be asked to write summaries of articles,

career coach

Ten Tips for Designing Better Documents

Desktop publishing packages, high-level word processing programs, and advanced printers now make it possible for you to turn out professional-looking documents and promotional materials. The temptation, though, is to overdo it by incorporating too many features in one document. Here are ten tips for applying good sense and good design principles in "publishing" your documents.

- **Analyze your audience.** Sales brochures and promotional letters can be flashy—with colour print, oversized type, and fancy borders—to attract attention. But such effects are out of place for most conservative business documents. Also consider whether your readers will be reading painstakingly or merely browsing. Lists and headings help those readers who are in a hurry.

- **Avoid amateurish effects.** Strive for simple, clean, and forceful effects. Many beginning writers, eager to display every graphic device a program offers, produce busy, cluttered documents. Too many typefaces, ruled lines, oversized headlines, and images will overwhelm readers.

- **Choose an appropriate type size.** For most business memos, letters, and reports, the body text should be 11 to 12 points tall (a point is 0.35 mm). Larger type looks amateurish, and smaller type is hard to read.

- **Use a consistent type font.** Although your software may provide a variety of fonts, stay with a single family of type within one document—at least until you become more expert. The most popular fonts are Times New Roman and Arial. For emphasis and contrast, you can vary the font size and weight with **bold**, *italic*, ***bold italic,*** and other selections.

- **Do not justify right margins.** Textbooks, novels, newspapers, magazines, and other long works are usually set with justified (even) right margins. However, for shorter works ragged-right margins are recommended because such margins add white space and help readers locate the beginnings of new lines. Slower readers find ragged-right copy more legible.

- **Separate paragraphs and sentences appropriately.** In most business documents, the first line of a paragraph is preceded by a blank line, but some writers like to indent the first line five spaces from the left margin. To separate sentences, most writers follow printers' standards and leave only one space. Be sure to maintain consistency throughout your document.

- **Design readable headings.** If you choose to present headings in all caps, use them sparingly because solid blocks of capital letters interfere with recognition of word patterns. To further improve readability, select a sans serif typeface (one without cross strokes or embellishment), such as Arial.

- **Strive for an attractive page layout.** In designing title pages or graphics, provide a balance between print and white space. Also consider placing the focal point (something that draws the reader's eye) at the optical centre of a page—about three lines above the actual centre. Moreover, remember that the average reader scans a page from left to right and top to bottom in a Z pattern. Plan your graphics accordingly.

- **Use graphics and clip art with restraint.** Charts, original drawings, photographs, and clip art can be scanned into documents. Use such images, however, only when they are well drawn, relevant, purposeful, and appropriately sized.

- **Develop expertise.** Learn to use the desktop publishing features of your current word processing software, or investigate one of the special programs, such as QuarkXPress, Adobe's InDesign, and Corel's Ventura. Although the learning curve for many of these programs is steep, such effort is well spent if you will be producing newsletters, brochures, announcements, visual aids, and promotional literature.

---

chapters, or books to sharpen their writing skills and to confirm their knowledge of reading assignments. In writing a summary, you will follow these general guidelines:

- Present the goal or purpose of the document being summarized. Why was it written?

- Highlight the research methods (if appropriate), findings, conclusions, and recommendations.

- Omit illustrations, examples, and references.

- Organize for readability by including headings and bulleted or enumerated lists.

- Include your reactions or an overall evaluation of the document if asked to do so.

An *executive summary* summarizes a long report, proposal, or business plan. It concentrates on what management needs to know from a longer report. How to prepare an executive summary is covered in Chapter 13

Periodic (Activity) Reports

Periodic reports keep management informed of operations and activities.

Most businesses—especially larger ones—require periodic reports (sometimes called activity reports) to keep management informed of operations. These recurring reports are written at regular intervals—weekly, monthly, yearly—so that management can monitor and, if necessary, remedy business strategies. Some periodic reports simply contain numbers, such as sales volume, number and kind of customer service calls, shipments delivered, accounts payable, and personnel data. More challenging periodic reports require descriptions and discussions of activities. In preparing a narrative description of their activities, employees writing periodic reports usually do the following:

- Summarize regular activities and events performed during the reporting period

- Describe irregular events deserving the attention of management

- Highlight special needs and problems

Managers naturally want to know that routine activities are progressing normally. Employees today enjoy a great deal of independence and shoulder much responsibility because of flattened hierarchies on the job. They often work flexible hours in far-flung locations. Keeping track of their activities and the tasks they were assigned is crucial in such an environment. Increasingly, routine reports are sent by e-mail and take the form of efficient bulleted lists without commentary.

Figure 12.7 shows a weekly activity report prepared by Siddharth Singh, a senior Web producer at the information technology firm Sygnal Macro in Ottawa. Sid is responsible for his firm's Web presence in Asian countries or territories, mainly Japan, China, Hong Kong, and Vietnam. In his weekly reports to his supervisor, Thomas LeClerc, Sid neatly divides his projects into *completed*, *in progress*, and *ongoing*. Thomas, the manager, then combines the activity reports from all his subordinates into a separate periodic report detailing the department's activities to his superiors.

Sid justifies the use of jargon, missing salutation and complimentary close, and ultra-short bulleted items as follows: "We e-mail our reports internally, so some IT jargon can be expected. The readers will understand it. Thomas and upper management all want reporting to be brief and to the point. Bullets fit us just fine." Periodic reports ensure that information within the company flows steadily and that supervisors know the status of current and pending projects. This efficient information flow is all the more important because Sid works at home two days a week. Several of his co-workers also telecommute.

Trip, Convention, and Conference Reports

Employees sent on business trips or to conventions and conferences typically must submit reports when they return. Organizations want to know that their money was well spent in funding the travel. These reports inform management about new procedures, equipment, and laws, and they supply information affecting products, operations, and service.

The hardest parts of writing these reports are selecting the most relevant material and organizing it coherently. Generally, it is best not to use chronological sequencing (*in the morning we did X, at lunch we heard Y, and in the afternoon we did Z*). Instead, you should focus on three to five topics in which your reader will be interested. These items become the body of the report. Then simply add an introduction and a closing, and your report is organized. Here is a general outline for trip, conference, and convention reports:

Trip and conference reports identify the event, summarize three to five main points, itemize expenses separately, and express appreciation or suggest action to be taken.

- Begin by identifying the event (exact date, name, and location) and previewing the topics to be discussed.

- Summarize in the body three to five main points that might benefit the reader.

- Itemize your expenses, if requested, on a separate sheet.

- Close by expressing appreciation, suggesting action to be taken, or synthesizing the value of the trip or event.

FIGURE 12.7 Periodic (Activity) Report—E-Mail Format

Sends internal informational report by e-mail as required weekly by manager

To: Thomas LeClerc <tleclerc@sygnalmacro.com>
From: Siddharth Singh <ssingh@sygnalmacro.com>
Subject: Weekly Status Report (Siddharth / Week 3)
Cc:

Chooses bulleted lists and abbreviated project descriptions for high "skim value"

Completed Projects
– MCN 107786: Missing font installation sections (CN)
– MJP 107995: Update government page
– MVN108034: Remove mention of Sygnalimage Micro Edition (JP, HK)

– LJP12709: Post two new events on JP events main
– BT865: Add store links in (purchase) pages (JP)

Work in Progress
– 1215-01: Sygnalmacro.com Updates (JP, staged; live due date May 20)
– 1345-01: Sygnalimage AS Pro training page (JP, staged; live due date May 20)
– 1489-01: Manufacturing Redesign (JP, VN, HK,* due date July 1)
– 1677-01: PlayMode Player Security Bulletin (JP live, VN, HK,* due date July 2)

– LVN12698: Phone number updates related to Customer Care (JP, staged; live due date Aug. 1)
– LHK14867: JP menu edit (staged, waiting for approval; live due date March 1)

Ongoing Projects
– Broken links HK, JP external and internal

Other
– Worked with Andy Takamura and Sisi Lu on creating localized marketing badges for JP and SG
– Set up two registration forms for region on Wiley
– Continued to work on cdei script migration

Issues
– None

*Awaiting translations

SM Siddharth Singh | Senior Web Producer | Sygnal Macro | 367 Edison Ave., Ottawa, ON K1S 1B5 | +1 613.328.6800 | ssingh@sygnalmacro.com

Uses abbreviations for China (CN), Japan (JP), Hong Kong (HK), Singapore (SG), and Vietnam (VN) familiar to readers

Clearly labels the tasks as completed, pending, and ongoing

Includes internal project numbers to identify assignments

Provides full contact information in prepared signature block

---

Jack Horn was recently named employment coordinator in the Human Resources Department of an electronics appliance manufacturer headquartered in central Ontario. Recognizing his lack of experience in interviewing job applicants, he asked permission to attend a one-day conference on the topic. His boss, Elizabeth Greene, encouraged Jack to attend, saying, "We all need to brush up on our interviewing techniques. Come back and tell us what you learned." When he returned, Jack wrote the conference report shown in Figure 12.8. Here is how he described its preparation: "I know my boss values brevity, so I worked hard to make my report no more than a page and a quarter. The conference saturated me with great ideas, far too many to cover in one brief report. So, I decided to discuss three topics that would be most useful to our staff. Although I had to be brief, I nonetheless wanted to provide as many details—especially about common interviewing mistakes—as possible. By the third draft, I had compressed my ideas into a manageable size without sacrificing any of the meaning."

Progress and Interim Reports

Continuing projects often require progress or interim reports to describe their status. These reports may be external (advising customers regarding the headway of their projects) or internal (informing management of the status of activities). Progress reports typically follow this pattern of development:

● Specify in the opening the purpose and nature of the project.

● Provide background information if the audience requires filling in.

● Describe the work completed.

FIGURE 12.8 **Conference Report—Memo Format**

///TriCom
Total HR Services
Interoffice Memo

DATE: April 23, 2014
TO: Elizabeth Greene *JH*
FROM: Jack Horn
SUBJECT: Conference on Employment Interviews

I enjoyed attending the "Interviewing People" training conference sponsored by the National Business Foundation. This one-day meeting, held in Toronto on April 19, provided excellent advice that will help us strengthen our interviewing techniques. Although the conference covered many topics, this report concentrates on three areas: structuring the interview, avoiding common mistakes, and responding to new legislation.

Identifies topic and previews how the report is organized

Structuring the Interview

Job interviews usually have three parts. The opening establishes a friendly rapport with introductions, a few polite questions, and an explanation of the purpose for the interview. The body of the interview consists of questions controlled by the interviewer. The interviewer has three goals: (a) educating the applicant about the job, (b) eliciting information about the applicant's suitability for the job, and (c) promoting goodwill about the organization. In closing, the interviewer should encourage the applicant to ask questions, summarize main points, and indicate what actions will follow.

Sets off major topics with centred headings

Avoiding Common Mistakes

Probably the most interesting and practical part of the conference centred on common mistakes made by interviewers, some of which I summarize here:

1. Not taking notes at each interview. Recording important facts enables you to remember the first candidate as easily as you remember the last—and all those in between.

2. Not testing the candidate's communication skills. To be able to evaluate a candidate's ability to express ideas, ask the individual to explain some technical jargon from his or her current position.

3. Having departing employees conduct the interviews for their replacements. Departing employees may be unreliable as interviewers because they tend to hire candidates not quite as strong as they are.

4. Failing to check references. As many as 45 percent of all résumés may contain falsified data. The best way to check references is to network: ask the person whose name has been given to suggest the name of another person.

Covers facts that will most interest and help reader

Elizabeth Greene   Page 2   April 23, 2014

Responding to Employment Legislation

Provisions of the Human Rights Code prohibit interviewers from asking candidates—or even their references—about candidates' disabilities. A question we frequently asked ("Do you have any physical limitations that would prevent you from performing the job for which you are applying?") would now break the law. Interviewers must also avoid asking about medical history; prescription drug use; prior workers' compensation claims; work absenteeism due to illness; and past treatment for alcoholism, drug use, or mental illness.

Sharing This Information

Concludes with offer to share information

This conference provided me with valuable training that I would like to share with other department members at a future staff meeting. Let me know when it can be scheduled.

- Explain the work currently in progress, including personnel, activities, methods, and locations.

- Describe current problems and anticipate future problems and possible remedies.

- Discuss future activities and provide the expected completion date.

As a location manager for Maple Leaf Video Productions, Gina Genova frequently writes progress reports, such as the one shown in Figure 12.9. Producers

FIGURE 12.9 Progress Report—Letter Format

Maple Leaf Productions, Inc.

100 Front Street, Toronto, ON M5J 1E3 (416) 539-8922
FAX (416) 539-8649

January 9, 2014

Mr. Jeffrey S. Sears
Executive Producer
Toronto Film Studios
629 Eastern Avenue
Toronto, ON M4M 1E4

Dear Jeff:

Identifies project and previews report → This letter describes the progress of my search for an appropriate rustic home, villa, or farm to be used for the wine country sequences in the telefilm *Boodga Bay*. Three sites will be available for you to inspect on January 20, as you requested.

Background: In preparation for this assignment, I consulted Director Dave Durslag, who gave me his preferences for the site. He suggested a picturesque home situated near vineyards, preferably with woods in the background. I also consulted Producer Teresa Silva, who told me that the site must accommodate 55 to 70 production crew members for three weeks. Ben Waters, telefilm accountant, requested that the cost of the site not exceed $30,000 for a three-week lease.

Saves space by integrating headings into paragraphs → **Work Completed:** For the past eight days I have searched the Niagara Escarpment area in Southern Ontario's wine country. Possible sites include turn-of-the-century estates, Victorian mansions, and rustic farmhouses in the Welland/St. Catharines area. One exceptional site is the Country Meadow Inn, a 97-year-old farmhouse nestled among vineyards with a breathtaking view of the Escarpment.

Work to Be Completed: In the next five days, I'll search the Niagara countryside. Many old wineries contain charming structures that may present exactly the degree of atmosphere and mystery we need. I will also inspect possible structures in and around Niagara-on-the-Lake. I've made an appointment with the director of provincial parks to discuss our project, use of public lands, restrictions, and costs.

Tells the bad news as well as the good → **Anticipated Problems:** Two complications may affect filming. (1) Property owners are unfamiliar with filmmaking and are suspicious of short-term leases. (2) Most trees won't have leaves again until May.

Concludes by giving completion date and describing what follows → By January 13 you'll have my final report describing the three most promising locations. Arrangements will be made for you to visit these sites January 20.

Sincerely,

Gina

Gina Genova
Production Scout

Tips for Writing Progress Reports

- Identify the purpose and the nature of the project immediately.
- Supply background information only if the reader must be educated.
- Describe the work completed.
- Discuss the work in progress, including personnel, activities, methods, and locations.
- Identify problems and possible remedies.
- Consider future activities.
- Close by telling the expected date of completion.

want to be informed of what she is doing, and a phone call does not provide a permanent record. Here is how she described the reasoning behind her progress report: "I usually include background information in my reports because a director does not always know or remember exactly what specifications I was given for a location search. Then I try to hit the high points of what I have completed and what I plan to do next, without getting bogged down in tiny details. Although it would be easier to skip them, I have learned to be upfront with any problems that I anticipate. I do not tell how to solve the problems, but I feel duty-bound to at least mention them."

Investigative Reports

Investigative or informational reports deliver data for a specific situation—without offering interpretation or recommendations. These nonrecurring reports are generally arranged in a direct strategy with three segments: introduction, body, and summary. The body—which includes the facts, findings, or discussion—may be organized by time, component, importance, criteria, or convention. What is important is dividing the topic into logical segments, say, three to five areas that are roughly equal and do not overlap.

Investigative reports provide information without interpretation or recommendations.

Beth Givens, an information specialist for a Maritime health care consulting firm, was given the task of researching and writing an investigative report for a St. John's Hospital. Her assignment: study the award-winning patient-service program at Good Samaritan Hospital and report how it improved its patient satisfaction rating from 6.2 to 7.8 in just one year. Beth collected data and then organized her findings into four parts: management training, employee training, patient services, and follow-up program. Although we do not show Beth's complete report here, you can see a similar informational report in Figure 11.2 in Chapter 11.

Whether you are writing a periodic, a trip, a conference, a progress, or an investigative report, you will want to review the suggestions found in the Checklist box.

Checklist

Writing Informational Reports

Introduction

- **Begin directly.** Identify the report and its purpose.
- **Provide a preview.** If the report is more than a page long, give the reader a brief overview of its organization.
- **Supply background data selectively.** When readers are unfamiliar with the topic, briefly fill in the necessary details.
- **Divide the topic.** Strive to group the facts or findings into three to five roughly equal segments that do not overlap.

Body

- **Arrange the subtopics logically.** Consider organizing by time, component, importance, criteria, or convention.
- **Use clear headings.** Supply functional or talking headings (at least one per page) that describe each important section.

- **Determine the degree of formality.** Use an informal, conversational writing style unless the audience expects a more formal tone.
- **Enhance readability with graphic highlighting.** Make liberal use of bullets, numbered and lettered lists, headings, underlined items, and white space.

Summary/Concluding Remarks

- **When necessary, summarize the report.** Briefly review the main points and discuss what action will follow.
- **Offer a concluding thought.** If relevant, express appreciation or describe your willingness to provide further information.

Preparing Short Analytical Reports

Analytical reports differ significantly from informational reports. Although both seek to collect and present data clearly, analytical reports also analyze the data and typically try to persuade the reader to accept the conclusions and act on the recommendations. Informational reports emphasize facts; analytical reports emphasize reasoning and conclusions.

For some readers you may organize analytical reports directly with the conclusions and recommendations near the beginning. Directness is appropriate when the reader has confidence in the writer, based on either experience or credentials. Frontloading the recommendations also works when the topic is routine or familiar and the reader is supportive.

Directness can backfire, though. If you announce the recommendations too quickly, the reader may immediately object to a single idea. You may have had no suspicion that this idea would trigger a negative reaction. Once the reader is opposed, changing an unfavourable mind-set may be difficult or impossible. A reader may also think you have oversimplified or overlooked something significant if you lay out all the recommendations before explaining how you arrived at them. When you must lead the reader through the process of discovering the solution or recommendation, use the indirect method: present conclusions and recommendations last.

Most analytical reports answer questions about specific problems and aid in decision making. *How can we use a Web site most effectively? Should we close the Bradford plant? Should we buy or lease company cars? How can we improve customer service?* Three typical analytical reports answer business questions: justification/recommendation reports, feasibility reports, and yardstick reports. Because these reports all solve problems, the categories are not mutually exclusive. What distinguishes them are their goals and organization.

Justification/Recommendation Reports

Both managers and employees must occasionally write reports that justify or recommend something, such as buying equipment, changing a procedure, hiring an employee, consolidating departments, or investing funds. These reports may also be called internal proposals because their persuasive nature is similar to that of external proposals (presented in Chapter 13). Large organizations sometimes prescribe how these reports should be organized; they use forms with conventional headings. When you are free to select an organizational plan yourself, however, let your audience and topic determine your choice of direct or indirect strategy.

Direct Strategy. For nonsensitive topics and recommendations that will be agreeable to readers, you can organize directly according to the following sequence:

- Identify the problem or need briefly.

- Announce the recommendation, solution, or action concisely and with action verbs.

- Explain more fully the benefits of the recommendation or steps necessary to solve the problem.

- Include a discussion of pros, cons, and costs.

- Conclude with a summary specifying the recommendation and necessary action.

Here is how Cory Black applied the process in justifying a purchase. Cory is operations manager in charge of a fleet of trucks for a large parcel delivery company in Quebec. When he heard about a new Goodyear smart tire with an electronic chip, Cory thought his company should give the new tire a try. Because new tires would represent an irregular purchase and because they would require a pilot test, he wrote the justification/recommendation report, shown in Figure 12.10, to his boss. Cory described his report in this way: "As more and more parcel delivery companies crop up, we have to find ways to cut costs so that we can remain competitive. Although more expensive initially, smart tires may solve many of our problems and save us money in the long

Analytical reports present information but emphasize reasoning, conclusions, and recommendations.

Justification/ recommendation reports follow the direct or indirect strategy depending on the audience and the topic.

The direct strategy is appropriate for justification/ recommendation reports on nonsensitive topics and for receptive audiences.

FIGURE 12.10 Justification/Recommendation Report: Direct Strategy

1 Prewriting

Analyze: The purpose of this report is to persuade the manager to authorize the purchase and pilot testing of smart tires.

Anticipate: The audience is a manager who is familiar with operations but not with this product. He will probably be receptive to the recommendation.

Adapt: Present the report data in a direct, straightforward manner.

2 Writing

Research: Collect data on how smart tires could benefit operations.

Organize: Discuss the problem briefly. Introduce and justify the recommendation by noting its cost-effectiveness and paperwork benefits. Explain the benefits of smart tires. Describe the action to be taken.

Compose: Write and print the first draft.

3 Revising

Revise: Revise to break up long paragraphs about benefits. Isolate each benefit in an enumerated list with headings.

Proofread: Double-check all figures. Be sure all headings are parallel.

Evaluate: Does this report make its request concisely but emphatically? Will the reader see immediately what action is required?

DATE: July 19, 2014
TO: Jim Jordan
FROM: Cory Black, Operations Manager
SUBJECT: Goodyear Smart Tires—Pilot Test

Next to fuel, truck tires are our biggest operating cost. Last year we spent $236,000 replacing and retreading tires for 495 trucks. This year the costs will be greater because prices have jumped at least 12 percent and because we've increased our fleet to 550 trucks. Truck tires are an additional burden because they require labour-intensive paperwork to track their warranties, wear, and retread histories. To reduce our long-term costs and to improve our tire tracking system, I recommend that we do the following:

Introduces problem briefly

■ Purchase 24 Goodyear smart tires.
■ Begin a one-year pilot test on six trucks.

Presents recommendations immediately

How Smart Tires Work

Smart tires have an embedded computer chip that monitors wear, performance, and durability. The chip also creates an electronic fingerprint for positive identification of a tire. By passing a handheld sensor next to the tire, we can learn where and when a tire was made (for warranty and other identification), how much tread it had originally, and its serial number.

Justifies recommendation by explaining product and benefits

How Smart Tires Could Benefit Us

Although smart tires are initially more expensive than other tires, they could help us improve our operations and save us money in four ways:

1. **Retreads.** Goodyear believes that the wear data is so accurate that we should be able to retread every tire three times, instead of our current two times. If that's true, in one year we could save at least $27,000 in new tire costs.
2. **Safety.** Accurate and accessible wear data should reduce the danger of blowouts and flat tires. Last year, drivers reported six blowouts.
3. **Record keeping and maintenance.** Smart tires could reduce our maintenance costs considerably. Currently, we use an electric branding iron to mark serial numbers on new tires. Our biggest headache is manually reading those serial numbers, decoding them, and maintaining records to meet safety regulations. Reading such data electronically could save us thousands of dollars in labour.
4. **Theft protection.** The chip can be used to monitor each tire as it leaves or enters the warehouse or yard, thus discouraging theft.

Enumerates items for maximum impact and readability

Summary and Action

Specifically, I recommend that you do the following:

Explains recommendation in more detail

■ Authorize the special purchase of 24 Goodyear smart tires at $500 each, plus one electronic sensor at $1,500.
■ Approve a one-year pilot test in our Quebec territory that equips six trucks with smart tires and tracks their performance.

Specifies action to be taken

run. I knew Jim Jordan, operations vice president, would be most interested in what they could do for us, so I concentrated on benefits. In my first draft the benefits were lost in a couple of long paragraphs. Only after I read what I had written did I see that I was really talking about four separate benefits. Then I looked for words to summarize each one as a heading. So that Jim would know exactly what he should do, I concluded with specifics. All he had to do was say 'Go.'"

Indirect Strategy. When a reader may oppose a recommendation or when circumstances suggest caution, do not rush to reveal your recommendation. Consider using the following sequence for an indirect approach to your recommendations:

The indirect strategy is appropriate for justification/recommendation reports on sensitive topics and for potentially unreceptive audiences.

- Refer to the problem in general terms, not to your recommendation, in the subject line.

- Describe the problem or need your recommendation addresses. Use specific examples, supporting statistics, and authoritative quotations to lend credibility to the seriousness of the problem.

- Discuss alternative solutions, beginning with the least likely to succeed.

- Present the most promising alternative (your recommendation) last.

- Show how the advantages of your recommendation outweigh its disadvantages.

- Summarize your recommendation. If appropriate, specify the action it requires.

- Ask for authorization to proceed if necessary.

Lara Brown, an executive assistant at a large petroleum and mining company near Calgary, Alberta, received a challenging research assignment. Her boss, the director of human resources, asked her to investigate ways to persuade employees to quit smoking. Here is how she described her task: "We banned smoking many years ago inside our buildings, but we never tried very hard to get smokers to actually kick their habits. My job was to gather information about the problem and how other companies have helped workers stop smoking. The report would go to my boss, but I knew he would pass it along to the management council for approval. If the report were just for my boss, I would put my recommendation right up front because I'm sure he would support it. But the management council is another story. They need persuasion because of the costs involved—and because some of them are smokers. Therefore, I put the alternative I favoured last. To gain credibility, I documented my sources. I had enough material for a ten-page report, but I kept it to two pages in keeping with our company report policy."

Lara single-spaced her report, shown in Figure 12.11, because her company prefers this style. Some companies prefer the readability of double-spacing. Be sure to check with your organization for its preference before printing out your reports.

Documenting sources lends added credibility to justification/ recommendation reports.

Feasibility Reports

Feasibility reports examine the practicality and advisability of following a course of action. They answer this question: Will this plan or proposal work? Feasibility reports typically are internal reports written to advise on such matters as consolidating departments, offering a wellness program to employees, or hiring an outside firm to handle a company's accounting or computing operations. These reports may also be written by consultants called in to investigate a problem. The focus in these reports is on the decision: stopping or proceeding with the proposal. Because your role is not to persuade the reader to accept the decision, you will want to present the decision immediately. In writing feasibility reports, consider these suggestions:

Feasibility reports analyze whether a proposal or plan will work.

A typical feasibility report presents the decision, background information, benefits, problems, costs, and a schedule.

- Announce your decision immediately.

- Provide a description of the background and problem necessitating the proposal.

FIGURE 12.11 Justification/Recommendation Report: Indirect Strategy, MLA Style

DATE: October 11, 2014

TO: Gordon McClure, Director, Human Resources

FROM: Lara Brown, Executive Assistant

SUBJECT: Smoking Cessation Programs for Employees

At your request, I have examined measures that encourage employees to quit smoking. As company records show, approximately 23 percent of our employees still smoke, despite the antismoking and clean-air policies we adopted in 2009. To collect data for this report, I studied professional and government publications; I also inquired at companies and clinics about stop-smoking programs.

This report presents data describing the significance of the problem, three alternative solutions, and a recommendation based on my investigation.

Significance of Problem: Health Care and Productivity Losses

Employees who smoke are costly to any organization. The following statistics show the effects of smoking for workers and for organizations:

- Absenteeism is 40 to 50 percent greater among employees who smoke.
- Accidents are two to three times greater among smokers.
- Bronchitis, lung and heart disease, cancer, and early death are more frequent among smokers (Arhelger 4).

Although our clean-air policy prohibits smoking in the building, shop, and office, we have done little to encourage employees to stop smoking. Many workers still go outside to smoke at lunch and breaks. Other companies have been far more proactive in their attempts to stop employee smoking. Many companies have found that persuading employees to stop smoking was a decisive factor in reducing their extended health insurance premiums. Below is a discussion of three common stop-smoking measures tried by other companies, along with a projected cost factor for each (Rindfleisch 1).

Alternative 1: Literature and Events

The least expensive and easiest stop-smoking measure involves the distribution of literature, such as "The Ten-Step Plan" from Smokefree Enterprises and government pamphlets citing smoking dangers. Some companies have also sponsored events, such as Weedless Wednesday, a one-day event intended to develop group spirit in spurring smokers to quit. "Studies show, however," says one expert, "that literature and company-sponsored events have little permanent effect in helping smokers quit" (Mendel 108).

Cost: Negligible

[Margin annotations:]

Introduces purpose of report, tells method of data collection, and previews organization

Avoids revealing recommendation immediately

Uses headings that combine function and description

Documents data sources for credibility; uses MLA style citing author and page number in the text

Discusses least effective alternative first

FIGURE 12.11 *(continued)*

Alternative 2: Stop-Smoking Programs Outside the Workplace

Local clinics provide treatment programs in classes at their centres. Here in Calgary we have the Smokers' Treatment Centre, ACC Motivation Centre, and New-Choice Program for Stopping Smoking. These behaviour-modification stop-smoking programs are acknowledged to be more effective than literature distribution or incentive programs. However, studies of companies that off-workplace programs show that many employees fail to attend regularly and do not complete the programs.

Cost: $1,200 per employee, three-month individual program   *Highlights costs for*
          (New-Choice Program)   *easy comparison*
          $900 per employee, three-month group session

Alternative 3: Stop-Smoking Programs at the Workplace

Many clinics offer workplace programs with counsellors meeting employees *Arranges alternatives* in company conference rooms. These programs have the advantage of *so that most* keeping a firm's employees together so that they develop a group spirit and *effective is last* exert pressure on each other to succeed. The most successful programs are on company premises and also on company time. Employees participating in such programs had a 72 percent greater success record than employees attending the same stop-smoking program at an outside clinic (Honda 65). A disadvantage of this arrangement, of course, is lost work time—amounting to about two hours a week for three months.

Cost: $900 per employee, three-month program for two hours per
          week release time for three months

Conclusions and Recommendation   *Summarizes findings*
       and ends with specific
       recommendation

Smokers require discipline, counselling, and professional assistance in kicking the nicotine habit, as explained at the Alberta Health Services Web site (Quit Smoking). Workplace stop-smoking programs on company time are more effective than literature, incentives, and off-workplace programs. If our goal is to reduce health care costs and lead our employees to healthful lives, we should invest in a workplace stop-smoking program with release time for smokers. Although the program temporarily reduces productivity, we can expect to recapture that loss in lower health care premiums and healthier employees.

Therefore, I recommend that we begin a stop-smoking treatment program on   *Reveals recommendation* company premises with two hours per week of release time for participants   *only after discussing all* for three months.   *alternatives*

Lists all references in MLA style

3

Works Cited

Magazine — Arhelger, Zack. "The End of Smoking." *The World of Business* 5 Nov.
       2012: 3–8. Print.

Journal — Honda, Emeline Maude. "Managing Anti-Smoking Campaigns: The Case for
       Company Programs." *Management Quarterly* Mar. 2013: 52–69. Print.

Book — Mendel, I. A. The *Puff Stops Here.* Chicago: Science Publications, 2012. Print.

Database — Rindfleisch, Terry. "Smoke-Free Workplaces Can Help Smokers Quit, Expert
       Says." *Knight Ridder Tribune Business News* 4 Jan. 2013.
       ABI/INFORM. Web. 2 July 2013.

Web site — "Quit Smoking." *Alberta Health Services.* 20 Apr. 2011. Web. 1 Oct. 2014.

FIGURE 12.12 Feasibility Report

Outlines organization of the report →

Reveals decision immediately

Describes problem and background

Evaluates positive and negative aspects of proposal objectivity

Presents costs and schedule; omits unnecessary summary

BROWN ENGINEERING, INC.

MEMORANDUM

Date: May 12, 2014

To: Eileen Heffernan, Vice President

From: Ashley Denton-Tait, Human Resources Manager *ADT*

Subject: Feasibility of an E-Mail and Internet Monitoring Program

The plan calling for implementing an employee e-mail and Internet monitoring program is workable and could be fully implemented by July 1. This report discusses the plan's background, benefits, problems, costs, and time frame.

Background: Current Misuse of E-Mail and the Internet. E-mail is efficient and cost-effective when used correctly. We allow employees Internet access for job-related tasks. However, we know that many employees are using their access for personal reasons, resulting in lowered productivity, higher costs, and a strain on our network. We hired an outside consultant who suggested an e-mail and Internet monitoring program.

Benefits of Plan: Appropriate Use of E-Mail and the Internet. The proposed plan calls for installing e-mail and Internet monitoring software, such as EmployeeMonitoring, UltraView Plus, or Spector CNE. We would fully disclose to employees that this software will be monitoring their online activity. We will also teach employees what e-mail and Internet use is appropriate. In addition to increased productivity, lowered costs, and improved network performance, this software will produce numerous other benefits. It can help protect our company against loss of intellectual property, trade secrets, and confidential information. The software will limit any liability for sexual harassment, workplace harassment, or cyberstalking.

Employee Acceptance. One of the biggest problems will be convincing employees to accept this new policy without them feeling as if their privacy is being violated. However, our consultant can help us communicate the reasons for this policy in such a way that employees will understand its need. In addition, adequate training will help employees understand appropriate use of e-mail and the Internet on the job.

Costs. Implementing the monitoring plan involves two direct costs. The first is the initial software cost of $400 to $900, depending on the package we choose. The second cost involves employee training and trainer fees. Initial training will cost about $1,000. However, the expenditures are within the budget planned for this project.

Time Frame. Selecting the software package will take about two weeks. Preparing a training program will require another three weeks. Once the program is started, I expect a breaking-in period of at least three months. By July 1 the e-mail and Internet monitoring program will be fully functional resulting in increased productivity, decreased costs, lowered liability, and improved network performance.

Please let me know by May 20 if you would like additional information about e-mail and Internet monitoring programs.

- Discuss the benefits of the proposal.

- Describe the problems that may result.

- Calculate the costs associated with the proposal, if appropriate.

- Show the time frame necessary for implementing the proposal.

Ashley Denton-Tait, human resources manager for a large public accounting firm, wrote the feasibility report shown in Figure 12.12. Because she discovered that the company was losing time and money as a result of personal e-mail and Internet use by employees, she talked with the vice president, Eileen Heffernan, about the problem. Eileen didn't want Ashley to take time away from her job to investigate what other companies were doing to prevent this type of problem. Instead, she suggested that they hire a consultant to investigate what other companies were doing to prevent or limit personal e-mail and Internet use. The vice president then wanted to know whether the consultant's plan was feasible. Although Ashley's report is only one page long, it provides all the necessary information: background, benefits, employee acceptance, costs, and time frame.

Yardstick Reports

Yardstick reports examine problems with two or more solutions. To evaluate the best solution, the writer establishes criteria by which to compare the alternatives. The criteria then act as a yardstick against which all the alternatives are measured. This yardstick approach is effective when companies establish specifications for equipment purchases and then compare each manufacturer's product with the established specs. The yardstick approach is also effective when exact specifications cannot be established.

For example, when a major aerospace firm considered relocating its global headquarters, it evaluated many cities, including Montreal, Toronto, and Vancouver. For each of these sites, the company compared geography, economic growth, airline service, training programs for labour, land availability and costs, zoning and environmental regulations, housing costs, and all-important tax breaks. Although the company did not set up exact specifications for each category, it compared each city in these various categories. The real advantage to yardstick reports is that alternatives can be measured consistently by using the same criteria. Reports that use a yardstick approach typically are organized this way:

- Begin by describing the problem or need.

- Explain possible solutions and alternatives.

- Establish criteria for comparing the alternatives; tell how the criteria were selected or developed.

- Discuss and evaluate each alternative in terms of the criteria.

- Draw conclusions and make recommendations.

Jenny Gardiner, benefits administrator for computer manufacturer CompuTech, was called on to write a report comparing outplacement agencies. These agencies counsel discharged employees and help them find new positions; fees are paid by the former employer. Jenny knew that times were bad for CompuTech and that extensive downsizing would take place in the next two years. Her task was to compare outplacement agencies and recommend one to CompuTech. After collecting information, Jenny found that her biggest problem was organizing the data and developing a system for making comparisons. All the outplacement agencies she investigated seemed to offer the same basic package of services. Here is how she described her report, shown in Figure 12.13:

"With the information I gathered about three outplacement agencies, I made a big grid listing the names of the agencies across the top. Down the side I listed general categories—such as services, costs, and reputation. Then I filled in the information for each agency. This grid, which began to look like a table, helped me organize all the bits and pieces of information. After studying the grid, I saw that all the information could be grouped into four categories: counselling services, administrative and research assistance, reputation, and costs. I made these the criteria I would use to compare agencies. Next, I divided my grid into two parts, which became Table 1 and Table 2. In writing the report, I could have made each agency a separate heading, followed by a discussion of how it measured up to the criteria. Immediately, though, I saw how repetitious that would become. So I used the criteria as headings and discussed how each agency met each criterion—or failed to meet it. Making a recommendation was easy once I had made the tables and could see how the agencies compared."

The Checklist box on page 337 summarizes the key steps to follow in writing successful analytical reports.

Yardstick reports consider alternative solutions to a problem by establishing criteria against which to weigh options.

Grids are a useful way to organize and compare data for a yardstick report.

FIGURE 12.13 Yardstick Report

<table>
<tr><td>DATE:</td><td>April 30, 2014</td></tr>
<tr><td>TO:</td><td>Graham T. Burnett, Vice President</td></tr>
<tr><td>FROM:</td><td>Jenny Gardiner, Benefits Administrator</td></tr>
<tr><td>SUBJECT:</td><td>Selecting Outplacement Services</td></tr>
</table>

Here is the report you requested April 2 investigating the possibility of CompuTech's use of outplacement services. It discusses the problem of counselling services for discharged staff and establishes criteria for selecting an outplacement agency. It then evaluates three prospective agencies and presents a recommendation based on that evaluation.

Introduces purpose and gives overview of report organization

Problem: Counselling Discharged Staff

In an effort to reduce costs and increase competitiveness, CompuTech will begin a program of staff reduction that will involve releasing up to 20 percent of our workforce over the next 12 to 24 months. Many of these employees have been with us for ten or more years, and they are not being released for performance faults. These employees deserve a severance package that includes counselling and assistance in finding new jobs.

Discusses background briefly because readers already know the problem

Solution and Alternatives: Outplacement Agencies

Numerous outplacement agencies offer discharged employees counselling and assistance in locating new jobs. This assistance minimizes not only the negative feelings related to job loss but also the very real possibility of litigation. Potentially expensive lawsuits have been lodged against some companies by unhappy employees who felt they were unfairly released.

Uses dual headings, giving function and description

In seeking an outplacement agency, we should find one that offers advice to the sponsoring company and to dischargees. Frankly, many of our managers need help in conducting termination sessions. CompuTech could unwittingly become liable to lawsuits because our managers are uninformed of specific procedures. Here in the metropolitan area, I have located three potential outplacement agencies appropriate to serve our needs: Gray & Associates, Right Access, and Careers Plus.

Announces solution and the alternatives it presents

Establishing Criteria for Selecting Agency

To choose among the three agencies, I established criteria based on professional articles, discussions with officials at other companies using outplacement agencies, and interviews with agencies. Here are the four groups of criteria I used in evaluating the three agencies:

Tells how criteria were selected

1. Counselling services—including job search advice, résumé help, crisis management, corporate counselling, and availability of full-time counsellors

2. Administrative and research assistance—including availability of administrative staff, librarian, and personal computers

3. Reputation—based on a telephone survey of former clients and listing with a professional association

4. Costs—for both group programs and executive services

Creates four criteria to use as yardstick in evaluating alternatives

FIGURE 12.13 (*continued*)

Vice President Burnett   Page 2   April 30, 2014

Discussion: Evaluating Agencies by Criteria

Each agency was evaluated using the four criteria just described. Data comparing the first three criteria are summarized in Table 1.

Table 1

A COMPARISON OF SERVICES AND REPUTATIONS
FOR THREE LOCAL OUTPLACEMENT AGENCIES

	Gray & Associates	Right Access	Careers Plus
Counselling services			
Résumé advice	Yes	Yes	Yes
Crisis management	Yes	No	Yes
Corporate counselling	Yes	No	No
Full-time counsellors	Yes	No	Yes
Administrative, research assistance			
Administrative staff	Yes	Yes	Yes
Librarian, research library	Yes	No	Yes
Personal computers	Yes	No	Yes
Listed by National Association of Career Consultants	Yes	No	Yes
Reputation (telephone survey of former clients)	Excellent	Good	Excellent

Counselling Services

All three agencies offered similar basic counselling services with job-search and résumé advice. They differed, however, in three significant areas.

Right Access does not offer crisis management, a service that puts the discharged employee in contact with a counsellor the same day the employee is released. Experts in the field consider this service especially important to help the dischargee begin "bonding" with the counsellor immediately. Immediate counselling also helps the dischargee through the most traumatic moments of one of life's great disappointments and helps him or her learn how to break the news to family members. Crisis management can be instrumental in reducing lawsuits because dischargees immediately begin to focus on career planning instead of concentrating on their pain and need for revenge. Moreover, Right Access does not employ full-time counsellors; it hires part-timers according to demand. Industry authorities advise against using agencies whose staff members are inexperienced and employed on an "as-needed" basis.

In addition, neither Right Access nor Careers Plus offers regular corporate counselling, which I feel is critical in training our managers to conduct terminal interviews. Careers Plus, however, suggested that it could schedule special workshops if desired.

Administrative and Research Assistance

Both Gray & Associates and Careers Plus offer complete administrative services and personal computers. Dischargees have access to staff and equipment to assist them in their job searches. These agencies also provide research libraries, librarians, and databases of company information to help in securing interviews.

(*Continued*)

Marginal annotations:
- Summarizes complex data in table for easy reading and reference
- Highlights the similarities and differences among the alternatives
- Places table close to spot where it is first mentioned
- Does not repeat obvious data from table

FIGURE 12.13 (*continued*)

Vice President Burnett   Page 3   April 30, 2014

Reputation

To assess the reputation of each agency, I checked its listing with the National Association of Career Consultants. This is a voluntary organization of outplacement agencies that monitors and polices its members. Gray & Associates and Careers Plus are listed; Right Access is not.

For further evidence I conducted a telephone survey of former agency clients. The three agencies supplied me with names and telephone numbers of companies and individuals they had served. I called four former clients for each agency. Most of the individuals were pleased with the outplacement services they had received. I asked each client the same questions so that I could compare responses.

Costs

All three agencies have two separate fee schedules, summarized in Table 2. The first schedule is for group programs intended for lower-level employees. These include off-site or on-site single-day workshop sessions, and the prices range from $1,200 a session (at Right Access) to $1,700 per session (at Gray & Associates). An additional fee of $50 to $60 is charged for each participant.

The second fee schedule covers executive services. The counselling is individual and costs from 10 to 18 percent of the dischargee's previous year's salary. Since CompuTech will be forced to release numerous managerial staff members, the executive fee schedule is critical. Table 2 shows fees for a hypothetical case involving a manager who earns $80,000 a year.

Table 2

A COMPARISON OF COSTS FOR THREE AGENCIES

	Gray & Associates	Right Access	Careers Plus
Group programs	$1,700/session $55/participant	$1,200/session $50/participant	$1,600/session $60/participant
Executive services	15% of previous year's salary	10% of previous year's salary	18% of previous year's salary plus $1,000 fee
Manager at $80,000/year	$12,000	$8,000	$15,400

Conclusions and Recommendations

Although Right Access charges the lowest fees, it lacks crisis management, corporate counselling, full-time counsellors, library facilities, and personal computers. Moreover, it is not listed by the National Association of Career Consultants. Therefore, the choice is between Gray & Associates and Careers Plus. Because they offer similar services, the deciding factor is costs. Careers Plus would charge $3,400 more for counselling a manager than would Gray & Associates. Although Gray & Associates has fewer computers available, all other elements of its services seem good. Therefore, I recommend that CompuTech hire Gray & Associates as an outplacement agency to counsel discharged employees.

Discusses objectively how each agency meets criteria

Selects most important data from table to discuss

Gives reasons for making recommendation

Narrows choice to final alternative

Checklist

Writing Analytical Reports

Introduction

- **Identify the purpose of the report.** Explain why the report is being written.

- **Describe the significance of the topic.** Explain why the report is important.

- **Preview the organization of the report.** Especially for long reports, explain to the reader how the report will be organized.

- **Summarize the conclusions and recommendations for receptive audiences.** Use the direct strategy only if you have the confidence of the reader.

Findings

- **Discuss pros and cons.** In recommendation/justification reports evaluate the advantages and disadvantages of each alternative. For unreceptive audiences, consider placing the recommended alternative last.

- **Establish criteria to evaluate alternatives.** In yardstick reports, create criteria to use in measuring each alternative consistently.

- **Support the findings with evidence.** Supply facts, statistics, expert opinion, survey data, and other proof from which you can draw logical conclusions.

- **Organize the findings for logic and readability.** Arrange the findings around the alternatives or the reasons leading to the conclusion. Use headings, enumerations, lists, tables, and graphics to focus emphasis.

Conclusions/Recommendations

- **Draw reasonable conclusions from the findings.** Develop conclusions that answer the research question. Justify the conclusions with highlights from the findings.

- **Make recommendations, if asked.** For multiple recommendations prepare a list. Use action verbs. Explain fully the benefits of the recommendation or steps necessary to solve the problem or answer the question

Summary of Learning Objectives

1 Tabulate information, use statistical techniques, and create decision matrices to sort and interpret business report data skillfully and accurately. Report data are more meaningful when sorted into tables or when analyzed by mean (the arithmetic average), median (the midpoint in a group of numbers), and mode (the most frequent response). Range represents a span between the highest and lowest numbers. Grids help organize complex data into rows and columns. Decision matrices employ a special grid with weights to help decision makers choose objectively among complex options. Accuracy in applying statistical techniques is crucial to gain and maintain credibility with the reader.

2 Draw meaningful conclusions and make practical report recommendations after sound and valid analysis. Conclusions tell what the survey data mean—especially in relation to the original report problem. They interpret key findings and may attempt to explain what caused the report problem. They are usually enumerated. In reports that call for recommendations, writers make specific suggestions for actions that can solve the report problem. Recommendations should be feasible, practical, and potentially agreeable to the audience. They should all relate to the initial problem. Recommendations may be combined with conclusions.

3 Organize report data logically and provide cues to aid comprehension. Reports may be organized in many ways, including by (a) time (establishing a chronology or history of events), (b) component (discussing a problem by geography, division, or product), (c) importance (arranging data from most important to least important or vice versa), (d) criteria (comparing items by standards), or (e) convention (using an already established grouping). To help guide the reader through the text, introductions, transitions, and headings serve as cues.

4 Write short informational reports that describe routine tasks. Periodic, trip, convention, progress, and investigative reports are examples of typical informational reports. Such reports include an introduction that may preview the report purpose and supply background data if necessary. The body of the report is generally divided into three to five segments that may be organized by time, component, importance, criteria, or convention. The body should include clear headings and may use an informal, conversational style, unless the audience expects a more formal tone. The summary or conclusion reviews the main points and discusses what action will follow. The conclusion may offer a final thought, express appreciation, or signal a willingness to provide further information. Like all professional business documents, a clear, concise, well-written report cements the writer's credibility with the audience. Because they are so important, reports require writers to apply all the writing techniques addressed in Chapters 4, 5, and 6.

5 **Compose short analytical reports that solve business problems.** Typical analytical reports include justification/recommendation reports, feasibility reports, and yardstick reports. Justification/recommendation reports organized directly identify a problem, immediately announce a recommendation or solution, explain and discuss its merits, and summarize the action to be taken. Justification/recommendation reports organized indirectly describe a problem, discuss alternative solutions, prove the superiority of one solution, and ask for authorization to proceed with that solution. Feasibility reports study the advisability of following a course of action. They generally announce the author's proposal immediately. Then they describe the background of, advantages and disadvantages of, costs of, and time frame for implementing the proposal. Yardstick reports compare two or more solutions to a problem by measuring each against a set of established criteria. They usually describe a problem, explain possible solutions, establish criteria for comparing alternatives, evaluate each alternative in terms of the criteria, draw conclusions, and make recommendations. The advantage to yardstick reports is consistency in comparing alternatives. Most reports serve as a basis for decision making in business.

Chapter Review

1. What is cross-tabulation, and when is it useful? (Obj. 1)
2. Calculate the mean, median, and mode for these numbers: 3, 4, 4, 4, 10. (Obj. 1)
3. What are correlations? (Obj. 1)
4. Why is a decision matrix a valuable managerial tool? (Obj. 1)
5. Why is the ability to conduct research and draw conclusions likely to increase your value to your employer? (Obj. 2)
6. How can you make your report conclusions as objective and bias free as possible? (Obj. 2)
7. Name five methods for organizing report data. Be prepared to discuss each. (Obj. 3)
8. What three devices can report writers use to prevent readers from getting lost in the text? (Obj. 3)
9. Name at least four guidelines for creating effective headings, and be prepared to explain them. (Obj. 3)
10. How do business writers organize most informational reports, and what can writers assume about the audience? (Obj. 4)
11. Describe periodic reports and what they generally contain. (Obj. 4)
12. What should progress reports include? (Obj. 4)
13. When is the indirect strategy appropriate for justification/recommendation reports? (Obj. 5)
14. What is a feasibility report? Are such reports generally intended for internal or external audiences? (Obj. 5)
15. What is a yardstick report? (Obj. 5)

Critical Thinking

1. When tabulating and analyzing data, you may discover relationships among two or more variable that help explain the findings. Can you trust these correlations and assume that their relationship is one of cause and effect? (Obj. 1)
2. Researchers can draw various conclusions from a set of data. How do you know how to shape conclusions and recommendations? (Obj. 2)
3. How can you increase your chances that your report recommendations will be implemented? (Obj. 2)
4. Should all reports be organized so that they follow the sequence of investigation—that is, a description of the initial problem, an analysis of the issues, data collection, data analysis, and conclusions? Why or why not? (Obj. 3)
5. What are the major differences between informational and analytical reports? (Objs. 4, 5)
6. **Ethical Issue:** You have learned that drawing conclusions involves subjectivity, although your goal is to remain objective. Even the most even-handed researchers bring their goals, background, and frame of reference to bear on the inferences they make. Consider the contentious issue of climate change. Most mainstream scientists now believe climate change to be real and induced by human activity. However, some scientists cast doubt on the extent to which global warming is human-made and constitutes an imminent threat. How can something objectively measurable be so contentious? (Obj. 2)

12.1 Tabulation and Interpretation of Survey Results (Obj. 1)

TEAM

Your business communication class at North Shore College was asked by the college bookstore manager, Harry Locke, to conduct a survey. Concerned about the environment, Locke wants to learn students' reactions to eliminating plastic bags, of which 45,000 are given away annually by the bookstore. Students answered questions about a number of proposals, resulting in the following raw data:

For major purchases the bookstore should do the following:

	Agree	Undecided	Disagree
1. Continue to provide plastic bags	132	17	411
2. Provide no bags; encourage students to bring their own bags	414	25	121
3. Provide no bags; offer cloth bags at a reduced price (about $3)	357	19	184
4. Give a cloth bag with each major purchase, the cost to be included in registration fees	63	15	482

Your Task. In groups of four or five, do the following:

a. Convert the data into a table (see Figure 12.1) with a descriptive title. Arrange the items in a logical sequence.

b. How could these survey data be cross-tabulated? Would cross-tabulation serve any purpose?

c. Given the conditions of this survey, name at least three conclusions that could be drawn from the data.

d. Prepare three to five recommendations to be submitted to Mr. Locke. How could they be implemented?

e. Role-play a meeting in which the recommendations and implementation plan are presented to Mr. Locke. One student plays the role of Mr. Locke; the remaining students play the role of the presenters.

12.2 Distinguishing Between Conclusions and Recommendations (Obj. 2)

A study of red light traffic violations produced the following findings: Red light traffic violations were responsible for more than 25,000 crashes in several metropolitan areas. Crashes from running red lights decreased by 10 percent in areas using camera programs to cite offenders. Two out of seven local governments studied showed a profit from the programs; the others lost money.[3]

Your Task. Based on the preceding facts, indicate whether the following statements are conclusions or recommendations:

a. Red light violations are dangerous offences.

b. Red light cameras are an effective traffic safety tool.

c. Local governments should be allowed to implement red light camera programs.

d. Although red light camera programs are expensive, they prevent crashes and are, therefore, worthwhile.

e. The city of Centreville should not implement a red light program because of the program's cost.

f. Red light programs are not necessarily profitable for local governments.

12.3 Buying a Car: Create a Decision Matrix (Objs. 1, 2)

David, an outrigger canoe racer, needs to buy a new car. He wants a vehicle that will carry his disassembled boat and outrigger. At the same time, he will need to travel long distances on business. His passion is soft-top sports cars, but he is also concerned about gas mileage. These four criteria are impossible to find in one vehicle.

David has the following choices:

- Station wagon
- SUV with or without a sunroof
- Four-door sedan, a fuel-efficient "family car"
- Sports car, convertible

He wants to consider the following criteria:

- Price
- Ability to carry cargo, such as a canoe
- Fuel efficiency
- Comfort over long distances
- Good looks and fun
- Quality build/manufacturer's reputation

Your Task. Follow the steps outlined in Figure 12.3 to determine an assessment scale and to assign a score to each feature. Then consider which weights are probably most important to David, given his needs. Calculate the totals to find the vehicle that is most suitable for David.

12.4 Organizing Data (Obj. 3)

Your Task: In groups of three to five, discuss how the findings in the following reports could be best organized. Consider these methods: time, component, importance, criteria, and convention.

a. A monthly sales report submitted to the sales manager.

b. A progress report submitted six months into the process of planning the program for your organization's convention.

c. A report comparing three locations for a fast-food company's new restaurant. The report presents data on real estate values, construction costs, traffic patterns, competition, provincial and territorial taxes, labour availability, and population demographics.

d. A report describing the history of the development of dwarf and spur apple trees, starting with the first genetic dwarfs discovered about 100 years ago and progressing to today's grafted varieties on dwarfing rootstocks.

e. An informational brochure for job candidates that describes your company's areas of employment: accounting, finance, information systems, operations management, marketing, production, and computer-aided design.

f. A recommendation report to be submitted to management presenting four building plans to improve access to your building, in compliance with federal regulations. The plans range considerably in feasibility and cost.

g. An informational report describing a company's expansion plans in South America, Europe, Australia, and Southeast Asia.

h. An employee performance appraisal submitted annually.

12.5 Writing a Survey: Studying Employee Use of Instant Messaging (Obj. 1)

WEB

Instant messaging (IM) is a popular way to exchange messages in real time. It offers the convenience of telephone conversations and e-mail. Best of all, it allows employees to contact anyone in the world while retaining a written copy of the conversation—without a whopping telephone bill! But IM is risky for companies. They may lose trade secrets or confidential information over insecure lines. They also may be liable if inappropriate material is exchanged. Moreover, IM opens the door to viruses that can infect a company's entire computer system.

Your boss just read an article stating that 40 percent of companies now use IM for business and up to 90 percent of employees use IM *without* their manager's knowledge or authorization. She asks you to prepare a survey of your 48-member staff to learn how many are using IM. She wants to know what type of IM software they have downloaded, how many hours a day they spend on IM, what the advantages of IM are, and so forth. The goal is not to identify those using or abusing IM. Instead, the goal is to learn when, how, and why employees use IM so that appropriate policies can be designed.

Your Task. Use the Web or an electronic database to learn more about IM. Then prepare a short employee survey. Include an appropriate introduction that explains the survey and encourages a response. Should you ask for names on the survey? How can you encourage employees to return the forms? Your instructor may want to expand this survey into a report by having you produce fictitious survey results, analyze the findings, draw conclusions, and make recommendations.

12.6 Executive Summary: Condensing the Facts for Your Boss (Obj. 4)

WEB

Like many executives, your boss is too rushed to read long journal articles. But she is eager to keep up with developments in her field. Assume she has asked you to help her stay abreast of research in her field. She asks you to submit to her one summary every month on an article of interest.

Your Task. In your field of study, select a professional journal, such as *Landscape Management*. Using an electronic database search or a Web search, look for articles in your target journal. Select an article that is at least five pages long and is interesting to you. Write an executive summary in memo format. Include an introduction that might begin with *As you requested, I am submitting this executive summary of. . . .* Identify the author, article name, journal, and date of publication. Explain what the author intended to do in the study or article. Summarize three or four of the most important findings of the study or article. Use descriptive rather than functional headings. Summarize any recommendations you make. Your boss would also like a concluding statement indicating your reaction to the article. Address your memo to Susan Wright.

12.7 Periodic Report: Filling in the Boss (Obj. 4)

E-MAIL

You work hard at your job, but you rarely see your boss. Keeping him or her informed of your activities and accomplishments is difficult.

Your Task. For a job that you currently hold or a previous one, describe your regular activities, discuss irregular events that management should be aware of, and highlight any special needs or problems. Use a memo format in writing a periodic e-mail report to your boss.

12.8 Progress Report: Checking In (Obj. 4)

E-MAIL

Students writing a long report described in Chapter 13 must keep their instructors informed of their progress.

Your Task. Write a progress report informing your instructor of your work. Briefly describe the project (its purpose, scope, limitations, and methodology), work completed, work yet to be completed, problems encountered, future activities, and expected completion date. Address the e-mail report to your instructor.

12.9 Investigative Report: Marketing Abroad (Obj. 4)

INTERCULTURAL

WEB

You have been asked to prepare a training program for Canadian companies doing business outside the country.

Your Task. Select a country to investigate. Check to see whether your school or library subscribes to CultureGrams, an online resource with rich data about the daily lives and cultures of the world's peoples. Collect data from CultureGrams files, CountryWatch, or the country's embassy in Ottawa. Interview on-campus international students. Use the Web to discover data about the country. See Activity 13.6 and Figure 13.5 in Chapter 13 for additional ideas on gathering information on intercultural communication. Collect information about formats for written communication, observance of holidays, customary greetings, business ethics, and other topics of interest to businesspeople. Remember that your report should promote business, not tourism. Prepare a memo report addressed to Kelly Johnson, editor for the training program materials.

12.10 Justification/Recommendation Report: Developing an Organizational Media Use Policy (Obj. 5)

TEAM

WEB

As a manager in a mid-sized engineering firm, you are aware that members of your department frequently use e-mail, social networking sites, instant messaging, and texting for private messages, shopping, and games. In addition to the strain on computer facilities, you worry about declining productivity and security problems. When you walked by one worker's computer and saw what looked like pornography on the screen, you knew you had to do something. Although workplace privacy is a hot-button issue for unions and employee-rights groups, employers have legitimate reasons for wanting to know what is happening on their computers. A high percentage of lawsuits involve the use and abuse of e-mail, and increasingly, other media as well. You think that the executive council should establish some kind of media use policy. The council is generally receptive to sound suggestions, especially if they are inexpensive. At present no media policy exists, and you fear that the executive council is not fully aware of the dangers. You decide to talk with other managers about the problem and write a justification/recommendation report.

Your Task. In teams discuss the need for a comprehensive media use policy. Using the Web and electronic databases, find information about other firms' use of such policies. Look for examples of companies struggling with lawsuits over abuse of technology on the job. In your report should you describe suitable policies? Should you recommend computer monitoring and surveillance software? Should the policy cover instant messaging, social networking sites, blogging, and smartphone use? Each member of the team should present and support his or her ideas regarding what should be included in the report. Individually or as a team, write a convincing justification/recommendation report to the executive council based on the conclusions you draw from your research and discussion. Decide whether you should be direct or indirect.

12.11 Feasibility Report: Improving Employee Fitness (Obj. 5)

Your company is considering ways to promote employee fitness and morale.

Your Task. Select a possible fitness program that seems reasonable for your company. Consider a softball league, bowling teams, basketball league, lunchtime walks, lunchtime fitness speakers and demos, company-sponsored health club membership, a workout room, a fitness centre, a fitness director, and so on. Assume that your boss has tentatively agreed to one of the programs and has asked you to write a memo report investigating its feasibility.

12.12 Yardstick Report: Measuring the Alternatives (Obj. 5)

Your Task. Identify a problem or procedure that must be changed at your work or in an organization you know. Consider challenges, such as poor scheduling of employees, outdated equipment, slow order processing, failure to encourage employees to participate fully, restrictive rules, inadequate training, or disappointed customers. Consider several solutions or courses of action (retaining the present status could be one alternative). Develop criteria that you could use to evaluate each alternative. Write a report measuring each alternative by the yardstick you have created. Recommend a course of action to your boss or to the organization head.

Grammar and Mechanics C.L.U.E. Review 12

Total Review

The first ten chapters reviewed specific guides from Appendix A, Grammar and Mechanics Guide. The exercises in this and the remaining chapters are total reviews, covering all of the grammar and mechanics guides and confusing words and frequently misspelled words.

Each of the following sentences has a total of **three** errors in grammar, punctuation, capitalization, usage, or spelling. On a separate sheet, write a correct version. Avoid adding new phrases, starting new sentences, or rewriting in your own words. When finished, compare your responses with the key beginning on page Key-1.

Example: After our supervisor and her returned from their meeting at 2:00 p.m. we were able to sort the customers names more quickly.

Revision: After our supervisor and **she** returned from their meeting at **2 p.m.**, we were able to sort the **customers'** names more quickly.

1. Toyota, the best-selling japanese carmaker, had enjoyed a strong favourable perception of high quality therefore it long remained unharmed by a string of much-publicized recalls.

2. The auditors report, which my boss and me read very closely, featured the following three main flaws, factual inaccuracies, omissions, and incomprehensible language.

3. 8 of the 20 workers in my department were fired, as a result, we had to work much harder to acheive our objectives.

4. As a matter of principal, we offer some form of financial support to more than sixty percent of our current MBA candidates. Which proves our commitment to executive education.

5. To post easily to your blog on the Web you could use Mozilla's web browser firefox and an add-on called ScribeFire.

6. Peters presentation to a nonprofit group on advanced Internet marketing netted him only two hundred dollars, a fifth of his usual honorarium but he believes in pro bono work.

7. The old company manual covers the basics of: searching, selecting interpreting and organizing data.

8. Our latest press release which was written in our Corporate Communication Department announces the opening of 3 Canadian offices.

9. Letter reports usualy has side margins of one and a half to two centimetres.

10. The CEO and Manager, who had went to a meeting in the West, delivered a report to Jeff and I when they returned.

Endnotes

1 Androich, A., & Laird, K. (2011, March 28). Secrets of Canada's top loyalty programs. *Marketing,* pp. 19–24.

2 Ewing, J. (2007, May 4). First mover in mobile: How Nokia is selling cell phones to the developing world. *BusinessWeek Online*. Retrieved June 5, 2007, from http://www.businessweek.com

3 Red light camera reform. (2003, May/June). *WestWays,* 19.

CHAPTER 13

Proposals, Business Plans, and Formal Business Reports

OBJECTIVES

After studying this chapter, you should be able to

1. Discuss the general uses and basic components of informal proposals and grasp their audience and purpose.

2. Discuss formal proposals and their specific components.

3. Identify the components of typical business plans and ethically create buy-in for your business ideas.

4. Describe the components of the front matter in formal business reports, and show how they further the purpose of your report.

5. Describe the body and back matter of formal business reports and how they serve the purpose of your report.

6. Specify tips that aid writers of formal business reports.

© Jose Luis Pelaez, Inc./CORBIS

Procrastination expert Piers Steel reports that although at least 95 percent of the population procrastinates, only 15 to 20 percent are regular offenders. To manage this negative tendency, he suggests limiting your access to e-mail and making your passwords for gaming and social media Web sites 50-character strings to make logging in difficult.[1] Why do you think people procrastinate? What strategies work for you to avoid procrastination?

Preparing Informal Proposals

Proposals are written offers to solve problems, provide services, or sell equipment. Some proposals are internal, often taking the form of justification and recommendation reports. You learned about these reports in Chapter 12. Most proposals, however, are external and serve as a critical means of selling equipment and services that generate income for many organizations.

Proposals can be divided into two categories: solicited and unsolicited. When government agencies or firms know exactly what they want, they prepare a request for proposal (RFP), specifying their requirements. Government agencies and private businesses use RFPs to solicit competitive bids from vendors. Most proposals are solicited, such as those presented by provincial, territorial, or federal government agencies. Enterprising companies looking for work might submit unsolicited proposals and are watchful for business opportunities.

LEARNING OBJECTIVE 1

Discuss the general uses and basic components of informal proposals and grasp their audience and purpose.

Government agencies and many companies use requests for proposals (RFPs) to solicit competitive bids on projects.

Components of Informal Proposals

Informal proposals may be presented in short (two- to four-page) letters. Sometimes called *letter proposals*, they may contain six principal components: introduction, background, proposal, staffing, budget, and authorization request. As you can see in Figure 13.1, both informal and formal proposals contain these six basic parts.

FIGURE 13.1 Components of Formal and Informal Proposals

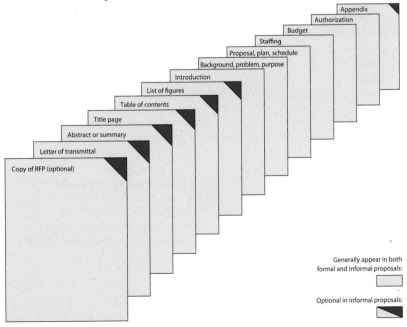

Appendix
Authorization
Budget
Staffing
Proposal, plan, schedule
Background, problem, purpose
Introduction
List of figures
Table of contents
Title page
Abstract or summary
Letter of transmittal
Copy of RFP (optional)

Generally appear in both formal and informal proposals:

Optional in informal proposals:

Introduction. Most proposals begin by briefly explaining the reasons for the proposal and by highlighting the writer's qualifications. To make your introduction more persuasive, you need to provide a "hook," such as the following:

- Hint at extraordinary results with details to be revealed shortly.

- Promise low costs or speedy results.

- Mention a remarkable resource (well-known authority, new computer program, well-trained staff) available exclusively to you.

- Identify a serious problem (worry item) and promise a solution, to be explained later.

- Specify a key issue or benefit that you feel is the heart of the proposal.

Although writers may know what goes into the proposal introduction, many face writer's block before they can get started. Writer's block can be a barrier because the writer simply doesn't know how to get started. It is often a good idea to put off writing the proposal introduction until after you have completed other parts. In longer proposals the introduction also describes the scope and limitations of the project, as well as outlining the organization of the material to come.

> In the background section of a proposal, the writer discusses the problem and goals of the project.

Background, Problem, and Purpose. The background section identifies the problem and discusses the goals or purposes of the project. In an unsolicited proposal, your goal is to convince the reader that a problem exists. Thus, you must present the problem in detail, discussing such factors as monetary losses, failure to comply with government regulations, or loss of customers. In a solicited proposal, your aim is to persuade the reader that you understand the problem completely. Thus, if you are responding to an RFP, this means repeating its language.

> The actual proposal section must give enough information to secure the contract but not so much detail that the services are no longer needed.

Proposal, Plan, and Schedule. In the proposal section itself, you should discuss your plan for solving the problem. In some proposals this is tricky because you want to disclose enough of your plan to secure the contract without giving away so much information that your services aren't needed. Without specifics, though, your proposal has little chance, so you must decide how much to reveal. Tell what you propose to do and how it will benefit the reader. Remember, too, that a proposal is a sales presentation. Sell your methods, product, and "deliverables" (items that will be left with the client). In this section some writers specify how the project will be managed and how its progress will be audited. Most writers also include a schedule of activities or timetable showing when events will take place.

> The staffing section promotes the credentials and expertise of the project leaders and support staff.

Staffing. The staffing section of a proposal describes the credentials and expertise of the project leaders. It may also identify the size and qualifications of the support staff, along with other resources, such as computer facilities and special programs for analyzing statistics. The staffing section is a good place to endorse and promote your staff and to demonstrate to the client that your company can do the job. Some firms follow industry standards and include staff qualifications in an appendix.

> Because a proposal is a legal contract, the budget must be carefully researched.

Budget. A central item in most proposals is the budget, a list of proposed project costs. You need to prepare this section carefully because it represents a contract; you cannot raise the price later—even if your costs increase. You can—and should—protect yourself from rising costs with a deadline for acceptance. In the budget section, some writers itemize hours and costs; others present a total sum only. Your analysis of the project will help you decide what kind of budget to prepare.

Authorization Request. Informal proposals often close with a request for approval or authorization. In addition, the closing should remind the reader of key benefits and motivate action. It might also include a deadline beyond which the offer is invalid. Authorization information can be as simple as naming in the letter of transmittal the company official who would approve the contract resulting from the proposal. However, in most cases, a *model contract* is sent along that responds to the requirements specified by the RFP. This model contract almost always results in negotiations before the final project contract is awarded.

Preparing Formal Proposals

Proposals became a staple in the aerospace industry in the 1950s to streamline the bidding for government defence projects. Because proposals are vital to their success, high-tech companies and defence contractors maintain specialists who do nothing but write proposals. Such proposals typically tell how a problem can be solved, what procedure will be followed, who will do it, how long it will take, and how much it will cost. When receiving bids, companies today want to be able to "compare apples with apples." They also want the protection offered by proposals, which are legal contracts. As you can imagine, writing a formal proposal to bid on a multimillion-dollar contract requires careful preparation, expertise, and countless staff hours.

LEARNING OBJECTIVE 2

Discuss formal proposals and their specific components.

Special Components of Formal Proposals

Formal proposals differ from informal proposals not in style but in size and format. Formal proposals respond to big projects and may range from 5 to 200 or more pages. To facilitate comprehension and reference, they are organized into many parts, as shown in Figure 13.1. In addition to the six basic components described for informal proposals, formal proposals may contain some or all of the following front and end parts.

Copy of the RFP. A copy of the RFP may be included in the opening parts of a formal proposal. Large organizations may have more than one RFP circulating, and identification is necessary.

Letter of Transmittal. A letter of transmittal, usually bound inside formal proposals, addresses the person who is designated to receive the proposal or who will make the final decision. The letter describes how you learned about the problem or confirms that the proposal responds to the enclosed RFP. This persuasive letter briefly presents the major features and benefits of your proposal. Here you should assure the reader that you are authorized to make the bid and mention the time limit for which the bid stands. You may also offer to provide additional information and ask for action, if appropriate.

Formal proposals might also contain a copy of the RFP, a letter of transmittal, an abstract, a title page, a table of contents, a list of figures, and an appendix.

Abstract or Executive Summary. An abstract is a brief summary (typically one page) of a proposal's highlights intended for specialists or for technical readers. An executive summary also reviews the proposal's highlights, but it is written for managers and should be less technically oriented. Formal proposals may contain either or both. For more information about writing executive summaries and abstracts, use a search engine, such as Google.

An abstract summarizes a proposal's highlights for specialists; an executive summary does so for managers.

Title Page. The title page includes the following items, generally in this order: title of proposal, name of client organization, RFP number or other announcement, date of submission, authors' names, and the name of their organization.

Table of Contents. Because most proposals do not contain an index, the table of contents is quite important. A table of contents should include all headings and their beginning page numbers. Items that appear before the contents (copy of RFP, letter of transmittal, abstract, and title page) typically are not listed in the contents. However, any appendices should be listed.

List of Figures. Proposals with many tables and figures often contain a list of figures. This list includes each figure or table title and its page number. If you have just a few figures or tables, however, you may omit this list.

Appendix. Ancillary material of interest to some readers goes in appendices. Appendix A might include résumés of the principal investigators or testimonial letters. Appendix B might include examples or a listing of previous projects. Other appendices could include audit procedures, technical graphics, or professional papers cited in the body of the proposal.

Proposals in the past were always paper-based and delivered by mail or special messenger. Today, however, companies increasingly prefer *online proposals*. Receiving companies may transmit the electronic proposal to all levels of management without ever printing a page, thus appealing to many environmentally conscious organizations.

Well-written proposals win contracts and business for companies and individuals. Many companies depend entirely on proposals to generate their income, so proposal writing is extremely important. The Checklist box summarizes important elements to remember in writing proposals.

Checklist

Writing Proposals

Introduction

- **Indicate the purpose.** Specify why you are making the proposal.
- **Develop a persuasive "hook."** Suggest excellent results, low costs, or exclusive resources. Identify a serious problem or name a key issue or benefit.

Background, Problem, Purpose

- **Provide necessary background.** Discuss the significance of the proposal and its goals or purposes.
- **Introduce the problem.** For unsolicited proposals convince the reader that a problem exists. For solicited proposals show that you fully understand the problem and its ramifications.

Proposal, Plan, Schedule

- **Explain the proposal.** Present your plan for solving the problem or meeting the need.
- **Discuss plan management and evaluation.** If appropriate, tell how the plan will be implemented and evaluated.

- **Outline a timetable.** Furnish a schedule showing what will be done and when.

Staffing

- **Promote the qualifications of your staff.** Explain the specific credentials and expertise of the key personnel for the project.
- **Mention special resources and equipment.** Show how your support staff and resources are superior to those of the competition.

Budget

- **Show project costs.** For most projects itemize costs. Remember, however, that proposals are contracts.
- **Include a deadline.** Here or in the conclusion, present a date beyond which the bid figures are no longer valid.

Authorization

- **Ask for approval.** Make it easy for the reader to authorize the project (for example, *Sign and return the duplicate copy*).

Creating Effective Business Plans

Another form of proposal is a business plan. Let's say you want to start your own business. Unless you can count on the Bank of Mom and Dad, you will need financial backing, such as a bank loan or venture capital supplied by investors. A business plan is critical for securing financial support of any kind. Such a plan also ensures that you have done your homework and know what you are doing in launching your business. It provides you with a detailed road map to chart a course to success.

According to the Small Business Administration, most entrepreneurs spend about 400 hours writing a good business plan. The average consultant can do it in about 40 hours.[2] Increasingly sophisticated software, such as Business Plan Pro, PlanWrite, and PlanMagic, is available for those who have done their research, assembled the relevant data, and just want formatting help. Free shareware can also be found on the Internet.[3]

LEARNING OBJECTIVE 3

Identify the components of typical business plans and ethically create buy-in for your business ideas.

Components of Typical Business Plans

If you are serious about starting a business, the importance of a comprehensive, thoughtful business plan cannot be overemphasized. Your business plan is more likely to secure the funds you need if it is carefully written and includes the following elements:

- **Letter of transmittal or executive summary with mission statement.** Explain your reason for writing. Provide your name, address, telephone number, and e-mail address, along with contact information for all principals. Include a concise mission statement for your business. Describe your business, explaining the reasons it will succeed. Because potential investors will be looking for this mission statement, consider highlighting it with a paragraph heading (*Mission statement*) or use bolding or italics. Some consultants say that you should be able to write your mission statement on the back of a business card. Others think that one or two short paragraphs might be more realistic. To give it special treatment, you could make the mission statement a section of its own following the table of contents. Your executive summary is a business plan in miniature and should not exceed two pages. It should conclude by introducing the parts of the plan that follows and asking for financial support.

- **Table of contents.** List the page numbers and topics included in your plan.

- **Company description.** Identify the form of your business (proprietorship, partnership, or corporation) and its type (merchandising, manufacturing, or service). For existing companies, describe the company's founding, growth, sales, and profit.

- **Product or service description.** In jargon-free language, explain what you are providing, how it will benefit customers, and why it is better than existing products or services. For start-ups explain why the business will be profitable. Investors aren't always looking for a unique product or service. Instead, they are searching for a concept whose growth potential distinguishes it from others competing for funds.

- **Market analysis.** Discuss market characteristics, trends, projected growth, customer behaviour, complementary products and services, and barriers to entry. Identify your customers and how you will attract, hold, and increase your market share. Discuss the strengths and weaknesses of your direct and indirect competitors.

- **Operations and management.** Explain specifically how you will run your business, including location, equipment, personnel, and management. Highlight experienced and well-trained members of the management team and your advisers. Many investors consider this the most important factor in assessing business potential. Can your management team implement this business plan?

- **Financial analysis.** Outline a realistic start-up budget that includes fees for legal and professional services, occupancy, licences or permits, equipment, insurance, supplies, advertising and promotions, salaries and wages, accounting, income, and utilities. Also present an operating budget that projects costs for personnel, insurance, rent, depreciation, loan payments, salaries, taxes, repairs, and so on. Explain how much money you have, how much you will need to start up, and how much you will need to stay in business.

- **Appendices.** Provide necessary extras, such as managers' résumés, promotional materials, and product photos. Most appendices contain tables that exhibit the sales forecast, a personnel plan, anticipated cash flow, profit and loss, and a balance sheet.

Seeing Sample Business Plans on the Web

Writing a business plan is easier if you can see examples and learn from experts' suggestions. On the Web you will find many sites devoted to business plans. Some sites want to sell you something; others offer free advice. The Atlantic Canada Opportunities Agency site (**www.acoa-apeca.gc.ca/English/publications/FactSheetsAndBrochures/Pages/How_to_prepare_a_marketing_Plan.aspx**) provides a complete guide to preparing successful business plans. A quick Google search will reveal many other sites offering free and pay-for-service advice.

The Business Development Bank of Canada (BDC), a financial institution owned by the Government of Canada, provides financial and consulting services to small and medium-sized Canadian businesses. At the BDC Web site (**www.bdc.ca/en/home.htm**), you will find business plan advice and templates. In addition to suggestions for writing and using a business plan, the BDC site provides tools for self-assessments, continuity planning, and information about marketing and financing. This site provides a wide range of resources and tools for the budding entrepreneur.

Writing Formal Business Reports

LEARNING OBJECTIVE **4**

Describe the components of the front matter in formal business reports, and show how they further the purpose of your report.

Formal reports are similar to formal proposals in length, organization, and serious tone. Instead of making an offer, however, formal reports represent the end product of thorough investigation and analysis. They present ordered information to decision makers in business, industry, government, and education. In many ways formal reports are extended versions of the analytical business reports presented in Chapter 12. Figure 13.2 shows the components of typical formal reports, their normal sequence, and parts that might be omitted in informal reports.

Front Matter Components of Formal Business Reports

A number of front and end items lengthen formal reports but enhance their professional tone and serve their multiple audiences. Formal reports may be read by many levels of managers, along with technical specialists and financial consultants. Therefore, breaking a long, formal report into small segments makes its information more accessible and easier to understand for all readers. These segments are discussed here and also illustrated in the model report shown later in the chapter (Figure 13.3 on pages 355–364). This analytical report studies the economic impact of an industrial park on Winnipeg, Manitoba, and makes recommendations for increasing the city's future revenues.

Cover. Formal reports are usually enclosed in vinyl or heavy paper binders to protect the pages and to give a professional, finished appearance. Some companies have binders imprinted with their name and logo. The title of the report may appear through a cutout window or may be applied with an adhesive label. Good stationery and office supply stores usually stock an assortment of report binders and labels.

> Like proposals, formal reports are divided into many segments to make information comprehensible and accessible.

FIGURE 13.2 Components of Formal and Informal Reports

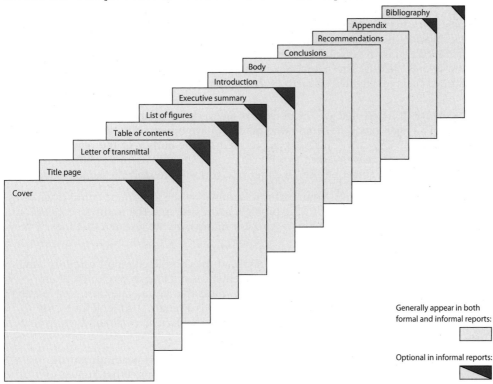

Labels (from bottom to top): Cover, Title page, Letter of transmittal, Table of contents, List of figures, Executive summary, Introduction, Body, Conclusions, Recommendations, Appendix, Bibliography

Generally appear in both formal and informal reports:

Optional in informal reports:

Title Page. A report title page, as illustrated in the Figure 13.3 model report, begins with the name of the report typed in upper-case letters (no underscore and no quotation marks). Next comes *Presented to* (or *Submitted to*) and the name, title, and organization of the individual receiving the report. Lower on the page is *Prepared by* (or *Submitted by*) and the author's name plus any necessary identification. The last item on the title page is the date of submission. All items after the title are typed in a combination of upper-case and lowercase letters.

Letter or Memo of Transmittal. Generally written on organization statio-nery, a letter or memorandum of transmittal introduces a formal report. You will recall that letters are sent to outsiders and memos to insiders. A transmittal letter or memo follows the direct pattern and is usually less formal than the report itself (for example, the letter or memo may use contractions and the first-person pronouns *I* and *we*). The transmittal letter or memo typically (a) announces the topic of the report and tells how it was authorized; (b) briefly describes the project; (c) highlights the report's findings, conclusions, and recommendations, if the reader is expected to be supportive; and (d) closes with appreciation for the assignment, instruction for the reader's follow-up actions, acknowledgment of help from others, or offers of assistance in answering questions. If a report is going to various readers, a spe-cial transmittal letter or memo should be prepared for each, anticipating how each reader will use the report.

> A letter or memo of transmittal gives a personalized overview of a formal report.

Table of Contents. The table of contents shows the headings in the report and their page numbers. It gives an overview of the report topics and helps readers locate them. You should wait to prepare the table of contents until after you've completed the report. For short reports you should include all headings. For longer reports you might want to list only first- and second-level headings. Leaders (spaced or unspaced dots) help guide the eye from the heading to the page number. Items may be indented in outline form or typed flush with the left margin.

List of Illustrations. For reports with several figures or tables, you may want to include a list to help readers locate them. This list may appear on the same page as the table of contents, space permitting. For each figure or illustration, include a title and page number. Some writers distinguish between tables and all other illustrations, which are called figures. If you make the distinction, you should prepare separate lists of tables and figures. Because the model report in Figure 13.3 has few illustrations, the writer labelled them all "figures," a method that simplifies numbering.

An executive summary supplies an overview of a longer report.

Executive Summary. The purpose of an executive summary is to present an overview of a longer report to people who may not have time to read the entire document. Generally, an executive summary is prepared by the author of the report. However, occasionally you may be asked to write an executive summary of a published report or article written by someone else. In either case you will probably do the following:

- **Summarize key points.** Your goal is to summarize the important points, including the purpose of the report; the problem addressed; and the findings, conclusions, and recommendations. You might also summarize the research methods, if they can be stated concisely.

- **Look for strategic words and sentences.** Read the completed report carefully. Pay special attention to the first and last sentences of paragraphs, which often contain summary statements. Look for words that enumerate (*first, next, finally*) and words that express causation (*therefore, as a result*). Also look for words that signal essentials (*basically, central, leading, principal, major*) and words that contrast ideas (*however, consequently*).

- **Prepare an outline with headings.** At a minimum, include headings for the purpose, findings, and conclusions or recommendations. What kernels of information would your reader want to know about these topics?

- **Fill in your outline.** Some writers use their computers to cut and paste important parts of the text. Then they condense with careful editing. Others find it more efficient to create new sentences as they prepare the executive summary.

- **Begin with the purpose.** The easiest way to begin an executive summary is with the words *The purpose of this report is to. . . .* Experienced writers may be more creative.

- **Follow the report sequence.** Present all your information in the order in which it is found in the report.

- **Eliminate nonessential details.** Include only main points. Do not include anything not in the original report. Use minimal technical language.

- **Control the length.** An executive summary is usually no longer than 10 percent of the original document. Thus, a 100-page report might require a 10-page summary. A 10-page report might need only a 1-page summary—or no summary at all. The executive summary for a long report may also include graphics to adequately highlight main points.

To see a representative executive summary, look at Figure 13.3. Although it is only one page long, this executive summary includes headings to help the reader see the main divisions immediately. Let your organization's practices guide you in determining the length and form of an executive summary.

The introduction to a formal report describes the background, explains the purpose, and discusses the significance, scope, and organization of the topic.

Introduction. Formal reports begin with an introduction that sets the scene and announces the subject. Because they contain many parts serving different purposes, formal reports are somewhat redundant. The same information may be included in the letter of transmittal, summary, and introduction. To avoid sounding repetitious, try to present the data slightly differently. However, do not skip the introduction because you've included some of its information elsewhere. You cannot be sure that your reader saw the information earlier. A good report introduction typically covers the following elements, although not necessarily in this order:

- **Background.** Describe events leading up to the problem or need.

- **Problem or purpose.** Explain the report topic and specify the problem or need that motivated the report.

- **Significance.** Tell why the topic is important. You may want to quote experts or cite newspapers, journals, books, and other secondary sources to establish the importance of the topic.

- **Scope.** Clarify the boundaries of the report, defining what will be included or excluded.

- **Organization.** Orient readers by giving them a road map that previews the structure of the report.

Beyond these minimal introductory elements, consider adding any of the following information that is relevant to your readers:

- **Authorization.** Identify who commissioned the report. If no letter of transmittal is included, also tell why, when, by whom, and to whom the report was written.

- **Literature review.** Summarize what other authors and researchers have published on this topic, especially for academic and scientific reports.

- **Sources and methods.** Describe your secondary sources (periodicals, books, databases). Also explain how you collected primary data, including survey size, sample design, and statistical programs used.

- **Definitions of key terms.** Define words that may be unfamiliar to the audience. Also define terms with special meanings, such as *small business* when it specifically means businesses with fewer than 30 employees.

Body and Back Matter Components of Formal Business Reports

LEARNING OBJECTIVE 5

Describe the body and back matter of formal business reports and how they serve the purpose of your report.

The body of a formal report is the "meat" of the document. In this longest and most substantive section of the text, the author or team discusses the problem and findings, before reaching conclusions and making recommendations. Extensive and bulky materials that don't fit in the text belong in the appendix. Although some very long reports may have additional components, the back matter usually concludes with a list of sources. The body and back matter of formal business reports are discussed in this section. Figure 13.2 shows the parts of typical reports, the order in which they appear, and elements usually found only in formal reports.

Because formal business reports can be long and complex, they usually include more sections than routine informal business reports do. These components are standard and conventional; that is, the audience expects to see them in a professional report. Documents that conform to such expectations are easier to read and deliver their message more effectively. You will find most of the components addressed here in the model report in Figure 13.3, the analytical report studying the economic impact of an industrial park in Winnipeg, Manitoba.

Body. The principal section in a formal report is the body. It discusses, analyzes, interprets, and evaluates the research findings or solution to the initial problem. This is where you show the evidence that justifies your conclusions. Organize the body into main categories by following your original outline or by using one of the patterns described earlier (such as time, component, importance, criteria, or convention).

Although we refer to this section as the body, it does not carry that heading. Instead, it contains clear headings that explain each major section. Headings may be functional or talking. Functional heads (such as *Results of the Survey, Analysis of Findings,* or *Discussion*) help readers identify the purpose of the section but do not reveal what is in it. Such headings are useful for routine reports or for sensitive topics that may upset readers. Talking heads (for example, *Findings Reveal Revenue* and *Employment Benefits*) are more informative and interesting, but they do not help readers see the organization of the report. The model report in Figure 13.3 uses combination headings; as the name suggests, they combine functional heads for organizational sections (*Introduction, Conclusions and Recommendations*) with talking heads that reveal the content. The headings divide the body into smaller parts.

Conclusions. This important section tells what the findings mean, particularly in terms of solving the original problem. Some writers prefer to intermix their conclusions with the analysis of the findings—instead of presenting the conclusions separately. Other writers place the conclusions before the body so that busy readers can examine the significant information immediately. Still others combine the conclusions and recommendations. Most writers, though, present the conclusions after the body because readers expect this structure. In long reports this section may include a summary of the findings. To improve comprehension, you may present the conclusions in a numbered or bulleted list. See Chapter 12 for more suggestions on drawing conclusions.

Recommendations. When asked, you should submit recommendations that make precise suggestions for actions to solve the report problem. Recommendations are most helpful when they are practical and reasonable. Naturally, they should evolve from the findings and conclusions. Do not introduce new information in the conclusions or recommendations sections. As with conclusions, the position of recommendations is somewhat flexible. They may be combined with conclusions, or they may be presented before the body, especially when the audience is eager and supportive. Generally, though, in formal reports they come last.

> The recommendations section of a formal report offers specific suggestions for solving a problem.

Recommendations require an appropriate introductory sentence, such as *The findings and conclusions in this study support the following recommendations.* When making many recommendations, number them and phrase each as a command, such as *Begin an employee fitness program with a workout room available five days a week.* If appropriate, add information describing how to implement each recommendation. Some reports include a timetable describing the who, what, when, where, and how for putting each recommendation into operation. Chapter 12 provides more information about writing recommendations.

Appendix. Incidental or supporting materials belong in appendices at the end of a formal report. These materials are relevant to some readers but not to all. They may be too bulky to include in the text. Appendices may include survey forms, copies of other reports, tables of data, large graphics, and related correspondence. If several appendices are necessary, they would be named Appendix A, Appendix B, and so forth.

Works Cited or References. If you use the MLA (Modern Language Association) referencing format, all sources of information would be listed alphabetically in the *Works Cited.* If you use the APA (American Psychological Association) format, your list would be called *References.* Your listed sources must correspond to the in-text citations in the report whenever you are borrowing words or ideas from published and unpublished resources.

> The Works Cited or References section of a formal report identifies the sources of ideas mentioned in the report.

Regardless of the documentation format, you must include the author, title, publication, date of publication, page number, and other significant data for all ideas or quotations used in your report. For electronic references include the preceding information plus a description of the electronic address or URL leading to the citation. Also include the retrieval date on which you located the electronic reference. To see electronic and other citations, examine the list of references at the end of Figure 13.3. Appendix B of the text contains additional documentation information.

Final Writing Tips

Formal reports are not undertaken lightly. They involve considerable effort in all three phases of writing, beginning with analysis of the problem and anticipation of the audience (as discussed in Chapter 4). Researching the data, organizing it into a logical presentation, and composing the first draft (Chapter 5) make up the second phase of writing. Revising, proofreading, and evaluating (Chapter 6) are completed in the third phase. Although everyone approaches the writing process somewhat differently, the following tips offer advice in problem areas faced by most writers of formal reports:

- **Allow sufficient time.** The main reason given by writers who are disappointed with their reports is "I just ran out of time." Develop a realistic timetable and stick to it.

- **Finish data collection.** Do not begin writing until you've collected all the data and drawn the primary conclusions. Starting too early often means backtracking. For reports based on survey data, complete the tables and figures first.

- **Work from a good outline.** A big project, such as a formal report, needs the order and direction provided by a clear outline, even if the outline has to be revised as the project unfolds.

- **Provide a proper writing environment.** You will need a quiet spot where you can spread out your materials and work without interruption. Formal reports demand blocks of concentration time.

- **Use the features of your computer wisely.** Your word processor enables you to keyboard quickly, revise easily, and check spelling, grammar, and synonyms readily. A word of warning, though: save your document often and print occasionally so that you have a hard copy. Take these precautions to guard against the grief caused by lost files, power outages, and computer malfunctions.

- **Write rapidly; revise later.** Some experts advise writers to record their ideas quickly and save revision until after the first draft is completed. They say that quick writing avoids wasted effort spent in polishing sentences or even sections that may be cut later. Moreover, rapid writing encourages fluency and creativity. However, a quickly written first draft does not work for everyone. Many business writers prefer a more deliberate writing style, so consider this advice selectively and experiment with the method that works best for you.

- **Save difficult sections.** If some sections are harder to write than others, save them until you've developed confidence and a rhythm from working on easier topics.

- **Be consistent in verb tense.** Use past-tense verbs to describe completed actions (for example, *the respondents said* or *the survey showed*). Use present-tense verbs, however, to explain current actions (*the purpose of the report is, this report examines, the table shows,* and so forth). When citing references, use past-tense verbs (*Jones reported that*). Do not switch back and forth between present- and past-tense verbs in describing related data.

Formal reports require careful attention to all phases of the 3-x-3 writing process.

Smart report writers allow themselves plenty of time, research thoroughly, and draw up a useful outline.

Effective formal reports maintain parallelism in verb tenses, avoid first-person pronouns, and use the active voice.

- **Generally avoid *I* and *we*.** To make formal reports seem as objective and credible as possible, most writers omit first-person pronouns. This formal style sometimes results in the overuse of passive-voice verbs (for example, *periodicals were consulted* and *the study was conducted*). Look for alternative constructions (*periodicals indicated* and *the study revealed*). It is also possible that your organization may allow first-person pronouns, so check before starting your report.

- **Let the first draft sit.** After completing the first version, put it aside for a day or two. Return to it with the expectation of revising and improving it. Do not be afraid to make major changes.

- **Revise for clarity, coherence, and conciseness.** Read a printed copy out loud. Do the sentences make sense? Do the ideas flow together naturally? Can wordiness and flabbiness be cut out? Make sure that your writing is so clear that a busy manager does not have to reread any part. See Chapter 6 for specific revision suggestions.

- **Proofread the final copy three times.** First, read a printed copy slowly for word meanings and content. Then read the copy again for spelling, punctuation, grammar, and other mechanical errors. Finally, scan the entire report to check its formatting and consistency (page numbering, indenting, spacing, headings, and so forth).

The Checklist box on page 365 summarizes the process and components of formal reports.

Putting It All Together

Formal reports in business generally aim to study problems and recommend solutions. Brigitte Morceaux, senior research consultant with Petit, Morceaux Industrial Consultants, was asked to study the economic impact of a local industrial park on the city of Winnipeg, Manitoba, resulting in the formal report shown in Figure 13.3.

FIGURE 13.3 **Model Formal Report**

Title Page

Includes report title in all caps with longer line above shorter line

**ECONOMIC IMPACT OF ROXBURY INDUSTRIAL PARK
ON THE CITY OF WINNIPEG**

Prepared for
The Standing Committee on Property and Development
Winnipeg City Council
Winnipeg, Manitoba

Highlights name of report recipient

Prepared by
Brigitte Morceaux
Senior Research Consultant
Petit, Morceaux Industrial Consultants

Identifies report writer

March 12, 2014

Omits page number

The title page is usually arranged in four evenly balanced areas. If the report is to be bound on the left, move the left margin and centre point 0.5 cm to the right. Notice that no page number appears on the title page, although it counts as "page i." In designing the title page, be careful to avoid anything unprofessional—such as too many type fonts, italics, oversized print, and inappropriate graphics. Keep the title page simple and professional.

(Continued)

FIGURE 13.3 (*continued*) **Letter of Transmittal**

PETIT, MORCEAUX INDUSTRIAL CONSULTANTS

588 Main Street
Winnipeg, Manitoba R2L 1E6

www.petitmorceaux.com
(204) 549-1101

March 12, 2014

Councillor Richard Moody
Chairperson
Standing Committee on Property and Development
City of Winnipeg
Winnipeg, MB R2L 1E9

Dear Councillor Moody:

Announces report and identifies authorization —

The attached report, requested by the Standing Committee on Property and Development in a letter dated September 20, describes the economic impact of Roxbury Industrial Park (RIP) on the City of Winnipeg. We believe you will find the results of this study useful in evaluating future development of industrial parks within the city limits.

This study was designed to examine economic impact in three areas:

Gives broad overview of report purposes —

(1) Current and projected tax and other revenues accruing to the city from Roxbury Industrial Park

(2) Current and projected employment generated by the park

(3) Indirect effects on local employment, income, and economic growth

Describes primary and secondary research —

Primary research consisted of interviews with 15 Roxbury Industrial Park tenants and managers, in addition to a 2010 survey of over 5,000 RIP employees. Secondary research sources included the Annual Budget of the City of Winnipeg, other government publications, periodicals, books, and online resources. Results of this research, discussed more fully in this report, indicate that Roxbury Industrial Park exerts a significant beneficial influence on the Winnipeg metropolitan economy.

Offers to discuss report; expresses appreciation —

I would be pleased to discuss this report and its conclusions with you at your request. My firm and I thank you for your confidence in selecting our company to prepare this comprehensive report.

Sincerely,

Brigitte Morceaux

Brigitte Morceaux
Senior Research Consultant

BM:mef

Attachment

A letter or memo of transmittal announces the report topic and explains who authorized it. It briefly describes the project and previews the conclusions, if the reader is supportive. Such messages generally close by expressing appreciation for the assignment, suggesting follow-up actions, acknowledging the help of others, or offering to answer questions. The margins for the transmittal should be the same as for the report, about 3 cm on all sides.

FIGURE 13.3 (*continued*) **Table of Contents and List of Figures**

TABLE OF CONTENTS

LIST OF FIGURES

Figure

iii

Uses leaders to guide eye from heading to page number

Indents secondary headings to show levels of outline

Includes tables and figures in one list for simplified numbering

Because the table of contents and the list of figures for this report are small, they are combined on one page. Notice that the titles of major report parts are in all caps, while other headings are a combination of upper- and lowercase letters. The style duplicates those within the report. Word processing programs enable you to generate a contents page automatically, including leaders and accurate page numbering—no matter how many times you revise. Notice that the page numbers are right-justified. Multiple-digit page numbers must line up properly (say, the number 9 under the 0 of 10).

FIGURE 13.3 (*continued*) **Executive Summary**

Opens directly with major research findings

Identifies data sources

Summarizes organization of report

Condenses recommendations

EXECUTIVE SUMMARY

Winnipeg can benefit from the development of industrial parks like the Roxbury Industrial Park. Both direct and indirect economic benefits result, as shown by this in-depth study conducted by Petit, Morceaux Industrial Consultants. The study was authorized by the Standing Committee on Property and Development when Goldman-Lyon & Associates sought City Council's approval for the proposed construction of a G-L industrial park. The City Council requested evidence demonstrating that an existing development could actually benefit the city.

Our conclusion that Winnipeg benefits from industrial parks is based on data supplied by a survey of 5,000 Roxbury Industrial Park employees, personal interviews with managers and tenants of RIP, city and provincial documents, and professional literature.

Analysis of the data revealed benefits in three areas:

(1) **Revenues.** The City of Winnipeg earned nearly $1 million in tax and other revenues from the Roxbury Industrial Park in 2013. By 2017 this income is expected to reach $1.7 million (in constant 2013 dollars).

(2) **Employment.** In 2010 RIP businesses employed a total of 7,035 workers, who earned an average wage of $28,120. By 2017 RIP businesses are expected to employ directly nearly 15,000 employees who will earn salaries totalling over $450 million.

(3) **Indirect benefits.** Because of the multiplier effect, by 2017 Roxbury Industrial Park will directly and indirectly generate a total of 38,362 jobs in the Winnipeg area.

On the basis of these findings, it is recommended that development of additional industrial parks be encouraged to stimulate local economic growth.

iv

An executive summary or abstract highlights report findings, conclusions, and recommendations. Its length depends on the report it summarizes. A 100-page report might require a ten-page summary. Shorter reports may contain one-page summaries, as shown here. Unlike letters of transmittal (which may contain personal pronouns and references to the writer), summaries are formal and impersonal. They use the same margins as the body of the report.

FIGURE 13.3 (*continued*) Introduction

ECONOMIC IMPACT OF ROXBURY INDUSTRIAL PARK

PROBLEM

This study was designed to analyze the direct and indirect economic impact of Roxbury Industrial Park on the City of Winnipeg. Specifically, the study seeks answers to these questions:

(1) What current tax and other revenues result directly from this park? What tax and other revenues may be expected in the future?

(2) How many and what kind of jobs are directly attributable to the park? What is the employment picture for the future?

(3) What indirect effects has Roxbury Industrial Park had on local employment, incomes, and economic growth?

BACKGROUND

The Standing Committee on Property and Development commissioned this study of Roxbury Industrial Park at the request of Winnipeg City Council. Before authorizing the development of a proposed Goldman-Lyon industrial park, the City Council requested a study examining the economic effects of an existing park. Members of Council wanted to determine to what extent industrial parks benefit the local community, and they chose Roxbury Industrial Park as an example.

For those who are unfamiliar with it, Roxbury Industrial Park is a 40 hectare industrial park located in Winnipeg about 2.5 km from the centre of the city. Most of the area lies within a specially designated area known as Redevelopment Project No. 2, which is part of the Winnipeg Capital Region Development Commission's planning area. Planning for the park began in 1993; construction started in 1995.

1

Lists three problem questions

Describes authorization for report and background of study

The introduction of a formal report contains the title printed 5 cm from the top edge. Titles for major parts of a report (such as Problem, Background, Findings, *and* Conclusions) *are centred in all caps. First-level headings (such as* Revenues *on page 2 of this report) are printed with bold upper- and lowercase letters. Second-level headings (such as* Sales and Use Revenues *on page 3) begin at the left side.*

FIGURE 13.3 (*continued*) Introduction and Discussion

The park now contains 14 building complexes with over 25,000 square metres of completed building space. The majority of the buildings are used for office, research and development, marketing and distribution, or manufacturing uses. Approximately 5 hectares of the original area are yet to be developed.

Data for this report came from a 2013 survey of more than 5,000 Roxbury Industrial Park employees, interviews with 15 RIP tenants and managers, the Annual Budget of the City of Winnipeg, current books, articles, journals, and online resources. Projections for future revenues resulted from analysis of past trends and *Estimates of Revenues for Debt Service Coverage, Redevelopment Project No. 2* (Miller 78–79).

Provides specifics for data sources

MLA-style parenthetical citation

DISCUSSION OF FINDINGS

The results of this research indicate that major direct and indirect benefits have accrued to the City of Winnipeg and surrounding municipal areas as a result of the development of Roxbury Industrial Park. The research findings presented here fall into three categories: (a) revenues, (b) employment, and (c) indirect effects.

Previews organization of report

Revenues

Uses topical arrangement

Roxbury Industrial Park contributes a variety of tax and other revenues to the City of Winnipeg. Figure 1 summarizes revenues.

Places figure close to textual reference

Figure 1

REVENUES RECEIVED BY THE CITY OF WINNIPEG
FROM ROXBURY INDUSTRIAL PARK

Current Revenues and Projections to 2017

	2013	2017
Property taxes	$604,140	$1,035,390
Revenues from licences	126,265	216,396
Business taxes	75,518	129,424
Provincial service receipts	53,768	92,134
Licences and permits	48,331	82,831
Other revenues	64,039	111,987
Total	$972,061	$1,668,162

Source: City of Winnipeg Chief Financial Officer. 2013 *Annual Financial Report.* City of Winnipeg, Jan. 2014. Web. 16 Jan. 2014.

2

Notice that this formal report is single-spaced. Many businesses prefer this space-saving format. However, some organizations prefer double-spacing, especially for preliminary drafts. If you single-space, do not indent paragraphs. If you double-space, do indent the paragraphs. Page numbers may be centred near the bottom of the page or placed near the upper right corner at the margin. Strive to leave comfortable top, bottom, and side margins. References follow the MLA citation style. Notice that the citations appear as references in the "Works Cited" section with a corresponding parenthetical reference to the author in the text of the report at the appropriate location.

FIGURE 13.3 (*continued*) Discussion

Sales and Use Revenues

As shown in Figure 1, the city's largest source of revenues from RIP is the property tax. Revenues from this source totalled $604,140 in 2013, according to the City of Winnipeg Standing Committee on Finance (City of Winnipeg 103). Property taxes accounted for more than half of the park's total contribution to the City of $972,061.

Continues interpreting figures in table

Other Revenues

Other major sources of City revenues from RIP in 2013 include revenues from licences such as motor vehicle in lieu fees, trailer coach licences ($126,265), business taxes ($75,518), and provincial service receipts ($53,768).

Projections

Total City revenues from RIP will nearly double by 2017, producing an income of $1.7 million. This projection is based on an annual growth rate of 1.4 percent in constant 2013 dollars.

Employment

One of the most important factors to consider in the overall effect of an industrial park is employment. In Roxbury Industrial Park the distribution, number, and wages of people employed will change considerably in the next five years.

Sets stage for next topics to be discussed

Distribution

A total of 7,035 employees currently work in various industry groups at Roxbury Industrial Park, as shown in Figure 2. The largest number of workers (58 percent) is employed in manufacturing and assembly operations. In the next largest category, the computer and electronics industry employs 24 percent of the workers. Some overlap probably exists because electronics assembly could be included in either group. Employees also work in publishing (9 percent), warehousing and storage (5 percent), and other industries (4 percent).

Although the distribution of employees at Roxbury Industrial Park shows a wide range of employment categories, it must be noted that other industrial parks would likely generate an entirely different range of job categories.

3

Only the most important research findings are interpreted and discussed for readers. The depth of discussion depends on the intended length of the report, the goal of the writer, and the expectations of the reader. Because the writer wants this report to be formal in tone, she avoids I *and* we *in all discussions.*

FIGURE 13.3 (*continued*) **Discussion**

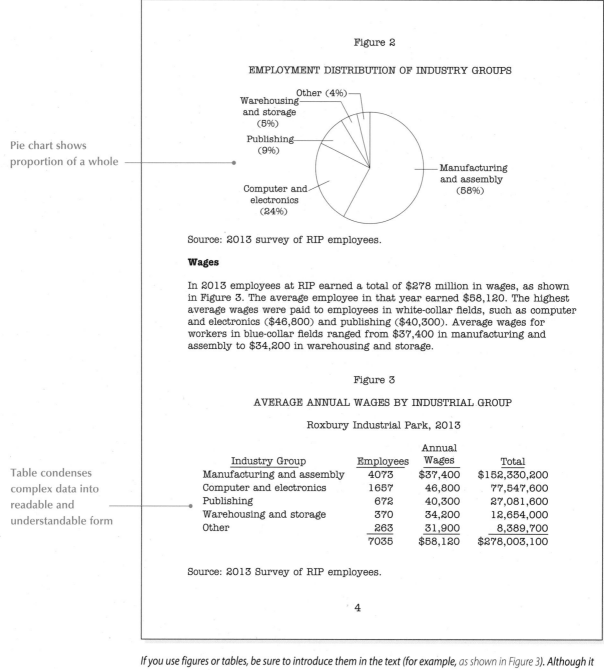

Pie chart shows proportion of a whole

Figure 2

EMPLOYMENT DISTRIBUTION OF INDUSTRY GROUPS

Other (4%)
Warehousing and storage (5%)
Publishing (9%)
Manufacturing and assembly (58%)
Computer and electronics (24%)

Source: 2013 survey of RIP employees.

Wages

In 2013 employees at RIP earned a total of $278 million in wages, as shown in Figure 3. The average employee in that year earned $58,120. The highest average wages were paid to employees in white-collar fields, such as computer and electronics ($46,800) and publishing ($40,300). Average wages for workers in blue-collar fields ranged from $37,400 in manufacturing and assembly to $34,200 in warehousing and storage.

Figure 3

AVERAGE ANNUAL WAGES BY INDUSTRIAL GROUP

Roxbury Industrial Park, 2013

Table condenses complex data into readable and understandable form

Industry Group	Employees	Annual Wages	Total
Manufacturing and assembly	4073	$37,400	$152,330,200
Computer and electronics	1657	46,800	77,547,600
Publishing	672	40,300	27,081,600
Warehousing and storage	370	34,200	12,654,000
Other	263	31,900	8,389,700
	7035	$58,120	$278,003,100

Source: 2013 Survey of RIP employees.

4

If you use figures or tables, be sure to introduce them in the text (for example, as shown in Figure 3). Although it is not always possible, try to place them close to the spot where they are first mentioned. To save space, you can print the title of a figure at its side. Because this report contains few tables and figures, the writer named them all "Figures" and numbered them consecutively.

FIGURE 13.3 (*continued*) Discussion, Conclusions, and Recommendations

Projections

By 2017 Roxbury Industrial Park is expected to more than double its number of employees, bringing the total to over 15,000 workers. The total payroll in 2017 will also more than double, producing more than $450 million (using constant 2012 dollars) in salaries to RIP employees. These projections are based on an 8 percent growth rate, along with anticipated increased employment as the park reaches its capacity (Miller 78–79).

Clarifies information and tells what it means in relation to original research questions

Future development in the park will influence employment and payrolls. As Ivan Novak, RIP project manager, stated in an interview, much of the remaining five hectares is planned for medium-rise office buildings, garden offices, and other structures for commercial, professional, and personal services (September 2013). Average wages for employees are expected to increase because of an anticipated shift to higher-paying white-collar jobs. Industrial parks often follow a similar pattern of evolution (Badri 38–45). Like many industrial parks, RIP evolved from a warehousing centre into a manufacturing complex.

CONCLUSIONS AND RECOMMENDATIONS

Summarizes conclusions and recommendations

Analysis of tax revenues, employment data, personal interviews, and professional literature leads to the following conclusions and recommendations about the economic impact of Roxbury Industrial Park on the City of Winnipeg:

1. Property tax and other revenues produced nearly $1 million in income to the City of Winnipeg in 2013. By 2017 revenues are expected to produce $1.7 million in city income.

2. RIP currently employs 7,035 employees, the majority of whom are working in manufacturing and assembly. The average employee in 2013 earned $38,120.

3. By 2017 RIP is expected to employ more than 15,000 workers producing a total payroll of over $450 million.

4. Employment trends indicate that by 2017 more RIP employees will be engaged in higher-paying white-collar positions.

On the basis of these findings, we recommend that the City Council of Winnipeg authorize the development of additional industrial parks to stimulate local economic growth.

5

After discussing and interpreting the research findings, the writer articulates what she considers the most important conclusions and recommendations. Longer, more complex reports may have separate sections for conclusions and resulting recommendations. In this report they are combined. Notice that it is unnecessary to start a new page for the conclusions.

FIGURE 13.3 (***continued***) **Works Cited**

Arranges references in
alphabetical order

Follows MLA
documentation style

WORKS CITED

Badri, Mahmood A. "Infrastructure, Trends, and Economic Effects of Industrial
Parks."*www.industryweek.com.* Penton Media, Inc., 1 Apr. 2013: 38–45. Web.
15 Dec. 2013.

City of Winnipeg Chief Financial Officer 2013 *Annual Financial Report* City of
Winnipeg, Jan. 2014. Web. 16 Jan. 2014.

Miller, Arthur M. *Estimates of Revenues for Debt Service Coverage, Redevelopment Project No. 2.* Winnipeg, Rincon Press, 2013. Print.

Novak, Ivan M. E-mail interview. 30 Sept. 2013.

*On this page the writer lists all references cited in the text as well as others that she examined during her research.
The writer lists these citations following the MLA referencing style. Notice that all entries are arranged alphabetically. Book and periodical titles are italicized, but they could be underlined. When referring to online items, she
shows the full name of the citation and identifies the date on which she accessed the electronic reference. This
references page is shown with single-spacing, which is preferable for business reports. However, MLA style recommends double-spacing for research reports, including the references page. MLA style also shows "Works Cited" in
upper- and lowercase letters. However, the writer preferred to use all caps to be consistent with other headings in
this business report.*

Checklist

Preparing Formal Reports

Report Process

- **Analyze the report and purpose.** Develop a problem question (*How is e-mail affecting productivity and security at MegaTech?*) and a purpose statement (*The purpose of this report is to investigate the use of e-mail at MegaTech and recommend policies and procedures that enhance company productivity and security*).

- **Anticipate the audience and issues.** Consider primary and secondary audiences. What do they already know? What do they need to know? Divide the major problem into subproblems for investigation.

- **Prepare a work plan.** Include problem and purpose statements, as well as a description of the sources and methods of collecting data. Prepare a tentative project outline and work schedule with anticipated dates of completion for all segments of the project.

- **Collect data.** Begin by searching secondary sources (electronic databases, books, magazines, journals, newspapers) for information on your topic. Then, if necessary, gather primary data by surveying, interviewing, observing, and experimenting.

- **Document data sources.** Establish a system for keeping track of your sources. When saving files from business databases or the Internet, be sure to record the complete publication information. Some researchers like to prepare note cards or separate sheets of paper citing all references (author, date, source, page, and quotation). Select a documentation format and use it consistently.

- **Interpret and organize the data.** Arrange the collected information in tables, grids, or outlines to help you visualize relationships and interpret meanings. Organize the data into an outline (Chapter 5).

- **Prepare graphics.** Make tables, charts, graphs, and illustrations—but only if they serve a function. Use graphics to help clarify, condense, simplify, or emphasize your data.

- **Compose the first draft.** At a computer write the first draft from your outline. Use appropriate headings and transitional expressions (such as *however, on the contrary,* and *in addition*) to guide the reader through the report.

- **Revise and proofread.** Revise to eliminate wordiness, ambiguity, and redundancy. Look for ways to improve readability, such as bulleted or numbered lists. Proofread three times for (a) word and content meaning, (b) grammar and mechanical errors, and (c) formatting.

- **Evaluate the product.** Examine the final report. Will it achieve its purpose? Encourage feedback so that you can learn how to improve future reports.

Report Components

- **Title page.** Balance the following lines on the title page: (a) name of the report (in all caps); (b) name, title, and organization of the individual receiving the report; (c) author's name, title, and organization; and (d) date submitted.

- **Letter of transmittal.** Announce the report topic and explain who authorized it. Briefly describe the project and preview the conclusions, if the reader is supportive. Close by expressing appreciation for the assignment, suggesting follow-up actions, acknowledging the help of others, or offering to answer questions.

- **Table of contents.** Show the beginning page number where each report heading appears in the report. Connect the page numbers and headings with leaders (spaced dots) by using your word processing software. In MS Word 2007, for example, click on the **Home** tab, open the **Paragraph menu** and click **Tabs** at the bottom left of the window.

- **List of illustrations.** Include a list of tables, illustrations, or figures showing the title of the item and its page number. If space permits, put these lists on the same page with the table of contents.

- **Executive summary.** Summarize the report purpose, findings, conclusions, and recommendations. Gauge the length of the summary by the length of the report and by your organization's practices.

- **Introduction.** Explain the problem motivating the report; describe its background and significance. Clarify the scope and limitations of the report. Optional items include a review of the relevant literature and a description of data sources, methods, and key terms. Close by previewing the report's organization.

- **Body.** Discuss, analyze, and interpret the research findings or the proposed solution to the problem. Arrange the findings in logical segments that follow your outline. Use clear, descriptive headings.

- **Conclusions and recommendations.** Explain what the findings mean in relation to the original problem. If asked, make enumerated recommendations that suggest actions for solving the problem.

- **Appendix.** Include items of interest to some but not all readers, such as questionnaires, transcripts of interviews, data sheets, or other information that is not essential to explain your findings, but that supports your analysis. Add large graphics—pictures, maps, figures, tables, charts, and graphs—that are not discussed directly in the text.

- **Works Cited or References.** If footnotes are not provided in the text, list all references in a section called "Works Cited" or "References."

Summary of Learning Objectives

1 **Discuss the general uses and basic components of informal proposals and grasp their audience and purpose.** Although they may vary, most proposals have certain standard parts in common. Informal proposals contain the following: (a) a persuasive introduction that explains the purpose of the proposal and qualifies the writer; (b) background material identifying the problem and project goals; (c) a proposal, plan, or schedule outlining the project; (d) a section describing staff qualifications; (e) a budget showing expected costs; and (f) a request for approval or authorization.

2 **Discuss formal proposals and their specific components.** Beyond the six components generally contained in informal proposals, formal proposals may include these additional parts: (a) a copy of the RFP (request for proposal), (b) a letter of transmittal, (c) an executive summary, (d) a title page, (e) a table of contents, (f) a list of illustrations, and (g) an appendix.

3 **Identify the components of typical business plans and ethically create buy-in for your business ideas.** Business plans help entrepreneurs secure start-up funding and also provide a road map to follow as a business develops. Typical business plans include the following: letter of transmittal or executive summary, table of contents, company description, product or service description, market analysis, description of operations and management, financial analysis, and appendices. For start-up businesses seeking financial backing, the product or service description as well as the operations and management analyses are particularly important. They must promote growth potential and promise a management team capable of implementing the business plan.

4 **Describe the components of the front matter in formal business reports, and show how they further the purpose of your report.** Formal business reports may include these beginning components: a vinyl or heavy paper cover, a title page, a letter of transmittal, a table of contents, a list of illustrations, and an executive summary. The introduction to a formal report sets the scene by discussing some or all of the following topics: background material, problem or purpose, significance of the topic, scope and organization of the report, authorization, review of relevant literature, sources and methods, and definitions of key terms.

5 **Describe the body and back matter of formal business reports and how they serve the purpose of your report.** The body of a report discusses, analyzes, interprets, and evaluates the research findings or solution to a problem. The conclusion tells what the findings mean and how they relate to the report's purpose. The recommendations tell how to solve the report problem. The last portions of a formal report are the appendix and references.

6 **Specify tips that aid writers of formal business reports.** Before writing, develop a realistic timetable and collect all necessary data. During the writing process, work from a good outline, work in a quiet place, and use a computer. Also, try to write rapidly, revising later. While writing, use verb tenses consistently and avoid *I* and *we*. A few days after completing the first draft, revise to improve clarity, coherence, and conciseness. Proofread the final copy three times.

Chapter Review

1. What purpose do proposals serve? (Objs. 1, 2)
2. Who uses requests for proposals (RFPs), and why? (Objs. 1, 2)
3. What are the six principal components of an informal letter proposal? (Obj. 1)
4. Why is the budget section in a proposal particularly important? (Obj. 2)
5. Why does an entrepreneur need to write a business plan? (Obj. 3)
6. Name eight components of typical business plans. (Obj. 3)
7. What should a business plan mission statement include, and how long should it be? (Obj. 3)
8. Why are formal reports written in business? Give an original example of a business-related formal report. (Obj. 4)
9. What is a letter or memorandum of transmittal? (Obj. 4)
10. How long should a typical executive summary be? (Obj. 4)
11. Name the steps necessary to write an executive summary in a formal business report. (Obj. 4)
12. What should be included in the introduction to a formal report? (Obj. 4)
13. What should the writer strive to do in the body of a formal report? (Obj. 5)
14. Why must writers list their sources and identify them in the text? (Obj. 5)
15. In your view, what are six of the most important tips for the writer of a formal report? Explain each of your choices. (Obj. 6)

Critical Thinking

1. Which category of proposal, solicited or unsolicited, is more likely to succeed, and why? (Obj. 1)
2. Compare proposals and business plans. (Objs. 1–3)
3. What is the purpose of a business plan, and what should it communicate to investors? (Obj. 3)
4. How do formal business reports differ from informal business reports? (Objs. 4–6)
5. **Ethical Issue:** How can a team of writers ensure that each member shoulders an equal or fair amount of the work on an extensive writing project, such as a formal proposal or report?

Activities

13.1 Proposals: Solving a Workplace Problem in an Unsolicited Informal Proposal (Obj. 1)

The ability to spot problems before they turn into serious risks is prized by most managers. Draw on your internship and work experience. Can you identify a problem that could be solved with a small to moderate financial investment? Look for such issues as missing lunch or break rooms for staff; badly needed health initiatives, such as gyms or sports club memberships; low-gas-mileage, high-emission company vehicles; or lack of recycling efforts.

Your Task. Discuss with your instructor the workplace problem that you have identified. Make sure you choose a relatively weighty problem that can nevertheless be lessened or eliminated with a minor expenditure. Be sure to include a cost-benefit analysis. Address your unsolicited letter or memo proposal to your current or former boss and copy your instructor.

13.2 Proposals: Comparing Real Proposals (Objs. 1, 2)

Many new companies with services or products to offer would like to land corporate or government contracts. However, they are intimidated by the request for proposal (RFP) process. You have been asked for help by your friend Mikayla, who has started her own designer uniform company. Her goal is to offer her colourful yet functional uniforms to hospitals and clinics.

Before writing a proposal, however, she wants to see examples and learn more about the process.

Your Task. Use the Web to find at least two examples of business proposals. Do not waste time on sites that want to sell templates or books. Find actual examples. Then prepare a memo to Mikayla in which you do the following:

a. Identify two sites with sample business proposals.

b. Outline the parts of each proposal.

c. Compare the strengths and weaknesses of each proposal.

d. Draw conclusions. What can Mikayla learn from these examples?

13.3 Proposals: Medicus Associates Solicits Your Proposal (Obj. 1)

> TEAM

In university towns, sports medicine is increasingly popular. A new medical clinic, Medicus Associates, is opening its doors in your community. A friend recommended your small business to the administrator of the clinic, and you received a letter asking you to provide information about your service. The new medical clinic specializes in sports medicine, physical therapy, and cardiac rehabilitation services. It is interested in retaining your company rather than hiring its own employees to perform the service your company offers.

Your Task. Working in teams, first decide what service you will offer. It could be landscaping, uniform supply, laundry of uniforms, general cleaning, computerized no-paper filing systems, online medical supplies, patient transportation, supplemental hospice care, temporary office support, or food service. As a team, develop a letter proposal outlining your plan, staffing, and budget. Use persuasion to show why contracting your services is better than hiring in-house employees. In the proposal letter, request a meeting with the administrative board. In addition to a written proposal, you may be expected to make an oral presentation that includes visual aids or handouts. Send your proposal to Dr. Pat Leigh, Director, Medicus Associates. Supply a local address.

13.4 Proposal and Grant Writing: Learning From the Nonprofits (Objs. 1, 2)

`WEB`

You would like to learn more about writing business proposals and especially about writing grants. Grants are written to solicit funding from institutions, foundations, or the government. You might one day even decide to become a professional grant or proposal writer. However, first you need experience.

Your Task. Volunteer your services for a local nonprofit organization, such as a United Way (**www.unitedway.ca**) member agency, an educational institution, or your local religious community. To learn more about writing grants, use a search engine to look up *proposal*. Try such categories as *business proposal writing* and *grant proposal writing*. In the browser window, enclose the search terms in quotation marks. Your instructor may ask you to submit a preliminary memo report outlining ten or more pointers you learn about writing proposals and grants for nonprofit organizations.

13.5 Business Plans: Can Your Team Write a Winning Plan? (Obj. 3)

`TEAM`   `WEB`

Business plans at many schools are more than classroom writing exercises. They have won regional, national, and worldwide prizes. Although some contests are part of MBA programs, other contests are available for undergraduates. Enterprize Canada, the largest student-run business competition in Canada, is hosted and organized under the leadership of students from the Sauder School of Business at the University of British Columbia. At the 2009 national competition and conference, which hosted more than 450 delegates, the winning business plan from VSM Technologies was a spinoff of the cofounder's award-winning Ph.D. work.

VSM Technologies offers two types of products. The first is a novel wireless vital signs monitoring integrated circuit that improves patients' safety by continuously monitoring their vital signs. In an emergency, it can communicate the data to the medical staff through Bluetooth and WiFi-enabled personal communication devices, such as cellphones and PDAs. It is a miniaturized, low-cost device that can measure blood pressure, heart rate, and body temperature continuously and simultaneously. The design is revolutionary as its wireless circuits use on-chip antennas, which reduce the overall size of the module immensely.

The second product is a groundbreaking 3D package for wireless circuits, which reduces the power consumption of the wireless circuits drastically. This design has recently been acclaimed internationally and has received a lot of media attention.[4]

As part of a business plan project, you and your team are challenged to come up with an idea for a new business or service. It doesn't need to be as sophisticated as the above example. For example, you might want to offer a lunch service with fresh sandwiches or salads delivered to office workers' desks. You might propose building a better Web site for an organization. You might want to start a document preparation business that offers production, editing, and printing services. You might have a terrific idea for an existing business to expand with a new product or service.

Your Task. Working in teams, explore entrepreneurial ventures based on your experience and expertise. Conduct team meetings to decide on a product or service, develop a work plan, assign responsibilities, and create a schedule. Your goal is to write a business plan proposal that will convince potential investors (sometimes your own management) that you have an excellent business idea and that you can pull it off. Check out sample business plans on the Web. The two "deliverables" from your project will be your written business plan and an oral presentation. Your written report should include a cover, transmittal document (letter or memo), title page, table of contents, executive summary, proposal (including introduction, body, and conclusion), appendix items, optional glossary, and sources. In the body of the proposal, be sure to explain your mission and vision, the market, your marketing strategy, operations, and financial information. Address your business plan proposal to your instructor.

13.6 Formal Reports: Intercultural Communication (Objs. 4–6)

`INTERCULTURAL`   `TEAM`

North American businesses are expanding into foreign markets with manufacturing plants, sales offices, and branches abroad. Most North Americans, however, have little knowledge of or experience with people from other cultures. To prepare for participation in the global marketplace, you are to collect information for a report focused on an Asian, Latin American, or European country where English is not regularly spoken. Before selecting the country, though, consult your campus international student program for volunteers who are willing to be interviewed. Your instructor may make advance arrangements with international student volunteers.

Your Task. In teams of three to five, collect information about your target country from the library and other sources. Then invite an international student representing your target country to be interviewed by your group. As you conduct primary and secondary research, investigate the topics listed in Figure 13.4. Confirm what you learn in your secondary research by talking with your interviewee. When you complete your research, write a report for the CEO of your company (make up a name and company). Assume that your company plans to expand its operations abroad. Your report should advise the company's executives of the social customs, family life, attitudes, religions, education, and values in the target country. Remember that your company's interests are business oriented; do not dwell on tourist information. Write your report individually or in teams.

13.7 Business Plans: Studying Samples and Selecting the Best (Obj. 3)

`WEB`

As a member of a group of venture capitalists with money to invest in start-up companies, you must make a choice. Assume your group has received three business plan proposals.

FIGURE 13.4 **Intercultural Interview Topics and Questions**

Social Customs
- How do people react to strangers? Are they friendly? Hostile? Reserved?
- How do people greet each other?
- What are the appropriate manners when you enter a room? Bow? Nod? Shake hands with everyone?
- How are names used for introductions? Is it appropriate to inquire about one's occupation or family?
- What are the attitudes toward touching?
- How does one express appreciation for an invitation to another's home? Bring a gift? Send flowers? Write a thank-you note? Are any gifts taboo?
- Are there any customs related to how or where one sits?
- Are any facial expressions or gestures considered rude?
- How close do people stand when talking?
- What is the attitude toward punctuality in social situations? In business situations?
- What are acceptable eye contact patterns?
- What gestures indicate agreement? Disagreement?

Family Life
- What is the basic unit of social organization? Basic family? Extended family?
- Do women work outside of the home? In what occupations?

Housing, Clothing, and Food
- Are there differences in the kinds of housing used by different social groups? Differences in location? Differences in furnishings?
- What occasions require special clothing?
- Are some types of clothing considered taboo?
- What is appropriate business attire for men? For women?
- How many times a day do people eat?
- What types of places, food, and drink are appropriate for business entertainment? Where is the seat of honour at a table?

Class Structure
- Into what classes is society organized?
- Do ethnic, religious, or economic factors determine social status?
- Are there any minority groups? What is their social standing?

Political Patterns
- Are there any immediate threats to the political survival of the country?
- How is political power manifested?
- What channels are used for expressing political opinions?
- What information media are important?
- Is it appropriate to talk politics in social situations?

Religion and Folk Beliefs
- To which religious groups do people belong? Is one predominant?
- Do religious beliefs influence daily activities?
- Which places are considered sacred? Which objects? Which events?
- How do religious holidays affect business activities?

Economic Institutions
- What are the country's principal products?
- Are workers organized in unions?
- How are businesses owned? By family units? By large public corporations? By the government?
- What is the standard work schedule?
- Is it appropriate to do business by telephone? By computer?
- How has technology affected business procedures?
- Is participatory management used?
- Are there any customs related to exchanging business cards?
- How is status shown in an organization? Private office? Secretary? Furniture?
- Are businesspeople expected to socialize before conducting business?

Value Systems
- Is competitiveness or cooperation more prized?
- Is thrift or enjoyment of the moment more valued?
- Is politeness more important than factual honesty?
- What are the attitudes toward education?
- Do women own or manage businesses? If so, how are they treated?
- What are your people's perceptions of Canadians? What has been hardest for you to adjust to in Canada? How could Canadians make this adjustment easier for you?

Your Task. Visit either Bplans.com at **www.bplans.com** or one of the sites mentioned in this chapter. Search for sample business plans. Browse the list and select three business plans to study. Analyze all parts of each plan. Then select one that you will recommend for funding. Prepare a memo to your investor group explaining why you think this start-up business will succeed. Also comment on the organization, format, and writing style of the business plan. What are its strengths and weaknesses? Address your memo to your instructor.

13.8 Proposal, Business Plan, and Report Topics (Objs. 1–6)

A list with nearly 100 report topics is available at **www.guffeybrief4e.nelson.com**. The topics are divided into the following categories: accounting, finance, personnel/human resources, marketing, information systems, management, and general business/education/campus issues. You can collect information for many of these reports by using electronic databases and the Web. Your instructor may assign them as individual or team projects. All involve critical thinking in organizing information, drawing conclusions, and making recommendations. The topics include assignments appropriate for proposals, business plans, and formal reports.

13.9 Executive Summary: Locating Expert Information About Business Plans (Obj. 3)

WEB TEAM E-MAIL

To supplement your knowledge of business plans and draw on various sources, search electronic databases to find recent articles about business plans and business models. This activity can be completed in teams, with each member contributing valuable tips and insights about business plans from an article or two.

Your Task. Using ProQuest, Factiva, EBSCO, or some other business database, search for the keywords *business plan,* and if you want more sources, for *business model.* You may also try searching business publications on the Internet. Select an article that is at least 1,200 words long and discusses business plans fully. Write an executive summary in memo format, or write an e-mail, if requested by your instructor. Identify the author, article title, periodical, and date of publication. Summarize the most important findings of the article. Use talking rather than functional headings, if helpful.

13.10 Unsolicited Proposal: Thwarting Residence Room Thievery (Objs. 1, 2)

CONSUMER   **TEAM**

As an enterprising postsecondary student, you recognized a problem as soon as you arrived on campus. Residence rooms filled with pricey digital equipment were very attractive to thieves. Some students move in with more than $3,000 in gear, including laptop computers, flat-screen TVs, digital cameras, MP3 players, video game consoles, PDAs, and DVD players. You solved the problem by buying an extra-large steel footlocker

to lock away your valuables. However, shipping the footlocker was expensive (nearly $100), and you had to wait for it to arrive from a catalogue company. Your bright idea is to propose to the Campus Student Organization (CSO) that it allow you to offer these steel footlockers to students at a reduced price and with campus delivery. Your footlocker, which you found by searching the Web, is extremely durable and works great as a coffee table, nightstand, or card table. It comes with a smooth interior liner and two compartments.

Your Task. Working individually or with a team, imagine that you have made arrangements with a manufacturer to act as an intermediary selling footlockers on your campus at a reduced price. Consult the Web for manufacturers and make up your own figures. However, how can you get the CSO's permission to proceed? Give that organization a cut? Use your imagination in deciding how this plan might work on a college or university campus. Then prepare an unsolicited proposal to your CSO. Outline the problem and your goals of protecting students' valuables and providing convenience. Check the Web for statistics regarding on-campus burglaries. Such figures should help you develop one or more persuasive "hooks." Then explain your proposal, project possible sales, discuss a timetable, and describe your staffing. Submit your proposal to Billie White, President, Campus Student Organization.

Grammar and Mechanics C.L.U.E. Review 13

Total Review

Each of the following sentences has a total of three errors in grammar, punctuation, capitalization, usage, or spelling. On a separate sheet, write a correct version. Avoid adding new phrases, starting new sentences, or rewriting in your own words. When finished, compare your responses with the key beginning on page Key-1.

Example: The following 3 statistical terms frequently describe data, Mean, median, and mode.

Revision: The following **three** statistical terms frequently describe **data: mean**, median, and mode.

1. Lack of job security and high unemployment is here to stay. Even if we do our work really good.

2. Managers in 3 departments' complained that there departments were over budget for supplies.

3. After sending many e-mails to Frank and I, the client felt badly about barraging us with messages to solicit a response from our two teams'.

4. The new vice president and her decided to move up the launch to May 3rd, as a result, the software was buggy.

5. Managers of big corporations' sometimes do not know how to motivate, consequently, the executives miss an opportunity to develop their worker's.

6. The Director of marketing wanted to speak to you and I about the poor moral in our division.

7. Laura and him decided to except assistance with their proposal, therefore, they completed the project by the deadline.

8. We invited seventy-five employees to hear 2 experts disberse information about wellness.

9. Memo's usually contain four necessary parts, subject line, opening, body and action closing.

10. Darrin Jizmejian who was recently evaluated, wondered whether his formal report would be presented at the March 13th meeting?

Endnotes

[1] Jordan, T. (2011, January 19–February 14). How to get things done now (well, soon). *Canadian Business, 84,* p. 73.

[2] MasterPlans: Professional Business Plan Writers. (n.d.) Rapid development cycle. Retrieved March 5, 2010, from http://www.masterplans.com

[3] Turner, M. L. (2007). Guide to business plan consultants: Hiring help is the next best thing to writing your plan

yourself. *Work.com.* Retrieved March 5, 2010, from http://www.work.com/business-plan-consultants-880/

[4] Enterprize Canada. (2009). Enterprize Canada business competition results 2009. Retrieved July 10, 2009, from http://www.enterprizecanada.org/competition/past-winners

CHAPTER 14

Business Presentations

OBJECTIVES

1. Discuss two important first steps in preparing effective oral presentations.

2. Explain the major elements in organizing the content of a presentation, including the introduction, body, and conclusion.

3. Identify techniques for gaining audience rapport, including (a) using effective imagery, (b) providing verbal signposts, and (c) sending appropriate nonverbal messages.

4. Discuss designing visual aids, handouts, and multimedia presentations and using presentation technology competently.

5. Specify delivery techniques for use before, during, and after a presentation and apply reflective thinking skills.

6. Organize team-based written and oral presentations and understand how to communicate in teams.

7. Explain effective techniques for adapting oral presentations to intercultural audiences and demonstrate intercultural and diversity understanding.

8. List techniques for improving telephone and voice mail skills to project a positive image.

Rob Melnychuk/Getty Images

What is the going rate for a high-profile Canadian speaker? According to All American Talent & Celebrity Network, The Great One, Wayne Gretzky, commands up to $100,000 per speaking engagement. And not only athletes receive such paycheques. All American Speakers reports that Kim Cattrall and Howie Mandel charge more than $50,000 per engagement and Jim Carrey and Martin Short cost more than $100,000.[1] Why are organizations willing to pay such fees for these speakers? If you were in attendance for one of these speakers, what would your expectations be?

Preparing Effective Oral Presentations

LEARNING OBJECTIVE 1

Discuss two important first steps in preparing effective oral presentations.

At some point everyone in business has to sell an idea, and such persuasion is often done in person. Many of us do not consider ourselves to be professional speakers, nor do we take advantage of opportunities in college or university and elsewhere to develop speaking skills. However, such skills often play an important role in a successful career and are useful at every career stage. You might, for example, have to make a sales pitch before customers or speak to a professional gathering. You might need to describe your company's expansion plans to your banker, or you might need to persuade management to support your proposed marketing strategy. This chapter prepares you to use speaking skills in making oral presentations, whether alone or as part of a team.

For any presentation you can reduce your fears and lay the foundation for a professional performance by focusing on five areas: preparation, organization, audience rapport, visual aids, and delivery.

Knowing Your Purpose

The most important part of your preparation is deciding what you want to accomplish. Whether your goal is to persuade or to inform, you must have a clear idea of where you are going. At the end of your presentation, what do you want your listeners to remember or do?

Preparing for an oral presentation means identifying the purpose and knowing the audience.

Mark Miller, a loan officer at Dominion Trust, faced such questions as he planned a talk for a class in small-business management. Mark's former business professor had asked him to return to campus and give the class advice about borrowing money from banks to start new businesses. Because Mark knew so much about this topic, he found it difficult to extract a specific purpose statement for his presentation. After much thought he narrowed his purpose to this: *To inform potential entrepreneurs about three important factors that loan officers consider before granting start-up loans to launch small businesses.* His entire presentation focused on ensuring that the class members understood and remembered three principal ideas.

Knowing Your Audience

A second key element in preparation is analyzing your audience, anticipating its reactions, and making appropriate adaptations. Audiences may fall into four categories, as summarized in Figure 14.1. By anticipating your audience, you have a better idea of how to organize your presentation. A friendly audience, for example, will respond to humour and personal experiences. A neutral audience requires an even, controlled delivery style. The talk would probably be filled with facts, statistics, and expert opinions. An uninterested audience that is forced to attend requires a brief presentation. Such an audience might respond best to humour, cartoons, colourful visuals, and startling statistics. A hostile audience demands a calm, controlled delivery style with objective data and expert opinion.

FIGURE 14.1 **Succeeding With Four Audience Types**

Audience Members	Organizational Pattern	Delivery Style	Supporting Material
Friendly			
They like you and your topic.	Use any pattern. Try something new. Involve the audience.	Be warm, pleasant, and open. Use a lot of eye contact and smiles.	Include humour, personal examples, and experiences.
Neutral			
They are calm, rational; their minds are made up, but they think they are objective.	Present both sides of the issue. Use pro/con or problem/solution patterns. Save time for audience questions.	Be controlled. Do nothing showy. Use confident, small gestures.	Use facts, statistics, expert opinion, and comparison and contrast. Avoid humour, personal stories, and flashy visuals.
Uninterested			
They have short attention spans; they may be there against their will.	Be brief—no more than three points. Avoid topical and pro/con patterns that seem lengthy to the audience.	Be dynamic and entertaining. Move around. Use large gestures.	Use humour, cartoons, colourful visuals, powerful quotations, and startling statistics.
	Avoid darkening the room, standing motionless, passing out handouts, using boring visuals, or expecting the audience to participate.		
Hostile			
They want to take charge or to ridicule the speaker; they may be defensive, emotional.	Organize using a noncontroversial pattern, such as a topical, chronological, or geographic strategy.	Be calm and controlled. Speak evenly and slowly.	Include objective data and expert opinion. Avoid anecdotes and humour.
	Avoid a question-and-answer period, if possible; otherwise, use a moderator or accept only written questions.		

Other elements, such as age, gender, education, experience, and the size of the audience, will affect your style and message content. Analyze the following questions to help you determine your organizational pattern, delivery style, and supporting material.

> **Audience analysis issues include size, age, gender, experience, attitude, and expectations.**

- How will this topic appeal to this audience?

- How can I relate this information to my listeners' needs?

- How can I earn respect so that they accept my message?

- What would be most effective in making my point? Facts? Statistics? Personal experiences? Expert opinion? Humour? Cartoons? Graphic illustrations? Demonstrations? Case histories? Analogies?

- What measures must I take to ensure that this audience remembers my main points?

If you have agreed to speak to an audience with which you are unfamiliar, ask for the names of a half dozen people who will be in the audience. Contact them and learn about their backgrounds and expectations for the presentation. This information can help you answer questions about what they want to hear and how deeply you should explore the subject. You will want to thank these people when you start your speech. Doing this kind of homework will impress the audience.

Organizing the Content for a Powerful Impact

Once you have determined your purpose and analyzed the audience, you are ready to collect information and organize it logically. Good organization and intentional repetition are the two most powerful keys to audience comprehension and retention. In fact, many speech experts recommend the following admittedly repetitious but effective plan:

- **Step 1:** Tell them what you're going to say.

- **Step 2:** Say it.

- **Step 3:** Tell them what you have just said.

In other words, repeat your main points in the introduction, body, and conclusion of your presentation. Although it seems redundant, this strategy works surprisingly well. Let's examine how to construct the three parts of an effective presentation.

Capturing Attention in the Introduction

How many times have you heard a speaker begin with, *It's a pleasure to be here*. Or, *I'm honoured to be asked to speak*. Boring openings, such as these, get speakers off to a dull start. Avoid such banalities by striving to accomplish three goals in the introduction to your presentation:

- Capture listeners' attention and get them involved.

- Identify yourself and establish your credibility.

- Preview your main points.

Attention-grabbing openers include questions, startling facts, jokes, anecdotes, and quotations.

If you are able to appeal to listeners and involve them in your presentation right from the start, you are more likely to hold their attention until the finish. Consider some of the same techniques that you used to open sales letters: a question, a startling fact, a joke, a story, or a quotation. Some speakers achieve involvement by opening with a question or command that requires audience members to raise their hands or stand up. To establish your credibility, you need to describe your position, knowledge, or experience—whatever qualifies you to speak. Try also to connect with your audience. Listeners respond particularly well to speakers who reveal something of themselves and identify with them.

After capturing attention and establishing yourself, you will want to preview the main points of your topic, perhaps with a visual aid. You may want to put off actually writing your introduction, however, until after you have organized the rest of the presentation and crystallized your principal ideas.

Take a look at Mark Miller's introduction, shown in Figure 14.2, to see how he integrated all the elements necessary for a good opening.

Organizing the Body

The best oral presentations focus on a few key ideas.

The biggest problem with most oral presentations is a failure to focus on a few principal ideas. Thus, the body of your short presentation (20 or fewer minutes) should include a limited number of main points, say, two to four. Develop each main point with adequate but not excessive explanation and details. Too many details can obscure the main message, so keep your presentation simple and logical. Remember, listeners have no pages to leaf back through should they become confused.

When Mark Miller began planning his presentation, he realized immediately that he could talk for hours on his topic. He also knew that listeners are not good at separating major and minor points. Thus, instead of submerging his listeners in a sea of information, he sorted out a few main ideas. In the banking industry, loan officers generally ask the following three questions of each applicant for a small business loan: (1) Are you ready to "hit the ground running" in starting your business? (2) Have you done your homework? and (3) Have you made realistic projections of potential sales, cash flow, and

FIGURE 14.2 Oral Presentation Outline

What Makes a Loan Officer Say *Yes*?

I. INTRODUCTION

Captures attention —— A. How many of you expect one day to start your own businesses? How many of you have all the cash available to capitalize that business when you start?

Involves audience —— B. Like you, nearly every entrepreneur needs cash to open a business, and I promise you that by the end of this talk you will have inside information on how to make a loan application that will be successful.

Identifies speaker —— C. As a loan officer at Dominion Trust, which specializes in small-business loans, I make decisions on requests from entrepreneurs like you applying for start-up money.
Transition: Your professor invited me here today to tell you how you can improve your chances of getting a loan from us or from any other lender. I have suggestions in three areas: experience, preparation, and projection. —— *Previews three main points*

II. BODY

A. First, let's consider experience. You must show that you can hit the ground running.
  1. Demonstrate what experience you have in your proposed business.
  2. Include your résumé when you submit your business plan.
  3. If you have little experience, tell us whom you would hire to supply the skills that you lack.
  Transition: In addition to experience, loan officers will want to see that you have researched your venture thoroughly. ——

Establishes main points —— B. My second suggestion, then, involves preparation. Have you done your homework?
  1. Talk to local businesspeople, especially those in related fields.
  2. Conduct traffic counts or other studies to estimate potential sales.
  3. Analyze the strengths and weaknesses of the competition.
  Transition: Now that we've discussed preparation, we're ready for my final suggestion. —— *Develops coherence with planned transitions*

C. My last tip is the most important one. It involves making a realistic projection of your potential sales, cash flow, and equity.
  1. Present detailed monthly cash-flow projections for the first year.
  2. Describe *What-if* scenarios indicating both good and bad possibilities.
  3. Indicate that you intend to supply at least 25 percent of the initial capital yourself.
  Transition: The three major points I've just outlined cover critical points in obtaining start-up loans. Let me review them for you. ——

III. CONCLUSION

Summarizes main points —— A. Loan officers are most likely to say *yes* to your loan application if you do three things: (1) prove that you can hit the ground running when your business opens; (2) demonstrate that you've researched your proposed business seriously; and (3) project a realistic picture of your sales, cash flow, and equity.

B. Experience, preparation, and projection, then, are the three keys to launching your business with the necessary start-up capital so that you can concentrate on where your customers, not your funds, are coming from. —— *Provides final focus*

---

equity investment? These questions would become his main points, but Mark wanted to streamline them further so that his audience would be sure to remember them. He capsulized the questions in three words: *experience, preparation*, and *projection*. As you can see in Figure 14.2, Mark prepared a sentence outline showing these three main ideas. Each is supported by examples and explanations.

How to organize and sequence main ideas may not be immediately obvious when you begin working on a presentation. The following methods, which review and amplify those discussed in Chapter 12, provide many possible strategies and examples to help you organize a presentation:

- **Chronology.** Example: A presentation describing the history of a problem, organized from the first sign of trouble to the present.

- **Geography/space.** Example: A presentation about the changing diversity of the workforce, organized by regions in the country (East Coast, West Coast, and so forth).

- **Topic/function/conventional grouping.** Example: A report discussing mishandled airline baggage, organized by names of airlines.

- **Comparison/contrast (pro/con).** Example: A report comparing organic farming methods with those of modern industrial farming.

- **Journalistic pattern.** Example: A report describing how identity thieves can ruin your good name. Organized by *who, what, when, where, why,* and *how.*

- **Value/size.** Example: A report describing fluctuations in housing costs, organized by prices of homes.

- **Importance.** Example: A report describing five reasons that a company should move its headquarters to a specific city, organized from the most important reason to the least important.

- **Problem/solution.** Example: A company faces a problem, such as declining sales. A solution, such as reducing the staff, is offered.

- **Simple/complex.** Example: A report explaining genetic modification of plants, such as corn, organized from simple seed production to complex gene introduction.

- **Best case/worst case.** Example: A report analyzing whether two companies should merge, organized by the best-case result (improved market share, profitability, employee morale) as opposed to the worst-case result (devalued stock, lost market share, employee malaise).

In the presentation shown in Figure 14.2, Mark arranged the main points by importance, placing the most important point last, where it had maximum effect. When organizing any presentation, prepare a little more material than you think you will actually need. Experienced speakers always have something useful in reserve, such as an extra handout, transparency, or idea—just in case they finish early. At the same time, most speakers go about 25 percent over the allotted time as opposed to their practice runs at home in front of the mirror. If your speaking time is limited, as it usually is in your classes, aim for less than the limit when rehearsing so that you don't take time away from the next presenters.

Summarizing in the Conclusion

Nervous speakers often rush to wrap up their presentations because they can't wait to flee the stage. However, listeners will remember the conclusion more than any other part of a speech. That's why you should spend some time to make it most effective. Strive to achieve three goals:

- Summarize the main themes of the presentation.

- Leave the audience with a specific and memorable "take-away."

- Include a statement that allows you to leave the podium gracefully.

Some speakers end limply with such comments as, *I guess that's about all I have to say* or *That's it.* Such lame statements show little enthusiasm and are not the culmination of the talk that listeners expect. Skilled speakers alert the audience that they are finishing. They use phrases such as, *In conclusion, as I end this presentation,* or, *It's time for me to sum up.* Then they proceed immediately to the conclusion. Audiences become justly irritated with a speaker who announces the conclusion but then digresses with one more story or talks for ten more minutes.

A straightforward summary should review major points and focus on what you want the listeners to do, think, or remember. You might say, *In bringing my presentation to a close, I will restate my major purpose . . . ,* or, *In summary, my major purpose has been to. . . . In support of my purpose, I have presented three major points. They are (1). . . , (2) . . . , and (3). . . .* Notice how Mark Miller, in the conclusion shown in Figure 14.2, summarized his three main points and provided a final focus to listeners.

If you are promoting a recommendation, you might end as follows: *In conclusion, I recommend that we retain Matrixx Marketing to conduct a telemarketing campaign beginning September 1 at a cost of X dollars. To complete this recommendation, I suggest that we (a) finance this campaign from our operations budget, (b) develop a persuasive message describing our new product, and (c) name Lisa Beck to oversee the project.*

A conclusion is similar to a punch line and must be memorable. Think of it as the high point of your presentation, a valuable kernel of information to take away. The valuable kernel of information, or take-away, should tie in with the opening or present a forward-looking idea. Avoid merely rehashing, in the same words, what you said before but ensure that the audience will take away very specific information or benefits and a positive impression of you and your company. The so-called take-away is the value of the presentation to the audience and the benefit audience members believe they have received. The tension that you built in the early parts of the talk now culminates in the close.

In your conclusion you might want to use an anecdote, an inspiring quotation, or a statement that ties in the opener and offers a new insight. Whatever you choose, be sure to include a closing thought that indicates you are finished. For example, *This concludes my presentation. After investigating many marketing firms, we are convinced that Matrixx is the best for our purposes. Your authorization of my recommendations will mark the beginning of a very successful campaign for our new product. Thank you.*

Building Audience Rapport Like a Pro

Good speakers are adept at building audience rapport. They form a bond with the audience; they entertain as well as inform. How do they do it? Based on observations of successful and unsuccessful speakers, we learn that the good ones use a number of verbal and nonverbal techniques to connect with the audience. Their helpful techniques include providing effective imagery, supplying verbal signposts, and using body language strategically.

Effective Imagery

You will lose your audience quickly if you fill your talk with abstractions, generalities, and dry facts. To enliven your presentation and enhance comprehension, try using some of the following techniques. However, beware of exaggeration or distortion. Keep your imagery realistic and credible.

- **Analogies.** A comparison of similar traits between dissimilar things can be effective in explaining and drawing connections.

- **Metaphors.** A comparison between otherwise dissimilar things without using the words *like* or *as* results in a metaphor.

- **Similes.** A comparison that includes the words *like* or *as* is a simile.

- **Personal anecdotes.** Nothing connects you faster *or* better with your audience than a good personal story.

- **Personalized statistics.** Although often misused, statistics stay with people—particularly when they relate directly to the audience.

- **Worst- and best-case scenarios.** Hearing the worst that could happen can be effective in driving home a point.

Verbal Signposts

Speakers must remember that listeners, unlike readers of a report, cannot control the rate of presentation or flip back through pages to review main points. As a result, listeners get lost easily. Knowledgeable speakers help the audience recognize the organization and main points in an oral message with verbal signposts. They keep listeners on track by including helpful previews, summaries, and transitions, such as these:

Knowledgeable speakers provide verbal signposts to indicate when they are previewing, summarizing, or switching directions.

- **Previewing**

  The next segment of my talk presents three reasons for . . .

  Let's now consider the causes of . . .

- **Summarizing**

  Let me review with you the major problems I have just discussed . . .

  You see, then, that the most significant factors are . . .

- **Switching directions**

  Thus far we have talked solely about . . . ; now let's move to . . .

  I have argued that . . . and . . . , but an alternative view holds that . . .

You can further improve any oral presentation by including appropriate transitional expressions, such as *first, second, next, then, therefore, moreover, on the other hand, on the contrary,* and *in conclusion.* These transitional expressions, which you learned about in Chapter 5, build coherence, lend emphasis, and tell listeners where you are headed. Notice in Mark Miller's outline in Figure 14.2 the specific transitional elements designed to help listeners recognize each new principal point.

Nonverbal Messages

A speaker's appearance, movement, and speech affect the success of a presentation.

Although what you say is most important, the nonverbal messages you send can also have a potent effect on how well your audience receives your message. How you look, how you move, and how you speak can make or break your presentation. The following suggestions focus on nonverbal tips to ensure that your verbal message is well received.

- **Look terrific!** Like it or not, you will be judged by your appearance. For everything but small in-house presentations, be sure you dress professionally. The rule of thumb is that you should dress at least as well as the best-dressed person in the audience.

- **Animate your body.** Be enthusiastic and let your body show it. Emphasize ideas to enhance points about size, number, and direction. Use a variety of gestures, but don't consciously plan them in advance.

- **Speak extemporaneously.** Do not read from notes or a manuscript but speak freely. Use your presentation slides to guide your talk. You will come across as more competent and enthusiastic if you are not glued to your notes or manuscript. Use note cards or a paper outline only if presenting without an electronic slideshow.

- **Punctuate your words.** You can keep your audience interested by varying your tone, volume, pitch, and pace. Use pauses before and after important points. Allow the audience to take in your ideas.

- **Get out from behind the podium.** Avoid being glued to the podium. Movement makes you look natural and comfortable. You might pick a few places in the room to walk to. Even if you must stay close to your visual aids, make a point of leaving them occasionally so that the audience can see your whole body.

- **Vary your facial expression.** Begin with a smile but change your expressions to correspond with the thoughts you are voicing. You can shake your head to show disagreement, roll your eyes to show disdain, look heavenward for guidance, or wrinkle your brow to show concern or dismay. To see how speakers convey meaning without words, mute the sound on your TV and watch the facial expressions of a talk show personality.

Planning Visual Aids and Multimedia Presentations

Before you make a business presentation, consider this wise proverb: "Tell me, I forget. Show me, I remember. Involve me, I understand." Your goals as a speaker are to make listeners understand, remember, and act on your ideas. To get them interested and involved, include effective visual aids. Some experts say that we acquire 85 percent of all our knowledge visually. Therefore, an oral presentation that incorporates visual aids is far more likely to be understood and retained than one lacking visual enhancement.

Good visual aids have many purposes. They emphasize and clarify main points, thus improving comprehension and retention. They increase audience interest, and they make the presenter appear more professional, better prepared, and more persuasive. Well-designed visual aids illustrate and emphasize your message more effectively than words alone; therefore, they may help shorten a meeting or achieve your goal faster. Visual aids are particularly helpful for inexperienced speakers because the audience concentrates on the aid rather than on the speaker. However, experienced speakers work hard at not being eclipsed or upstaged by their slideshows. Good visuals also serve to jog the memory of a speaker, thus improving self-confidence, poise, and delivery.

LEARNING OBJECTIVE 4

Discuss designing visual aids, handouts, and multimedia presentations and using presentation technology competently.

Types of Visual Aids

Fortunately for today's speakers, many forms of visual media are available to enhance a presentation. Figure 14.3 describes the pros and cons of a number of visual aids that can guide you in selecting the best visual aid for any speaking occasion. Three of the most popular visuals are multimedia slides, overhead transparencies, and handouts.

Visual aids clarify points, improve comprehension, and aid retention.

Multimedia Slides. With today's excellent software programs—such as Microsoft PowerPoint, Apple Keynote, Lotus Freelance Graphics, Corel Presentations, and Adobe Presenter or Adobe Ovation—you can create dynamic, colourful presentations with your PC. The output from these programs is generally shown on a computer monitor, a TV monitor, an LCD (liquid crystal display) panel, or a screen. With a little expertise and advanced equipment, you can create a multimedia presentation that includes stereo sound, videos, and hyperlinks, as described shortly in the discussion of multimedia presentations.

Overhead Transparencies. Some speakers still rely on the overhead projector for many reasons. Most meeting areas are equipped with projectors and screens. Moreover, acetate transparencies for the overhead are cheap, easily prepared on a computer or copier, and simple to use. Because rooms need not be darkened, a speaker using transparencies can maintain eye contact with the audience. Many experienced speakers create overhead slides in addition to their electronic slides to have a backup plan in the case of malfunctioning presentation technology. A word of caution, though, when using transparencies: stand to the side of the projector so that you don't obstruct the audience's view.

Handouts. You can enhance and complement your presentations by distributing pictures, outlines, brochures, articles, charts, summaries, or other supplements. Speakers who use presentation software often prepare a set of their slides along with notes to hand out to viewers. Timing the distribution of any handout, though, is tricky. If given out during a presentation, your handouts tend to distract the audience, causing you to lose control. Therefore, you should discuss handouts during the presentation but delay distributing them until after you finish.

To maintain control, distribute handouts after you finish speaking.

Speaker's Notes. You have a variety of options for printing hard-copy versions of your presentation. You can, for example, make speaker's notes, which are a wonderful aid for practising your talk. Beneath the miniature image of each slide is space for you to key in your supporting comments for the abbreviated material in your slides. You

FIGURE 14.3 Pros and Cons of Visual Aid Options

Medium		Pros	Cons
Multimedia slides 		Create professional appearance with many colour, art, graphic, and font options. Easy to use and transport via removable storage media, Web download, or e-mail attachment. Inexpensive to update.	Present potential incompatibility issues. Require costly projection equipment and practice for smooth delivery. Tempt user to include features that may fail to add value.
Transparencies 		Give professional appearance with little practice. Easy to (1) prepare, (2) update and maintain, (3) locate reliable equipment, and (4) limit information shown at one time.	Appear to some as an outdated presentation method. Hold speaker captive to the machine. Provide poor reproduction of photos and some graphics.
Handouts 		Encourage audience participation. Easy to maintain and update. Enhance recall because audience keeps reference material.	Increase risk of unauthorized duplication of speaker's material. Can be difficult to transport. May cause speaker to lose audience's attention.
Flipcharts or whiteboards 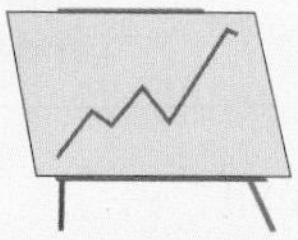		Provide inexpensive option available at most sites. Easy to (1) create, (2) modify on the spot, (3) record comments from the audience, and (4) combine with more high-tech visuals in the same presentation.	Require graphics talent. Difficult for larger audiences to see. Prepared flipcharts are cumbersome to transport and easily worn with use.
Video 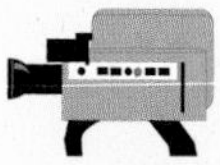		Gives an accurate representation of the content; strong indication of forethought and preparation.	Creates potential for compatibility issues related to computer video formats. Expensive to create and update.
Props 		Offer a realistic reinforcement of message content. Increase audience participation with close observation.	Lead to extra work and expense in transporting and replacing worn objects. Limited use with larger audiences.

can also include up to nine miniature versions of your slides per printed page. These miniatures are handy if you want to preview your talk to a sponsoring organization or if you want to supply the audience with a summary of your presentation. However, resist the temptation to read from your notes during the slide presentation. It might turn off your audience and make you appear insecure and incompetent.

Designing an Impressive Multimedia Presentation

Few corporate types or entrepreneurs would do without the razzle-dazzle of colourful images to make their point. Electronic slideshows, PowerPoint in particular, have become a staple of business presentations. However, overuse or misuse may be the downside of the ever-present multimedia slideshow. Over the two decades of the software program's existence, millions of poorly created and badly delivered PowerPoint presentations have tarnished PowerPoint's reputation as an effective communication tool. Tools are helpful only when used properly.

Imagine those who sit through the more than 30 million PowerPoint presentations that Microsoft estimates are made each day.[2] No doubt, many of them would say this "disease" has reached epidemic proportions. As a result, PowerPoint is often ridiculed as an ineffective communication tool. If you looked up "death by PowerPoint" in your favourite search engine, you would score hundreds of thousands of hits. However, text-laden, amateurish slides that distract and bore audiences are the fault of their creator and not the software program itself. Former Apple "Chief Evangelist" Guy Kawasaki became tired of lousy PowerPoint pitches, so he created the 10/20/30 Rule of PowerPoint, which is explained in the Career Coach box.

In the sections that follow, you will learn to create an impressive multimedia presentation using the most widely used presentation software program, PowerPoint. With any software program, of course, gaining expertise requires an investment of time and effort. You could take a course, or you could teach yourself through an online tutorial, such as that at http://office.microsoft.com/en-us/training/default.aspx. Another way to master PowerPoint is to read a book, such as Doug Lowe's *Microsoft Office PowerPoint for Dummies*. If operated by a proficient slide preparer and a skillful presenter, PowerPoint can add a distinct visual impact to any presentation.

> PowerPoint has become the business standard for presenting and selling ideas.

career coach

The 10/20/30 Rule of PowerPoint

Would you like to pitch a business idea to a successful venture capitalist? If yes, you had better whip your PowerPoint skills into shape. Former Apple "Chief Evangelist" and a founding partner of Garage Technology Ventures Guy Kawasaki is tired of lousy pitches from would-be entrepreneurs and their endless slides laden with fuzzy jargon. An early advocate of customer evangelism in high tech, Kawasaki decided to evangelize the 10/20/30 Rule of PowerPoint: 10 slides, 20 minutes, and 30-point typeface. In his blog, Kawasaki writes that this rule applies to any presentation aiming to reach agreement:

Ten slides. Ten is the optimal number of slides in a PowerPoint presentation because a normal human being cannot comprehend more than ten concepts in a meeting—and venture capitalists are very normal. (The only difference between you and a venture capitalist is that he is getting paid to gamble with someone else's money.) If you must use more than ten slides to explain your business, you probably don't have a business. The ten topics that a venture capitalist cares about are:

1. Problem
2. Your solution
3. Business model
4. Underlying magic/technology
5. Marketing and sales
6. Competition
7. Team
8. Projections and milestones
9. Status and timeline
10. Summary and call to action

Twenty minutes. You should give your ten slides in twenty minutes. . . . [P]eople will arrive late and have to leave early. In a perfect world, you give your pitch in twenty minutes, and you have forty minutes left for discussion.

Thirty-point font. The reason people use a small font is twofold: first, they don't know their material well enough; second, they think that more text is more convincing. Force yourself to use no font smaller than thirty points. I guarantee it will make your presentations better because it requires you to find the most salient points and to know how to explain them well. If "thirty points" is too dogmatic, then I offer you an algorithm: find out the age of the oldest person in your audience and divide it by two. That's your optimal font size.

To visit Guy Kawasaki's blog, go to **www.blog.guykawasaki.com** or follow him on Twitter: **http://twitter.com/Guykawasaki**.

Applying the 3-x-3 Writing Process to Creating a Visually Appealing PowerPoint Presentation

Some presenters prefer to create their slides first and then develop the narrative around their slides. Others prefer to prepare their content first and then create the visual component. The risk associated with the first approach is that you may be tempted to spend too much time making your slides look good and not enough time preparing your content. Remember that great-looking slides never compensate for thin content. In the following discussion, we review the three phases of the writing process and show how they help you develop a visually appealing PowerPoint presentation. In the prewriting phase, you analyze, anticipate, and adapt. In the second phase, you research, organize, and compose. In the third phase, you revise, edit, and evaluate.

Analyzing the Situation.

Analyzing and anticipating how your audience will react determines your choice of content and design.

Making the best content and design choices for your slides depends greatly on your analysis of the presentation situation. Will your slides be used during a live presentation? Will they be part of a self-running presentation, such as in a store kiosk? Will they be saved on a server so that those with Internet access can watch the presentation at their convenience? Will they be sent as a PowerPoint show or a PDF document—also sometimes called a "deck"—to a client instead of a hard-copy report? Are you converting PowerPoint slideshows for viewing on video iPods or BlackBerry devices?[3]

If you are e-mailing the presentation or posting it online as a self-contained file, the slides will typically feature more text than if they were delivered orally. If, however, you are creating slides for a live presentation, your analysis will prompt you to choose powerful, telling images over boring text-laden slides.

Anticipating Your Audience.

Think about how you can design your presentation to get the most positive response from your audience. Audiences respond, for example, to the colours you use. Primary ideas are generally best conveyed with bold colours, such as blue, green, and purple. Because the messages that colours convey can vary from culture to culture, colours must be chosen carefully.

Just as you anticipate audience members' reactions to colour, you can usually anticipate their reaction to special effects. Using animation and sound effects—flying objects, swirling text, clashing cymbals, and the like—only because they are available is not a good idea. Special effects distract your audience, drawing attention away from your main points. You should add animation features only if doing so helps convey your message or adds interest to the content. When your audience members leave, they should be commenting on the ideas you conveyed—not the cool swivels and sound effects.

Adapting Text and Colour Selections.

Follow the 6-x-6 rule and select background and text colours based on the lightness of the room.

Adapt the amount of text on your slide to how your audience will use the slides. As a general guideline, most graphic designers encourage the 6-x-6 rule: "six bullets per screen, max; six words per bullet, max."[4] You may find, however, that breaking this rule is sometimes necessary, particularly when your users will be viewing the presentation on their own with no speaker assistance. For most purposes, though, strive to break free from bulleted lists whenever possible and minimize the use of text.

Adapt the colours based on where the presentation will be given. Use light text on a dark background for presentations in darkened rooms. Use dark text on a light background for presentations in lighted rooms. Avoid using a dark font on a dark background, such as red text on a dark blue background. In the same way, avoid using a light font on a light background, such as white text on a pale blue background. Dark on dark or light on light results in low contrast, making the slides difficult to read.

Researching Your PowerPoint Options.

You may need to present a complicated idea and will have to learn more about PowerPoint to determine the best way to clarify and simplify its visual presentation. Besides using online tutorials and studying books on the subject, be on the lookout as you view other people's presentations to learn fresh ways to illustrate your content more effectively. Chances are you will learn the most from fellow students and team members who have truly mastered the software.

Organizing Your Slides. When you prepare your slides, translate the major headings in your presentation outline into titles for slides. Then build bullet points by using short phrases. In Chapter 5 you learned to improve readability by using graphic highlighting techniques, including bullets, numbers, and headings. In preparing a PowerPoint presentation, you will use those same techniques.

The slides you create to accompany your spoken ideas can be organized with visual elements that will help your audience understand and remember what you want to communicate. Let's say, for example, that you have three points in your presentation. You can create a blueprint slide that captures the three points in a visually appealing way, and then you can use that slide several times throughout your presentation. Near the beginning the blueprint slide provides an overview of your points. Later it will provide transitions as you move from point to point. For transitions you can direct your audience's attention by highlighting the next point you will be talking about. Finally, the blueprint slide can be used near the end to provide a review of your key points.

Working With Templates. All presentation programs require you to (a) create a template that will serve as the background for your presentation and (b) make each slide by selecting a layout that best conveys your message. When you craft your template, be cautious about selecting the slide templates that came with the program. They have been seen by millions and amount to what one expert has labelled "visual clichés."[5] Overused templates and even clip art that ship with PowerPoint can weary viewers who have seen them repeatedly in presentations. Instead of using a standard template, search for *PowerPoint template* in Google or your favourite search engine. You will see hundreds of template options available as free downloads. Unless your employer requires that presentations all have the same look, your audience will most likely appreciate fresh templates that complement the purpose of your presentation and provide visual variety.

> Overused templates and clip art produce "visual clichés" that bore audiences.

Office PowerPoint 2007 presentation templates replace the **AutoContent Wizard**. They come with new and familiar layouts and themes you can modify. Templates get you started quickly. They allow you to add your own images or a logo and delete or modify text. Relying only on templates, however, generally leads to text-heavy presentations that lack visual elements. Nevertheless, it's a good start for a PowerPoint newbie. With more experience, you can create backgrounds and layouts from scratch by adding your own elements to each slide.

Composing Your Slideshow. During this composition stage, many users fall into the trap of excessive formatting and programming. They fritter away precious time fine-tuning their slides. They don't spend enough time on what they are going to say and how they will say it. To avoid this trap, set a limit for how much time you will spend making your slides visually appealing. Your time limit will be based on how many "bells and whistles" (a) your audience expects and (b) your content requires to make it understandable. Remember that not every point or every thought requires a visual. In fact, it's smart to switch off the slides occasionally and direct the focus to yourself. Darkening the screen while you discuss a point, tell a story, give an example, or involve the audience will add variety to your presentation.

Create a slide only if the slide accomplishes at least one of the following purposes:

- Generates interest in what you are saying and helps the audience follow your ideas

- Highlights points you want your audience to remember

- Introduces or reviews your key points

- Provides a transition from one major point to the next

- Illustrates and simplifies complex ideas

In a later section of this chapter, you will find very specific steps to follow as you create your presentation.

FIGURE 14.4 Revising and Enhancing Slides for Greater Impact

Before Revision
After Revision

The slide on the left contains bullet points that are not parallel and that overlap in meaning. The second and sixth bullet points say the same thing. Moreover, some bullet points are too long. After revision, the slide on the right has a more convincing title illustrating the "you" view. The bullet points are shorter, and each begins with a verb for parallelism and an emphasis on action. The photo adds interest.

Designing for Optimal Effect. Try to avoid long, boring bulleted lists in a presentation. You can alter layouts by repositioning, resizing, or changing the fonts for the placeholders in which your title, bulleted list, organization chart, video clip, photograph, or other elements appear. Figure 14.4 illustrates two of the many layout and design options for creating your slides. The figure shows you can make your slides visually more appealing and memorable

Notice that the bulleted items on the first slide in Figure 14.4 are not parallel. The slide looks as if the author had been brainstorming or freewriting a first draft. The second and sixth bullet points express the same thought, that shopping online is convenient and easy for customers. Some bullet points are too long. As opposed to that, the bullets on the improved slide are very short, well within the 6-x-6 rule, even though they are complete sentences. The photograph in the revised slide adds interest and illustrates the point. You may use stock photos that you can download from the Web for personal or school use without penalty or consider taking your own pictures if you own a digital camera.

Figure 14.5 shows how to add variety and pizzazz to your slides. Notice that the same information that appeared as bullet points in Figure 14.4 now appears as exciting spokes radiating from the central idea: Why You Should Sell Online. This spoke diagram is just one of the numerous **SmartArt graphics** in the **Illustrations** tab in PowerPoint. You can also animate each item in the diagram. Occasionally, try to convert pure text and bullet points to diagrams, charts, and other images to add punch to your slideshow. You will keep your audiences interested and help them retain the information you are presenting.

You can add pizzazz to your slides by animating some items and using SmartArt graphics from the Illustrations tab.

Revising, Proofreading, and Evaluating Your Slideshow. Use PowerPoint's **Slide Sorter View** to rearrange, insert, and delete slides during the revision process. This is the time when you will focus on making your presentation as clear and concise as possible. If you are listing items, be sure that all items use parallel grammatical form. Figure 14.6 shows how to revise a slide to improve it for conciseness, parallelism, and other features. Study the design tips described in the first slide and determine which suggestions were not followed. Then compare it with the revised slide.

FIGURE 14.5 Converting a Bulleted Slide Into a Diagram

Revised With a SmartArt Graphic **SmartArt Graphics Options**

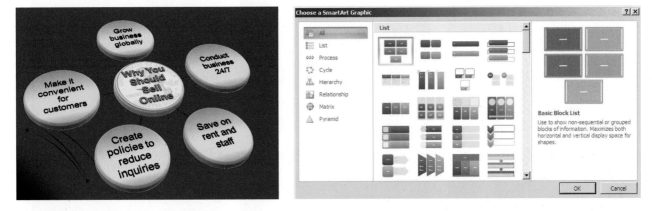

The same content that appears in the Figure 14.4 slides takes on a totally different look when arranged as spokes radiating from a central idea. Add a 3-D effect and a muted background image to the middle shape, for example, and you depart from the usual boring template look. When presenting this slide, you can animate each item and control when it is revealed, further enlivening your presentation. PowerPoint 2007 provides SmartArt graphics with many choices of diagrams and shapes for arranging information.

As you are revising, check carefully to find spelling, grammar, punctuation, and other errors. Use the PowerPoint spell check, but don't rely on it without careful proofing, preferably from a printed copy of the slideshow. Nothing is as embarrassing as projecting errors on a huge screen in front of an audience. Also check for consistency in how you capitalize and punctuate points throughout the presentation.

The final stage in applying the 3-x-3 writing process to developing a PowerPoint presentation involves evaluation. Consider whether you have done all you can to use the tools PowerPoint provides to communicate your message in a visually appealing way. In addition, test your slides on the equipment and in the room you will be using during your presentation. Do the colours you selected work in this new setting? Are the font styles and sizes readable from the back of the room? Figure 14.7 shows examples of slides that incorporate what you have learned in this discussion.

FIGURE 14.6 Designing More Effective Slides

Before Revision

DESIGN TIPS FOR SLIDE TEXT

1. STRIVE TO HAVE NO MORE THAN SIX BULLETS PER SLIDE AND NO MORE THAN SIX WORDS PER BULLET.
2. IF YOU USE UPPER- AND LOWERCASE TYPE, IT IS EASIER TO READ
3. IT IS BETTER TO USE PHRASES RATHER THAN SENTENCES.
4. USING A SIMPLE, HIGH-CONTRAST TYPEFACE IS EASIER TO READ AND DOES NOT DETRACT FROM YOUR PRESENTATION
5. BE CONSISTENT IN YOUR SPACING, CAPITALIZATION, AND PUNCTUATION.

After Revision

Design Tips for Slide Text

- Limit: 6 bullets per slide
- Limit: 6 words per bullet
- Use upper- and lowercase type
- Use concise phrases, not sentences
- Use simple typeface
- Use consistent spacing, capitalization, and punctuation

The slide on the left is difficult to read and understand because it violates many slide-making rules. How many violations can you spot? The slide on the right illustrates an improved version of the same information. Which slide do you think viewers would rather read?

FIGURE 14.7 PowerPoint Slides That Summarize and Illustrate Multimedia Presentations

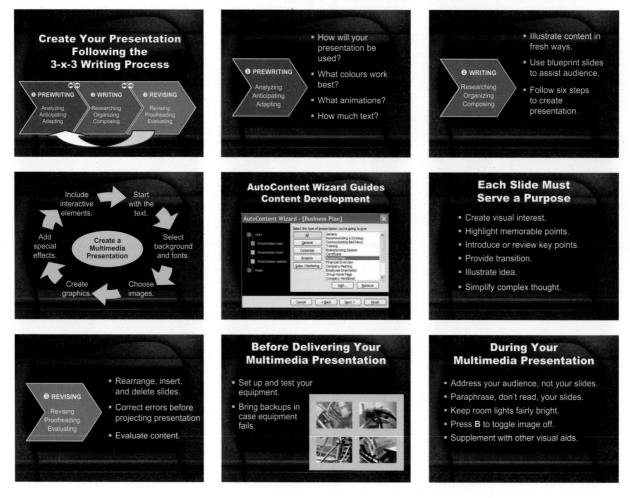

The dark purple background and the green and blue hues in the slideshow shown in Figure 14.7 are standard choices for many business presentations. With an unobtrusive dark background, white fonts are a good option for maximum contrast and, hence, readability. The creator of the presentation varied the slide design to break the monotony of bulleted or numbered lists. Images and animated diagrams add interest and zing to the slides.

Using PowerPoint Effectively With Your Audience

> A fabulous slideshow can be ruined if you are unfamiliar with the equipment.

Many promising presentations have been sabotaged by technology glitches or by the presenter's unfamiliarity with the equipment. Fabulous slides are of value only if you can manage the technology expertly

Practising and Preparing

Allow plenty of time before your presentation to set up and test your equipment (see the PowerPoint preshow checklist at **www.tlccreative.com/images/tutorials/PreShowChecklist.pdf**). Confirm that the places you plan to stand are not in the line of the projected image. Audience members do not appreciate having part of the slide displayed on your body. Make sure that all links to videos or the Web are working and that you know how to operate all features the first time you try. No matter how much time you put into preshow setup and testing, you still have no guarantee that all will go smoothly. Therefore, you should always bring backups of your presentation. Overhead transparencies or handouts of your presentation provide good substitutes. Transferring your presentation to a CD or a USB flash drive that could run from any available note-book might prove useful as well.

Keeping Your Audience Engaged

In addition to using technology to enhance and enrich your message, here are additional tips for performing like a professional and keeping the audience engaged.

- Know your material. This will free you to look at your audience and gaze at the screen, not your practice notes. Maintain genuine eye contact to connect with individuals in the room.

- As you show new elements on a slide, allow the audience time to absorb the information. Then paraphrase and elaborate on what the listeners have seen. Do not insult your audience's intelligence by reading verbatim from a slide.

- Leave the lights as bright as you can. Make sure the audience can see your face and eyes.

- Use a radio remote control (not infrared) so you can move freely rather than remain tethered to your computer. Radio remotes will allow you to be up to 15 metres away from your laptop.

- Maintain a connection with the audience by using a laser pointer to highlight slide items to discuss. Be aware, however, that a dancing laser point in a shaky hand may make you appear nervous. Steady your hand.

- Don't leave a slide on the screen when you have finished discussing it. In **Slide Show, View Show** mode, strike *B* on the keyboard to turn on or off the screen image by blackening it. Pushing *W* will turn the screen white.

Some presenters allow their PowerPoint slides to "steal their thunder." In developing a presentation, don't expect your slides to carry the show. You can avoid being upstaged by not relying totally on your slides. Help the audience visualize your points by using other techniques, such as, drawing a diagram on a whiteboard or flipchart, or demonstrating or displaying real objects or props. Remember that slides should be used only to help your audience understand the message and to add interest. Your audience came to see and hear *you*.

Eight Steps to Making a Powerful Multimedia Presentation

We have now discussed many suggestions for making effective PowerPoint presentations, but you may still be wondering how to put it all together. Here is a step-by-step process for creating a powerful multimedia presentation:

1. **Start with the text.** The text is the foundation of your presentation. Express your ideas by using words that are clear, concise, and understandable. Once the entire content of your presentation is in place, you are ready to begin adding colour and all the other elements that will make your slides visually appealing.

2. **Select background and fonts.** Select a template that will provide consistent font styles, font sizes, and a background for your slides. You can create your own template or use one included with PowerPoint. You can also download free templates or pay for templates from many online sites. You can't go wrong selecting a basic template design with an easy-to-read font, such as Times New Roman or Arial. As a general rule, use no more than two font styles in your presentation. The point size should be between 24 and 36. Title fonts should be larger than the text font. The more you use PowerPoint and find out what works and does not work, the more you can experiment with bolder, more innovative background and font options that effectively convey your message.

> To keep your audience interested, maintain eye contact, don't read from your slides, use a radio remote and a laser pointer, and turn off an image when it has been discussed.

> For a powerful presentation, first write the text and then work on templates, font styles, and colours.

3. **Choose images that help communicate your message.** Images, such as clip art, photographs, and maps, should complement the text. Never use an image that is not immediately relevant. *Microsoft Office Online* is accessed in PowerPoint and contains thousands of clip art images and photographs, most of which are in the public domain and require no copyright permissions. Before using images from other sources, determine whether permission from the copyright holder is required. Bear in mind that some people consider clip art amateurish, so photographs are usually preferable. In addition, clip art is available to any user, so it tends to become stale fast.

Learn to simplify complex information in visually appealing graphics.

4. **Create graphics.** PowerPoint includes a variety of tools to help you simplify complex information or transform a boring bulleted list into a visually appealing graphic. You can use PowerPoint's **Illustrations** tools in the **Insert** tab to create a timeline or a flowchart. The **SmartArt** graphic will help you create an organization chart or a cycle, radial, pyramid, Venn, or target diagram. With the **Chart** function, you can select from more than a dozen chart types including line, pie, and bar charts. All these tools require practice before you can create effective graphics. Remember that graphics should be easy to understand without overloading your audience with unnecessary details or too much text. In fact, put such details in handouts rather than cluttering your slides with them.

5. **Add special effects.** To keep your audience focused on what you are discussing, use PowerPoint's **Animations** tab to control when objects or text appear on the screen. Animate points in a bulleted list to appear one at a time, for example, or the boxes in a radial diagram to appear as each is discussed. Keep in mind that the first thing your audience sees on every slide should describe the slide's content. With motion paths and other animation options, you can move objects to different positions on the slide, or, to minimize clutter, you can dim or remove them once they have served their purpose.

   In addition, as you move from slide to slide in a presentation, you can select transition effects, such as *wipe down*. The animation and transition options range from subtle to flashy—choose them with care so that the visual delivery of your presentation doesn't distract from the content of your message. An option at this step is to purchase a PowerPoint add-in product, such as Ovation, that can add professional-looking special effects to your presentation with very little effort.[6]

6. **Create hyperlinks to approximate the Web-browsing experience.** Make your presentation more interactive and intriguing by connecting your PowerPoint presentation, via hyperlinks, to other sources that provide content that will enhance your presentation. You can hyperlink to (a) other slides within the presentation or in other PowerPoint files; (b) other programs that will open a second window that displays items, such as spreadsheets, documents, videos; and (c) if you have an Internet connection, Web sites.

   Once you have finished discussing the hyperlinked source or watching the video that opened in a second window, you close that window, and your hyperlinked PowerPoint slide is in view. In this way, you can break up the monotony of typical linear PowerPoint presentations. Instead, your hyperlinked show approximates the viewing experience of a Web user who enters a site through a main page or portal and then navigates at will to reach second- and third-level pages.

7. **Engage your audience by asking for interaction.** When audience response and feedback are needed, interactive tools are useful. Audience response systems may be familiar to you from game shows, but they are also used for surveys and opinion polls, group decision making, voting, quizzes and tests, and many other applications. To interact with your audience, present polling questions. Audience members submit their individual or team responses by using handheld devices read by a PowerPoint add-in program. The audience immediately sees a bar chart that displays the response results (For more information, go to **http://intl.turningtechnologies.com or www.optiontechnologies.com**).

8. **Move your presentation to the Internet.** You have a range of alternatives, from simple to complex, for moving your multimedia presentation to the Internet or your company's intranet. The simplest option is posting your slides online for others to access. Even if you are giving a face-to-face presentation, attendees appreciate these electronic handouts because they don't have to lug them home. The most complex option for moving your multimedia presentation to the Internet involves a Web conference or broadcast.

Internet options for slide presentations range from posting slides online to conducting a live Web conference with slides, narration, and speaker control.

Web presentations with slides, narration, and speaker control have emerged as a way for anyone who has access to the Internet to attend your presentation without leaving the office. For example, you could initiate a meeting via a conference call, narrate by using a telephone, and have participants see your slides from the browsers on their computers. If you prefer, you could skip the narration and provide a prerecorded presentation. Web-based presentations have many applications, including providing access to updated training or sales data whenever needed.[7]

Some businesses convert their PowerPoint presentations to PDF documents or send PowerPoint shows (file extension *.PPSX), which open directly in **Slide Show View**, ready to run. Both types of documents are highly suitable for e-mailing. Among their advantages, they start immediately, can't be easily changed, and typically result in smaller, less memory-intensive files.

Polishing Your Delivery and Following Up

Once you have organized your presentation and prepared visuals, you are ready to practise delivering it. You will feel more confident and appear more professional if you know more about various delivery methods and techniques to use before, during, and after your presentation.

LEARNING OBJECTIVE 5
Specify delivery techniques for use before, during, and after a presentation and apply reflective thinking skills.

Choosing a Delivery Method

Inexperienced speakers often feel that they must memorize an entire presentation to be effective. Unless you are an experienced performer, however, you will sound wooden and unnatural. What's more, forgetting your place can be disastrous! That is why we don't recommend memorizing an entire oral presentation. However, memorizing significant parts—the introduction, the conclusion, and perhaps a meaningful quotation—can be dramatic and impressive.

If memorizing your business presentation won't work, is reading from a manuscript the best plan? Definitely not! Reading to an audience is boring and ineffective. Because reading suggests that you don't know your topic very well, the audience loses confidence in your expertise. Reading also prevents you from maintaining eye contact. You can't see audience reactions; consequently, you can't benefit from feedback.

Neither memorizing nor reading creates very convincing business presentations. The best plan, by far, is to present extemporaneously, especially when you are displaying an electronic slideshow, such as PowerPoint. *Extemporaneous delivery* means speaking freely, generally without notes, after preparation and rehearsing. It means that in your talk you comment on the electronic slideshow you have prepared and rehearsed several times. Remember, PowerPoint and other presentation software have replaced traditional outlines and notes. Reading notes or a manuscript in addition to PowerPoint slides will damage your credibility.

Extemporaneous delivery results in more convincing presentations than those that are memorized or read.

If you give a talk without PowerPoint, however, you may use note cards or an outline containing key sentences and major ideas, but beware of reading from a script. By preparing and then practising with your notes, you can talk to your audience in a conversational manner. Your notes should be neither entire paragraphs nor single words. Instead, they should contain a complete sentence or two to introduce each major idea. Below the topic sentence(s), outline subpoints and illustrations. Note cards will keep you on track and prompt your memory, but only if you have rehearsed the presentation thoroughly.

career coach

How to Avoid Stage Fright

Ever get nervous before making a presentation? Everyone does! And it's not all in your head, either. When you face something threatening or challenging, your body reacts in what psychologists call the *fight-or-flight response*. This physical reflex provides your body with increased energy to deal with threatening situations. It also creates those sensations—dry mouth, sweaty hands, faster heartbeat, and stomach butterflies—that we associate with stage fright. The fight-or-flight response arouses your body for action—in this case, making a presentation.

Because everyone feels some form of apprehension before speaking, it's impossible to eliminate the physiological symptoms altogether. However, you can reduce their effects with the following techniques:

- **Breathe deeply.** Use deep breathing to ease your fight-or-flight symptoms. Inhale to a count of ten, hold this breath to a count of ten, and exhale to a count of ten. Concentrate on your counting and your breathing; both activities reduce your stress.

- **Convert your fear.** Don't view your sweaty palms and dry mouth as evidence of fear. Interpret them as symptoms of exuberance, excitement, and enthusiasm to share your ideas.

- **Know your topic and come prepared.** Feel confident about your topic. Select a topic that you know well and that is relevant to your audience. Test your equipment and arrive with time to spare.

- **Use positive self-talk.** Remind yourself that you know your topic and are prepared. Tell yourself that the audience is on your side—because it is! Moreover, most speakers appear to be more confident than they feel. Make this apparent confidence work for you.

- **Take a sip of water.** Drink some water to alleviate your dry mouth and constricted voice box, especially if you are talking for more than 15 minutes.

- **Shift the spotlight to your visuals.** At least some of the time, the audience will be focusing on your slides, transparencies, handouts, or whatever you have prepared—and not totally on you.

- **Ignore any stumbles.** Don't apologize or confess your nervousness. If you keep going, the audience will forget any mistakes quickly.

- **Feel proud when you finish.** You will be surprised at how good you feel when you finish. Take pride in what you have accomplished, and your audience will reward you with applause and congratulations. Your body, of course, will call off the fight-or-flight response and return to normal!

Overcoming Stage Fright

Stage fright is both natural and controllable.

Nearly everyone experiences some degree of stage fright when speaking before a group. "If you hear someone say he or she isn't nervous before a speech, you're talking either to a liar or a very boring speaker," says corporate speech consultant Dianna Booher.[8] Being afraid is quite natural and results from actual physiological changes occurring in your body. Faced with a frightening situation, your body responds with the fight-or-flight response, discussed more fully in the Career Coach box. You can learn to control and reduce stage fright, as well as to incorporate techniques for effective speaking, by using the following strategies and techniques before, during, and after your presentation.

Before Your Presentation

Thorough preparation, extensive rehearsal, and stress-reduction techniques can lessen stage fright.

Speaking in front of a group will become less daunting if you allow for adequate preparation, sufficient practice, and rehearsals. Interacting with the audience and limiting surprises, such as malfunctioning equipment, will also add to your peace of mind. Review the following tips for a smooth start:

- **Prepare thoroughly.** One of the most effective strategies for reducing stage fright is knowing your subject thoroughly. Research your topic diligently and prepare a careful sentence outline. Those who try to "wing it" usually suffer the worst butterflies—and make the worst presentations.

- **Rehearse repeatedly.** When you rehearse, practise your entire presentation, not just the first half. In PowerPoint you may print out speaker's notes, an outline, or a handout featuring miniature slides, which are excellent for practice. If you don't use an electronic slideshow, place your outline sentences on separate note cards. You may also want to include transitional sentences to help you move to the next topic as you practise. Rehearse alone or before friends and family. Also try an audio or a video recording of your rehearsals so that you can evaluate your effectiveness.

- **Time yourself.** Most audiences tend to get restless during longer talks. Thus, try to complete your presentation in no more than 20 minutes. Set a simple kitchen timer during your rehearsal to keep track of time. Better yet, PowerPoint offers a function called **Rehearse Timings** in the **Slide Show** tab that can measure the length of your talk as you practise.

- **Check the room.** If you are using a computer, a projector, or sound equipment, be certain they are operational. Before you start, check electrical outlets and the position of the viewing screen. Ensure that the seating arrangement is appropriate to your needs.

- **Greet members of the audience.** Try to make contact with a few members of the audience when you enter the room, while you are waiting to be introduced, or when you walk to the podium. Your body language should convey friendliness, confidence, and enjoyment.

- **Practise stress reduction.** If you feel tension and fear while you are waiting your turn to speak, use stress-reduction techniques, such as deep breathing. Additional techniques to help you conquer stage fright are presented in the Career Coach box.

During Your Presentation

To stay in control during your talk, to build credibility, and to engage your audience, follow these time-tested guidelines for effective speaking:

- **Begin with a pause.** When you first approach the audience, take a moment to make yourself comfortable. Establish your control of the situation.

- **Present your first sentence from memory.** By memorizing your opening, you can immediately establish rapport with the audience through eye contact. You will also sound confident and knowledgeable.

- **Maintain eye contact.** If the size of the audience overwhelms you, pick out two individuals on the right and two on the left. Talk directly to these people. Don't ignore listeners in the back of the room.

> Eye contact, a moderate tone of voice, and natural movements enhance a presentation.

- **Control your voice and vocabulary.** This means speaking in moderated tones but loudly enough to be heard. Eliminate verbal static, such as *ah, er, you know,* and *um.* Silence is preferable to meaningless fillers when you are thinking of your next idea.

- **Put the brakes on.** Many novice speakers talk too rapidly, displaying their nervousness and making it very difficult for audience members to understand their ideas. Slow down and listen to what you are saying.

- **Move naturally.** If you have a lectern, don't remain glued to it. Move about casually and naturally. Avoid fidgeting with your clothing, hair, or items in your pockets. Do not roll up your sleeves or put your hands in your pockets. Learn to use your body to express a point.

- **Use visual aids effectively.** You should discuss and interpret each visual aid for the audience. Move aside as you describe it so that it can be seen fully. Use a pointer if necessary, but steady your hand if it is shaking.

- **Avoid digressions.** Stick to your outline and notes. Don't suddenly include clever little anecdotes or digressions that occur to you on the spot. If it is not part of your rehearsed material, leave it out so that you can finish on time. Remember, too, that your audience may not be as enthralled with your topic as you are.

- **Summarize your main points and arrive at the high point of your talk.** Conclude your presentation by reiterating your main points or by emphasizing what you want the audience to think or do. Once you have announced your conclusion, proceed to it directly.

After Your Presentation

The time to answer questions, distribute handouts, and reiterate main points is after a presentation.

As you are concluding your presentation, handle questions and answers competently and provide handouts if appropriate. Try the following techniques:

- **Distribute handouts.** If you prepared handouts with data the audience will need, pass them out when you finish.

- **Encourage questions.** If the situation permits a question-and-answer period, announce it at the beginning of your presentation. Then, when you finish, ask for questions. Set a time limit for questions and answers.

- **Repeat questions.** Although the speaker may hear the question, audience members often do not. Begin each answer with a repetition of the question. This also gives you thinking time. Then direct your answer to the entire audience.

- **Reinforce your main points.** You can use your answers to restate your primary ideas (*I'm glad you brought that up because it gives me a chance to elaborate on . . .*). In answering questions, avoid becoming defensive or debating the questioner.

- **Keep control.** Don't allow one individual to take over. Keep the entire audience involved.

- **Avoid "Yes, but" answers.** The word *but* immediately cancels any preceding message. Try replacing it with *and*. For example, *Yes, X has been tried. And Y works even better because. . . .*

- **End with a summary and appreciation.** To signal the end of the session before you take the last question, say something like, *We have time for just one more question.* As you answer the last question, try to work it into a summary of your main points. Then express appreciation to the audience for the opportunity to talk with them.

Organizing Team-Based Written and Oral Presentations

LEARNING OBJECTIVE 6

Organize team-based written and oral presentations and understand how to communicate in teams.

Companies form teams for many reasons, as discussed in Chapter 2. The goal of some teams may be an oral presentation to pitch a new product or to win a high-stakes contract. The goal of other teams may be to investigate a problem and submit recommendations to decision makers in a report. The outcome of any team effort is often (a) a written report; (b) a series of self-contained electronic slides, also called a slide deck; or (c) an oral presentation delivered live. The boundaries are becoming increasingly blurred between flat, two-dimensional hard-copy reports and multimedia, hyperlinked slideshows. Both hard-copy reports and multimedia presentations are delivered to clients in business today. This is why team writing and speaking appear side by side in this chapter.

Whether your team's project produces written reports, slide decks, or oral presentations, you generally have considerable control over how the project is organized and completed. If you have been part of any team efforts before, you also know that such projects can be very frustrating—particularly when some team members don't carry their weight or when members cannot resolve conflict. Conversely, team projects can be harmonious and productive when members establish ground rules and follow guidelines related to preparing, planning, collecting information for, organizing, rehearsing, and evaluating team projects.

Preparing to Work Together

Before any group begins to talk about a specific project, members should get together and establish basic ground rules. One of the first tasks is naming a meeting leader to conduct meetings, a recorder to keep a record of group decisions, and an evaluator to determine whether the group is on target and meeting its goals. The group should decide whether it will be governed by consensus (everyone must agree), by majority rule, or by some other method.

The most successful teams make meetings a top priority. They compare schedules to set up the best meeting times, and they meet often. They avoid other responsibilities that might disrupt these meetings.

When teams first organize, they should consider the value of conflict. By bringing conflict into the open and encouraging confrontation, teams can prevent personal resentment and group dysfunction. Confrontation can actually create better final products by promoting new ideas and avoiding groupthink. Conflict is most beneficial when team members can air their views fully. Another important topic to discuss during team formation is how to deal with team members who are not doing their share of the work. Teams should decide whether they will "fire" members who are not contributing or take some other action in dealing with slackers.

Teams must decide whether they will be governed by consensus, by majority rule, or by some other method.

Planning the Document or Presentation

Once teams have established ground rules, members are ready to discuss the target document or presentation. During these discussions, they must be sure to keep a record of all decisions. They should establish the specific purpose for the document or presentation and identify the main issues involved. They must decide on the final format. For a collaborative business report, they should determine what parts it will include, such as an executive summary, figures, and an appendix. They should consider how the report or presentation will be delivered—in person, online, or by e-mail. For a team oral presentation, they should decide on its parts, length, and graphics. For either written or oral projects, they should profile the audience and focus on the questions audience members would want answered. If the report or presentation involves persuasion, they must decide what appeals would achieve the team's purpose.

Next the team should develop a work plan (see Chapter 11), assign jobs, and set deadlines. Members should work backward from the due date, particularly if time is short. For oral presentations teams must schedule time for content and creative development, as well as for a series of rehearsals. The best-planned presentations can fall apart if they are poorly rehearsed.

For oral presentations all team members should have written assignments. These assignments should detail each member's specific responsibilities for researching content, producing visuals, developing handout materials, building transitions between segments, and showing up for rehearsals. For written reports members must decide how the final document will be composed: individuals working separately on assigned portions, one person writing the first draft, the entire group writing the complete document together, or some other method.

In planning a team document or presentation, develop a work plan, assign jobs, and set deadlines.

Collecting Information

One of the most challenging jobs for team projects is generating and collecting information. Unless facts are accurate, the most beautiful report or the most high-powered presentation will fail. As you brainstorm ideas, consider cluster diagramming (see Chapter 5). Assign topics and decide who will be responsible for gathering what information. Establishing deadlines for collecting information is important if a team is to remain on schedule. Team members should also discuss ways to ensure the accuracy of the information collected.

Unless facts are accurate, reports and presentations will fail.

Organizing, Writing, and Revising

When a project progresses into the organizing and writing stages, a team may need to modify some of its earlier decisions. Team members may review the proposed organization of the final document or presentation and adjust it if necessary. In composing the first draft of a written report or presentation, team members will probably write separate segments. As they work on these segments, they should use the same version of word processing or presentation graphics program to facilitate combining files.

As individuals work on separate parts of a written report, the team should decide on one person (probably the best writer) to coordinate all the parts. The writer strives for a consistent style, format, and tone in the final product. For oral presentations team members must try to make logical connections between segments. Each presenter builds a bridge to the next member's topic to create a smooth transition. Team members should also agree to use the same template, and they should allow only one person to make global changes in colour, font, and other formatting on the slide and title masters.

Editing, Rehearsing, and Evaluating

The last stage in a collaborative project involves editing, rehearsing, and evaluating. For a written report, one person should assume the task of merging the various files, running a spell checker, and examining the entire document for consistency of design, format, and vocabulary. That person is responsible for finding and correcting grammatical and mechanical errors. Then the entire group meets as a whole to evaluate the final document. Does it fulfill its purpose and meet the needs of the audience?

For oral presentations one person should also merge all the files and be certain that they are consistent in design, format, and vocabulary. Teams making presentations should practise together several times. If that is not feasible, experts say that teams must schedule at least one full real-time rehearsal with the entire group.[9] Whenever possible, practise in a room that is similar to the location of your talk. Consider video recording one of the rehearsals so that each presenter can critique his or her own performance. Schedule a dress rehearsal with an audience at least two days before the actual presentation. Practise fielding questions.

Successful group documents emerge from thoughtful preparation, clear definition of contributors' roles, commitment to a group-approved plan, and a willingness to take responsibility for the final product. More information about writing business reports appeared in previous chapters of this book.

Adapting Presentations to International and Cross-Cultural Audiences

Every good speaker adapts to the audience, and cross-cultural presentations call for special adjustments and sensitivity. Most people understand that they must speak slowly, use short sentences, and pause frequently when communicating with nonnative speakers of English.

Beyond these basic language adaptations, however, more fundamental sensitivity is often necessary. In organizing a presentation for a cross-cultural audience, you may need to anticipate and adapt to different speaking conventions, values, and nonverbal behaviour. You may also need to contend with limited language skills and a certain reluctance to voice opinions openly.

Understanding Different Values and Nonverbal Behaviour

In addressing cross-cultural audiences, anticipate expectations and perceptions that may differ significantly from what you may consider normal. Remember, for example, that the North American emphasis of getting to the point quickly is not equally prized across the globe. Therefore, think twice about delivering your main idea upfront.

When working with an interpreter or speaking before individuals whose English is limited, you must be very careful about your language. For example, you will need to express ideas in small chunks to give the interpreter time to translate. You may need to slow down as you speak and stop after each thought to allow time for the translation that will follow. Even if your presentation or speech is being translated simultaneously, remember to speak slowly and to pause after each sentence to ensure that your message is rendered correctly in the target language.

The same advice is useful in organizing presentations. Consider breaking your presentation into short, discrete segments. Such organization enables participants to ask questions and digest what has been presented. This technique is especially effective in cultures where people communicate in "loops." Match your presentation and your nonverbal messages to the expectations of your audience. Constant smiling is not as valued in Europe as it is in North America. Many Europeans distrust a speaker who is cracking jokes, smiling, or laughing in a business presentation. Their expectation is of a rational—that is, "serious"—fact-based delivery. North American–style enthusiasm is often interpreted abroad as hyperbolic exaggeration or, worse, as dishonesty and can lead to misunderstandings.

Remember, too, that some cultures prefer greater formality than North Americans exercise. Instead of first names, use only honorifics (*Mr.* or *Ms.*) and last names, as well as academic or business titles—such as *Doctor* or *Director*. Writing on a flipchart or transparency seems natural and spontaneous in this country. Abroad, though, such informal techniques may suggest that the speaker does not value the audience enough to prepare proper visual aids in advance.[10]

Adjusting Visual Aids to International and Multicultural Audiences

Although you may have to exercise greater caution with culturally diverse audiences, you will still want to use visual aids to help communicate your message. Find out from your international contact whether you can present in English or whether you will need an interpreter. In many countries listeners are too polite to speak up when they don't understand you. One expert advises explaining important concepts in several ways by using different words and then requesting members of the audience to relay their understanding of what you have just said back to you. Another expert suggests packing more text on PowerPoint slides and staying closer to its literal meaning. After all, most nonnative speakers of English understand written text much better than they comprehend spoken English. In North America presenters may spend 90 seconds on a slide, whereas in other countries they may need to slow down to two minutes per slide.[11]

To ensure clarity and show courtesy, provide handouts in English and the target language. Never use numbers without projecting or writing them out for all to see. If possible, say numbers in both languages, but only if you can pronounce or even speak the target language well enough to avoid embarrassment. Distribute translated handouts, summarizing your important information, when you finish.

Whether you are speaking to familiar or cross-cultural audiences, your presentation requires attention to content and strategy. The Checklist box on page 396 summarizes suggestions for preparing, organizing, and illustrating oral presentations.

Improving Telephone and Voice Mail Skills

One form of business presentation involves presenting yourself on the telephone, a skill that is still very important in today's workplace. Despite the heavy reliance on e-mail, the telephone remains an extremely important piece of equipment in offices. With the addition of today's wireless technology, it doesn't matter whether you are in or out of the office. You can always be reached by phone, and making a positive first impression is very important. This section focuses on traditional telephone techniques and voice mail—both opportunities for making a good impression. As a business communicator, you can be more productive, efficient, and professional by following some simple suggestions.

Making Telephone Calls Efficiently

Before making a telephone call, decide whether the intended call is really necessary. Could you find the information yourself? If you wait a while, will the problem resolve itself? Perhaps your message could be delivered more efficiently by some other means. Some companies have found that telephone calls are often less important than the work they interrupt. Alternatives to telephone calls include instant messaging, e-mail,

LEARNING OBJECTIVE 8

List techniques for improving telephone and voice mail skills to project a positive image.

Making productive telephone calls means planning an agenda, identifying the purpose, being courteous and cheerful, and avoiding rambling.

memos, or calls to automated voice mail systems. If you must make a telephone call, consider using the following suggestions to make it fully productive.

- **Plan a mini-agenda.** Have you ever been embarrassed when you had to make a second telephone call because you forgot an important item the first time? Before placing a call, jot down notes regarding all the topics you need to discuss. Following an agenda guarantees not only a complete call but also a quick one. You will be less likely to wander from the business at hand while rummaging through your mind trying to remember everything.

Checklist

Getting Ready to Speak

- **Identify your purpose.** Decide what you want your audience to believe, remember, or do when you finish. Aim all parts of your talk toward this purpose.
- **Analyze the audience.** Consider how to adapt your message (its organization, appeals, and examples) to your audience's knowledge and needs.

Organizing the Introduction

- **Get the audience involved.** Capture the audience's attention by opening with a promise, story, startling fact, question, quotation, relevant problem, or self-effacing joke.
- **Establish yourself.** Demonstrate your credibility by indentifying your position, expertise, knowledge, or qualifications.
- **Preview your main points.** Introduce your topic and summarize its principal parts.

Organizing the Body

- **Develop two to four main points.** Streamline your topic so that you can concentrate on its major issues.
- **Arrange the points logically.** Sequence your points chronologically, from most important to least important, by comparison and contrast, or by some other strategy.
- **Prepare transitions.** Between major points, write bridge statements that connect the previous item to the next one. Use transitional expressions as verbal signposts (first, second, then, however, consequently, on the contrary, and so forth).
- **Have extra material ready.** Be prepared with more information and visuals in case you have additional time to fill.

Organizing the Conclusion

- **Review your main points.** Emphasize your main ideas in your closing so that your audience will remember them.
- **Provide a strong, final focus.** Tell how your listeners can use this information, why you have spoken, or what you

want them to do. As the culmination of your talk, end with a specific audience benefit or thought-provoking final thought (a "take-away"), not just a lame rehash.

Designing Visual Aids

- **Select your medium carefully.** Consider the pros and cons of each alternative.
- **Highlight main ideas.** Use visual aids to illustrate major concepts only. Keep them brief and simple.
- **Try to replace bullets whenever possible.** Use flowcharts, diagrams, timelines, and so forth to substitute for bulleted lists when suitable.
- **Use aids skillfully.** Talk to the audience, not to the visuals. Paraphrase their contents.

Developing Multimedia Presentations

- **Learn to use your software program.** Study template and slide layout designs to see how you can adapt them to your purposes.
- **Select colours based on the light level in the room.** Consider how mixing light and dark fonts and backgrounds affects their visibility. Use templates and preset slide layouts if you are new to PowerPoint.
- **Use bulleted points for major ideas.** Make sure your points are all parallel and observe the 6-x-6 rule.
- **Include multimedia options that will help you convey your message.** Use moderate animation features and hyperlinks to make your talk more interesting and to link to files with related content in the same document, in other documents, or on the Internet.
- **Make speaker's notes.** Jot down the narrative supporting each slide and use these notes to practise your presentation. Do not read from notes while speaking to an audience, however.
- **Maintain control.** Don't let your slides upstage you. Engage your audience by using additional techniques to help them visualize your points.

- **Use a three-point introduction.** When placing a call, immediately (a) name the person you are calling, (b) identify yourself and your affiliation, and (c) give a brief explanation of your reason for calling. This kind of introduction enables the receiving individual to respond immediately without asking further questions.

- **Be brisk if you are rushed.** For business calls when your time is limited, avoid such questions as, *How are you?* Instead, say, *Lisa, I knew you would be the only one who could answer these two questions for me.* Another efficient strategy is to set a "contract" with the caller: *Lisa, I have only ten minutes, but I really wanted to get back to you.*

- **Be cheerful and accurate.** Let your voice show the same kind of animation that you radiate when you greet people in person. In your mind try to envision the individual answering the telephone. A smile can certainly affect the tone of your voice, so smile at that person. Keep your voice and throat relaxed by keeping your head straight. Don't squeeze the phone between your shoulder and your ear. Obviously, don't eat food or chew gum while on the phone. Moreover, be accurate about what you say. *Hang on a second; I will be right back* rarely is true. It is better to say, *It may take me two or three minutes to get that information. Would you prefer to hold or have me call you back?*

- **Bring it to a close.** The responsibility for ending a call lies with the caller. This is sometimes difficult to do if the other person rambles on. You may need to use suggestive closing language, such as *I have certainly enjoyed talking with you*, and *I have learned what I needed to know, and now I can proceed with my work*

- **Avoid telephone tag.** If you call someone who is not in, ask when it would be best for you to call again. State that you will call at a specific time—and do it. If you ask a person to call you, give a time when you can be reached—and then be sure you are in at that time.

- **Leave complete voice mail messages.** Remember that there is no rush when you leave a voice mail message. Always enunciate clearly and speak slowly when giving your telephone number or spelling your name. Be sure to provide a complete message, including your name, telephone number, and the time and date of your call. Explain your purpose so that the receiver can be ready with the required information when returning your call.

> In making telephone calls, plan a mini-agenda, use a three-point introduction, and be brisk if you have little time.

Receiving Telephone Calls Professionally

With a little forethought you can project a professional image and make your telephone a productive, efficient work tool. Developing good telephone manners and techniques will also reflect well on you and on your organization.

- **Identify yourself immediately.** In answering your telephone or someone else's, provide your name, title or affiliation, and, possibly, a greeting. For example, *Larry Lopez, Proteus Software. How may I help you?* Force yourself to speak clearly and slowly. Remember that the caller may be unfamiliar with what you are saying and fail to recognize slurred syllables.

- **Be responsive and helpful.** If you are in a support role, be sympathetic to callers' needs. Instead of *I don't know*, try *That's a good question; let me investigate.* Instead of *We can't do that*, try *That's a tough one; let's see what we can do.* Avoid *No* at the beginning of a sentence. It sounds especially abrasive and displeasing because it suggests total rejection.

- **Practise telephone confidentiality.** When answering calls for others, be courteous and helpful, but don't give out confidential information. Better to say *She's away from her desk* or *He's out of the office* than to report a colleague's exact whereabouts.

- **Take messages carefully.** Few things are as frustrating as receiving a potentially important phone message that is illegible. Repeat the spelling of names and verify telephone numbers. Write messages legibly and record their time and date. Promise to give the messages to intended recipients, but don't guarantee return calls.

> Receiving productive telephone calls means identifying yourself, acting responsive, being helpful, and taking accurate messages.

- **Explain what you are doing when transferring calls.** Give a reason for transferring, and indicate the extension to which you are directing the call in case the caller is disconnected.

Making the Best Use of Voice Mail

Because telephone calls can be disruptive, many businesspeople are making extensive use of voice mail to intercept and screen incoming calls. Voice mail links a telephone system to a computer that digitizes and stores incoming messages. Some systems also provide such functions as automated attendant menus, allowing callers to reach any associated extension by pushing specific buttons.

Voice mail is quite efficient for message storage. Because as many as half of all business calls require no discussion or feedback, the messaging capabilities of voice mail can mean huge savings for businesses. Incoming information is delivered without interrupting potential receivers and without all the niceties that most two-way conversations require. Stripped of superfluous chitchat, voice mail messages allow communicators to focus on essentials. Voice mail also eliminates telephone tag, inaccurate message taking, and time zone barriers.

However, voice mail should not be overused. Individuals who screen all incoming calls cause irritation, resentment, and needless telephone tag. Here are some ways to make voice mail work most effectively for you:

- **Announce your voice mail.** If you rely principally on a voice mail message system, identify it on your business stationery and cards. Then, when people call, they will be ready to leave a message.

- **Prepare a warm and informative greeting.** Make your mechanical greeting sound warm and inviting, both in tone and in content. Identify yourself and your organization so that callers know they have reached the right number. Thank the caller and briefly explain that you are unavailable. Invite the caller to leave a message or, if appropriate, call back.

- **Test your message.** Call your number and assess your message. Does it sound inviting? Sincere? Understandable? Are you pleased with your tone? If not, says one consultant, have someone else, perhaps a professional, record a message for you.

This chapter has provided valuable tips for preparing and delivering first-rate oral presentations. You have also learned effective techniques for adapting oral presentations to intercultural audiences. Finally, we illustrated techniques for improving telephone and voice mail skills. All these techniques and tips can help you be a successful business communicator in an increasingly challenging workplace.

> Voice mail eliminates telephone tag, inaccurate message taking, and time zone barriers; it also allows communicators to focus on essentials.

Summary of Learning Objectives

1 Discuss two important first steps in preparing effective oral presentations. First, identify what your purpose is and what you want the audience to believe or do so that you can aim the entire presentation toward your goal. Second, know your audience so that you can adjust your message and style to its knowledge and needs.

2 Explain the major elements in organizing the content of a presentation, including the introduction, body, and conclusion. The introduction of a good presentation should capture the listener's attention, identify the speaker, establish credibility, and preview the main points. The body should discuss two to four main points, with appropriate explanations, details, and verbal signposts to guide listeners. The conclusion should review the main points, provide a final focus or take-away, and allow the speaker to leave the podium gracefully.

3 Identify techniques for gaining audience rapport, including (a) using effective imagery, (b) providing verbal signposts, and (c) sending appropriate nonverbal messages. You can improve audience rapport by using effective imagery, including analogies, metaphors, similes, personal anecdotes, statistics, and worst-case or best-case scenarios. Rapport is also gained by including verbal signposts that tell the audience when you are previewing, summarizing, and switching directions. Nonverbal messages have a powerful effect on the way your message is received. You should look terrific, animate your body, punctuate your words, get out from behind the podium, and vary your facial expressions.

4 **Discuss designing visual aids, handouts, and multimedia presentations and using presentation technology competently.** Use simple, easily understood visual aids to emphasize and clarify main points. Choose multimedia slides, transparencies, flipcharts, or other visuals. Generally, it is best to distribute handouts after a presentation. Speakers employing a program, such as PowerPoint, use templates, layout designs, and bullet points to produce effective slides. A presentation may be enhanced with slide transitions, hyperlinks, sound, animation, video elements, and other multimedia effects. Speaker's notes and handouts may be generated from slides. Web-based presentations allow speakers to narrate and show slides without leaving their home bases. Increasing numbers of speakers are using the Internet to e-mail or post their slides as electronic shows or report deliverables instead of generating paper copies.

5 **Specify delivery techniques for use before, during, and after a presentation and apply reflective thinking skills.** Before your talk, prepare a sentence outline on note cards or speaker's notes and rehearse repeatedly. Check the room, lectern, and equipment. During the presentation consider beginning with a pause and presenting your first sentence from memory. Speak freely, extemporaneously, commenting on your slides but using no other notes. Make eye contact, control your voice, speak and move naturally, and avoid digressions. After your talk distribute handouts and answer questions. End gracefully and express appreciation.

6 **Organize team-based written and oral presentations and understand how to communicate in teams.** In preparing to work together, teams should name a leader and decide how they will make decisions (by consensus, majority rule, or some other method). They should work out a schedule, discuss the benefits of conflict, and determine how they will deal with members who fail to do their share. They should decide on the purpose, form, and procedures for preparing the final document or presentation. They must brainstorm ideas, assign topics, and establish deadlines. In composing the first draft of a report or presentation, they should use the same software version and meet to discuss the drafts and rehearsals. For written reports one person should probably compose the final draft, and the group should evaluate it. For group presentations team members need to work for consistency of design, format, and wording. Several rehearsals, one of which should be videotaped, will enhance the final presentation.

7 **Explain effective techniques for adapting oral presentations to intercultural audiences and demonstrate intercultural and diversity understanding.** In presentations before groups whose English is limited, speak slowly, use simple English, avoid jargon and clichés, and opt for short sentences. Pause often to allow an interpreter to keep up with you. Consider building up to your main idea rather than announcing it immediately. Also consider breaking the presentation into short segments to allow participants to ask questions and digest small parts separately. Beware of appearing too spontaneous and informal. Use visual aids to help communicate your message but also distribute translated handouts summarizing the most important information.

8 **List techniques for improving telephone and voice mail skills to project a positive image.** You can improve your telephone calls by planning a mini-agenda and using a three-point introduction (name, affiliation, and purpose). Be cheerful and responsive and use closing language to end a conversation. Avoid telephone tag by leaving complete messages. In answering calls, identify yourself immediately, avoid giving out confidential information when answering for others, and take careful messages. For your own message, prepare a warm and informative greeting. Tell when you will be available. Evaluate your message by calling it yourself.

Chapter Review

1. Can speaking skills be improved, or do we have to be "born" communicators? (Obj. 1)

2. Why are analyzing an audience and anticipating its reactions particularly important before business presentations, and how would you adapt to the four categories of listeners? (Obj. 1)

3. In preparing an oral presentation, you can reduce your fears and lay a foundation for a professional performance by focusing on what five areas? (Obj. 1)

4. In the introduction of an oral presentation, you can establish your credibility by using what two methods? (Obj. 2)

5. What is Guy Kawasaki's 10/20/30 rule, and what is it good for? (Obj. 2)

6. List six techniques for creating effective imagery in a presentation. Be prepared to discuss each. (Obj. 3)

7. List suggestions that would ensure that your nonverbal messages reinforce your verbal messages effectively. (Obj. 3)

8. Why are visual aids particularly useful to inexperienced speakers? (Obj. 4)

9. Name specific advantages and disadvantages of multimedia presentation software. (Obj. 4)

10. How is the 6-×-6 rule applied in preparing bulleted points? (Obj. 4)

11. What delivery method is most effective for speakers? (Obj. 5)

12. Why should speakers deliver the first sentence from memory? (Obj. 5)

13. Which five issues should be resolved before a team can collaborate productively? (Obj. 6)

14. How might presentations before intercultural audiences be altered to be most effective? (Obj. 7)

15. How can you avoid telephone tag? (Obj. 8)

Critical Thinking

1. What is extemporaneous speaking, and what makes it the best delivery method for business presentations? (Obj. 5)

2. How can a speaker make the most effective use of visual aids? (Obj. 4)

3. How can speakers prevent multimedia presentation software from stealing their thunder? (Obj. 4)

4. Discuss effective techniques for reducing stage fright. (Obj. 5)

5. **Ethical Issue:** Careful business writers always document their sources in written reports; however, when the report findings are presented by using PowerPoint, the sources are often omitted. Should information in PowerPoint presentations be sourced? If so, how? Is omitting this information unethical? (Obj. 4)

Activities

14.1 Critiquing a Speech (Objs. 1–4)

Your Task. Search online or your library for a speech that was delivered by a significant businessperson or a well-known political figure. Write a memo report to your instructor critiquing the speech in terms of the following:

a. Effectiveness of the introduction, body, and conclusion

b. Evidence of effective overall organization

c. Use of verbal signposts to create coherence

d. Emphasis of two to four main points

e. Effectiveness of supporting facts (use of examples, statistics, quotations, and so forth)

14.2 Knowing Your Audience (Objs. 1–2)

Your Task. Select a recent issue of *Fortune, Canadian Business, BusinessWeek,* or another business periodical approved by your instructor. Based on an analysis of your classmates, select an

article that will appeal to them and that you can relate to their needs. Submit to your instructor a one-page summary that includes (a) the author, article title, source, issue date, and page reference; (b) a one-paragraph article summary; (c) a description of why you believe the article will appeal to your classmates; and (d) a summary of how you can relate the article to their needs.

14.3 Overcoming Stage Fright (Obj. 5)

TEAM

What makes you most nervous when making a presentation before class? Being afraid of becoming tongue-tied? Having all eyes on you? Messing up? Forgetting your ideas and looking silly?

Your Task. Discuss the previous questions as a class. Then, in groups of three or four, talk about ways to overcome these fears. Your instructor may ask you to write a memo (individually or collectively) summarizing your suggestions, or you may break out of your small groups and report your best ideas to the entire class.

14.4 Investigating Oral Communication in Your Field (Objs. 1, 5)

Your Task. Interview one or two individuals in your professional field. How is oral communication important in this profession? Does the need for oral skills change as a person advances? What suggestions can these people make to newcomers to the field for developing proficient oral communication skills? Discuss your findings with your class.

14.5 Outlining an Oral Presentation (Objs. 1, 2)

One of the hardest parts of preparing an oral presentation is developing the outline.

Your Task. Select an oral presentation topic from the list in Activity 14.7 or suggest an original topic. Prepare an outline for your presentation by using the following format:

Title
Purpose
             I. INTRODUCTION
State your name   A.
Gain attention and
involve audience   B.
Establish credibility   C.
Preview main points D.
Transition
           II. BODY
Main point   A.
Illustrate, clarify, contrast 1.
                 2.
                 3.

Transition
Main point   B.
Illustrate, clarify, contrast 1.
                 2.
                 3.

Transition
Main point   C.
Illustrate, clarify, contrast 1.
                 2.
                 3.

Transition
          III. CONCLUSION
Summarize main points A.
Provide final focus
or "take-away"   B.
Encourage questions C.

14.6 Researching Best Employer List Information (Objs. 1–5)

Your Task. Using an electronic database, perform a search to learn how MediaCorp Canada determines which companies make its Canada's Top 100 Employers annual lists. Research the following lists. Then organize and present a five- to ten-minute informative talk to your class.

a. Best Employers for New Canadians

b. 50 Best Employers in Canada (*The Globe and Mail*)

c. Canada's Best Diversity Employers

14.7 Choosing a Topic for an Oral Presentation (Objs. 1–6)

WEB

Your Task. Select a topic from the following list or from the report topics at the ends of Chapters 11 and 12. For an expanded list of report topics, go to **www.guffeybrief4e. nelson.com**. Individually or as a team, prepare a five- to ten-minute oral presentation. Consider yourself an expert or a team of experts called in to explain some aspect of the topic before a group of interested people. Because your time is limited, prepare a concise yet forceful presentation with effective visual aids.

If this is a group presentation, form a team of three or four members and conduct thorough research on one of the following topics, as directed by your instructor. Follow the tips on team presentations in this chapter. Divide the tasks fairly, meet for discussions and rehearsals, and crown your achievement with a 15- to 20-minute presentation to your class. Make your PowerPoint presentation interesting and dynamic.

a. What are the top five career opportunities for your college or university major? Consider job growth, compensation, and benefits. What kind of academic and other experience is typically required to apply for each?

b. What information and tools are available at Web job banks to postsecondary students searching for full-time employment after graduation? Consider Workopolis.com and other job banks.

c. How can attendance be improved in a minor sports field (your choice) at your school?

d. What simple computer security tips can your company employ to avoid problems?

e. What is telecommuting, and for what kind of workers is it an appropriate work alternative?

f. What criteria should parents use in deciding whether their young children should attend parochial, private, public, or home school?

g. What travel location would you recommend for postsecondary students at winter break or in summer?

h. What is the economic outlook for a given product, such as domestic cars, laptop computers, digital cameras, fitness equipment, or a product of your choice?

i. How can your organization or institution improve its image?

j. What are the Webby Awards, and what criteria do the judges use to evaluate Web sites?

k. What brand and model of computer and printer represent the best buy for postsecondary students today?

l. What franchise would offer the best investment opportunity for an entrepreneur in your area?

14.8 Consumer: Will Maxing Out My Credit Cards Improve My Credit Rating? (Objs. 1, 2)

CONSUMER
WEB

The program chair for the campus business club has asked you to present a talk to the group about consumer credit. He saw a newspaper article saying that very few people know their credit scores. Many consumers, including students, have dangerous misconceptions about their scores. Not knowing your score could result in a denial of credit and difficulty obtaining needed services and even a job.

Your Task. Using electronic databases and the Web, learn more about credit scores and typical misconceptions. For example, is a higher or lower credit score better? Can you improve your credit score by marrying well? If you earn more money, will you improve your score? If you have a low score, is it impossible to raise it? Can you raise your score by maxing out all your credit cards? (One survey reported that 28 percent of consumers believed the latter statement was true!) Prepare an oral presentation appropriate for a student audience. Conclude with appropriate recommendations.

14.9 Improving Telephone Skills by Role-Playing (Obj. 8)

Your Task. Your instructor will divide the class into pairs. For each scenario take a moment to read and rehearse your role silently. Then play the role with your partner. If time permits, repeat the scenarios, changing roles.

Partner 1	Partner 2
a. You are the personnel manager of Datatronics, Inc. Call Elizabeth Franklin, office manager at Computers Plus. Inquire about a job applicant, Chelsea Chaisson, who listed Ms. Franklin as a reference. Respond to Partner 2.	a. You are the receptionist for Computers Plus. The caller asks for Elizabeth Franklin, who is home sick today. You don't know when she will be able to return. Answer the call appropriately.
b. Call Ms. Franklin again the following day to inquire about the same job applicant, Chelsea Chaisson. Ms. Franklin answers today, but she talks on and on, describing the applicant in great detail. Tactfully close the conversation.	b. You are now Ms. Franklin, office manager. Describe Chelsea Chaisson, an imaginary employee. Think of someone with whom you have worked. Include many details, such as her ability to work with others, her appearance, her skills at computing, her schooling, her ambition, and so forth.
c. You are now the receptionist for Tom Wing, of Wing Imports. Answer a call for Mr. Wing, who is working in another office, at Extension 134, where he will accept calls.	c. You are now an administrative assistant for attorney Michael Murphy. Call Tom Wing to verify a meeting date Mr. Murphy has with Mr. Wing. Use your own name in identifying yourself.
d. You are now Tom Wing, owner of Wing Imports. Call your attorney, Michael Murphy, about a legal problem. Leave a brief, incomplete message.	d. You are now the receptionist for attorney Michael Murphy. Mr. Murphy is skiing in Aspen and will return in two days, but he doesn't want his clients to know where he is. Take a message.
e. Call Mr. Murphy again. Leave a message that will prevent telephone tag.	e. Take a message again.

14.10 Presenting Yourself Professionally on the Telephone and in Voice Mail (Obj. 8)

Practise the phone skills you learned in this chapter. Leave your instructor a professional voice mail message. Prepare a mini-agenda before you call. Introduce yourself. If necessary, spell your name and indicate the course and section. Speak slowly and clearly, especially when leaving your phone number. Think of a comment you could make about an intriguing fact, peer discussion, or your business writing class.

Grammar and Mechanics C.L.U.E. Review 14

Total Review

Each of the following sentences has a total of **three** errors in grammar, punctuation, capitalization, usage, or spelling. On a separate sheet, write a correct version. Avoid adding new phrases, starting new sentences, or rewriting in your own words. When finished, compare your responses with the key beginning on page Key-1.

Example: She said that a list of our customers names and addresses were all ready available.

Revision: She said that a list of our **customers'** names and addresses **was already** available.

1. If you are planning a short presentation you should focus on about 3 main points and limit yourself to twenty minutes.

2. Because he was President of the company Mr. Yost made at least 6 major presentations every year.

3. The companys CGA asked me to explain the principle ways we planned to finance the thirty-year mortgage.

4. My accountant and me are greatful to be able to give a short presentation, however, we may not be able to cover the entire budget.

5. The introduction to a presentation should accomplish three goals, (a) Capture attention, (b) establish credibility, and (3) preview main points.

6. Steven wondered whether focusing on what the audience is to remember, and summarizing main points was equally important?

7. A list of suggestions for a speakers ideas are found in the article titled "How To Improve Your Listening Skills."

8. The appearance and mannerisms of a speaker definately effects a listeners evaluation of the message.

9. Melody Hobson, who is an expert speaker said that reading from slides is the Kiss of Death in a presentation.

10. In a poll of three thousand workers only one third felt that there companies valued their opinions.

Endnotes

1 Deane, M. (2010, June 8). Costs for speaking. *Investopedia.com*. Retrieved April 4, 2011, from http://financialedge.investopedia.com/financial-edge/0610/Canadian-Celebs-Outrageous-Speaking-Fees.aspx

2 Lewis, A. (2005, July 5). So many meetings, so little point, *Denver Post*, p. C1. Retrieved July 18, 2007, from LexisNexis database; Paradi, D. (2003). Are we wasting $250 million per day due to bad PowerPoint? Retrieved July 18, 2007, from http://thinkoutsidetheslide.com

3 Bajaj, G. (2006, November 22). Impatica ShowMate. Retrieved July 18, 2007, from http://www.indezine.com

4 Bates, S. (2005). *Speak like a CEO: Secrets for commanding attention and getting results*. New York: McGraw-Hill Professional, p. 113.

5 Bergells, L. (2007, May 2). Top nine visual clichés. *Maniactive.com Blog*. Retrieved July 18, 2007, from http://www.maniactive.com. See also How to avoid the 7 deadly sins of PowerPoint. (2004, July 30). *Yearbook of Experts News Release Wire*. Retrieved October 11, 2004, from LexisNexis Academic database.

6 Ozer, J. (2006, January 11). Ovation for PowerPoint. *PC Magazine*. Retrieved July 18, 2007, from http://www.pcmag.com/article2/0,1759,1921436,00.asp. See more information at http://www.adobe.com/products/ovation/

7 Boeri, R. J. (2002, March). Fear of flying? Or the mail? Try the Web conferencing cure. *Emedia Magazine*, 49.

8 Booher, D. (2003). *Speak with confidence*. New York: McGraw-Hill Professional, p. 14; Booher, D. (1991). *Executive's portfolio of model speeches for all occasions*. Englewood Cliffs, NJ: Prentice Hall, p. 259.

9 Peterson, R. (n. d.). Presentations: Are you getting paid for overtime? Presentation Coaching Institute. Retrieved July 29, 2007, from http://passociates.com; Marken Communications. (2001, March 14). The sales presentation: The bottom line is selling. Retrieved July 29, 2007, from http://www.markencom.com

10 Dulek, R. E., Fielden, J. S., & Hill, J. S. (1991, January/February). International communication: An executive primer. *Business Horizons*, 22.

11 Davidson, R., & Rosen, M. Cited in Brandel, M. (2006, February 20). Sidebar: Don't be the ugly American. *Computerworld*. Retrieved July 20, 2007, from http://www.computerworld.com

UNIT 5

Employment Communication

Chapter 15
The Job Search, Résumés, and Cover Letters

Chapter 16
Interviewing and Following Up

Digital Vision/Getty Images

CHAPTER 15

The Job Search, Résumés, and Cover Letters

OBJECTIVES

1. Prepare for a successful job search by identifying your interests, evaluating your assets, recognizing the changing nature of jobs, and choosing a career path.

2. Apply both online and traditional job search techniques.

3. Appreciate the need to customize your résumé and know whether to choose a chronological or a functional résumé style.

4. Organize your qualifications and information into effective résumé segments.

5. Describe techniques that optimize a résumé for today's technologies, including preparing a scannable résumé, a plain-text résumé, and an e-portfolio.

6. Write a customized cover letter to accompany a résumé.

Terry Vine/Getty Images

With more than 200 million users in 2010, Twitter is known for both the quantity and the quality of its users. Public figures, such as Stephen Harper, Steve Nash, Margaret Atwood, U.S. President Barack Obama, and countless celebrities, engage directly with the public through their accounts.[1] Twitter has also become a tool for job searchers by creating the TwitJob Search application (**www.twitjobsearch.com**). Following a company and its management via Twitter can help you research companies when preparing for a job search or an interview. Certainly, social media has changed the job search. In what other innovative ways can you widen your job search?

Preparing for a Successful Job Search

LEARNING OBJECTIVE 1

Prepare for a successful job search by identifying your interests, evaluating your assets, recognizing the changing nature of jobs, and choosing a career path.

The Web has changed the way we look for jobs today, making the process easier but also more challenging. Because hundreds and perhaps thousands of candidates may be applying for an advertised position, you must do everything possible to be noticed and to outshine the competition. You must also look beyond the Web.

The better prepared you are, the more confident you will feel during your search. This chapter provides expert advice on preparing for employment, searching the job market, writing a customized résumé, and developing an effective cover letter. What you learn here can lead to a successful job search and maybe even to your dream job.

You may think that the first step in finding a job is writing a résumé. However, the job-search process actually begins long before you are ready to prepare your résumé. Regardless of the kind of employment you seek, you must invest time and effort getting ready. You can't hope to find the position of your dreams without (a) knowing yourself, (b) knowing the job market, and (c) knowing the employment process.

Finding a satisfying career requires learning about yourself, the job market, and the employment process.

Begin the job search by identifying your interests and goals and evaluating your qualifications. This self-evaluation will help you choose a suitable career path and a job objective. At the same time, you should be studying the job market and becoming aware of significant changes in the workplace and hiring techniques. You will want to understand how to use the latest Web resources in your job search. Use these Web resources and traditional resources to search the open and hidden job markets for positions. Once you know what jobs are available in your field, you will need to design a résumé and cover letter that can be customized for small businesses and for larger organizations that may be using résumé-scanning programs. Following these steps, summarized in Figure 15.1 and described in this chapter, gives you a master plan for securing a job you really want.

Identifying Your Interests and Goals

The employment process begins with introspection. This means looking inside yourself to analyze what you like and dislike so that you can make good employment choices. Career counsellors charge large sums for helping individuals learn about themselves. You can do the same kind of self-examination—without spending a dime. For guidance in choosing a field that eventually proves to be satisfying, answer the following questions. If you have already chosen a field, think carefully about how your answers relate to that choice.

Answer specific questions to help yourself choose a career.

- *What are you passionate about? Can you turn this passion into a career?*
- *Do you enjoy working with people, data, or things?*
- *Would you like to work for someone else or be your own boss?*
- *How important are salary, benefits, technology support, and job stability?*
- *How important are working environment, colleagues, and job stimulation?*
- *Would you rather work for a large or small company?*
- *Must you work in a specific city, geographic area, or climate?*

FIGURE 15.1 The Employment Search

START HERE

Identify your interests and goals.

Reevaluate your progress.

or

Accept the best offer.

Interview companies.

Design a customized résumé and cover letter.

Search the hidden job market.

Search the open job market.

Choose a career path and job objective.

Evaluate your qualifications.

Know the Process

Know Yourself

Know the Job Market

- *Are you looking for security, travel opportunities, money, power, or prestige?*
- *How would you describe the perfect job, boss, and co-workers?*

Evaluating Your Qualifications

In addition to your interests, assess your qualifications. Employers today want to know what assets you have to offer them. Your responses to the following questions will target your thinking and prepare a foundation for your résumé. Remember, though, that employers seek more than empty assurances: they will want proof of your qualifications.

Decide what qualifications you possess and how you can prove them.

- *What technology skills can you offer?* Employers are often interested in specific software programs, Web experience, and social media skills.
- *What other skills have you acquired in school, on the job, or through activities? How can you demonstrate these skills?*
- *Do you work well with people? Do you enjoy teamwork?* What proof can you offer? Consider extracurricular activities, clubs, class projects, and jobs.
- *Are you a leader, self-starter, or manager? What evidence can you offer?*
- *Do you speak, write, or understand another language?* In today's global economy, being able to communicate in more than one language is an asset.
- *Do you learn quickly? Are you creative?* How can you demonstrate these characteristics?
- *Do you communicate well in speech and in writing? How can you verify these talents?*
- *What are the unique qualifications you can offer that will make you stand out among other candidates?* Think about what you offer that will make you memorable during your job search.

Recognizing Employment Trends in Today's Workplace

As you learned in Chapter 1, the nature of the workplace is changing. One of the most significant changes involves the concept of the "job." Following the downsizing of corporations and the outsourcing and offshoring of jobs in recent years, companies are employing fewer people in permanent positions.

Other forms of employment are replacing traditional jobs. In many companies teams complete special projects and then disband. Work may also be outsourced to a group that's not even part of the organization. Because new technologies can spring up overnight, making today's skills obsolete, employers are less willing to hire people into jobs with narrow descriptions. Instead, they are hiring contingency employees who work temporarily and then leave. What's more, big companies are no longer the main employers. People work for smaller companies, or they start their own businesses.

What do these changes mean for you? For one thing, you should probably forget about a lifelong career with a single company. Don't count on regular pay raises, promotions, and a comfortable retirement income. You should also become keenly aware that a career that relies on yesterday's skills is headed for trouble. You are going to need updated, marketable skills that serve you well as you move from job to job. Upgrading your skills and retraining yourself constantly are the best career strategies for the twenty-first century. People who learn quickly and adapt to change will always be in demand even in a climate of surging change.[2]

Choosing a Career Path

The job picture in Canada is extraordinarily dynamic and flexible. Individuals just entering the workforce will make at least three to four career changes in their lives.[3] Although you may be frequently changing jobs in the future, you still need to train for a specific career area now. In choosing an area, you will make the best decisions when you can match your interests and qualifications with the requirements and rewards in specific careers. Where can you find the best career data? Here are some suggestions:

- **Visit your campus career centre.** Most campus career centres have resources that allow you to investigate various fields. They may also have well-trained counsellors who can assist you with workshops, seminars, résumé assistance, and mock interviews.

- **Search the Web.** Many job search sites on the Web offer career-planning information and resources.

- **Use your library.** Print and online resources in your library are especially helpful. Consult the *Blue Book of Canadian Business, Canadian Key Business Directory,* and *The Financial Post 100 Best Companies to Work for in Canada* for information about career duties, qualifications, salaries, and employment trends.

- **Take a summer job, internship, or part-time position in your field.** Nothing is better than trying out a career by actually working in it or a related area. Many companies offer internships and temporary or part-time jobs to begin training and developing relationships with students.

- **Interview someone in your chosen field.** People are usually flattered when asked to describe their careers. Inquire about needed skills, required courses, financial and other rewards, benefits, working conditions, future trends, and entry requirements.

- **Volunteer with a nonprofit organization.** Many postsecondary institutions encourage service learning opportunities. In volunteering their services, students gain valuable experience, and nonprofit organizations appreciate the expertise and fresh ideas that students bring.

- **Monitor the classified ads.** Early in your postsecondary career, begin monitoring want ads and Web sites of companies in your career area. Check job availability, qualifications sought, duties, and salary range.

- **Join professional and student organizations in your field.** Frequently, professional organizations offer student membership status and reduced rates. You will receive inside information on issues, career news, and possibly jobs.

Conducting a Successful Job Search

Searching for a job today is vastly different as a result of the Web. Until fairly recently, a job seeker browsed the local classified ads, found a likely sounding job listing, prepared an elegant résumé on bond paper, and sent it out via Canada Post. The Web has changed that. The challenge today is realizing how to use the Web to your advantage. Like other smart job seekers, you can combine both electronic and traditional job-search tactics to land the job of your dreams.

Searching for a Job Online

Searching for a job electronically has become a common but not always fruitful approach. With all the publicity given to Web-based job boards, you might think that electronic job searching has totally replaced traditional methods. Although Web sites, such as *WowJobs.ca* and *Monster.ca*, shown in Figure 15.2, list millions of jobs, actually landing a job is much harder than just clicking a mouse. In addition, these job boards now face competition from social networking sites, such as LinkedIn, Facebook, and Twitter.[4]

Both recruiters and job seekers complain about job boards. Corporate recruiters say that the big job boards bring a flood of candidates, many of whom are not suited for the listed jobs. Workplace experts estimate that the average Fortune 500 Company is inundated with 2,000 résumés a day.[5] Job candidates grumble that listings are frequently outdated and fail to produce leads. Some career advisers call these sites black holes,[6] into which résumés vanish without a trace. Applicants worry about the privacy of information posted at big boards. Most important, a recent study has shown that the percentage of external hires resulting from job boards is astonishingly low—3.95 percent at CareerBuilder.com, 3.14 percent at Monster.com, and 1.35 percent at HotJobs.com.[7]

Despite these gloomy prospects, many job seekers use job boards to gather job-search information, such as résumé, interviewing, and salary tips. Job boards also serve as a jumping-off point in most searches. They can inform you about the kinds of jobs that are available and the skill sets required. With tens of thousands of job boards and employment Web sites deluging the Internet, it's hard to know where to start. A few of the best-known Canadian online job sites are listed here:[8]

- Workopolis (**www.workopolis.com**).

- Public Service Commission of Canada (**http://jobs-emplois.gc.ca**).

Job boards list many jobs, but finding a job requires more work than merely clicking a mouse.

The best-known job boards provide job-search, résumé, interviewing, and salary tips.

FIGURE 15.2 Job Boards Jump-Start a Job Search

Courtesy Monster.ca

- Monster.ca (**www.monster.ca**)
- HotJobs.ca
- Human Resources Development Canada Job Bank (**www.jobbank.gc.ca**)

Beyond the Big Job Boards.
Disillusioned job seekers may turn their backs on job boards but not on electronic job-searching tactics. Wise candidates know how to use their computers to search for jobs at Web sites such as the following:

- **Company Web sites.** Probably the best way to find a job online is at a company's own Web site. Many companies now post job openings only on their own Web sites to avoid being inundated by the volume of applicants that respond to online job boards.

- **Professional organization Web sites.** Online job listings have proved to be the single-most popular feature of many professional organizations. Although you may pay a fee to join a professional organization in your career field, the benefits are enormous.

- **Local employment Web sites.** Although the big job boards allow you to search for jobs geographically, many job seekers have luck in using local employment Web sites, such as Craigslist and Kijiji.

- **Niche Web sites.** If you want a job in a specialized field, look for a niche Web site, such as *HealthCareerWeb.com* or *SixFigureJobs.com*.

- **Social media sites.** Perhaps you already use social media sites, such as Facebook, to communicate with family and friends. Users are also increasingly tapping into social media sites to prospect for jobs, and recruiters also use these sites to find potential employees. LinkedIn, TwitJobSearch, and YouTube are sites that are being used by employers and employees. Of course, most successful job seekers understand the necessity of maintaining a professional online appearance at all times.

You need to be aware of the dangers associated with using online job boards and other employment sites. Your current boss might see your résumé posted online, or a fraudster could use the information in your résumé to steal your identity. The following tips can help you conduct a safe, effective Web job search:

- **Use reputable sites.** Stick to the well-known, reputable job boards.

- **Be selective.** Limit the number of sites on which you post your résumé.

- **Use a dedicated e-mail address.** Set up a separate e-mail account with a professional-sounding e-mail address for your job search.

- **Limit personal information.** Never include social insurance information or other identification numbers on your résumé.

- **Post privately.** If given the option, choose to post your résumé privately.

- **Count the days.** Renew your résumé posting every 14 days. If you haven't received a response in 45 days, pull your résumé from the site and post it elsewhere.

- **Keep careful records.** Record every site on which you post your résumé. At the end of your job search, remove all posted résumés.

- **Protect your references.** Omit your references when posting your résumé online.

- **Don't respond to a "blind" job posting.** Respond only to job postings that include a company name or contact information.

Despite the dangers, job seekers use online sites to search millions of openings. The harsh reality, however, is that landing a job still depends largely on personal contacts.

Searching for a Job by Using Traditional Techniques

Finding the perfect job requires an early start and a determined effort. One study of college graduates revealed that those with proactive personalities were the most successful in securing interviews and jobs. Successful candidates were not passive; they were driven to "make things happen."[9]

Whether you use traditional or online job-search techniques, you should be prepared to launch an aggressive campaign—and you can't start too early. In addition to maintaining good grades, remember the importance of experience, such as internships. Traditional job-search techniques, such as those described here, continue to be critical in landing jobs.

- Check classified ads in local and national newspapers.
- Check announcements in publications of professional organizations.
- Contact companies in which you are interested, even if you know of no current opening.
- Sign up for campus interviews with visiting company representatives.
- Attend career fairs.
- Ask for advice from your instructors.
- Develop your own network of contacts.

> The most successful job seekers are those who launch aggressive, proactive campaigns.

Creating a Customized Résumé

After using both traditional and online resources to learn about the employment market and to develop job leads, you will focus on writing a customized résumé. This means you will prepare a special résumé for every position you want. The competition is so stiff today that you cannot get by with a generic, all-purpose résumé. Although you can start with a basic résumé, you should customize it to fit each company and position if you want your résumé to stand out from the crowd. Include many keywords that describe the skills, traits, tasks, and job titles associated with your targeted job. You will learn more about keywords shortly.

The Web has made it so easy to apply that recruiters are swamped with applications. As a job seeker, you have about five seconds to catch the recruiter's eye—if your résumé is even read by a person. Many companies use computer scanning technologies to weed out unqualified candidates.[10] Your goal is to make your résumé fit the targeted position and be noticed. Such a résumé does more than merely list your qualifications. It packages your assets into a convincing advertisement that sells you for a specific job.

The goal of a résumé is winning an interview. Even if you are not in the job market at this moment, preparing a résumé now has advantages. Having a current résumé makes you look well organized and professional should an unexpected employment opportunity arise. Moreover, preparing a résumé early can help you recognize weak areas and give you time to bolster them. Even after you have accepted a position, it's a good idea to keep your résumé up to date. You never know when an opportunity might come along!

LEARNING OBJECTIVE 3

Appreciate the need to customize your résumé and know whether to choose a chronological or a functional résumé style.

> Winning an interview is the goal of a customized résumé.

Choosing a Résumé Style

Résumés usually fall into two categories: chronological and functional. In this section we present basic information and insider tips on how to choose an appropriate résumé style, how to determine its length, and how to arrange its parts. You will also learn about adding a summary of qualifications, which busy recruiters increasingly want to see. Models of the résumés in the following discussion are shown in our comprehensive résumé section beginning on page 418.

> See our comprehensive collection of résumé models and styles beginning on page 418.

Chronological. The most popular résumé format is the chronological résumé, shown in Figures 15.6 through 15.10 in our résumé collection. It lists work history job by job, starting with the most recent position. Recruiters favour the chronological format because such résumés quickly reveal a candidate's education and experience record. Recruiters are familiar with the chronological résumé, and as many as 85 percent of employers prefer to see a candidate's résumé in this format.[11] The chronological style works well for candidates who have experience in their field of employment and for those who show steady career growth, but it is less appropriate for people who have changed jobs frequently or who have gaps in their employment records. For postsecondary students and others who lack extensive experience, the functional résumé format may be preferable.

Functional. The functional résumé, shown in Figure 15.10 on page 422, focuses on a candidate's skills rather than on past employment. Like a chronological résumé, the functional résumé begins with the candidate's name, address, telephone number, job objective, and education. Instead of listing jobs, though, the functional résumé groups skills and accomplishments in special categories, such as *Supervisory and Management Skills* or *Retailing and Marketing Experience*. This résumé style highlights accomplishments and can de-emphasize a negative employment history. People who have changed jobs frequently, who have gaps in their employment records, or who are entering an entirely different field may prefer the functional résumé. Recent graduates with little or no related employment experience often find the functional résumé useful. Older job seekers who want to downplay a long job history and job hunters who are afraid of appearing overqualified may also prefer the functional format. Be aware, though, that online job boards may insist on the chronological format. In addition, some recruiters are suspicious of functional résumés, thinking the candidate is hiding something.

Deciding on Length

Experts simply do not agree on how long a résumé should be. Conventional wisdom has always held that recruiters prefer one-page résumés. A carefully controlled study of 570 recruiters, however, revealed that while they claimed they preferred one-page résumés, the recruiters actually chose to interview the applicants with two-page résumés.[12] Recruiters who are serious about candidates often prefer a full picture with the kind of details that can be provided in a two-page résumé. Conversely, recruiters are said to be extremely busy and prefer concise résumés.

Perhaps the best advice is to make your résumé as long as needed to sell your skills to recruiters and hiring managers. Individuals with more experience will naturally have longer résumés. Those with fewer than ten years of experience, those making a major career change, and those who have had only one or two employers will likely have one-page résumés. Those with ten years or more of related experience may have two-page résumés. Finally, some senior-level managers and executives with a lengthy history of major accomplishments might have résumés that are three pages or longer.[13]

Organizing Your Information Into Effective Résumé Categories

Although résumés have standard categories, their arrangement and content should be strategically planned. A customized résumé emphasizes skills and achievements aimed at a particular job or company. It shows a candidate's most important qualifications first, and it de-emphasizes any weaknesses. In organizing your qualifications and information, try to create as few headings as possible; more than six generally looks cluttered. No two résumés are ever exactly alike, but most writers consider including some or all of these categories: main heading, career objective, summary of qualifications, education, experience, capabilities and skills, awards and activities, personal information, and references.

Chronological résumés focus on job history with the most recent positions listed first.

Because functional résumés focus on skills, they may be more advisable for graduates with little experience.

Recruiters may say they prefer one-page résumés, but many choose to interview candidates with longer résumés.

LEARNING OBJECTIVE 4

Organize your qualifications and information into effective résumé segments.

Main Heading

Your résumé, whether it is chronological or functional, should always start with your name. Format your name so that it stands out on the page. Following your name, list your contact information, including your complete address, area code and phone number, and e-mail address. Be sure to include a telephone number where you can receive messages. The outgoing message at this number should be in your voice, it should mention your full name, and it should be concise and professional. If you include your cellphone number and are expecting a call from a recruiter, pick up only when you are in a quiet environment and can concentrate.

For your e-mail address, be sure it sounds professional instead of something like *2sexy4you@hotmail.com* or *sixpackguy@yahoo.com*. Also be sure that you are using a personal e-mail address. Putting your work e-mail address on your résumé announces to prospective employers that you are using your current employer's resources to look for another job. If you have a Web site where an e-portfolio or samples of your work can be viewed, include the address in the main heading.

Career Objective

Opinion is divided about the effect of including a career objective on a résumé. Recruiters think such statements indicate that a candidate has made a commitment to a career and is sure about what he or she wants to do. Career objectives, of course, make the recruiter's life easier by quickly classifying the résumé. Such declarations, however, can also disqualify a candidate if the stated objective doesn't match a company's job description.[14] A well-written objective—customized for the job opening—can add value to either a chronological or a functional résumé.

Your objective should focus on the employer's needs. Therefore, it should be written from an employer's perspective, not your own. Focus on how you can contribute to the organization, not what the organization can do for you. A typical self-serving objective is *To obtain a meaningful and rewarding position that enables me to learn more about the graphic design field and allows for advancement.* Instead, show how you can add value to the organization with such an objective as *Position with an advertising firm designing Web sites, publications, logos, and promotional displays for clients, where creativity, software knowledge, and proven communication skills can be used to build client base and expand operations.*

Also be careful that your career objective doesn't downplay your talents. For example, some consultants warn against using the words *entry-level* in your objective, as these words emphasize lack of experience or show poor self-confidence. Finally, your objective should be concise. Try to limit your objective to no more than three lines. Avoid using complete sentences and the pronoun *I*.

If you choose to omit the career objective, be sure to discuss your objectives and goals in your cover letter. Wise job seekers are also incorporating their objectives into a summary of qualifications, which is discussed next.

> Career objectives are most appropriate for specific, targeted positions; they may limit a broader job search.

Summary of Qualifications

Recruiters are busy, and smart job seekers add a summary of qualifications to their résumés to save the time of recruiters and hiring managers. A summary at the top of your résumé makes it easier to read and ensures that your most impressive qualifications are not overlooked by a recruiter, who skims résumés quickly. A well-written summary motivates the recruiter to read further.

A summary of qualifications (also called *career profile, job summary or professional highlights*) should include three to eight bulleted statements that prove you are the ideal candidate for the position. When formulating these statements, consider your experience in the field, your education, your unique skills, awards you have won, certifications, and any other accomplishments that you want to highlight. Include numbers wherever possible. Target the most important qualifications an employer will be looking for in the person hired for this position. Examples of summaries of qualifications appear in Figures 15.6, 15.7, 15.8, 15.9, and 15.11 in the résumé models.

> A summary of qualifications section lists your most impressive accomplishments and qualifications in one concise bulleted list.

Education

The next component in a chronological résumé is your education—if it is more noteworthy than your work experience. In this section you should include the name and location of schools, dates of attendance, major fields of study, and degrees or diplomas received. Once you have attended college or university, you don't need to list secondary school information on your résumé. Your grade-point average (GPA) or class ranking may be important to prospective employers. One way to enhance your GPA is to calculate it in your major courses only (for example, *3.6/4.0 in major*). It is not unethical to showcase your GPA in your major—as long as you clearly indicate what you are doing. If your GPA is low, you might choose to omit it. Remember, however, that many employers will assume your GPA is lower than a 3.0 if you omit it.[15]

Under *Education* you might be tempted to list all the courses you took, but such a list makes for very dull reading. Refer to courses only if you can relate them to the position sought. When relevant, include certificates earned, seminars attended, workshops completed, and honours earned. If your education is incomplete, include such statements as *B.S. degree expected 6/14* or *80 units completed in 120-unit program*. Title this section *Education, Academic Preparation,* or *Professional Training*. If you are preparing a functional résumé, you will probably put the education section below your skills summaries, as Kevin Touhy has done in Figure 15.10.

Work Experience or Employment History

When your work experience is significant and relevant to the position sought, this information should appear before education. List your most recent employment first and work backward, including only those jobs that you think will help you win the targeted position. A job application form may demand a full employment history, but your résumé may be selective. Be aware, though, that time gaps in your employment history will probably be questioned in the interview. For each position show the following:

- Employer's name, city, and province or territory

- Dates of employment (month and year)

- Most important job title

- Significant duties, activities, accomplishments, and promotions

Describe your employment achievements concisely but concretely to make what résumé consultants call "a strong value proposition."[16] Avoid generalities, such as *Worked with customers*. Be more specific, with such statements as *Served 40 or more retail customers a day, Successfully resolved problems about custom stationery orders*, or *Acted as intermediary among customers, printers, and suppliers*. If possible, quantify your accomplishments, such as *Conducted study of equipment needs of 100 small businesses in Brampton, Personally generated orders for sales of $90,000 annually*, or *Keyed all the production models for a 250-page employee procedures manual*. One professional recruiter said, "I spend a half hour every day screening 50 résumés or more, and if I don't spot some [quantifiable] results in the first 10 seconds, the résumé is history."[17]

Your employment achievements and job duties will be easier to read if you place them in a bulleted list. When writing these bullet points, don't try to list every single thing you have done on the job; instead, customize your information so that it relates to the target job. Make sure your list of job duties shows what you have to contribute and how you are qualified for the position you are applying for. Do not make your bullet points complete sentences, and avoid using personal pronouns (*I, me, my*).

In addition to technical skills, employers seek individuals with communication, management, and interpersonal capabilities. This means you will want to select work experiences and achievements that illustrate your initiative, dependability, responsibility, resourcefulness, flexibility, and leadership. Employers also want people who can work in teams. Thus, include such statements as *Collaborated with interdepartmental task force in developing ten-page handbook for temporary workers* and *Headed student government team that conducted most successful voter registration in campus history*.

Statements describing your work experience can be made forceful and persuasive by using action verbs, such as those listed in Figure 15.3 and illustrated in Figure 15.4. Starting each of your bullet points with an action verb will help ensure that your bulleted lists are parallel.

FIGURE 15.3 Use Action Verbs in Statements That Quantify Achievements

The underlined words are especially good for pointing out accomplishments.

Communication Skills
arbitrated
arranged
authored
clarified
collaborated
convinced
corresponded
defined
developed
directed
drafted
edited
enlisted
explained
formulated
influenced
integrated
interpreted
mediated
moderated
negotiated
participated
persuaded
promoted
publicized
reconciled
recruited
resolved
spoke
specified
suggested
summarized
translated
wrote

Teamwork, Supervision Skills
adapted
advised

assessed
assisted
clarified
coached
collaborated (with)
communicated
coordinated
counselled
demonstrated
demystified
developed
enabled
encouraged
evaluated
expedited
explained
facilitated
guided
informed
instructed
motivated
persuaded
set goals
stimulated
teamed (with)
trained

Management, Leadership Skills
administered
analyzed
assigned
attained
authorized
chaired
consolidated
contracted
coordinated
delegated
developed
directed

evaluated
executed
handled
headed
implemented
improved
increased
led
modelled
organized
oversaw
planned
prioritized
produced
recommended
reorganized
reviewed
scheduled
strengthened
supervised
trained

Research Skills
analyzed
clarified
collected
critiqued
diagnosed
evaluated
examined
experimented
extracted
formulated
gathered
identified
informed
inspected
interpreted
interviewed
invented
investigated

located
measured
observed
organized
researched
reviewed
searched
solved
studied
summarized
surveyed
systematized

Clerical, Detail Skills
activated
approved
arranged
catalogued
classified
collected
compiled
edited
executed
generated
implemented
inspected
logged
maintained
monitored
operated
organized
prepared
processed
proofread
purchased
recorded
retrieved
screened
specified
streamlined

systematized
tabulated
updated
validated

Creative Skills
acted
conceptualized
created
customized
designed
developed
directed
established
fashioned
founded
illustrated
initiated
instituted
integrated
introduced
invented
originated
performed
planned
revitalized
shaped

Technical Skills
assembled
built
calculated
computed
configured
designed
devised
engineered
fabricated
installed
maintained
operated

overhauled
performed troubleshooting
programmed
remodelled
repaired
retrieved
solved
upgraded

Financial Skills
administered
allocated
analyzed
appraised
audited
balanced
budgeted
calculated
computed
developed
forecast
managed
marketed
planned
projected
researched

More Accomplishment Verbs
achieved
expanded
improved
pioneered
reduced (losses)
resolved (problems)
restored
revamped
spearheaded
transformed

FIGURE 15.4 Use Action Verbs in Statements That Quantify Achievements

- **Identified** weaknesses in internships and researched five alternate programs
- **Reduced** delivery delays by an average of three days per order
- **Streamlined** filing system, thus reducing 400-item backlog to zero
- **Organized** holiday awards program for 1200 attendees and 140 workers
- **Designed** three pages in HTML for company Web site
- **Represented** 2,500 students on committee involving university policies and procedures
- **Calculated** shipping charges for overseas deliveries and recommended most economical rates
- **Managed** 24-station computer network linking data in three departments
- **Distributed and explained** voter registration forms to more than 500 prospective voters
- **Praised** by top management for enthusiastic teamwork and achievement
- **Secured** national recognition from Communities in Bloom Foundation for tree project

Capabilities and Skills

Recruiters want to know specifically what you can do for their companies. Therefore, list your special skills, such as *Proficient in preparing federal, provincial, and local payroll tax returns, as well as franchise and personal property tax returns*. Include your ability to use the Web, software programs, social media, office equipment, and communication technology tools. If you speak a foreign language or use sign language, include it on your résumé. Describe proficiencies you have acquired through training and experience, such as *Certified in computer graphics and Web design through an intensive 350-hour classroom program*. Use such expressions as *competent in, skilled in, proficient with, experienced in*, and *able to*; for example, *Competent in writing, editing, and proofreading reports, tables, letters, memos, manuscripts, and business forms*.

> Emphasize the skills and aptitudes that prove you are qualified for a specific position.

You will also want to highlight exceptional aptitudes, such as working well under stress, learning computer programs quickly, and interacting with customers. If possible, provide details and evidence that back up your assertions, such as *Mastered PhotoShop in 25 hours with little instruction*. Include examples of your writing, speaking, management, organizational, and interpersonal skills—particularly those talents that are relevant to your targeted job. For recent graduates this section can be used to give recruiters evidence of your potential. Instead of *Capabilities*, the section might be called *Skills and Abilities*.

Those job hunters preparing a functional résumé will place more focus on skills than on any other section. A well-written functional résumé groups skills into categories, such as *Accounting/Finance Skills, Management/Leadership Skills, Communication/Teamwork Skills*, and *Computer/Technology Skills*. Each skills category includes a bulleted list of achievements and experience that demonstrate the skill, including specific numbers whenever possible. These skills categories should be placed in the beginning of the résumé, where they will be highlighted, followed by education and work experience. The action verbs shown in Figures 15.3 and 15.4 can also be used when constructing a functional résumé.

Awards, Honours, and Activities

If you have three or more awards or honours, highlight them by listing them under a separate heading. If not, put them in the education or work experience section if appropriate. Include awards, scholarships (financial and other), fellowships, dean's list, honours, recognition, commendations, and certificates. Be sure to identify items clearly. Your reader may be unfamiliar, for example, with different groups or awards; tell what they mean. Instead of saying *Recipient of Star award*, give more details: *Recipient of Star award given by Mount Allison University to outstanding graduates who combine academic excellence and extracurricular activities*.

> Awards, honours, and activities are appropriate for the résumé.

It is also appropriate to include school, community, volunteer, and professional activities. Employers are interested in evidence that you are a well-rounded person. This section allows you to demonstrate leadership and interpersonal skills. Strive to use action statements. For example, instead of saying *Treasurer of business club*, explain more fully: *Collected dues, kept financial records, and paid bills while serving as treasurer of 35-member business club*.

Personal Data

Today's résumés generally omit personal data, such as birth date, marital status, height, weight, national origin, health, and religious affiliation. Such information doesn't relate to genuine occupational qualifications, and recruiters are legally barred from asking for such information. Some job seekers do, however, include hobbies or interests (such as skiing or photography) that might grab the recruiter's attention or serve as conversation starters. Naturally, you shouldn't mention time-consuming interests or dangerous pastimes (such as rock climbing, scuba diving, caving, bungee jumping, or motorcycle racing). You could also indicate your willingness to travel or to relocate since many companies will be interested.

> Omit personal data not related to job qualifications.

References

Listing references directly on a résumé takes up valuable space. Moreover, references are not normally instrumental in securing an interview—few companies check them before the interview. Instead, recruiters prefer that you bring to the interview a list of individuals willing to discuss your qualifications. Therefore, you should prepare a separate list, such as that in Figure 15.5, when you begin your job search. Ask three to five individuals—instructors, your current employer or previous employers, colleagues or subordinates, and other professional contacts—whether they would be willing to answer inquiries regarding your qualifications for employment. Be sure,

> References are unnecessary for the résumé, but they should be available for the interview.

FIGURE 15.5 Sample Reference List

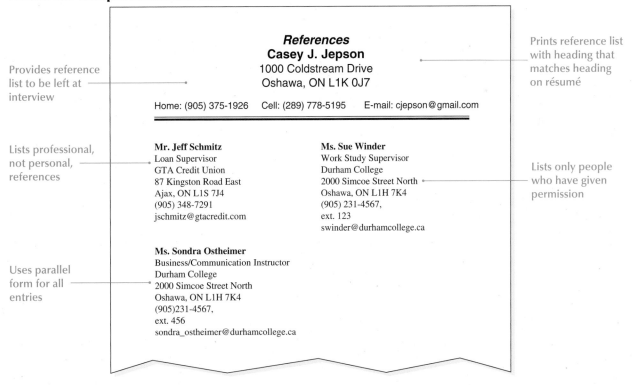

Provides reference list to be left at interview

Lists professional, not personal, references

Uses parallel form for all entries

References
Casey J. Jepson
1000 Coldstream Drive
Oshawa, ON L1K 0J7

Home: (905) 375-1926   Cell: (289) 778-5195   E-mail: cjepson@gmail.com

Mr. Jeff Schmitz
Loan Supervisor
GTA Credit Union
87 Kingston Road East
Ajax, ON L1S 7J4
(905) 348-7291
jschmitz@gtacredit.com

Ms. Sue Winder
Work Study Supervisor
Durham College
2000 Simcoe Street North
Oshawa, ON L1H 7K4
(905) 231-4567,
ext. 123
swinder@durhamcollege.ca

Ms. Sondra Ostheimer
Business/Communication Instructor
Durham College
2000 Simcoe Street North
Oshawa, ON L1H 7K4
(905)231-4567,
ext. 456
sondra_ostheimer@durhamcollege.ca

Prints reference list with heading that matches heading on résumé

Lists only people who have given permission

FIGURE 15.6 Chronological Résumé: Recent College Graduate With Related Experience

Rebecca Chowdhry used a chronological résumé to highlight her work experience, most of which is related directly to the position she seeks. Although she is a recent graduate, she has accumulated experience in two part-time jobs and one full-time job. She included a summary of qualifications to highlight her skills, experience, and interpersonal traits aimed at a specific position.

Notice that Rebecca designed her résumé in two columns with five major categories listed in the left column. In the right column, she included bulleted items for each of the five categories. Conciseness and parallelism are important in writing an effective résumé. In the Experience *category, she started each item with an action verb, which improved readability and parallel form.*

Lists most impressive qualifications ————

Arranges jobs in reverse chronological order ————

Uses bulleted lists to make résumé easier to read ————

Shows job titles in bold for readability ————

Rebecca L. Chowdhry
680 Mountain View Avenue, Victoria, BC V9B 2B9   (614) 479-1982   rlchowdhry@hotmail.com

OBJECTIVE
Position with financial services organization installing accounting software and providing user support, where computer experience and proven communication and interpersonal skills can be used to improve operations.

SUMMARY OF QUALIFICATIONS
- More than five years' experience in the accounting field
- Experienced in designing, installing, and providing technical support for accounting software, including SAP, Great Plains, Peachtree, and Oracle
- Proficient in Word, Access, PowerPoint, Excel, and QuickBooks
- Skilled in technical writing, including proposals, user manuals, and documentation
- Commended for tactful, professional, and friendly communication skills
- Fluent in speaking and writing French

EXPERIENCE
Accounting software consultant. West Coast Software, Victoria, B.C.
June 2011 to present
- Design and install accounting systems for businesses, such as Century 21 Butler Realty, Capital Financial Services, Pacific Lumber, and others
- Provide ongoing technical support and consultation for regular clients
- Help write proposals such as successful $400,000 government contract

Office manager (part-time). Coastal Productions, Oak Bay, B.C.
June 2010 to May 2011
- Conceived and implemented improved order processing and filing system
- Designed and integrated module code pieces to export and convert data from an inhouse SQL database to QuickBooks format for automated cheque printing and invoice billing
- Trained three employees to operate QuickBooks software

Bookkeeper (part-time). Home Roofing, Victoria, B.C.
August 2006 to May 2010
- Kept books for roofing and repair company with $240,000 gross income
- Performed all bookkeeping tasks including quarterly internal audit and payroll

EDUCATION
Camosun College, Victoria, B.C.
Bachelor of Business Administration, June 2010
GPA in major 3.6 (4.0 = A)

Oracle University—currently enrolled in database training seminars leading to Oracle certification

HONOURS AND ACTIVITIES
- Dean's list, three semesters
- Elected to executive committee, student goverment

Includes detailed objective in response to advertisement

Uses present-tense verbs for current job and past-tense verbs for previous jobs

Specifies relevant activities for targeted position

Provides white space around headings to create open look

however, to provide them with an opportunity to refuse. No reference is better than a negative one.

Do not include personal or character references, such as friends, family, or neighbours, because recruiters rarely consult them. Companies are more interested in the opinions of objective individuals who know how you perform professionally and academically. One final note: most recruiters see little reason for including the statement *References furnished upon request.*

In Figures 15.6 through 15.10, you will find models for chronological and functional résumés. Use these models to help you organize the content and format of your own persuasive résumé.

To highlight her skills and capabilities, Casey placed them in the summary of qualifications at the top of her résumé. She used the tables feature of her word processing program to help her format. Because she wanted to describe her skills and experience fully, she used two pages.

Casey J. Jepson
1000 Coldstream Drive
Oshawa, ON L1K 0J7

Home: (905) 375-1926   Cell: (289) 778-5195   E-mail: cjepson@gmail.com

SUMMARY OF QUALIFICATIONS
- More than three years' experience in administrative positions, working with business documents and interacting with customers
- Ability to keyboard (65 wpm) and use ten-key calculator (150 kpm)
- Proficient with Microsoft Word, Excel, Access, PowerPoint, FrontPage, and Publisher (passed MOS certification exam)
- Competent in Web research, written and oral communication, records management, desktop publishing, computer software troubleshooting, and proofreading and editing business documents
- Trained in QuickBooks, Flash, Photoshop, Dreamweaver
- Experienced in planning all-day seminars and travel arrangements

Omits objective to keep all options open

Focuses on skills and aptitudes that employers seek

EXPERIENCE

Administrative Assistant, Work Study
Durham College, Oshawa, Ontario
August 2011–present
- Create letters, memos, reports, and forms in Microsoft Word
- Develop customized reports and labels using Microsoft Access
- Maintain departmental Microsoft Excel budget

Uses present-tense verbs for current job

Loan Support Specialist
GTA Credit Union, Ajax, Ontario
May 2009–September 2011
- Prepared loan documents for consumer, residential, mortgage, agricultural, and commercial loans
- Ensured compliance with federal, provincial, and bank regulations
- Originated correspondence (both oral and written) with customers and insurance agencies
- Ordered and interpreted appraisals, titles, and credit reports
- Created and maintained paper and electronic files for customers
- Protected the confidentiality of all clients

Arranges employment by job title for easy recognition

Customer Sales Representative
Wal-Mart, Whitby, Ontario,
Winter seasons 2009–2011
- Answered phones and assisted customers with orders
- Resolved customers' merchandise questions and problems
- Enjoyed working in teams to achieve company goals

Includes second-page heading

Casey J. Jepson   Page 2

EDUCATION
Durham College, Oshawa, Ontario
Major: Office Administration - Executive Program
Ontario College Diploma expected May 2013. GPA in major: 3.8 (4.0 = A)

ACTIVITIES AND AWARDS
- Assisted student president in all functions and coordinated all activities of the APS (Administrative Professionals Society) Torch Awards Program while serving as student vice president
- Placed first in provincial APS Administrative Assistant competition
- Earned second place in Bill Wolfe Writing Contest
- Served as Durham College Student Association (DCSA) Representative for Office Administration program
- Nominated for DCSA Ambassador Award (recognizes outstanding students for excellence in and out of classroom)

Combines activities and awards to fill out section

FIGURE 15.8 Chronological Résumé: Current College Student With Limited Related Experience

Rick's résumé answers an advertisement specifying skills for a staff accountant. In responding to the ad, he targeted his objective and shaped his statements to the precise job requirements mentioned by the employer.

To produce this attractive print-based résumé, he employed italics, bold, and scalable font features from his word processing program. He realized that this résumé might not be scannable and could not be embedded in an e-mail message. That's why he was ready with a scannable version that shortened the line length and stripped the fancy formatting in case he had to submit it electronically.

Uses italics, larger type size, and bold underline to enhance appearance

RICK M. JAMESON

732 Balmoral Street
Medicine Hat, AB T1A 0W4
Phone: (403) 479-1982
Cell: (403) 412-5540
E-mail: rmjameson@west.net

Objective: Position as Staff Accountant with progressive firm, where my technical, computer, and communication skills will be useful in managing accounts and acquiring new clientele

Responds to specific job advertisement

SUMMARY OF QUALIFICATIONS

Accounting
- Able to journalize entries accurately in general and specialized journals
- Proficient in posting to general ledger, preparing trial balance, and detecting discrepancies
- Trained in preparing and analyzing balance sheet and other financial statements

Computer
- Experienced in using Word, Excel, HTML, and Dreamweaver
- Comfortable in Windows and Internet environments
- Able to learn new computer programs and applications quickly, with little instruction

Communication and Interpersonal
- Enjoy working with details and completing assignments accurately and on time
- Demonstrate sound writing and speaking skills acquired and polished in business letter writing, report writing, and speech classes
- Interact well with people as evidenced in my successful sales, volunteer, and internship work; enjoy meeting new people

Highlights skills named in advertisement

EXPERIENCE

Tax Preparer, Tax Clinic Program
Sponsored by the Chartered Accountants of Alberta. Prepare provincial and federal tax returns for individuals with incomes of less than $25,000. Conduct interviews with more than 50 individuals to elicit data regarding taxes. Determine legitimate tax deductions and record them accurately. (Tax seasons, 2010 to present)

Accounting Intern, Software, Inc., Accounting Department, Medicine Hat, AB
Assisted in analyzing data for weekly accounts payable aging report. Prepared daily cash activity report for sums up to $10,000. Calculated depreciation on 12 capital asset accounts with a total valuation of more than $900,000. Researched and wrote report analyzing one division's budget of $150,000. (Spring 2010)

Salesperson, Wal-Mart, Medicine Hat, AB
Helped customers select gardening and landscaping supplies. Assisted in ordering merchandise, stocking the department, and resolving customer problems. (Summers 2009, 2010)

Uses paragraph style instead of bulleted items to pack more data into a small space

Quantifies descriptions of experience

EDUCATION

Medicine Hat College, Medicine Hat, AB. Business Administration diploma expected June 2012
Major: Accounting
GPA: 3.2 (A = 4.0)
Participated as member of Accounting Club for two years
Received Award of Merit for volunteer work as orientation guide and peer tutor

Includes activities and awards with education because of limited space

FIGURE 15.9 **Chronological Résumé: University Graduate With Substantial Experience**

Because Rachel has many years of experience and seeks executive-level employment, she highlighted her experience by placing it before her education. Her summary of qualifications highlighted her most impressive experience and skills. This chronological two-page résumé shows the steady progression of her career to executive positions, a movement that impresses and reassures recruiters.

RACHEL M. JOHNSON
395 Noble Street
Sudbury, ON P3C 3R9

E-mail: rachel.johnson395@hotmail.com
(705) 490-3310

OBJECTIVE Senior Financial Management Position

SUMMARY OF QUALIFICATIONS
- 12 years' comprehensive experience in the accounting industry, including 8 years as a controller
- Certified General Accountant (CGA)
- Demonstrated ability to handle all accounting functions for large, midsized, and small firms
- Able to isolate problems, reduce expenses, and improve the bottom line, resulting in substantial cost savings
- Proven talent for interacting professionally with individuals at all levels, as demonstrated by performance review comments
- Experienced in P&L, audits, taxation, interal control, inventory management, A/P, A/R, cash management

Lists most impressive credentials

PROFESSIONAL HISTORY AND ACHIEVEMENT

11/08 to present   CONTROLLER
Apex Business Machines and Supplies, Sudbury, ON
- Direct all facets of accounting and cash management for 60-employee, $3 million business
- Supervise inventory and production operations for tax compliance
- Convinced owner to lower sales prices, resulting in doubling first-quarter 2011 sales
- Created cost accounting by product and pricing based on gross margin
- Increased line of credit with 12 major suppliers

Uses action verbs but includes many good nouns for possible computer scanning

1/06 to 10/08   CONTROLLER
Burgess Inc., Sudbury, ON (major manufacturer of flashlight and lantern batteries)
- Managed all accounting, cash, payroll, credit, and collection operations for 75-employee business
- Implemented a new system for cost accounting, inventory control, and accounts payable, resulting in a $100,000 annual savings
- Reduced staff from 10 persons to 5 with no loss in productivity
- Successfully reduced inventory levels from $1.1 million to $600,000

Explains nature of employer's business because it is not immediately recognizable

Emphasizes steady employment history by listing dates FIRST

8/04 to 11/05   TREASURER/CONTROLLER
The Builders of Sudbury, ON (manufacturer of modular housing)
- Supervised accounts receivable/payable, cash management, payroll, insurance
- Directed monthly and year-end closings, banking relations, and product costing
- Refinanced company with long-term loan, ensuring stability

Describes and quantifies specific achievements

Rachel M. Johnson   Page 2

4/00 to 6/04   SUPERVISOR OF GENERAL ACCOUNTING
Levin National Batteries, Sudbury, ON (local manufacturer of flashlight batteries)
- Completed monthly and year-end closing of ledgers for $1 million business
- Audited freight bills, acted as interdepartmental liaison, prepared financial reports

ADDITIONAL INFORMATION

Education: Bachelor of Business and Computer Science degree, Laurentian University, Major: Accounting, 1999
Certification: Certified General Accountant (CGA), 2003
Personal: Will travel and/or relocate

Deemphasizes education because work history is more important for mature candidates

FIGURE 15.10 Functional Résumé: Recent University Graduate With Unrelated Part-Time Experience

Recent graduate Kevin Touhy chose this functional format to deemphasize his meagre work experience and emphasize his potential in sales and marketing. This version of his résumé is more generic than one targeted for a specific position. Yet it emphasizes his strong points with specific achievements and includes an employment section to satisfy recruiters.

The functional format presents ability-focused topics. It illustrates what the job seeker can do for the employer instead of narrating a history of previous jobs. Although recruiters prefer chronological résumés, the functional format is a good choice for new graduates, career changers, and those with employment gaps.

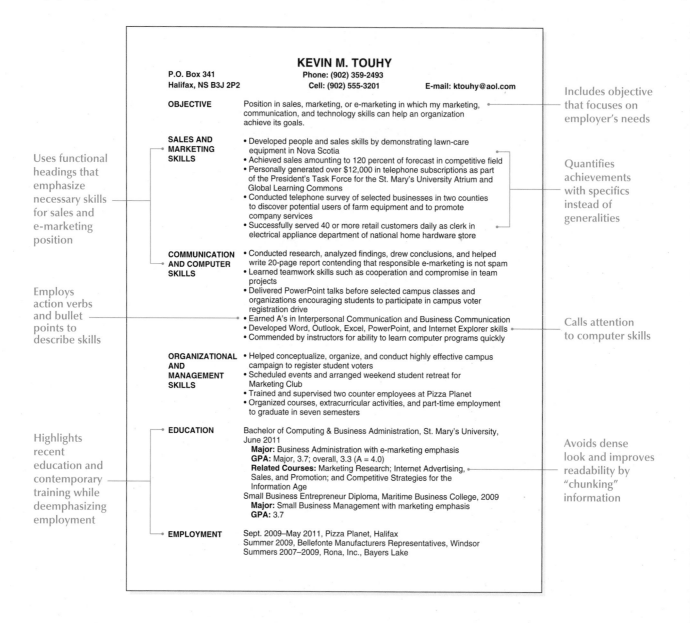

KEVIN M. TOUHY

P.O. Box 341
Halifax, NS B3J 2P2

Phone: (902) 359-2493
Cell: (902) 555-3201

E-mail: ktouhy@aol.com

OBJECTIVE
Position in sales, marketing, or e-marketing in which my marketing, communication, and technology skills can help an organization achieve its goals.

Includes objective that focuses on employer's needs

SALES AND MARKETING SKILLS
- Developed people and sales skills by demonstrating lawn-care equipment in Nova Scotia
- Achieved sales amounting to 120 percent of forecast in competitive field
- Personally generated over $12,000 in telephone subscriptions as part of the President's Task Force for the St. Mary's University Atrium and Global Learning Commons
- Conducted telephone survey of selected businesses in two counties to discover potential users of farm equipment and to promote company services
- Successfully served 40 or more retail customers daily as clerk in electrical appliance department of national home hardware store

Uses functional headings that emphasize necessary skills for sales and e-marketing position

Quantifies achievements with specifics instead of generalities

COMMUNICATION AND COMPUTER SKILLS
- Conducted research, analyzed findings, drew conclusions, and helped write 20-page report contending that responsible e-marketing is not spam
- Learned teamwork skills such as cooperation and compromise in team projects
- Delivered PowerPoint talks before selected campus classes and organizations encouraging students to participate in campus voter registration drive
- Earned A's in Interpersonal Communication and Business Communication
- Developed Word, Outlook, Excel, PowerPoint, and Internet Explorer skills
- Commended by instructors for ability to learn computer programs quickly

Employs action verbs and bullet points to describe skills

Calls attention to computer skills

ORGANIZATIONAL AND MANAGEMENT SKILLS
- Helped conceptualize, organize, and conduct highly effective campus campaign to register student voters
- Scheduled events and arranged weekend student retreat for Marketing Club
- Trained and supervised two counter employees at Pizza Planet
- Organized courses, extracurricular activities, and part-time employment to graduate in seven semesters

EDUCATION
Bachelor of Computing & Business Administration, St. Mary's University, June 2011
Major: Business Administration with e-marketing emphasis
GPA: Major, 3.7; overall, 3.3 (A = 4.0)
Related Courses: Marketing Research; Internet Advertising, Sales, and Promotion; and Competitive Strategies for the Information Age
Small Business Entrepreneur Diploma, Maritime Business College, 2009
Major: Small Business Management with marketing emphasis
GPA: 3.7

Highlights recent education and contemporary training while deemphasizing employment

Avoids dense look and improves readability by "chunking" information

EMPLOYMENT
Sept. 2009–May 2011, Pizza Planet, Halifax
Summer 2009, Bellefonte Manufacturers Representatives, Windsor
Summers 2007–2009, Rona, Inc., Bayers Lake

Optimizing Your Résumé for Today's Technologies

Thus far we have aimed our résumé advice at human readers. However, the first reader of your résumé may well be a computer. Hiring organizations today use a variety of methods to process incoming résumés. Some organizations still welcome traditional print-based résumés that may include attractive formatting. Larger organizations, however, must deal with thousands of incoming résumés. Increasingly, they are placing those résumés directly into searchable databases. So that you can optimize your chances, you may need three versions of your résumé: (1) a traditional print-based résumé, (2) a scannable résumé, and (3) a plain-text résumé for e-mailing or online posting. This does not mean that you have to write different résumés. You are merely preparing different versions of your traditional résumé. With all versions you should also be aware of the significant role of résumé keywords. You may decide to create an e-portfolio to showcase your qualifications. You may also decide to prepare a professional video résumé to describe your skills. However, a video résumé is generally used as a supplement to, not a substitute for, a traditional résumé.

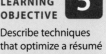

LEARNING OBJECTIVE 5

Describe techniques that optimize a résumé for today's technologies, including preparing a scannable résumé, a plain-text résumé, and an e-portfolio.

Designing a Print-Based Résumé

Print-based résumés (also called *presentation résumés*) are attractively formatted to maximize readability. You can create a professional-looking résumé by using your word processing program to highlight your qualifications. The examples in this chapter provide ideas for simple layouts that are easily duplicated. You can also examine résumé templates for design and format ideas. Their inflexibility, however, may lead to frustration as you try to force your skills and experience into a predetermined template sequence. What's more, recruiters who read hundreds of résumés can usually spot a template-based résumé. Instead, create your own original résumé that fits your unique qualifications.

Your print-based résumé should follow an outline format with headings and bullet points to present information in an orderly, uncluttered, easy-to-read format. An attractive print-based résumé is necessary (a) when you are competing for a job that does not require electronic submission, (b) to present in addition to an electronic submission, and (c) to bring with you to job interviews. Even if a résumé is submitted electronically, nearly every job candidate should have an attractive printed résumé handy for human readers.

> Because résumés are increasingly becoming part of searchable databases, you may need three versions.

> A print-based résumé should be attractive, readable, and outlined with headings in an orderly, uncluttered format.

Preparing a Scannable Résumé

A scannable résumé is one that is meant to be printed on plain white paper and scanned by a computer. To screen incoming résumés, many mid- and large-sized companies use automated applicant-tracking software. These systems scan an incoming résumé with optical character recognition (OCR) looking for keywords. The most sophisticated programs enable recruiters and hiring managers to search for keywords, rank résumés based on the number of "hits," and generate reports. Information from your résumé is stored, usually from six months to a year.

Before sending your résumé, find out whether the recipient uses scanning software. If you can't tell from the job announcement, call the company to ask whether it scans résumés electronically. If you don't get a clear answer and you have even the slightest suspicion that your résumé might be read electronically, you will be smart to prepare a plain, scannable version as shown in Figure 15.11. Although current scanning software can read a résumé in any format, many companies still use older versions that have difficulty with complex fonts and formatting. Therefore, it pays to follow these tips for maximizing scannability and hits.

> Applicant-tracking software scans incoming résumés searching for keywords.

Tips for Maximizing Scannability. A scannable résumé must sacrifice many of the graphic enhancements you might have used to make your print résumé attractive. To maximize scannability:

- **Use 10- to 14-point type.** Use a well-known font, such as Times New Roman or Arial. The font size in the body of your résumé should be 10-, 11-, or 12-point, and headings should be no larger than 14-point.

FIGURE 15.11 Scannable Résumé

Leticia P. Lorimar prepared this plain résumé free of graphics and fancy formatting so that it would scan well if read by a computer. Within the résumé she included many job titles, skills, traits, and other descriptive key words that scanners are programmed to recognize. To improve accurate scanning, she avoided bullets, italics, underlining, and columns. If she had had more information to include, she could have gone on to a second page since a résumé to be scanned need not be restricted to one page.

Places name alone at top of résumé where scanner expects to find it

LETICIA P. LORIMAR
49 South Edgewater Road
St. Thomas, ON N5P 2H5
519 742-5839
LLorimar@i-zoom.net

OBJECTIVE
Customer-oriented, fast-learning, detail-oriented individual seeks teller position with financial institution.

Uses asterisks to list most impressive qualifications; includes many key words for target position

SUMMARY OF QUALIFICATIONS
* Over three years' experience as a bank teller
* Proven ability to interact professionally, efficiently, and pleasantly with customers
* Reputation for accuracy and ability to work well under pressure
* Speak French fluently
* Experience using Excel, Word, PowerPoint, accounting software, banking CRT, and the Internet
* Member of First Bank's Diversity Committee
* Received First Bank Certificate of Merit as an outstanding new employee

Uses typical headings for easy recognition

EXPERIENCE
First Bank, London, ON
July 2010 to present
Teller

    Cheerfully greet customers, make deposits and withdrawals, accurately enter on computer. Balance up to $10,000 in cash with computer journal tape daily within 15-minute time period. Solve customer problems and answer questions patiently. Issue cashier's cheques, savings bonds, and traveller's cheques. Complete tasks under pressure with speed, accuracy, and special attention to positive customer service. Communicate well with customers who speak English or French.

Prevents inaccurate scanning by using Arial type font in which letters do not touch

Elgin Community Development Corporation, St. Thomas, ON
June 2008 to June 2010
Bookkeeper

    Managed all bookkeeping functions, including accounts payable, accounts receivable, payroll, and tax reports for a small business. Demonstrated ability to work independently, took responsibility for establishing and meeting deadlines, and learned new computer programs without instruction. Commended for honesty as well as being a self-starter who could handle multiple priorities and deadlines.

EDUCATION
University of Western Ontario, London, ON
Bachelor of Management and Organizational Studies expected in 2013

Fanshawe College, London, ON
Business Administration Diploma, 2010
Major: Accounting

Provides ample white space for accurate scanning

Scannable résumés use plain formatting, large fonts, quality printing, and white space.

- **Avoid fancy formatting.** Don't use borders, shading, underlining, italics, or other graphics to highlight text. These features don't scan well. Most applicant-tracking programs, however, can accurately read bold print, solid bullets, and asterisks.

- **Place your name on the first line.** Reports generated by applicant-tracking software usually assume that the first line of a résumé contains the applicant's name.

- **List each phone number on its own line.** Your landline and cellphone numbers should appear on separate lines to improve recognition.

- **Avoid double columns.** When listing job duties, skills, computer programs, and so forth, don't tabulate items into two- or three-column lists. Scanners read across and may convert tables into nonsensical output.

- **Take care when printing and mailing.** When printing your scannable résumé for mailing, use smooth white paper and black ink and print it on a quality printer. Mail your résumé in a large envelope to avoid folding it. If your résumé is longer than one page, do not staple it.

Tips for Maximizing Hits. In addition to paying attention to the physical appearance of your résumé, you must also be concerned with keywords that produce hits or recognition by the scanner. To maximize hits, follow these suggestions:

- **Focus on specific keywords or keyword phrases.** Study carefully any advertisements and job descriptions for the position you want. Describe your experience, education, and qualifications in terms associated with the job advertisement or job description for this position. Select keywords or phrases that describe specific skills, traits, expertise, tasks, and job titles.

- **Use accurate names.** Spell out complete names of schools, degrees or diplomas, and dates. Include specific names of companies, products, and services as appropriate.

- **Be careful of abbreviations and acronyms.** Spell out unfamiliar abbreviations but maximize easily recognized abbreviations and acronyms—especially those within your field, such as CAD, JPG, or JIT.

- **Describe interpersonal traits and attitudes.** Hiring managers look for keywords and phrases that describe interpersonal traits and attitudes that are related to a specific position.

> Scanners produce hits when they recognize targeted keywords, such as nouns describing skills, traits, tasks, and job titles.

Preparing a Plain-Text Résumé

A plain-text résumé is an electronic version suitable for e-mailing or pasting into online résumé bank submission forms. Employers prefer plain-text résumés because they avoid possible e-mail viruses and word processing incompatibilities. Usually embedded within an e-mail message, a plain-text résumé, shown in Figure 15.12, is immediately searchable. You should prepare a plain-text résumé if you want the fastest and most reliable way to contact potential employers. To create a plain-text résumé, follow these suggestions:

- **Observe all the tips for a scannable résumé.** A plain-text résumé requires the same attention to content, formatting, and keywords as that recommended for a scannable résumé.

- **Reformat with shorter lines.** Many e-mail programs wrap lines longer than 65 characters. To avoid having your résumé look as if a chain saw attacked it, use a short line length.

- **Think about using keyboard characters to enhance format.** In addition to using capital letters and asterisks, you might use spaced equals signs (= = =) and tildes (~ ~ ~) to create lines that separate résumé categories.

- **Move all text to the left.** Do not centre items; start all text at the left margin. Remove tabs.

- **Save your résumé in plain text (.txt) or rich text format (.rtf).** Saving your résumé in one of these formats will ensure that it can be read when pasted into an e-mail message.

- **Test your résumé before sending it to an employer.** After preparing and saving your résumé, copy and paste a copy of it into an e-mail message and send it to yourself. Make any necessary changes.

When sending a plain-text résumé to an employer, be sure that your subject line clearly describes the purpose of your message.

> Employers prefer plain-text documents because they are immediately searchable and they do not require employers to open attachments, which might carry viruses or create software incompatibilities.

Showcasing Your Qualifications in an E-Portfolio or Video Résumé

As the workplace becomes increasingly digitized, you have yet another way to display your qualifications to prospective employers—the digitized e-portfolio. Resourceful job candidates in other fields—particularly writers, models, artists, and graphic artists—have

Chapter 15: The Job Search, Résumés, and Cover Letters

FIGURE 15.12 Plain-Text Résumé

To be sure her résumé would transmit well when embedded within an e-mail message, Leticia prepared a special version with all lines starting at the left margin. She used a 10 cm line length to avoid awkward line breaks. To set off her major headings, she used the tilde character on her keyboard. She saved the document as a text file (.txt or .rtf) so that it could be read by various computers. At the end she included a statement saying that an attractive, fully formatted hard copy of her résumé was available on request.

Starts all lines at left margin

Sets off headings with the tilde (~) but could have omitted this attempt to improve readability

Uses asterisks instead of bullets, which do not scan well

Shortens lines to avoid awkward line wrapping

Creates large empty space that is unavoidable in this format

```
LETICIA P. LORIMAR
49 South Edgewater Road
St. Thomas, ON N5P 2H5
Phone: 519 742-5839
E-Mail: LLorimar@i-zoom.net

~ ~ ~ ~ ~ ~
OBJECTIVE
~ ~ ~ ~ ~ ~

Customer-oriented, fast-learning, detail-oriented individual
seeks teller position with financial institution.

~ ~ ~ ~ ~ ~ ~ ~ ~ ~ ~ ~ ~ ~ ~ ~ ~ ~ ~
SUMMARY OF QUALIFICATIONS
~ ~ ~ ~ ~ ~ ~ ~ ~ ~ ~ ~ ~ ~ ~ ~ ~ ~ ~

* More than three years' experience as a bank teller
* Proven ability to interact professionally, efficiently, and
  pleasantly with customers
* Reputation for accuracy and ability to work well under
  pressure
* Speak French fluently
* Experience using Excel, Word, PowerPoint, accounting
  software, banking CRT, and the Internet
* Member of First Bank's Diversity Committee
* Received First Bank Certificate of Merit as an
  outstanding new employee

~ ~ ~ ~ ~ ~ ~ ~
EXPERIENCE
~ ~ ~ ~ ~ ~ ~ ~

First Bank, London, ON
July 2010 to present
Teller
* Cheerfully greet customers, make deposits and withdrawals
* Balance up to $10,000 in cash with computer journal tape
  daily within 15-minute time period
* Solve customer problems and answer questions patiently
* Issue cashier's cheques, savings bonds, and traveller's cheques
* Complete tasks under pressure with speed, accuracy, and
  attention to positive customer service
* Communicate well with customers speaking English or French
```

been creating print portfolios to illustrate their qualifications and achievements for some time. Now business and professional job candidates are using electronic portfolios to show off their talents.

An e-portfolio is a collection of digital files that can be navigated with the help of menus and hyperlinks much like a personal Web site. An e-portfolio provides viewers with a snapshot of a candidate's performance, talents, and accomplishments. A digital portfolio may include a copy of your résumé, reference letters, commendations for special achievements, awards, certificates, work samples, a complete list of your courses, thank-you letters, and anything else that touts your accomplishments. An e-portfolio might include links to electronic copies of your artwork, film projects, videos, blueprints, photographs, multimedia files, and blog entries that might otherwise be difficult

An e-portfolio offers links to examples of a job candidate's performance, talents, and accomplishments in digitized form.

to share with potential employers. E-portfolios are generally accessed at Web sites, where they are available around the clock to employers. Some colleges and universities not only make Web site space available for student e-portfolios but also provide instruction and resources for scanning photos, digitizing images, and preparing graphics. E-portfolios may also be burned onto CDs and DVDs to mail to prospective employers.

E-portfolios have many advantages. At Web sites they can be viewed at employers' convenience. Let's say you are talking on the phone with an employer in another city who wants to see a copy of your résumé. You can simply refer the employer to the Web address where your résumé resides. E-portfolios can also be seen by many individuals in an organization without circulating a paper copy. But the real reason for preparing an e-portfolio is that it shows off your talents and qualifications more thoroughly than a print résumé does.

Job candidates generally offer e-portfolios at Web sites, but they may also burn them onto CDs or DVDs.

You might want to consider creating a video to profile your skills. A professional-grade video résumé may open doors and secure an interview when other techniques have failed.[18] However, some recruiters are skeptical about digital or video portfolios because they fear that such applications will take more time to view than paper-based résumés do. Experts agree that the new medium will need to mature before smart guidelines can be established. You can learn more about video résumés by searching the Web.

A video résumé may be useful in applying to a far-off company.

Applying the Final Touches to Your Résumé

Because your résumé is probably the most important message you will ever write, you'll revise it many times. With so much information in concentrated form and with so much riding on its outcome, your résumé demands careful polishing, proofreading, and critiquing.

As you revise, be certain to verify all the facts, particularly those involving your previous employment and education. Don't be caught in a mistake or, worse, distortion of previous jobs and dates of employment. These items likely will be checked, and the consequences of puffing up a résumé with deception or flat-out lies are simply not worth the risk. The Ethical Insights box on page 428 outlines dangerous areas to avoid.

Polishing Your Résumé

While you continue revising, look for other ways to improve your résumé. For example, consider consolidating headings. By condensing your information into as few headings as possible, you'll produce a clean, professional-looking document. Study other résumés for valuable formatting ideas. Ask yourself what graphic highlighting techniques you can use to improve readability: capitalization, underlining, indenting, and bulleting. Experiment with headings and styles to achieve a pleasing, easy-to-read message. Moreover, look for ways to eliminate wordiness. For example, instead of *Supervised two employees who worked at the counter*, try *Supervised two counter employees*. Review Chapter 5 for more tips on writing concisely.

Study résumé models for ideas on improving your format.

In addition to making your résumé concise, make sure that you haven't included any of the following information, which doesn't belong on a résumé:

- Any basis for discrimination (age, marital status, gender, national origin, religion, race, number of children, disability)

- A photograph

- Reasons for leaving previous jobs

- The word *résumé*

- Social insurance number

- Salary history or requirements

- High school information

- References

- Full addresses of schools or employers (include city and province only)

Are Inflated Résumés Worth the Risk?

A résumé is expected to showcase a candidate's strengths and minimize weaknesses. For this reason recruiters expect a certain degree of self-promotion. Some résumé writers, however, step over the line that separates honest self-marketing from deceptive half-truths and flat-out lies. Distorting facts on a résumé is unethical; lying is illegal. Most important, either practice can destroy a career.

Given the competitive job market, it might be tempting to puff up your résumé. You would not be alone in telling fibs or outright whoppers. One study found that 44 percent of applicants lied about their work histories, 23 percent fabricated licences or credentials, and 41 percent falsified their educational backgrounds.[19] Although recruiters can't check everything, most will verify previous employment and education before hiring candidates. More than half will require official transcripts.

After hiring, the checking process may continue. If hiring officials find a discrepancy in GPA or prior experience and the error is an honest mistake, they meet with the new hire to hear an explanation. If the discrepancy wasn't a mistake, they will likely *fire* the person immediately. No job seeker wants to be the unhappy position of explaining résumé errors or defending misrepresentation. Avoiding the following problems can keep you off the hot seat:

- **Inflated education, grades, or honours.** Some job candidates claim degrees or diplomas from colleges or universities when in fact they merely attended classes. Others increase their GPAs or claim fictitious honours. Any such dishonest reporting is grounds for dismissal when discovered.

- **Enhanced job titles.** Wanting to elevate their status, some applicants misrepresent their titles. For example, one technician called himself a "programmer" when he had actually programmed only one project for his boss. A mail clerk who assumed added responsibilities conferred on herself the title of "supervisor." Even when the description seems accurate, it's unethical to list any title not officially granted.

- **Puffed-up accomplishments.** Some job seekers inflate their employment experience or achievements. One clerk, eager to make her photocopying duties sound more important, said that she assisted the vice president in communicating and distributing employee directives. A graduate who spent the better part of six months watching rented videos on his DVD player described the activity as *Independent Film Study*. The latter statement may have helped win an interview, but it lost him the job. In addition to avoiding puffery, guard against taking sole credit for achievements that required many people. When recruiters suspect dubious claims on résumés, they nail applicants with specific—and often embarrassing—questions during their interviews.[20]

- **Altered employment dates.** Some candidates extend the dates of employment to hide unimpressive jobs or to cover up periods of unemployment and illness. Let's say that several years ago Cindy was unemployed for 14 months between working for Company A and being hired by Company B. To make her employment history look better, she adds seven months to her tenure with Company A and seven months to Company B. Now her employment history has no gaps, but her résumé is dishonest and represents a potential ethical trap for her.

- **Hidden keywords.** One of the latest sneaky tricks involves inserting invisible keywords into electronic résumés. To fool scanning programs into ranking their résumés higher, some job hunters use white type on a white background or they use Web coding to pack their résumés with target keywords. However, newer recruiter search tools detect such mischief, and those résumés are tossed.[21]

If your honest qualifications aren't good enough to get you the job you want, start working now to improve them. No job seeker should want to be hired based on lies.

Above all, make sure your print-based résumé looks professional. Avoid anything humorous or "cute," such as a help-wanted poster with your name or picture inside. Eliminate the personal pronoun *I* to ensure an objective style. Use high-quality paper in a professional colour, such as white, off-white, or light grey. Print your résumé by using a first-rate printer. Be prepared with a résumé for people to read and versions for computer scanning, sending by e-mail, and posting to Web sites.

Proofreading Your Résumé

After revising, you must proofread, proofread, and proofread again for spelling, mechanics, content, and format. Then have a knowledgeable friend or relative proofread it yet again. This is one document that must be perfect. Because the job market is so competitive, one typo, misspelled word, or grammatical error could eliminate you from consideration.

By now you may be thinking that you'd like to hire someone to write your résumé. Don't! First, you know yourself better than anyone else could know you. Second, you

In addition to being well written, a résumé must be carefully formatted and meticulously proofread.

will end up with either a generic or a one-time résumé. A generic résumé in today's highly competitive job market will lose out to a customized résumé nine times out of ten. Equally useless is a one-time résumé aimed at a single job. What if you don't get that job? Because you will need to revise your résumé many times as you seek a variety of jobs, be prepared to write (and rewrite) it yourself.

The Checklist box summarizes the key points to consider when preparing for employment and submitting a customized résumé.

Checklist

Preparing for Employment and Submitting a Customized Résumé

Preparation

- **Research the job market.** Learn about available jobs, common qualifications, and potential employers. The best résumés are customized for specific jobs with specific companies.
- **Analyze your strengths.** Determine what aspects of your education, experience, and personal characteristics will be assets to prospective employers.
- **Study models.** Look at other résumés for formatting and element placement ideas. Experiment with headings and styles to achieve a creative, readable product.

Headings and Objectives

- **Identify yourself.** List your name, address, and telephone numbers.
- **Include a career objective for a targeted job.** Use an objective only if it is intended for a specific job (*Objective: Junior cost accountant position in the petroleum industry*).
- **Prepare a summary of qualifications.** Include a list of three to eight bulleted statements that prove you are the ideal candidate for the position.

Education

- **Name your degree or diploma, date of graduation, and institution.** Emphasize your education if your experience is limited.
- **List your major and GPA.** Give information about your studies, but don't inventory all your courses.

Work Experience

- **Itemize your jobs.** Start with your most recent job. Give the employer's name and city, dates of employment (month, year), and most significant job title.
- **Describe your experience.** Use action verbs to summarize achievements and skills relevant to your targeted job.
- **Promote your "soft" skills.** Give evidence of communication, management, and interpersonal talents. Employers want more than empty assurances; try to quantify your skills and accomplishments (*Developed teamwork skills while collaborating with six-member task force in producing 20-page mission statement*).

Special Skills, Achievements, and Awards

- **Highlight your technology skills.** Remember that nearly all employers seek employees who are proficient in using the Web, e-mail, word processing, databases, spreadsheets, and presentation programs.
- **Show that you are a well-rounded individual.** List awards, experiences, and extracurricular activities—particularly if they demonstrate leadership, teamwork, reliability, loyalty, industry, initiative, efficiency, and self-sufficiency.

Final Tips

- **Look for ways to condense your data.** Omit all street addresses except your own. Consolidate your headings. Study models and experiment with formats to find the most readable and efficient groupings.
- **Double-check for parallel phrasing.** Be sure that all entries have balanced construction, such as similar verb forms (*Organized files, trained assistants, scheduled events*).
- **Make your résumé computer friendly.** If there's a chance your résumé will be read by a computer, be sure to remove graphics and emphasize keywords.
- **Consider omitting references.** Have a list of references available for the interview, but don't include them or refer to them unless you have a specific reason to do so.
- **Project professionalism and quality.** Avoid personal pronouns and humour. Use quality paper and a high-performance printer.
- **Resist the urge to inflate your qualifications.** Be accurate in listing your education, grades, honours, job titles, employment dates, and job experience.
- **Proofread, proofread, proofread!** Make this important document perfect by proofreading at least three times. Ask a friend to check it, too.

Submitting

- **Follow instructions for submitting.** Learn whether the employer wants candidates to send a print résumé, a plain-text version, a PDF file, or a fax.
- **Practise sending plain-text résumés.** Before submitting a plain-text résumé, try sending it to yourself or friends. Perfect your skill in achieving an attractive format.

Submitting Your Résumé

If you are responding to a job advertisement, be sure to read the listing carefully to make sure you know how the employer wants you to submit your résumé. Not following the prospective employer's instructions can eliminate you from consideration before your résumé is even reviewed. Employers will probably ask you to submit your résumé in one of the following ways:

Send your résumé in the format the employer requests.

- **Word document.** Recruiters may still ask candidates to send their résumés and cover letters by surface mail. They may also allow applicants to attach their résumés as MS Word documents to e-mail messages, despite the fear of viruses.

- **Plain-text document.** As discussed earlier, many employers expect applicants to submit résumés and cover letters as plain-text documents. This format is widely used for posting to an online job board or for sending by e-mail. Plain-text résumés may be embedded within or attached to e-mail messages.

- **PDF document.** For safety reasons, many employers prefer PDF (portable document format) files. A PDF résumé will look exactly like the original and cannot be altered. Most computers come with Adobe Acrobat Reader for easy reading of PDF files. Converting your résumé to a PDF file, however, requires software, such as Adobe Acrobat.

- **Company database.** Some organizations prefer that you complete an online form with your résumé information. This enables them to plug your data into their formats for rapid searching. You might be able to cut and paste your information into the form.

- **Fax.** Although still a popular way of sending résumés, faxing presents problems in blurring and lost information. If you must fax your résumé, use at least a 12-point font to improve readability. Thinner fonts—such as Times, Palatino, New Century Schoolbook, Arial, and Bookman—are clearer than thicker ones. Avoid underlines, which may look broken or choppy when faxed. Follow up with your polished, printed résumé.

Creating a Customized, Persuasive Cover Letter

LEARNING OBJECTIVE 6

Write a customized cover letter to accompany a résumé.

Job candidates often labour over their résumés but treat the cover letter as an afterthought. Some send out résumés without including a cover letter at all. These critical mistakes could destroy a job search. Even if an advertisement doesn't request one, be sure to distinguish your application with a customized cover letter (also called a *letter of application*). It has three purposes: (1) introducing the résumé, (2) highlighting your strengths in terms of benefits to the reader, and (3) gaining an interview. In many ways your cover letter is a sales letter; it sells your talent and tries to beat the competition. It will, accordingly, include many of the techniques you learned for sales letters in Chapter 9, especially if your letter is unsolicited.

Recruiting professionals disagree about how long to make a cover letter. Many prefer short letters with no more than three paragraphs. Others desire longer letters that supply more information, thus giving them a better opportunity to evaluate a candidate's qualifications. These recruiters argue that hiring and training new employees is expensive and time consuming; therefore, they welcome extra data to guide them in making the best choice the first time. Follow your judgment in writing a brief or a longer cover letter. If you feel, for example, that you need space to explain in more detail what you can do for a prospective employer, do so.

Regardless of its length, a cover letter should have three primary parts: (1) an opening that introduces the message and identifies the position, (2) a body that sells the candidate and focuses on the employer's needs, and (3) a closing that requests an interview and motivates action. When putting your cover letter together, remember

that the biggest mistake job seekers make when writing cover letters is making them sound too generic. You should, therefore, write a personalized, customized cover letter for every position you apply for.

Gaining Attention in the Opening

Your cover letter will be more appealing and will more likely be read if it begins by addressing the reader by name. Rather than sending your letter to the Hiring Manager or Human Resources Department, try to identify the name of the appropriate individual. Call the organization for the name of the person in charge of hiring for the position. If that fails, look on the company Web site under About Us or use professional networking sites, such as LinkedIn, to locate a contact working in the organization. If you still cannot find the name of any person to address, you might replace the salutation of your letter with a subject line such as *Application for Position of* . . . .

> The opening in a cover letter gains attention by addressing the receiver by name.

How you open your cover letter depends largely on whether the application is solicited or unsolicited. If an employment position has been announced and applicants are being solicited, you can use a direct approach. If you do not know whether a position is open and you are prospecting for a job, use an indirect approach. Whether direct or indirect, the opening should attract the attention of the reader. Strive for openings that are more imaginative than *Please consider this letter an application for the position of* . . . or *I would like to apply for.* . . .

Openings for Solicited Jobs.
Here are some of the best techniques to open a cover letter for a job that has been announced:

- **Refer to the name of an employee in the company.** Remember that employers always hope to hire known quantities rather than complete strangers. *Mitchell Sims, a member of your Customer Service Department, told me that IntriPlex is seeking an experienced customer service representative. The enclosed summary of my qualifications demonstrates my preparation for this position.*

> Openers for solicited jobs refer to the source of the information, the job title, and qualifications for the position.

- **Refer to the source of your information precisely.** If you are answering an advertisement, include the exact position advertised and the name and date of the publication. For large organizations it is wise to mention the section of the newspaper where the ad appeared: *The job you advertised in Section C-3 of the June 1* Daily News *for an accounting administrator greatly appeals to me. With my accounting training and computer experience, I believe I could serve Quad Graphics well.*

- **Refer to the job title and describe how your qualifications fit the requirements.** Human resources directors are looking for a match between an applicant's credentials and the job's needs: *Will an honours graduate with a degree in recreation and two years of part-time experience organizing social activities for a convalescent hospital qualify for your position of activity director?*

Openings for Unsolicited Jobs.
If you are unsure whether a position actually exists, you might use a more persuasive opening. Because your goal is to convince this person to read on, try one of the following techniques:

- **Demonstrate an interest in and knowledge of the reader's business.** Show the hiring officer that you have done your research and that this organization is more than a mere name to you: *Because Signa HealthNet, Inc., is organizing a new information management team for its recently established group insurance division, could you use the services of a well-trained information systems graduate who seeks to become a professional systems analyst?*

- **Show how your special talents and background will benefit the company.** Human resources managers need to be convinced that you can do something for them: *Could your rapidly expanding publications division use the services of an editorial assistant who offers exceptional language skills, an honours degree from the University of Prince Edward Island, and two years' experience in producing a campus literary publication?*

> Openers for unsolicited jobs show interest in and knowledge of the company and spotlight reader benefits.

FIGURE 15.13 Solicited Cover Letter

Kendra A. Hawkins

8011 Davies Road NW, Edmonton, AB T6E 4Z6
(780) 492-1244 khawkins@webworx.ca — *Uses personally designed letterhead*

May 23, 2014

Ms. Courtney L. Donahue
Director, Human Resources — *Addresses proper person by name and title*
Premier Enterprises
57 Bedford Drive NE
Calgary, AB T3K 1L2

Dear Ms. Donahue:

Your advertisement for an assistant product manager, appearing May 22 in — *Identifies job and exact page where ad appeared*
Section C of the *Calgary Herald*, immediately caught my attention because my
education and training closely parallel your needs.

According to your advertisement, the job includes "assisting in the coordination
of a wide range of marketing programs as well as analyzing sales results and
tracking marketing budgets." A recent internship at Ventana Corporation — *Relates writer's experiences to job requirements*
introduced me to similar tasks. Assisting the marketing manager enabled me
to analyze the promotion, budget, and overall sales success of two products
Ventana was evaluating. My ten-page report examined the nature of the
current market, the products' life cycles, and their sales/profit return. In
addition to this research, I helped formulate a product merchandising plan and
answered consumers' questions at a local trade show.

Intensive course work in marketing and management, as well as proficiency — *Discusses schooling*
in computer spreadsheets and databases, has given me the kind of marketing
and computer training that Premier probably demands in a product manager.
Moreover, my recent retail sales experience and participation in campus — *Discusses experience*
organizations have helped me develop the kind of customer service and
interpersonal skills necessary for an effective product manager.

After you have examined the enclosed résumé for details of my qualifications, — *Refers reader to résumé*
I would be happy to answer questions. Please call me at (780) 492-1244 to
arrange an interview at your convenience so that we may discuss how my
marketing experience, computer training, and interpersonal skills could — *Asks for interview and repeats main qualifications*
contribute to Premier Enterprises.

Sincerely,

Kendra A. Hawkins

Kendra A. Hawkins

Enclosure

In applying for an advertised job, Kendra Hawkins wrote the solicited cover letter shown in Figure 15.13. Notice that her opening identifies the position and the newspaper completely so that the reader knows exactly what advertisement Kendra means. Using features on her word processing program, Kendra designed her own letterhead that uses her name and looks like professionally printed letterhead paper.

More challenging are unsolicited cover letters, such as Donald Vinton's shown in Figure 15.14. Because he hopes to discover or create a job, his opening must grab the reader's attention immediately. To do that, he capitalizes on company information appearing in an online article. Donald purposely kept his cover letter short and to the point because he anticipated that a busy executive would be unwilling to read a long, detailed letter. Donald's unsolicited letter "prospects" for a job. Some job candidates feel that such letters may be even more productive than efforts to secure advertised jobs since "prospecting" candidates face less competition and show initiative. Notice that Donald's letter uses a personal business letter format with his return address above the date.

FIGURE 15.14 Unsolicited Cover Letter

Uses personal business style with return address above date

2250 Beaver Creek Drive
Aurora, ON L4G 0B4
May 29, 2014

Mr. Richard M. Jannis
Vice President, Operations
Sports World, Inc.
694 Wellington Avenue
Toronto, ON M5G 7K6

Dear Mr. Jannis:

Shows resourcefulness and knowledge of company

Today's *Toronto Star* reports that your organization plans to expand its operations to include national distribution of sporting goods, and it occurs to me that you will be needing highly motivated, self-starting sales representatives and marketing managers. Here are three significant qualifications I have to offer:

Uses bulleted list to make letter easier to read

- Four years of formal training in business administration, including specialized courses in sales management, retailing, marketing promotion, and consumer behaviour

- Practical experience in demonstrating and selling consumer products, as well as successful experience in telemarketing

- Excellent communication skills and a strong interest in most areas of sports (which helped me become a sportscaster at the campus radio station GCNF)

Keeps letter brief to retain reader's attention

Refers to enclosed résumé

May we talk about how I can put these qualifications, and others summarized in the enclosed résumé, to work for Sports World as it develops its national sales force? I'll call during the week of June 5 to discuss your company's expansion plans and the opportunity for an interview.

Takes initiative for follow-up

Sincerely yours,

Donald W. Vinton

Donald W. Vinton

Enclosure

Selling Your Strengths in the Body

Once you have captured the attention of the reader and identified your purpose in the letter opening, you should use the body of the letter to promote your qualifications for this position. If you are responding to an advertisement, you'll want to explain how your preparation and experience fill the stated requirements. If you are prospecting for a job, you may not know the exact requirements. Your employment research and knowledge of your field, however, should give you a reasonably good idea of what is expected for this position.

It's also important to stress reader benefits. In other words, you should describe your strong points in relation to the needs of the employer. Hiring officers want you to tell them what you can do for their organizations. This is more important than telling what courses you took in college or university or what duties you performed in your

> The body of the cover letter promotes the candidate's qualifications for the targeted job.

previous jobs. Instead of *I have completed courses in business communication, report writing, and technical writing,* try this:

> *Courses in business communication, report writing, and technical writing have helped me develop the research and writing skills required of your technical writers.*

Choose your strongest qualifications and show how they fit the targeted job. Remember that students with little experience are better off spotlighting their education and its practical applications, as these candidates did:

> *Because you seek an architect's apprentice with proven ability, I submit a drawing of mine that won second place in the Sinclair College drafting contest last year.*

> *Composing e-mail messages, business letters, memos, and reports in my business communication and office technology courses helped me develop the writing, language, proofreading, and computer skills mentioned in your ad for an administrative assistant.*

Employers seek employees who are team players, take responsibility, show initiative, and learn easily.

In the body of your letter, you may choose to discuss relevant personal traits. Employers are looking for candidates who, among other things, are team players, take responsibility, show initiative, and learn easily. Don't just list several personal traits, though; instead, include documentation that proves you possess these traits. Notice how the following paragraph uses action verbs to paint a picture of a promising candidate:

> *In addition to developing technical and academic skills at Dalhousie University, I have gained interpersonal, leadership, and organizational skills. As vice president of the business students' organization, I helped organize and supervise two successful fundraising events. These activities involved conceptualizing the tasks, motivating others to help, scheduling work sessions, and coordinating the efforts of 35 diverse students in reaching our goal. I enjoyed my success with these activities and look forward to applying such experience in your management trainee program.*

Finally, in this section or the next, you should refer the reader to your résumé. Do so directly or as part of another statement, as shown here:

> *As you will notice from my enclosed résumé, I will graduate in June with a bachelor's degree in business administration.*

Motivating Action in the Closing

The closing of a cover letter confidently requests an interview and makes it easy to respond.

After presenting your case, you should conclude by asking confidently for an interview. Don't ask for the job. To do so would be presumptuous and naïve. In requesting an interview, you might suggest reader benefits or review your strongest points. Sound sincere and appreciative. Remember to make it easy for the reader to agree by supplying your telephone number and the best times to call you. In addition, keep in mind that some hiring officers prefer that you take the initiative to call them. Avoid expressions like *I hope,* which will weaken your closing. Here are possible endings:

> *To add to your staff an industrious, well-trained administrative assistant with proven word processing and communication skills, call me at (905) 492–1433 to arrange an interview. I can meet with you at any time convenient to you.*

> *Next week, after you have examined the enclosed résumé, I will call you to discuss the possibility of arranging an interview.*

Sending Your Cover Letter

Many applicants using technology make the mistake of not including cover letters with their résumés submitted by e-mail, fax, or on corporate Web sites. A résumé that arrives without a cover letter makes the receiver wonder what it is and why it was sent. Recruiters want you to introduce yourself, and they also are eager to see some evidence that you can write. Some candidates either skip the cover letter or think they can get by with one-line cover letters such as this: *Please see attached résumé, and thanks for your consideration.*

FIGURE 15.15 E-Mail Cover Letter

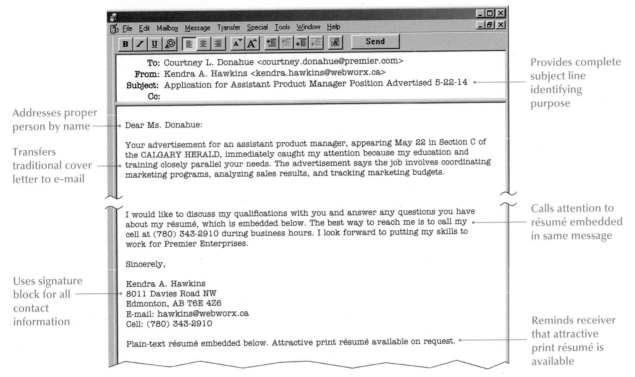

Provides complete subject line identifying purpose

Addresses proper person by name

Transfers traditional cover letter to e-mail

Calls attention to résumé embedded in same message

Uses signature block for all contact information

Reminds receiver that attractive print résumé is available

To: Courtney L. Donahue <courtney.donahue@premier.com>
From: Kendra A. Hawkins <kendra.hawkins@webworx.ca>
Subject: Application for Assistant Product Manager Position Advertised 5-22-14
Cc:

Dear Ms. Donahue:

Your advertisement for an assistant product manager, appearing May 22 in Section C of the CALGARY HERALD, immediately caught my attention because my education and training closely parallel your needs. The advertisement says the job involves coordinating marketing programs, analyzing sales results, and tracking marketing budgets.

I would like to discuss my qualifications with you and answer any questions you have about my résumé, which is embedded below. The best way to reach me is to call my cell at (780) 343-2910 during business hours. I look forward to putting my skills to work for Premier Enterprises.

Sincerely,

Kendra A. Hawkins
8011 Davies Road NW
Edmonton, AB T6E 4Z6
E-mail: hawkins@webworx.ca
Cell: (780) 343-2910

Plain-text résumé embedded below. Attractive print résumé available on request.

If you are serious about landing the job, take the time to prepare a professional cover letter. If you're sending your résumé via e-mail, you may use the same cover letter you would send by surface mail but shorten it a bit. As illustrated in Figure 15.15, an inside address is unnecessary for an e-mail recipient. Also move your return address from the top of the letter to just below your name. Include your e-mail address and phone number. Remove tabs, bullets, underlining, and italics that might be problematic in e-mail messages. If you are submitting your résumé by fax, send the same cover letter you would send by surface mail. If you are submitting your résumé as a PDF file, do the same for your cover letter.

Final Tips for Successful Cover Letters

As you revise your cover letter, notice how many sentences begin with *I*. Although it's impossible to talk about yourself without using *I*, you can reduce "I" domination with this writing technique. Make activities and outcomes and not yourself the subjects of sentences. For example, rather than *I took classes in business communication and computer applications*, say *Classes in business communication and computer applications prepared me to . . . .* Instead of *I enjoyed helping customers*, say *Helping customers was a real pleasure.*

Like the résumé, your cover letter must look professional and suggest quality. This means using a traditional letter style, such as block. Also, be sure to print it on the same quality paper as your résumé. As with your résumé, proofread it several times yourself, then have a friend read it for content and mechanics. Don't rely on spell check to find all the errors. Just like your résumé, your cover letter must be perfect.

Before preparing a customized cover letter, refer to the Checklist box for tips.

> A cover letter should look professional and suggest quality.

Checklist

Preparing and Sending a Customized Cover Letter

Opening

- **Use the receiver's name.** Whenever possible, address the proper individual by name.

- **Identify your information source, if appropriate.** In responding to an advertisement, specify the position advertised, the date, and the publication name. If someone referred you, name that person.

- **Gain the reader's attention.** Use one of these techniques: (a) tell how your qualifications fit the job specifications, (b) show knowledge of the reader's business, (c) describe how your special talents will be assets to the company, or (d) use an original and relevant expression.

Body

- **Describe what you can do for the reader.** Demonstrate how your background and training fill the job requirements.

- **Highlight your strengths.** Summarize your principal assets in terms of education, experience, and special skills. Avoid repeating specific data from your résumé.

- **Refer to your résumé.** In this section or the closing, direct the reader to the attached résumé. Do so directly or incidentally as part of another statement.

Closing

- **Ask for an interview.** Also consider reviewing your strongest points or suggesting how your assets will benefit the company.

- **Make it easy to respond.** Tell when you can be reached during office hours or announce when you will call the reader. Note that some recruiters prefer that you call them.

Sending

- **Include a cover letter with your résumé.** Send your cover letter along with your résumé as a Word attachment, embedded in an e-mail message, as a plain-text attachment, or as a PDF file.

- **If you e-mail your cover letter, put your contact information in the signature area.** Move your return address from the top of the letter to the signature block. Include your phone number and e-mail address.

Summary of Learning Objectives

1 **Prepare for employment by identifying your interests, evaluating your assets, recognizing the changing nature of jobs, and choosing a career path.** The employment process begins with an analysis of your preferences and your qualifications. Because the nature of jobs is changing, your future work may include flexible work assignments, multiple employers, and constant retraining. You can learn more about career opportunities through your campus career centre, the Web, your library, internships, part-time jobs, interviews, classified ads, and professional organizations.

2 **Apply both online and traditional job search techniques.** Electronic job-search techniques include visiting the big commercial sites (such as Monster, Yahoo HotJobs, and Workopolis) and corporations' sites, professional organizations' sites, and niche sites. To establish online networking, job seekers are joining social sites such as LinkedIn and Facebook. Traditional job-search techniques include checking classified ads, studying announcements in professional organizations, contacting companies directly, signing up for campus interviews, attending career fairs, asking for advice from instructors, and developing a personal network of contacts.

3 **Appreciate the need to customize your résumé and know whether to choose a chronological or a functional résumé style.** Because of intense competition, job seekers must customize their résumés for every position sought. Chronological résumés, listing work and education by dates, rank highest with recruiters. Functional résumés, highlighting skills instead of jobs, appeal to people changing careers or those having negative employment histories. Functional résumés are also effective for recent graduates who have little work experience.

Get more practice at **www.guffeybrief4e.nelson.com**

4 Organize your qualifications and information into effective résumé segments. In preparing a résumé, organize your skills and achievements so that they aim at a particular job or company. Study models to arrange most effectively your main heading, career objective (optional), summary of qualifications, education, work experience, capabilities, awards and activities, personal data (optional), and references (optional). Use action verbs to show how your assets will help the target organization.

5 Describe techniques that optimize a résumé for today's technologies, including preparing a scannable résumé, a plain-text résumé, and an e-portfolio. Candidates should consider preparing a scannable résumé that limits line length, avoids fancy formatting, and emphasizes keywords and keyword phrases. Keywords are nouns that an employer might use to describe a position and its requirements. Plain-text résumés are stripped of all formatting and prepared as text files so that they may be embedded within e-mail messages or submitted online. An e-portfolio is a collection of digitized materials that illustrate a candidate's performance, talents, and accomplishments. E-portfolios may be posted at Web sites or burned onto CDs or DVDs.

6 Write a customized cover letter to accompany a résumé. Gain attention in the opening by addressing the receiver by name and mentioning the job or a person who referred you. Build interest in the body by stressing your strengths in relation to the stated requirements. Explain what you can do for the targeted company. Refer to your résumé, request an interview, and make it easy for the receiver to reach you. If you send your cover letter by e-mail, shorten it a bit and include complete contact information in the signature block. Remove tabs, bullets, underlining, and italics that could be problematic in e-mail.

Chapter Review

1. You are about to begin your job search. What should you do first? (Obj. 1)

2. List five sources of career information. (Obj. 1)

3. Has searching for a job online replaced traditional job-search methods? Explain. (Obj. 2)

4. Using the Web, where should job candidates look in addition to searching the big job board sites? (Obj. 2)

5. What is a customized résumé, and why should a job seeker have one? (Obj. 3)

6. What is a chronological résumé, and what are its advantages and disadvantages? (Obj. 3)

7. What is a functional résumé, and what are its advantages and disadvantages? (Obj. 3)

8. List five tips for writing an effective career objective on your résumé. (Obj. 4)

9. Describe a summary of qualifications and explain why it is increasingly popular on résumés. (Obj. 4)

10. In addition to technical skills, what traits and capabilities are employers seeking? (Obj. 4)

11. To optimize your résumé for today's technologies, how many versions of your résumé should you expect to make? What are they? (Obj. 5)

12. What changes must be made in a typical résumé to make it effective for computer scanning? (Obj. 5)

13. What are the three purposes of a cover letter? (Obj. 6)

14. What information goes in the body of a cover letter? (Obj. 6)

15. When you send a cover letter within an e-mail message, what changes should you make to the format of the letter? (Obj. 6)

Critical Thinking

1. How has the Internet changed job searching for individuals and recruiters? Has the change had a positive or a negative effect? Why? (Obj. 1)

2. How is a résumé different from a company employment application? (Objs. 1, 2)

3. Some job candidates think that applying for unsolicited jobs can be more fruitful than applying for advertised openings. Discuss the advantages and disadvantages of letters that "prospect" for jobs. (Obj. 5)

4. In regard to hiring, conventional wisdom holds that it's all about whom you know. How can job candidates find an insider to refer them for a job opening? (Obj. 2)

5. **Ethical Issue:** Job candidate Karen accepts a position with Company A. One week later she receives a better offer from Company B. She wants very much to accept it. What should she do?

Activities

Note: All Documents for Analysis may be downloaded from **www.guffeybrief4e.nelson.com** so that you do not have to rekey the entire message.

15.1 Document for Analysis: Résumé (Obj. 4)

One effective way to improve your writing skills is to critique and edit the résumé of someone else.

Your Task. Analyze the following poorly organized résumé. Discuss its weaknesses. Your instructor may ask you to revise sections of this résumé before showing you an improved version.

Résumé of Brenda Ann Trudell
9 Franklin Terrace
Timmins, ON
Home: 834-4583 Cell: 594-2985
E-mail: supahsnugglykitty@aol.com

OBJECTIVE: I would like to find an entry-level position with a large corporation that offers opportunity for advancement

SKILLS: Word processing, spreadsheet, QuickBooks, Internet, Excel, PowerPoint, Excel, database.

EDUCATION
Northern College, Timmins, ON. Now working on diploma in Business Administration.

Major: Accounting. My GPA in major is 3.5. Expected diploma date: June 2013. Very interested in forensic accounting. Took courses in: Analysis and Application of Accounting Data and Financial Reporting.

EXPERIENCE
Assistant bookkeeper, 2011 to present. Marsh and McLennan, Inc., Timmins. I work with many small businesses to keep their bookkeeping records. I have to be accurate, and I get little supervision. I prepare income tax returns, I monitor and update A/R records for Overland Truck Lines. I am responsible for the payroll records at three firms. The owner of Marsh and McLennan said I was reliable and painstaking.

Peterson Controls Inc., Timmins. I held a data processing internship from July to October 2010. I worked with spreadsheets and also kept information for production uptime and downtime. Prepared graphs, answered phones; helped people with collecting and photocopying their data.

2009–2011. Northern College, Timmins. I was coordinator of Student Tax Clinic Project. I marketed the program to Northern students. I scheduled volunteers, got the supplies, and kept track of all appointments.

Community Service: March of Dimes Drive at Central Park High School; All Souls Unitarian Church, assistant director of Children's Choir.

15.2 Document for Analysis: Cover Letter (Obj. 6)

The following cover letter accompanies Brenda Trudell's résumé (Activity 15.1).
Your Task. Analyze each section of the following cover letter written by Brenda and list its weaknesses. Your instructor may

ask you to revise this letter before showing you an improved version.

Dear Human Resources Director:

I would like you to consider me for the accounting position that I saw for Mead Products. I am working part time and trying to finish my diploma program, but I think a position at your industry-leading firm would be beneficial and would certainly look good on my résumé.

I have been studying accounting at Northern College for two years, and I have taken courses in business law, management, finance, accounting, and marketing. I am most interested in my accounting courses, especially in forensic accounting.

I have worked at Marsh and McLennan as an assistant bookkeeper. I should mention that I have had another internship, which was at Peterson Controls. I worked on spreadsheets at Peterson. I also was coordinator of the Student Tax Clinic Program at Northern, which helped me develop leadership and interpersonal skills. I think that all of these positions gave me the skills needed to be a good intern for you.

I am a competent, reliable, well-organized person who gets along pretty well with others. I feel that I have a strong foundation in accounting as a result of my course work and my experience. I hope you will agree that, along with my personal qualities and my desire to succeed, I qualify for the open accounting position with your company.

Yours very truly,

15.3 Identifying Your Employment Interests (Obj. 1)

Your Task. In an e-mail or a memo addressed to your instructor, answer the questions in the section "Identifying Your Interests" at the beginning of the chapter. Draw a conclusion from your answers. What kind of career, company, position, and location seem to fit your self-analysis?

15.4 Evaluating Your Qualifications (Objs. 1, 2, and 3)

Your Task. Prepare four worksheets that inventory your qualifications in these areas: employment, education, capabilities and skills, and honours and activities. Use active verbs when appropriate.

a. **Employment.** Begin with your most recent job or internship. For each position list the following information: employer, job title, dates of employment, and three to five duties, activities, or accomplishments. Emphasize activities related to your job goal. Strive to quantify your achievements.

b. **Education.** List degrees, diplomas, certificates, and training accomplishments. Include courses, seminars, or skills that are relevant to your job goal. Calculate your GPA in your major.

c. **Capabilities and skills.** List all capabilities and skills that recommend you for the job you seek. Use words like *skilled, competent, trained, experienced,* and *able to.* Also list five or more qualities or interpersonal skills necessary for a successful individual in your chosen field. Write action statements demonstrating that you possess some of these qualities. Empty assurances aren't good enough; try to show evidence (*Developed teamwork skills by working with a committee of eight to produce a. . . .*)

d. **Awards, honours, and activities.** Explain any awards so that the reader will understand them. List campus, community, and professional activities that suggest you are a well-rounded individual or possess traits relevant to your target job.

15.5 Choosing a Career Path (Obj. 1)

> **WEB**

Many people know amazingly little about the work done in various occupations and the training requirements.
Your Task. Use Working in Canada (**www.workingincanada. gc.ca**) to learn more about an occupation of your choice. Find the description of a position for which you could apply in two to five years. Learn about what workers do on the job, working conditions, training and education needed, earnings, and expected job prospects. Print the pages that describe employment in the area in which you are interested. If your instructor directs, attach these copies to the cover letter you will write in Activity 15.9.

15.6 Locating Salary Information (Obj. 1)

> **WEB**

What salary can you expect in your chosen career?
Your Task. Visit Working In Canada's Wages and Outlook Reports section at **www.workingincanada.gc.ca** (select Researchers from the menu at left, and then click Wages and Outlook Report). Select an occupation based on the kind of employment you are seeking now or will be seeking after you graduate. What wages can you expect in this occupation? Print a copy of the wage information. Click to learn more about this occupation. Take notes on three or four interesting bits of information you learned about this occupation. Bring a printout of the wage information to class and be prepared to discuss what you learned about this occupation.

15.7 Searching the Job Market (Obj. 1)

Where are the jobs? Even though you may not be in the market at the moment, become familiar with the kinds of available positions because job awareness should become an important part of your education.
Your Task. Clip or print a job advertisement or announcement from (a) the classified section of a newspaper, (b) a job board on the Web, (c) a company Web site, or (d) a professional association listing. Select an advertisement or announcement describing the kind of employment you are seeking now or plan to seek when you graduate. Save this advertisement or announcement to attach to the résumé you will write in Activity 15.8.

15.8 Writing Your Résumé (Obj. 4)

Your Task. Using the data you developed in Activity 15.4, write your résumé. Aim it at a full-time job, part-time position, or internship. Attach a job listing for a specific position (from Activity 15.7). Also prepare a list of references. Revise your résumé until it is perfect.

15.9 Preparing Your Cover Letter (Obj. 6)

Your Task. Write a cover letter introducing your résumé. Again, revise until it is perfect.

15.10 Swapping Résumés (Obj. 2)

A terrific way to get ideas for improving your résumé is seeing how other students have developed their résumés.
Your Task. Bring your completed résumé to class. Attach a plain sheet with your name at the top. In small groups exchange your résumés. Each reviewer should provide at least two supportive comments and one suggestion for improvement on the cover sheet. Reviewers should sign their names with their comments.

Grammar and Mechanics C.L.U.E. Review 15

Total Review

Each of the following sentences has a total of **three** errors in grammar, punctuation, capitalization, usage, or spelling. On a separate sheet, write a correct version. Avoid adding new phrases or rewriting sentences in your own words. When finished, compare your responses with the key beginning on page Key-1.
Example: One West coast company found that e-mail consumed about 24% of staff members workdays.
Revision: One West **Coast** company found that e-mail consumed about **24 percent** of staff **members'** workdays.

1. Many employers use sights like Facebook to learn about potential employees. Which mean job seekers must maintain a professional online presence.

2. To conduct a safe online job search, you must: (a) Use only reputable job boards, (2) keep careful records, and (c) limit the number of sites on which you post your résumé.

3. When Melissas job search was complete she had received 4 job offers.

4. If you loose your job dont become discouraged by the thought of having to find another.

5. Joseph wondered whether it was alright to ask his professor for employment advise?

6. At last months staff meeting team members examined several candidates résumés.

7. Rather then schedule face to face interviews the team investigated videoconferencing.

8. 12 applicants will be interviewed on April 10th, consequently, we may need to work late to accommodate them.

9. Professional e-mail manners reflects on you and your company, however, to few employees are trained properly.

10. In the last issue of *Newsweek* did you see the article titled "Should a résumé include a Career Objective?"

Endnotes

1. Twitter. (January/February 2011). *Canadian Business,* p. 31

2. Financial outlook. (1999, March 22). *Maclean's,* p. 37.

3. Catano, V. M., Wiesner, W. H., Hackett, R. D., & Methot, L. (2010). *Recruitment and Selection in Canada,* 4th ed. Toronto: Nelson, p. 149.

4. Levy, R. (2010). How to use social media in your job search. *About.com.* Retrieved February 12, 2010, from http://jobsearch.about.com/od/networking/a/socialmedia.htm

5. Korkki, P. (2007, July 1). So easy to apply, so hard to be noticed. *The New York Times.* Retrieved July 8, 2008, from LexisNexis database.

6. Marquardt, K. (2008, February 21). 5 tips on finding a new job. *U.S. News & World Report.* Retrieved February 16, 2010, from http://www.usnews.com/articles/business/careers/2008/02/21/5-tips-on-finding-a-new-job.html

7. Crispin, G., & Mehler, M. (2009, February). CareerXroads 8th annual source of hire study. *CareerXroads.com.* Retrieved February 12, 2010, from http://www.careerxroads.com/news/SourcesOfHire09.pdf

8. Zee InfoTech. (2009). *Links to top Canadian job sites.* Retrieved August 6, 2009, from http://www.zeeinfotech.com/zee_visa/info Canada/working/links.html

9. Brown, J., Cober, R. T., Kane, K., Levy, P. E., & Shalhoop, J. (2006). Proactive personality and the successful job search: A field investigation with college graduates. *Journal of Applied Psychology, 91*(3), 717–726. Retrieved July 15, 2007, from Business Source Premier (EBSCO) database.

10. Korkki, P. (2007, July 1). So easy to apply, so hard to be noticed. *The New York Times,* p. BU YT 16.

11. Medzilla. (2002, November 5). Résumé styles: Chronological versus functional? Best-selling author Richard H. Beatty joins in the résumé discussion [press release]. Retrieved July 21, 2007, from http://www.medzilla.com/press11502.html

12. Blackburn-Brockman, E., & Belanger, K. (2001, January). One page or two: A national study of CPA recruiters' preferences for résumé length. *Journal of Business Communication, 38*(1), 29–57.

13. Isaacs, K. (2007). *How to decide on résumé length.* Retrieved July 21, 2007, from http://www.resumepower.com/resume-length.html

14. Hansen, K. (2007). *Should you use a career objective on your résumé?* Retrieved July 21, 2007, from http://www.quintcareers.com/resume_objectives.html; Half, R. (2007). Some résumé objectives do more harm than good. Retrieved July 21, 2007, from http://www.careerjournal.com/jobhunting/resumes/19971231-half3.html

15. Build the résumé employers want. (n.d.). Retrieved July 21, 2007, from http://www.jobweb.com/resources/library/Interviews

16. Locke, A. (2008, June 18). Is your resume telling the wrong story? *The Ladders.com.* Retrieved February 15, 2010, from http://www.theladders.com/career-advice/Is-Your-Resume-Telling-the-Wrong-Story

17. Washington, T. (2007). Effective résumés bring results to life. Retrieved July 21, 2007, from http://www.careerjournal.com/jobhunting/resumes/ 20000913-washington. html

18. The video résumé technique. (2007). Retrieved July 20, 2007, from http://www.collegegrad.com/jobsearch/Guerrilla-Insider-Techniques/The-Video-Résumé-Technique

19. Kidwell, R. E., Jr. (2004, May). "Small" lies, big trouble: The unfortunate consequences of résumé padding from Janet Cooke to George O'Leary. *Journal of Business Ethics, 51*(2), 175–184.

20. Rigdon, J. E. (1992, June 17). Deceptive résumés can be door-openers but can become an employee's undoing. *The Wall Street Journal,* p. B1. See also Solomon, B. (1998, April). Too good to be true? *Management Review,* 28.

21. Needleman, S. E. (2007, March 6). Why sneaky tactics may not help résumé. *The Wall Street Journal,* p. B8.

CHAPTER 16

Interviewing and Following Up

OBJECTIVES

After studying this chapter, you should be able to

1. Understand the importance of a job interview, its purposes, and its forms, including screening, hiring or placement, and one-on-one, panel, group, sequential, stress, and online interviews.

2. Describe what to do before an in-person interview, including researching the target company, rehearsing success stories, practising answers to possible questions, and cleaning up digital dirt.

3. Explain how to perform during an interview, including sending positive nonverbal messages and using good techniques in answering questions.

4. Describe how to answer typical interview questions, such as those that seek to get acquainted, gauge your interest, probe your experience, explore your accomplishments, look to the future, and inquire about salary expectations.

5. Understand how to close an interview positively, including asking meaningful questions.

6. Outline the activities that take place after an interview, including thanking the interviewer and contacting references.

7. Understand how to complete employment applications and write résumé follow-up, rejection follow-up, job acceptance, and job rejection messages.

Image Source/Getty Images

When hiring managers were interviewed regarding the most common mistakes prospective employees make, answering a cellphone or texting during the interview topped the list, followed by dressing inappropriately and appearing uninterested. However, they also cited more outrageous actions, including hugging the hiring manager at the end of the interview and providing a copy of a college diploma with the original name blanked out and the interviewee's name added.[1] What unusual interview stories have you heard?

The Job Interview: Understanding Its Importance, Purposes, and Types

LEARNING OBJECTIVE **1**

Understand the importance of a job interview, its purposes, and its forms, including screening, hiring or placement, and one-on-one, panel, group, sequential, stress, and online interviews.

A job interview can change your life. Because employment is a major part of everyone's life, the job interview takes on enormous importance. Interviewing is equally significant whether you are completing your education and searching for your first serious position or in the workforce and striving to change jobs.

Everyone agrees that job interviews are extremely stressful. However, the more you learn about the process and the more prepared you are, the less stress you will feel. It's also important to realize that a job interview is a two-way street. It's not just about being judged by the employer. You, the applicant, will be using the job interview to evaluate the employer. Do you really want to work for this organization?

This chapter will increase your interviewing effectiveness and confidence by explaining the purposes and kinds of interviews and how to prepare for them. You will learn how to gather information about an employer and how to reduce nervousness, control body language, and fight fear during an interview. You will pick up tips for responding to recruiters' favourite questions and learn how to cope with illegal questions and salary matters. Moreover, you will receive pointers on significant questions you can ask during an interview. Finally, you will learn what you should do as a successful follow-up to an interview.

Yes, job interviews can be intimidating and stressful. However, you can expect to ace an interview when you know what's coming and when you prepare thoroughly. It's often the degree of preparation that determines who gets the job. First you need to know the purposes of employment interviews and what types of interviews you might encounter in your job search.

Purposes of Employment Interviews

During job interviews candidates try to (a) convince an employer of their potential, (b) learn about the job, and (c) amplify résumé information.

An interview has several purposes for you as a job candidate. It is an opportunity to (a) convince the employer of your potential, (b) find out more about the job and the company, and (c) expand on the information in your résumé. This is the time for you to gather information about whether you would fit into the company culture. You should also be thinking about whether this job suits your career goals.

From the employer's perspective, the interview is an opportunity to (a) assess your abilities in relation to the requirements for the position; (b) discuss your training, experience, knowledge, and abilities in more detail; (c) see what drives and motivates you; and (d) decide whether you would fit into the organization.

Types of Employment Interviews

Job applicants generally face two kinds of interviews: screening interviews and hiring or placement interviews. You must succeed in the first to proceed to the second. Once you make it to the hiring or placement interview, you will find a variety of interview styles, including one-on-one, panel, group, sequential, stress, and online interviews. You will be better prepared if you know what to expect in each type of interview.

Screening Interviews. Screening interviews do just that—they screen candidates to filter those who fail to meet minimum requirements. Companies use screening interviews to save time and money by eliminating less qualified candidates before scheduling face-to-face interviews. Although some screening interviews are conducted during job fairs or on campuses, most screening interviews take place on the telephone, and some take place online.

During a screening interview, you will likely be asked to provide details about education and experience listed on your résumé; therefore, you must be prepared to sell your qualifications. Remember that the person conducting the screening interview is trying to determine whether you should move on to the next step in the interview process.

Hiring or Placement Interviews. The most promising candidates selected from screening interviews will be invited to hiring or placement interviews. Hiring managers want to learn whether candidates are motivated, qualified, and a good fit for the position. Their goal is to learn how the candidate would fit into their organization. Conducted in depth, hiring or placement interviews may take many forms.

One-on-One Interviews. In one-on-one interviews, which are the most common type, you can expect to sit down with a company representative and talk about the job and your qualifications. If the representative is the hiring manager, questions will be specific and job related. If the representative is from human resources, the questions will probably be more general.

Panel Interviews. Panel interviews are usually conducted by people who will be your supervisors and colleagues. Usually seated around a table, interviewers take turns asking questions. Panel interviews are advantageous because they save time and show you how the staff works together. In answering questions, keep eye contact with the questioner and with the others. Try to take notes during the interview so that you can remember each person's questions and what was important to that individual.[2]

Group Interviews. Group interviews occur when a company interviews several candidates for the same position at the same time. Some employers use this technique to measure leadership skills and communication styles. During a group interview, stay focused on the interviewer, and treat the other candidates with respect.

Sequential Interviews. Sequential interviews allow a candidate to meet with two or more interviewers on a one-on-one basis over several hours or days. You must listen carefully and respond positively to all interviewers. Sell your qualifications to each one; don't assume that any interviewer knows what was said in a previous interview.

Stress Interviews. Stress interviews are meant to test your reactions during nerve-racking situations. You may be forced to wait a long time before being greeted by the interviewer, you may be given a test with an impossible time limit, or you may be treated rudely by one or more of the interviewers. Another stress interview technique is to have interviewers ask questions at a rapid rate. If you are asked rapid-fire questions from many directions, take the time to slow things down. The best way to handle stress questions is to remain calm and give carefully considered answers.

> Screening interviews are intended to eliminate those who fail to meet minimum requirements.

> In hiring or placement interviews, recruiters try to learn how the candidate would fit into their organization.

> The various kinds of hiring interviews include one-on-one, panel, group, sequential, stress, and online.

Online Interviews. Many companies today use technology to interview job candidates from a distance. Although conference call interviews have long been used, some companies use webcams to conduct interviews. Webcam interviews save job applicants and companies time and money, especially when applicants are not in the same geographic location as the company. Even though your interview may be online via a webcam, don't take it any less seriously than a face-to-face interview.

No matter what interview structure you encounter, you will feel more comfortable and be better prepared if you know what to do before, during, and after the interview.

Before the Interview

LEARNING OBJECTIVE **2**

Describe what to do before an in-person interview, including researching the target company, rehearsing success stories, practising answers to possible questions, and cleaning up digital dirt.

Once you have sent out at least one résumé or filled out at least one job application, you must consider yourself an active job seeker. Being active in the job market means that you should be prepared to be contacted by potential employers. As discussed earlier, employers use screening interviews to narrow the list of candidates. If you do well in the screening interview, you will be invited to an in-person or online job interview.

Ensuring Professional Phone Techniques

Even with the popularity of e-mail, most employers contact job applicants by phone to set up interviews. Employers can judge how well applicants communicate by hearing their voices and expressions over the phone. Therefore, once you are actively looking for a job, anytime the phone rings, it could be a potential employer. Don't make the mistake of letting an unprofessional voice mail message or a lazy roommate ruin your chances. To make the best impression, try these tips:

- Invest in a good answering machine or voice mail service. Make sure that your outgoing message is concise and professional, with no distracting background sounds. It should be in your own voice and include your full name for clarity.

- Tell those who might answer your phone at home about your job search. Explain to them the importance of acting professionally and taking complete messages.

- If you have children, prevent them from answering the phone during your job search. Children of all ages are not known for taking good messages!

- If you have put your cellphone number on your résumé, don't answer it unless you are in a good location to carry on a conversation with an employer.

- Use voice mail to screen calls. By screening incoming calls, you can be totally in control when you return a prospective employer's call. Organize your materials and ready yourself psychologically for the conversation.

Making the First Conversation Impressive

Whether you answer the phone directly or return an employer's call, make sure you are prepared for the conversation. Remember that this is the first time the employer has heard your voice. How you conduct yourself on the phone will create a lasting impression. To make that first impression a positive one, follow these tips:

- Keep a list near the telephone of positions for which you have applied.

- Treat any call from an employer just like an interview. Use a professional tone and businesslike language. Be polite and enthusiastic, and sell your qualifications.

- If caught off guard by the call, ask whether you can call back in a few minutes. Take that time to organize your materials and yourself.

- Have a copy of your résumé available so that you can answer any questions that come up. Also have your list of references, a calendar, and a notepad handy.

- Be prepared for a screening interview. As discussed earlier, this might occur during the first phone call.

- Take good notes during the phone conversation. Obtain accurate directions, and verify the spelling of your interviewer's name. If you will be interviewed by more than one person, get all their names.

Before you hang up, reconfirm the date and time of your interview. You could say something like *I look forward to meeting with you next Wednesday at 2 p.m.*

Researching the Target Company

After scheduling an in-person interview, it's time to begin in-depth research. One of the most important steps in effective interviewing is gathering detailed information about a prospective employer. Never enter an interview cold. Recruiters are impressed by candidates who have done their homework.

Visit the library or search the Web for information and articles about the target company or its field, service, or product. Visit the company's Web site and read everything. Call the company to request annual reports, catalogues, or brochures. Ask about the organization and possibly the interviewer. Learn something about the company's history, mission and goals, size, geographic locations, number of employees, customers, competitors, culture, management structure, names of leaders, reputation in the community, financial condition, strengths and weaknesses, and future plans. Also learn what you can about the industry in which the company operates and take some time to analyze the company's advertising, including sales and marketing brochures. Talking with company employees is always a good idea, if you can manage it. They are probably the best source of inside information. Try to be introduced to someone who is currently employed—but not working in the immediate area where you want to be hired. Be sure to seek out someone who is discreet.

Blogs are also good sources for company research. Many employees maintain both formal and informal blogs, where they share anecdotes and information about their employers. You can use these blogs to learn about a company's culture, its current happenings, and its future plans. Many job seekers find that they can get a more realistic picture of a company's day-to-day culture by reading blogs than they would by reading news articles or company Web site information.[3] Also join the company's Facebook page, and start following the company on Twitter to gather even more information before your interview.

In learning about a company, you may uncover information that convinces you that this is not the company for you. It's always better to learn about negatives early in the process. More likely, though, the information you collect will help you tailor your application and interview responses to the organization's needs. You know how flattered you feel when an employer knows about you and your background. That feeling works both ways. Employers are pleased when job candidates take an interest in them. Be ready to put in plenty of effort in investigating a target employer because this effort really pays off at interview time.

Preparing and Practising

After you have learned about the target organization, study the job description or job listing. Knowing as much as you can about the position enables you to practise your best response strategies before the interview.

The most successful job candidates never go into interviews unprepared. They rehearse success stories and practise answers to typical questions. They also clean up digital dirt and plan their responses to any problem areas on their résumés. As part of

Before an interview, take time to research the target company and learn about its goals, customers, competitors, reputation, and so forth.

Blogs can provide authentic information about a company's culture, current happenings, and future plans.

their preparation before the interview, they decide what to wear, and they gather the items they plan to take with them.

Rehearse Success Stories.

To feel confident and be able to sell your qualifications, prepare and practise success stories. These stories are specific examples of your educational and work-related experience that demonstrate your qualifications and achievements. Look over the job description and your résumé to determine what skills, training, personal characteristics, and experience you want to emphasize during the interview. Then prepare a success story for each one. Incorporate numbers, such as dollars saved or percentage of sales increase, whenever possible. Your success stories should be detailed but brief. Think of them as 30-second sound bites.

Practise telling your success stories until they fluently roll off your tongue and sound natural. Then in the interview be certain to find places to insert them. Tell stories about (a) dealing with a crisis, (b) handling a tough interpersonal situation, (c) successfully juggling many priorities, (d) changing course to deal with changed circumstances, (e) learning from a mistake, (f) working on a team, and (g) going above and beyond expectations.[4]

Practise Answers to Possible Questions.

Imagine the kinds of questions you may be asked and work out sample answers. Although you can't anticipate precise questions, you can expect to be asked about your education, skills, experience, and availability. Recite answers to typical interview questions in front of a mirror, with a friend, while driving in your car, or in spare moments. Keep practising until you have the best responses down pat. Consider recording a practise session to see and hear how you answer questions. Do you look and sound enthusiastic?

Clean Up Any Digital Dirt.

Many companies that recruit on college and university campuses are now using Google and Yahoo to screen applicants. Review your online presence, and clean it up by using the following steps.

- **Remove questionable content.** Remove any incriminating, provocative, or distasteful photos, content, and links that could make you look unprofessional to potential employers.

- **Stay positive.** Don't complain about things in your professional or personal life online.

- **Be selective about who is on your list of friends.** You don't want to miss out on an opportunity because you seem to associate with negative, immature, or unprofessional people. Your best bet is to make your personal networking pages private.

- **Avoid joining groups or fan pages that may be viewed negatively.** Remember that online searchers can turn up your online activities, including group memberships, blog postings, and so on. If you think any activity you are involved with might show poor judgment, remove yourself immediately.

- **Don't discuss your job search if you are still employed.** Employees can find themselves in trouble with their current employers by writing status updates or sending tweets about their job search.

- **Set up a professional social networking page.** Use Facebook, LinkedIn, or other social networking sites to create a professional page.

Expect to Explain Problem Areas on Your Résumé.

Interviewers are certain to question you about problem areas on your résumé. If you have little or no experience, you might emphasize your recent training and up-to-date skills. If you have gaps in your résumé, be prepared to answer questions about them positively and truthfully. If you were fired from a job, accept some responsibility for what happened and explain what you gained from the experience. Don't criticize a previous employer and don't hide the real reasons. If you received low grades for one term, explain why and point to your improved grades in subsequent terms.

Decide How to Dress. What you wear to a job interview still matters. Even if some employees in the organization dress casually, you should look qualified, competent, and successful. Avoid loud colours; strive for a coordinated, natural appearance. Favourite "power" colours for interviews are grey and dark blue. Cover tattoos and conceal body piercings; these can be a turnoff for many interviewers. Don't overdo jewellery, and make sure that what you do wear is clean, pressed, odour free, and lint free. Shoes should be polished and scuff free. To summarize, ensure that what you wear projects professionalism and shows your respect for the interview situation.

Gather Items to Bring. Decide what you should bring with you to the interview and get everything ready the night before. You should plan to bring copies of your résumé, your reference lists, a notebook and pen, money for parking, and samples of your work, if appropriate. Place everything in a businesslike briefcase to add that final professional touch to your look.

During the Interview

On the day of your interview, arrive a little early so that you have time to park and do some last-minute grooming. As you enter the office, be courteous and congenial to everyone. You are being judged not only by the interviewer but also by the receptionist and anyone else who sees you before and after the interview. They will notice how you sit, what you read, and even whether you washed your hands after using the restroom. Introduce yourself to the receptionist and wait to be invited to sit. You may be asked to fill out a job application while you wait. Tips for completing job applications effectively appear later in this chapter.

LEARNING OBJECTIVE 3

Explain how to perform during an interview, including sending positive nonverbal messages and using good techniques in answering questions.

Sending Positive Nonverbal Messages and Acting Professionally

You have already sent nonverbal messages to your interviewer by arriving on time, being courteous, dressing professionally, and greeting the receptionist confidently. You will continue to send nonverbal messages throughout the interview. Remember that what comes out of your mouth and what is written on your résumé are not the only messages an interviewer receives from you. Nonverbal messages also create powerful impressions on people. Here are suggestions that will help you send the right nonverbal messages during interviews:

- **Control your body movements.** Keep your hands, arms, and elbows to yourself. Don't lean on a desk. Keep your feet on the floor. Don't cross your arms in front of you. Keep your hands out of your pockets.

- **Exhibit good posture.** Sit erect, leaning forward slightly. Don't slouch in your chair; at the same time, don't look too stiff and uncomfortable. Good posture demonstrates confidence and interest.

- **Practise appropriate eye contact.** A direct eye gaze, at least in North America, suggests interest and trustworthiness. If you are being interviewed by a panel, remember to maintain eye contact with all interviewers.

- **Use gestures effectively.** Nod to show agreement and interest. Gestures should be used as needed, but don't overdo it.

- **Smile enough to convey a positive attitude.** Have a friend give you honest feedback on whether you generally smile too much or not enough.

- **Listen attentively.** Show the interviewer you are interested and attentive by listening carefully to the questions being asked. This will also help you answer questions appropriately.

- **Turn off your cellphone or other electronic devices.** Avoid the embarrassment of allowing your cellphone to ring or your BlackBerry to buzz during an interview by turning it completely off, not just switching it to vibrate.

- **Don't chew gum.** Chewing gum during an interview is distracting and unprofessional.

- **Sound enthusiastic and interested—but sincere.** The tone of your voice has an enormous effect on the words you say. Avoid sounding bored, frustrated, or sarcastic during an interview. Employers want employees who are enthusiastic and interested.

- **Avoid "empty" words.** Filling your answers with verbal pauses, such as *um, uh, like,* and *basically,* communicates that you are unprepared. Also avoid annoying distractions, such as clearing your throat repeatedly or sighing deeply.

Projecting a Professional Demeanour

Greet the interviewer confidently, and don't be afraid to initiate a handshake. Doing so exhibits professionalism and confidence. Extend your hand, look the interviewer directly in the eye, smile pleasantly, and say, *I'm pleased to meet you, Mr. Thomas. I am Constance Ferraro.* In this culture a firm, not crushing, handshake sends a nonverbal message of poise and assurance. Once introductions have taken place, wait for the interviewer to offer you a chair. Make small talk with upbeat comments, such as *This is a beautiful headquarters,* or, *I'm very impressed with the facilities you have here.* Don't immediately begin rummaging in your briefcase for your résumé. Being at ease and unrushed suggests that you are self confident.

The way you answer questions can be almost as important as what you say. Use the interviewer's name and title from time to time when you answer. *Ms. Lyon, I would be pleased to tell you about. . . .* People like to hear their own names. Be sure you are pronouncing the name correctly, and don't overuse this technique. Avoid answering questions with a simple *yes* or *no;* elaborate on your answers to better sell yourself. Keep your answers positive; don't criticize anything or anyone.

During the interview it may be necessary to occasionally refocus and clarify vague questions. Some interviewers are inexperienced and ill at ease in the role. You may even have to ask your own question to understand what was asked: *By ___, do you mean ___?* Consider closing some of your responses with, *Does that answer your question?* or *Would you like me to elaborate on any particular experience?*

Always aim your answers at the key characteristics interviewers seek: expertise, competence, motivation, interpersonal skills, decision-making skills, enthusiasm for the job, and a pleasing personality. Remember to stay focused on your strengths. Don't reveal weaknesses, even if you think they make you look human. You won't be hired for your weaknesses, only for your strengths. Be sure to use good English and enunciate clearly. Avoid slurred words, such as *gonna* and *din't,* as well as slangy expressions, such as *yeah, like,* and *ya know.*

You cannot expect to be perfect in an employment interview. No one is. However, you can avert sure disaster by avoiding certain topics and behaviours, such as those described in Figure 16.1.

FIGURE 16.1 Twelve Interview Actions to Avoid

1. **Don't be late or too early.** Arrive five to ten minutes before your scheduled interview.

2. **Don't be rude.** Treat everyone you come into contact with warmly and respectfully.

3. **Don't ask for the job.** Asking for the job is naive, undignified, and unprofessional. Wait to see how the interview develops.

4. **Don't criticize anyone or anything.** Don't criticize your previous employer, supervisors, colleagues, or job. The tendency is for interviewers to wonder whether you would speak about their companies similarly.

5. **Don't be a threat to the interviewer.** Avoid suggesting directly or indirectly that your goal is to become head honcho, a path that might include the interviewer's job.

6. **Don't act unprofessionally.** Don't discuss controversial subjects and don't use profanity. Don't talk too much.

7. **Don't emphasize salary or benefits.** Don't bring up salary, vacation, or benefits early in an interview. Leave this up to the interviewer.

8. **Don't focus on your imperfections.** Never dwell on your liabilities or talk negatively about yourself.

9. **Don't interrupt.** Interrupting not only is impolite but also prevents you from hearing a complete question or remark.

10. **Don't bring someone along.** Don't bring a friend or relative with you to the interview. If someone must drive you, ask that person to drop you off and come back later.

11. **Don't appear impatient.** Your entire focus should be on the interview. Don't glance at your watch, which can imply that you're late for another appointment.

12. **Don't act desperate.** A sure way to turn off an interviewer is to act too desperate. Don't focus on why you need the job; focus on how you will add value to the organization.

Answering Typical Interview Questions

Employment interviews are all about questions, and many of the questions interviewers ask are not new. You can anticipate a large percentage of questions that will be asked before you ever walk into an interview room. Although you cannot anticipate every question, you can prepare for different types.

This section presents questions that may be asked during employment interviews. Some questions are meant to help the interviewer become acquainted with you. Others are aimed at measuring your interest, experience, and accomplishments. Still others will probe your future plans and challenge your reactions. Some will inquire about your money expectations. Your interviewer may use situational or behavioural questions and may even occasionally ask an illegal question. To get you thinking about how to respond, we have provided an answer or discussion for one or more of the questions in each of the following groups. As you read the remaining questions in each group, think about how you could respond most effectively.

How you answer questions can be as important as the answers themselves.

LEARNING OBJECTIVE 4

Describe how to answer typical interview questions, such as those that seek to get acquainted, gauge your interest, probe your experience, explore your accomplishments, look to the future, and inquire about salary expectations.

Questions to Get Acquainted

After opening introductions recruiters generally try to start the interview with personal questions that put you at ease. They are also striving to gain an overview to see whether you will fit into the organization's culture. When answering these questions, keep the employer's needs in mind and try to incorporate your success stories.

1. Tell me about yourself.

Experts agree that you must keep this answer short (one to two minutes tops) but on target. Use this chance to promote yourself. Stick to educational, professional, or business-related strengths; avoid personal or humorous references. Be ready with at least three success stories illustrating characteristics important to this job. Demonstrate responsibility you have been given; describe how you contributed as a team player. Try practising this formula: *I have completed a ___ degree with a major in ___. Recently I worked for ___ as a ___. Before that I worked for ___ as a ___. My strengths are ___ (interpersonal) and ___ (technical).* Try rehearsing your response in

> Prepare for get-acquainted questions by practising a short formula response.

Chapter 16: Interviewing and Following Up

30-second segments devoted to your education, work experience, qualifications, and skills.

2. What are your greatest strengths?

   Stress your strengths that are related to the position, such as *I am well organized, thorough, and attentive to detail.* Tell success stories and give examples that illustrate these qualities: *My supervisor says that my research is exceptionally thorough. For example, I recently worked on a research project in which I. . . .*

3. Do you prefer to work by yourself or with others? Why?

   This question can be tricky. Provide a middle-of-the-road answer that not only suggests your interpersonal qualities but also reflects an ability to make independent decisions and work without supervision.

4. What was your major in college [or university], and why did you choose it?

5. What are some things you do in your spare time? Hobbies? Sports?

Questions to Gauge Your Interest

Recruiters want to know how interested you are in this organization and in this specific position.

Interviewers want to understand your motivation for applying for a position. Although they will realize that you are probably interviewing for other positions, they still want to know why you are interested in this particular position with this organization. These types of questions help them determine your level of interest.

1. Why do you want to work for this company?

   Questions like this illustrate why you must research an organization thoroughly before the interview. The answer to this question must prove that you understand the company and its culture. This is the perfect place to bring up the company research you did before the interview. Show what you know about the company and discuss why you want to become a part of this organization. Describe your desire to work for this organization not only from your perspective but also from its point of view. What do you have to offer that will benefit the organization?

2. Why are you interested in this position?

3. What do you know about our company?

4. Why do you want to work in the _____ industry?

5. What interests you about our products (or services)?

Questions About Your Experience and Accomplishments

After questions about your background and education and questions that measure your interest, the interview generally becomes more specific with questions about your experience and accomplishments. Remember to show confidence when you answer these questions. If you are not confident in your abilities, why should an employer be?

Employers will hire a candidate with less experience and fewer accomplishments if he or she can demonstrate the skills required.

1. Why should we hire you when we have applicants with more experience or better credentials?

   In answering this question, remember that employers often hire people who present themselves well instead of others with better credentials. Emphasize your personal strengths that could be an advantage with this employer. Are you a hard worker? How can you demonstrate it? Have you had recent training? Some people have had more years of experience but actually have less knowledge because they have done the same thing over and over. Stress your experience in using the latest methods and equipment.

   Be sure to mention your computer training and use of the Web. Tell success stories. Emphasize that you are open to new ideas and learn quickly. Above all, show that you are confident in your abilities.

2. Describe the most rewarding experience of your career so far.

3. How have your education and professional experiences prepared you for this position?

4. What were your major accomplishments in each of your past jobs?

5. What was a typical workday like?

6. What job functions did you enjoy most? Least? Why?

7. Tell me about your computer skills.

8. Who was the toughest boss you ever worked for, and why?

9. What were your major achievements in college [or university]?

10. Why did you leave your last position? OR: Why are you leaving your current position?

Questions about your experience and accomplishments enable you to work in your practised success stories.

Questions About the Future

Questions that look into the future tend to stump some candidates, especially those who have not prepared adequately. Employers ask these questions to see whether you are goal oriented and to determine whether your goals are realistic.

When asked about the future, show ambition and interest in succeeding with this company.

1. Where do you expect to be five (or ten) years from now?

   Formulate a realistic plan with respect to your present age and situation. The important thing is to be prepared for this question. It's a sure kiss of death to respond that you would like to have the interviewer's job! Instead, show an interest in the current job and in making a contribution to the organization. Talk about the levels of responsibility you would like to achieve. Keep your answer focused on educational and professional goals, not personal goals.

2. If you got this position, what would you do to be sure you fit in?

3. This is a large [or small] organization. Do you think you would like that environment?

4. Do you plan to continue your education?

5. What do you predict for the future of the _____industry?

6. How do you think you can contribute to this company?

7. What would you most like to accomplish if you were to get this position?

8. How do you keep current with what is happening in your profession?

Challenging Questions

The following questions may make you uncomfortable, but the important thing to remember is to answer truthfully without dwelling on your weaknesses. As quickly as possible, convert any negative response into a discussion of your strengths.

Strive to convert a discussion of your weaknesses to topics that show your strengths.

1. What is your greatest weakness?

   It's amazing how many candidates knock themselves out of the competition by answering this question poorly. Actually, you have many choices. You can present a strength as a weakness (*Some people complain that I'm a workaholic or too attentive to details*). You can mention a corrected weakness (*Because I needed to learn about designing Web sites, I took a course*). You could cite an unrelated skill (*I really need to brush up on my French*). You can cite a learning objective (*One of my long-term goals is to learn more about international management. Does your company have any plans to expand overseas?*). Another possibility is to reaffirm your qualifications (*I have no weaknesses that affect my ability to do this job*). Be careful that your answer doesn't sound too cliché (*I tend to be a perfectionist*) and instead shows careful analysis of your abilities.

Answer challenging
questions truthfully but
try to turn the discussion
into one that emphasizes
your strengths.

2. What type of people do you have no patience for?

Avoid letting yourself fall into the trap of sounding overly critical. One possible response is, *I have always gotten along well with others. But I confess that I can be irritated by complainers who don't accept responsibility.*

3. If you could live your life over, what would you change and why?

4. How would your former [or current] supervisor describe you as an employee?

5. What do you want the most from your job?

6. What is your grade-point average, and does it accurately reflect your abilities?

7. Have you ever used drugs?

8. Who in your life has influenced you the most, and why?

9. What are you reading right now?

10. Describe your ideal work environment.

11. Is the customer always right?

12. How do you define success?

Questions About Salary

Defer a discussion of
salary until later in the
interview when you know
more about the job and
whether it will be offered.

Remember that nearly all salaries are negotiable, depending on your qualifications. Knowing the typical salary range for the target position helps. The recruiter can tell you the salary ranges—but you will have to ask. If you have had little experience, you will probably be offered a salary somewhere between the low point and the midpoint in the range. With more experience you can negotiate for a higher figure. A word of caution, though. One personnel manager warns that candidates who emphasize money are suspect because they may leave if offered a few thousand dollars more elsewhere. Here are some typical money questions:

1. What salary are you looking for?

One way to handle salary questions is to ask politely to defer the discussion until it's clear that a job will be offered to you (*I'm sure when the time comes, we will be able to work out a fair compensation package. Right now, I'd rather focus on whether we have a match*). Another possible response is to reply candidly that you can't know what to ask until you know more about the position and the company. If you continue to be pressed for a dollar figure, give a salary range with an annual dollar amount. Be sure to do research before the interview so that you know what similar jobs are paying in your geographic region. For example, check a Web site, such as **http://salary.monster.ca** or **www.wowjobs.ca/salary.aspx**. When citing salary expectations, you will sound more professional if you cite an annual salary range rather than a dollar-per-hour amount.

2. How much are you presently earning?

3. How much do you think you're worth?

4. How much money do you expect to earn within the next ten years?

5. Are you willing to take a pay cut from your current (or previous) job?

Situational Questions

Questions related to situations help employers test your thought processes and logical thinking. When using situational questions, interviewers describe a hypothetical situation and ask how you would handle it. Situational questions differ based on the type of position for which you are interviewing. Knowledge of the position and the company culture will help you respond favourably to these questions.

Even if the situation sounds negative, keep your response positive. Here are just a few examples:

Employers find that situational and behavioural interview questions give them useful information about job candidates.

1. You receive a call from an irate customer who complains about the service she received last night at your restaurant. She is demanding her money back. How would you handle the situation?

2. If you were aware that a co-worker was falsifying data, what would you do?

3. Your supervisor has just told you that she is dissatisfied with your work, but you think it's acceptable. How would you resolve the conflict?

4. Your supervisor has told you to do something a certain way, and you think that way is wrong and that you know a far better way to complete the task. What would you do?

5. Assume that you are hired for this position. You soon learn that one of the staff is extremely resentful because she applied for your position and was turned down. As a result, she is being unhelpful and obstructive. How would you handle the situation?

Behavioural Questions

Instead of traditional interview questions, you may be asked to tell stories. The interviewer may say, *Describe a time when* or *Tell me about a time when.* . . . To respond effectively, learn to use the storytelling or STAR technique. Ask yourself what the **S**ituation or **T**ask was, what **A**ction you took, and what the **R**esults were.[5] Practise using this method to recall specific examples of your skills and accomplishments. To be fully prepared, develop a coherent and articulate STAR narrative for every bullet point on your résumé. When answering behavioural questions, describe only educational and work-related situations or tasks and try to keep them as current as possible. Here are a few examples of behavioural questions:

1. Tell me about a time when you solved a difficult problem.

   Tell a concise story explaining the situation or task, what you did, and the result. For example, *When I was at Ace Products, we continually had a problem of excessive back orders. After analyzing the situation, I discovered that orders went through many unnecessary steps. I suggested that we eliminate much paperwork. As a result, we reduced back orders by 30 percent.* Go on to emphasize what you learned and how you can apply that learning to this job. Practise your success stories in advance so that you will be ready.

2. Describe a situation in which you were able to use persuasion to successfully convince someone to see things your way.

   When answering behavioural questions, describe only educational and work-related situations or tasks.

   The recruiter is interested in your leadership and teamwork skills. You might respond, *I have learned to appreciate the fact that the way you present an idea is just as important as the idea itself. When trying to influence people, I put myself in their shoes and find some way to frame my idea from their perspective. I remember when I.* . . .

3. Describe a time when you had to analyze information and make a recommendation.

4. Describe a time that you worked successfully as part of a team.

5. Tell me about a time you dealt with confidential information.

6. Give me an example of a time when you were under stress to meet a deadline.

7. Tell me about a time when you had to go above and beyond the call of duty to get a job done.

8. Tell me about a time you were able to successfully deal with another person even when that individual may not have personally liked you (or vice versa).

9. Give me an example of when you showed initiative and took the lead.

10. Tell me about a recent situation in which you had to deal with an upset customer or co-worker.

Illegal and Inappropriate Questions

Employment laws that prohibit discrimination in the workplace also apply to interviews. Questions regarding race, national origin, sexual orientation, religion, age, marital status, family situation, arrest record, illnesses or diseases, personal information (such as height or weight), or disabilities are not allowed in an interview. Therefore, it is inappropriate for interviewers to ask any question related to these areas. These questions become illegal, though, only when a court of law determines that the employer is asking them with the intent to discriminate. Most illegal interview questions are asked innocently by inexperienced interviewers. Some are only trying to be friendly when they inquire about your personal life or family. Regardless of the intent, how should you react?

If you find the question harmless and if you want the job, go ahead and answer it. If you think that answering it would damage your chance to be hired, try to deflect the question tactfully with such a response as, *Could you tell me how my marital status relates to the responsibilities of this position?* or *I prefer to keep my personal and professional lives separate.* If you are uncomfortable answering a question, try to determine the reason behind it; you might answer, *I don't let my personal life interfere with my ability to do my job,* or *Are you concerned with my availability to work overtime?* Another option, of course, is to respond to any inappropriate or illegal question by confronting the interviewer and threatening a lawsuit or refusing to answer. However, you could not expect to be hired under these circumstances. In any case, you might want to reconsider working for an organization that sanctions such procedures.

Here are some inappropriate and illegal questions that you may or may not want to answer:[6]

1. What is your marital status? Are you married? Do you live with anyone? Do you have a boyfriend [or girlfriend]? (However, employers can ask your marital status after hiring for tax and insurance forms.)

2. Do you have any disabilities? Have you had any recent illnesses? (But it is legal to ask if the person can perform specific job duties, such as, *Can you carry a 22.5-kilogram sack up a 3-metre ladder five times daily?*)

3. I notice you have an accent. Where are you from? What is the origin of your last name? What is your native language? (However, it is legal to ask what languages you speak fluently if language ability is related to the job.)

4. Have you ever filed a worker's compensation claim or been injured on the job?

5. Have you ever had a drinking problem or been addicted to drugs? (But it is legal to ask if a person uses illegal drugs.)

6. Have you ever been arrested? (But it is legal to ask, *Have you ever been convicted of ___?* when the crime is related to the job.)

7. How old are you? What is your date of birth? When did you graduate from high school? (But it is legal to ask, *Are you 16 years (or 18 years or 21 years) old or older?* depending on the age requirements for the position.)

8. Of what country are you a citizen? Where were you born? (But it is legal to ask, *Are you a Canadian citizen?* or, *Can you legally work in Canada?*)

9. What is your maiden name? (But it is legal to ask, *What is your full name?* or, *Have you worked under another name?*)

> Candidates who are asked illegal questions must decide whether to answer, deflect the question tactfully, or confront the interviewer.

> You may respond to an inappropriate or illegal question by asking tactfully how it relates to the responsibilities of the position.

10. Do you have any religious beliefs that would prevent you from working weekends or holidays? (An employer can, however, ask you if you are available to work weekends and holidays.)

11. Do you have children? Do you plan to have children? Do you have adequate child-care arrangements? (However, employers can ask for dependent information for tax and insurance purposes after you are hired.)

12. How much do you weigh? How tall are you? (However, employers can ask you about your height and weight if minimum standards are necessary to safely perform a job.)

Closing the Interview

Once the interview nears conclusion, start thinking about how to end on a positive note. It's easy to become flustered after a challenging interview, so be sure to practise questions that you plan to ask. Also, focus on how to leave a lasting positive impression.

Asking Your Own Questions

At some point in the interview, usually near the end, you will be asked whether you have any questions. The worst thing you can do is say *No*, which suggests that you are not interested in the position. Instead, ask questions that will help you gain information and will impress the interviewer with your thoughtfulness and interest in the position. Remember that this interview is a two-way street. You must be happy with the prospect of working for this organization. You want a position for which your skills and personality are matched. Use this opportunity to learn whether this job is right for you. Be aware that you don't have to wait for the interviewer to ask you for questions. You can ask your own questions throughout the interview to learn more about the company and position. Here are some questions you might ask:

1. What will my duties be (if not already discussed)?

2. Tell me what it's like working here in terms of the people, management practices, workloads, expected performance, and rewards.

3. What training programs are available from this organization? What specific training will be given for this position?

4. Who would be my immediate supervisor?

5. What is the organizational structure, and where does this position fit in?

6. Is travel required in this position?

7. How is job performance evaluated?

8. Assuming my work is excellent, where do you see me in five years?

9. How long do employees generally stay with this organization?

10. What are the major challenges for a person in this position?

11. What do you see in the future of this organization?

12. What do you like best about working for this organization?

13. May I have a tour of the facilities?

14. When do you expect to make a decision?

LEARNING OBJECTIVE 5

Understand how to close an interview positively, including asking meaningful questions.

Your questions should impress the interviewer but also provide valuable information about the job.

Ending Positively

When you end the interview, summarize your strongest qualifications, thank the interviewer, and ask for the interviewer's card.

After you have asked your questions, the interviewer will signal the end of the interview, usually by standing up or by expressing appreciation that you came. If not addressed earlier, you should at this time find out what action will follow. Demonstrate your interest in the position by asking when it will be filled or what the next step will be. Too many candidates leave the interview without knowing their status or when they will hear from the recruiter. Don't be afraid to say that you want the job!

Before you leave, summarize your strongest qualifications, show your enthusiasm for obtaining this position, and thank the interviewer for a constructive interview and for considering you for the position. Ask the interviewer for a business card, which will provide the information you need to write a thank-you letter, which is discussed later. Shake the interviewer's hand with confidence and acknowledge anyone else you see on the way out. Be sure to thank the receptionist. Leaving the interview gracefully and enthusiastically will leave a lasting impression on those responsible for making the final hiring decision.

After the Interview

LEARNING OBJECTIVE 6

Outline the activities that take place after an interview, including thanking the interviewer and contacting references.

After leaving the interview, immediately make notes of what was said in case you are called back for a second interview. Write down key points that were discussed, the names of people you spoke with, and other details of the interview. Ask yourself what went really well and what could have been improved. Note your strengths and weaknesses during the interview so that you can work to improve in future interviews. Next, write down your follow-up plans. To whom should you send thank-you letters? Will you contact the employer by phone? If so, when? Then be sure to follow up on those plans, beginning with writing a thank-you letter and contacting your references.

Thanking Your Interviewer

A follow-up thank-you letter shows your good manners and your enthusiasm for the job.

After a job interview you should always send a thank-you letter, also called a follow-up letter. This courtesy sets you apart from other applicants, most of whom will not bother. Your letter also reminds the interviewer of your visit and suggests your good manners and genuine enthusiasm for the job. Follow-up letters are most effective if sent immediately after the interview. In your letter refer to the date of the interview, the exact job title for which you were interviewed, and specific topics discussed. Avoid worn-out phrases, such as *Thank you for taking the time to interview me*. Be careful, too, about overusing I, especially to begin sentences. Most important, show that you really want the job and that you are qualified for it. Notice how the letter in Figure 16.2 conveys enthusiasm and confidence.

If you have been interviewed by more than one person, send a separate letter to each interviewer. It's also a good idea to send a thank-you letter to the receptionist and to the person who set up the interview. Your thank-you letter will probably make more of an impact if prepared in proper business format and sent by regular mail. However, if you know the decision will be made quickly, send your follow-up message by e-mail.

Contacting Your References

Thoughtful candidates alert the people who are acting as references so that they will be prepared to be contacted by the target company.

Once you have thanked your interviewer, it's time to alert your references that they may be contacted by the employer. You might also have to request a letter of recommendation to be sent to the employer by a certain date. As discussed in Chapter 15, you should have already asked permission to use these individuals as references, and you should have supplied them with a copy of your résumé and information about the types of positions you are seeking.

To provide the best possible recommendation, your references need information. What position have you applied for with what company? What should they stress to the prospective employer? Write your reference describing the position, its requirements, and the recommendation deadline. Include a copy of your résumé. You might remind her of a positive experience with you that she could use in the recommendation. Remember that recommenders need evidence to support generalizations. Give them appropriate ammunition.

FIGURE 16.2 **Interview Follow-Up Letter**

Christopher D. Wiley

2250 Tupper Street, Thunder Bay, ON P7A 4A5
(807) 483-6734, cwiley@mail.com

May 28, 2013

Mr. Eric C. Nielsen
Comstock Images & Technology
245 Maitland Street
London, ON N6B 2Y2

Dear Mr. Nielsen:

Talking with you Thursday, May 27, about the graphic designer position was both informative and interesting.

Thanks for describing the position in such detail and for introducing me to Ms. Ouchi, the senior designer. Her current project designing an annual report in four colours sounds fascinating as well as quite challenging.

Now that I have learned in greater detail the specific tasks of your graphic designers, I'm more than ever convinced that my computer and creative skills can make a genuine contribution to your graphic productions. My training in design and layout using PhotoShop and InDesign ensures that I could be immediately productive on your staff.

You will find me an enthusiastic and hardworking member of any team effort. As you requested, I'm enclosing additional samples of my work. I'm eager to join the graphics staff at your London headquarters, and I look forward to hearing from you soon.

Sincerely,

Christopher D. Wiley

Christopher D. Wiley

Enclosures

Callout labels (left):
- Mentions the interview date and specific job title
- Highlights specific skills for the job
- Shows appreciation, good manners, and perseverance—traits that recruiters value

Callout labels (right):
- Personalizes the message by referring to topics discussed in the interview
- Reminds reader of interpersonal skills as well as enthusiasm and eagerness for this job

Following Up

If you don't hear from the interviewer within five days, or at the specified time, call him or her. Practise saying something like, *I'm wondering what else I can do to convince you that I'm the right person for this job*, or, *I'm calling to find out the status of your search for the ___ position.* You could also e-mail the interviewer to find out how the decision process is going. When following up, it's important to sound professional and courteous. Sounding desperate, angry, or frustrated that you have not been contacted can ruin your chances.

Depending on the response you get to your first follow-up request, you may have to follow up additional times. Keep in mind, though, that some employers will not tell you about their hiring decision unless you are the one hired. Don't harass the interviewer and don't force a decision. If you don't hear back from an employer within several weeks after following up, it's best to assume that you didn't get the job and to continue with your job search.

To review the important actions you can take to perform effectively before, during, and after a job interview, see the Checklist box on page 458.

Checklist

Performing Effectively Before, During, and After a Job Interview

Before the Interview

- **Expect to be screened by telephone.** Near your telephone, keep your résumé, a list of references, a calendar, and a notepad. Also have a list of companies where you applied.

- **Research the target company.** Once an interview is scheduled, conduct in-depth research about the company's mission, goals, size, customers, competitors, culture, management structure, names of leaders, financial condition, future plans, strengths, and weaknesses. Talk to company employees if possible.

- **Prepare success stories.** Organize and practice many success stories with specific examples of your educational and work-related experiences that demonstrate your accomplishments and achievements. Be ready to recite them in 30-second sound bites.

- **Practise answers to possible questions.** Recite answers to typical questions in a mirror, with a friend, or in spare moments. Consider recording a practice session to evaluate your performance. Be ready to explain problem areas on your résumé.

- **Clean up your digital dirt.** Remove any incriminating, provocative, or distasteful photos, contents, and links that could make you look unprofessional to potential employers.

- **Get ready.** Take a trial trip to locate the employer. Select professional-looking clothes for the interview. Gather items to take with you: copies of your résumé, your reference lists, a notebook and pen, money for parking, and work samples, if appropriate. Use a presentable briefcase to carry your items.

During the Interview

- **Send positive nonverbal messages.** Control your body movements, use good posture, maintain appropriate eye contact, use gestures effectively, smile enough to convey a positive attitude, listen attentively, turn off your cellphone, don't chew gum, sound enthusiastic and interested, and avoid *um, uh, like,* and *ya know*.

- **Fight fear.** Remind yourself that you are thoroughly prepared, breathe deeply, know that your fear is typical, and remember that the interviewer has to please you as well.

- **Be confident.** Use the interviewer's name, refocus and clarify vague questions, and aim your answers at key characteristics interviewers seek.

- **Incorporate your success stories.** As you answer questions, work in your success stories that emphasize your skills and accomplishments. Keep the employer's needs in mind for this particular position.

- **Express enthusiasm for working for this company.** Show what you know about the company and explain why you want to become part of this organization.

Closing the Interview

- **Ask your own questions.** Be prepared with meaningful, thoughtful questions to help you determine whether this job is right for you.

- **End the interview positively.** Summarize your strongest qualifications, show your enthusiasm for the job, and thank the interviewer. Ask for the interviewer's business card. Shake hands and acknowledge anyone else on the way out.

After the Interview

- **Make notes.** Immediately record key points and note what you could improve for your next interview.

- **Send a thank-you message.** Thank the interviewer in a message that notes the date of the interview, the exact title of the position, and specific topics discussed. Express your enthusiasm for the job and thank the interviewer for sharing information about the position and the organization. E-mail notes are increasingly acceptable.

- **Contact your references.** Alert your references that they may be contacted by the employer. Provide any additional information that will help them make supportive statements.

Other Employment Documents and Follow-Up Messages

Although the résumé and cover letter are your major tasks, other important documents and messages are often required during the employment process. You may need to complete an employment application form and write follow-up letters. You might also have to write a letter of resignation when leaving a job. Because each of these tasks reveals something about you and your communication skills, you will want to put your best foot forward. These documents often subtly influence company officials to offer a job.

LEARNING OBJECTIVE 7

Understand how to complete employment applications and write résumé follow-up, rejection follow-up, job acceptance, and job rejection messages.

Application Form

Some organizations require job candidates to fill out job application forms instead of or in addition to submitting résumés. This practice permits them to gather and store standardized data about each applicant. Whether the application is on paper or online, follow the directions carefully and provide accurate information. The following suggestions can help you be prepared:

> **When applying for jobs, keep with you a card summarizing your important data.**

- Carry a card summarizing vital statistics not included on your résumé. If you are asked to fill out an application form in an employer's office, you will need a handy reference to the following data: graduation dates; beginning and ending dates of all employment; salary history; full names, titles, and present work addresses of former supervisors; full addresses and phone numbers of current and previous employers; and full names, occupational titles, occupational addresses, and telephone numbers of persons who have agreed to serve as references.

- Look over all the questions before starting.

- Fill out the form neatly, using blue or black ink. Many career counsellors recommend printing your responses; cursive handwriting can be difficult to read.

- Answer all questions honestly. Write *Not applicable* or *N/A* if appropriate.

- Use accurate spelling, grammar, and punctuation.

- If asked for the position desired, give a specific job title or type of position. Don't say, *Anything* or *Open*. These answers make you look unfocused; moreover, they make it difficult for employers to know what you're qualified for or interested in.

- Be prepared for a salary question. Unless you know what comparable employees are earning in the company, the best strategy is to suggest a salary range or to write *Negotiable* or *Open*.

- Be prepared to explain the reasons for leaving previous positions. Use positive or neutral phrases, such as *Relocation, Seasonal, To accept a position with more responsibility, Temporary position, To continue education,* or *Career change.* Avoid such words or phrases as *Fired, Quit, Didn't get along with supervisor,* or *Pregnant.*

- Look over the application before submitting to make sure it is complete and that you have followed all instructions. Sign and date the application.

Application or Résumé Follow-Up Letter

If your résumé or application generates no response within a reasonable time, you may decide to send a short follow-up letter such as the following. Doing so (a) jogs the memory of the personnel officer, (b) demonstrates your serious interest, and (c) allows you to emphasize your qualifications or to add new information.

Rejection Follow-Up Letter

If you didn't get the job and you think it was perfect for you, don't give up. Employment specialists encourage applicants to respond to a rejection. The candidate who was offered the position may decline, or other positions may open up. In a rejection follow-up letter, it's acceptable to admit you are disappointed. Be sure to add, however, that you are still interested and will contact the company again in a month in case a job opens up. Then follow through for a couple of months—but don't overdo it. You should be professional and persistent but not a pest.

Job Acceptance and Rejection Letters

When all your hard work pays off, you will be offered the position you want. Although you will likely accept the position over the phone, it's a good idea to follow up with an acceptance letter to confirm the details and to formalize the acceptance.

If you must turn down a job offer, show your professionalism by writing a sincere letter. This letter should thank the employer for the job offer and explain briefly that you are turning it down. Taking the time to extend this courtesy could help you in the future if this employer has an opening.

Resignation Letter

After you have been in a position for a period of time, you may find it necessary to leave. Perhaps you have been offered a better position, or maybe you have decided to return to school full-time. Whatever the reason, you should leave your position gracefully and tactfully. Although you will likely discuss your resignation in person with your supervisor, it is a good idea to document your resignation by writing a formal letter. Some resignation letters are brief, while others contain great detail. Remember that many resignation letters are placed in personnel files.

The amount of time that you have been with a company may also dictate the amount of notice you should provide. The higher and more responsible your position, the longer the notice you should give your employer. You should, however, always give some notice as a courtesy.

Writing job acceptance, job rejection, and resignation letters requires effort. That effort, however, is worth it because you are building bridges that later may carry you to even better jobs in the future.

Summary of Learning Objectives

1 **Understand the importance of a job interview, its purposes, and its forms, including screening, hiring or placement, one-on-one, panel, group, sequential, stress, and online interviews.** Job interviews are extremely important because they can change your life. As a job candidate, you have the following purposes in an interview: (a) convince the employer of your potential, (b) find out more about the job and the company, and (c) expand on the information in your résumé. From the employer's perspective, the interview is an opportunity to (a) assess your abilities in relation to the requirements for the position; (b) discuss your training, experience, knowledge, and abilities in more detail; (c) see what drives and motivates you; and (d) decide whether you would fit into the organization. Screening interviews seek to eliminate less qualified candidates. Hiring or placement interviews may be one-on-one, panel, group, sequential, stress, or online.

2 **Describe what to do before an in-person interview, including researching the target company, rehearsing success stories, practising answers to possible questions, and cleaning up digital dirt.** If you are lucky enough to be selected for an in-person interview, you should research the target company by learning about its products, mission, customers, competitors, and finances. Before your interview, prepare 30-second success stories that demonstrate your qualifications and achievements. Practise answers to typical interview questions. Clean up any digital dirt. Expect to explain any problem areas on your résumé. If you are not sure where the employer is located, take a trial trip the day before your interview. Decide how to dress so that you will look qualified, competent, and professional. On the day of your interview, make sure you arrive on time and make a good first impression.

3 **Explain how to perform during an interview, including sending positive nonverbal messages and using good techniques in answering questions.** During your interview send positive nonverbal messages by controlling body movements, showing good posture, maintaining eye contact, using gestures effectively, and smiling enough to convey a positive attitude. Listen attentively, turn off your cellphone or other electronic devices, don't chew gum, and sound enthusiastic and sincere. If you feel nervous, breathe deeply and remind yourself that you are well prepared. Tell yourself that you control part of this interview and that interviews are a two-way street.

4 **Describe how to answer typical interview questions, such as those that seek to get acquainted, gauge your interest, probe your experience, explore your accomplishments, look to the future, and inquire about salary expectations.** Interviewers often ask the same types of questions. Be prepared to respond to inquiries, such as *Tell me about yourself*. Practise answering questions about why you want to work for the organization, why you should be hired, how your education and experience have prepared you for the position, where you expect to be in five or ten years, what your greatest weaknesses are, and how much money you expect to earn. Be ready for situational questions that ask you to respond to a hypothetical situation. Expect behavioural questions that begin with *Tell me about a time when you. . . .* Think about how you would respond to possible illegal or inappropriate questions.

5 **Understand how to close an interview positively, including asking meaningful questions.** Toward the end of an interview, you should be prepared to ask your own questions, such as, *What will my duties be?* and *When do you expect to make a decision?* After asking your questions and the interviewer signals the end of the meeting, find out what action will follow. Summarize your strongest qualifications, show your enthusiasm for obtaining this position, and thank the interviewer. Ask for the interviewer's business card. Shake the interviewer's hand with confidence and acknowledge anyone else you see on the way out.

6 **Outline the activities that take place after an interview, including thanking the interviewer and contacting references.** After leaving the interview, immediately make notes of the key points discussed. Note your strengths and weaknesses during the interview so that you can work to improve in future interviews. Write a thank-you letter that includes the date of the interview, the exact job title for which you were interviewed, and specific topics discussed. Show that you really want the job. Alert your references that they may be contacted.

7 **Understand how to complete employment applications and write résumé follow-up, rejection follow-up, job acceptance, and job rejection messages.** If you don't hear from the interviewer within five days or at the specified time, call him or her. You could also e-mail to learn how the decision process is going. Sound professional, not desperate, angry, or frustrated. If asked to fill out an application form, look over all the questions before starting. If asked for a salary figure, provide a salary range or write *Negotiable* or *Open*. If you don't get the job, consider writing a letter that expresses your disappointment but your desire to be contacted in case a job opens up. If you are offered a job, write a letter that confirms the details and formalizes your acceptance. When resigning a position, write a letter that confirms the date of resignation, offers assistance to prepare for your resignation, and expresses thanks.

Chapter Review

1. What are the main purposes of a job interview for a job candidate and for the employer? (Obj. 1)

2. What is a screening interview, and why is it so important? (Obj. 1)

3. Briefly describe the types of hiring or placement interviews you may encounter. (Obj. 1)

4. You have scheduled an interview with a large local company. What kind of information should you seek about this company and where can you expect to find it? (Obj. 2)

5. What are success stories, and how can you use them during a job interview? (Obj. 2)

6. What is digital dirt, and what should you do to clean it up during the employment process? (Obj. 2)

7. How can you send positive nonverbal messages during an interview? (Obj. 3)

8. What should you do if an interview question is vague or unclear? (Obj. 3)

9. What is the best way to answer the question *Tell me about yourself?* (Obj. 4)

10. How could you respond to the question *Why should we hire you when we have applicants with more experience or better credentials?* (Obj. 4)

11. What should you do if asked a salary question early in an interview? (Obj. 4)

12. What is the difference between a situational and a behavioural question? (Obj. 4)

13. What kinds of questions should you ask during an interview? (Obj. 5)

14. List the steps you should take immediately following your job interview. (Obj. 6)

15. If you are offered a position, why is it important to write an acceptance letter, and what should it include? (Obj. 7)

Critical Thinking

1. Is it normal to be nervous about an employment interview, and what can be done to overcome this fear? (Obj. 1)

2. What can you do to improve the first impression you make at an interview? (Objs. 2, 3)

3. Do you think behavioural questions (such as *Tell me about a business problem you have had and how you solved it*) are more effective than traditional questions (such as *Tell me what you are good at*)? Why? (Obj. 4)

4. If you are asked an illegal interview question, why is it important to first assess the intentions of the interviewer? (Obj. 4)

5. **Ethical Issue:** When asked about his previous salary in a job interview, Jeremy boosts his salary a bit. He reasons that he was about to get a raise, and he also felt that he deserved to be paid more than he was actually earning. Even his supervisor said that he was worth more than his salary. Is Jeremy justified in inflating his previous salary? (Obj. 4)

Activities

16.1 Researching an Organization (Obj. 2)

`WEB`

An important part of your preparation for an interview is finding out about the target company.

Your Task. Select an organization where you would like to be employed. Assume you have been selected for an interview. Using resources described in this chapter, locate information about the organization's leaders and their business philosophies. Learn about the organization's history, accomplishments, setbacks, finances, products, customers, competition, and advertising. Prepare a summary report documenting your findings.

16.2 Learning What Jobs Are Really About Through Blogs, Facebook, and Twitter (Obj. 2)

`WEB`

Blogs and social media sites, such as Facebook and Twitter, are becoming more important tools in the employment search

process. By accessing blogs, company Facebook pages, and Twitter feeds, job seekers can learn additional information about a company's culture and day-to-day activities.

Your Task. Using the Web, locate a blog that is maintained by an employee of a company where you would like to work. Monitor the blog for at least a week. Also access the company's Facebook page and monitor Twitter feeds for at least a week. Prepare a short report summarizing what you learned about the company through reading the blog postings, status updates, and tweets. Include a statement of whether this information would be valuable during your job search.

16.3 Building Interview Skills (Objs. 2, 3)

Successful interviews require diligent preparation and repeated practice. To be well prepared, you need to know what skills are required for your targeted position. In addition to computer and communication skills, employers generally want to know whether a candidate works well with a team, accepts responsibility, solves problems, is efficient, meets deadlines, shows leadership, saves time and money, and is a hard worker.

Your Task. Consider a position for which you are eligible now or one for which you will be eligible when you complete your education. Identify the skills and traits necessary for this position. If you prepared a résumé in Chapter 15, be sure that it addresses these targeted areas. Now prepare interview worksheets listing at least ten technical and other skills or traits you think a recruiter will want to discuss in an interview for your targeted position.

16.4 Preparing Success Stories (Obj. 2)

You can best showcase your talents if you are ready with your own success stories that show how you have developed the skills or traits required for your targeted position.

Your Task. Using the worksheets you prepared in Activity 16.3, prepare success stories that highlight the required skills or traits. Select three to five stories to develop into answers to potential interview questions. For example, here's a typical question: *How does your* background *relate to the position we have open?* A possible response: *As you know, I have just completed an intensive training program in ___. In addition, I have over three years of part-time work experience in a variety of business settings. In one position I was selected to manage a small business in the absence of the owner. I developed responsibility and customer-service skills in filling orders efficiently, resolving shipping problems, and monitoring key accounts. I also inventoried and organized products worth over $200,000. When the owner returned from a vacation to Florida, I was commended for increasing sales and was given a bonus in recognition of my efforts.* People relate to and remember stories. Try to shape your answers into memorable stories.

16.5 Polishing Answers to Interview Questions (Obj. 4)

Practice makes perfect in interviewing. The more often you rehearse responses to typical interview questions, the closer you are to getting the job.

Your Task. Select three questions from each of these question categories discussed in this chapter: Questions to Get Acquainted, Questions to Gauge Your Interest, Questions About Your Experience and Accomplishments, Questions About the Future, and Challenging Questions. Write your answers to each set of questions. Try to incorporate skills and traits required for the targeted position and include success stories where appropriate. Polish these answers and your delivery technique by practising in front of a mirror or by making an audio or video recording.

16.6 Learning to Answer Situational Interview Questions (Obj. 4)

TEAM
WEB

Situational interview questions can vary widely from position to position. You should know enough about a position to understand some of the typical situations you would encounter on a regular basis.

Your Task. Use your favourite search tool to locate typical job descriptions of a position in which you are interested. Based on these descriptions, develop a list of six to eight typical situations someone in this position would face; then write situational interview questions for each of these scenarios. In pairs of two students, role-play interviewer and interviewee, alternating with your listed questions.

16.7 Developing Skill With Behavioural Interview Questions (Obj. 4)

TEAM
WEB

Behavioural interview questions are increasingly popular, and you will need a little practice before you can answer them easily.

Your Task. Use your favourite search tool to locate lists of behavioural questions on the Web. Select five skill areas such as communication, teamwork, and decision making. For each skill area, find three behavioural questions that you think would be effective in an interview. In pairs of two students, role-play interviewer and interviewee, alternating with your listed questions. You goal is to answer effectively in one or two minutes. Remember to use the STAR method when answering.

16.8 Knowing What to Ask (Obj. 5)

When it is your turn to ask questions during the interview process, be ready.

Your Task. Decide on three to five questions that you would like to ask during an interview. Write these questions out and practise asking them so that you sound confident and sincere.

16.9 Saying Thanks for the Interview (Objs. 6, 7)

You have just completed an exciting employment interview, and you want the interviewer to remember you.

Your Task. Write a follow-up thank-you letter to Ronald T. Ranson, Human Resources Development, Domosys Corporation, 43 rue Sainte-Ursule, Vieux Québec, Québec G1R 4E4 (or a company of your choice). Make up any details needed.

16.10 Searching for Advice (Objs. 1–7)

WEB

You can find wonderful, free, and sometimes entertaining information about job-search strategies and career tips and interview advice on the Web.

Your Task. Use the Web to locate articles or links to sites with job-search, résumé, and interview information. Make a list of at least five good interview pointers—ones that were not covered in this chapter. Send an e-mail message to your instructor describing your findings or post your findings to a class discussion board to share with your classmates.

Grammar and Mechanics C.L.U.E. Review 16

Total Review

Each of the following sentences has a total of **three** errors in grammar, punctuation, capitalization, usage, or spelling. On a separate sheet, write a correct version. Avoid adding new phrases, starting new sentences, or rewriting in your own words. When finished, compare your responses with the key beginning on page Key-1.

1. Before going to a job interview you should research the following—company size, competitors, reputation, strengths and weaknesses.

2. I wonder how many companys use software to scan candidates résumés and search for keywords?

3. Even with the popularity of e-mail most employers' will contact job applicants by telephone to set up there interviews.

4. Initial contacts by employers will usualy be made by telephone, therefore, insure that you keep important information nearby.

5. If you have gaps in your employment history explain what you did during this time, and how you kept up to date in your field.

6. Interviewees should not criticise anyone or anything and they should not focus on there imperfections.

7. Evan was asked whether he had a Bachelors degree, and whether he had five years experience.

8. If you are hopping to create a good impression be sure to write a thank you letter after a job interview.

9. When Robins interview was over she told friends that she had done good.

10. Robin was already to send a thank-you message, when she realized she could not spell the interviewers name.

Endnotes

[1] CareerBuilder. (2011, January 12). Career expert offers tips on how to ace an interview [press release]. Retrieved September 15, 2011, from http://www.prnewswire.com/news-releases/employers-reveal-outrageous-and-common-mistakes-candidates-made-in-job-interviews-according-to-new-careerbuilder-survey-113341389.html

[2] Panel interview. (2007). Job-Employment-Guide.com. Retrieved August 12, 2007, from Job-Employment-Guide.com at http://www.job-employment-guide.com/panel-interview.html

[3] Maher, K. (2004, October 5). Job seekers and recruiters pay more attention to blogs. Retrieved August 12, 2007, from http://www.careerjournal.com/jobhunting/usingnet/20041005-maher.html

[4] Ryan, L. (2007, May 6). Job seekers: Prepare your stories. Retrieved August 12, 2007, from http://ezinearticles.com/?Job-Seekers:-Prepare-Your-Stories&id=142327

[5] Wright, D. (2004, August/September). Tell stories, get hired. *OfficePro*, pp. 32–33.

[6] Illegal interview questions. (2001, January 29). *USA Today*. Retrieved August 10, 2007, from http://www.usatoday.com/careers/resources/interviewillegal.htm; Washington, T. (2007). Advice on answering illegal interview questions. Retrieved August 10, 2007, from http://www.careerjournal.com/jobhunting/interviewing/19971231-washington.htm; Illegal interview questions. (2007). FindLaw. Retrieved August 10, 2007, from http://employment.findlaw.com/employment/employment-employee-hiring/employment-employee-hiring-interview-questions.html; Keep the interview legal. Resource centre: Recruiting and hiring advice. (2009). Monster.ca. Retrieved July 12, 2009, from http://hiring.monster.ca/hr/hr-best-practices/recruiting-hiring-advice/acquiring-job-candidates/legal-job-interview-questions-canada.aspx

Competent Language Usage Essentials (C.L.U.E.)

In the business world, people are often judged by the way they speak and write. Using the language competently can mean the difference between individual success and failure. Often a speaker sounds accomplished, but when that same individual puts ideas in print, errors in language usage destroy his or her credibility. One student observed, "When I talk, I get by on my personality, but when I write, the flaws in my communication show through. That's why I'm in this class."

How This Grammar and Mechanics Guide Can Help You

This grammar and mechanics guide contains 54 guidelines covering sentence structure, grammar, usage, punctuation, capitalization, number style, and the use of abbreviations. These guidelines focus on the most frequently used—and abused—language elements. Frequent checkpoint exercises enable you to try out your skills immediately. In addition to the 54 language guides in this appendix, you'll find a list of 165 frequently misspelled words and a quick review of selected confusing words.

The concentrated materials in this guide help novice business communicators focus on the major areas of language use. The guide is not meant to teach or review *all* the principles of English grammar and punctuation. It focuses on a limited number of language guidelines and troublesome words. Your objective should be mastery of these language principles and words, which represent a majority of the problems typically encountered by business writers.

How to Use This Grammar and Mechanics Guide

Your instructor may give you the short C.L.U.E. language diagnostic test (located in the Instructor's Manual) to help you assess your competency. This test will give you an idea of your language competence. After taking the diagnostic test, read and work your way through the 54 guidelines. You should also use the self-teaching Trainer exercises, all of which correlate with this Grammar and Mechanics Guide. Concentrate on areas in which you are weak. Memorize the spelling list and definitions for the confusing words located at the end of this appendix.

Within these materials you will find two kinds of exercises for your practice. (1) *Checkpoints*, located in this appendix, focus on a small group of language guidelines. Use them to test your comprehension as you complete each section. (2) *Review exercises*, located in the text chapters, cover all guidelines, spelling words, and confusing words. Use the review exercises to reinforce your language skills at the same time you are learning about the processes and products of business communication. As you complete the review exercises, you may want to use the standard proofreading marks shown on the inside front cover.

- **Reference books.** More comprehensive treatment of grammar and punctuation guidelines can be found in Clark and Clark's *HOW 12: A Handbook for Office Professionals*, ISBN 978-0-324-66239-4; Joanne Buckley's *Checkmate: A Writing Reference for Canadians*, ISBN 978-0-17-650256-0; and *The Harbrace Handbook for Canadians* by John Hodges and Andrew Stubbs, ISBN 978-0-17-622509-4.

Grammar and Mechanics Guidelines

Sentence Structure

GUIDE 1: Avoid sentence fragments. A fragment is an incomplete sentence. You can recognize a complete sentence because it (a) includes a subject (a noun or pronoun that interacts with a verb), (b) includes a verb (a word expressing action or describing a condition), and (c) makes sense (comes to a closure). A complete sentence is an independent clause. One of the most serious errors a writer can make is punctuating a fragment as if it were a complete sentence.

Fragment	Improved
Because 90 percent of all business transactions involve written messages. Good writing skills are critical.	Because 90 percent of all business transactions involve written messages, good writing skills are critical.
The recruiter requested a writing sample. Even though the candidate seemed to communicate well.	The recruiter requested a writing sample, even though the candidate seemed to communicate well.

Tip. Fragments often can be identified by the words that introduce them—such words as *although, as, because, even, except, for example, if, instead of, since, so, such as, that, which,* and *when.* These words introduce dependent clauses. Make sure such clauses are always connected to independent clauses.

DEPENDENT CLAUSE   INDEPENDENT CLAUSE

After she became supervisor, she had to write more memos and reports.

GUIDE 2: Avoid run-on (fused) sentences. A sentence with two independent clauses must be joined by a coordinating conjunction (*and, or, nor, but*) or by a semicolon (;). Without a conjunction or a semicolon, a run-on sentence results.

Run-on	Improved
Robin visited resorts of the rich and the famous he also dropped in on luxury spas.	Robin visited resorts of the rich and famous, and he also dropped in on luxury spas.
	Robin visited resorts of the rich and famous; he also dropped in on luxury spas.

GUIDE 3: Avoid comma-splice sentences. A comma splice results when a writer joins (splices together) two independent clauses without using a coordinating conjunction (*and, or, nor, but*).

Comma Splice	Improved
Disney World operates in Orlando, EuroDisney serves Paris.	Disney World operates in Orlando; EuroDisney serves Paris.
	Disney World operates in Orlando, and EuroDisney serves Paris.
Visitors wanted a resort vacation, however they were disappointed.	Visitors wanted a resort vacation; however, they were disappointed.

Tip. In joining independent clauses, beware of using a comma and such words as *consequently, furthermore, however, therefore, then, thus,* and so on. These conjunctive adverbs require semicolons.

✓ Checkpoint

Revise the following to rectify sentence fragments, comma splices, and run-ons.

1. Although it began as a side business for Disney. Destination weddings now represent a major income source.

2. About 2,000 weddings are held yearly. Which is twice the number just ten years ago.

3. Weddings may take place in less than one hour, however the cost may be as much as $5,000.

4. Limousines line up outside Disney's wedding pavilion, they are scheduled in two-hour intervals.

5. Most couples prefer a traditional wedding, others request a fantasy experience.

For all the Checkpoint sentences, compare your responses with the answers at the end of this appendix.

Grammar

Verb Tense

GUIDE 4: Use present tense, past tense, and past participle verb forms correctly.

Present Tense (Today I _____)	Past Tense (Yesterday I _____)	Past Participle (I have _____)
am	was	been
begin	began	begun
break	broke	broken
bring	brought	brought
choose	chose	chosen
come	came	come
do	did	done
give	gave	given
go	went	gone
know	knew	known
pay	paid	paid
see	saw	seen
steal	stole	stolen
take	took	taken
write	wrote	written

The package *came* yesterday, and Kevin *knew* what it contained.

If I *had seen* the shipper's bill, I *would have paid* it immediately.

I *know* the answer now; I wish I *had known* it yesterday.

Tip. Probably the most frequent mistake in tenses results from substituting the past participle form for the past tense. Notice that the past participle requires auxiliary verbs, such as *has, had, have, would have,* and *could have.*

Faulty

When he *come* over last night, he *brung* pizza.

If he *had came* earlier, we *could have saw* the video.

Correct

When he *came* over last night, he *brought* pizza.

If he *had come* earlier, we *could have seen* the video.

Verb Mood

GUIDE 5: Use the subjunctive mood to express hypothetical (untrue) ideas.
The most frequent misuse of the subjunctive mood involves using *was* instead of *were* in clauses introduced by *if* and *as though* or containing *wish.*

If I *were* (not *was*) you, I would take a business writing course.

Sometimes I wish I *were* (not *was*) the manager of this department.

He acts as though he *were* (not *was*) in charge of this department.

Tip. If the statement could possibly be true, use *was.*

If I *was* to blame, I accept the consequences.

✓ Checkpoint

Correct faults in verb tenses and mood.

6. If I was you, I would have went to the ten o'clock meeting.

7. The manager could have wrote a better report if he had began earlier.

8. When the vice president seen the report, he immediately come to my office.

9. I wish the vice president was in your shoes for just one day.

10. If the manager had knew all that we do, I'm sure he would have gave us better reviews.

Verb Voice

For a discussion of active- and passive-voice verbs, see pages 113–114 in Chapter 5.

Verb Agreement

GUIDE 6: Make subjects agree with verbs despite intervening phrases and clauses.
Become a detective in locating *true* subjects. Don't be deceived by prepositional phrases and parenthetical words that often disguise the true subject.

Our study of annual budgets, five-year plans, and sales proposals *is* (not *are*) progressing on schedule. (The true subject is *study*.)

The budgeted item, despite additions proposed yesterday, *remains* (not *remain*) as submitted. (The true subject is *item*.)

A vendor's evaluation of the prospects for a sale, together with plans for follow-up action, *is* (not *are*) what we need. (The true subject is *evaluation*.)

Tip. Subjects are nouns or pronouns that control verbs. To find subjects, cross out prepositional phrases beginning with such words as *about, at, by, for, from, of,* and *to.* Subjects of verbs are not found in prepositional phrases. Also, don't be tricked by expressions introduced by *together with, in addition to,* and *along with.*

GUIDE 7: Subjects joined by *and* require plural verbs. Watch for true subjects joined by the conjunction *and*. They require plural verbs.

The CEO and one of his assistants *have* (not *has*) ordered a limo.

Considerable time and money *were* (not *was*) spent on remodelling.

Exercising in the gym and jogging every day *are* (not *is*) how he keeps fit.

GUIDE 8: Subjects joined by *or* or *nor* may require singular or plural verbs. The verb should agree with the closest subject.

Either the software or the printer *is* (not *are*) causing the glitch. (The verb is controlled by the closer subject, *printer*.)

Neither Montréal nor Calgary *has* (not *have*) a chance of winning. (The verb is controlled by *Calgary*.)

Tip. In joining singular and plural subjects with *or* or *nor*, place the plural subject closer to the verb. Then the plural verb sounds natural. For example, *Either the manufacturer or the distributors are responsible*.

GUIDE 9: Use singular verbs for most indefinite pronouns. The following pronouns all take singular verbs: *anyone, anybody, anything, each, either, every, everyone, everybody, everything, neither, nobody, nothing, someone, somebody,* and *something*.

Everyone in both offices *was* (not *were*) given a bonus.

Each of the employees *is* (not *are*) being interviewed.

GUIDE 10: Use singular or plural verbs for collective nouns, depending on whether the members of the group are operating as a unit or individually. Such words as *faculty, administration, class, crowd,* and *committee* are considered collective nouns. If the members of the collective are acting as a unit, treat them as singular subjects. If they are acting individually, it's usually better to add the word *members* and use a plural verb.

Correct

The Finance Committee *is* working harmoniously. (*Committee* is singular because its action is unified.)

The Planning Committee *are* having difficulty agreeing. (*Committee* is plural because its members are acting individually.)

Improved

The Planning Committee members *are* having difficulty agreeing. (Add the word *members* if a plural meaning is intended.)

Tip. In North America collective nouns are generally considered singular. In Britain these collective nouns are generally considered plural.

✓ Checkpoint

Correct the errors in subject–verb agreement.

11. The agency's time and talent was spent trying to develop a blockbuster ad campaign.

12. Your e-mail message, along with both of its attachments, were not delivered to my computer.

13. Each of the Fortune 500 companies are being sent a survey regarding women in management.

14. A full list of names and addresses are necessary before we can begin.

15. Either the judge or the lawyer have asked for a recess.

Pronoun Case

GUIDE 11: Learn the three cases of pronouns and how each is used. Pronouns are substitutes for nouns. Every business writer must know the following pronoun cases.

Subjective (Nominative) Case	Objective Case	Possessive Case
Used for subjects of verbs and subject complements	Used for objects of prepositions and objects of verbs	Used to show possession
I	me	my, mine
we	us	our, ours
you	you	your, yours
he	him	his
she	her	her, hers
it	it	its
they	them	their, theirs
who, whoever	whom, whomever	whose

GUIDE 12: Use subjective-case pronouns as subjects of verbs and as complements. Complements are words that follow linking verbs (such as *am, is, are, was, were, be, being*, and *been*) and rename the words to which they refer.

She and *I* (not *her* and *me*) are looking for entry-level jobs. (Use nominative-case pronouns as the subjects of the verb phrase *are looking*.)

We hope that Marci and *he* (not *him*) will be hired. (Use a nominative-case pronoun as the subject of the verb phrase *will be hired*.)

It must have been *she* (not *her*) who called last night. (Use a nominative-case pronoun as a subject complement.)

Tip. If you feel awkward using nominative pronouns after linking verbs, rephrase the sentence to avoid the dilemma. Instead of *It is she who is the boss*, say *She is the boss*.

GUIDE 13: Use objective-case pronouns as objects of prepositions and verbs.

Send the e-mail to *her* and *me* (not *she* and *I*). (The pronouns *her* and *me* are objects of the preposition *to*.)

The CEO appointed Rick and *him* (not *he*) to the committee. (The pronoun *him* is the object of the verb *appointed*.)

Tip. When a pronoun appears in combination with a noun or another pronoun, ignore the extra noun or pronoun and its conjunction. Then the case of the pronoun becomes more obvious.

Jason asked Jennifer and *me* (not *I*) to lunch. (Ignore *Jennifer and*.)

The waiter brought hamburgers to Jason and *me* (not *I*). (Ignore *Jason and*.)

Tip. Be especially alert to the following prepositions: *except, between, but,* and *like.* Be sure to use objective pronouns as their objects.

> Just between you and *me* (not *I*), that mineral water comes from the tap.
>
> Everyone except Robert and *him* (not *he*) responded to the invitation.

GUIDE 14: Use possessive pronouns to show ownership. Possessive pronouns (such *as hers, yours, whose, ours, theirs,* and *its*) require no apostrophes.

> All reports except *yours* (not *your's*) have to be rewritten.
>
> The apartment and *its* (not *it's*) contents are *hers* (not *her's*) until June.

Tip. Don't confuse possessive pronouns and contractions. Contractions are shortened forms of subject–verb phrases (such as *it's* for *it is, there's* for *there is, who's* for *who is,* and *they're* for *they are*).

✓ Checkpoint

Correct errors in pronoun case.

16. My partner and me have looked at many apartments, but your's has the best location.

17. We thought the car was her's, but it's licence plate doesn't match.

18. Just between you and I, do you think there printer is working?

19. Theres not much the boss or me can do if its broken, but its condition should have been reported to him or I earlier.

20. We received several applications, but your's and her's were missing.

GUIDE 15: Use pronouns ending in self only when they refer to previously mentioned nouns or pronouns.

> The president *himself* ate all the M&Ms.
>
> Send the package to Mike or *me* (not *myself*).

Tip. Trying to sound less egocentric, some radio and TV announcers incorrectly substitute *myself* when they should use *I.* For example, "Jerry and *myself* (should be *I*) are cohosting the telethon."

GUIDE 16: Use who or whoever for subjective-case constructions and whom or whomever for objective-case constructions. In determining the correct choice, it's helpful to substitute *he* for *who* or *whoever* and *him* for *whom* or *whomever.*

> For *whom* was this software ordered? (The software was ordered for *him.*)
>
> *Who* did you say called? (You did say *he* called?)
>
> Give the supplies to *whoever* asked for them. (In this sentence the clause *whoever asked for them* functions as the object of the preposition *to.* Within the clause, *whoever* is the subject of the verb *asked.* Again, try substituting *he: he asked for them.*)

✓ Checkpoint

Correct any errors in the use of *self*-ending pronouns and *who/whom.*

21. The boss herself is willing to call whoever we decide to honour.

22. Who have you asked to develop ads for our new products?

23. I have a pizza for whomever placed the telephone order.

24. The meeting is set for Wednesday; however, Matt and myself cannot attend.

25. Incident reports must be submitted by whomever experiences a personnel problem.

Pronoun Reference

GUIDE 17: Make pronouns agree in number and gender with the words to which they refer (their antecedents). When the gender of the antecedent is obvious, pronoun references are simple.

One of the boys lost *his* (not *their*) new tennis shoes. (The singular pronoun *his* refers to the singular *One*.)

Each of the female nurses was escorted to *her car* (not *their cars*). (The singular pronoun *her* and singular noun *car* are necessary because they refer to the singular subject *Each*.)

Somebody on the girls' team left *her* (not *their*) headlights on.

When the gender of the antecedent could be male or female, sensitive writers today have a number of options.

Faulty	Improved
Every employee should receive *their* cheque Friday. (The plural pronoun *their* does not agree with its singular antecedent *employee*.)	All employees should receive *their* cheques Friday. (Make the subject plural so that the plural pronoun *their* is acceptable. This option is preferred by many writers today.)
	All employees should receive cheques Friday. (Omit the possessive pronoun entirely.)
	Every employee should receive *a* cheque Friday. (Substitute *a* for a pronoun.)
	Every employee should receive *his or her* cheque Friday. (Use the combination *his or her*. However, this option is wordy and should be avoided.)

GUIDE 18: Be sure that pronouns, such as *it*, *which*, *this*, and *that*, refer to clear antecedents. Vague pronouns confuse the reader because they have no clear single antecedent. The most troublesome are *it, which, this,* and *that.* Replace vague pronouns with concrete nouns, or provide these pronouns with clear antecedents.

Faulty	Improved
Our office recycles as much paper as possible because it helps the environment. (Does *it* refer to *paper, recycling,* or *office*?)	Our office recycles as much paper as possible because such efforts help the environment. (Replace *it* with *such efforts*.)
The disadvantages of local area networks can offset their advantages. That merits further evaluation. (What merits evaluation: advantages, disadvantages, or offsetting of one by the other?)	The disadvantages of local area networks can offset their advantages. That fact merits further evaluation. (*Fact* supplies a concrete noun for the vague pronoun *that*.)
Negotiators announced an expanded health care plan, reductions in dental coverage, and a proposal of on-site child-care facilities. This caused employee protests. (What exactly caused employee protests?)	Negotiators announced an expanded health care plan, reductions in dental coverage, and a proposal of on-site child-care facilities. This reduction in dental coverage caused employee protests. (The pronoun *This* now has a clear reference.)

Tip. Whenever you use the words *this, that, these,* and *those* by themselves, a red flag should pop up. These words are dangerous when they stand alone. Inexperienced writers often use them to refer to an entire previous idea rather than to a specific antecedent, as shown in the preceding example. You can usually solve the problem by adding another idea to the pronoun (such as *this reduction*).

✅ **Checkpoint**

Correct the faulty and vague pronoun references in the following sentences. Numerous remedies exist.

26. Every employee must wear their picture identification badge.

27. Flexible working hours may mean slower career advancement, but it appeals to many workers.

28. Any renter must pay his rent by the first of the month.

29. Someone in this office reported that his computer had a virus.

30. Obtaining agreement on job standards, listening to co-workers, and encouraging employee suggestions all helped to open lines of communication. This is particularly important in team projects.

Adjectives and Adverbs

GUIDE 19: Use adverbs, not adjectives, to describe or limit the action of verbs. Use adjectives after linking verbs.

Andrew said he did *well* (not *good*) on the exam. (The adverb *well* describes how he did.)

After its tune-up, the engine is running *smoothly* (not *smooth*). (The adverb *smoothly* describes the verb *is running.*)

Don't take the manager's criticism *personally* (not *personal*). (The adverb *personally* tells how to take the criticism.)

She finished her homework *more quickly* (not *quicker*) than expected. (The adverb *more quickly*) explains how she finished her homework.)

Liam felt *bad* (not *badly*) after he heard the news. (The adjective *bad* follows the linking verb *felt.*)

GUIDE 20: Hyphenate two or more adjectives that are joined to create a compound modifier before a noun.

Follow the *step-by-step* instructions to construct the *low-cost* bookshelves.

A *well-designed* keyboard is part of this *state-of-the-art* equipment.

Tip. Don't confuse adverbs ending in *-ly* with compound adjectives: *newly enacted* law and *highly regarded* CEO would not be hyphenated.

✅ **Checkpoint**

Correct any problems in the use of pronouns, adjectives, and adverbs.

31. My manager and me could not resist the once in a lifetime opportunity.

32. Because John and him finished their task so quick, they made a fast trip to the recently opened snack bar.

33. If I do good on the exam, I qualify for many part time jobs and a few full time positions.

34. The vice president told him and I not to take the announcement personal.

35. In the not too distant future, we may enjoy more practical uses of robots.

Punctuation

GUIDE 21: Use commas to separate three or more items (words, phrases, or short clauses) in a series. (CmSer)

Downward communication delivers job instructions, procedures, and appraisals.

In preparing your résumé, try to keep it brief, make it easy to read, and include only job-related information.

The new ice cream flavours include cookie dough, chocolate raspberry truffle, cappuccino, and almond amaretto.

Tip. Some professional writers omit the comma before *and*. However, most business writers prefer to retain that comma because it prevents misreading the last two items as one item. Notice in the previous example how the final two ice cream flavours could have been misread if the comma had been omitted.

GUIDE 22: Use commas to separate introductory clauses and certain phrases from independent clauses. (CmIntro) This guideline describes the comma most often omitted by business writers. Sentences that open with dependent clauses (often introduced by words such as *since, when, if, as, although,* and *because*) require commas to separate them from the main idea. The comma helps readers recognize where the introduction ends and the big idea begins. Introductory phrases of four or more words or phrases containing verbal elements also require commas.

If you recognize introductory clauses, you will have no trouble placing the comma. (A comma separates the introductory dependent clause from the main clause.)

When you have mastered this rule, half the battle with commas will be won.

As expected, additional explanations are necessary. (Use a comma even if the introductory clause omits the understood subject: *As we expected*.)

In the spring of last year, we opened our franchise. (Use a comma after a phrase containing four or more words.)

Having considered several alternatives, we decided to invest. (Use a comma after an introductory verbal phrase.)

To invest, we needed $100,000. (Use a comma after an introductory verbal phrase, regardless of its length.)

Tip. Short introductory prepositional phrases (three or fewer words) require no commas. Don't clutter your writing with unnecessary commas after such introductory phrases as *by 2014, in the fall,* or *at this time.*

GUIDE 23: Use a comma before the coordinating conjunction in a compound sentence. (CmConj) The most common coordinating conjunctions are *and, or, nor,* and *but.* Occasionally *for, yet,* and *so* may also function as coordinating conjunctions. When coordinating conjunctions join two independent clauses, commas are needed.

The investment sounded too good to be true, *and* many investors were dubious. (Use a comma before the coordinating conjunction *and* in a compound sentence.)

Niagara Falls is the honeymoon capital of the world, *but* some newlyweds prefer to go to more exotic destinations.

Tip. Before inserting a comma, test the two clauses. Can each of them stand alone as a complete sentence? If either is incomplete, skip the comma.

Promoters said the investment offer was for a limited time and couldn't be extended by even one day. (Omit a comma before *and* because the second part of the sentence is not a complete independent clause.)

Lease payments are based largely on your down payment and on the value of the car at the end of the lease. (Omit a comma before *and* because the second half of the sentence is not a complete clause.)

✓ Checkpoint

Add appropriate commas.

36. Before she enrolled in this class Erin used to sprinkle her writing with commas semicolons and dashes.

37. After studying punctuation she learned to use commas more carefully and to reduce her reliance on dashes.

38. At this time Erin is engaged in a serious yoga program but she also finds time to enlighten her mind.

39. Next fall Erin may enroll in communication and merchandising or she may work for a semester to earn money.

40. When she completes her junior year she plans to apply for an internship in Montréal Edmonton or Toronto.

GUIDE 24: Use commas appropriately in dates, addresses, geographic names, degrees, and long numbers. (CmDate)

September 30, 1963, is his birthday. (For dates use commas before and after the year.)

Send the application to James Kirby, 3405 120th Ave. N.W., Edmonton, AB T5W 1M3, as soon as possible. (For addresses use commas to separate all units except the two-letter province abbreviation and the postal code.)

Lisa expects to move from Calgary, Alberta, to Sarnia, Ontario, next fall. (For geographic areas use commas to enclose the second element.)

Karen Munson, CGA, and Richard B. Larsen, PhD, were the speakers. (For professional designations and academic degrees following names, use commas to enclose each item.)

The latest census figures show the city's population to be 342,000. (Although the metric system uses space separators instead of commas in large numbers, most businesspeople continue to include them as they make the numbers easier to read and understand.)

GUIDE 25: Use commas to set off internal sentence interrupters. (CmIn)
Sentence interrupters may be verbal phrases, dependent clauses, contrasting elements, or parenthetical expressions (also called transitional phrases). These interrupters often provide information that is not grammatically essential.

Medical researchers, working steadily for 18 months, developed a new cancer therapy. (Use commas to set off an interrupting verbal phrase.)

The new therapy, which applies a genetically engineered virus, raises hopes among cancer specialists. (Use commas to set off nonessential dependent clauses.)

Dr. James C. Morrison, who is one of the researchers, made the announcement. (Use commas to set off nonessential dependent clauses.)

It was Dr. Morrison, not Dr. Arturo, who led the team effort. (Use commas to set off a contrasting element.)

This new therapy, by the way, was developed from a herpes virus. (Use commas to set off a parenthetical expression.)

Tip. Parenthetical (transitional) expressions are helpful words that guide the reader from one thought to the next. Here are typical parenthetical expressions that require commas:

as a matter of fact	in addition	of course
as a result	in the meantime	on the other hand
consequently	nevertheless	therefore
for example		

Tip. Always use *two* commas to set off an interrupter, unless it begins or ends a sentence.

 Checkpoint

Insert necessary commas.

41. James listed 222 George Henry Blvd. Toronto ON M2J 1E6 as his forwarding address.

42. This report is not however one that must be classified.

43. Employment of paralegals which is expected to increase 32 percent next year is growing rapidly because of the expanding legal services industry.

44. The contract was signed May 15 2010 and remains in effect until May 15 2015.

45. As a matter of fact the average North American drinks enough coffee to require 5 kilograms of coffee beans annually.

GUIDE 26: Avoid unnecessary commas.
Do not use commas between sentence elements that belong together. Don't automatically insert commas before every *and* or at points where your voice might drop if you were saying the sentence out loud.

Faulty

Growth will be spurred by the increasing complexity of business operations, and by large employment gains in trade and services. (A comma unnecessarily precedes *and.*)

All students with high grades, are eligible for the honour society. (A comma unnecessarily separates the subject and verb.)

One of the reasons for the success of the business honour society is, that it is very active. (A comma unnecessarily separates the verb and its complement.)

Our honour society has, at this time, more than 50 members. (Commas unnecessarily separate a prepositional phrase from the sentence.)

✓ Checkpoint

Remove unnecessary commas. Add necessary ones.

46. Car companies promote leasing because it brings customers back into their showrooms sooner, and gives dealers a steady supply of late-model used cars.

47. When shopping for a car you may be offered a fantastic leasing deal.

48. The trouble with many leases is, that the value of the car at the end of the lease may be less than expected.

49. We think on the other hand, that you should compare the costs of leasing and buying, and that you should talk to a tax adviser.

50. Many North American automakers are, at this time, offering intriguing lease deals.

Semicolons and Colons

GUIDE 27: Use a semicolon to join closely related independent clauses.
Experienced writers use semicolons to show readers that two thoughts are closely associated. If the ideas are not related, they should be expressed as separate sentences. Often, but not always, the second independent clause contains a conjunctive adverb (such as *however, consequently, therefore,* or *furthermore*) to show the relation between the two clauses.

> Learning history is easy; learning its lessons is almost impossible. (A semicolon joins two independent clauses.)

> He was determined to complete his degree; consequently, he studied diligently. (A semicolon precedes the conjunctive adverb and a comma follows it.)

> Serena wanted a luxury apartment located near campus; however, she couldn't afford the rent. (A semicolon precedes the conjunctive adverb and a comma follows it.)

Tip. Don't use a semicolon unless each clause is truly independent. Try the sentence test. Omit the semicolon if each clause could not stand alone as a complete sentence.

Faulty	Improved
There's no point in speaking; unless you can improve on silence. (The second half of the sentence is a dependent clause. It could not stand alone as a sentence.)	There's no point in speaking unless you can improve on silence.
Although I cannot change the direction of the wind; I can adjust my sails to reach my destination. (The first clause could not stand alone.)	Although I cannot change the direction of the wind, I can adjust my sails to reach my destination.

GUIDE 28: Use a semicolon to separate items in a series when one or more of the items contains internal commas.

> Representatives from as far away as Longueuil, Quebec; Vancouver, British Columbia; and Whitehorse, Yukon, attended the conference.

> Stories circulated about Henry Ford, founder, Ford Motor Company; Lee Iacocca, former CEO, Chrysler Motor Company; and Kiichiro Toyoda, founder, Toyota Motor Corporation.

GUIDE 29: Use a colon after a complete thought that introduces a list of items.
Such words as *these, the following,* and *as follows* may introduce the list or they may be implied.

> The following cities are on the tour: Toronto, Ottawa, and Winnipeg.

> An alternative tour includes several West Coast cities: Vancouver, Nanaimo, and Victoria.

Tip. Be sure that the statement before a colon is grammatically complete. An introductory statement that ends with a preposition (such as *by, for, at,* and *to*) or a verb (such as *is, are,* or *were*) is incomplete. The list following a preposition or a verb actually functions as an object or as a complement to finish the sentence.

Faulty	Improved
Three Big Macs were ordered by: Pam, Jim, and Lee. (Do not use a colon after an incomplete statement.)	Three Big Macs were ordered by Pam, Jim, and Lee.
Other items that they ordered were: fries, Cokes, and salads. (Do not use a colon after an incomplete statement.)	Other items that they ordered were fries, Cokes, and salads.

GUIDE 30: Use a colon after business letter salutations and to introduce long quotations.

Dear Mr. Duran: Dear Lisa:

The Asian consultant bluntly said: "North Americans tend to be too blabby, too impatient, and too informal for Asian tastes. To succeed in trade with Pacific Rim countries, North Americans must become more willing to adapt to native cultures."

Tip. Use a comma to introduce short quotations. Use a colon to introduce long one-sentence quotations and quotations of two or more sentences.

 Checkpoint

Add appropriate semicolons and colons.

51. Marco's short-term goal is an entry-level job his long-term goal however is a management position.

52. Speakers included the following professors Rebecca Hilbrink University of Western Ontario Lora Lindsey McGill University and Michael Malone Durham College.

53. The recruiter was looking for three qualities loyalty initiative and enthusiasm.

54. Microsoft seeks experienced individuals however it will hire recent graduates who are skilled.

55. Mississauga is an expanding region therefore many business opportunities are available.

Apostrophe

GUIDE 31: Add an apostrophe plus *s* to an ownership word that does not end in an *s* sound.

We hope to show a profit in one year's time. (Add *'s* because the ownership word *year* does not end in an *s*.)

The company's assets rose in value. (Add *'s* because the ownership word *company* does not end in *s*.)

All the women's votes were counted. (Add *'s* because the ownership word *women* does not end in *s*.)

GUIDE 32: Add only an apostrophe to an ownership word that ends in an *s* sound—unless an extra syllable can be pronounced easily.

Some workers' benefits will cost more. (Add only an apostrophe because the ownership word *workers* ends in an *s*.)

Several months' rent are now due. (Add only an apostrophe because the ownership word *months* ends in an *s*.)

The boss's son got the job. (Add *'s* because an extra syllable can be pronounced easily.)

Tip. To determine whether an ownership word ends in an *'s*, use it in an *of* phrase. For example, *one month's salary* becomes *the salary of one month*. By isolating the ownership word without its apostrophe, you can decide whether it ends in an *s*.

GUIDE 33: Use a possessive pronoun or add 's to make a noun possessive when it precedes a gerund (a verb form used as a noun).

We all protested *Laura's* (not *Laura*) smoking. (Add *'s* to the noun preceding the gerund)

His (not *Him*) talking on his cellphone angered moviegoers. (Use a possessive pronoun before the gerund).

I appreciate *your* (not *you*) answering the telephone while I was gone. (Use a possessive pronoun before the gerund.)

✓ Checkpoint

Correct any problems with possessives.

56. Both companies executives received huge bonuses, even when employees salaries were falling.

57. In just one weeks time we promise to verify all members names and addresses.

58. The manager and I certainly appreciate you bringing this matter to our CGAs attention.

59. All beneficiaries names must be revealed when insurance companies write policies.

60. Is your sister-in-laws job downtown?

Other Punctuation

GUIDE 34: Use one period to end a statement, command, indirect question, or polite request. Never use two periods.

Matt worked at BioTech, Inc. (Statement. Use only one period.)

Deliver it before 5 p.m. (Command. Use only one period.)

Stacy asked whether she could use the car next weekend. (Indirect question)

Will you please send me an employment application. (Polite request)

Tip. Polite requests often sound like questions. To determine the punctuation, apply the action test. If the request prompts an action, use a period. If it prompts a verbal response, use a question mark.

Faulty

Could you please correct the balance on my next statement? (This polite request prompts an action rather than a verbal response.)

Improved

Could you please correct the balance on my next statement.

GUIDE 35: Use a question mark after a direct question and after statements with questions appended.

Are they hiring at BioTech, Inc.?

Most of their training is in-house, isn't it?

GUIDE 36: Use a dash to (a) set off parenthetical elements containing internal commas, (b) emphasize a sentence interruption, or (c) separate an introductory list from a summarizing statement. The dash has legitimate uses. However, some writers use it whenever they know that punctuation is necessary, but they're not sure exactly what. The dash can be very effective, if not misused.

Three top students—Gene Engle, Donna Hersh, and Mika Sato—won awards. (Use dashes to set off elements with internal commas.)

Executives at IBM—despite rampant rumours in the stock market—remained quiet regarding dividend earnings. (Use dashes to emphasize a sentence interruption.)

Japan, Taiwan, and Turkey—these were areas hit by recent earthquakes. (Use a dash to separate an introductory list from a summarizing statement.)

GUIDE 37: Use parentheses to set off nonessential sentence elements, such as explanations, directions, questions, or references.

Researchers find that the office grapevine (see Chapter 1 for more discussion) carries surprisingly accurate information.

Only two dates (February 15 and March 1) are suitable for the meeting.

Tip. Careful writers use parentheses to de-emphasize and the dash to emphasize parenthetical information. One expert said, "Dashes shout the news; parentheses whisper it."

GUIDE 38: Use quotation marks to (a) enclose the exact words of a speaker or writer; (b) distinguish words used in a special sense, such as slang; or (c) enclose titles of articles, chapters, or other short works.

"If you make your job important," said the consultant, "it's quite likely to return the favour."

The recruiter said that she was looking for candidates with good communication skills. (Omit quotation marks because the exact words of the speaker are not quoted.)

This office discourages "rad" hair styles and clothing. (Use quotation marks for slang.)

In *Businessweek* I saw an article entitled "Communication for Global Markets." (Use quotation marks around the title of an article; use all caps, underlines, or italics for the name of the publication.)

Tip. Never use quotation marks arbitrarily, as in *Our "spring" sale starts April 1.*

✓ Checkpoint

Add appropriate punctuation.

61. Will you please send your print catalogue as soon as possible

62. (Direct quotation) Our Stanley Cup promotion said the CEO will cost nearly $500,000

63. (De-emphasize) Two kinds of batteries see page 16 of the instruction booklet may be used in this camera.

64. Tim wondered whether sentences could end with two periods

65. All computers have virus protection don't they

Capitalization

GUIDE 39: Capitalize proper nouns and proper adjectives. Capitalize the *specific* names of persons, places, institutions, buildings, religions, holidays, months, organizations, laws, races, languages, and so forth. Don't capitalize common nouns that make *general* references.

Proper Nouns	Common Nouns
Michelle Deluca	the manufacturer's rep
Algonquin Provincial Park	the wilderness park
College of the Rockies	the community college
CN Tower	the downtown building
Environmental Assessment Agency	the federal agency
Persian, Armenian, Hindi	modern foreign languages

Proper Adjectives

Hispanic markets	Italian dressing
Xerox copy	Japanese executives
Swiss chocolates	Red River economics

GUIDE 40: Capitalize only specific academic courses and degrees.

Professor Donna Howard, PhD, will teach Accounting 121 next spring.

James Barker, who holds bachelor's and master's degrees, teaches marketing.

Jessica enrolled in classes in management, English, and business law.

GUIDE 41: Capitalize courtesy, professional, religious, government, family, and business titles when they precede names.

Mr. Jameson, Mrs. Alvarez, and Ms. Robinson (Courtesy titles)

Professor Andrews, Dr. Lee (Professional titles)

Rabbi Cohen, Pastor Williams, Pope John (Religious titles)

Senator Tom Harrison, Mayor Jackson (Government titles)

Uncle Edward, Aunt Teresa, Cousin Vinny (Family titles)

Vice President Morris, Budget Director Lopez (Business titles)

Do not capitalize a title when it is followed by an appositive (that is, when the title is followed by a noun that renames or explains it).

Only one professor, Jonathan Marcus, favoured a tuition hike.

Local candidates counted on their premier, Lorne Calvert, to raise funds.

Do not capitalize titles following names unless they are part of an address.

Mark Yoder, president of Yoder Enterprises, hired all employees.

Paula Beech, director of Human Resources, interviewed all candidates.

Send the package to Amanda Harr, Advertising Manager, Cambridge Publishers, 20 Park Plaza, Saint John, NB E2L 1G2.

Generally, do not capitalize a title that replaces a person's name.

Only the prime minister, his chief of staff, and one senator made the trip.

The director of marketing and the sales manager will meet at 1 p.m.

Do not capitalize family titles used with possessive pronouns.

my mother, his father, your cousin

GUIDE 42: Capitalize the main words in the titles, subject lines, and headings. Main words are all words except (a) the articles *a, an, the*; (b) the conjunctions *and, but, or, and nor*; (c) prepositions containing two or three letters (e.g.,

of, *in, to, by, on, for*); (d) the word *to* in infinitives (such as *to run, to say, and to write*); the word *as*—unless any of these words are the first or last words in the title, subject line, or heading.

> I enjoyed the book *A Customer Is More Than a Name.* (Book title)
>
> Team Meeting to Discuss Deadlines Rescheduled for Friday (Subject line)
>
> We liked the article titled "Advice From a Pro: How to Say It With Pictures." (Article)
>
> Check the Advice and Resources link at the *CareerBuilder* Web site.

(Note that the titles of books are underlined or italicized but the titles of articles are enclosed in quotation marks.)

GUIDE 43: Capitalize north, south, east, west, and their derivatives only when they represent specific geographic regions.

from the Pacific Northwest	heading northwest on the highway
living in the East	east of the city
moving to the West Coast	western Quebec, southern Manitoba

GUIDE 44: Capitalize the main words in the specific names of departments, divisions, or committees within business organizations. Do not capitalize general references.

> All forms are available from our Department of Human Resources.
>
> The Consumer Electronics Division launched an upbeat marketing campaign.
>
> We volunteered for the Employee Social Responsibility Committee.
>
> You might send an application to the company's personnel department.

GUIDE 45: Capitalize product names only when they refer to trademarked items. Don't capitalize the common names following manufacturers' names.

Dell laptop computer	Skippy peanut butter	NordicTrack treadmill
Energizer batteries	Norelco razor	Kodak colour copier
Coca-Cola	Apple computer	Big Mac sandwich

GUIDE 46: Capitalize most nouns followed by numbers or letters (except in page, paragraph, line, and verse references).

Room 14	Exhibit A	Flight 12, Gate 43
Figure 2.1	Plan No. 1	Model Z2010

✓ Checkpoint

Capitalize all appropriate words.

66. vice president moore bought a new nokia cellphone before leaving for the east coast.

67. when you come on tuesday, travel west on highway 5 and exit at mt. pleasant street.

68. The director of our human resources department called a meeting of the company's building security committee.

69. our manager and president are flying on air canada flight 34 leaving from gate 69 at mirabel international airport.

70. my father read a *canadian business* article titled "can you build loyalty with bricks and mortar?"

Number Usage

GUIDE 47: Use word form to express (a) numbers ten and under and (b) numbers beginning sentences.
General references to numbers *ten* and under should be expressed in word form. Also use word form for numbers that begin sentences. If the resulting number involves more than two words, however, recast the sentence so that the number does not fall at the beginning.

> We answered *six* telephone calls for the *four* sales reps.
>
> *Fifteen* customers responded to the *three* advertisements today.
>
> A total of 155 cameras were awarded as prizes. (Avoid beginning the sentence with a long number, such as *one hundred and fifty-five*.)

GUIDE 48: Use figures to express most references to numbers 11 and over.

> Over *150* people from *53* companies attended the two-day workshop.
>
> A *120* mL serving of Haagen-Dazs toffee crunch ice cream contains *300* calories and *19* grams of fat.

GUIDE 49: Use figures to express money, dates, clock time, decimals, and percents.

> One item cost only *$1.95*; most, however, were priced between *$10* and *$35*. (Omit the decimals and zeros in even sums of money.)
>
> A meeting is scheduled *May 12*. (Notice that we do not write *May 12th*.)
>
> Deliveries are made at *10:15* a.m. and again at 4 p.m. (Use lowercase *a.m.* and *p.m.*)
>
> All packages must be ready by *4 o'clock*. (Do *not* write 4:00 o'clock.)
>
> When sales dropped *4.7* percent, net income fell *9.8* percent. (Use the word *percent* instead of the symbol %.)

GUIDE 50. Use a combination of words and figures to express sums of 1 million and over. Use words for small fractions.

> Orion lost *$62.9 million* in the latest fiscal year on revenues of *$584 million*. (Use a combination of words and figures for sums of 1 million and over.)
>
> Only *one half* of the registered voters turned out. (Use words for small fractions.)

Tip. To ease your memory load, concentrate on the numbers normally expressed in words: numbers *ten* and under, numbers at the beginning of a sentence, and small fractions. Nearly everything else in business is generally written with figures.

✓ Checkpoint

Correct any inappropriate expression of numbers.

71. Although he budgeted fifty dollars, Jake spent 94 dollars and 34 cents for his cellphone.

72. Is the meeting on November 7th or November 14th?

73. UPS deliveries arrive at nine AM and again at four fifteen PM.

74. The company applied for a fifty thousand dollar loan at six %.

75. The Canadian population is close to 33,000,000 and the world population is estimated to be nearly 6,600,000,000.

Abbreviations

Abbreviations should be used only when they are clear and appropriate. Be aware that every field (such as technology and engineering) has its own specialized abbreviations. Therefore, be certain before you use such abbreviations that the receiver of your information is familiar with them.

GUIDE 51: Use abbreviations for titles before and after proper names.

Mr. Peter Mansbridge	Joshua Paul, *Jr.*
Rev. Simon Brownsley	*Hon.* Diane Finley
Samford Amhas, *MD*	Ronny Muntroy, *PhD*

GUIDE 52: Learn when to use periods with abbreviations.

Use a period with conventional abbreviations.

Mrs.	Ms.	Mr.	Dr.	Hon.	Prof.

Acronyms (shortened forms), which are pronounced as a word, do not have periods.

AIDS	scuba	laser	UNICEF	NAFTA

Latin abbreviations have periods.

e.g.	i.e.	etc.	vs.

GUIDE 53: Use abbreviations for familiar institutions, organizations, associations, corporations, and people.

Institutions

UBC	UWO	WLU	CNIB

Organizations and Associations

NDP	CIA	YMCA	CAW	CAPIC	CMA
OPEC	G8	OSSTF	NHLPA	CHRP	CSIS

Corporations

IBM	CTW	CBC

People

PET	FDR	LBJ	JFK

GUIDE 54: Remember your audience when using abbreviations. If the short form or abbreviation is not well known, spell it out it before using it throughout the discussion.

The CBE (Council of Biology Editors) documentation style is used primarily in the sciences. Consult a reference text for information about how to use CBE documentation.

✓ Checkpoint

Correct any inappropriate use of abbreviations.

76. My dr., Samnik Shanban, m.d., has wonderful credentials.

77. To save both money and time, the specialist recommended l.a.s.e.r. surgery.

78. The question was addressed to Prof Antle.

79. You should remember to use a large-sized font when preparing overheads, eg, 24 point or larger.

80. Mrs. Cathrick was n.a. for comment.

Key to Grammar and Mechanics Checkpoint Exercises in Appendix A

This key shows all corrections. If you marked anything else, double-check the appropriate guideline.

1. Disney, destination

2. yearly, which

3. hour; however,

4. pavilion;

5. wedding;

6. If I *were* you, I would have *gone* . . . .

7. could have *written* . . . had *begun* earlier.

8. vice president *saw* . . . immediately *came*

9. vice president *were*

10. manager had *known* . . . would have *given*

11. time and talent *were* spent (note that two subjects require a plural verb.)

12. attachments, *was* (Note that the subject is *message.)*

13. Each of . . . companies *is* (Note that the subject is *Each.)*

14. list of names and addresses *is* (Note that the subject is *list.)*

15. lawyer *has*

16. My partner and *I* . . ., but *yours*

17. was *hers*, but *its*

18. you and *me* . . . *their* printer

19. *There's* not much the boss or *I* can do if *it's* broken, . . . reported to him or *me* earlier.

20. but *yours* and *hers*

21. *whomever*

22. *Whom* have you asked . . ..

23. for *whoever*

24. Matt and *I*

25. by *whoever*

26. Every employee must wear *a* picture identification badge, OR *All employees* must wear picture identification *badges.*

27. slower career advancement, but *flexible scheduling* appeals to many workers. (Revise to avoid the vague pronoun *it.)*

28. Any renter must pay *the* rent . . .. OR *All renters must pay their rent* . . ..

29. reported that *a* computer . . .. OR: reported that *his or her* computer . . ..

30. communication. *These techniques are* particularly important (Revise to avoid the vague pronoun *This.)*

31. My manager and *I* could not resist the *once-in-a-lifetime* opportunity.

32. John and *he* finished their task so *quickly* (Do not hyphenate *recently opened.)*

33. do *well* . . . *part-time* jobs and a few *full-time*

34. told him and *me* . . . *personally.*

35. *not-too-distant* future

36. class, Erin . . . with commas, semicolons,

37. studying punctuation,

38. program,

39. merchandising,

40. junior year, . . . in Montréal, Edmonton,

41. Blvd., Toronto, ON M2J 1E6

42. not, however,

43. paralegals, . . . next year,

44. May 15, 2010, . . . May 15, 2015.

45. fact,

46. sooner [delete comma]

47. car,

48. is [delete comma]

49. think, on the other hand, . . . buying [delete comma]

50. automakers are [delete comma] at this time [delete comma]

51. entry-level job; his long-term goal, however,

52. professors: Rebecca Hilbrink, University of Western Ontario; Lora Lindsey, McGill University; and Michael Malone, Durham College.

53. qualities: loyalty, initiative,

54. individuals; however,

55. region; therefore,

56. companies' . . . employees'

57. one week's time, . . . members'

58. appreciate your . . . CGA's

59. beneficiaries'

60. sister-in-law's

61. possible.

62. "Our Stanley Cup promotion," said the CEO, "will cost nearly $500,000."

63. Two kinds of batteries (see page 16 of the instruction booklet)

64. two periods.

65. protection, don't they?

66. Vice President Moore . . . Nokia . . . East Coast

67. When . . . Tuesday, . . . Highway 5 . . . Mt. Pleasant Street.

68. Human Resources Department . . . Building Security Committee

69. Our . . . Air Canada Flight 34 . . . Gate 69 at Mirabel International Airport

70. *Canadian Business* article titled, "Can You Build Loyalty With Bricks and Mortar?"

71. $50 . . . $94.34

72. November 7 or November 14 [delete th]

73. 9 a.m . . . 4:15 p.m. (Note only one period at the end of the sentence.)

74. $50,000 . . . 6 percent.

75. 33 million . . . 6.6 billion

76. doctor . . . MD,

77. laser

78. Professor

79. e.g.

80. not available

Confusing Words

accede:	to agree or consent	*affect:*	to influence
exceed:	to go over a limit	*effect:*	(n) outcome, result; (v) to bring about, to create
accept:	to receive		
except:	to exclude; (prep) but	*all ready:*	prepared
adverse:	opposing; antagonistic	*already:*	by this time
averse:	unwilling; reluctant	*all right:*	satisfactory
advice:	suggestion, opinion	*alright:*	unacceptable variant spelling
advise:	to counsel or recommend	*altar:*	structure for worship

alter:	to change
appraise:	to estimate
apprise:	to inform
ascent:	(n) rising or going up
assent:	(v) to agree or consent
assure:	to promise
ensure:	to make certain
insure:	to protect from loss
capital:	(n) city that is seat of government; wealth of an individual; (adj) chief
Capitol:	building that houses U.S. state or national lawmakers
cereal:	breakfast food
serial:	arranged in sequence
cite:	to quote; to summon
sight:	a view; to see
site:	location
coarse:	rough texture
course:	a route; part of a meal; a unit of learning
complement:	that which completes
compliment:	(n) praise, flattery; (v) to praise or flatter
conscience:	regard for fairness
conscious:	aware
council:	governing body
counsel:	(n) advice, lawyer, consultant; (v) to give advice
credible:	believable
creditable:	good enough for praise or esteem; reliable
desert:	(n) arid land; (v) to abandon
dessert:	sweet food
device:	invention or mechanism
devise:	to design or arrange
disburse:	to pay out
disperse:	to scatter widely
elicit:	to draw out
illicit:	unlawful
envelop:	(v) to wrap, surround, or conceal
envelope:	(n) a container for a written message
every day:	each single day
everyday:	ordinary
farther:	a greater distance
further:	additional
formally:	in a formal manner
formerly:	in the past

grate:	(v) to reduce to small particles; to cause irritation; (n) a frame of crossed bars blocking a passage
great:	(adj) large in size; numerous; eminent or distinguished
hole:	an opening
whole:	complete
imply:	to suggest indirectly
infer:	to reach a conclusion
lean:	(v) to rest against; (adj) not fat
lien:	(n) a legal right or claim to property
liable:	legally responsible
libel:	damaging written statement
loose:	not fastened
lose:	to misplace
miner:	person working in a mine
minor:	(adj) lesser; (n) a person under age
patience:	calm perseverance
patients:	people receiving medical treatment
personal:	private, individual
personnel:	employees
plaintiff:	(n) one who initiates a lawsuit
plaintive:	(adj) expressive of suffering or woe
populace:	(n) the masses; population of a place
populous:	(adj) densely populated
precede:	to go before
proceed:	to continue
precedence:	priority
precedents:	events used as an example
principal:	(n) capital sum; school official; (adj) chief
principle:	rule of action
stationary:	immovable
stationery:	writing material
than:	conjunction showing comparison
then:	adverb meaning "at that time"
their:	possessive form of they
there:	at that place or point
they're:	contraction of *they are*
to:	a preposition; the sign of the infinitive
too:	an adverb meaning "also" or "to an excessive extent"
two:	a number
waiver:	abandonment of a claim
waver:	to shake or fluctuate

165 Frequently Misspelled Words

absence
accommodate
achieve
acknowledgment
across
adequate
advisable
analyze
annually
appointment
argument
automatically
bankruptcy
becoming
beneficial
budget
business
calendar
cancelled
catalogue
centre
changeable
column
committee
congratulate
conscience
conscious
consecutive
consensus
consistent
control
convenient
correspondence
courteous
criticize
decision
deductible
defendant
definitely
dependant (n)
dependent (adj)
describe

desirable
destroy
development
disappoint
dissatisfied
division
efficient
embarrass
emphasis
emphasize
employee
envelope
equipped
especially
evidently
exaggerate
excellent
exempt
existence
extraordinary
familiar
fascinate
feasible
February
fibre
fiscal
foreign
forty
fourth
friend
genuine
government
grammar
grateful
guarantee
harass
height
hoping
immediate
incidentally
incredible
independent

indispensable
interrupt
irrelevant
itinerary
judgment
knowledge
legitimate
library
licence (n)
license (v)
maintenance
manageable
manufacturer
mileage
miscellaneous
mortgage
necessary
nevertheless
ninety
ninth
noticeable
occasionally
occurred
offered
omission
omitted
opportunity
opposite
ordinarily
paid
pamphlet
permanent
permitted
pleasant
practical
prevalent
privilege
probably
procedure
profited
prominent
qualify

quantity
questionnaire
receipt
receive
recognize
recommendation
referred
regarding
remittance
representative
restaurant
schedule
secretary
separate
similar
sincerely
software
succeed
sufficient
supervisor
surprise
tenant
therefore
thorough
though
through
truly
undoubtedly
unnecessarily
usable
usage
using
usually
valuable
vigorous (but vigour)
volume
weekday
writing
yield

For many reasons business writers are careful to properly document report data. Citing sources strengthens a writer's argument, as you learned in Chapter 11. Acknowledging sources also shields writers from charges of plagiarism. Moreover, good references help readers pursue further research.

Before we discuss specific documentation formats, you must understand the difference between *source* notes and *content* notes. Source notes identify quotations, paraphrased passages, and author references. They lead readers to the sources of cited information, and they must follow a consistent format. Content notes, however, enable writers to add comments, explain information not directly related to the text, or refer readers to other sections of a report. Because content notes are generally infrequent, most writers identify them in the text with a raised asterisk (*). At the bottom of the page, the asterisk is repeated with the content note following. If two content notes appear on one page, a double asterisk identifies the second reference.

Your real concern will be with source notes. These identify quotations or paraphrased ideas in the text, and they direct readers to a complete list of references (a bibliography) at the end of your report. Researchers have struggled for years to develop the perfect documentation system, one that is efficient for the writer and crystal clear to the reader. As a result, many systems exist, each with its advantages. The important thing for you is to adopt one system and use it consistently.

Students frequently ask, "But what documentation system is most used in business?" Actually, no one method dominates. Many businesses have developed their own hybrid systems. These companies generally supply guidelines illustrating their in-house style to employees. Before starting any research project on the job, you will want to inquire about your organization's preferred documentation style. You can also look in the files for examples of previous reports.

References are usually cited in two places: (1) a brief citation appears in the text, and (2) a complete citation appears in a bibliography at the end of the report. The two most common formats for citations and bibliographies in academic work are those of the Modern Language Association (MLA) and the American Psychological Association (APA). Each has its own style for textual references and bibliography lists. The citations in this textbook are adapted from the APA style, which is increasingly the standard in business communication.

Modern Language Association Format

Writers in the humanities and liberal arts frequently use the MLA format, which is illustrated in Figure B.1. In parentheses close to the textual reference appears the author's name and page cited. If no author is known, a shortened version of the source title is used. At the end of the report, the writer lists alphabetically all references in a bibliography called "Works Cited." The MLA no longer requires the use of URLs in Web citations because Web addresses change and most readers can find Web addresses by using a Web browser and searching for the publication title. In another recent change, MLA style now requires identification of the publication medium, such as *Print* or *Web*. For more information consult *MLA Handbook for Writers of Research Papers*, 7e (New York: The Modern Language Association of America, 2009) or Rossiter's *The MLA Pocket Handbook* (DW Publishing).

Portions of MLA Text Page and Works Cited

Peanut butter was first delivered to the world by a St. Louis physician in 1890. As discussed at the Peanut Advisory Board's Web site, peanut butter was originally promoted as a protein substitute for elderly patients ("History"). However, it was the 1905 Universal Exposition in St. Louis that truly launched peanut butter. Since then, annual peanut butter consumption has zoomed to 1.5 kilograms a person in the United States (Barrons).

America's farmers produce 1.6 million metric tons of peanuts annually, about half of which is used for oil, nuts, and candy. Lisa Gibbons, executive secretary of the Peanut Advisory Board, says that "peanuts in some form are in the top four candies: Snickers, Reese's Peanut Butter Cups, Peanut M & Ms, and Butterfingers" (Meadows 32).

Works Cited

Barrons, Elizabeth Ruth. "A Comparison of Domestic and International Consumption of Legumes." *Journal of Economic Agriculture* 23 (2010): 45–49. Print.

"History of Peanut Butter." *Peanut Advisory Board.* Alabama Peanut Producers Association. (n.d.) Web. Retrieved 19 Jan. 2011.

Meadows, Mark Allen. "Peanut Crop Is Anything but Peanuts at Home and Overseas." *Business Monthly* May 2011: 31–34. Print.

MLA In-Text Format

In-text citations generally appear close to the point where the reference is mentioned or at the end of the sentence inside the closing period. Follow these guidelines:

- Include the last name of the author(s) and the page number. Do not use a comma, as (Smith 310).

- If the author's name is mentioned in the text, cite only the page number in parentheses. Do not include either the word *page* or the abbreviations *p.* or *pp.*

- If no author is known, refer to the document title or a shortened version of it, as ("Facts at Fingertips" 102).

MLA Bibliographic Format

In the "Works Cited" bibliography, list all references cited in a report. Some writers include all works consulted. A portion of an MLA bibliography is shown in Figure B.1. A more complete list of model references appears in Figure B.2. Following are selected guidelines summarizing important points regarding MLA bibliographic format:

- Use italics for the titles of books, magazines, newspapers, journals, and Web sites. Capitalize all main words.

- Enclose the titles of magazine, newspaper, and journal articles in quotation marks. Include volume and issue numbers for journals only.

- Use the following sequence for electronic sources: author; article name in quotation marks; title of Web site, project, or book in italics; name of institution, organization, or publisher affiliated with the site; page numbers if available; URL (only if necessary for retrieval); publication medium (such as *Web, Print,* or *PDF*); and access date.

FIGURE B.2 MLA Sample Works Cited

Works Cited

Air Canada. *2012 Annual Report*. Dorval, QC: Air Canada. Print. — Annual report, print

Atamian, Richard A., and Ellen Ferranto. *Driving Market Forces*. New York: — Book, two authors, print
  HarperCollins, 2010. Print.

"Audio Conferencing." *Encyclopaedia Britannica*. 2010. *Britannica.com*. Web. 19 — Encyclopedia, Web
  Oct. 2010.

Austin, Anthony. Personal interview. 16 Jan. 2012. — Interview

Balcazar, Saul. "The Future of Investing," *Fortune* 1 Mar. 2010: 62–67. *ABI/Inform*. — Magazine article, Web database
  Web. 15 Mar. 2010.

Berss, Marcia. "Protein Man," *Forbes* 24 Oct. 2011: 65–66. Print. — Magazine article, print

Cantrell, Mark R., and Hilary Watson. "Violence in Today's Workplace." *Office* — Magazine article, PDF file
  Review 10 Jan. 2010: 24–27. PDF file. 23 May 2011.

"Globalization Often Means That the Fast Track Leads Overseas." *National Post* — Newspaper article, no author, print
  16 June 2011: A1, A4. Print.

Grover, Hal. "When Taking a Tip From a Job Network, Proceed With Caution." *The* — Newspaper article, one author, print
  Globe and Mail 7 Feb. 2011: B1. Print.

Gutzman, Debra. "Corporate Ghostwriting," *Financial Times* 14 Apr. 2011: n.pag. — Newspaper article, Web, no page
  FT.com. Web. 20 Apr. 2011.

Lynch, Diane. "Wired Women: Gender in High-Tech Workplace." *abcnews.go.com* — Web document without print version
  Technology. n.d. Web. 24 Apr. 2011.

Statistics Canada. A Portrait of Persons With Disabilities: Target Groups Project. — Government publication
  Ottawa: Ministry of Industry, Science and Technology, 2006. Print.

Vitalari, Nicholas P., James C. Patton, and Andrew Milner. "Key Trends in Systems — Journal article with volume and issue numbers, print
  Development in Europe and North America." *Journal of Global Information
  Management* 3.2 (2010): 5–20. Print. [*3.2* signifies volume 3, issue 2]

Walker, Robyn C., and Jolanta Aritz. "Cognitive Organization and Identity
  Maintenance in Multicultural Teams," *Journal of Business Communication* 47.1 — Journal, electronic database
  (2010): 20–41. Business Source Complete database. Web. 15 Mar. 2011.

"Writing With Inferential Statistics." *The OWL at Purdue*. Purdue University Online — Web document, no author, no date
  Writing Lab, n.d. Web. 20 Feb. 2011.

Yellin, Mike. "Re: Managing Managers and Cell Phones." 9 Sept. 2011. *Yahoo* — Listserv, discussion group, blog posting
  Groups. E-commerce. Web. 15 Sept. 2011.

American Psychological Association Format

Popular in the social and physical sciences, the American Psychological Association (APA) documentation style uses parenthetic citations. That is, each author reference is shown in parentheses when cited in the text, as shown in Figure B.3. At the end of the report, all references are listed alphabetically in a bibliography called "References." Because online materials can change, APA now recommends providing a digital object identifier (DOI) when available rather than the URL. In another departure from previous advice, APA style no longer requires the date of retrieval. For more information about APA formats, see the *Publication Manual of the American Psychological Association*, 6e (Washington, DC: American Psychological Association, 2009) or Rossiter's *The APA Pocket Handbook* (DW Publishing).

Peanut butter was first delivered to the world by a St. Louis physician in 1890. As discussed at the Peanut Advisory Board's Web site, peanut butter was originally promoted as a protein substitute for elderly patients (History, n.d.). However, it was the 1905 Universal Exposition in St. Louis that truly launched peanut butter. Since then, annual peanut butter consumption has zoomed to 1.5 kilograms a person in the United States (Barrons, 2010, p. 46).

America's farmers produce 1.6 million metric tons of peanuts annually, about half of which is used for oil, nuts, and candy. Lisa Gibbons, executive secretary of the Peanut Advisory Board, says that "peanuts in some form are in the top four candies: Snickers, Reese's Peanut Butter Cups, Peanut M & Ms, and Butterfingers" (Meadows, 2011, p. 32).

References

Barrons, E. R. (2010, November). A comparison of domestic and international consumption of legumes. *Journal of Economic Agriculture, 23*(3), 45–49.

History of peanut butter. (n.d.). Peanut Advisory Board. Alabama Peanut Producers Association. Retrieved from http://www.alpeanuts.com/consumer_interest/articles.phtml?articleID=102

Meadows, M. A. (2011, May). Peanut crop is anything but peanuts at home and overseas. *Business Monthly,* 31–34.

APA In-Text Format

Within the text, document each specific textual source with a short description in parentheses. Following are selected guidelines summarizing important elements of APA style:

- For a direct quotation, include the last name of the author(s), date of publication, and page number, as (Jones, 2012, p. 36). Use *n.d.* if no date is available.

- If no author is known, refer to the first few words of the reference list entry and the year, as (Computer Privacy, 2013).

- Include page numbers only for direct quotations.

APA Reference Format

List all citations alphabetically in a section called "References." A portion of an APA reference page is shown in Figure B.3. A more complete list of model references appears in Figure B.4. APA style requires specific capitalization and sequencing guidelines, some of which are summarized here:

- Include an author's name with the last name first followed by initials, such as *Smith, M. A.* First and middle names are not used.

- Show the date of publication in parentheses immediately after the author's name, as *Smith, M. A. (2013, March 2).*

- Italicize the titles of books. Use "sentence-style" capitalization. This means capitalize only the first word of a title, proper nouns, and the first word after an internal colon.

- Do not italicize or underscore the titles of magazine and journal articles. Use sentence-style capitalization for article titles.

- Italicize the names of magazines, newspapers, and journals. Capitalize the initial letters of all main words.

FIGURE B.4 APA Sample References

References

Air Canada. (2012). *2012 annual report*. Dorval, QC: Author. — Annual report

Atamian, R. A., & Ferranto, E. (2010). *Driving market forces*. New York: HarperCollins. — Book, two authors

Audio conferencing. (2010). In *Encyclopaedia Britannica*. Retrieved October 19, 2011, from Encyclopaedia Britannica Online: http//www.britannica.com/eb/article-61669 — Encyclopedia, online

Balcazar, S. (2010, March 1). The future of investing. [Electronic version]. *Fortune*, 62–67. — Magazine article, online, without DOI, print version available

Beardsley, E. (2011, April 6). Building gone wild in China. [Electronic version]. *Asia Today*, 102, pp. 42–44. doi: 10.1090/14733300410001676403 — Magazine article, with DOI

Berss, M. (2008, October 24). Protein man. *Forbes*, 65–66. — Magazine article, print

Clay, R. (2008, June). Science vs. ideology: Psychologists fight back about the misuse of research. *Monitor on Psychology*, 39(6). Retrieved from http://www.apa.org.monitor/ — Magazine article, online

Globalization often means that the fast track leads overseas. (2011, June 16). *National Post*, pp. A1, A4. — Newspaper article, no author, print

Guzman, D. (2011, April 20). Corporate ghostwriting. *Financial Times*. Retrieved from http://www.ft.com — Newspaper article, online

U.S. Department of Health and Human Services, National Institutes of Health, National Heart, Lung, and Blood Institute. (2003). *Managing asthma: A guide for schools* (NIH Publication No. 02-2650). Retrieved from http://www.nhlbi.nih.gov/health/prof/lung/asthma/asth_sch.pdf — Government report

Varma, P., Sivakumaran, B., and Marshall, R. (2010, March). Impulse buying and variety seeking: A trait-correlates perspective. *Journal of Business Research*, 63(3), 276–283. [63(3) signifies volume 63, series or issue 3] — Journal article from database (see Note 1 below)

Vitalari, N. P., Patton, J. C., & Milner, A. (2010, May). Key trends in systems development in Europe and North America. *Journal of Global Information Management*, 3(2), 5–20. — Journal article without DOI

Walker, R. D., & Aritz, J. (2010, January). Cognitive organization and identity maintenance in multicultural teams. [Electronic version]. *Journal of Business Communication*, 47(1): 20–41. doi: 10.1177/0021943609340669 — Journal article with DOI

Writing with inferential statistics. (n.d.). *The OWL at Purdue*. Retrieved from http://owl.english.purdue.edu/owl/resource/672/06/ — Web document, no author, no date

Yerkes, J. (2010, February 24). Re: Emerging business models [Online forum comment]. Retrieved from http://www1.wipo.int:8080/roller/trackback/ipisforum/Weblog/theme_nine_emerging_business_models — Web posting to newsgroup, online forum, or discussion group

Note 1: Database identification is unnecessary if the article is easily located through its primary publication.
Note 2: Do not include retrieval dates unless the source material may change over time (e.g., wikis).
Note 3: Although APA style prescribes double-spacing for the References page, we show single spacing to conserve space and to represent preferred business usage.

- Include the document object identifier (DOI) when available for online periodicals. If no DOI is available, include the URL but no date of retrieval.

- For an online periodical that also appears in a printed version, include *Electronic version* in brackets after the article's title. Do not include a URL.

- For articles easily obtained from an online database (such as that in a school library), provide print information. The database need not be identified. You may include an accession number in parentheses at the end, but APA style does not require it.

Key to Grammar and Mechanics C.L.U.E. Exercises

Chapter 1

1. Whether you are already working or about to enter today's **workplace, communication** skills are critical to your career success. [Guide 1. Fragment]

2. Surveys of employers consistently show that communication skills are important to **job success; job** advertisements often request excellent oral and written communication skills. [Guide 3. Comma splice]

3. *C*

4. We cannot predict future **jobs;** however, they will undoubtedly require brainpower and education. [Guide 3. Comma splice]

5. Face-to-face conversations have many **advantages, even** though they produce no written record and sometimes waste time. [Guide 1. Fragment]

6. A vital part of the communication process is **feedback. It** helps the sender know that the message was received and understood. [Guide 3. Comma splice]

7. Knowledge workers must be critical **thinkers. They** must be able to make decisions and communicate those decisions. [Guide 2. Run-on sentence]

8. Management uses many methods to distribute information **downward, such** as newsletters, announcements, meetings, videos, and company intranets. [Guide 1. Fragment]

9. *C*

10. You may be expected to agree to a company's code of **ethics. You** will also be expected to know the laws applying to your job. [Guide 3. Comma splice]

Chapter 2

1. Our recruiter must **choose** from among four strong candidates. [Guide 4]

2. The use of smartphones and laptops during meetings **is** prohibited. [Guide 6]

3. If I **were** you, I would finish my degree program. [Guide 5]

4. Considerable time and money **were** spent on communication training for employees. [Guide 7]

5. Neither the president nor the operations manager **has** read the complete report. [Guide 8]

6. Disagreement and dissension **are** normal and should be expected in team interactions. [Guide 7]

7. Everything in the meeting minutes and company reports **is** open to public view. [Guide 9]

8. A committee of three employees and two managers **is** working to establish office priorities. [Guide 10]

9. Greg said that he **saw** the report before it was distributed to management. [Guide 4]

10. Each of the office divisions **is** expected to work together to create common procedures. [Guide 9]

Chapter 3

1. Direct the visitors to my boss and **me**; she and I will give them a tour of our facility. [Guide 13]

2. Judging by you and **me** alone, this department will be the most productive one in the company. [Guide 13]

3. The team knew that **its** project was doomed once the funding was cut. [Guide 14]

4. You and **I** did the work of three; she only did hers and poorly so. [Guide 12]

5. The shift manager and I will work overtime tonight, so please direct all calls to him or **me**. [Guide 15]

6. Each new job candidate must be accompanied to **his or her** interview by a staff member. *OR:* All new job candidates must be accompanied to **their** interviews by a staff member. [Guide 17]

7. Please deliver the printer supplies to **whoever** ordered them. [Guide 16]

8. Most applications arrived on time, but **yours** and **hers** were not received. [Guide 14]

9. *C* [Guide 13]

10. **Who** did you say left messages for Connie and me? [Guide 16]

Chapter 4

1. Business writers strive to use **easy-to-understand** language and familiar words. [Guide 20]

2. Luis said he did **well** in his employment interview. [Guide 19]

3. Having prepared for months, we won the contract **easily**. [Guide 19]

4. Collaboration on **team-written** documents is necessary for big projects. [Guide 20]

5. Jenna felt **bad** when her team project was completed. [Guide 19]

6. The 3-×-3 writing plan provides **step-by-step** instructions for writing messages. [Guide 20]

7. Our **recently revised** office handbook outlined all recommended document formats. [Guide 20]

8. The project ran **smoothly** after Maria organized the team. [Guide 19]

9. **Locally installed** online collaboration tools are **easy to use** and work well. [Guide 20]

10. **Well-written** safety messages include short, familiar words. [Guide 20]

Chapter 5

1. The 3-×-3 writing process includes prewriting, **writing**, and revising. [Guide 21, CmSer]

2. Before asking others for **information**, see what you can find yourself. [Guide 22, CmIntr]

3. Formal research methods include accessing electronically, searching **manually**, and investigating primary sources. [Guide 21, CmSer]

4. If a project is **complex**, consider organizing it by outlining the major points. [Guide 22, CmIntr]

5. Careful writers define the main **topic**, and they divide it into three to five components. [Guide 23, CmConj]

6. We decided that Jill **Hawkins**, who is the best writer on the **team**, should prepare the final draft. [Guide 25, CmIn]

7. The company's executives expected new office construction to be finished by September 1, **2013**, in **Whistler**, B.C. [Guide 24, CmDate]

8. Grammar **checkers**, by the **way**, often highlight passive voice as a grammar fault. [Guide 25, CmIn]

9. When you must be tactful and avoid naming the doer of an **action**, the passive voice can be helpful. [Guide 22, CmIntr]

10. *C* [Guide 26]

Chapter 6

1. Successful product names may appear to have been named by **magic; however,** the naming process is methodical and deliberate. [Guide 27]

2. Choosing the right name and tagline is **critical; consequently,** companies are eager to hire specialists. [Guide 27]

3. Naming is a costly **endeavour;** fees may range up to $70,000 for a global name. [Guide 27]

4. Expanding markets are in **Paris, France; Beijing, China;** and **Dubai City**, United Arab Emirates. [Guide 28]

5. As she was about to name a fashion product, Rachel Hermes **said:** "If I am launching a new fashion label, the task becomes very difficult. I have to find a name that communicates the creative style that the brand is to embody." [Guide 30]

6. For a new unisex perfume, Hermes considered the following **names:** Declaration, Serenity, and Earth. [Guide 29]

7. Naming is not a problem for small **companies; however,** it is a big problem for global brands. [Guide 27]

8. Hermes started with a thorough competitive **analysis;** it included quantifying the tone and strength of competing names. [Guide 27]

9. Attending the naming sessions were James Harper, marketing **director;** Reva Cruz, product **manager;** and Cheryl Chang, vice president. [Guide 28]

10. Distribution of goods has become **global; therefore,** names have to be registered in many countries. [Guide 27]

Chapter 7

1. Facebook **users'** accounts will be suspended if the members don't abide by the **site's** policies. [Guides 32, 31]

2. **James's** performance review was outstanding again. [Guide 32]

3. Would you please give me directions to your downtown **headquarters. [Use period, not question mark.** Guide 34]

4. The shipping supervisor resented **Barbara's** being late almost every morning. [Guide 33]

5. Is it true that the CEO decided to write a weekly **blog?** [Guide 35]

6. You must replace the ink cartridge **(see** page 8 in the **manual)** before printing. [Guide 37]

7. Justin wondered whether all the sales **managers'** databases needed to be updated. [Guide 32]

8. (Direct quotation) "**Health** care **costs,**" said the CEO, "**will** increase substantially this **year.**" [Guide 38]

9. In just two **months'** time, we expect to interview five candidates for the opening. [Guide 32]

10. The meeting starts at 10 a.m. sharp, doesn't **it?** [Guide 35]

Chapter 8

1. Once the **management team** and the **union** members finally agreed, **Mayor Knox** signed the **agreement.** [Guides 39, 41]

2. All **WestJet Airlines** passengers must exit the **plane** at Gate 14 when they reach **Pearson International Airport.** [Guides 39, 46]

3. The vice president of the **United States** urged members of the **European Union** to continue to seek peace in the **Middle East.** [Guides 39, 43]

4. My **uncle**, who lives in the **West**, has Skippy **peanut butter** and Coca-Cola for **breakfast.** [Guides 41, 43, 45]

5. Our **marketing manager** and **director** of **sales** thought that the **company** should purchase BlackBerry **smartphones** for all **sales reps.** [Guides 41, 45]

6. Personal **tax rates** for **Japanese** citizens are low by **international** standards, according to **Professor Yamaguchi** at **Osaka University.** [Guides 39, 41]

7. Jinhee Kim, who heads our **Customer Communication Division**, has a **master's degree** in social psychology from the **University** of **Calgary.** [Guides 44, 40, 39]

8. Please consult **Figure** 4.5 in **Chapter** 4 to obtain **Statistics Canada** population figures for the **Pacific Northwest.** [Guides 46, 39, 43]

9. Last **fall** did you see the article titled "The **Global Consequences** of **Using Crops** for **Fuel**"? [Guides 39, 42]

10. Toby plans to take courses in **marketing, business law,** and **English** in the **spring.** [Guides 40, 39]

Chapter 9

1. Included in her bad-news message was a **compliment** and valuable **advice.**

2. His **principal** reason for declining the invitation was his busy **calendar.**

3. In her damage-control message, the manager made a **conscious** effort to regain the customer's confidence.

4. In your **everyday** business affairs, you must show **patience** even when irritated.

5. Before you **proceed** with the report, please check those **embarrassing** statistics.

6. Although we will look into this matter **further**, I am not **surprised** at your report.

7. The judge declared that the comments of **their** attorneys were **irrelevant** to the case at hand.

8. Because the property was **too** difficult to **appraise**, its value was unrecorded.

9. Meredith hoped to **elicit** advice from her counsellor, but she was **disappointed**.

10. The manager **recommended** that we switch to an annual **maintenance** schedule.

Chapter 10

1. Susan showed me **five** different customer messages with the same **two** complaints. [Guide 47]

2. **Twenty-eight** employees indicated they would change their health benefits. [Guide 47]

3. Did Mike request **$300** to attend the **one**-day seminar? [Guides 49, 47]

4. Most deliveries arrive before **10 a.m.** [Guide 49]

5. Personal income tax returns must be mailed by April **15**. [Guide 49]

6. We earned 2.5 **percent** dividends on our **$3,000** investment. [Guide 49]

7. Our company applied for a **$100,000** loan at **6 percent**. [Guide 49]

8. Average attendance at Major League Baseball games totalled **80 million** in the United States and Canada. [Guide 50]

9. I bought the item on eBay for **$1.50** and sold it for **$15**. [Guide 49]

10. That store offers a **30-day** customer satisfaction return policy. [Guide 48]

Chapter 11

1. The recruiter cited **studies** showing that **managers** leave [delete comma] when they lose their autonomy.

2. As they work more than **40 hours** a week without overtime pay, most **professionals** today are wondering **whether** their jobs can survive the recession.

3. One organization paid **$3,000** each for **12** employees to attend a **one-week** workshop in communication training.

4. My company **spends $500** on ink cartridges every month, but the cost doesn't worry my partner and **me** because our printed materials look sharp and professional.

5. If you find **an** open document on a colleague's computer **screen**, **it's** inappropriate to peek.

6. **Today's** workers should brush up their marketable **skills; otherwise**, they may not find another job after being laid off.

7. On June **1** our company **president** revealed a **$4 million** drop in profits, which was bad news for everyone.

8. Most of us prefer to be let down **gently** [delete comma] when we are being refused **something;** that is why the **reasons-before-refusal** pattern is effective.

9. Between you and **me**, if we **were** to share a ride each **morning**, we would save a lot of money.

10. Despite the recent economic **downturn**, our **president** and CEO gave an optimistic assessment of the **company's** outlook.

Chapter 12

1. Toyota, the best-selling **Japanese** carmaker, has enjoyed a strong favourable perception of high **quality; therefore**, it long remained unharmed by a string of much-publicized recalls.

2. The **auditor's** report, which my boss and **I** read very closely, featured the following three main **flaws:** factual inaccuracies, omissions, and incomprehensible language.

3. **Eight** of the 20 workers in my department were **fired;** as a result, we had to work much harder to **achieve** our objectives.

4. As a matter of **principle**, we offer some form of financial support to more than **60** percent of our current MBA **candidates, which** proves our commitment to executive education.

5. To post easily to your blog on the **Web**, you could use Mozilla's **Web** browser **Firefox** and an add-on called ScribeFire.

6. **Peter's** presentation for a nonprofit group on advanced Internet marketing netted him only **$200**, a fifth of his usual **honorarium**, but he believes in pro bono work.

7. The old company manual covers the basics **of** [delete colon] searching, **selecting, interpreting,** and organizing data.

8. Our latest press **release**, which was written in our Corporate Communication **Department**, announces the opening of **three** Canadian offices.

9. Letter reports **usually have** side margins of 1.5–2 centimetres.

10. The CEO and **manager**, who had **gone** to a meeting in the West, delivered a report to Jeff and **me** when they returned.

Chapter 13

1. Lack of job security and high unemployment **are** here to **stay** [delete period] even if we do our work **well**.

2. Managers in **three departments** complained that **their** departments were over budget for supplies.

3. After sending many e-mails to Frank and **me**, the client felt **bad** about barraging us with messages to solicit a response from our two **teams**.

4. The new vice president and **she** decided to move up the launch to **May 3;** as a result, the software was buggy.

5. Managers of big **corporations** sometimes do not know how to **motivate;** consequently, the executives miss an opportunity to develop their **workers**.

6. The **director** of marketing wanted to speak to you and **me** about the poor **morale** in our division.

7. Laura and **he** decided to **accept** assistance with their **proposal**; therefore, they completed the project by the deadline.

8. We invited **75** employees to hear **two** experts **disperse** information about wellness.

9. **Memos** usually contain four necessary **parts**: subject line, opening, **body**, and action closing.

10. Darrin **Jizmejian**, who was recently evaluated, wondered whether his formal report would be presented at the **March 13 meeting**.

Chapter 14

1. If you are planning a short **presentation**, you should focus on about **three** main points and limit yourself to **20** minutes.

2. Because he was **president** of the **company**, Mr. Yost made at least **six** major presentations every year.

3. The **company's** CGA asked me to explain the **principal** ways we planned to finance the 30-year mortgage.

4. My accountant and **I** are **grateful** to be able to give a short **presentation**; however, we may not be able to cover the entire budget.

5. The introduction to a presentation should accomplish three **goals**: (a) **capture** attention, (b) establish credibility, and (c) preview main points.

6. Steven wondered whether focusing on what the audience is to **remember** [delete comma] and summarizing main points **were** equally **important**. [delete question mark]

7. A list of suggestions for a **speaker's** ideas **is** found in the article titled "How **to** Improve Your Listening Skills."

8. The appearance and mannerisms of a speaker **definitely affect** a **listener's** evaluation of the message.

9. Melody Hobson, who is an expert **speaker**, said that reading from slides is the **kiss** of **death** in a presentation.

10. In a poll of **3,000 workers**, only one third felt that **their** companies valued their opinions.

Chapter 15

1. Many employers use **sites** like Facebook to learn about potential employees, **which means** job seekers must maintain a professional online presence.

2. To conduct a safe online job search, you **must** [delete colon] (a) **use** only reputable job boards, (b) keep careful records, and (c) limit the number of sites on which you post your résumé.

3. When **Melissa's** job search was **complete**, she had received **four** job offers.

4. If you **lose** your **job, don't** be discouraged by the thought of having to find another.

5. Joseph wondered whether it was **all right** to ask his professor for employment **advice**. [change question mark to period]

6. At last **month's** staff **meeting**, team members examined several **candidates'** résumés.

7. Rather **than** schedule **face-to-face interviews**, the team investigated videoconferencing.

8. **Twelve** applicants will be interviewed on **April 10**; consequently, we may need to work late to accommodate them.

9. Professional e-mail manners **reflect** on you and your **company**; however, **too** few employees are trained properly.

10. In the last issue of *Newsweek*, did you see the article titled "Should a **Résumé Include** a Career Objective?"

Chapter 16

1. Before going to a job **interview**, you should research the **following**: [delete hyphen] company size, competitors, reputation, strengths, and weaknesses.

2. I wonder how many **companies** go online to find out more about **candidates' backgrounds**. [delete question mark]

3. Even with the popularity of **e-mail**, most **employers** [delete apostrophe] contact job applicants by telephone to set up **their** interviews.

4. Initial contacts by employers are **usually** made by **telephone**; therefore, **ensure** that you keep important information nearby.

5. If you have gaps in your employment **history**, explain what you did during this **time** [delete comma] and how you stayed **up-to-date** in your field.

6. Interviewees should not **criticize** anyone or **anything**, and they should not focus on **their** imperfections.

7. Evan was asked whether he had a **bachelor's degree** [delete comma] and whether he had five **years'** experience.

8. If you are **hoping** to create a good **impression**, be sure to write a **thank-you** message after a job interview.

9. When **Robin's** interview was **over**, she told friends that she had done **well**.

10. Robin was **all ready** to send a thank-you **message** [delete comma] when she realized she could not spell the **interviewer's** name.

Acknowledgments

Chapter 1

p. 8 Figure 1.1 based on Chickowski, E. (2006, January 9). Phones offer more than call option; e-mail, text messaging, ability to play music among bells, whistles. *San Diego Business Journal*, p. 17; Quittner, J. (2006, September 4). Wikis offer quick way to collaborate; software acts like intranet, letting widely scattered staffers pool knowledge. *Crain's New York Business*, p. 34; Blogs, podcasts pushed as enterprise tools. (2006, January 12). *Information Week*; Brandon, J. (2006, June 6). Reworking the office: How will you be working—one, five, twenty years down the road? *PC Magazine*, p. 97; Open source VoIP takes a few steps forward. (2006, November 7). *Information Week*; Tricker, J. (2005, September). Office design trends: Bring on the boomerang-shaped table. *Indiana Business Magazine*, p. 4; Mirel, D. Wide open spaces: Cubicle-ridden offices transition to more open-offices formats, a result of advanced mobile technology and innovative office design. (2006, May-June). *Journal of Property Management*, 30; Held, S. (2006, March). Office tech update: From "print and distribute" to "distribute and print." *Indiana Business Magazine*, p. 64; Gardyasz, J. (2006, April 24). CustomerVision bringing wikis to business. *Business Record* (Des Moines), p. 3; The future of tech. (2005, June 20). *BusinessWeek*, p. 81; Mann, A. (2006, November 1). Enterprise content now encompassing wikis, blogs, podcasts and more. *Network World*; Klein, K. E. (2006, August 21). A company blog keeps people connected. (2006, August 21). *BusinessWeek Online*. Retrieved November 12, 2006, from InfoTrac College Edition database; Brynko, B. (2006, March). Top ten technology trends. *Information Today*, p. 1; Totty, M. (2005, September 12). Prime time for videoconferences. *The New York Times*, p. R6; Hof, R. H. (2006, June 19). Web 2.0: The new guy at work. *BusinessWeek*, p. 58.

Chapter 2

p. 31 Plugged In based on Schindler, E. (2008, February 1 5). Running an effective teleconference or virtual meeting. *CIO*. Retrieved June 28, 2009, from http://www.cio.com; Gordon, J. (2005, June). Do your virtual teams deliver only virtual performance? *Training*, 20; Brown-Johnston, N. (2005, January-February). Virtual teamwork: Smart business leaders need high-performance virtual teams. *Detroiter*, p. 55; Managing virtual teams. (2004, March 16). *Info-Tech Advisor Newsletter*; Snyder, B. (2003, May).Teams that span time zones face new work rules. *Stanford Business Magazine*. Retrieved April 15, 2007, from http://www.gsb.stanford.edu/news/bmag/sbsm0305/feature_virtual_teams.shtml; Loudin, K. H. (2003, June). Building bridges: Virtual teamwork in the 21st century. *Contract Management*; Armstrong, D. (2000, March). Building teams across borders. *Executive Excellence*, 10.

pp. 31–32 Discussion of Tuckman's model based on Robbins, H. A., & Finley, M. (1995). *Why teams don't work*. Princeton, NJ: Peterson's/Pacesetter Books, Chapter 22.

p. 32 Figure 2.1. Portions reprinted with permission of Peterson's, a division of International Thomson Publishing, FAX 800-730-2215. Adapted from *Why teams don't work*. © 1995 by Harvey A. Robbins and Michael Finley.

p. 33 Discussion of conflict and groupthink based on Toledo, R. (2008, June). Conflict is everywhere. *PM Network*. Retrieved June 28, 2009, from Business Source Complete database; McNamara, P. (2003, August/September). Conflict resolution strategies. *OfficePro*, p. 25; Weiss, W. (2002, November). Building and managing teams. *SuperVision*, p. 19; Eisenhardt, K. (1997, July/August). How management teams can have a good fight. *Harvard Business Review*, pp. 77–85; Brockmann, E. (1996, May). Removing the paradox of conflict from group decisions. *Academy of Management Executives*, pp. 61–62; Beebe, S., & Masterson, J. (1999). *Communicating in small groups*. New York: Longman, pp. 198–200.

p. 40 Figure 2.6 Courtesy of MeetingSense Software Corporation, http://www.meetingsense.com

pp. 51–53 Discussion of etiquette based on Gaining an etiquette edge. (2005, December). *Office Professional*, p. 6; The power of politeness. (2006, August). *Journal of Accountancy*. Retrieved November 30, 2006, from Business Source Premier (EBSCO) database.

Chapter 3

p. 64 Figure 3.1 based on Chaney, L. H., & Martin, J. S. (2000). *Intercultural business communication*, 2nd ed. Upper Saddle River, NJ: Prentice Hall, Chapter 5; J. Chung's analysis appearing in Chen, G. M., & Starosta, W. J. *Foundations of intercultural communication*. Boston: Allyn and Bacon, 1998, p. 51; O'Hara-Devereaux, M., & Johansen, R. (1994). *Globalwork: Bridging distance, culture, and time*. San Francisco: Jossey-Bass, p. 55.

Chapter 4

p. 91 Discussion of online collaboration tools based on the following: Beyond Google Docs: 7 Web-based collaboration tools. (2009, July 6). *Information Week*. Retrieved July 19, 2009, from InfoTrac College Edition database; Dahl, D. (2009, June). Connecting the dots: How to choose the right collaboration software for your company. *Inc.*, p. 103. Retrieved July 19, 2009, from InfoTrac College Edition database; Fichter, D. (2005, July/August). The many forms of e-collaboration: Blogs, wikis, portals, groupware, discussion boards, and instant messaging. *Online*, pp. 48–50. Retrieved July 18, 2009, from Business Source Complete database.

p. 92 Information on adapting to legal responsibilities based in part on Walter, R. J., & Sleeper, G. J. (2002, Spring). Employee recruitment and retention: When company inducements trigger liability. *Review of Business*, 17; Cordier, P. J. (2003, May). Essentials of good safety communications. (2003, May). *Pulp & Paper*, p. 25; Woolever, K. R. (1990, June 2). Corporate language and the law: Avoiding

liability in corporate communications. *IEE Transactions on Professional Communication*, 95–98.

Chapter 7

p. 145 Plugged In box (Cloud Computing) based on Hamm, S. (2009, June 15). Cloud computing's big bang for business. *BusinessWeek*, pp. 43–44; Wildstrom, S. H. (2009, April 6). What to entrust to the cloud. *BusinessWeek*, pp. 89–90; Burrows, P. (2009, August 1 7). Apple and Google: Another step apart. *BusinessWeek*, pp. 24–25; Hamm, S. (2009, April 6). IBM reaches for the clouds. *BusinessWeek*, p. 34.

p. 161 The five main uses of wikis based on Nations, D. (2009). The business wiki. About. com: Web Trends. Retrieved February 13, 2010, from http://webtrends.about.com/od/wiki/a/business-wiki.htm

p. 152 Figure 7.2 Using E-Mail Smartly and Safely is based on Totty, M. (2007, March 26). Rethinking the inbox. *The Wall Street Journal*, p. R8; Minzesheimer, B. (2007, April 10). Check your e-mail—before you hit send. *USA Today*, p. 1D; Derbyshire, J. (2007, April 21). To: emailers, subject: etiquette. *The Wall Street Journal*, p. 10; Munter, M., Rogers, P. S., & Rymer, J. (2003, March). Business e-mail: Guidelines for users. *Business Communication Quarterly*, 66(1), 26; E-mail acceptable use: An enforceable policy. (2003, September 30). *Info-Tech Advisor Newsletter*; Maney, K. (2003, July 24). How the big names tame e-mail. *USA Today*, p. 1A; Email: The DNA of office crimes. (2003, September/October). *Electric Perspectives*, 4; Hughes, L. (2003, July/August). E-mail etiquette: Think before you send. *Women in Business*, p. 29.

p. 159 Tips for Creating a Professional Blog based on Wuorio, J. (n.d.). Blogging for business: 7 tips for getting started. Microsoft Small Business Center. Retrieved January 14, 2010, from http://www.microsoft.com/smallbusiness/resources/marketing/online-marketing/small-business-blog.aspx#Smallbusinessblog

p. 161 The five main uses of wikis based on Nations, D. (2009). The business wiki. About. com: Web Trends. Retrieved February 13, 2010, from http://webtrends.about.com/od/wiki/a/business-wiki.htm

Chapter 8

pp. 188–194 Discussion of claim and adjustment letters based on McCartney, S. (2007, March 20). What airlines do when you complain. *The Wall Street Journal*, p. D5; Liao, H. (2007, March). Do it right this time: The role of employee service recovery performance in customer-perceived justice and customer loyalty after service failures. *Journal of Applied Psychology*, 92(2), 475. Retrieved January 12, 2007, from Business Source Premier (EBSCO) database; Davidow, M. (2003, February). Organizational responses to customer complaints: What works and what doesn't. *Journal of Service Research*, 5(3), 31. Retrieved June 3, 2007, from Business Source Premier (EBSCO) database; Michelson, M. W., Jr.

(2003, December). Turning complaints into cash. *American Salesman*, p. 22; Torp, J. R. (2003, March/April). In person, by phone, by mail, or online: Managing customer complaints. *ABA Bank Compliance*, p. 10; Kim, C., Kim, S., Im, S., & Shin, S. (2003). The effect of attitude and perception on consumer complaint intentions. *Journal of Consumer Marketing, 20*, 352; Lawrence, K. (2000, Fall). How to profit from customer complaints: Turning problems into opportunities. *Canadian Manager*, 25; David, D., & Baker, M. A. (1994). Rereading bad news: Compliance-gaining features in management memos. *Journal of Business Communications*, 267–290; Smart, D. T., & Martin, C. L. (1993, Spring). Consumers who correspond with business: A profile and measure of satisfaction with responses. *Journal of Applied Business Research*, 30–42; Clark, G. L., Kaminski, P. F., & Rink, D. R. (1992, Winter). Consumer complaints: Advice on how companies should respond based on an empirical study. *Journal of Services Marketing*, 41–50.

Chapter 9

p. 217 Plugged In box based on Weber, H. R. (2009, October 13). Social sites new conduits for customer service. Retrieved January 21, 2010, from, http://www.crmbuyer.com; Social networking and customer service. (n.d.) Retrieved January 21, 2010, from http://www.allthingscrm.com; Baker, L. (2008, July 24). How to combat complaints sites in Google. Retrieved January 21, 2010, from http://www.searchenginejournal.com; Whitehead, J. (2009, December 9). Are customer complaints on Twitter good for brands? Retrieved January 22, 2010, from http://www.brandrepublic.com; Miles, S. (2009, October 26). Complain, complain, complain. Retrieved January 22, 2010, from http://www. recessionwire.com

Chapter 10

p. 235 Effective Persuasion Techniques based on Hoar, R. (2005, March 1). Be more persuasive. *Management Today*, 56; Venter, D. (2006). Negotiation persuasion. Retrieved June 29, 2006, from http://www.calumcoburn.co.uk/articles/articles-persuasion.html; Muir, G. (2006). *All presenting is persuasive*. *Link&Learn eNewsletter*. Retrieved June 29, 2006, from http://www.linkageinc.com/company/news_events/link_learn/enewsletter/archive/2006/01; Master the art of persuasion to boost your managerial effectiveness. (2006,

February). *Payroll Manager's Report*, 15; Cialdini, R. B. (2002, April). The science and practice of persuasion. *Cornell Hotel & Restaurant Administration Quarterly*, 40; Francaro, K. E. (2004, August). Managing by persuasion. *Contract Management*, 4.

p. 254 Figure 10.8 Media Release used with permission of the Antique and Classic Boat Society – Toronto Chapter. Photo courtesy of Timothy Du Vernet.

Chapter 11

p. 280 Figure 11.7's image published with permission of ProQuest. Further reproduction is prohibited without permission. Image produced by ProQuest. Inquires may be made to: ProQuest, P.O. Box 1346, 789 E. Eisenhower Parkway, Ann Arbor, MI 48106-1346 USA. Telephone (734)761-7400; E-mail: info@proquest.com; Web-page: www.proquest.com

p. 286 Figure 11.9 based on Search Engine Watch (2009, September 15). Top search providers for August 2009. SearchEngineWatch.com. Retrieved January 29, 2010, from http://searchenginewatch.com/3634991; Sullivan, D. (2006, August 21). ComScore media metrix search engine ratings. Retrieved January 28, 2010, from http://searchenginewatch.com/reports/article. php/2156431

Chapter 12

p. 321 Career Coach box based on Booher, D. (2001, April). E-writing. *Executive Excellence*, 16; Bernstel, J. B., & Thomases, H. (2001, March). Writing words for the Web. *Bank Marketing*, 16–21; Graves, P. R., & Murry, J. E. (1990, Summer). Enhancing communication with effective page design and typography. *Delta Pi Epsilon* Instructional Strategies Series.

Chapter 13

p. 369 Figure 13.4 based on Sokuvitz, S., & George, A. M. (2003, June). Teaching culture: The challenges and opportunities of international public relations. *Business Communication Quarterly*, 97; Koh, A. C. (2003). Teaching understanding cultural differences for business in an internet-based economy. *Journal of Teaching in International Business, 15*(2), 27; Sterkel, K. S. (1988, September). Integrating intercultural communication and report writing in the communication class. *Bulletin of the Association for Business Communication*, pp. 13–16.

Chapter 14

p. 373 Figure 14.1 based on Elsea, J. G. (1985, September). Strategies for effective presentations. *Personnel Journal*, 31–33, in Hamilton, C. (2001). *Communicating for results*. Belmont, CA: Wadsworth/Thomson Learning, p. 340.

p. 380 Figure 14.3 based on Booher, D. (2003). *Speak with confidence*. New York: McGraw-Hill Professional, pp. 131–143; U.S. Department of Labor. (1996, May). Presenting effective presentations with visual aids. Retrieved July 29, 2007, from http://www.osha.gov/doc/outreachtraining/htmlfiles/traintec.html; McConnon, S. (2002). *Presenting with power*. Oxford: How To Books, pp. 38–43.

p. 381 Career Coach (Guy Kawasaki) based on Kawasaki, G. (2005, December 30). The10/20/30 rule of PowerPoint. *How to Change the World*. Retrieved March 20, 2010, from http://blog. guykawasaki.com/2005/12/the_102030_rule.html and on personal communication by e-mail on April 8, 2010.

Chapter 15

p. 409 Searching for a Job Electronically partially based on Farquharson, L. (2003, September 15). Technology special report: The best way to find a job. *The Wall Street Journal*, p. R8; Maher, K., & Silverman, R. E. (2002, January 2). Your career matters: Online job sites yield few jobs, users complain. *The Wall Street Journal*, p. A7; Goodrich, E., & George, M. (2002, February 25). Employer-backed job site lets companies avoid Monster. *Information Week*, p. 24.

p. 423 Optimizing Your Résumé for Today's Technologies partially based on All you need to know about the electronic résumé. Retrieved July 27, 2007, from http://www.brooklyn.liu.edu/bbut07/car/career_articles/electronic_resume.html; Scannable résumés. Retrieved July 27, 2007, from http://www.career.vt.edu/JOBSEARC/Resumes/scannable.htm; Wheeler, K. (2006, October 26). The video résumé. Retrieved July 21, 2007, from http://www.ere.net/articles/db/02FEE6D607B142E68D2F80310EDBCCEC.asp; Fisher, A. (2004, June 28). How to ruin an online job hunt. *Fortune*, p. 43; Conlin, M. (2003, July 14). The résumé doctor is in. *Business-Week*, p. 116; Hansen, R. (2007). Scannable résumé fundamentals: How to write text résumés. Retrieved July 27, 2007, from http://www.quintcareers.com/scannable_resumes.html

Index

Note: Page references followed by "f" refer to figures.